HOLD, PLEASE

"I've watched Richard create order out of chaos for years, so it comes as no surprise when he was able to do it again with these beautiful posts. Together they create a powerful reminder of where we've been as well as a thoughtful and compassionate guide for moving ahead."
— *Bernadette Peters*

"It is no surprise to me that Richard Hester is an exquisite companion as he insightfully guides us on the journey through the strange isolation of that endless pandemic. The Elizabethan theatre was frequently shut down because of the Black Death, and I've often tried to imagine how the players of that time managed to cope with the stress. Richard's book makes it vividly clear."
— *Des McAnuff, Director*

"Said simply, Richard Hester's HOLD PLEASE is the reflection of a good man. Hester is the consummate theatre artist, a stalwart friend, trustworthy colleague, and brilliant collaborator. His epic, personal memoir of the historic COVID 19 shutdown and cautious re-opening is proof of that in ways he may not have intended but with which we now have been unexpectedly blessed. Daily personal journaling has been compiled now into an epic history of minute detail, personal insight, shared fears, and wonder. It shines light on our darkest hours in a way that is both formidable, intimate, and deeply generous, personally and professionally."
— *Tom Viola*

"I am so grateful that Richard wrote all of this down so that I don't have to remember it myself."
— *Patti LuPone*

"Thank you for taking my suggestion seriously (Imaa need you to file these and publish a book good sir.) because we are all better for it."
— *Ariana DeBose*

"Richard Hester is a saint as far as I'm concerned. Anything he writes I would read, however I haven't had the time to read his book yet as my first grandchild was just born. As soon as I stop changing diapers, Richard's book is the first thing I'm reading!"
— *Mandy Patinkin*

"I have always been in awe of Richard Hester's gift as a storyteller. He has beautifully crafted a diary that reminds us of the journey we have been on for the past two years, and with this book given us the courage to carry on with hope and faith."
— *Sergio Trulillo, Director/Choreographer*

"(Hester's) lyrical writing about the natural world adds dimension to humorous stories about working—and not working—from home…Hester interweaves descriptions of living through Covid-19 with stories of his colorful theatrical career…"
— *Kirkus Reviews*

Hold, Please: Stage Managing A Pandemic

Copyright © 2022 by Richard Hester

Cover painting by Sue Pendleton
Cover design by littleBULL

This work depicts actual events in the life of the author as truthfully as recollection permits and/or can be verified by research. All opinions belong to the author. The information in this book is true and complete to the best of the author's knowledge. The author and publisher disclaim any liability in connection with the use of this information.

All rights reserved. No part of this book may be reproduced in any form by any electronic or mechanical means including photocopying, recording, or information storage and retrieval without permission in writing from the author.

ISBN-13: 978-1944540999

Published by Sordelet Ink
www.sordeletink.com

HOLD, PLEASE

STAGE MANAGING A PANDEMIC

RICHARD HESTER

Introduction by Rick Elice

FOREWORD BY RICK ELICE—XI

INTRODUCTION—XIII

SPRING 2020—3

SUMMER 2020—113

FALL 2020—245

WINTER 2020-2021—379

SPRING 2021—503

AFTERWORD—551

ACKNOWLEGEMENTS—553

REFERENCES—555

For Michael. And the cat.

Foreword
by Rick Elice

If a Martian anthropologist were to appear at my door (fully vaccinated, of course), and ask for the name of one person who represented everything that a modern civilized, committed, thoughtful person ought to represent—oh, come on, let's face it, I would unhesitatingly say: Frankie Valli. (How could I not? Family is everything, after all.)

But if that same Martian were to ask me who I'd want around to help re-start the civilization if it suddenly went belly-up, who I would want in my lifeboat, who I would want to stage-manage my show or even better my life—or just someone I'd want around in general, I would say: That's easy. Richard Hester.

And then I'd say: Just living in the same city as Richard Hester gives me comfort beyond all understanding. Because Richard Hester knows stuff nobody else knows. If I need to have my deck painted, my lights brightened, my lines spoken verbatim; or if I suddenly require a hydraulic lift (never mind what for); or if I have an anxiety attack at rehearsal and get sent out of the room by the director (not that such a thing has ever happened to me, you understand), Richard Hester always knows what to do.

Richard is not only a stage manager and production supervisor, he's a consummate student. He makes it his business to understand every aspect of what happens onstage, backstage, and off stage, because he knows all of that is his business. And he's fast. Richard Hester can tech a two-part, seven-hour play in just under 43 minutes.

But, as you're already aware, we are not here to honor Richard's decades of telling the rest of the world what to do and how to do it. Well, actually, maybe we are.

Because at the very moment most of us hung up our rehearsal togs and pulled down the blinds—I mean, on that fateful 12th day of March 2020, when our entire industry abruptly and indefinitely shuttered—Richard Hester, alone among us, rushed into the breach and wrote. And because he's who he is and does what he does, his daily missives were more than mere observational meanderings. He told us what to do and how to do it.

I found myself, in that endless line of dark days, looking forward to his next entry, curling up with each one as with a good book. Richard's words became comforting and comprehensive survival guides, step-by-step instruction manuals, veritable how-to-face-the-unknown columns. Now, collected in these pages, they still are.

When Richard asked me to write this foreword, he said "Don't feel as though you need to read it all again." But once I started, I couldn't stop. Because Richard's daily columns didn't just help all of us make it through that thing called COVID. Today, collectively, they form a blueprint for stage-managing our post-COVID lives.

Certainly, the full range of Richard's skills are only hinted at in this book. Richard makes theater. He does plays, revivals, concerts. He'll even take a chance on a spanking new musical about four guys from Jersey. (And I'm real glad he did.)

But in these pages, Richard's insights are a show unto themselves. In his words, you'll hear the beating of a great and giving heart. And his observations, like all the best writing, are not merely the grace notes of life, but the very stuff and texture of a melody that, thanks to Richard, we can all learn by heart.

Rick Elice
Co-Author of Jersey Boys
November 2021

Introduction

For our opening night in Toronto, the crew of the First National Tour of the musical *Wicked* gave me a T-shirt printed with the words, "Hold, please."

When you are putting up a musical there is a period after the studio rehearsals and before the first performance that's referred to as tech. During that time, the cast is on the actual stage for the first time. They are shown the real props for the first time having had four weeks using pretend versions of them made of cardboard and gaffer's tape. Costumes show up for the first time. Lighting, sound, projections, and set moves are programmed into the computers or taught to the crew and the show slowly starts to come together. Very slowly. Sometimes glacially slowly.

My job as the stage manager is to keep everything moving forward. Coordinating each of the different departments, I make sure that they are all integrating and working together. I constantly push, nudge, cajole, tease, and sometimes even beg everyone to keep going ahead. Until I stop them.

"Hold, please."

Something's gone wrong. Something's not working. Yelling, "stop" in a crowded theatre is almost as bad as yelling, "fire." Automated scenery has something called an e-stop that the operator can hit and instantly shut everything down. In an emergency, that's what you need to happen. Somebody is in danger of being hurt so everything must stop on a dime, and it does. Often the scenery then bangs into itself. Everything needs to be reset because cues have been interrupted in mid execution. So, when it's not an emergency, you need to find a way to stop the forward action without throwing everything into chaos. I will wait until cues are almost completed and as gently and forcefully as possible slowly drone out a, "and… hold, please." Then everybody stops smoothly and calmly and whatever has gone wrong can be fixed or worked on and we can then move forward again.

Throughout that tech, I said the words, "Hold, please," a lot.

The past year and a few months of the COVID-19 pandemic were much like a hold during tech. Our forward action was halted, but plenty of work was going on behind the scenes to get us back up and running again.

My husband Michael and I, along with our cat, spent most of that time in our apartment on the Upper West Side of Manhattan. Neither of us had ever spent that much time in one place in our adult lives nor even with each other.

During the inevitable pauses during a tech, I am called upon to keep everyone posted as to what is going on. There is nothing more frustrating than sitting in the dark, waiting in silence, without having any idea of what the problem is. When everything shut down in March of 2020, it wasn't always easy to understand what was happening. I started writing about what was going on as a way for me to understand it and to put it into some sort of perspective and order. I posted them on social media and people started reading, so I kept going.

I didn't set out to write every day, but that's what I did for a full year. It turned out that there was a lot to talk about and a lot to work through. We are moving forward, again, now, but we discovered over this strange time just how much work is left to do on the machinery that drives us.

We all experienced this period in different ways. The advantages and disadvantages that each of us has in life seemed to get magnified. I wouldn't presume to speak for anyone's experience other than my own—not Michael's or even our cat's for that matter.

What follows is my year and mine, alone. There was a lot of loss but a lot of joy, too. Some relationships fell away but some strengthened and grew. Kept from doing what we usually did, we came up with new things—some good enough to keep doing and some, maybe not so much. So much of what happened to us was unfamiliar and anxiety-provoking. Some of what we learned changed how we look at the world around us and how we choose to live our lives.

It was, in short, a year.

Hold, Please

SPRING 2020

MARCH–MAY

MARCH 12, 2020
125,000 Reported Cases Worldwide. 4,500 Deaths.
296 Total Reported Cases in New York. 1 Death.

Last night, after weeks of his downplaying and ridiculing the virus, we were finally told by our President, that it is, in fact, serious.

There are over a thousand cases of it on the US mainland.

The solution put forth today by our President is to ban all flights from Europe starting on Friday—passenger and cargo alike. According to him, this "foreign" virus has been mismanaged in Europe and we don't want it here. Within seconds of his address, tweets went out that the President misspoke. This ban won't affect cargo. The ban is for mainland Europe only, not the United Kingdom. The ban doesn't apply to US citizens or permanent residents who have been properly screened, just EU passport holders.

OK, so then, what does this mean practically? Do US and Permanent Residents need to be tested at the airport? Some people carrying the virus are completely asymptomatic. They are still carrying it and you just can't tell. I am guessing that European airports are a mess this morning with everybody scrambling to get home. There does not appear to be any sort of plan to ensure that everyone gets home by Friday. If the restrictions don't apply to the UK, surely everyone will just flee from Europe by going to England via the Chunnel.

Italy is in lockdown. Nobody can move from town to town and all businesses except grocery stores and other essential services have been closed.

Nobody thinks that can happen here because we only have 1,000 cases. Is that true, though? There has been no testing. Kits aren't available. We are far more likely to already have tens of thousands of cases on the US mainland that simply haven't been identified yet. This ban is already too late. The virus is here.

In response to last night's address to the nation, the stock market is plunging again today. Trading has just been halted. Again. Non-perishable food is disappearing from grocery stores.

This travel ban, whatever else it does, is going to keep tourists away from the US in droves. That will severely impact, hotels, entertainment, transportation, restaurants... you name it. Gatherings need to be curtailed. The NBA canceled its entire season yesterday, can Broadway be far behind?

We need to think these next few weeks through. Without panic. Make sure that you can get through them in terms of food and medication. Don't hoard, be smart about it. Wash your hands. Really. Stay away from crowds—both for your sake and theirs. Act as if you already have it. We need to be smart about how we move around it and interact with each other for the next few weeks. God-willing, this will pass and turn out to be nothing. Let's take it seriously NOW so that is exactly what happens. Breathe.

Be safe.
Be kind.
Be smart.

It seems that we are unlikely to get any real guidance from the federal government. They have not realized that this is a real thing and are still factoring politics into their every response. Try and be clear about where you are getting your information from.

Doctors are saying to wash your hands and practice social distancing.
Be safe.
Be kind.
Be smart.

March 13, 2020

17,660 cases reported in Italy. 1,266 Deaths—250 in the last 24 hours.

Yesterday we watched as the way we live our lives changed. Hourly.

Most of us, especially those of us in the entertainment and foodservice industries make our livings in large groups. We require a crowd. We can't do crowds now. We are all going to have to figure out how to live in this new life unfolding around us.

It seems that we are not going to get any sort of meaningful guidance from the federal government or the current administration. In fact, what we are already getting from the top is a bunch of misinformation and outright lies. We are getting a far more coordinated response on the state level. It isn't perfect, but they appear to have at least one foot somewhat firmly planted in reality.

How are we all going to pay rent? I don't have the slightest idea, but we will. Let's look out for each other. Please do not be afraid to reach out. Nobody needs to suffer alone when we are all going through this. Nobody.

MARCH 14, 2020
175 additional deaths in Italy.

Both Michael and I have been sick with something these last couple of days. Between the two of us, we do have some of the coronavirus symptoms but by no means all. Cough. Bouts of feverishness. Aches. Now on day three, we've both woken up feeling like ourselves although Michael can't taste anything.

We spent a good part of yesterday morning trying to figure out if there was any way we could get tested here in New York City. The short answer is no. There aren't any tests available.

There is an almost complete lack of communication between 311 and the NY Department of Health and Hospitals. The NY Coronavirus hotline and 311 both send you to the same place without giving out any reliable information.

In the face of that, what we decided to do is to just live our lives. Until we are completely asymptomatic (which might be today) we are sleeping in separate places. (We are fortunate enough to have a good sofa bed in the living room and are taking turns sleeping on it.) Spending two weeks together in this apartment without being able to go to the theatre or museums and without attending any social events is an interesting challenge.

Today, I feel well enough to do something. We live close to Central Park, so we are going to take a walk there today. Until there is any information there doesn't seem to be anything more that we can do. The hardest thing to do is to just sit around and wait.

The news doesn't help. Every single word out of the president's mouth is an out-and-out lie. The only thing he is concerned about is stopping the free fall of the stock market. We're tuning him out.

All my jobs have stopped. Norwegian Cruise Lines has now halted its cruising. Both the *Jersey Boys* tour and its Off-Broadway production are suspended for the moment. I hope that everyone in those companies is safe and healthy and stays that way.

The last few days have been a roller coaster ride. Welcome to our new normal. For now. I like the occasional day of doing nothing in my bathrobe but two weeks of this is going to be endless unless we set ourselves some goals.

Let's see what happens next.

MARCH 15, 2020
633 Total Reported Cases in New York. 10 Deaths.

We got some much-needed exercise and fresh air yesterday in the Park. Whatever it was that we might have had seems to have passed. It was a beautiful day in NY—cold but crystal clear and bright.

Lots of people were still out and about as if nothing was going on. Large group picnics and touch football games were very much in evidence. People don't seem concerned about getting it. Everyone thinks that they're healthy, they're young, and that it's survivable.

American Airlines has just announced that they are suspending most of their international long-haul flights starting tomorrow through to the beginning of May. The rest will soon follow and I am sure it will start to impact domestic travel as well.

We are truly looking at the most monumental societal change that any of us have ever lived through. 9-11 changed things for us, but the immediate disruption was only a couple of days. We've ended up with some permanent changes (taking off your shoes at airports and enhanced screenings for example) but life continued. This is going to be a much greater disruption and a much longer one.

Sporting events, theatrical events, church services have all been or will soon be stopped. This is not just happening here in NY, but all over the world. The West End in London has been much slower to react than the US, Canada, and Australia, but it's coming. Nike is closing its stores until May which means that a lot of other major US retailers are going to follow suit. Restaurants are also going to close either out of caution or because nobody will be going to them.

We have never been through anything like this before. Everything is changing extremely quickly. Most of these changes have come about in just the last three days.

So, moving forward, we need to be safe. We need to take care of ourselves but almost more importantly, take care of those around us. We should stop being sure that we can survive it and start thinking of ourselves as the person who could give it to someone who can't.

Be kind. Let's not add to anyone's anxiety if we can help it.

Be smart. With the ever-changing rulebook, the only way to stay on top of it all is to stay calm and take in new changes as they roll in. We need to try and put the facts together without taking in the spin. It's time to plan. When you have something concrete to concentrate on, it will quell the anxiety and the fear.

Be safe.
Be kind.
Be smart.

March 16, 2020
961 Total Reported Cases in New York. 21 Deaths.

What to do?

We have very little money coming in. We are essentially at zero earnings. I know that a lot of people are in the same boat.

We are all going to see how long our hair can get and what color it all really is! We are going to become better cooks. Michael and I are making sure that we have enough non-perishable food (canned goods, grains, protein sources) to allow us to stay home for a couple of weeks. We need SOME toilet paper but not ALL the toilet paper.

We've created a routine. We get up in the morning, take a shower, make the bed, get dressed. Michael cooks, I do the dishes. We throw out the garbage. It is extremely hard not to get paralyzed by the enormity of this. We are trying to focus on what we need to improve our lives for the future.

There are thousands of us going through the same thing. It's like we are in an earthquake right now. The ground beneath our feet is moving. Everything is changing and evolving radically by the hour. You can't deal with the after-effects of the earthquake until the ground stops moving. We are still shaking—it's not done yet.

We will all get through this. How? I don't have a blessed clue, but I know we will.

"The natural condition is one of insurmountable obstacles on the road to imminent disaster. Strangely enough, it all works out in the end... it's a mystery." —Tom Stoppard

March 17, 2020
1,407 Total Reported Cases in New York. 35 Deaths.

I discovered today that the entire company of *Jersey Boys* on the Norwegian Cruise Lines ship Bliss is still on board. They have been sitting in the middle of the Hudson River here in New York for many days, but they are now heading to Norfolk, VA. There they will all be held in quarantine for two weeks before being able to go home.

To the amazing JB NCL Bliss company: you are now leaderless throughout this time. Given the fact that I know all of you, here are some ready-made responses to the great ideas that I know you are all going to come up with about the show while you are trapped on the boat:

1) No.
2) I don't think that's a good idea.
3) No.
4) Have you thought that idea all the way through?

5) You only came up with that idea because you are bored. Go to the gym, (with wipes) work out, and think about it.
6) No.
7) If you've really thought about it, and that's what you've decided to do, for heaven's sake please don't tell me about it. (and don't post.)
8) Definitely no.

Yesterday, the President got on a call with the State Governors and told them to take care of themselves. He's abdicated responsibility. Fortunately for those of us here in NY, Governor Cuomo seems to be emerging as a real leader during this. I'm not so sure about the mayor of our city.

Mayor de Blasio announced that NYC is likely to enact a "Shelter in Place" order in the next 48 hours. You will only be able to leave your homes for groceries, health care, and exercise. (The exercise seems a gray area to me.) You will be required to stay at least 6 feet away from people you don't live with. That has sparked a panic run on groceries. Lines are out the door all over the neighborhood.

Meanwhile in Washington, the White House announcements are getting more and more blunt and dire, but they are missing the point. All we want to know is what is going on and what we should do.

"Shelter in Place" could easily expand to lockdown if people don't start changing their behaviors. We don't know where the virus is. We aren't doing any testing. That's what we should be doing. We need to be prepared to be in our homes for a while. Our new normal is being created daily. Stay open to it. Let's live our lives and respect the people around us enough to let them live theirs as well.

March 18, 2020
2,507 Total Reported Cases in New York. 60 Deaths.

The Norwegian Bliss is now not heading to Norfolk but instead "south." A two-year-old passenger from two cruises ago tested positive for the virus but there is no way of knowing if said passenger had it while they were on the ship. So far, everyone on board reports feeling fine.

Several days ago, friends in Germany told me that our President had been in contact with a German company about creating a vaccine for the virus and promised them a fortune if they would develop it for the sole use of the US. Presumably, he would then market it to other countries in the world at a huge profit. Yesterday, this came out in the news here. This is called profiteering. Bertolt Brecht wrote a whole play about it called *Mother Courage and her Children*.

Another friend of mine is attempting to get back home to Australia. Flights that were once hundreds of dollars are now over two thousand. Does that seem like a good public relations ploy—gouge your loyal customers when they need help the most?

Because of my job, and because of my family, my sphere of friends encircles the globe. Every single one of us is going through this.

London is facing an imminent lockdown. Schools across Britain are expected to close by the weekend. Much like here, it seems that their national government is not fully communicating with their local governments in terms of coordinating. The Mayor of London is complaining that he is being left in the dark. The West End has shut down. The Olivier Awards have been postponed.

South Africa has suddenly enacted a whole series of emergency measures almost overnight. Friends and family there say that they feel as if they are several weeks behind the rest of us on the timeline but are catching up.

There is an interesting debate going on around the world about "Herd Immunity." Herd immunity occurs when enough people have the antibodies that it creates an effective firewall against the spread of a virus. A vaccine can create immunity, but so can getting and surviving it.

Holland appears to be advocating that the country NOT go into lockdown so that 50-60% of the population will get it and achieve herd immunity that way. The problem with all our social distancing, they argue, is that as soon as we come out of isolation, the virus can begin to spread anew. Given what the resulting death count will be, the Dutch are being slammed for this approach.

In Australia, the AFL (Footy) season is starting as scheduled, which seems a bit ridiculous because indoor gatherings of over 100 people are banned. Schools in Australia are staying open—the argument being that if they close then the parents of those kids won't be able to work. Qantas has stopped 90% of its regular flights and Virgin Australia has stopped all of theirs.

Then there are our friends to the north in Canada. The announcement came today that we are closing the US/Canadian border to all non-essential activity. Trade will still be allowed to happen, but no non-essential people will be able to travel back and forth. Bars and Restaurants are now closed to everything except take-out. Gyms are closing. Museums and theatres are all closed.

Strangely, the one thing that everyone seems to be experiencing no matter where they are, is panic hoarding of toilet paper. My friends in Germany can't find any. None of us can.

Everyone, everywhere, is trying to make sense of this without really knowing the best way to combat it.

The leaders of the world are people. They aren't saints. Even the great ones have flaws. We need to let them learn from mistakes and change their minds. We must hope that they talk to each other and share whatever information they have. This is a crisis that requires us to become educated and listen and evolve our behaviors. When all of this is over, we are truly going to look back and applaud those who did their all without profit or greed. Now is not the time to amass a fortune, now is the time to take care of each other and get each other through this—calmly, safely, intelligently, and hopefully with as much humor as we can.

March 19, 2020
4,221 Total Reported Cases in New York. 88 Deaths.

The earth is getting a breather because of this crisis. With tourism halted, everything is going to get a chance to grow back. Less travel means far less pollution is going to be pumped into the atmosphere. Over-visited places have emptied.

According to reports, the water in Venice is clearing up. You can look down into the canals and see fish.

Governor Cuomo just suspended mortgage payments for 90 days for those out of work. That's a relief. That's the kind of decision that helps people. Next step, rents.

March 20, 2020
7,660 Total Reported Cases in New York. 143 Deaths.

NY is forecasting that we could potentially need 30,000 ventilators and we currently only have about 5,000-6,000 of them. Ventilators are a necessary tool for the treatment of people who have contracted the virus and are experiencing serious respiratory symptoms like pneumonia. The entire federal government's emergency stockpile of ventilators which is meant to supply the whole country is just 12,000. If we run out, doctors are going to have to choose which patients get them and which patients don't. That might seem unthinkable, but that's what's already happening in Italy.

A couple of days ago when the President had his phone meeting with the State Governors and told them that they should take care of themselves, what he did was put 50 different states at odds with each other. Each of them, now, is going out into the Global Marketplace on the hunt for ventilators. New York now has people in China looking for ventilators. Every other country in the world and even other states are doing the same thing.

Our federal government has the power to force manufacturers to start creating them. Car and appliance manufacturers could be making more ventilators as we speak.

What do we do? How do we fix this? We do exactly what we are doing. We let the people who we elected to represent us—our public servants—go out there and do their jobs. If there are ventilators to be found, our Governor will find them. We all feel like we must do something, ourselves. Well, right now, as ridiculous as that sounds, we just need to keep each other safe by following the guidelines as best we can.

The Norwegian Bliss is due to arrive at the Port of Miami at 5 pm. Here's hoping.

MARCH 21, 2020
10,410 Total Reported Cases in New York. 195 Deaths.

Michael and I have been going back and forth about where we think the best place to ride this out is. Should we stay in NY or get out?

Staying in NY is what feels right to me. When 9/11 happened, I was stuck out in Pennsylvania. I couldn't get back into the city for three days because the bridges and tunnels were closed. It felt wrong not to be here,

It will be rough here in the coming weeks because of the concentration of cases. But there are also more resources here than in rural areas. I don't know that this is the right answer, but it's the one we are going with... for now.

New Yorkers are nothing if not resilient and resourceful. Out of protective masks? We will make them! IATSE union wardrobe members and stitchers have teamed up with Governor Cuomo to make face masks for medical personnel. We got no federal help in 9/11 and we managed to sort it out. Getting no help now, we are on it. This is why I want to stay in NY.

Jersey Boys has suspended the rest of this season's US tour. Two incoming Broadway plays, *The Hangman*, and the revival of *Who's Afraid of Virginia Woolf*, have closed for good. Without any income from ticket sales, there is no way for them to cover any expenses such as the ongoing rental of equipment.

Once this is over, most shows will need to start again from scratch. Not only will they need to recapitalize to fund the restart, but they are going to have to somehow convince theatregoers that it is safe to return.

In my experience, it takes about 6 weeks for an actor to get stuck in a bad habit and then forget that they have ever done whatever the moment is, in a different way.

Sometimes, after a while, and for whatever reason, an actor will start moving onstage a few words earlier or a few words later than they were directed to do in a particular moment. I then need to remind them when they are supposed to do it.

If it has been a couple of months since I've seen them, though, the response from the actor sometimes the response is more along the lines of, "So that's a change?" They've been doing it the "wrong" way for so long that they have forgotten that it was ever any other way.

As a country, we are now all doing things differently. We are eating at home—exclusively. We will all soon be shopping from home, online—exclusively. We are not gathering in groups of more than 10. We are setting up FaceTime dinner dates and Zoom meetings. It all seems strange now, but in 6 weeks it isn't going to feel so odd. We are going to get used to this.

When the pandemic is over, (and it will be) we won't be the same. We are going to have to either re-learn past behaviors or leave those behind and move forward with the new ones that we've created. We are going to have to consciously learn how to get close again—how to be comfortable in a crowd.

Human beings are incredibly adaptable. Look around. Could anyone have predicted just how radically our society would change in so short a time? We are living through history. We are in one of those moments that become markers on the timeline for one reason or another. WWI, the Spanish Flu, WWII, 9/11.

The NCL Bliss is now in the Port of Miami. The *Jersey Boys* company and crew are still awaiting disembarking instructions. Given the travel restrictions and the fact that they live all over the world, it is going to take a minute to repatriate everybody. Welcome back to the world.

March 22, 2020

15,191 Total Reported Cases in New York. 249 Deaths.

It's been two full weeks.

We all need to stop listening to the daily White House briefings. They are not helpful. The President is not able to hold in-person rallies, so his White House briefings have become a substitute for him. Despite having experts with him, he is still spreading dangerous misinformation. He lacks clarity and coherence. Lacking empathy, there is nothing about how he addresses us that is comforting or constructive. We can't do anything about them happening except to stop watching them.

On the other hand, Governor Cuomo is clearly outlining the obstacles that are in the way. He is knowledgeable on the virus, how government works and what can be done.

This is going to go on for a while… "4 months—6 months—9 months," said the Governor this morning. Nine months takes us to the end of the year. This could be what our lives are like for the entire rest of the year.

Rest assured that you are not alone in being terrified that you're going to run out of money. We are all terrified of that. The fact that we are all in the same boat should, however, be a cause for comfort. Because we are all experiencing the same thing there will have to be a national economic response to this. It's just simple basic common sense.

Life is going on. We are figuring this all out and we have each other. That's not nothing. That's everything.

MARCH 23, 2020
First case reported in Belize.

This is now boring. The president is bored. He's looking at the economic numbers and he's panicking. He's indicating that he's leaning towards relaxing social distancing at the end of the week. The medical experts working with him, agree that these strictures cannot be relaxed yet.

The wave of infections hasn't happened yet. We can't stop it, but we can do some things to manage its effects once it gets here. That is what social distancing is designed to do. We cannot stop this behavior too early. Hong Kong learned that lesson the hard way. They relaxed restrictions and in return got a whole new wave of infections. The problem, of course, is that every step that we take to minimize the coming spike in cases is bad for the economy.

The White House only cares about the economy. This morning Governor Cuomo announced that at the end of the week, he would be looking at what relaxing social distancing here in NY would mean. He's being a politician. We need the federal government's help. He's trying not to annoy the president. He's not really going to relax social distancing.

The Republicans are resisting invoking the Defense Production Act to make ventilators because it removes those manufacturers' ability to make a profit. They would rather lose lives than money.

Washington does not believe that this is happening or that it can happen to them. Most federal lawmakers are in the most vulnerable parts of the population and they don't seem to realize it. Senator Rand Paul tested positive for the virus yesterday. This was after he had spent the morning, despite all the warnings, in the Senate gym.

The Republican economic stimulus bill that the Democrats voted against yesterday only helped businesses. It contained large corporate bailouts with no strings attached. It would have allowed the administration to bail out companies on their own without Congressional oversight. It even snuck in abortion restrictions and limitations on not-for-profits' ability to receive support. The Republican Senate is looking at this as an opportunity. It's not an opportunity, it's a crisis.

We are going to see the fight between the health of the population vs. the health of the economy escalate. Both need to remain healthy. For the moment, though, both just need to remain alive.

As somebody posted yesterday, "We can save the world by staying on the couch and watching TV? Let's not screw this up!" It's going to get much more boring than it already is before this is all over.

March 24, 2020
First cases reported in Laos, Libya, and on Easter Island.

6 out of 7 of the President's top seven revenue-producing clubs and resorts had to close because of the coronavirus restrictions so the President announced yesterday that he was considering a move to reopen businesses next week.

We got some further clarification on the rest of the Republican's stand on the matter, too. Dan Patrick, the Lt. Governor of Texas said yesterday that grandparents should be willing to sacrifice themselves for the good of the economy. Let that sink in.

The good news is that neither the President nor the Federal government can reopen anything because they didn't close anything down in the first place. The states did. This isn't under federal control.

The President is now touting "cures" that are not only not proven therapies but are also, in fact, sometimes dangerous. There were reports of somebody dying yesterday because they took too much of one of the unproven drugs, he erroneously announced yesterday would cure COVID-19.

I just heard that Julia Miles, the founder of The Women's Project passed away this week.

While I was still in college, I was lucky enough to work on several projects with Julia. She started The Women's Project to give women a chance to tell stories that mattered to them and that were created by them. In the 1970s this was a novel idea. The most notable of the shows I did was the revue *A…My Name is Alice*.

Alice was a revue of songs and skits—each written by a different team—by or about women. It was directed by Julianne Boyd (who now runs The Berkshire Theatre Company) and Joan Micklin Silver (a noted film director of movies such as *Hester Street*, *Chilly Scenes of Winter*, and *Crossing Delancey*). We started it in the basement of the American Place Theatre on 46th Street and then ran it for about a year and a half downtown at the Village Gate in Greenwich Village.

Throughout my career, I have been lucky enough to work for a whole array of truly accomplished women who taught me much of what I know of the business: Stage Managers, Directors, and Producers. And I've worked for performers—Patti LuPone and Bernadette Peters for example—who have each created incredible careers that have lasted decades and kept me employed for years. These women, and countless, countless others that I have been privileged to work for and with, owe something to women like Julia Miles who led the charge.

I can't help but think what would be happening in the country now if we were being led by a woman.

March 25, 2020
30,841 Total Reported Cases in New York. 632 Deaths.

Today is hard. Jackson Browne has the virus. Prince Charles has it. Friends have it.

We lost Terrance McNally yesterday to complications from this virus. He was the man who became the powerful and uplifting voice of the last huge global pandemic in the 1980s. He was the man whose play *Love! Valour! Compassion!* gave my husband his Broadway debut. He's gone.

For those of you not here in New York, who are concerned, it is not carnage in the streets here. Quite the opposite. It is extremely quiet. There are people outside. Walking dogs. I can see them from our windows. Individuals, not groups. It's much easier to stay inside when the weather is as bleak as this and more and more people are doing just that. The Mayor is talking about closing some of the city's streets to traffic to give people more room to walk around and still maintain social distancing.

The estimates are that the virus in New York will spike three weeks from now. We currently have the most cases in the country here in NY. One of the reasons for that is that we have, by far, done the most testing compared to other states. So, what this means is that we have the most known cases of this virus.

Living like this is very hard and it's really getting old. What we are doing now would have been considered the plot of a science fiction thriller two weeks ago. What will things be like two weeks from now?

In the meantime, all we can do is stay where we are. Hunker down. Love each other. Take a shower. Get dressed. Make our beds. Eat well. We've got this.

March 26, 2020
37,397 Total Reported Cases in New York. 867 Deaths.

The USNC Ship Comfort is about to be deployed to NY. It will have 1000 beds and will deal with what the hospitals overrun with virus cases cannot. It is the largest trauma facility on the planet.

Almost everything in the city is closed. Grocery stores are open. People are lining up on the street to get in while staying 6 feet apart. They are only letting a limited number of people in at a time. For the most part, shelves are stocked. Cleaning products, however, are in short supply. Somewhere downtown, I scored a couple of large cans of Lysol. They have a Mango-Hibiscus scent that is truly disgusting. But if that's why they were sitting on the shelf, I'm not going to complain.

We have a couple of little bottles of Purell leftover from swag bags and international flight bags. We are using it while we have it, but it's one of the things that you cannot get anywhere in the city. When we get home, we take off our shoes at the door and wash our hands. We disinfect each thing that we bought by wiping them down with Lysol and then wash our hands again.

Here's what I have learned about the virus:

The COVID virus is not a living organism, but a protein molecule (DNA) covered by a protective layer of fat, which, when absorbed by the cells of the eye, nose, or mouth changes their genetic code and converts them into aggressor and multiplier cells. Since the virus is not a living organism, but a protein molecule, it can't be killed, but it can decay. The disintegration time depends on the temperature, humidity, and type of material upon which it rests.

The virus is very fragile—the only thing that protects it is that layer of fat. That's why we are all washing our hands with soap. Soap dissolves the fat layer and destroys the protein molecule.

While the virus is lying on cloth it is quite inert. After 3-6 hours it will degenerate on its own. For copper surfaces, it takes about 4 hours. (Copper is naturally antiseptic—SO glad we went with copper kitchen counters when we redid the kitchen!) It can also last up to 4 hours on wood, but up to 24 hours on cardboard and 42 hours on metals other than copper, and 72 hours on plastics.

We should all keep our living spaces clean and well-ventilated and open our blinds. UV light from the sun also breaks this molecule down. We should be washing our hands several times a day for 20 seconds at a time. Groceries and packages that come into our living spaces should be wiped down.

People are staying at home especially because yesterday was cold and rainy. Despite the gloom, however, there were signs of spring everywhere. Everything is in bloom—flowers are up, all of New York City's trees are in full flower. Because the city is so quiet, you can hear the birds.

People are starting to call what we are doing Physical Distancing rather than Social Distancing. This is a much better idea. This is not the time to be apart from each other in any way other than physically. Check-in. People who seem fine one day can freak out the next. Let's pick up the phone and stay in contact with each other.

March 27, 2020
44,701 Total Reported Cases in New York. 1,139 Deaths.

I haven't woken up to an alarm in weeks. While I have showered every day, I haven't used any hair product in days. Who's looking at me? I haven't put in any contact lenses. I need them for seeing detail at a distance. I'm not looking at anything at a distance. I haven't been to a show. I'm not driving.

Our spending is now a fraction of what it once was. We aren't buying theatre tickets. We aren't eating out. We aren't going out for drinks. We aren't buying clothes. We aren't buying snacks or coffee or any one of a hundred things that you pick up over a day. I'm not traveling anywhere. I'm not going to museums. I'm not renting cars. I'm not buying ridiculous things in other countries that we have no room for back in the apartment. We are just buying food and cleaning supplies.

Things around the apartment that were broken are getting fixed. Slowly, but it's happening.

Those little pieces of things that sit around in dishes—for years—are now getting glued back to the things they fell or broke off of. The piles of papers and miscellaneous nonsense that seem to be everywhere are getting worked through. It started slowly, but now that I am seeing results, it's going faster. Stuff is getting tossed. Or filed. Or just put away.

I have a 4' stack of books next to the bed to be read and I'm back to reading a bit each day.

There are currently seven living things residing in our apartment: Michael, Me, the cat, a thirty-year-old rubber plant, an orchid in the middle of its glorious third blooming, a new pot of daffodils, and the yeast starter for the sourdough bread that Michael has started baking. He has named it Booboo. The bread-making gives Michael the structure for his day. It requires constant attention between timed gaps. The result is good. Unfortunately, too good. The neighbors are getting some of it so that we don't eat it all ourselves.

We watch the news of the world unfold on TV until we can't stand it anymore.

Mark Blum who Michael spent a year with on Broadway in *12 Angry Men* passed away yesterday. The British Prime Minister Boris Johnson tested positive for the virus yesterday.

The government in Washington continues to fail us. Badly. There are now more and more Republicans who are calling upon the older generation to sacrifice themselves for the good of our economy. These people are the same people who wailed that Obamacare would lead to Death-Panels that would decide who would live and who would die.

Our Governor is not always easy to hear, but what he's saying will help us all get through this. As someone who has been through cancer, I can tell you that what gets you through it is a plan. When everything is unknown, it's scary. When you know what's against you, you can move forward.

In New York, we are three weeks away from what they think will be the highest point of this spike. The rest of the country is probably going to peak sometime after that. In the meantime, we just need to keep living our weird new lives—cleaning, sorting, reading, watching, eating, and baking, and loving each other.

March 28, 2020
52,400 Total Reported Cases in New York. 1,492 Deaths.

The two parties are fighting over a stimulus package. It is a $2.2 trillion coronavirus and relief bill called the CARES Act. (The Corona Virus Aid, Recover and Economic Securities Act—HR 748.)

The primary point of contention over it has been a provision that allowed Treasury Secretary Steven Mnuchin sole discretion to disburse $500 billion in revenue to whichever corporation he feels should get it. Those disbursements would remain secret for six months. After a lot of back and forth, the Democrats have managed to add in an independent inspector and an oversight board to monitor the funds,

The President then lied to the public about what else the Democrats had added to the bill—there was no "Green New Deal" and no windmills. Nonetheless, he signed it, but he included a "signing statement."

Under past Presidents, these used to be innocuous statements of thanks and support but under G.W. Bush they started being a way for the President to challenge items in the Bill without deciding to veto the whole thing. What the President said in this signing statement was that he would ignore the oversight provisions. Nancy Pelosi has said that she anticipated this move (Remember that the President is looking for some of that bailout money for his own companies) and that there are many levels of oversight included in the Bill to countermand this.

On the plus side, the President is now finally forcing General Motors to make ventilators under the Defense Production Act. They say they can build them in 100 days which is all well and good, but projections put our peak need here in New York City in 20 days.

The President is denying assistance to states whose Governors aren't being "nice" to him. He reportedly recently said to his Vice-President, "Don't call the woman in Michigan." Michigan's Governor Gretchen Whitmer has said that shipments of medical supplies that were coming to her state were canceled and are now going to the Federal government instead.

States with decent leadership are in far better shape than states with ineffective leaders. Florida Governor, Ron DeSantis, has been extremely slow to respond to this crisis and shut things down. I wonder how many people he killed by allowing the beaches to remain open for Spring Break.

Dealing with all of this is not easy. We have a long way to go, but we are getting there. Stay the course. Breathe and be safe. Be kind. Love.

March 29, 2020
59,648 Total Reported Cases in New York. 1,874 Deaths.

I have no idea what day of the week it is.

Five or six years ago, *Jersey Boys* played in Tokyo for two weeks. While I was there, I bought some Luwak Coffee as a gift for Michael. In Indonesia, there is a small animal called a Civet cat. It's a bit bigger than a house cat. This animal eats coffee beans and then poops them out. These beans are collected from the forest floor, roasted, and then brewed to make what is the world's smoothest cup of coffee. Or so they claim. Some people cruelly keep these cats in captivity to generate this coffee, but I was assured by the people I bought this coffee from that these beans were not farmed, they were collected in the wild.

It is the most expensive coffee on the planet. I spent well over $100 for enough of these beans to make a single pot of coffee. The little handful of beans were shrink-wrapped and the box they were in has sat in the kitchen ever since I gave them to Michael. We kept waiting for the perfect occasion to grind and brew up the beans. Well, this morning we made the pot of Luwak coffee. Whatever day of the week this is seemed to us to be occasion enough.

Verdict? Good… It was, indeed, very smooth—none of coffee's usual acidity. Was it worth the money? Who can say what a unique experience is worth? I certainly wouldn't spend that kind of money on something so ridiculous now but I'm glad we were able to try it.

We are all going to experience the worst of this pandemic at different times in different parts of the country and around the world. New York City is going to peak before many other places. Some places around the world are where we were two weeks ago. Three weeks ago, a month ago. We are not going to be able to resume traveling as usual until everybody has passed their peaks.

The President yesterday threatened to officially quarantine New York, by force if necessary. That turned out to be completely illegal so today he backed off but not before he panicked a lot of people. So far nearly 70,000 people with health care experience have volunteered to assist in New York State hospitals. Over 6,000 mental health professionals have volunteered to help as well. They are offering their services without charge.

None of us are in this alone. Do not suffer in silence. Reach out. Organizations that can help are almost everywhere. We will get through this—if you're reading this, we are getting through this.

MARCH 30, 2020
66,663 Total Reported Cases in New York. 2,286 Deaths.

This morning the USNS Comfort sailed into New York's harbor, made its way up the Hudson, and is now, for the immediate and foreseeable future, docked in midtown Manhattan.

It is what is called a Mercy-class hospital ship and is the 2nd of its kind to join the US Navy's fleet. It is a non-commissioned ship that is crewed by civilians from something called the Military Sealift Command. Its purpose here in NY during the pandemic is to relieve NYC hospitals of patients with non-coronavirus-related issues.

I am sure there far are more than the usual amounts of home accidents these days: people changing lightbulbs in lamps that have been out for months and getting shocked or falling off step ladders reaching for the ones in the ceiling, people drilling a hole through their hands as they finally try and fix something that has been broken for years, and people crushing their hands as they reach between the mechanism of the sofa bed trying to retrieve the skinny remote that has slipped in. (Of course, those are all things that have almost happened to me during this last week, alone. Almost...)

People with other medical issues are still battling those through all of this, too. They still need to go to hospitals for transfusions and radiation treatments and chemo sessions, check-ups. It's not as if those things have just been put on hold along with everything else. The people who need to go through them are particularly at risk from this virus given their reduced immune systems.

In addition to getting help from the USNS Comfort, a Christian relief organization called Samaritan's Purse in partnership with the Mount Sinai Health System has been setting up a mobile field hospital on the East Meadow in Central Park. Samaritan's Purse is a missionary group, and they provide aid to people in physical need as their way of accomplishing that. Their president is Billy Graham's son Franklin Graham. Their encampment looks like something out of a science-fiction movie.

The streets are very quiet. Some cars are out but not a lot. There are occasional buses. The fancy high-end stores on Madison Avenue are closed. Some of them have been emptied of their stock, some are just sitting there fully stocked with the lights off.

As I walked down Madison Avenue this morning, I could hear birds. It feels like we are waiting for the tsunami to strike. We are at that weird time when the water has all gone out and we are looking in wonder at an empty seabed.

I surely hope that wall of water isn't coming.

MARCH 31, 2020
75,853 Total Reported Cases in New York. 2,775 Deaths.

The Samaritan's Purse emergency field hospital that is opening in Central Park seems to be raising more and more questions with each passing hour. The leader of this organization, Franklin Graham, has stated his belief is that marriage is defined as "exclusively the union of one genetic male and one genetic female" and the unrighteous who disagree will be sentenced to "everlasting punishment in hell."

They are a huge organization with $650 million in assets. One of their programs is called Operation Christmas Child. Under that, they deliver gifts to kids in Muslim countries as a kind of conversion scheme. There are reports that the volunteers who are setting this camp up agree to follow their stance on homosexuality before being allowed to help. One wonders what kind of care the patients who don't conform to this narrow, bigoted view will receive.

At a time when New Yorkers are pulling together and working as one, this seems like a blight. I wish that the Mayor had given this some better consideration before agreeing to let them continue. I am surprised that Mount Sinai agreed to work with them. Help for "some" is not what this city is about. The whole undertaking has taken on a far more sinister air.

A doctor named Dave Price who is a Pulmonary Medicine and Critical Care Fellow at Weill Cornell Medical Center in NY posted that you are going to get COVID-19 almost exclusively from your hands touching your face—eyes, nose, mouth. If you assume that everyone around you, has it and behave accordingly, you can protect yourself. The main thing that wearing a mask does for the general population, in his opinion, is to keep you from touching your face.

I'm happy to add that to the ever-expanding list of things we are learning about this virus. We will all be experts when this is behind us.

APRIL 1, 2020
90,377 Total Reported Cases in New York. 3,411 Deaths.

As we head into our fourth week of this, it feels like we are being inundated with numbers. At any time of the day or night when you turn on the television, that's what you'll get.

Yesterday, the White House claimed that the best-case scenario for the US would be 100,000—240,000 deaths. They then blamed NY for its "slow start" as a reason for the issues we are facing here.

By the end of January and beginning of February, the Washington Post reported that most Intelligence included in the President's daily briefings was about the virus. That means that for many weeks, knowing what was going on, he was still proclaiming the virus a hoax. He is now blaming his delay in responding to the crisis on the distraction his impeachment trial caused. It should be noted that he was acquitted on February 6.

On February 7—which we now know is long after he had been warned about the virus coming here—the US State Department facilitated the delivery of 17.8 TONS of PPE supplies to China which included masks, gowns, gauze, respirators, and other materials. We are now facing extreme shortages here, in this country, of all those things.

The first case of the virus in NY was reported on March 1—just two days after the President publicly declared that the virus was non-existent and a Democratic ruse. Following that, Governor Cuomo called a crisis meeting with what he called "a SWAT team of government officials." He had a three-page memo that he'd drafted that outlined a basic plan. The Governor then pushed for legislation that gave him unilateral executive powers for any declared state emergency. Before this, he did not have the power to order home quarantines or mandate testing, etc. Now, because of that bill, he does.

It turns out that the *Jersey Boys* company took over a week to disembark from the Norwegian Bliss and head home. Despite that delay, they were extremely lucky. There are still many ships out there floating around with not only their crews on board but also their passengers. Today, the U.S. Coast Guard has directed all cruise ships to remain at sea indefinitely. They directed the cruise lines to send any severely ill passengers to the countries where the ships are registered. For most of the major U.S. lines, that means the Bahamas. The Bahamas is in no fit state to be able to care for those people. They have still not recovered from last year's hurricanes.

Cruise ships register in places like the Bahamas (NCL), Panama, and Malta purely to avoid paying US taxes. The Cruise companies get to keep a massive amount of their profits as a result. Well, now we are experiencing the downside to that. In terms of the law, because of this practice, these aren't our ships.

Most people who get this virus will get sick to varying degrees, and recover. Completely. Many people who get the virus will never have any symptoms. They may never know they've had it. Here's a good number: over 6,000 people suffering from coronavirus in New York hospitals have been discharged and sent home. That's comforting news.

Let's concentrate on that. Not the idiocy coming out of the White House. Not the stuff we can't control. Let's concentrate on what we can do for each other. For now, that's simply to keep our distance.

APRIL 2, 2020
100,780 Total Reported Cases in New York. 4,138 Deaths.

The city is in full glorious bloom. There are beautiful trees screaming color up and down New York's streets and avenues. Every meridian and every flower box have in them a riot of color from crowds of spring bulbs. I'm sure that this is something that happens every year at this time, but until now, I am sad to say that I don't think that I have never fully noticed it.

These days, there is a level of quiet in New York that is mind-boggling. Buses are still running and there is the occasional taxi and car, but then there are vast stretches of time when even the largest avenues are empty.

All non-essential construction has been put on hold. That steady thumping of digging, building, and demolition equipment that it almost seems like the heartbeat of the city has stopped.

Crowded sidewalks have drastically thinned out. People aren't screaming at each other trying to rise above the usual rave-level decibels of the city. There is nobody to listen to the poor man out in the middle of 72nd Street screaming and ranting.

Periodically the silence is broken by a siren from a fire truck or an ambulance. The level of volume from them seems completely unnecessary. In some ways, hearing how loud they really are and realizing how easy they usually are to ignore makes you understand just how loud the city usually is.

There's none of that noise these days, so when you walk down the empty city streets nothing is distracting you from looking at all our trees. It's overwhelming.

As New Yorkers, we have an innate sense of spatial relationships. Without thinking, we can walk down the street and never bump into anybody no matter how crowded it might be. We can tell from 30 feet away, based on how fast somebody is walking across the street whether we are going to collide, and we can adjust long before we get there. We often cross within inches of each other but both of us know exactly where we are and know that we aren't going to hit. This alarms tourists who come from far less crowded places and are not at all comfortable with what we all just take for granted.

The advent of cell phones has screwed a lot of this up. People lose all sense of where they are in relation to other people when they are glued to their phones. They behave like drunk drivers on a jammed freeway. Now, though, out on the streets, we are staying extremely far away from each other. 6 feet is the minimum mandated by government guidelines but lots of people are staying much farther away from each other than that. Walking down the street yesterday, for the first time, I was aware of people *instinctively* veering out of each other's way starting from as far as 20 feet away. It's getting into our subconscious. In a few more weeks we are going to forget that it was ever any other way.

The English have an expression, supposedly based on a Chinese curse (although there doesn't seem to be any such curse) that says, "May you live in interesting times." We are certainly living in interesting times. We have never experienced anything like this.

Like anything new, some of it is anxiety-provoking, but it is also amazing. The whole world is going through the same thing. The whole world. We shouldn't let fear stop us from seeing it and experiencing the "Wow."

April 3, 2020
111,455 Total Reported Cases in New York. 4,899 Deaths.

The 1,000 bed USNS Comfort that was meant to relieve our hospitals currently has only 20 patients on board. The other ship that was sent to Los Angeles, the Mercy, has only 15 patients on board.

These ships are wartime trauma hospitals. If you are a 20-year-old soldier who has just been shot in the leg, they can help. However, if you are an older citizen suffering from something else, then the narrow military-style bunks the patients are bedded in are probably not going to help. There are 49 conditions, including COVID-19, that the ship will not accept. On top of that, ambulances are required to take patients to local hospitals first for testing for these other conditions before patients can be transferred to the ship.

So much for relieving local hospitals but thank you for the message of hope.

Arizona Governor Doug Ducey finally issued some stay-at-home guidelines and issued the order that non-essential services close. NOT included in those orders are, strangely, nail and hair salons and golf courses. Under Arizona law, the mayors of Phoenix and other Arizona cities are powerless to close these businesses themselves. This means that if the nail and hair salons close voluntarily that they will not be eligible for any state aid so, in effect, are being forced to stay open.

Governor Rick DeSantis of Florida finally issued a state-wide stay-at-home order except that he exempted Churches. There are 2,900 Baptist churches in Florida. That's just the Baptists. Seven of the 100 largest churches in the country with attendance at greater than 5,500 are in Florida. Yesterday, he then issued a second order which takes away individual cities' ability to put in stronger restrictions than the state has mandated. In other words, those Mayors who are trying to properly fight against the virus in their cities now, like in Arizona, have their hands tied.

There is a meme working its way through Facebook which says, "Having some states lockdown, and some states not, is like having a peeing section in a swimming pool."

The President's son-in-law Jared Kushner appeared at the White House press briefing yesterday and said, (referring to medical supplies) "The notion of the federal stockpile is that it is supposed to be our stockpile. It's not supposed to be state's stockpiles that they then use."

The federal government is an umbrella structure connecting the states. It isn't a thing or a population in and of itself. It has no population. Does Kushner think that the stockpile of supplies is for his family in the White House?

Andrew Yang, the erstwhile Democratic Presidential candidate said this yesterday, "We Asian Americans need to embrace and show our American-ness in ways we never have before. We need to step up, help our neighbors, donate gear, vote, wear red, white, and blue, volunteer, fund aid organizations, and do everything in our power to accelerate the end of this crisis. We should show without a shadow of a doubt that we are Americans who will do our part for our country in this time of need."

Do Asian-American citizens need to prove to the rest of the population that they aren't the virus? I imagine that if the President keeps referring to the virus as the China flu that the answer might be yes.

There's not very much we can do about the failings of our government except to speak up about them. Do better. We're watching.

April 4, 2020
1.1 million cases reported worldwide.

Every night at 7 pm New York City erupts in an explosion of sound. Out on our balconies or leaning out of our windows, we make noise. We applaud, bang on saucepans, and hoot and holler. That sound is for the hospital workers and first responders who are putting their lives on the line every day.

When I was a kid in New Jersey, the town siren would go off at 6 or 7 pm and we all knew that was when we needed to get on our bikes and go home. Now, every night for the last week or so, the joyful noise starts at 7 pm and it marks the beginning of our evening with a moment of gratitude. Wherever we are and whatever we are doing we stop and join in.

I cannot begin to imagine what they are all dealing with out there today, but I do know that this is not the first time that they have had to fight an unknown and terrifying enemy.

In August of 1793, there was an outbreak of Yellow Fever in Philadelphia. Nobody knew what caused it and people panicked. At that time, Philadelphia had a population of 50,000 people. 20,000 people fled the city. Some neighboring towns refused to let these refugees in. Major port cities like New York and Baltimore instituted quarantines against people and goods from Philadelphia.

Philadelphia was then the capital of the United States. The federal government had no power to act in this crisis, so they didn't. Washington, who was President, continued to meet with his cabinet until September 10 when he left to go on a scheduled vacation. The rest of the legislature cut their meetings short a few days later when a dead body was discovered on the steps of the State House and they all panicked.

The epidemic burned out by itself by the beginning of November of that year after 10% of the population of Philadelphia perished. There were subsequent epidemics of Yellow fever—Baltimore in 1794, New York in 1795 and 1798, and Wilmington in 1798, and many more through the years. It was nearly a century later, though, in 1881 before it was finally discovered that the fever was transmitted by mosquitoes.

There is now a vaccine for Yellow Fever. It still occurs around the world—mostly in tropical locations. About 30,000 people lost their lives to it last year—mostly in Africa. Given how much I travel, I've been vaccinated against it.

In January of 1918, the H1N1 virus caused a pandemic that came to be known as the Spanish Flu. By the time the pandemic was over, it had infected about 500,000,000 people or about 25% of the world's population at the time. As many as 100,000,000 people lost their lives around the world to this flu.

World War I would not fully stop until November of 1918 when the Germans signed the Armistice. Ostensibly to maintain morale considering the brutality of the war, US censors minimized and clamped down on early reports of the virus's mortality. Germany, the US, France, and the UK all avoided factual reporting.

Spain, which had remained neutral, was free to report what was going on so the reports coming out of Spain were truly harrowing and included reports of the serious illness of their King. These reports created the false idea that Spain was particularly hard hit so that's why it started being called the Spanish Flu.

Researchers now believe that an early epicenter was a UK troop staging and hospital camp in Étaples, France, but there is some evidence that it had been circulating for months or even years before that. Some researchers even believe that it possibly began in China.

Like COVID-19, particles of the Spanish Flu or H1N1 virus are transmitted between people by coughing and sneezing. Those particles enter through the eyes, mouth, or nose. Crowded war-time conditions plus the lowered immune systems of the stressed-out soldiers in conjunction with massive troop movements across the world all contributed to the incredible spread.

In the US, the first case was reported in Haskell County, Kansas in January of 1918. By March 11, the virus had reached New York with the first case being reported in Queens. The pandemic came in two waves. The first wave was like a regular flu epidemic, the second wave which crested in October of 1918 was a result of the virus mutating. This second wave was devastating.

From what I can see, the people of the world did almost everything then that we are doing now. Public institutions were closed, and public gatherings were banned. Sporting venues and theatres were closed. Some schools were closed, some weren't. Some churches were closed, some weren't. People wore face masks.

This happened all over the world and how different countries responded, dictated how well they fared. New Zealand was slow to close its' ports and it got hammered as a result. This time around they are behaving in quite the opposite way, somehow remembering their history.

Here is a quote that I just read about the 1918 pandemic, "Cities where public health officials imposed multiple social containment measures within a few days after the first local cases were recorded cut peak weekly death rates by up to half compared with cities that waited just a few weeks to respond."

There was a complete lack of leadership from Washington at the time. State and local governments stepped in, erratically, to fill the vacuum. Public officials lied and spouted made-up facts. Woodrow Wilson got the flu, but the White House kept it a secret. States received no help from the government. People could not trust what they read.

Then it passed. The virus seems to have mutated again and it just stopped. By the end, it had killed twice as many people as those who died in all of World War I.

On April 24, 1981, Ken Horne was reported to the CDC with a rare disease, Kaposi's sarcoma.

He became known as patient zero for the AIDS pandemic. Nobody knew what it was. Nobody knew how it was transmitted—was it passed by physical contact? Airborne? People were afraid to get anywhere near people who might have it. I was in college in NY when it started. We were all terrified, truly terrified.

The response from Washington? Nothing. President Ronald Reagan never once publicly referred to it by name while he was in office. Officials in the White House joked about it being the "gay plague". ACT UP and other groups eventually forced the Government to acknowledge HIV/AIDS. Broadway Cares and Equity Fights Aids were both started to help people suffering from this disease because nobody else was. Since then, 75 million people have been infected with AIDS worldwide. 32 million people have died.

In 2009 another H1N1 virus appeared from the same family as the so-called Spanish flu: SARS.

8,000 people became infected with it and 10% of them died. There have been others. A lot of others. Epidemics have been a part of human life since time immemorial. They will be going forward too. With the current ease of global travel, the outbreaks have grown to pandemics.

There is nothing new about COVID-19 except its molecular make-up. It is just the latest in a very long line. These outbreaks happen and then we forget. Do you think we haven't forgotten about AIDS? Ask a 20-something. As impossible as it seems, once COVID-19 has passed, we will forget about this one, too.

In February of 2018, the President proposed deep budget cuts to both the CDC and WHO.

In May of 2018, National Security Advisor John Bolton dissolved the NSC's Office of Global Health Security and Biodefense that had been set up after the Ebola outbreak in 2016 by President Obama. The White House's response to COVID-19 was to appoint the Vice-President to head the task force. This is a man who not only has no medical expertise whatsoever, but also the man who is responsible for a sizable increase in HIV/AIDS cases in his home state of Indiana due to his actions as Governor.

Now, for some reason, the President's son-in-law Jared Kushner who has no government experience, let alone medical experience is addressing us about the response to the coronavirus. When Kushner misspoke about the purpose of the national stockpile, a reporter pointed out that the Government's website contradicted him. Rather than correct Kushner's remarks, the Administration has simply re-written the description. Given the ineptitude of this White House, they of course only rewrote it in one location and left the original description in others.

The take-away from all of this? We've been here before. Not only have we been here before, but we've been here before with the same kind of seemingly total Governmental incompetence that we are experiencing now. The people who have gotten us through them all have been our health care workers—working through the nights, putting themselves in harm's way, facing the un-faceable every day.

What I've learned from all the reading I've done this morning on global pandemics is that like all the others, this one, too, will pass. Every couple of decades we are going to repeat something like this because there seems to be something in us as a species that makes it impossible for us to remember. Maybe, in some regards, it's a blessing. It allows us to go through life with less anxiety.

Our health care workers won't forget though. Tonight at 7 pm, lean out your window and make some noise for the incredibly brave and dedicated people who are fighting the good fight right out there on the front lines. We are in the hands of those doctors and nurses who are risking their lives. For us. With us. Every day.

Let's make a LOT of noise.

April 5, 2020
132,700 Total Reported Cases in New York. 6,596 Deaths.

To wear a mask or not to wear one?

The World Health Organization officially says that you only need to wear a mask under certain conditions. The CDC has gone back and forth. Our President's inspiring recommendation is, and I quote, "You can do it—you don't have to do it. It's only a recommendation. I don't think I'm going to be doing it."

Dr. Anthony Fauci, the director of the National Institute of Allergy and Infectious Diseases said of the issue, "The thing that has inhibited that a bit (recommending that the public wear masks) is to make sure that we don't take away the supply of masks from the health-care workers who need them, But when we get in a situation when we have enough masks, I believe there will be some very serious consideration about broadening this recommendation of using masks. We're not there yet, but we're close."

Governor Cuomo says it couldn't hurt. Mayor de Blasio says that we should wear something.

The Japanese have been wearing masks when they are ill for years and the rest of us have all rolled our eyes.

New York City has a population of 8.6 million people in a very small physical area. If you include the greater metropolitan area that number goes up to 20.1 million people. Tokyo proper has a population of 13.9 million and when you add in their metropolitan area that number goes up to over 38 million people—almost twice as many people as we have here. The Japanese have learned that they must take care of each other. They are just too close together. That's a lesson we should probably learn too.

A couple of weeks ago we were talking to friends who have friends in Italy who had reported that despite recommendations to the contrary that Italians had started wearing masks out on the streets. At the time, we thought that was overkill. The Italians said that's what they all had thought a couple of weeks before, too.

Last week, I wasn't wearing a mask. This week, I am. I've started wearing a mask even when I'm completely by myself out on the street.

It couldn't hurt and it might just help.

April 6, 2020
142,561 Total Reported Cases in New York. 7,657 Deaths.

The President's news conference yesterday was followed by the network's usual post-conference Presidential fact-checking segment. How has that become a regular and expected part of this crisis?

It turned out that there was plenty to fact check. The President, again, was relentlessly pushing the completely untested anti-malarial drug hydroxychloroquine as something that people should try. "Why not, it couldn't hurt." When Dr. Anthony Fauci attempted to answer a reporter's question about the dangers of using this drug, the President interrupted and wouldn't let him finish. One person has already died from using this drug improperly. The assumed reason for his relentless pushing of this is that either the President himself or somebody else close to him owns stock in the company that makes the drug. How has that come to be an expected rationale to explain the President's actions?

It had been long enough since I'd last listened to him live that I had forgotten just how incoherent he is. He absolutely cannot string a sentence together that makes sense from beginning to end.

Governor Cuomo's news conferences continue to be informative and easy to follow. He is a comforting presence. Tough and direct. He is coherent. He has a sense of humor. Everything he says is broadcast with easy-to-read bullet points that follow along on the right of the screen. When he doesn't know he says, "I don't know." It's a relief.

The longer this goes on, the more we learn. Nobody recommended wearing masks, now they are. We can't let the changes in the rules throw us. Guidelines need to remain fluid as we learn more. Nobody knows everything however much we might want them to. That's OK. We're good.

April 7, 2020
149,974 Total Reported Cases in New York. 8,930 Deaths.

In Chicago, as of two days ago, it has been reported that 68% of the city deaths have involved African Americans.

Mayor de Blasio said Sunday that there is "a striking overlap of where this virus is doing the most damage and where we've had historic health care disparities."

A group called Lawyers' Committee for Civil Rights Under Law has issued a letter to the Federal Department of Health and Human Services as well as a freedom of information request to the CDC demanding that they release demographic data relating to the virus but thus far have not gotten a response.

It is hardly surprising that the racial disparity in our country would also affect health care during the pandemic but seeing the written evidence for it is chilling.

Countries around the world are not learning from each other. Despite what was happening in Italy, Boris Johnson in England was inclined to let the virus take its course thinking that in time enough people will have survived it that they will, in essence, protect the rest. Now the virus is running rampant in England and Boris Johnson is now in the ICU suffering from it, seriously, himself. This leaves the country without leadership right when it needs it the most.

To temporarily fill the vacuum, the Queen took the rare step of addressing the nation herself.

Her speech was, well, fantastic. Love her or hate her, you cannot deny that she has immense power as a person and perhaps as an institution. The thing she said that I found particularly moving was, "And though self-isolating may at times be hard, many people of all faiths, and of none, are discovering that it presents an opportunity to slow down, pause and reflect, in prayer or meditation." It's the "and of none" that I think is kind of remarkable. With those three words, whatever her own beliefs (she is the head of the Church of England), she included everybody.

Then Spain. Poor Spain. They are truly suffering although the number of deaths has now fallen for four days in a row which is a hopeful sign. They, too, were extremely slow to respond, thinking, like the United States, like England, that it was a THEM problem, not an OUR problem.

Every single country around the world and every single race and every single creed are susceptible to this virus. As of a couple of days ago, only 18 countries on the planet have no reported cases: Comoros, Kiribati, Lesotho, the Marshall Islands, Micronesia, Nauru, North Korea, Palau, Samoa, Sao Tome, and Principe, the Solomon Islands, South Sudan, Tajikistan, Tonga, Turkmenistan, Tuvalu, Vanuatu, and Yemen. Some of those may be able to avoid this as they are tiny remote island republics. Others like North Korea and some of the others probably do have cases, they just aren't being acknowledged.

This is not about them. This is about us. When will we begin to acknowledge that, as a planet, we are one group of people? This virus has done more to make us equal than anything else possibly could have and yet, we still find a way to favor one group over another when it comes to treating it.

April 8, 2020

160,185 Total Reported Cases in New York. 9,879 Deaths.

Are we still doing this?

Wuhan's 11 million residents were released from total lockdown this morning after 76 days.

Social distancing measures are still very much in effect there. Masks are mandatory. Travel restrictions are still very much in place. This morning, the only thing that changed was that they are now actually allowed to leave their homes because for the first time since this started there, 76 days ago, nobody died yesterday.

Here in NY, on the other hand, we may just be experiencing the beginning of our peak. You'd never know it from looking out the window and seeing people going about their lives. A friend of mine who lives near a hospital, however, just posted that a 2nd white refrigerator truck is now parked outside as a temporary morgue.

In 1918 during the Spanish Flu pandemic people who were quarantined at home did not have television. It hadn't been invented yet. People did not have radios in their homes—that only started to happen a few years later. Some people had telephones. The old candlestick-type phones. Often those phones were party lines—if you were lucky enough (and economically secure enough) to have a phone, you probably shared the phone with the rest of the people in your building.

What people did have were newspapers. Many papers, however, were following the Federal government's blackout on spreading news about the flu ostensibly to maintain morale.

We still have newspapers, but we rely far more on our televisions. As I write this, Senator Bernie Sanders is dropping out of the Presidential race. Vice-President Joe Biden is now the presumptive Democratic nominee. If we want to change how we are being led, the path forward now appears clear. But that's for later.

For now, we are home and to answer the question, yes, we are still doing this.

April 9, 2020

172,256 Total Reported Cases in New York. 10,929 Deaths.

Every crisis that we have faced in the past has changed us. Just think about how travel changed after 9/11. Having to take off our shoes started right after 9/11 in December when a terrorist tried to ignite explosives in his shoes on a flight from Paris to Miami. Not being able to carry water through security happened after an attempted attack in 2006 when a terrorist tried to mix two liquid chemicals on a flight out of the Philippines. We don't think about doing either thing anymore. They are an unremarkable and normal part of our lives.

What will our lives be like after COVID-19?

Reports coming out today are now suggesting that most New York coronavirus cases came from Europe rather than Asia.

The first case reported in the US was on January 21. The President imposed travel restrictions against China on February 2. 10 days later. The restrictions were geared toward non-US Chinese nationals only. Americans and permanent residents could continue to travel freely. In other words, the restrictions didn't stop anything. A friend of mine who lives on the west coast was working in China at the end of January and flew home. He got sick. He thought it was just a particularly bad case of the flu. He recovered and it was only later that he realized what it was that he'd probably had.

I flew to London on February 28. On March 1, I flew to the Isle of Jersey then back to London on March 2. I was in London until March 8 when I flew back to NY. During that week, I was on four flights, involving eight airports. We auditioned over 100 people in London that week for *Jersey Boys* on the NCL Bliss. I then saw six performances of West End plays that were either sold out or very close to it. On March 9, the day I got back, Michael and I went to a Gala dinner that was packed with people.

On the 10th, Michael developed a cough and aches. By the 11th, he had a fever. I was in auditions in New York on the 9th, 10th, and 11th. The night of the 11th, I sent an email to the folks I was doing the auditions with saying that I didn't feel great (sore throat, flushed, and achy) but that I'd come in if people were comfortable with me possibly being ill. The immediate response was that we should continue and that I should come in. By later that evening we decided to postpone my part of the *Jersey Boys* auditions on the 12th but continue with the music sessions.

We were scheduled to do Off-Broadway auditions on March 13th but canceled those as well. My body aches were bad enough at that point that I was having trouble sleeping. Michael was still feeling ill and by then he had lost his sense of smell.

Travel restrictions from Europe went into effect on the 13th but, like the Chinese travel restrictions, exempted US nationals and permanent residents rendering the restrictions pointless. When I returned from Europe on March 8, I wasn't stopped or questioned about anything when I landed. During the SARS pandemic, I remember landing in Hong Kong and going through a monitor that was there to detect people with fevers. Nothing like that was anywhere in evidence here in the US.

I was one of the thousands of people who came into NY from Europe during that period. Hundreds of thousands. And not one of us was monitored or tested. As late as March 25, a friend of mine's mother flew into San Francisco from Singapore and she, too, went through the airport with absolutely no screenings and no questions.

Michael and I were both fully recovered by about March 16th or 17th, but we were never able to get tested. How are we going to be able to responsibly start to reopen the US economy without really knowing where the virus is and how many of us have had it or have it? 16.8 million people have filed for unemployment in the last 3 weeks. That pressure is going to make everyone want to get back to business as usual long before we should.

This will change us. How doesn't matter, we'll know when it happens. Let's focus on now and doing our part to stop the spread. Honestly, what else can we do?

April 10, 2020
183,729 Total Reported Cases in New York. 11,850 Deaths.

In some ways, it feels like the world is doing a reboot. Everything is getting turned off and we are waiting for it all to be turned back on again. The screen is black, and we are just waiting until the prompt box pops up. We should probably all just get a cup of coffee and do something else until it's back.

It is being reported this morning that the US is now in a recession. It is an election year so all of Washington is understandably panicking. If the White House wants to reopen the economy, and it seems obvious that they do, they need to coordinate a nationwide testing mandate. We need to know where the virus is to be able to fight it. It's just that simple.

Yesterday, it was reported that the White House was going to stop funding mobile testing sites.

After the overwhelmingly negative response to this announcement, the White House has today extended support for the testing through May.

New York is well ahead of the nation, not to mention other countries, on per-capita testing. The New York State testing lab is now able to process 300 tests a day, they are hoping to get up to 2,000 tests a day by next week. New York State has a population of nearly 20 million people. It's still not nearly enough yet.

Last night, Michael and I attended a virtual Seder. It was a joyous, fantastic celebration with some wonderful people. Here's my favorite quote from the evening from a piece written by Rabbi David Hartman, "Passover is the night for reckless dreams; for visions about what a human being can be, what society can be, what people can be, what history may become."

We are rebooting. We are soon going to start again.

Let's take this opportunity to dream, recklessly dream, about what our new lives are going to look like. About what we can do to make our lives, here, together on this small beautiful green planet better. We have been given the chance. The prompt screen isn't even back up yet.

Dream.

לשנה הבאה בירושלים
L'shana haba-ah biy'rushalayim

APRIL 11, 2020
192,262 Total Reported Cases in New York. 12,772 Deaths.

The White House is going to try to push us out of our homes and back to work before it's fully safe to do so.

The economy does need to start up again. Millions upon millions of people are unemployed. At the height of the depression in the early 1930s, the unemployment rate was nearly 25%. We are currently at about 13% which is the worst since then. Even after the 2008 financial crisis we only got to about 10%.

They are going to push us back to the point where they feel that the level of resulting death will be acceptable. Companies are going to start gearing advertising towards us to convince us that everything is fine. They will urge us to relax and buy their product. Relax and go to the gym or pick up a latte. Chill out and go to a game or a show. They are going to downplay just how serious this virus is to get us to go out and spend. And, wow, do we all want that.

What do we all feel is an acceptable level of resulting death for coming back this soon? Is there such a thing?

The White House is launching a task force to decide how this will happen, while their expert, Dr. Fauci, is saying that the peak is still ahead of us. You don't plan for recovery from a war when you are in the middle of fighting it. Yes, we are going to need to recover, but we need to win the fight first.

There has been a 30% drop in pollution over the northeastern United States. It is at the lowest point that has ever been recorded since NASA started monitoring it. The air quality index in New Delhi was at 45 last month—this time last year it was 160. There are blue skies in India's major cities for the first time in recent memory. The air around the world is cleaner. The water is cleaner. Do we want to give all of that up?

For the last month, my spending has gone way down. We're buying food and supplies. On a usual pre-virus day, I would come home with a wallet full of receipts for all sorts of other things. The basis of our economy is that we, the citizens, spend money. It requires us to pay for transportation and to eat out. It needs us to buy clothes and disposable consumer products.

The Consumer Price Index is one of the major numbers that economists look at to judge the health of our economy and it's down. The price of oil, another key economic indicator, is way down. Who's going anywhere?

We used to make fun of my Dad for being a Depression baby. He was born in 1923 and came of age in Virginia during the worst financial crisis that the country had ever seen. He was a generous man in later years but loathe to spend frivolously. It went against everything he learned growing up. The rest of the family was all about spending frivolously. We didn't live through that time.

Maybe we should rethink some of how we were living before we dive back unthinking to exactly the way it was. We can all now choose how we return to "normal" and what that "normal" will look like. We have the time to think about it. Governor Cuomo just offered this quote from Winston Churchill, "Now this is not the end. It is not even the beginning of the end. But it is, perhaps the end of the beginning."

Nick Cordero is a Tony-nominated actor who has been in a coma for the last 12 days. His wife tweeted out last night that he needs our prayers now as he has taken a turn for the worse. Nick is a strapping healthy-looking guy with a beautiful wife and a young kid. He is only 41 years old. This is real. None of us are safe from this.

Let's stop for a minute and think about how we want to come back.

April 12, 2020
200,635 Total Reported Cases in New York. 13,710 Deaths.

Today, as marked in the Christian calendar, is Easter. The 40 days before Easter is called Lent. It is customary during this time to give up certain luxuries to honor Christ's 40-day journey into the desert. It seems that we've all done that.

This year Lent began on February 26 and lasted through this past Thursday, April 9. February 26 was the day that California announced the first case in the US with no clear source of exposure. It was the realization that the virus was here and the beginning of what led to us all giving up the luxury of freely living our lives.

Easter is typically celebrated as a time of hope and there are, indeed, signs of hope. Hospitalizations in New York City seem to have truly plateaued. The rate of new patients admitted has significantly dropped.

That said, the US has now passed Italy with the highest number of reported deaths. Despite that, some people don't believe that this is happening. There are churches across the country that are taking the stay-at-home orders as a violation of their right of freedom of assembly and their right to practice religion. There are churches across this country that plan on holding Easter services today as usual and people will die as a result.

So, what will be the signal that we can go back to our lives? I think realistically it's going to be the development and production of a vaccine. That could be six months away. Or less. Or more. Nobody knows yet.

Whatever your faith, let's celebrate the renewal of the season together. Download Zoom. The basic app is free. Not all our elderly friends and family have a working knowledge of the internet. Call them and listen to their voices and let them listen to yours. You don't need to go to church in person. For now, join in online.

There are signs of renewal everywhere. Happy Easter. Happy Passover. Happy Spring.

April 13, 2020
208,488 Total Reported Cases in New York. 14,728 Deaths.

We live on the 5th floor of our building in the back away from the street, but even so, there is usually a level of city noise that obliterates almost everything else. This morning, the only sound I could hear when I woke up was the rain hitting against the window and tapping on the air conditioner.

A couple of days ago, I was walking through Central Park, and I became aware of just how many kinds of birds make their homes there. I can identify the basic ones by sight—sparrows, chickadees, starlings, cardinals, blue jays—but there are plenty there that I have no idea what they are.

This isn't news to anyone who lives outside the city, but for the rest of us living here, I have an announcement: They all make their own sounds. At the same time. Starlings have a kind of chirping shriek—that's not a very good description, but up until now, I had never noticed it. I walked through the park, listening to the birds, and trying to find new ones. I sat on a bench and just listened, and I could pick about ten different bird calls without really trying.

The skyscrapers are still there poking above the tree line, but the traffic isn't. The birds have taken over.

Every night at 7 pm as I'm banging away on my frying pan and Michael is yelling, "Thank you!" out our living room window, we take in our neighbors.

There's the old lady in the red bathrobe. She's on her terrace in the building next to us to the left on the floor above. She also bangs on a frying pan (she gave me the idea). Sometimes she is late coming out and both Michael and I get worried that something's happened to her. On the other side of 97th Street from us is a tall building that looks like it was built in the '70s or '80s. It's about 20 stories tall. When this started only a couple of people would come out. Now, all the terraces are full every night. There is a family that always waves a New York State flag—they've been there from the beginning.

To the right of us, there is a young couple who have a terrace a floor below who come out with their dog. He loves the noise—his tail wags like it's going to fall off. Above them directly across from us is a guy who has the messiest terrace in the neighborhood. It is packed with discarded junk all stacked up. Now, we check in with him every night—nodding as we make noise together.

Not only does New York not look the same, but it also doesn't sound the same these days either.

April 14, 2020
The US State Department reports the first death of a staff member.

During an additional 2 pm briefing yesterday, Governor Cuomo announced that the six Democratic North-Eastern states that form the main population corridor are forming a consortium to discuss how they would reopen.

Governor Phil Murphy of New Jersey, Governor Tom Wolf of Pennsylvania, Governor Ned Lamont of Connecticut, Governor Gina Raimondo of Rhode Island, and Governor John Carney of Delaware all participated in the briefing by Governor Andrew Cuomo of New York to express their solidarity and willingness to work together.

The corridor that these states occupy stretches from Boston to Washington D.C. and should by rights also include both Massachusetts and Maryland who have Republican Governors. A few hours later it was announced that Governor Charlie Baker, the Republican from Massachusetts had joined the consortium making it a total of seven states. That was an impressive and wise move on Governor Baker's part. I imagine he is going to get a whole lot of party blowback coming his way as a result.

On the west coast, the three states of Washington, Oregon, and California did the same thing. Governor Gavin Newsom of California, Governor Kate Brown of Oregon, and Governor Jay Inslee of Washington formed a coalition. They are all Democrats as well.

The idea behind these consortiums is that absent any sensible Federal guidance, the States will need to figure out how to reopen on their own. In the Northeast, millions of people every single day commute between this cluster of States. You can't open one of them without being able to open all of them.

No timeline has been put forth and no guidelines have been put forth. These two separate consortiums of States have been created just to discuss and plan. They have made no announcements yet.

I cannot think of another moment in our history when states have banded together on their own to deal with something that is affecting the entire country—Banded together in opposition to the President. Of course, there was the Civil War… Individual states have certainly resisted Federal laws—think of the Civil Rights Movement—but have clusters of them come together like this before?

The White House response did not disappoint. I'm not sure I have ever seen anything like it. During his news conference, the President was completely unhinged. He did not speak about the victims of the virus. He did not reassure the country. He was only interested in how he thinks the media has been attacking HIM.

He is desperately trying to re-write the history of his response to this virus because he thinks the criticism being levied against him is unfair. He kept pushing that he put the Chinese travel ban in place well before there was a single death in the US. Now, of course, testing seems to show that most of the U.S. cases came in from Europe, not China. Regardless, hundreds of thousands of people traveled to the U.S. from both China and Europe during that period ban or no ban. There was never a proper ban and there isn't one now.

In response, Paula Reid, the CBS White House Correspondent, asked him what he had done to prepare for the pandemic during the time he'd bought with his travel ban. Where was the testing? Where was the support for hospitals? The President erupted. He never answered any of her questions but, instead, lashed out and called her a "fake" and "disgraceful."

Moving on from that, he made it clear that he wants to be the one to reopen the country and he wants to do it soon. When challenged on his authority to do this by reporters, his response was, "When somebody is President of the United States, the authority is total."

After the briefing, Governor Cuomo said, "The constitution says we don't have a king. To say, 'I have total authority over the country because I'm the president, it's absolute, that is a king. We didn't have a king. We didn't have King George Washington—we had President George Washington."

Our Governors are going to reopen the country, not the White House. The White House didn't shut it down. The Governors have made it clear that they would welcome Federal support doing this but, ultimately, they say that it's up to them.

I don't think we should hide from what's going on, but we shouldn't panic either. What's happening around us is unprecedented. I try to stay fascinated and not be terrified. When I can't do that, I just turn off the TV, make some lunch and call a friend.

April 15, 2020

222,617 Total Reported Cases in New York. 16,394 Deaths.

Every morning right when I wake up, I do a kind of inventory. Throat's a little scratchy. Allergies or is it IT? Sniffles…? Blow my nose. No. Aches? No, not really. OK—today, I'm OK.

Yesterday, several health experts said that they thought that Social Distancing guidelines might need to remain in place in some form until 2022. That took my breath away for a minute.

Governor Newsom of California in his daily briefing described what that might look like.

As some businesses reopen, masks and gloves would become ubiquitous. You'd walk into a restaurant and your server would be wearing a mask and gloves. There would be fewer tables and they would be further apart from each other so the six-foot limits could be observed. The menus would be disposable.

How would that affect my business, theatre? If you sold fewer seats—say every third one—and staggered the rows, would people come? What would that be like?

I took a lot of survey classes in college and one of the things that stuck with me from my Philosophy classes was a concept put forth by a Sociologist named Émile Durkheim called "Collective Effervescence." This is what happens when a group or a society comes together to experience the same thing together. The physically closer we are to each other, the more the group "effervesces." As our emotions are shared, the experience becomes exponentially greater.

It's what happens at a game when everybody rooting for the same team sits tightly together and starts to react as one. It's what happens in a church or a synagogue or a mosque or a temple or a meeting house when people gather to worship. It's what happens at the theatre when we all sit tightly together and start to experience the roller coaster ride of emotions together.

The experience bubbles up. We feel it more deeply and more profoundly when we are together—the energy transfers between us and becomes greater than the sum of its parts. That's what we are all hungry for.

That's one of the reasons why every day at 7 pm we all lean out of our windows and scream and clap together for our brave health care workers. We are social creatures. We need that collective experience—that rush—that only comes when we are together.

I am more convinced than ever that the game-changer will be a vaccine.

When? There is no way to tell. An effective vaccine requires an enormous amount of research and testing, and it also requires something somewhat unquantifiable—luck. Researchers say 6-18 months. Maybe more, maybe less. That's where luck will play its part.

I don't want to go to a restaurant and sit alone at an isolated table and I don't want to watch a Broadway show sitting by myself, either, isolated from everyone else. But if that's the only way we can even approximate getting together for the next while, then I'll do it.

We will all do it. We will adjust because we must.

APRIL 16, 2020
230,506 Total Reported Cases in New York. 17,137 Deaths.

In March of 2014, WHO reported that there had been an outbreak of Ebola in Guinea, West Africa. It spread and case numbers continued to grow mostly in Guinea and nearby Sierra Leone and Liberia. By summer, there were 1,000 new cases every day.

The international community felt that the US was slow to respond, but by August of 2014, the US under President Obama started to pay attention. By December of that year—now nine months later, Congress appropriated $5.4 billion in emergency Ebola funding—most of which was spent outside of the US. By the time the breakout was contained, 28,000 cases were reported with 11,000 deaths.

President Obama led a coordinated US effort. What he did was oversee the work each of these different agencies did. Each of these agencies was empowered to do the job that they were qualified to do. 3,000 DOD, CDC and USAID, and other health officials were sent to the affected region. At the end of the outbreak, twelve people were treated for the deadly disease on US soil and two died. There was no pandemic. It was stopped. It could have gone global. It could have been devastating.

Using what they learned from battling the Ebola outbreak, the Obama Administration created a color-coded 69-page National Security Council playbook on how to deal with a pandemic. It was officially called, *The Playbook for Early Response to High-Consequence Emerging Infectious Disease Threats and Biological Incidents.* The current administration was apparently briefed on it in 2017. The playbook was kept by NSC officials in the global health security directorate which was disbanded by the current President in 2018.

Departments that had been created by past administrations to solve specific problems remain unstaffed and all but abandoned under this Administration. Resources like the Pandemic playbook lie forgotten on shelves in empty offices. Instead of relying on people who have dedicated their lives to the study of a specific topic, the President, instead, makes up facts that suit him and his immediate needs and then sometimes, hours later, denies he ever said them. He often sends out conflicting messages or no message at all.

The trade embargoes against China put in place by the current administration are preventing basic supplies like swabs needed for testing from being able to enter the US. We are fighting ourselves rather than working together to combat this. We have already learned valuable lessons from the past. The cost of us having to be taught them again is too great.

Meanwhile, here at home, it is yet another stunningly beautiful day in New York City. It is a little chilly maybe, and breezy, but it is sunny and bright, and the sky is indescribably blue. The building across the way from us on 97th Street has a patch of green grass in front of it. This morning we woke up to the sound of a lawnmower being run over it. It took me back to being in the 'burbs as a kid.

In the middle of this global crisis, the virus, the economy, and the terror there are still many moments of utter simplicity and genuine beauty. It's time to open windows and look out and up at them. And breathe the day in, deeply.

April 17, 2020
237,492 Total Reported Cases in New York. 17,614 Deaths.

Store windows along Madison Avenue and up and down Columbus are full of the latest spring fashions that are now gathering dust. The designs probably began their lives in a designer's notebook a couple of years ago. The ideas were pitched. The ones that were accepted got mocked up. Notes were given, the mock-ups were adjusted. Versions were built for a runway show. The ones that were received well went into design revisions and production for mass-market distribution. Clothes based on those designs were made in factories (mostly overseas) by an army of workers (probably underpaid) and transported back here to the US in huge container ships. Stores who decided that they could sell those designs ordered quantities of them and put them on display.

Now they are just sitting there.

When this is over, we are probably not going to want the same things that we did before this started. Our tastes are changing. Are we going to want to see all the dark, gritty shows that were in rehearsal or previews before Broadway closed, or, instead, like after 9/11 are we going to want to escape to an island in Greece and listen to ABBA songs?

Those new shows that we now may never see, have been in development for years. Producers and creatives bet on what they think people are going to want to see several years ahead before they start putting a show together. Many dollars, sometimes millions, have been spent and countless weeks and months of development and rehearsal have happened before a single theatregoer walks in and sits down in a seat to wait for the show to start.

Whatever they decided then is what we are going to be told is what we want now. The great advertising machine will get behind the ideas that are just starting to come to light and push them relentlessly our way to convince us that it was our idea to want these things in the first place. Some will be successful and some we will resist no matter how hard we are sold on the idea.

In the rural areas of the US, not yet hard-hit by COVID-19, people are starting to protest the stay-at-home orders. In Michigan, a group of unmasked angry protesters rallied at the State Capitol building in Lansing demanding that the restrictions be lifted. They carried confederate flags and banners with swastikas on them. They packed in together and chanted, "Lock her up" about Governor Gretchen Whitmer.

More protests have erupted around the country. The pressure on Governors to reopen their states is going to be enormous. It's going to get worse. How do you tell people that live in rural areas far away from other people that they have to be shut down for the good of all?

On FOX TV Dr. Oz advocated the re-opening of schools yesterday, saying that the resulting 2-3% mortality rate would be acceptable. That's anywhere between six and nine million people in the US that he is saying would be an acceptable loss. By late afternoon, he'd backtracked and apologized but he'd already said it and he's not the only one thinking it by far.

We all want to go back to work. We all want to be able to start planning again. Summer's coming, but if we don't stay this course summer will come and go and we will be right back to where we are now.

I am living on the Upper West Side in Manhattan in a comfortable apartment. We have the mortgage money. For now, anyway. We have food on the table. It's all very easy for me to say.

I do understand that. So, how do we convince everybody who is truly suffering and in need that they need to be patient? We can't blame them for being in a hurry. They are terrified.

Six to nine million people dead, however, is just not anything we should be even considering.

The bottom line is that's the choice. Hold on or kill six to nine million people.

April 18, 2020
244,369 Total Reported Cases in New York. 18,175 Deaths.

Yesterday, the President tweeted that states should rebel against their Democratic Governors.

"LIBERATE MINNESOTA!"
"LIBERATE MICHIGAN!"
"LIBERATE VIRGINIA!"

In the middle of a global pandemic, our President is encouraging the population to rebel against their leadership. He is telling people that their issue is not with the virus but with their Governors and that they should revolt against these oppressors. There is an implicit call to violence in those tweets and it is being heard.

In our large urban areas, we are privy to a whole array of information and reporting that isn't necessarily trickling down into other areas. People who are only listening to the White House, or their Republican Governors who are, themselves, parroting the White House, are getting a skewed version of reality. Is it any wonder that they all think that the pandemic is a hoax? To these people, the stay-at-home orders seem to be designed to destroy our economy and by extension, America.

If one state opens back up and the rest of us don't, it doesn't take a rocket scientist to see what is going to result. You can't partially shut down and expect that to work.

Flying in the face of simple common sense, the Governor of Florida started reopening the beaches last night. What do they honestly think is going to happen?

Food plants in rural areas of the United States are starting to have to close because intense clusters of new cases are breaking out. Food workers, who are keeping us all fed are getting sick because they are all working on top of each other and passing the virus around to each other.

Governors in those states MUST deal with this. As those food plants continue to close, we could potentially start seeing food shortages. Again, it doesn't take a scientist to take that problem forward to a very unpleasant conclusion for the nation.

"Every kingdom divided against itself will be ruined, and every city or household divided against itself will not stand." Matthew 12:25

"A house divided against itself, cannot stand." Abraham Lincoln.

If something seems too good to be true then, sadly, it is probably too good to be true. Anybody who tells you that there are simple solutions to a complex and multilayered intersecting issue is someone who should not be listened to no matter how much we want to believe them. We are all smart enough to take in the information we get and take it forward to see what the result will be. There simply aren't that many paths ahead of us, the way that we are heading, that end well.

April 19, 2020
251,013 Total Reported Cases in New York. 18,699 Deaths.

Even though nothing about this life we are now living is normal, I'm not sure labeling this the "new normal" is helpful. It is not normal, new or otherwise, and we don't need to pretend that it is. This is a time of unprecedented crisis, and we are dealing with it.

During World War II, stockings were in extremely short supply. They started being traded on the black market. People used cigarettes to barter for them and, I am sure, sexual favors. Everybody wanted them badly because having them made it seem as if things were normal.

Stockings back in the day had a seam that ran down the back of the leg. When they couldn't find stockings, women started drawing a line down the back of their legs with an eyebrow pencil. It made it look like they were wearing stockings when really, their legs were bare.

At some point, after World War II was over, stockings became available again and life went on.

In 1953, eight years after the end of the war, Allen Gant invented pantyhose in North Carolina and stockings became a thing of the past. Nobody needed or even wanted them anymore. We moved on. Stockings are a silly example, maybe, but people were making do.

That's what we are doing. We are making do.

I think that it's worth pointing out that not everything has ground to a halt in these weird times. In the middle of the greatest crisis the planet has faced in our lifetimes, three days ago, the Administration changed the EPA rules and created a new method to calculate the costs and benefits of curbing mercury pollution. These changes are designed to undermine the controls on mercury and many other pollutants by, on paper, reducing the positive health effects and raising the costs. It makes it APPEAR that these regulations are not being effective and, therefore, can be loosened.

While none of us are paying attention, the President is getting legislation passed to further help his rich friends.

Brexit is moving forward in England. They left the European Union on January 31. They don't participate in any EU decision-making now, but they are still bound by its rules until the end of the year. Two days ago, Boris Johnson doubled down on his firm intention to press forward. The combined financial impact of leaving the EU plus the COVID-19 costs are mind-blowing. Skeptics are saying that the reason Downing St. is moving forward is that there is hope that the overwhelming costs of the virus will mask the costs of leaving the EU. More smoke and mirrors. Politics are getting in the way and making all this worse.

Yesterday, I finally hit a kind of wall. I don't know how much more I can take in from Washington without exploding. I started looking things up. This is what our founding fathers put into the *Declaration of Independence* in 1776, "We hold these truths to be self-evident, that all men are created equal, that they are endowed by their Creator with certain unalienable Rights, that among these are Life, Liberty and the pursuit of Happiness.— That to secure these rights, Governments are instituted among Men, deriving their just powers from the consent of the governed,—That whenever any Form of Government becomes destructive of these ends, it is the Right of the People to alter or to abolish it, and to institute new Government, laying its foundation on such principles and organizing its powers in such form, as to them shall seem most likely to affect their

Safety and Happiness."

The current administration is not honoring its pact with the people of the United States.

They are not looking out for our safety.

"Governments are instituted among Men, deriving their just powers from the consent of the governed."

I will continue to sacrifice the freedoms I once had to live my life as I chose. I will not consent to do it forever, but I will consent to do it for now. I will not accept any of this as normal, but I will, in total solidarity with all my fellow humans around the globe do everything in my power to uphold my part of our social bargain. I will keep myself separate. Not forever, but for now.

We can wait this out. Washington D.C. is not interested in our safety and well-being. They are willing to trade that for money. For the moment, we are stuck with the people in charge who are making these decisions. We can change this. And we will.

"We have to open for a better future than we have ever had."

Governor Andrew Cuomo—April 19, 2020

April 20, 2020
257,399 Total Reported Cases in New York. 19,670 Deaths.

It has been forty days since Michael, and I hunkered down. Many of the world's religions consider forty an important number.

In Christianity, Christ fasted and walked through the desert for forty days and nights. Lent, which honors this, lasts for forty days. In both Christianity and Judaism, in the story of Noah, it rained for forty days and forty nights and when that was over, Noah waited for forty days after the tops of the mountains could be seen before he released the raven. Islam also believes that Moses (Musa) spent forty days on Mt. Sinai before he received the Ten Commandments. The fortieth day after death has significance for both some Russians and Serbs as well as some Filipinos. In Hinduism, several popular fasting periods last for forty days.

There are other far more mundane references to forty: Ali Baba had forty thieves, we use WD40 to stop things squeaking, a typical Western workweek is forty hours. It takes forty weeks to bring a pregnancy to term.

The word quarantine, itself, derives from the Venetian version of the Italian 'quaranta giorni' which means forty days. That was the length of time that Venetian officials required arriving ships to be isolated in the harbor during the Black Death. There are countless more references to the number forty both in our religions as well as in our secular lives.

Forty days ago, I hadn't heard of Zoom. I had never worn a mask. We used white vinegar to clean surfaces. We didn't make jokes about toilet paper. Forty days ago, I wasn't aware of anything that Governor Andrew Cuomo was doing. Up to the point that we hit forty days ago, I typically spent about a third of my life traveling and when I was home, my suitcase was always semi-packed. Up until forty days ago, Michael made a meal maybe once or twice a week. We ate out a lot. I got my hair cut every couple of weeks. I wore button-down shirts. The list goes on and on. Forty days ago, I thought that what was happening in Italy was terrible.

We have had a forty-day crash course in how to live through a pandemic. For all of us now, though, I'm not sure that the number forty really means anything more than the number after thirty-nine and the one before forty-one.

It is worth noting, I think, though, that we have gotten through this past forty days. Yes, we have lost people, tragically, people we shouldn't have lost, but in the last forty days we have changed how we go about our daily lives and those changes have saved many other lives. What we are all doing together is making a difference. We are still here.

April 21, 2020
262,032 Total Reported Cases in New York. 20,341 Deaths.

Yesterday, while I was taking a walk, I needed a restroom, so after a few blocks, I found a boutique coffee store and bakery and went in. The masked and gloved guy behind the counter was kind enough to let me use the bathroom even though they were take-out only and pointed me towards the back. I ordered a decaf americano as I went thinking that it was only fair and that I was at least supporting a small local business.

Public restrooms are an interesting challenge these days. Suddenly those signs that say "Employees Must Wash Their Hands Before Returning to Work" really mean something.

I paid for my decaf and left. The decaf was $4.50. That startled me. I paid by credit card as I almost always do these days, (who wants to pass money back and forth?) left a dollar tip and I left the store feeling like I'd wasted a fortune. $5.50 for a cup of coffee when a whole bag of ground beans costs $10.00? I have been buying ridiculously expensive cups of coffee the world over for almost as long as I can remember, and I have never given it much of a thought.

Almost exactly a year ago, on April 15, Notre Dame Cathedral in Paris caught fire. In a single night, 850 years of history went up in flames. All of us, all over the world, watched and grieved.

Yes, it was just an old church, but it meant something to countless millions of people.

In the weeks and months following, there was a lot of discussion about how it was to be rebuilt.

Should it be the same or should it be reimagined as something new? Architects submitted ideas with all sorts of modernistic revisions. Ideas like using the structure of the old building but then branching out in bold new directions ala I.M. Pei's now-iconic glass pyramid in the middle of the Louvre.

Many heated public arguments and lots of angry dissent followed. Ultimately, it was decided to build back the cathedral exactly as it had been. Recently, studies have even shown that the 800-year-old wood of the ceiling may have been what saved the structure from collapsing—steel would have melted and brought the whole thing down—so they are now thinking that they will replace the wood ceiling... with wood. The way it was originally.

There will be changes, however, but changes that will be hard to see—a sprinkler system for one. They are structural changes that will make the new Cathedral stronger and better able to withstand calamity. The old building used a lot of lead and all of that will need to be replaced with a safer material. The new Notre Dame will look the same, but it will be, in theory, stronger and safer.

Our economy also burnt down. Our economy also must be restored—I think we can take that as a given—but should it go back exactly as it was or should we stop and think about how we can make it better?

Our old economy relied on us spending like crazy people, buying everything in sight. It relied on us being fine with spending $5.50 on a cup of coffee. And we all did it. Are we still going to want to do it?

Crude oil has fallen BELOW zero per barrel. Take that in. Below zero. How is that possible? Well, largely because nobody needs it. It costs more to get it out of the ground than they can sell it for. Most storage facilities in the US are full. There isn't room for any more of it. We aren't using it. We aren't suddenly all going to go on vacation. Or hop in our cars to go to a sports arena. Oil trading is one of the huge indicators in terms of the health of the economy.

It's painful to say this, but I think that Broadway is unlikely to re-open before there is a vaccine. As much as I want to remain optimistic, I just don't see how that's going to work otherwise. You could argue that if you sold every other seat and left gaps between people that it might be safer, but you cannot pay the operating costs of running a show at 50% capacity. Period.

That's going to be the same with most so-called non-essential businesses. I am using theatre as my example because it's what I do. You could argue that theatre isn't necessary and that it can go away except that economically, it can't. Do you know why every town of a certain size in America has a theatre? Forget the basic innate need we, as human beings have, for stories and art. Towns across America have theatres to attract people to their other businesses. That's why these glorious old roadhouses get restored and re-opened. It's not because town councils with a soft spot in their hearts for the arts get all gooey and nostalgic, it's because somebody showed them a spreadsheet detailing the huge economic gains that would happen for the community if they invested money there.

Restaurants rely on theatre patrons to fill their seats. Parking garages rely on theatre patrons to fill their spaces. Then, there are the businesses that supply shows with costumes and sets and lights and everything else that goes into creating and maintaining a show. The list of businesses that have a symbiotic relationship with the Performing Arts is endless.

When I was on tour with *The Phantom of the Opera* a million years ago, we played Providence, Rhode Island for eight weeks. This was when *Phantom* was THE show to see. They estimated that our eight-week stop in Providence brought in over $50 million in ancillary revenue. $50 million was spent in downtown Providence at local businesses over and above the money that was spent by patrons to buy tickets to the show.

It took just days to stop the entire world's economic engine and it's likely to take months, if not years to reboot it. We are not going to be the same people coming out of this that we were going in. We are probably not going to want the same things. The longer this goes on, the more we are going to learn about ourselves. I, for one, don't think that I'm going to look at a $5.50 cup of coffee the same way again.

April 22, 2020
266,291 Total Reported Cases in New York. 20,859 Deaths.

Today marks the 50th anniversary of the first Earth Day that we observed in 1970. Earth Day celebrates support for environmental protection on an international level. It came to be after a 1969 oil spill off the coast of Santa Barbara when an oil platform blew out. From that horrific beginning, support has grown to where there are now events celebrated in support of the health of our beautiful fragile planet in 193 countries worldwide.

The Paris Agreement was signed on Earth Day in 2016 by 120 countries. Its support has since expanded to include 189 countries. To give you a barometer of what this means, as of this writing, there are 195 countries in total on our planet.

Under the Paris Agreement, each country agreed to plan and report on what it's doing to mitigate global warming. No country was forced to set dates or commit to any specific target, but the agreement encourages each country not to allow themselves to get worse. The Paris Agreement aims to try to limit global warming to C1.5 degrees above historic pre-Industrial levels.

Last year, the President announced that he planned to withdraw from this agreement. Under the terms of the 2016 agreement, however, the earliest that would be possible is November of 2020. Remember that come election time.

But I digress.

George Chidi, a political columnist, and public policy advocate from Georgia wrote an Op-ed piece yesterday that sheds some interesting light on why Governor Kemp is reopening non-essential businesses in Georgia.

To put his piece in the right context, for my pals overseas, there is a fundamental difference between Republicans and Democrats as to what the reach of our government should be.

Democrats tend towards so-called Big Government. This means that they tend to support many laws regulating corporations and other aspects of our financial lives. They enact laws that protect the environment against pollution and laws that protect workers from exploitation. Under Big Government, there are many social programs in place designed to assist people—in times of prosperity as well as in times of crisis. All these programs require large agencies that monitor and facilitate. These agencies require many people to staff them. Hence the term, 'Big Government'.

Republicans, on the other hand, lean towards the opposite way of thinking. This means that there is a belief that corporations should monitor themselves. The thought is that it is to the corporation's financial benefit to run their businesses properly—monitor pollution and the welfare of their workers so it behooves them to do it properly.

The trickle-down theory of economics theorizes that as those at the top succeed, benefits trickle down to the rest. Social programs are unnecessary because people can take care of themselves. The rich will take care of the poor. Republicans believe that government should be small and that all those agencies are a drain on the economy. Too many laws create obstacles that stifle economic growth. It is in the interest of large corporations to take care of their workers. They don't need government regulations to tell them to do that.

Under Obama, many programs, such as Obamacare, were created and agreements like the Paris Accord were initiated. Countless environmental protection regulations were either created or strengthened. On the other hand, under our current President, those programs have been dissolved and those agreements were withdrawn from. The Big Government agencies that were fully staffed under Obama were left vacant and unstaffed. Regulations that were in place monitoring and controlling corporate actions have been lifted and nullified. Environmental regulations have been erased across the board.

That's basically, and forgive me for grossly oversimplifying, what I think our current US vs THEM boils down to. Two separate points of view and two opposing opinions on what the role of Government should be.

In the past, the two sides have been able to reach compromises. In recent years—and I mean over the past 20 years or so—compromise has become more and more difficult to achieve as each side has dug in its heels.

OK, so—back to Georgia. Republican Georgia.

Fairly recently, Georgia imposed a constitutional limit on income tax at 6%. That can't be changed without now changing the constitution. This ensures that taxes cannot be raised by the state government. The citizens of Georgia will never need to give more than 6% of their incomes to the State. Republicans were all happy with this.

OK, fine. So now we have a crisis. The unemployment reserve fund in Georgia currently has a reserve of $2.6 billion. Last week, they paid out $42 million in unemployment claims. At the rate things are going, and there is nothing to indicate that it won't continue this way, this reserve will run out of funds in about 28 weeks. If unemployment continues to rise, maybe sooner. Georgia cannot, under its' Constitution, raise taxes to cover this. They do not have a way to replenish this fund.

So, facing this looming shortfall, Governor Kemp decided to re-open some businesses so that the workers will no longer be able to put in unemployment claims. Is it safe to go back to work? No. It's not remotely safe and the Governor knows that. Now, if workers decide not to go to work to protect themselves from COVID-19 it is their choice. Their businesses have not been closed by the State. They technically still have jobs. They are, therefore, not eligible to apply for unemployment if they stay home. That helps keep the fund solvent.

The businesses that Governor Kemp has chosen to reopen all employ people on the lower end of the earning spectrum. The higher-end workplaces, such as Banks, Software firms, and the like are all still closed. The people placed in harm's way by these decisions are far more likely to be of color or poor.

In the words of Mr. Chidi, "The purpose of this isn't to open up these businesses. It's to get the workers there off the dole. Work, and die. Or don't work … but you're on your own. Because we can't raise taxes to cover the time you spent trying to save your life and the lives of the people around you."

In other news yesterday, a Republican-led bi-partisan Senate committee review concurred with Intelligence findings that yes, Russia, interfered in the 2016 election. The Republican-led committee agrees that the Russians helped to elect this man as President of the United States in 2016. I think we'll be hearing a bit more on that.

In the meantime, this year, we are celebrating Earth Day by inadvertently giving our entire planet a much-needed break. We should always look for a silver lining it makes life more bearable. Happy Earth Day.

April 23, 2020
271,788 Total Reported Cases in New York. 21,516 Deaths.

While we are all going through the coronavirus pandemic, none of us are experiencing it in the same way. At no time in recent history has the social and economic divide been more apparent.

All the food that we are buying in stores relies on many people who are putting themselves in danger every single day before we ever pick it up off a shelf. The cashiers, who deal with hundreds of people a day are just the end of a long line of workers that get the food to us that we never see—meatpackers, farmworkers, truck drivers, packagers, distributors. Anybody out there still doing their jobs is putting themselves at a greater health risk than those of us who, without jobs, are staying home.

I don't want to suggest that staying at home is easy. Families with no resources at all are having to scramble to find food and necessities. Food banks across the country are doing all they can to ramp up their food distribution abilities but there is only so much they can do.

Unemployment websites are overwhelmed by new applicants. 4.4 million new claims were filed last week in the US bringing the national total up to 26 million people. WHO is warning that in the coming year that worldwide rates of famine could double.

Yesterday, the Mayor of Las Vegas gave one of the more remarkable interviews that we have seen yet from a politician. In the interview, Mayor Carolyn Goodman tells Anderson Cooper that she would be willing to re-open the casinos in Las Vegas and use her citizens as a control group to see how the virus is spreading. She is offering up her constituents to be used as canaries in the coal mine.

Yesterday, I decided to walk north. I don't usually ever have a reason to head that way, but I thought I would explore. What I found was that there were far fewer masks being worn north of where I live than there are to the south.

This virus is hitting communities of color HARD. Almost everywhere, people of color are losing their lives to COVID-19 at a far higher rate than white people are. The numbers have nothing to do with genetics and everything to do with economics and social stratification. The sad truth is if the people I passed on my walk north were wearing masks to protect themselves and each other, they would then be putting themselves at risk for even more racial harassment than they usually endure. Lose-lose.

Phillip Pullman, a beautiful writer and the author of the *His Dark*

Materials books wrote this yesterday, "The way we allow ourselves to be governed at the moment looks like the triumph of habit over putrefaction. We can't go on like this." We really can't and we don't have to. We can take care of ourselves.

April 24, 2020
278,456 Total Reported Cases in New York. 22,069 Deaths.

I don't pretend to have all the facts. The thing with facts is that none of them are absolute.

We accept things as facts until evidence comes to light to prove them wrong and then they are no longer considered facts.

The earth is flat, evil spirits live in brussels sprouts, and icepick lobotomies are an acceptable cure for mental illness. All of these were accepted as truth at some point in our history. Now we look at them and laugh at how silly we were to believe them. We look back at them in horror at what those "facts" did to people. Even though most of us don't give them credence anymore, I bet you can still find people who will think that they are true.

It has recently come to light that the first confirmed death on US soil from COVID-19 occurred on February 6 of this year rather than on the widely reported February 26. All the models about how this virus spread in the US were based on the February 26 date. The fact that we now have evidence that the virus was freely circulating a full three weeks before that, changes everything in terms of the projections. The models that we are basing our responses on, need to be reconstructed. Even so, they are just models of probability, they aren't cold hard facts.

A few days ago, there was a dust-up between the President and the Governor of NY when the former blamed the latter for over-reacting regarding how many ventilators the state would need to weather this crisis. The Governor shot back that his reactions were all based on the projections that the White House itself, through the CDC, had sent out. He was merely preparing for what he thought they would need based on what the White House thought would happen. Nobody knew. Not the CDC, not the Governor, not the President. They were all guessing. They were all doing their best to project based on what few facts they thought they knew.

In New York state alone there are a dozen or so different machines that can perform the COVID-19 test. Each of those machines requires different reagents and materials to function. Each of those machines takes a different amount of time to reach a result. Each of those machines and tests has a slightly different margin of error. Testing is not absolute. There are both false positives and false negatives—sometimes the error is as much as 15% or more. There is not enough information yet to even know whether once a person has developed antibodies in their blood from the virus, whether it will then give that person immunity from contracting the virus again. We do not know yet.

Hydroxychloroquine seemed like it might have some beneficial effect because it was used in a few places, and it seemed like it worked. Well, in the last weeks, it has been subjected to many trials. As a result, the mounting evidence now suggests that Hydroxychloroquine seems to do nothing to affect the virus. It also suggests that it seems to have negative, potentially fatal effects, in terms of how it affects the heart. Facts? Not really, just probability based on extensive testing. There is simply not enough known about COVID-19 to be able to make absolute choices about what the course of action should be to move us forward to getting us back to the lives we lead two months ago.

All the evidence that we have so far—taking in the lessons learned from the 1918 pandemic and other similar viruses from the past, taking in the lessons learned from other countries ahead of us in their curves, taking in what the trends seem to be from repeated clinical trials—all that evidence points towards the probability that reopening our businesses right now is unlikely to end well.

The odds are hugely stacked against a successful outcome. There is a tiny possibility, though, that it will be fine. That tiny, infinitesimal possibility is why people play Lotto and why almost all of them lose. Nothing in life is definite. We live with uncertainty every day of our lives in every aspect of our lives. Living through this crisis is no different.

None of us should listen to the President (or me for that matter) on any medical matter. We should be listening to our doctors. They may not have an answer either, but somebody who has devoted their life to the study of something probably has a more valuable idea of what to do than somebody who is just terrified of the unknown. The President's suggestion about injecting disinfectant to fight this virus is born out of desperation, impatience, and ignorance. He wants a simple black and white answer right away.

We've never really had answers like that, and we've been living quite happily without them all along.

April 25, 2020

287,898 Total Reported Cases in New York. 22,505 Deaths.

Yesterday, Michael and I decided that we would go downtown and get an antibody test. A friend of ours had gotten one at a walk-up clinic on 42nd Street the day before and said that the wait time wasn't too bad. It was the first time, since all of this started, that Michael and I had taken a long walk together through streets in Manhattan.

People are itching to get back. You can feel it. The government is also itching to get people back so that the economy can start to be rebuilt. All eyes are on Georgia where some hair salons have reopened, with every other seat being used, beauticians in masks, gowns, and gloves, and hand sanitizer available everywhere.

States are moving forward with bills that would stop people from being able to sue businesses for COVID-19 issues that arise from the workplace. In other words, if the state mandates that businesses re-open too early and you go back to work and, as a result, contract COVID-19, you would not be able to sue anybody. Utah passed that legislation yesterday.

At the testing site here in the city, Michael and I joined an orderly line of people outside—maybe six or seven of them—all responsibly masked and staggered at 6' intervals. We filled out our forms and waited.

Our insurance covered the testing, so it wouldn't cost us anything directly. After about 20 minutes, as other people left, we were able to go inside the waiting room and have a seat. One by one, we were called into the exam rooms in the back, and we had a small vial of blood drawn. Everybody there was very nice. It seemed clean and well managed. The whole thing took about five minutes. We left and walked home.

The World Health Organization (WHO) issued a warning yesterday that governments should not consider issuing "immunity passports" because there is not enough research available yet to support the idea that once you've had the virus that you are immune to getting it again.

The New York Times ran an article this morning about the efficacy of the antibody tests. They evaluated 14 of them using samples of blood that they knew either had or didn't have the antibodies. Only three of the tests were found to be accurate to any degree and even those three had an unacceptable rate of false-positive / false-negative. The test that Michael and I took was not mentioned by name in the article.

Whatever the results are from the antibody tests that we took yesterday (and we should get the results on Monday or Tuesday) there is currently nothing that we can do with them. We can't go back to work with the results. We can't hang out with any other like-resulted friends.

Ultimately, what Michael and I did yesterday was take a nice walk down to midtown and back.

For now, that's enough.

April 26, 2020
293,575 Total Reported Cases in New York. 22,910 Deaths.

I am guessing that almost everybody with kids is more than ready for our schools to reopen. Kids need time away from their parents as much as parents need time away from their kids.

It is hard enough to survive alone, during this, but the added responsibility of providing for children without the support umbrella offered by public schools must make it that much more daunting. Beyond actual education, the school lunch program is a lifeline that can mean the difference between eating that day or not for many underprivileged kids.

90% of the children in the United States attend public schools. Many come from single-parent families or families where both parents work. The Secretary of Education, Betsy DeVos believes that the Public School System should be dismantled, and that all education should be privatized. She has proposed massive cuts to after-school programs. She has proposed eliminating summer school programming. Her goal is to dismantle the entire system.

My husband and I, like most of our friends, work in the arts. What is sustaining people and getting them through this time? The Arts. People are watching movies and television programming created by artists and a whole host of craftspeople. The stories that we tell each other are the way that we process the world around us. If that's too airy-fairy for you, on an economic level, the television and motion picture industries are responsible for over $700 billion worth of annual revenue. Those industries employ over 2 million people annually.

Funding for the performing arts, much like school funding, has been eroding for decades.

Almost every single high school used to have a performing arts program. My high school had a band and a choir. We had a drama club that put on a big play and a big musical every single year in our high school's auditorium. I owe my career to what I learned in school and how it inspired me. My middle school and high school drama teachers lit the fire in me and encouraged it to grow.

The National Endowment for the Arts was formed under the Democratic President Lyndon B. Johnson in 1965. Johnson was not all that interested in the Arts himself, but he felt that the Arts had the power to improve the lives of ordinary Americans and could reduce the gap between the haves and the have-nots. The NEA has encouraged writers, performers, painters, sculptors, performing artists with exposure and with much-needed financial support. Because of that funding, artists from every medium have brought their work to a larger audience—inspiring thought and yes, some controversy. These artists have provided jobs and generated revenue for the people and institutions who presented them.

The National Endowment for the Arts has been deemed by Republican lawmakers as being unnecessary. Right-wing Christian groups have attacked it for encouraging what they consider to be "obscene." In 1981, the Republican President Ronald Reagan was already trying to dismantle it. A special task force (that included the right-leaning actor Charlton Heston) discovered that the "needs involved and the benefits of past assistance" didn't warrant dismantling it. Since taking office, our current President has already attempted to eliminate the NEA twice in his proposed budgets. Both times, Congress has defended the NEA and refused to let that happen.

So, fast forward to 2020 and COVID-19. We, as a nation, both left and right, agreed to shut everything down. We have put schooling and performing arts on hold trusting that they will still be there when we get back. If we learn anything from this period of enforced shutdown it should be how much we rely on those two institutions. They are a vital component of both our mental health as well as our basic economic health.

What an opportunity this is to make our schools better. What an opportunity this is to expand support for the Arts. Instead, I fear, the people in leadership positions are going to use this time to try to do the opposite. We owe it to ourselves and our kids to speak up and not to let them.

April 27, 2020
297,888 Total Reported Cases in New York. 23,391 Deaths.

Michael cooks and I do the dishes. That's our routine. Michael's an excellent cook so to do my part, I clean up. It seems only fair. In pre-COVID times, Michael would cook dinner once or twice a week and the rest of the time we would either eat out or not eat at all. Michael manages to use every pot and utensil that we have while he is prepping a meal. It is truly impressive. I'm not complaining at all. Much. The result is always worth it. As much as it probably feels to him as if he spends all day at the stove, I feel like I spend all day at the sink. We have a dishwasher, that I eye-rolled when we installed it but now count as one of my closest friends.

We aren't eating in restaurants, so demand for bulk food has all but evaporated. Farmers across the country are now actually having to plow their crops under. Food is rotting in the fields. Milk is just being dumped. The restaurant industry was responsible for a huge percentage of agricultural consumption—meat, dairy products, fruit, and vegetables.

Some of that demand has just shifted to grocery stores but food that goes to restaurants is not packaged in the same way that food that goes to grocery stores. We aren't going to buy 50lb sacks of flour at Whole Foods. Those tiny little cartons of milk that are consumed by students across the country are not usable anywhere else. With schools closed, what do you do with them? All that perishable food is just going to waste. It is going to waste while more and more people are in real danger of not having enough.

Last night, Broadway joined together online, from their homes, to celebrate the 90th birthday of Stephen Sondheim. It was an intensely moving night of some of the greatest living Broadway performers singing some of the most beautiful music ever written for the theatre. Technical glitches delayed the broadcast for over an hour, but it didn't matter. Last night I saw my industry pull it together and do the best they can. Those are the people I work with. That used to be my job. The pull to get back in the room with them and work is almost unendurable. Almost.

When Broadway reopens, it will cost each show more than a million dollars to get up and running again. That is money that is on top of usual weekly operating costs. Most shows won't survive having to do that twice. It's going to be hard enough the first time especially given that social distancing is going to have to be in effect. When Broadway reopens, there must be confidence that it's not just going to close again in a couple of months.

Oh good, Michael's calling. Our first meal of the day is served. Given the smells and noises coming out of the kitchen, happily, it's going to be a heavy dishwashing day.

April 28, 2020
300,796 Total Reported Cases in New York. 23,726 Deaths.

The President's suggestion that we all inject bleach to counteract the virus was the last straw. We need a break.

April 29, 2020
303,932 Total Reported Cases in New York. 24,172 Deaths.

Michael and I got our virus test results back. Drum roll… As we expected, both of us tested negative for the virus and positive for the antibodies—meaning we don't HAVE it, but we HAD it. Michael has more antibodies than I do, which I guess makes sense because he had a worse time of it than I did, though neither of us had it badly at all.

What do we do with this information? Well, first, these results are not fully reliable. The tests we were given are not yet approved by the FDA. As is being widely reported, there is no confirmation that having the antibodies protects you from getting the virus again. Nothing, yet I guess.

There is an interview in this week's New York Magazine with writer Emily St. John Mandel who wrote the novel *Station Eleven* about what life is like twenty years after a virus wipes out 99% of mankind. In the interview, Mandel says, "There's something almost tedious about disaster… At first, it's all dramatic, but then it just keeps collapsing."

Yesterday, my sister and I were talking about what we were doing, and we agreed that it was taking days to accomplish even ridiculously simple tasks.

One day, I wake up and notice from the bed that one of my socks is under the dresser. On the second day, I think, "I should pick that up." On day three, I decided to get it but as I start to crouch down, Michael calls from the other room that lunch is ready. On the fourth day, I resolve to finally get it, so I go into the bedroom, crouch down and pull the sock out. As I do, though, I notice that there's a pencil that's fallen down the back and is lying on the floor up against the wall and I think, "I should pick that up."

For those of us who are not working and just staying at home, there's an overwhelming sameness to every day.

Our current federal leadership continues to do a dangerously inadequate job. It's not just the Republicans. It's not as if the Democrats are doing anything other than running a kind of desperate defense against whatever is coming their way. Yesterday, Vice President Pence visited the Mayo Clinic and refused to wear a mask. That went contrary to every regulation the hospital has. That went contrary to everything that even the White House's health experts are saying we should all be doing. Pictures of the Vice President of the United States not wearing a mask in an actual hospital send the message that this virus isn't serious and that the safeguards can be ignored. Optics are everything. It is easier to look at a picture than it is to read an article.

Yesterday, we cleaned the bathroom. I mean we really cleaned it. Top to bottom. We were in the tub, on our knees, scrubbing. We completely disinfected the cat's litter box—brand new litter. All of it was long overdue. It felt good to do that. I am going to get something else done today, too. It's time.

First, though, there's a pencil underneath my dresser that I need to get.

April 30, 2020
308,309 Total Reported Cases in New York. 24,542 Deaths.

I can still remember where I was standing on campus at Columbia in 1983 when I first realized that the AIDS epidemic was serious and was going to affect me. I was very much in the closet, but I was experimenting. I was a senior in college, of course I was experimenting. I had slept with a choreographer of a show I was working on. He was older than I was and well established and somehow, because of his resume, I had assumed that because he was on his way to being well known that I was safe. That he was safe.

I was talking to a friend about it. We were standing next to the campus's eastern gate on Amsterdam Avenue, and he pointed out the obvious. The disease didn't care who it struck.

I remember that moment of realization as vividly as I remember anything.

AIDS is a very different disease than COVID-19. It isn't respiratory. You need to have actual physical contact with body fluids for them to transfer. We didn't know that at the beginning of that pandemic. In the beginning, people were terrified to even get close to each other let alone touch each other.

In 1987, Princess Diana visited an AIDS hospital in London and shook an AIDS patient's hand. If you want to know why people loved Diana so much, for a lot of us of a certain age who lived through that time, it was because of that and that alone. We were five years into the pandemic—FIVE YEARS—and nobody with anything like her visibility had ever done anything like that before. She held babies who were infected with AIDS and the pictures of her doing that gave everybody hope that maybe this disease wouldn't kill us all after all. It gave us hope that maybe we'd be able to live with it.

In 1992, nearly a full decade after the AIDS epidemic had started, Jerry Mitchell put together the first *Broadway Bares* event. He and seven of his friends who at the time were in the cast of the Broadway musical *The Will Rogers Follies* danced on a bar and raised $8,000 and some public awareness for a disease that had decimated the artistic community in New York. That disease had gone largely unnoticed and unfunded by the federal government.

One of the reasons Jerry started the *Broadway Bares* event is because the sheer terror of HIV/AIDS had changed how we behaved with each other. We were scared to touch one another. After ten long years of this, he wanted to show that there was a way that we could. Safely.

We are all now used to the idea of Safe Sex. Use a condom. Gay or straight, I don't care who you are, nobody goes into a sexual encounter without thinking about safe sex. We may ignore it, (at our peril) or scoff at it, but we all know it's there. The FDA finally approved Truvada or PrEP as an HIV prophylactic in 2012—thirty years after the AIDS epidemic started.

Safe Sex as a concept didn't exist before the early 1980s. Certainly, there were all sorts of other STDs that people got, and still get, but a shot of penicillin and you got rid of it. They weren't usually fatal. People just had sex and accepted the occasional consequence. 32 million people have died from HIV/AIDS since the start of the epidemic. 37.9 million people are currently living with it.

Hold, Please

The HIV/AIDS epidemic changed everything about our behavior. It has been nearly forty years since it started, and we have learned to live with it. It is no longer the death sentence it once was, but it hasn't gone away. It is manageable. It is a part of our everyday lives and we have had to make space for it. There is still no definitive cure for it.

COVID-19 is a novel coronavirus. Novel means new. It is not the same as the coronaviruses that have been circulating among us—like the common cold. It is similar, but we don't know enough about it yet to be able to predict with any confidence what it even does. In the last ten days or so, for example, we have now learned that it can cause blood-clotting in otherwise asymptomatic patients aged 20-40 that can lead to strokes. We have only just learned that. Nobody knows what our life after this virus is going to be like.

After millennia, there is still not a cure for the flu. There are some remedies that ease the symptoms, but once you get it, you've got it and you just need to get through it. 5% to 20% of all Americans get the flu every year. Many people die from it each year, but we don't report the deaths that way.

So, what do we do? Well, we are going to drag yet another chair up to an already crowded table of maladies that afflict us and make room for COVID. Throughout history, that's what we have always done.

We are madly starting to re-open everything without having a clue about what we are doing. It's only been about three months since we even became aware that COVID-19 existed. It's only been six weeks since everything started closing. We are going to figure out how to live with this thing, but for heaven's sake, take a breath. We aren't there yet.

We all want to get back to the way it was before COVID-19. Heck, we still all want to go back to the way it was before HIV/AIDS. We are going to learn to deal with COVID-19. There is nothing in our collective history that suggests that we won't. It is just going to take a minute.

May 1, 2020
312,799 Total Reported Cases in New York. 24,911 Deaths.

Yesterday, Michael and I reached a new milestone in our relationship. He let me cut his hair. I did a decent job if I do say so, myself. The news blared in the background as I did it and of course, there was the President.

A few weeks ago, our President loved China. Today, he wants us to believe that the Chinese created the virus in a lab and purposely released it. The virus is believed to have started in bats. A lab in Wuhan had been studying bats and how they carry and transmit viruses. A theory has been floated that scientists in Wuhan accidentally (or on purpose) allowed the virus to escape out into the population. The Chinese eat bats.

While much of this backlash against the Chinese is political hot potato-ing, the Chinese are not blameless in this. They have not been forthcoming at all during this crisis. Our relationship with the Chinese is complex and nuanced. After decades of isolation from the rest of the world, Richard Nixon visited China in 1972 with the express purpose of establishing a trade relationship and a political alliance against the U.S.S.R. That visit, for better or for worse, initiated the relationship that we now find ourselves in. It is a somewhat dysfunctional relationship, at best.

Over the last day or two, it has started to feel a bit like we are watching Thelma and Louise speed towards the abyss. The national social distancing guidelines expired yesterday, and the President does not plan to renew them. He is encouraging his supporters to resist. Armed protestors stormed the capitol in Michigan yesterday demanding to be set free from their homes. Ultimately, we need to take care of ourselves. None of us needs to be the first people back out into the world. If the idiots in Michigan want out so badly, let them. (The Governor just extended the stay-at-home order there until May 28.)

We don't have to do that yet here. Half of the Nation's states are starting to re-open while the case rate in the country has trended up in the last three days. The death toll keeps rising. If this rush to reopen works and two or three weeks from now, cases have trended down in those places then let's start to think about reopening ourselves. Texas is re-opening today after their largest single-day increase in deaths. Only 1% of the population of Texas has been tested. How reopening there now makes sense to anybody, I can't follow.

The next few weeks are going to be very telling. It's not necessarily going to be easy. In fact, it may get harder. If we, properly, do it now though, it may keep us from having to do it again later.

Michael's hair will need another cut in a couple of weeks. I might even let him cut mine. Might.

May 2, 2020
3.35 Million Cases Reported Worldwide. 239,000 Deaths.

Working in the theatre, we get thrown together with new groups of people all the time. In what we would call civilian life, people probably encounter much the same group every day. On a big musical, though, we encounter the same group of about 60 people every day, but just for a while.

Rehearsing a show and getting it up and running is an intense emotional experience that bonds the group much faster than other jobs usually do. When the show closes, though, despite those bonds, we move on to a new gig and we suddenly find ourselves with a whole new group of 60 people. Sometimes there is somebody in the new group that you've encountered in a previous group. If you are lucky enough to work in the same theatre building again, you already have a connection to the people running the theatre, but sometimes it is just a whole new cast of characters to get to know and quickly trust.

Last night Michael and I were part of a zoom session with a company from nearly 20 years ago that connected. We have remained in touch as a group ever since and, even though we have scattered, our connection has endured. It was beyond wonderful to see everybody's faces again if even only on a screen.

We are going to be among the last businesses to reopen. The Governor has put together a task force to explore how the startup should happen, but Broadway officials were not invited to be a part of it.

I think that there is a fear that if Broadway opens too soon that people from outside the city will start coming in. We aren't ready for visitors yet. As we get our numbers under control, we don't want to encourage people from other places who don't have a handle on their numbers from coming to the city. Beaches reopening in Florida means that people from elsewhere are going to travel there to play in the sand and water and sunshine and bring the virus with them. Broadway can't be responsible for doing the same thing. Despite that, we still need to be in on the planning. I don't understand why we aren't.

While we are more than ready to get back to our lives, that's not going to happen all that soon. So, while we wait, we will have to zoom in with those we love and be satisfied with looking deeply into each other's eyes. They are the window into the soul, after all.

May 3, 2020
First death reported in the State of Virginia.

Broadway runs like an artery down through the center of Manhattan. It runs through all manner of neighborhoods—high income, low income, residential, business. It runs past Columbia University on the Upper West Side and art galleries downtown in SoHo and in midtown it goes right through the heart of Times Square. You get to experience almost all of New York when you walk down Broadway.

During the first couple of weeks of the pandemic, nobody at all was out on the streets. Gradually, over these last few weeks, that terror of being outside seems to have lessened. As I walked downtown yesterday, I watched the people who were out there walking with me.

An overwhelming majority of my fellow New Yorkers finally seem to be observing the health guidelines. I would say that 90-95% of the people who were out on the street were wearing masks and staying away from each other.

All the stores that don't carry groceries or household goods are still closed. Most restaurants and bars are closed. Those that are open are only open for take-out or delivery. Outside some of those places that are open, people are standing in an orderly line, 6 feet apart. There are some places, though, where that isn't happening.

I got to Times Square and saw that the Naked Cowboy is back. I didn't realize that he is an ardent admirer of the President. His guitar is covered with stickers with the President's name on them. I will give him a shout-out for wearing a mask, but not for that.

From there, I walked over to 5th Avenue and headed back uptown alternating between 5th and Madison. In midtown, there are large stretches of these streets that are non-residential. They are all lined with "non-essential" retail stores that remain closed. Because of that, there are far fewer people walking along them. Madison Avenue still feels abandoned in the way that all of New York did during those first few weeks.

From there, I went into the park. Central Park was overwhelmed with people. The Great Lawn was crowded. Many large groups were having picnics and playing games. A few had masks, but many didn't. Some had masks on but wore them pointlessly under their chins. All through Central Park, there are signs, in red, that say, "Keep this far apart" with a six-foot arrow underneath. In Central Park, yesterday, I saw crowds of people clumped together right in front of the signs.

I live in a building with many fellow residents who are in the most "at-risk" category. I don't want to lose any of them. To help keep that from happening, I am choosing to wear a mask and stay away from everyone except my husband. I wonder how many of those people who are choosing not to do that are leaning out of their windows at 7 pm every night and applauding our frontline healthcare workers.

People who refuse to wear a mask should look at their masked neighbors sitting on their own who are inconveniencing themselves to try and protect everybody else. Look at them and then choose.

May 4, 2020
323,828 Total Reported Cases in New York. 25,837 Deaths.

New Zealand reported no new cases of the virus yesterday. At the beginning of this, before there was a single death reported, Prime Minister, Jacinda Arden, instituted a strict lockdown. Borders were quickly closed to all non-Residents on March 19. The lockdown went into place on March 25. The total death toll from the virus in New Zealand as of yesterday is 11.

New Zealand has the advantage of being a cluster of islands. The total population is only 4.8 million, a little bit more than half the population of New York City. In terms of a response to the virus, it seems that New Zealand has been the model of how to do it properly.

The rate of the virus in Australia seems to be dropping as well. If Australia can get to where New Zealand is, then the regular back and forth between those two countries can start up again but they will still need to keep their collective borders closed to all outsiders. As other countries around them start to get their numbers down and in control, then those countries can slowly be added into the bubble.

Here at home, forty states have already started re-opening even though new case rates in most of those states continue to rise. In some of those states, fewer than 1% of the population have been tested. They are reopening blindly. It is a huge gamble. They're playing lotto.

There is little or no coordination happening between most states. There is nothing in place at all stopping someone from a place with a very high rate, going somewhere where the case rate is low, and bringing the virus with them. Even the White House is now saying that the death rate by August will likely hit 100,000 people. That is up more than 20% from even a couple of days ago. And that's just the projection through August.

Yesterday, our consortium of seven states announced that they would be uniting to purchase and buy personal protection equipment for our hospitals. Rather than compete against each other, which is what has been happening, our group of eastern states will negotiate together and SHARE the proceeds as needed.

That is what we should be doing as a country. Instead, we are inexplicably doing the exact opposite. Every state is just doing whatever it wants to do regardless of what its neighbors are doing, and the President is encouraging this. Even his advisors are saying it's a bad idea.

When somebody like the Governor of Michigan holds their ground and keeps the closures in place, the citizens show up at the capitol armed to the teeth like an army in fury. On some level, how can you blame them? The President is encouraging them to reopen, and the Governor won't do it. Then to make the situation even worse, the President praises the Michigan armed protestors and calls them, "Very good people."

We are not seeing the sharp decline in cases that was hoped for in New York. Yes, we are trending down, but our numbers are still very high. Guidelines for reopening dictate is that there should be a 14-day drop in cases before we start to reopen. That is not happening in a single place in the US where businesses are reopening, instead, they are rising.

Michael is making our 55th brunch. I am going to wash my 55th batch of brunch dishes. We are going to have our 55th discussion about what we are going to have for dinner. Michael will then make our 55th dinner and I will then wash our 55th batch of dinner dishes. We will then go to sleep for the 55th time since this started. Then tomorrow, we will do it all again. And probably the day after. And the day after that.

This isn't as easy for many, many people who are truly suffering during this time. Michael and I, though, really do have everything we need right now. We have more than enough.

May 5, 2020
325,934 Total Reported Cases in New York. 26,119 Deaths.

I got off in my counting of days a few days ago and didn't notice until yesterday. I corrected it and I think I'm back on track. I'm forgiving myself for the mistake because there is almost nothing to differentiate one day from the next.

The President is heading to Arizona this morning—almost the textbook definition of non-essential travel—to tour a Honeywell factory. It's his first trip out since early March. As he leaves, I am listening to him trash Congress. He is trashing the Chinese. He is praising himself. He is praising our testing which is not close to being up to the task yet—not in numbers and not in reliability. He is praising the early re-opening. Arizona is an important state for him in the upcoming election. This visit is nothing more than a campaign stop.

There was a virtual global international vaccine summit yesterday that the US did not participate in. When questioned, the administration responded that the US already funds a lot of international research, so they didn't feel the need to attend. It doesn't matter if we are already funding some of those programs, not showing up sends the clear and very strongly stated signal that we are on our own.

Dr. Anthony Fauci has been the director of the National Institute of Allergy and Infectious Diseases since 1984. That's thirty-six years of service and experience. He took over the directorship during the height of the AIDS epidemic, he's been through SARS and Ebola and now he's going through this coronavirus pandemic. He is the person that the White House is using to base their response to COVID-19 on.

His response to what the White House is doing with his guidance is pretty much summed up in the question he asked this morning. "How many deaths and how much suffering are you willing to accept to get back to normal?"

"How much is human life worth?" Governor Cuomo asked this morning.

Having to choose between our economy and human lives is a terrible decision to make. It's a terrible decision because there is no possible answer. Like Sophie's choice, just trying to answer the question is going to cost.

For the rest of whatever day this is, I am going to try and get some stuff done. That will probably take me into whatever day tomorrow is and possibly the next. That's fine. I think I've got the time.

M AY 6, 2020
328,057 Total Reported Cases in New York. 26,689 Deaths.

It's been nearly two months since this whole thing started in earnest and yet every single night, we are still able to cheer on our troops who are still out there fighting the good fight. We haven't been beaten.

On Monday, I did our weekly grocery shop instead of Michael. I can't remember what he was doing that made me volunteer, but this week it was on me. He trusted me with The List. As usual, the line to get in stretched well around the block. We were all standing at the proscribed six-foot-intervals. We were all wearing masks. It took well over an hour to get inside the store (1:17:26 to be exact).

Once I got to the front of the line, I hit the, now, ubiquitous store traffic warden. It's a new job that's been created just for this crisis. The masked warden sits out in front of any popular store and makes sure that no more than the allowed amount of people are let inside. One out—One In. No mask? You can't enter.

Once inside, it's quite pleasant to shop these days. It's not crowded. The shelves are full. We have not started to feel the national meat shortage yet. I suppose that is yet to come. The only thing that seems to be hard to find in food stores is bread flour. With time on their hands, everybody has started baking bread.

At the checkout counters, there are now plastic guards separating the cashiers from each other.

The cashiers will pack your groceries into paper bags themselves, but they won't pack the groceries into bags that you've brought. If you have brought your own bags, they put the groceries back into your cart. It is up to you, now, to take the cart out onto the street and pack your groceries yourself.

At the wine store near us, you aren't allowed into the store at all. You stand online—6 feet apart—masked—and get to the front door where somebody takes your order (and your credit card) and comes back with your wine in a bag.

Over the last two months, we have changed the way we navigate through our days in ways we would never have imagined before. We have created workarounds for almost everything. Can't meet up? Let's do it virtually. Two months ago, I had never even heard of Zoom—now, it's a regular part of my week. Yes, it's all different, but so what?

We are a resilient species. We are blessed with something that gets us through times like this. Hope.

Hope allows us to believe that our lives can be better. That belief leads us ever forward towards a better life. Tonight at 7, when you lean out the window and clap for the incredibly brave people who are out there every single day working to keep us well, maybe spare a few claps for yourself. We are all "out there" every single day fighting our way through this pandemic. We all deserve some applause, too.

MAY 7, 2020
331,268 Total Reported Cases in New York. 26,916 Deaths.

The ex-Governor of New Jersey, Chris Christie just compared reopening the economy with the U.S. sending young men into battle during World War II. "Knowing that many of them would not come home alive…We decided to make that sacrifice because what we were standing up for was the American way of life," he said. "In the very same way now, we have to stand up for the American way of life."

During World War II, many soldiers who lost their lives were not from wealthy families. The grunts in the field were usually young working-class men and they gave their lives in unfathomable numbers. The sacrifices that Governor Christie is talking about are going to come from communities of people of color in far greater numbers than from people who look like him and his family.

This past week 3.1 million new people filed for unemployment. Michael and I were 2 of those people. We had delayed filing because the system was overloaded, and we figured that there were people out there who needed to get through more quickly than we did. We are having the same issues with the system that everybody else has had. Since the claims are retroactive, we aren't worried that we won't eventually figure it out but getting there is like making your way through the most complex labyrinth imaginable.

We join 33 million people in the United States who are currently on unemployment. Each one of us is an individual. Each tiny single part of that massively enormous number is somebody who matters to someone.

The Australian War Memorial in Canberra, Australia holds the most amazing nightly ceremony. Every day, just before they close, they honor a single person who gave their life for their country. It is called the Last Post. Rain or shine, a single fallen person's picture is placed on an easel. Family members come from all over Australia and the world to be there. They bring flowers. A bugle plays and everybody remembers.

Over 100,000 people over time have lost their lives to war in Australia. Every single night, the War Memorial puts an actual face to that number. Sadly, like everything else around the globe, the Last Post ceremony is temporarily on hold. When it starts up again, I would urge everyone to join in via their online live stream. If you are lucky enough to get there in person, someday, I can promise you that it is well worth the trip.

If I count, then so do you. Whoever you are. You aren't just a number, and neither am I.

Mᴀʏ 8, 2020
334,167 Total Reported Cases in New York. 27,233 Deaths.

New York, Massachusetts, and Connecticut are the last three states that have not yet moved to start to reopen. We are due to continue our stay-at-home directive here in New York until May 14. By then we will see what reopening has done to the numbers in the 47 other States and decide for ourselves whether we are going to start to reopen.

It is no longer as quiet in the city as it was six weeks ago. Early last week, work crews began appearing back on the streets. A few days ago, construction resumed on a building being put up in a lot down the street from us. The steady relentless thumping from the machines has been added back to the city's usual landscape of sound. Traffic, usually the main noise in the city, is still very low. There simply isn't anywhere to go.

There's a store on Columbus that sells Italian pottery. It's a beautiful little shop with beautiful things to buy in it. When we get to the point that shop can re-open, the owners, I'm sure, will take steps to ensure their customer's safety. They can make sure that only one or two people, wearing masks, are allowed into the shop at a time. They can wear masks themselves. That's all great, but who is going to shop, there? The April unemployment numbers are in and, as expected, we are now experiencing the worst unemployment numbers since the Great Depression. 14.7%.

Stores like the shop that sells pottery rely on people with disposable income. They rely on being in a well-trafficked area that ensures that plenty of people will walk by and look in. They need a certain number of the people who walk by and look every day to occasionally walk in and buy something.

Today is the 75th anniversary of V.E. Day. V.E. Day is the day that the Nazis unconditionally surrendered to the Allies, ending World War II in Europe. After the war ended in Europe, it took a long time for some country's economies to recover. People didn't want the same things they wanted before the war began. Nobody had any money. Countless millions of people had died, lost their lives in the war, or had been brutally murdered. The labor force of Europe's young able-bodied men had been decimated. It took a long time for all the interdependent pieces of the cogs of the European economies to be repaired and put back in place before the machine could be restarted. V.E. Day marked the day that all of that began.

We have not yet had our V.E. Day with this coronavirus. I'm not sure we are even all that close. The COVID-19 pandemic is still waging war on multiple fronts throughout the globe. Yes, we need to reopen. Yes, we all want to go back to work. It's just not that easy.

It is May 8, and we may see some snow here tomorrow. At least it will keep most of us inside. It will give us all another day to come up with workable ideas on how we get back once this virus subsides.

May 9, 2020
336,802 Total Reported Cases in New York. 27,454 Deaths.

I am used to having a lot of balls in the air at the same time. A typical pre-COVID day for me involved several concurrent work projects that often conflicted. I'd wake up some mornings not having the remotest idea of how I was going to get through everything on my plate.

I lived with a certain amount of anxiety. That anxiety was such a constant that I rarely noticed it. I focused on what needed to be done and, over the course of the day, I usually accomplished most of it. At some point in the evening, no matter how much was left to do, I'd call a halt and give myself a break for an hour or so before I went to bed. Over the course of a week, I'd try to make sure to leave time to walk or go to a museum, but while I was doing those things, I was usually letting what I need to do at work percolate underneath. Those "breaks" were just the time I needed for my internal webpage to load.

These days, that work-connected anxiety is simply not there. There is no work. Instead, I am working on a long series of "someday when I have time" projects.

My father collected coins. Not in an orderly sort of way, he just collected them. All of them were just piled loosely together in a big biscuit tin. That tin has been sitting in our storage unit for years. Some of them were things like old silver dollars from the days when they were made of silver. Those have a surprising amount of monetary value. Some of them, though, I think my dad just thought were interesting. Those are the ones that I am enjoying finding.

My father was interested in just about everything. Spotting these strange coins and looking up their history is exactly what my dad would have done. Going through them all and sorting them out has been like spending time with him again (he passed away about eight years ago).

Three people connected with the White House have now tested positive for the coronavirus.

The President's valet, the Vice President's Press Secretary (who is married to one of the President's chief advisors), and the personal assistant to the President's daughter have all tested positive for COVID-19.

The White House is determined to keep the President and Vice President safe. All three of the people infected have come into contact either with the President and Vice President themselves or with other people, who then in turn have been in contact with them. Thus far the President and Vice President have tested negative, but it is too soon to know for sure. The virus takes a while to replicate to the point that it is detectable.

The White House thought that they were invulnerable. The White House thought that this virus would spread among the greater "them" and not touch anyone "important" In Washington. The White House response has been swift and decisive. What they are doing now is what we, in the rest of the country have been clamoring for the government to do for us for months. We should have started doing all of this in January. They will take care of themselves, but not us.

When we do go back to work, there are changes, I think, that I will make in how I work and what I agree to take on. Really, though, I'm a juggler. I like being busy with multiple projects that mean something to me. I like working with different groups of people to figure out how to solve problems. More than anything, I like watching 1500 people crammed together in a room being moved by an experience that I helped create.

Apparently, today is Saturday. On this Saturday, instead of two shows and a meeting, I have several huge piles of coins that need sorting. I am going to spend this Saturday afternoon with my dad.

May 10, 2020
339,202 Total Reported Cases in New York. 27,627 Deaths.

My mother lives in Florida on the east coast up near Daytona Beach. She seems to have been responsible so far during this crisis. In normal times, she has a wide orbit of friends with whom she is socially active. They play mahjong, meet in book clubs, and they share meals.

These days, her contact with her friends is via the phone. Mom has figured out how to play mahjong online. Her local library has a whole process in place whereby she places her order for books, then when they come in, she gives them a call that she's coming. She drives up to the library, and somebody, masked, brings the books out in a bag, and then retreats. Mom gets the bag and drops off the books she's already read then heads home.

A very good friend of mine, here in the city, who has been socially distancing, wearing a mask, and behaving responsibly since the stay-at-home orders started, got sick the day before yesterday. My friend has no underlying conditions and falls outside the vulnerable age range. It is still not confirmed that what my friend has is COVID-19 but if they are still sick tomorrow, they are going to be tested. How could that happen if all the guidelines are being followed?

There is a very clear and interesting report by Dr. Erin Bromage, who is an Associate Professor of Biology at the University of Massachusetts, Dartmouth that tries to explain the theories behind how this virus moves. I will try and give it a short summary here.

To get infected, a person needs to be exposed to a certain amount of the virus. One or two particles of COVID-19 won't do it, you need to get a good dose of it. 1000 particles of SARS-CoV2 can potentially do the trick. If you are with a person who has it, you could get 1000 particles in one big breath or 100 particles per breath for ten smaller breaths or smaller amounts in more breaths. From studies of the regular flu, we know that 3-20 particles are released per minute of normal breathing. If you hang out with a person who has the virus for an hour, you could get more than enough.

That's true if they aren't speaking. Speaking increases the amount released by a factor of ten. You only need to be with an infected person who is speaking for five minutes for there to be enough COVID particles present to become infected. That's assuming normal breathing and speaking from a person with no visible symptoms to make you think that they are sick.

A single cough or sneeze from an infected person can release 200 million virus particles into the air. 200 MILLION. Remember, it could take a little as a thousand to infect you.

If an infected person sneezes in a small room and then leaves the room, the infected droplets from that sneeze can hang in the air for a couple of minutes. A healthy person can then walk into an otherwise empty room and easily inhale enough particles to get it without ever even having laid eyes on the infected person. Well, nobody's going to walk into a small room where a stranger might have been. Really? Think about a public restroom.

If somebody gets sick, five days before they had any symptoms, they could have been shedding virus particles. Some people shed more than others.

When you get people into groups, especially in an enclosed space, it becomes that much easier to share the virus. The largest outbreaks to date have happened in prisons, meatpacking plants, and churches. Weddings, funerals, and birthdays have also accounted for a big percentage of concentrated cases. In all those cases, people are in close enough contact with potentially ill people over a certain amount of time. Many of those people may have no visible symptoms whatsoever. ONE person infected in a 5,000-person megachurch during a service that lasts an hour or more—you don't need to have scored well on your math SATs to be able to figure out the potential results.

When your local restaurant reopens under the plans currently in place, not every table will be available for seating. There will be space between parties. That should be safe, right? Here's the thing, if you are having a meal in a restaurant, you are in an enclosed room. You cannot wear a mask while you are eating a meal. Chances are, if you are with even one other person, you are going to be speaking. If you are with a group, you are probably going to be speaking with some animation. Particles are going to be released into the air. The air in that restaurant is not going to be still. There will be some sort of air conditioning so that the room doesn't get stuffy. That means that the virus particles will travel on those air currents.

Keep in mind that my friend who is now sick has been doing everything "right". Even if it turns out that what they have is not COVID, they got something. Something jumped onto my friend even though my friend is living alone and keeping away from other people.

I called my mother this morning to wish her a happy Mother's Day. She was looking forward to finally getting her hair done now that the salons have reopened in Florida. I talked her out of it. At least I hope I did. You cannot distance yourself from somebody cutting your hair. It is a physical impossibility. When you get your hair done, you are in an enclosed salon. The person styling your hair will potentially have been in close contact with many other people—some of whom may be infected. It takes time to get your hair done. An hour?

Masks are a fence, not a wall. They don't stop everything. I love my mother. She's a smart woman. She's not going to get her hair done. Yet. She's not going to get her hair done yet because if she does, I am going to publicly call her out on it. Happy Mother's Day, mom. Messy hair and all, I love you.

May 11, 2020
341,026 Total Reported Cases in New York. 27,824 Deaths.

Bethany Mandel is a conservative writer who went to Rutgers University. She recently tweeted "I'm not sacrificing my home, food on the table, all of our docs and dentists, every form of pleasure (museums, zoos, restaurants), all my kids' teachers in order to make other people comfortable. If you want to stay locked down, do. I'm not."

This goes directly against what those on the left advocate. The left would term this selfishness and respond with virtue-signaling. She's doing the opposite. She is vice-signaling.

Vice-signaling is what elected the current Administration. Trying to point out the moral flaws in the actions of the government is not working because the community that has been formed around the vice-signaling that elected them is deaf to those types of arguments. To that community, "bleeding heart" liberalism is the enemy.

Bethany Mandel is an educated person. She is part of a large segment of society that is joining together and embracing their selfishness. "You can call me a Grandma killer", is how that tweet starts.

Shame is defined as a painful feeling of humiliation or distress caused by the consciousness of wrong or foolish behavior. Wrong or foolish behavior is defined by society. Something that causes shame in a person from one country might not register at all with an American. Something that causes shame in an American might be readily accepted by somebody in another country.

Our society in the United States is dividing. Some would say already divided. Up until now, what the left has been doing in response to the right has been to try and shame them into behaving in a virtuous way. The right has decided that what the left views as a virtue is a vice and what the left views as a vice is a virtue. The right can't be shamed by the left because the two groups no longer share the same accepted moral norms. We are now a society split in half with directly opposing ideologies.

Our President has embraced racism and greed and, in doing so, has created a community around him that believes the same things. Those things are no longer vices in that community because everybody in that community now considers them virtues. They may have always considered them virtues but kept that feeling hidden. Now that the President is on their side signaling his acceptance of their views, they can feel what they feel openly and without shame.

I fear that moving forward, science isn't moving fast enough to provide a solution to COVID-19, so people are panicking and looking elsewhere for answers, and they are finding them. They don't care if those answers make any rational sense or not. There is a difference between vice and virtue. As those around us start forgetting what that is, we must remember.

May 12, 2020
342,356 Total Reported Cases in New York. 28,042 Deaths.

The lady in the red bathrobe who comes out on her balcony every night at 7 to clap wasn't there yesterday. I wonder where she was. I think that the couple with the dog directly across from us and a floor down must have left the city. They haven't been out in a week. The guy with the messy balcony above them is still out almost every night and he now brings a kind of percussion instrument out with him when applauds.

I have no idea how any of these people are getting through this pandemic. These people are close enough to me that I can see them, but not close enough that I have a clue what their lives are like. Do they have enough food? Have they lost people? Are they scared? Are they angry?

My social media feed is full of noise and outright lies. Conspiracy theories, even though they offer answers that are bleak or terrifying, do offer answers. They provide a sense of certainty. If we are pre-disposed to believe that we are constantly under attack, a good conspiracy theory confirms that way of thinking. That confirmation of our worst fears, true or not, feels better than the alternative which is, "I don't know." Being certain of the worst can be better than not having an answer at all.

The President tweeted yesterday that "we have met the moment and we have prevailed."

As he tweeted this, we surpassed 80,000 people dead from the virus and those numbers are still rising. At a press conference yesterday, he announced a conspiracy theory called Obamagate, but then refused to say what it was. "It's obvious," was his response.

The President seems profoundly uncomfortable around "I don't know." Not only does he seem to not like "I don't know" he also seems terrified of demonstrable probability when it goes against what he wants. He appears to be grabbing blindly at conspiracy theories to keep from facing a hard truth—the truth being that there is no easy answer as to how to lead this country through this crisis.

Leadership requires taking in the available facts and opinions, weighing them, and deciding on a clear path forward. A good leader surrounds themselves with people who know more about their specific area than they do to advise them. The people that the President has surrounded himself with are mostly not experts in the fields their departments cover. Many of those people are businessmen like the president. The result of this is that the advice he is getting is almost completely from a business point of view.

When information that conflicts with that point of view comes his way from people who are professionals in other fields, such as Dr. Fauci, his chief health advisor, it's unsettling. So, he tries to ignore it or vilify it and distract from it.

"Obamagate" seems to be yet another desperate attempt at distraction. Nobody, not even his advisors seem to know what he is referring to.

In World War II we were fighting a relentless enemy that wanted to dominate the world. Terrible mistakes were made while we were fighting World War II, but we ultimately prevailed and ended the war. Was the horrific devastation caused by dropping the atom bombs on Hiroshima and Nagasaki worth it?

Last year I visited both of those cities while I was working in Japan. The memorials to the people who were lost and the museums that preserve the horrific images of the aftermath in both places are moving beyond comprehension. Both cities are now dedicated to Peace. Had we not dropped the bombs how much longer would the war have continued? Could we have won the war without dropping the bombs?

To fight this virus, we dropped an atom bomb on our economy. Was it worth it? Well, the war is still being fought so we don't know yet. The further away from the virus we get, the more we are going to learn and the more we are going to look back at the decisions that were made and be either horrified or relieved. Either way, we are going to forget that when these decisions were made, we just didn't know.

The discomfort of uncertainty is just that—a discomfort. We live with it every day because there are seldom any definitive answers to anything. We must be OK with that for now.

May 13, 2020
343,874 Total Reported Cases in New York. 28,247 Deaths.

On Tuesday, the Broadway League announced that the general shutdown of theatres would continue into September. That's four months from now. This doesn't mean that Broadway and Touring theatre is necessarily coming back in September, it just means that the date for which people can get refunds for tickets already bought has been extended from June to September. Honestly, none of the producers I have talked with these few weeks from all over the world feel that theatre will be able to resume until social distancing is over.

Theatre, especially Broadway has always been on the verge of total annihilation. In 1938, Kaufman and Hart wrote a play about the rise and decline of a theatre in NY entitled The Fabulous Invalid. That has been Broadway's nickname ever since.

Broadway was never going to survive the movies, or the depression, or the decline of the Times Square area in the '60s and '70s. Broadway was never going to survive 9/11.

In about 430 BCE, it seems that a plague struck Athens, Greece. There is not a lot of agreement among scholars as to what happened or, in fact, if it even happened. The only direct account of it that has survived the millennia comes from Thucydides. According to him, it arrived when the long war between Athens and Sparta that many of us dimly remember studying in school, started.

The Greeks believed in the healing power of theatre. Even their poetry was sung or chanted. During the years of this plague, a sanctuary to the healing god Asclepius was built next to the Theatre of Dionysus on the

Acropolis—the remains of which are still there.

There are countless references to plague and contagion throughout the Greek plays that remain from that period. Bernard Knox, a classicist, and author, makes the case that the broad setting of the Theban plague and details in the text of *Oedipus the King* does not make sense unless you consider that Sophocles composed it in light of or in response to the Athenian plague.

There doesn't appear to be anything that says whether theatres closed during that time but interestingly, Thucydides says that "nothing afflicted the Athenians or impaired their strength more" (than the plague.) He describes panic, defiance, desperation, and fatalism setting in. He reported that many of the city's inhabitants resisted quarantine and succumbed to lawlessness, indiscriminate spending, and a loss of faith in their gods. "Appalling too was the rapidity with which men caught the infection; dying like sheep if they attended on one another; and this was the principal cause of mortality..."

Stephen Greenblatt has a wonderful piece in the May 7 issue of the New Yorker about the bubonic plague and how it affected William Shakespeare. Parish records indicate that Shakespeare was baptized in Stratford on April 26, 1564. The first death from the plague that ultimately took a full fifth of the town's population was recorded a few months later in the same register. Throughout his life, the plague was a regular part of Shakespeare's life.

The plague would come and go. When it came, the government would track data from parishes and when those deaths reached a certain level, they would institute shut-down orders that sound a lot like what we are experiencing now. All forms of mass assembly except for church services were then banned. They believed that it was impossible to get infected during the act of worship.

Archery contests, feasts, and theatres were halted and closed. Sometimes these shutdowns lasted for months until the death rate came down to an acceptable level. People living in London during these times accepted the plague as a fact of life that they couldn't do anything about. When it came, people paused. When it went, they started up again.

A fresh outbreak of the plague in 1603-04 happened just as Elizabeth I died. Her successor, James I of Scotland postponed the celebrations surrounding his coronation and delayed his entry into London until it passed.

A theatre historian named J. Leeds Barroll III, concludes that in the years between 1606 and 1610, because of contagion, theatres in London were probably not open for more than a combined total of nine months in total. During those years Shakespeare wrote and produced, among others, *Macbeth*, *Anthony and Cleopatra*, *The Winter's Tale*, *The Tempest*... He seems to have kept himself busy.

References to plague occur throughout his work. "A plague on both your houses," says Mercutio in *Romeo and Juliet*. "O Lord! He will hang upon him like a disease. He is sooner caught than the pestilence, and the taker runs presently mad," says Beatrice of Benedick in *Much Ado About Nothing*.

Theatres closed in the US in 1918 during the Spanish Flu. By October of that year, the levels were bad enough that theatres and other venues that encouraged gatherings were closed.

Some theatres held out. The Marx Brothers opened a new show called *The Cinderella Girls* in Grand Rapids, Michigan that October. The audience wore masks. Whatever meager laughter there was, was muffled by the masks. Local health regulations allowed theatre owners to sell only every other seat and to keep every other row empty. There was no way, under those conditions, for the theatre to break even let alone turn a profit. After a miserable week, the show moved to Benton Harbor, Michigan for an equally terrible week before possibly going to New York. Whether or not it performed in New York, it closed almost immediately, and everyone went home. Producers reported huge losses which made headlines across the country. How could theatre possibly survive? Then the Flu passed and theatres, along with everything else, reopened. And everybody forgot all about it.

In the broad timeline that is our lives, this is just a short pause. The Fabulous Invalid isn't doomed by a longshot. As much as theatre has faced over the last several thousand years, it has ALWAYS come back.

Books didn't replace theatre, neither did Film or television. Artists, like Shakespeare in his time, are finding countless new ways to create and tell their stories. These new ways won't ever replace theatre, but once theatre is back, they will simply add to the ways in which we communicate with each other.

MAY 14, 2020
346,213 Total Reported Cases in New York. 28,408 Deaths.

I cut my own hair. My hair had gotten so long that the curly ends of it around my ears tickled me awake yesterday before the sun came up. That was it—I couldn't take it anymore.

Is it a great haircut? Well… I've had worse.

Across the country, people are crossing the thresholds of what they can bear every day. Everybody has their breaking point, and everybody has their own hill upon which they are willing to die. Some people are hitting those points because they are seeing their businesses die. Businesses that they or their parents or grandparents started, nurtured, and grew have been forced to close. These people are looking at a true abyss. How will they continue forward if their means of livelihood is no longer there? How will they feed their families? Some people are hitting those points just because they want to get their nails done.

Senate hearings were held yesterday to discuss how to implement coronavirus relief measures to re-open the country. The White House is trying to present a rosy picture of the state of the fight against the virus that is in direct opposition with what health professionals are saying. Health professionals, across the board, are warning, in no uncertain terms, that the effect of reopening too soon will end with a sharp rise in new cases and a sharp rise in new deaths.

Today, Richard Bright is being grilled by Congress. He was the former director of the Biomedical Advanced Research and Development Authority, and he believes that he was fired recently because he clashed with the Administration regarding the use of chloroquine and hydroxychloroquine. They are the existing malaria drugs that the President was encouraging the public to use against COVID-19. Bright's warnings of the dangers of using this drug were in direct opposition to what the Administration was saying.

A CNN poll yesterday revealed that 84% of Republicans say that they trust the health information that they are getting from the President. 72% of Republicans trust the information coming from the CDC. Only 61% of Republicans trust the information they are getting from Dr. Fauci. A CBS poll is even more alarming. According to their poll, 85% of Republicans trust the President, and only 51% trust Dr. Fauci. If you only listen to the news outlets that support the President, then of course that is what you are going to end up believing.

Two months ago, I would have laughed in your face if you suggested that I would ever cut my own hair. My attempt is not perfect. Of course, I needed to agree to let Michael fix the back where I couldn't see. I now understand what people are talking about when they talk about my cowlick. I wasn't even sure what it really was. Now having tried to cut it, I know and understand the problem. I do have a renewed appreciation for the skill of the people I've found over the years who know what they are doing.

All in all, though, I can now cross out "haircut" on my list of things that may lead me to a breaking point. A mere haircut won't be the thing that breaks me although hearing about people breaking for something even less than that just might.

MAY 15, 2020
348,461 Total Reported Cases in New York. 28,673 Deaths.

Today, parts of New York will begin phase one of re-opening. In five areas of the state, construction can start up again. Agriculture, fishing, forestry, and hunting in those five areas can pick up. Manufacturing and wholesale trade there can also restart. Those five areas do not include New York City.

The areas that are reopening phase one today, are rural areas that have been far less impacted than we have been in the city. The Western region where Buffalo is and the Capital region where Albany is will remain closed as will the downstate regions in which the greater New York City area is located. Rochester, in the Finger Lakes region, is the biggest urban area that can begin to reopen in the state.

The numbers of new cases and hospitalizations in those regions will be monitored. If those numbers start to rise too high, then some of the reopening will be scaled back so that local health facilities do not become overwhelmed. All of this seems clear, rational, and logical. The question is, will it work?

The aircraft carrier, USS Theodore Roosevelt, experienced an outbreak of the virus that infected 1,100 crew members. All 4,800 crew members have now gone through at least an initial round of testing. Personnel who either tested positive or seemed to have symptoms of COVID-19 were evacuated. As those crew members recovered, they were tested again. When they tested negative twice, they were then allowed to return to the carrier. Yesterday, it was reported that five sailors on USS Theodore Roosevelt who had gone through all that, have now tested positive for COVID-19. They seem to have gotten it again.

We are all assuming, on some level, that having the antibodies for the coronavirus provides some measure of immunity against getting it again. These new infections call that into question. This development doesn't mean that having the antibodies doesn't provide immunity, it just further supports the fact that we don't know yet. The tests are not 100% accurate. 5 out of 1,100 is .45% which falls within the margin of error for false negatives for the tests.

Europe is starting to discuss reopening for tourism. Most of what they are planning to try is regional tourism. If anyone is thinking that a wild summer in Mykonos is in any of our futures this year, they should probably think again. Greece looks like it may be one of the first countries to reopen but that will probably only be for European visitors and only from selected countries. Bars and restaurants will unlikely be open—it won't be a typical summer in the Greek islands.

After flattening their curve, South Korea eased restrictions and allowed bars and nightclubs to reopen. On May 6, a guy who had visited 5 nightclubs in one night in Seoul tested positive for the virus. Officials identified nearly 11,000 people who were in that area that night and have already tested over 7,000 of them. 100 new cases of the virus have been linked to that one guy. South Korea just reclosed all the bars and clubs.

Germany, after easing some of its restrictions is now seeing its numbers rise and may need to pull back as well. They have increased testing in a way that is well-coordinated and thorough and are, as a result, in a great position to be able to monitor well. Lebanon went back into complete lockdown a couple of days ago after cases spiked badly again there after they reopened too soon.

Here in the US, our testing is so uncoordinated that it is extremely difficult to tell what is happening. It is impossible to compare the numbers of a state that has tested 1% of its population with the numbers of a state that has tested more.

The President thinks that testing is overrated. "When you test, you have a case," he said. "When you test, you find something is wrong with people. If we didn't do any testing, we would have very few cases." How do we respond to a statement from the President of the United States that is that ludicrous?

As we all move to reopen, there are going to be surprising successes and tragic disasters. Nobody is going to be able to definitively predict what is going to happen in any one place.

New York City's "pause" has been extended to May 28. Beaches in the four-state area (New York, New Jersey, Delaware, and Connecticut) will reopen on Memorial Day. It's a little soon for Cuomo's taste, but the fear is that if we don't reopen the NY beaches then New Yorkers will just flood into areas that do. Nobody wants people to move around like that. Mayor de Blasio doesn't agree. He does not want New York City to ease its restrictions until June.

The further we go into this, the less we seem to know. Socrates said, "The only true wisdom is in knowing you know nothing." We are all blessed with common sense in some form or another. Now is the time to use it.

May 16, 2020

350,979 Total Reported Cases in New York. 28,845 Deaths.

Yesterday almost felt like a summer day in New York. It was 82 degrees and, like many days recently, crystal clear. I took my usual long walk down to Times Square and back and for the first time in two months had to stop at several corners and wait for traffic. There wasn't a lot of traffic, but enough that it felt like a usual, very chill, Sunday.

Ambient noise has started back, construction noise, of course. Air handling systems in the tall buildings of Manhattan are back with the noise of their exhaust systems blanketing the soundscape of the city. It felt like a normal day as I walked downtown. People were out—for the most part responsibly distant and masked—walking and shopping.

It is always easy to pick out what is different, but much harder to pick out what's become normal. Masks seem normal now. Emptiness in the city, while still compelling, has become normal enough that seeing people out yesterday seemed notable.

As I walked, I watched other people. Families navigating through the streets with their kids—some masked, some not. There were older New Yorkers pushing grocery carts and younger New Yorkers, excited to be together, walking and laughing. Homeless New Yorkers finally have a shot at getting something from people passing by. After being distracted by them all for a few blocks, I started noticing what was happening behind them.

We've all gotten used to our stores being closed. We've looked at the same dusty window displays for weeks. What I noticed yesterday, though, is that a lot of stores are now available for rent. Those stores are closed for good. All up and down Madison Avenue, there are empty storefronts, some boarded up with "for lease" signs on them. Some are just sitting there, vacant.

Even the large chains like Duane Reade/Walgreens are closing branches. I have never really understood how Duane Reade could support so many separate branches, but they have been a ubiquitous sight in Manhattan for years. I would say that in the last two months, about 50% of the branches between here on the Upper West Side, where we live, and Times Square are either closing or have already closed.

Jeff Bezos, the founder, and CEO of Amazon.com is on track to becoming the world's first trillionaire. During these two months at home, online ordering and delivery have skyrocketed. It is going to take far longer for people to get used to going back into stores to shop than it took for them to stop doing it. Fear stopped us. Hope will restart us. Fear is an immediate reaction. Hope is a slow, tentative process.

Disney just announced that when it reopens its Broadway shows, *Frozen* will not be among them. They are betting that as people start coming back to theatre that it will be in trickles, not in waves. They are thinking that it will be better to concentrate those few early theatregoers in fewer shows than to allow them to spread thinly across many different shows.

As we start to reopen, the landscape of our country is going to look very different. As much as the victims of this virus often have a glacially slow painful recovery, so will we as a city have. Reopening won't be like just diving into a heated pool. It will be much more like slowly creeping into a cold swimming pool—one tentative step at a time. The President is saying, "vaccine or no vaccine, we are back!" He can say that all he wants but it's not going to make most of us get into that freezing pool any faster.

A vaccine is going to take time for very good reason. It must be safe, and it must be effective. How is that safety determined? Time. Operation Warp Speed is going to move slowly whatever the White House chooses to call it.

Yes, we've got a long road back to being able to live in what we consider a normal fashion.

And yes, those we've lost will forever remain lost. Our lives, though, won't just magically resume at some mythical point in the future. They won't need to resume because they never stopped.

MAY 17, 2020
353,002 Total Reported Cases in New York. 28,971 Deaths.

When I was in high school and had to choose which college I wanted to attend, I ultimately chose where I went as much for where it was as for what I could learn there. I knew that I eventually wanted to live in New York City. I knew enough, however, from my sheltered upbringing in suburban New Jersey that I wasn't ready to live in New York City on my own. Going to school in New York would, I thought, be a great way to transition to the real world. And it was.

I had a perfectly good time in high school. Parts of it were miserable, but most of it was fine. I had great friends. I was a band and theatre kid so, of course, was picked on by the jocks and cheerleaders. Some of the jocks and cheerleaders, however, turned out to be as ambitious as the rest of us geeks were and ended up in our advanced classes.

By senior year, we all started studying together and became friends. Cheerleaders and band nerds and football players and theatre geeks would meet up after school and discuss life and write essays together. And laugh. I had some great teachers in high school that inspired me and set me firmly on the path that I am on today, but those friends did as much or more for me than my teachers did.

I was a smart, happy kid who was completely clueless about life. And I knew it. I showed up at Columbia University in New York City with a fair amount of basic knowledge and close to zero life experience.

(Mom, you may want to skip over this next bit.)

At Columbia, I had my first beer. By Thanksgiving of that year, I had lost my virginity to a Philosophy major. A woman.

Columbia College was a small part of Columbia University and was all-male until my senior year. My girlfriend went to Barnard across Broadway—an all-female college also within the University. She had a roommate who also had a boyfriend and the four of us lived together in their dorm room all year at Barnard. I have no idea how my girlfriend's roommate's boyfriend and I got past Barnard security every day, but we did. The four of us also had a friend named Peter who had graduated some years before. He had been living ever since then, secretly, in the basement of one of the campus theatre spaces.

Peter was a director—all of us had gotten to know each other working on a production of an Agatha Christie play that Peter directed that fall in the lobby of one of the dorms. Soon after that, Peter started sleeping on the floor at the foot of our beds after mysterious evenings of cruising and partying. He'd creep in during the night and we'd wake up in the morning to find him snoring on the floor.

Peter was a complete mess. He was a drug-addicted, sex-addicted, homeless person who couldn't move past his college years into the real world. We, of course, worshiped him. Peter got us all high one night and that made me decide to try all the drugs so that I could better understand what they did. Peter became my Professor of Illicit Substances. Every weekend, we would try something new. Peter would explain what each one would do, what the dangers were, and how to take them, and then we'd dive in.

From what I remember over that semester, we at least got through cocaine, mushrooms, and LSD. I refused to try heroin or anything else that needed injecting. I never really did anything more than once. Cocaine honestly didn't do much of anything for me. Mushrooms were hilarious and the LSD was amazing. The LSD was so amazing (we went to see *The Exorcist* on campus, and I wept with laughter all the way through) that I knew I should never do it again.

The rest of my years at school saw me volunteering at an Off-Broadway theatre downtown that soon led to me getting paid and beginning my entire career as a stage manager. I spent my junior year at school in London which began a life-long love affair with that city. On our semester breaks, we traveled throughout Europe—we skied in Switzerland, had a Seder in Rome, visited Dachau, and got drunk on retsina on a Greek Island. I started to sleep with guys. Peter became the first person I knew who died from AIDS.

By the time I finally graduated from Columbia I felt ready to live in New York. My point with all of that (and that was a lot of information—maybe too much. Sorry Mom.) is that College was far more than classes.

Last night, LeBron James created a virtual graduation for the Class of 2020. It was very inspiring. Some of the most popular performers and personalities in the country participated. President Obama delivered the Commencement Address, and it was spectacular. He gave the Class of 2020 three pieces of advice:

Don't be afraid. Do what you think is right. Build a community.

We watched, and were moved, but what did the Class of 2020 think? We have a niece who is graduating this year who didn't even know it was happening until we told her. I'm not sure whether she finally actually watched or not. Did she have the same experience watching a compassionate, articulate, and intelligent leader offer hope for the future that we did? I am certain she didn't.

What will college look like for her? She already knows that her classes will be virtual this fall.

Yes, she will get the information from her classes that she needs to know, but what about life experience? For her and kids her age, getting information online is a completely different experience than it would be for those of us of a certain age. She grew up with the internet. It has been a normal and expected part of her life since before she can remember.

Where the problem is going to be, I think, is in the life lessons they going to learn. None of them are going to be able to make the incredibly stupid mistakes and take the incredibly stupid risks that we all did when we were that age. I don't want to suggest that anything I did in college should be imitated in any way. That was my journey. How will these kids—young adults now—mess up and learn from it?

I am a firm believer in education. Education, however, must go beyond the walls of the classroom. We already have an entire generation of kids that seem more connected to each other on their phones than they appear to be with each other in person. COVID-19 might be a sometimes, terrifying pause for us, but it will likely be the defining moment at the beginning of this next generation's lives that will inform everything that follows for them.

Today is my husband Michael's birthday. Of all the people on the planet that I could be stuck with during this crisis, I can't imagine a better companion to get through it with. After an endless series of successes and mistakes and triumphs and wrong turns in my life, I've learned enough to be able to recognize something good when I have it. Now, all I need to do is not to screw it up. Hopefully, I have learned my lessons well enough to not mess it up TOO badly.

May the lessons that the Class of 2020 are learning, different though they may be, serve them just as well as the lessons I learned in 1984. Congratulations to my niece and to the entire Class of 2020—here and all around the world. Don't be afraid. Do what you think is right. Build a community. And, happy birthday, my love.

MAY 18, 2020

354,500 Total Reported Cases in New York. 29,454 Deaths.

A New York City Health Inspector traced an outbreak of cases in several wealthy households in the city back to a single person who had been working for each of them. It seems that each time, a short while after the person, who had, and continues to have, no symptoms themselves, started working in the house, the family got ill. When that happened, the person left for another job. So far, the Health Department has contact traced 53 cases back to this same person. Of those 53 people, three have died.

This was in 1906. The person's name was Mary Mallon. She worked as a cook. The disease in question was typhoid.

I find it surprising that nobody's made a real movie about Typhoid Mary yet. It has everything you'd want in a story—great characters, intrigue, and more than a touch of tragedy. It's even a perfect part for Saoirse Ronan.

One of the families who had gotten ill after Mary worked for them, hired a researcher named George Soper to investigate what had made them ill. It was he who put the pieces together and figured out that the one thing that all these afflicted families had in common was their cook. When he finally confronted her, she didn't believe him. She refused to give him either a stool or urine sample (the disease typically lodges in the gall bladder) and came after him with a meat cleaver. He convinced the authorities that she was a danger to the community and the Health Inspector had her quarantined. She was kept against her will for three years.

When questioned she admitted that she never washed her hands. In 1906, the concept of germs was still new. The theory that diseases were caused by germs that traveled between people was still not widely accepted. Her stool and urine samples, which she was forced to give, were, indeed, teeming with typhoid bacteria but, even so, she refused to believe that she carried the disease.

After three years the NY State Commissioner of Health released her after making her promise that she would not work as a cook again. A few years passed where she tried to work as a laundress, but she couldn't make enough money at it, so she secretly changed her name and went back to work as a cook.

Predictably, outbreaks of typhoid started up again and, after a long thrilling cat and mouse chase, the police finally tracked her down and arrested her. She spent the rest of her life—twenty-three years—in quarantine. She died under lock and key, a minor celebrity, in 1938.

At any point, she could have had her gallbladder removed and the source of the contagion would have gone, but she held firm to her belief that she wasn't carrying the disease and never allowed it. She preferred to remain imprisoned. She put her faith in God and the church and, by all accounts, found solace in that.

After her death, a post-mortem did indeed find evidence of the live bacteria in her gall bladder. They never did an actual autopsy on her. There is a theory that the authorities did not want to cause a city-wide panic with the results.

By the time she passed away, 400 other people had also been identified as typhoid carriers but none of them was ever incarcerated. It doesn't appear that anyone ever tried to educate Mary about the disease. A prickly and stubborn person, she was, instead, imprisoned and used as a lab rat by doctors.

Dimitri Ivanovsky first discovered that sap filtered from a diseased tobacco plant remained infectious to healthy plants in 1892. That was 128 years ago. Six years later, in 1898, Martinus Beijerinck called the filtered substance a virus. That was 122 years ago. It has now been 114 years since the concept of an asymptomatic carrier was first identified in the guise of Mary Mallon.

In as much as nothing can ever be known with total absolute surety, COVID-19 exists. Doctors didn't try and educate Mary. When that happened, an ignorant response was the only one possible.

You just need to look at Woodrow Wilson's reaction to the Spanish Flu pandemic to see that what we are doing now as a country is going to make getting through this much harder. He did a lot of the same things that our leadership is currently doing, and it didn't end well. Even with that, they did finally get through the Spanish Flu. They got through it and so will we.

I have faith in science. I have faith in history. I also have faith in some things that can't be so readily proved by science. I have faith in love.

Keeping each other safe is an act of love. If there is something that I can do that might help, then sign me up. Inconvenience is a small price to pay for keeping my community safe. If, as time passes, science tells us that some of the things we are doing now had no real effect, then I will get together with those I love, and we will laugh at our idiocy. For now, though, I am going to follow what the scientists are saying.

May 19, 2020
355,886 Total Reported Cases in New York. 29,652 Deaths.

Day after day
After day after day
After day after day after day

That's what song was in my head when I woke up this morning.

Merrily We Roll Along by George Furth and Stephen Sondheim is an interesting show because it is written backward. It starts with the final scene and works its way back to the first scene. You know how it ends from the beginning. The fun of the show is seeing, bit by bit (to quote another Stephen Sondheim musical) how the characters ended up the way that they do. How interesting it would be to know how all of this will end and then work our way back to where we are now.

Yesterday, we heard that a company named Moderna reported promising results with an experimental COVID-19 vaccine. The company tested 8 healthy volunteers and the vaccine caused all 8 of them to develop antibodies to the virus without immediate side effects.

My immediate reaction was the elation that this might soon be over. As the day went by, however, it became clear that while this development might indeed accelerate the speed with which we can all get back to work, that speed is still relative.

The next step for Moderna is to test the vaccine on a larger group of hundreds. Then, it will need to be tested on an even larger group of thousands to make sure that the vaccine is safe and, of course, effective. As the vaccine trials move forward, so will the studies that are determining how effective the COVID-19 antibodies are in terms of immunizing us. The test results of all these trials then need to be analyzed and, if the outcome is still positive, presented to the FDA for approval.

One immunologist on TV yesterday was optimistic that if all went well that the vaccine could be available as soon as the beginning of next year. That's great, but that's still eight months from now. If it all works. We have quite a way to go.

As we move along the path of this journey, I'm finding that there are moments where the reality of this sinks in. It's one thing to know something intellectually, but a completely different thing when you wake up to it on a deeper level.

Like everybody, Michael and I need to figure out how we are going to get through the next year. It's one thing to be unemployed and searching for a job, but a completely different thing to be unemployed when what you do isn't happening. Anywhere in the world. There are no jobs in our industry to be found. These next months are only going to be effective for a lot of us who work in businesses that are on hold if we create things to do ourselves.

As this crisis started, the fear and anxiety were overwhelming. We all just hid. Now, though, we have much more information. We've experienced living this way and we've learned to adjust. The days even seem longer now because they aren't being eaten up by terror.

As we move forward, there is going to be a LOT of political noise coming our way. After all, there's a big election coming up in November.

During one of his morning addresses, Governor Cuomo had the COVID swab test done on him on camera. A health care professional, in full PPE came on, stuck the swab in his nose, and left.

That moment did more towards alleviating the fear around this virus than talking about it ever has. It seemed easy and quick. A clear and effective presentation of facts.

On the other hand, yesterday, the President announced that he's been taking hydroxychloroquine to keep from getting the virus for about a week and a half. Hydroxychloroquine not only has no proven effect on the virus, but it also has some incredibly nasty side effects. The President latched onto this drug early on when it seemed like it might help somewhat, but since then, there is nothing that demonstrates that it can help at all.

Hydroxychloroquine is commonly used as a malaria prophylactic. I've taken it when I've traveled to places where there's malaria—Peru, parts of Africa, maybe Costa Rica. For me, it can cause headaches and vivid, sometimes, violent dreams. It can potentially cause a lot of other things in people including heart problems. It isn't something to be taken lightly. A week and a half ago, the point at which the President says he started taking the drug, was when one of his valets tested positive for the virus. The President, a reputed germaphobe, is clearly terrified of getting the virus. He's grasping at straws—taking a potentially dangerous drug with no proven application to the virus just because he's terrified.

Over the next months, we are going to get a lot angrier as more nonsense like this comes our way. It takes forever to wade through the noise to find out what's really being said, and it often just isn't worth it.

Maybe it was a result of that clear realization that we have so much more time in lockdown ahead of us, but yesterday, Michael and I did a massive clean-up in the apartment.

Our cat has several places in the apartment where he likes to sleep. These places change randomly over time. Recently, his favorite places have been under a sideboard kind of thing in the living room, on one of Michael's backpacks that has been, for the last two months, sitting on an armchair, and on a piece of cloth in the corner of the bedroom. He curls up in one of those places and after a few days or weeks, a nest-like circle of shed fur forms where he's been.

Michael and I do the same thing. We've established various places in the apartment where each of us likes to sit. In a tight circle around those areas, we've each formed nests made up of empty coffee cups, pencils, receipts, notepads, half-completed projects, future projects, paper clips, power cords—you name it.

Yesterday, we cleaned. Vacuumed. Dusted. Sorted. The piece of cloth Ziggy was sleeping on in the bedroom turned out to be one of Michael's shirts. We did laundry—clothes, towels, bathmats. The nests are gone. We have a clean slate.

Stephen Sondheim, who wrote *Merrily We Roll Along,* also wrote *Sunday in the Park with George* with James Lapine about the French pointillist painter Gorges Seurat. It is a musical about the creative process.

It ends with the words:

White.
A blank page or canvas.
His favorite.
So many possibilities.

Our apartment is clean. Our heads are clear. We are ready for anything.

May 20, 2020

357,052 Total Reported Cases in New York. 29,717 Deaths.

South Korea and the United States identified their first cases of COVID-19 on the same day.

In Seoul, restaurants, parks, and malls have reopened. When somebody tests positive, the government can trace and track almost anyone that person encountered. The government plans to keep these measures in place for months, or years, if necessary.

What is happening in South Korea won't happen here. We are a federation of 50 different states linked together by an overseeing federal government. All 50 states have a great deal of autonomy.

A strong President can offer leadership and guidance and federal legislation to keep the states in line with a coordinated effort, but we don't have that now. We have a President who has abdicated all responsibility for spearheading this effort, so the completely unsurprising result is that each of the 50 states is moving forward on their own, under their own rationales and guidelines.

What works in South Korea won't work here. We Americans have a knee-jerk reaction to anything that might even possibly infringe upon our rights. There are already people who have said that they won't get the vaccine when it comes because the government will use it to inject us all with tracking microchips. The government doesn't need to inject us with microchips. The government already has plenty of ability to track us. Every time we use a credit card, an ATM, pay a toll, go online, make a call, we are traceable.

If your computer is on and you discuss buying a car, car advertising will start to appear in some of your social media apps. Somebody's already listening. The government doesn't need to inject us with microchips, we've already done it ourselves. Willingly.

The CDC released their guidelines so late because they were trying to navigate through partisan politics. Releasing guidelines about how to get your horse slowly and carefully out of the barn is somewhat pointless when the horse is already out grazing in the field. We needed the testing two months ago when this all began.

When Michael and I got sick in early March, we did our best to get tested but they weren't available to be able to do that. Testing was limited to people with severe symptoms which we did not have. At that point, everybody should have been tested because we already knew that people without symptoms were carrying it.

What should be happening now, though, is that politicians, scientists, and human rights advocates, instead of fighting with each other, should all be working together to figure out a way through this pandemic. We must weigh where our greatest discomfort lies on the scale of virus containment vs. human rights vs. danger to the economy.

There's a saying that everyone's a socialist in a crisis. The ardent capitalists are, of course, the first ones to ask for government handouts when there's a problem. The stock market should rule... until it can't. The stock market is not going to solve this crisis.

I am not advocating that we should all be microchipped and give up more of our right to privacy. I think, though, that we need to be clear and honest about what rights we have already given up over the last few decades.

Virologists can only tell us how to fight the virus, not how to save the economy or our rights. We are getting more and more evidence with each passing day that we, the people, are not equipped to deal with this ourselves, either. We seem to be running amok.

South Korea is finding a way through this. That way is not open to us. If there is one way through, though, then there must be another one that will work for us.

May 22, 2020
360,818 Total Reported Cases in New York. 29,864 Deaths.

When I was a kid and living in suburban New Jersey, I lived on my bicycle. I rode everywhere—to school, to friends' houses, to towns that were miles away. Remember, this was a time when your mother would shoo you outside in the morning and tell you to come back for dinner when the town siren went off at 7. We'd wander home when we were hungry, but basically, we spent the day out playing somewhere. The whole day—on our own. We'd play in each other's yards or ride our bicycles three towns over. For me, my bike was freedom. And adventure. It let me dream about where I'd go when I grew up.

A few years ago, when we put *Jersey Boys* up in Holland, I was given a bicycle to get back and forth to rehearsal. Amsterdam is a city made for bicycles. There are bike lanes all through the city with their own traffic lights. My young teenage self would have thrilled to be in that city.

These days in New York City, public transportation is out of bounds. For one thing, it is almost impossible to maintain social distancing on either buses or subways. More importantly, however, essential workers need to travel to their jobs. Since the rest of us don't usually HAVE to go anywhere. Keeping off public transportation keeps them safer.

For Michael's birthday last Sunday, my gift to him was a bicycle helmet and a membership to Citi Bike, New York's bike-sharing system. Manhattan is just over 13 miles long. Now, with the bicycles, we can pretty much get anywhere on the island. What on earth were we waiting for?

We took our first ride in the park on Wednesday, I noticed something right away. Nobody out riding a bike follows the rules. They just go wherever and do whatever they want.

The Oxford dictionary defines rules as "one of a set of explicit or understood regulations or principles governing conduct within a particular activity or sphere." Almost none of us live completely alone. We are social creatures, and we form communities. We agree on rules to help us navigate along with each other in those communities. If everyone did exactly what they wanted, when they wanted, we'd be in constant conflict.

We have agreed that in this country anyway, that rather than make the rules ourselves that we will select people to represent us who will make them for us. We have also agreed that we are freely allowed to complain about the rules and about the people we have empowered to make them. Most importantly, though, we have agreed that until the rules change, we are not allowed to break them.

Now, there are rules we follow and those we don't. Sometimes, the rules we follow are in direct opposition to the rules that are in the books. For example, New York pedestrians don't wait for traffic signals to change before they cross. We cross when the coast is clear, regardless of whether the light is green or not. When you see somebody waiting at a street corner, following the rules, more likely than not, that person isn't from here.

I once got a ticket in Costa Mesa, California for jaywalking. Apparently, the people of Costa Mesa, as a community, had agreed to follow that rule. Nobody jaywalks in Tokyo either. Even at night when there's nobody around and no traffic. People wait for the light to change standing alone on a deserted street.

We chafe at rules all the time and we decide which ones we don't like, and which don't apply to us. I'm certainly as guilty of this as anyone. Remember though, in the broad picture, all the rules that we live under are made with our input and our tacit approval.

If we don't question that person whom we empowered to make the rules beforehand, or, even worse, don't participate in the choosing of that person, then we have lost our ability to have a say in what results. The choosing of that person is where we get our say. Once the person is chosen, our individual input is done. We can complain but the person we chose now makes the rules. That's what we agree to when we decide to live in this community.

Not participating in the choosing of the person you want always gives the advantage to the person you don't want. Sometimes the choice is clear, but sometimes you don't really like either person, so you choose the person you dislike the least. None of the choices are ever perfect. If you dislike everyone out there, and you feel that nobody is representing exactly what you want, then you can always try and get chosen to do the job yourself.

Short of that, we can't have everything we want, individually, every time. We have agreed, as part of our social contract with each other, to compromise some of our wishes for the good of all.

These days, the people we have chosen to lead us are facing a crisis that is new to them. Mistakes are being made. It's inevitable. These people are only human after all, and this is a particularly complicated problem. Some of the people who represent us are, however, failing quite badly.

We are coming up on a moment where we will have the opportunity to select other people to represent us at the highest level of our government. Many of the people who are currently holding these positions are trying to make rules that make it harder for anyone but them to be chosen. Rather than creating rules to help all of us, they are, instead, creating rules that only help themselves.

The people we have selected to make our rules in New York are asking us to keep social distancing measures in place and to wear masks. That is the decision that WE as a community has decided will help us through this health crisis. If you disagree with that rule, then, in a few months, you will have the ability to try and choose someone who will make another rule. In the meantime, you have agreed, as a member of this community, to follow those safety measures for everybody else—whether you believe in them or not.

Yes, I will continue to cross on the red, but only because, as a city, that is what we have collectively agreed to do. When I get back to Tokyo, though, or Costa Mesa, I will stand on that corner, for hours, if need be, until the light changes, because that is what they have decided to do there.

Today, I am going to request my absentee ballot. Then, with my helmet and my mask on, I'm going to go for a ride in the park. There's only one direction that we are supposed to go in, so that's the direction that I will take, no matter how many people I pass peddling the other way.

May 23, 2020

5.2 Million Cases Reported Worldwide. 340,000 Deaths.

"Jumping the Shark" is the term used to describe the point at which the writers of a TV show create a situation so ridiculous that you can look back and point to it as the thing that finally led to ending the show's run. The term came from an episode of *Happy Days* where the ultra-cool character, Fonzie, while still wearing his trademark leather jacket, is waterskiing and jumps over a fake shark.

It was a moment so removed from the original inspiration of the series that looking back on it, you could see that it was a clear harbinger of the end. The writers had run out of things to say. It was absurd. The COVID-19 pandemic has jumped the shark.

Yesterday, the White House did a particularly early briefing. At the top of it, the President marched forcefully up to the podium, announced that places of worship were essential services and that they needed to be reopened immediately. Churches, synagogues, and… mosques… (He choked a little on mosques.) He confidently announced that if Governors don't comply, he will override them. With that, he finished his little speech and marched right off again. The whole thing took less than a minute.

The President has no authority to force Governors to reopen houses of worship. Even if he did, some of the worst outbreaks of the virus that we've seen can be traced back to religious gatherings. Nothing about his little outburst made a lick of sense. Instead of being shocked, the response from TV commentators was more like, "Umm… No." and then they moved on to other topics.

The endless repetition of COVID coverage on TV is mind-numbing. We aren't really scared of it anymore. While waiting for the mayor to come on, I just watched 10 minutes of coverage of how Gatorland in Orlando is planning to reopen. The virus, in and of itself, is no longer even interesting.

In 1983, as the HIV/AIDS crisis raged, the only way we knew to fight it was to not have sex.

That's what we were told time and again by health officials, but they never told us how not to do that.

People are going to have sex regardless of whether they are allowed to or not. So, to try and deal with the issue in a way that took real human behavior into account, a group of activists came up with a document called *How to Have Sex in an Epidemic*. It provided some clear guidance on which sex acts were riskier than others and even provided early suggestions for condom use.

Staying at home forever is not going to work any better than refraining from sex did during the early HIV/AIDS era. It was never going to be the thing that cured the virus. In New York, staying at home for the last two months has seemingly accomplished what it was designed to do which was to keep our hospitals from being overrun. We cannot continue quarantining forever. The human psyche is not equipped for this much isolation.

Safe Sex is a myth. The only completely safe sex is no sex. Saf-ER Sex, however, is achievable. As we start interacting with each other again this summer, we are going to need to figure out how to achieve Saf-ER interaction. We are going to interact despite what anyone says. We NEED to interact. It's almost a miracle that we've been able to keep this up for as long as we already have.

The federal government has effectively muzzled the CDC, so we are going to need to rely on our state and city health departments to give us recommendations. Shaming people for breaking social guidelines, much like shaming people for unsafe sex practices, is just going to drive the behavior underground.

As painfully boring and depressing as this quarantine is, we need to stick with it a while longer. When we start reopening, maybe a few weeks from now, we should take it slow. The alternative is that we could all end right back where we started.

We all want out. I want it so badly that I can taste it. I miss you all.

May 24, 2020
Darnella Frazier remembers to charge her phone.

I got cruised out on the street yesterday. At least I think I was. The guy was wearing one of those sleek black fitted masks with a ridge down the center that follows the contours of the face but covers most of it. All I could see was the thin band of his face from the top of his mask to the bottom of his messy dark hair.

As we passed each other on opposite sides of the sidewalk, I noticed he was looking at me, and, for a moment, our eyes locked. I thought, at first, that he was a friend of mine that I'd recently had a texting conversation with, but then I realized that he was too tall for that to be him. I broke the eye lock and continued walking, feeling that brief pleasant rush of having been noticed.

As I walked past a closed store, I looked at my reflection in the empty window to see what he had seen. It wasn't very notable. What he had seen was a guy wearing a mask with a spider on it and a grey bicycle helmet. Most of what is identifiable about me was completely covered up. I really could have been almost anyone.

A week or two ago I was in a Duane Reade and a friend of mine said "Hi Richard!". Our eyes met, and he pulled down his mask so I could see who it was since I clearly didn't recognize him just from his eyes. Once he did that, I, of course, knew who it was, and he pulled his mask back up. We waggled elbows at each other and chatted for a while from 6 feet apart. Smiling is one of the few signals that are possible to convey through the eyes. We all seem to be getting the crinkle-eyed smile thing down—even exaggerating it to make sure it's being received.

Yesterday, I decided that I wanted to see the Little Red Lighthouse that sits under the George Washington Bridge. It's about four miles away from us and has been on my bucket list of things to see in New York for nearly 40 years. I hopped on a bike and headed up.

The lighthouse is built on a spit of land called Jeffrey's Hook which juts out into the Hudson River. It was originally in another location but moved to its current position in 1921 to help warn river traffic away from the rocks on the outcropping. Six years later, construction started on the George Washington Bridge and Jeffrey's Hook was used as the land that supported the eastern base of the bridge. They built the bridge right over the little lighthouse. Once the bridge was completed and lit the need for the lighthouse passed and it was decommissioned.

A truly beautiful children's picture book called *The Little Red Lighthouse, and the Great Gray Bridge* was written by Hildegarde Swift and Lynd Ward in 1942. When the city later proposed that the lighthouse be taken down, the public outcry was so great because of the book, that, instead, it was deeded to the New York Department of Parks and Recreation and allowed to remain. Years ago, friends of mine lost a child early on in their pregnancy and that is the spot where they chose to scatter the ashes. It's a beautiful little place in a remarkable spot.

While I was researching the history of the Little Red Lighthouse this morning, I came across a wonderful story of something that just happened there. A guy arranged with several teams from the New York Department of Parks and Recreation as well as the Historic House Trust of New York to let him propose at the top of the lighthouse. It was the first recorded proposal to ever occur at the top. This happened at the end of February just before everything shut down.

Oh yes, the other guy said yes.

Last year, Michael and I spent several months living and working in Tokyo. The Japanese have been wearing masks for years and they've never done anything to design or decorate them. After just a few weeks into mask-wearing here in New York, however, a whole new fashion industry has cropped up. People started making colorful masks for themselves and their friends. Now manufacturers have caught on and are mass producing them with an assortment of patterns and different designs. When did we start wearing masks?—end of March? Early April? It's only May and now they are ubiquitous. Now, we are all trying to figure out what is chic in a mask and what isn't. People are even getting different masks to go with their different outfits.

I am going to try and find out where I can get a black mask like the guy who may or may not have cruised me. I like the way it looked. Then I am going to have to assure Michael about the guy who may or may not have cruised me. I mean after all… it was just a look, right?

MAY 25, 2020
George Floyd murdered by Police Officer Derek Chauvin.

Today is Memorial Day.

Lila A. Fenwick, the first black woman to graduate from Harvard Law School.
Torin Jamal Howard, a young athlete, and a musician.
Kyra Swartz, who volunteered at animal rescue organizations.

Memorial Day started as Decoration Day which was to honor the Union and Confederate soldiers who died during the Civil War. By the early 1900s it had become a day in which we remember all of those who lost their lives while serving in the military in service of our country.

1967 was when the name Memorial Day was first used.

Antonio Checo, a social worker.
Coby Adolph, an entrepreneur, and an adventurer.
Lorena Borjas, a transgender immigrant activist.

Summer technically doesn't start until June, but many places use the day as the marker to reopen their businesses. When I was still in school, Memorial Day is when our town pool opened. The Memorial Day parade was a signal that the long endless winter was finally over, and classes were done. There was a feeling that we had an endless time of play and clear blue days ahead of us. No teachers. No obligations. We had the freedom to ride our bikes and swim and maybe go on a trip.

Helen Kafkis, a cook known for her chicken and stuffed peppers.
Doris Brown, a wife who passed on the same day as her husband.
Robert Charles Bazzell loved to drive along route 66.

This year is not quite the same.

Laneeka Barsdale, a ballroom dancer.
Howard Alexander Nelson, Jr., advocated for health care policy.
Melvin Pumphrey, a mentor.

This year, here in the US, we are going into a very different Memorial Day than we are used to. Health care workers are doing everything they can, short of screaming "fire" to urge people to wear masks and maintain social distancing.

Sean Christian Keville, a sports fan.
Cynthia Whiting, a doting grandmother.
Fredrick Brown Star, a businessman.

There are lessons that we can learn from parades that were held during earlier pandemics, but we seem to be ignoring them. Philadelphia decided not to cancel a Liberty Loan parade during the Spanish flu outbreak and that resulted in 1,000 deaths. Denver lifted restrictions to be able to celebrate Armistice Day and they saw a big spike, too.

Thomas Waters, a data analyst for affordable housing.
Bassey Offiong, a man who loved his friends.
Mary Desole, a literacy volunteer.

100,000 people have lost their lives to this virus already. This morning the New York Times filled the front page with their names. How many more will we have to lose because we can't keep up our responsible behavior.

We don't wish each other a happy Memorial Day. That's not what today is. Today is a day where we take a moment to offer thanks to the brave people who fought for us. The people that we are losing to this virus are not all soldiers. Some are, but these people are also health care workers and teachers, and law enforcement officers. These people are also wives and fathers and children and friends, bakers and cashiers and pilots and janitors, financiers and writers and gardeners and lawyers. Instead of turning today into a rave, maybe today we should honor those who have lost their lives by ensuring that more don't lose theirs.

Julia Maye Alexander, a math, English, and history teacher.
Dan Bellito, a town councilman.
Peggy Rakestraw, an avid reader.

We have fought many wars to preserve our way of life. Today, we honor those who didn't make it through their wars. Let's take some time today to think about all of them.

Lucius Hall, a preacher.
Kamal Ahmed, a hotel banquet worker, and Bangladeshi leader.
Alice Chavdarian, a loving, generous, and adventurous spirit.

May 26, 2020
367,349 Total Reported Cases in New York. 30,276 Deaths.

Since we never know which day it is, we tend to use things that happened to put events on a timeline. We have had the Day of the Haircut, the Day of the Pie, the Day of the Call with the Family, and many others like that. Yesterday, was The Day we Clipped the Cat's Claws.

Both Michael and I have had or been around cats for most of our lives. Growing up, we each went through many of them. At one point when I was a kid, we had seven. My father had reached his limit and found homes for three of them while we were away on a trip with my mother, and we went back down to four.

These days we are living with a cat that I got in San Francisco while I was doing *Jersey Boys*. Ziggy is a very chill cat. He's a very fluffy black and white mutt. While he started as mine, the Zig is now, being taken care of by both of us. If we come home at the same time, he still tends to come to me, but only because he knows that I am more of a pushover when it comes to feeding him. If someone is feeding him, he doesn't care who they are—he loves them.

The Zig is amenable to anything except getting his claws clipped. After all the cats that I've had, I know how to safely clip their claws. My last cat never complained at all. This one, though, even from the time he was tiny a kitten, he has hated it. The bigger he got the harder it was to do. It is as if we are impaling him with a glowing, hot poker. He hisses and yowls and desperately tries to claw his way away from us.

His claws had gotten long and sharp as needles. It had gotten to the point that he couldn't walk across our carpets anymore without getting stuck on them. It was time.

We have a method. It's imperfect, but it works. It is extremely traumatic for all three of us. Michael sits on the edge of the bed with his legs together and holds the cat on his back in the crevice between his knees. I then get behind Michael and get the back legs between Michael's back and his arm so the cat can't see what I'm doing. Once I get his back claws done, then he can't hurt Michael kicking with them as I do the front claws.

Because of the sound, we were expecting a call from Animal Care and Control for reported cruelty. The yowling and hissing and thrashing were epic, but we got through it. The second we were done the cat was totally fine. It was like a switch flicked off. He was completely calm, with no residual anxiety or trauma at all. He shook himself and casually sauntered over to his food dish knowing that he was going to get something good from his guilt-ridden caregivers. He got his treat. Ate it. And purred. Michael and I had to have a glass of sake. Possibly two.

The New York Stock Exchange opened for business this morning. They maintained only a 25% capacity with masks and distancing, but for the first time in two months, there will be live trading.

Health professionals are all warning about a second wave. The virus is still here. It hasn't gone anywhere. We slowed down its ability to spread somewhat for a moment, but we didn't get rid of it. Church services on Sunday and Memorial Day celebrations yesterday gave it a great chance to spread some more.

There are many more days ahead of us. It's going to be hard to follow The Day we Clipped the Cat's Claws, but I'm sure we will come up with something.

MAY 27, 2020
100,000 Total Reported Deaths in the United States.

One of the things that I have been able to do much more of during this strange period of forced inactivity away from the pressures of work, is read. I have always been an avid reader. My father wrote for a living and my mother was a librarian—it was somewhat inevitable. The newspaper in the town we lived in, in New Jersey once ran an article about my mother and father and sister and I being "the family that read together." We had to pose for a picture of all of us together reading. I can't imagine how I survived being teased about it in school.

Storytelling-wise, there is something a bit contrived about COVID-19 striking at the very moment we are facing a major election. Nonetheless, that's where we are and that's what we are facing. The pandemic seems to be crystallizing the views and positions of both parties as we head into November. Those positions were clearly differentiated over Memorial Day with pictures of Senator Joe Biden wearing a mask and pictures of the President, not. In a sense, those simple, clear images of the two men are emblematic of exactly what's dividing us.

On the one hand, you have a person wearing a mask, following the science. On the other hand, you have a person, not wearing a mask and not following the science. So, in a sense—good vs. evil. Science vs... what? If you look up what the opposite of science is, you get a whole bunch of words like ignorance, blindness, inexperience, immaturity, weak-mindedness, lack of knowledge, falsehoods, and unawareness. It is hard not to look at the pictures of mass gatherings over the weekend in places all over the country and not think about all those words.

For the moment, instead of all going out to party together, maybe we'd be better off just staying at home and diving into a good book.

MAY 28, 2020
369,438 Total Reported Cases in New York. 30,482 Deaths.

When I was five, my mother, sister, and I went to live with my grandfather in South Africa. At the time, apartheid was in full force. Black Africans were not allowed to live in white communities unless they had a passbook.

My Grandfather had several people working for him—a housekeeper named Maude and a gardener named Bennett. Behind my grandfather's house were the kiyas, or huts, where Maude and Bennett would stay, courtesy of their passbooks, for most of the week. Their actual homes were out of sight on the other side of a hill, in an area called Location. The kiyas had no windows and no electricity or plumbing. Kerosene heaters kept them warm, and an outhouse took care of their other needs. I think that there were floors in the kiyas—I have a memory of worn linoleum—but I wouldn't swear to it.

Maude and Bennett had worked for my grandfather for decades. When Maude became too old and finally retired, her daughter Agnes, took over her job. Agnes had a son named Jabulani who was four or five years older than I was. Bennett had a son named N'Kosinkulu who was two years older than my sister, and one year younger than me. My sister and I grew up with the two of them. I went to school down at the bottom of the road where we lived, and Jabulani and N'Kosinkulu went to school in Location. After school, we all played together.

I have a very vivid memory of playing with Jabulani one afternoon. I had a lot of nice toy cars. I still have one of my favorites—a Corgi Land rover. I also had a bunch of other much cheaper plastic ones. One afternoon, Jabulani suggested that he could make one of those cheaper cars run on its own, but he'd need to make a hole in the side of it. I readily agreed.

The car was light blue plastic and completely hollow inside. The wheels were two slag metal spool-shaped things that clicked into grooves in the plastic underneath. As Jabulani started drilling into the side of the car, he found it harder going than he thought it would be. He had gotten about halfway through the project when I turned on him.

I wailed into the house that Jabulani had ruined my toy. Yes, I had given my full consent to the operation, but it didn't matter. He had ruined my toy car. I KNEW that I would be believed. I KNEW that Jabulani would not be able to defend himself.

I knew all of this because I had more power than he did, even though I was younger. I knew my whiteness meant something more than his blackness did. I was six years old and, somehow, I already knew this. I also knew it was wrong. The shame I felt at watching Jabulani being punished for something that was not his fault has etched that memory deep into my psyche and I have never forgotten it.

Years later, I saw Athol Fugard's play *"Master Harold" ...and the Boys* on Broadway and there it was again. Fugard wrote a play about a boy whose mother owns a tea shop. The story recounts his relationship with the two middle-aged black men who work for his mother and who raised him. Hallie, the "Master Harold" of the title, turns on his friends in the end, unleashing the vicious racism that he has learned from his father. He also does it, knowing full well what he is doing.

Two days ago, a woman named Amy Cooper, seems to have done much the same thing in Central Park. Her dog was off its leash in an area where dogs are required to be leashed and when asked, politely, to put the leash back on by a black man, she called the police. Christian Cooper, the man in question, started filming the encounter.

She gets on the phone with the police and appears to consciously pitch her voice higher to pretend that she's in distress. Mr. Cooper stays calm and composed throughout. As a white woman, she can make a call knowing that Christian Cooper will be blamed, and she will be protected. As a white, middle-class woman, she is allowed to do whatever she wants—even if it's against the rules—and she will be believed. This isn't something that she has to think about. This is something that all people who are white know.

We have, by now, all watched George Floyd being killed by a white policeman in Minneapolis. The policeman asphyxiates him by kneeling on his neck. We are all at home watching TV during a global pandemic—it was hard to miss. George Floyd is handcuffed and not resisting, begging for his life and the white policeman, Derek Chauvin, does not stop. George Floyd dies in front of our eyes.

Even though we have now seen black George Floyd die at the hand of a white Derek Chauvin many times over, there is an extremely good chance that white Derek Chauvin will get away with it. White Derek Chauvin still hasn't even been charged with any wrongdoing.

African Americans constitute about 13% of the population of the United States. African Americans currently account for about 23% of the deaths from coronavirus. Are African Americans more susceptible to the coronavirus? Not genetically, no. African Americans are more susceptible to COVID-19 than white Americans because white Americans have better access to everything from information to resources.

Last August, there was a rally in Charlottesville, Virginia. White supremacists and neo-Nazis and Ku Klux Klan members marched to oppose the removal of a statue of Confederate General Robert E. Lee and to unify the white nationalist movement. A white supremacist rammed his car into a group of counter-protestors, killing one and injuring 19 others. The Governor, Terry McAuliffe, declared a state of emergency. The President's response to this was to say that there were "very fine people on both sides."

At six years old, I was able to take in the behavior of the society around me and act accordingly. At six, I was not making a judgment call, I was just acting in a way that I knew would work. The actions of those around us, particularly those people we have chosen to represent us, send us all the signals we need to live our lives. It doesn't matter what they say, it matters what they do. Kids growing up now, are taking careful note.

You can talk about the evils of racism all you want. Nothing is going to change until the behavior of those in charge changes. If Derek Chauvin is not tried and convicted of murder, then there is nothing whatsoever that is going to stop this from happening again. The signal will be sent, again, that it is OK to kill a black man.

Forget mask-wearing. The President has already, through his actions, told the entire country that they don't need to do that. This is murder we are talking about. More will die. Somebody else's father, cousin, friend, brother is going to die at the hands of a white man. How many black Americans do we bury before we get it?

I don't know what's going to happen to Derek Chauvin, but Amy Cooper has lost her job and had her dog taken away from her. It's a start, but we've still got a long way to go.

May 29, 2020
371,101 Total Reported Cases in New York. 30,578 Deaths.

There is rioting in Minneapolis. George Floyd's death is rightfully sparking demonstrations all over the country. The President does not seem to understand why. The rioting is a reaction to a much deeper systemic problem. Solve THAT problem and the rioting stops. But you need to be able to identify what that underlying problem is, first.

Last night POTUS tweeted "These THUGS are dishonoring the memory of George Floyd, and I won't let that happen. Just spoke to Governor Tim Walz and told him that the Military is with him all the way. Any difficulty and we will assume control but, when the looting starts, the shooting starts."

Twitter flagged the President's post today as an incitement to violence. In a long-overdue move, they have started to fact-check the President's tweets. A link was added to a tweet the President put out falsely claiming that there was widespread mail-in voting fraud. In response to that, the President immediately whipped off an unconsidered and ill-conceived executive order designed to remove liability protections from social media platforms. The order is unenforceable and, in any case, requires the approval of Congress who isn't going to give it. For their part, Twitter, says they plan to continue doing exactly what they are doing. The White House tried to retweet today's post on their official site and Twitter just flagged that one too.

The crisis of racism in this country is at least as dire as the crisis of COVID-19 and has been raging far longer. Our crisis of leadership may be the worst of all. All three have been largely ignored and all three are spreading unchecked—at the same time—with lethal consequences.

November is coming. This election, in the middle of this crisis matters. The people we elect in November are the people whom we are entrusting to lead us back to work—safely. We need to choose wisely.

May 30, 2020
372,473 Total Reported Cases in New York. 30,649 Deaths.

In 1773, to bail out the East India Company, the British Parliament passed a bill called the Tea Act. The Act granted the East India Company the right to be the sole importer of tea to the colonies in North America. The East India Company was one of the major corporations in England at that time and a key driver of the entire British economy and it was in danger of going under. England had amassed a crippling amount of national debt coming out of the French and Indian War a decade before and was using the colonies as an exploitable source of revenue to try and rise out of it.

Two years after that war had ended, Parliament passed the Stamp Act which taxed all paper goods sold in the colonies. The colonists protested, arguing that only their own representative governments had the right to levy taxes on them. The British countered that the war had directly benefited the colonies and, as a result, the colonists were being rightfully taxed to help pay for it. The colonies objected that they had no representation in Parliament, but Parliament argued that all British subjects enjoyed virtual representation even though they couldn't directly vote for their representatives.

Patrick Henry submitted a series of resolutions to the Virginia colony's local assembly that called upon colonists to resist the Stamp Act. Newspapers throughout the colonies then reprinted them for all to read. In Boston, a group that called themselves the Sons of Liberty incited a mob to march through the streets with an effigy of the local stamp collector that they then set on fire before ransacking the official's home. He subsequently quit. Similar protests sprung up in towns and cities throughout the colonies and, ultimately, Parliament had no choice but to repeal the act because they couldn't get anybody to agree to collect the taxes.

By the time the Tea Act came around, another seven years had passed. Another seven years of more kinds of taxation by the British Parliament without any representation from the colonies. Protests erupted in many places, the most famous being the one that happened in Boston. A well-organized mob of men, dressed as Native Americans, boarded the East India Company's ships in Boston Harbor and looted them, throwing the tea into the harbor. The violent reaction to this tea tax was not just about the tea. It was the inevitable result of an accumulation of a decade or more of injustice at the hands of the British. We celebrate that action every year as one of the triggers that led to the revolution that helped to birth our new country.

The rallying cry of freedom that inspired our Founding Fathers to break off on their own didn't quite extend to everybody. It wasn't meant to include enslaved people. It didn't include women, either. Or homosexuals. Throughout our national history, gay and transgendered people have been forced to live severely compromised lives. To this day, there are still laws on the books that discriminate against people for their sexual orientation.

Michael and I are not allowed to donate blood plasma, even though we have the COVID-19 antibodies, because we are gay. This outdated and discriminatory law, not based on any sort of science, dates from the early days of the HIV/AIDS plague when it was wrongly thought that only homosexual men were susceptible to the disease and were the sole transmitters of it.

In the 1950s and 1960s in this country, LGBTQ people faced a legal system that was completely stacked against them. It was a criminal offense to be and act as a gay person. Gay people went underground to live their lives. Bars were one of the few businesses that turned a blind eye to homosexuality. Why? Because there was money to be made. The bars and other kinds of establishments where gay people congregated were regularly raided by the police when their owners didn't pay them off. The Stonewall Inn in Greenwich Village, here in New York, was a gay bar that catered to some of the most marginalized, poor members of the LGBTQ community. It was owned and run by the mafia.

Early in the morning of June 28, 1969, during yet another police raid, someone threw a brick. That's all that was needed to light the fire. A spontaneous riot broke out and continued for several days. Each day, more and more people joined in. Those riots were the beginning of the movement that allows me to live an open life with my husband in this country fifty years later. The Stonewall Inn is now part of the National Park Service.

Yesterday, in many cities, all around the country, a whole series of sometimes violent protests erupted in response to the needless death of George Floyd. The protests are still going on. They are not only about George Floyd's murder by a police officer.

In the decades since the Civil Rights movement was fought in the 1960s, the change that struggle promised, has not come to be. There are certainly successes that can be pointed to, the most obvious being the Presidency of Barack Obama, but even so, nothing has truly changed for countless millions of African American people.

Michael and I went downtown to Foley Square to be part of the protest. Participating in a demonstration during a global pandemic was not something that we did lightly. We were careful, but despite the possible danger, we felt that we had an obligation to be there.

At 5 pm, the protest was still peaceful. Almost everybody was masked. "I can't breathe," was an oft-repeated chant. There was a huge police presence, but they were respectful and non-combative. And they were masked as well. There were just as many white people in the crowd as people of color. Michael and I did our best to stay on the edges.

"I can't breathe."

As time went on, and more of us gathered, the police started separating the crowd. Groups ended up fragmenting and going in different directions. One small faction, at the entrance to the Brooklyn Bridge, started confronting the police and pushing together, so Michael and I left them and went to another group. That group was in front of the NYC Criminal Court.

"I can't breathe."

While we were there, we saw some people getting arrested. The police started playing recordings over bullhorns telling people to get out of the street and onto the sidewalk.

"I can't breathe."

The police then started moving together in organized phalanxes. It looked as if things were going to erupt so Michael and I left and went home. We then watched the protests around the country get more and more intense. Newscasters on several stations took great pains to point out that the crowds were not just people of color.

These protests started in direct response to the death of George Floyd but what happened last night is about so much more than that. "A riot is the language of the unheard." So said Dr. Martin Luther King. He continued by asking, "What is it that America has failed to hear?"

"I can't breathe."

The President is talking about sending out the military to deal with the rioting. He is not listening.

"I can't breathe."

We sadly don't have a leader like Dr. King to guide us through this with intelligence and reason and compassion. Or a Nelson Mandela.

"I can't breathe."

We need to listen to why these riots are happening not just send out troops to quash them and put the fires out. The anger won't go away. The anger has been burning for decades. Centuries.

Over our entire history, it seems that the only way that change has happened has been through violent protest. Our country was founded on violent protests.

"I can't breathe."

Change will come. If this isn't the moment that we will look back and point to when that change came, then the next one will be.

"I can't breathe."

The question is, will change come out of violence or out of discussion and education.

"I can't breathe."

We need to listen.

May 31, 2020

373,682 Total Reported Cases in New York. 30,699 Deaths.

I hear a siren outside, this morning, but no sound of helicopters. Yet. Yesterday, there was a march organized in Harlem which is just north of us, so we started the day with more sirens on the street and helicopters in the air.

In the afternoon, I biked in the opposite direction, going downtown through Central Park. The trees in the park are in full leaf now, the spring flowers are largely gone. The Park is a dense thick cloud of green. As I rode downtown, I could hear a protest outside the wall on Central Park West. The group came into the park, near the Museum of Natural History. I continued downtown, riding with the group for a while and adding my voice to the chanting. The protest was strong, but not in any way out of control. It was organized, angry, and focused.

Every week, since the pandemic has shut us down, I've made a pilgrimage into Times Square to see what is happening there. Yesterday, much of Broadway in midtown was closed to vehicular traffic as part of a city program to give people a place to walk that allows them to spread out. Because of that, Times Square was extremely quiet. Very few pedestrians were out, and the whole area had the same desolate feel that it had had in the early weeks of the shutdown.

I wandered out of Times Square and walked down 45th Street to look at the theatres. Some still have their LED marquees running but a couple changed theirs to an image that says, "Only Intermission." I walked through Shubert Alley to 44th Street. The deli that we all used to use is closed. As is Sardi's. And of course, so are the theatres.

As I walked back into Times Square and was starting to head uptown I noticed that in the few minutes that I had been on 45th Street, groups of police officers, some in riot gear, were now standing stock still on several corners. Facing downtown. They were completely on alert. My stomach flipped.

In the distance, I could now see a dark smudge of what turned out to be the front edge of a tide of people walking north. As they got closer, I started being able to see individuals. A bus, two blocks down, had been stopped in the middle of making a turn, unable to proceed. It was being overwhelmed by a tsunami of people. White. Black. Hispanic. Asian.

They flowed into Times Square and filled it in a remarkably short time. I would guess that there were at least five or six thousand people in the group. This group was truly angry. The level of anger was very much escalated from that of the protest that Michael and I had been a part of the day before. The police stood their ground on the street corners and did not react to the protestors. The protesters screamed at them as they passed. I followed the crowd to the north edge of the square.

In the center of Times Square is a large red staircase, underneath which is the TKTS booth that sells ½ price tickets to Broadway shows on the day of. A large part of the crowd ended up on 47th Street, between the north end of the staircase and an Olive Garden. The protestors were largely situated to the west on 47th and a large group of 50-60 police officers had come together to the east. I stayed to the south of both groups in a looser mass of people who were watching. With everybody in this tight area, tension grew. The volume increased. Somebody threw something. Several people hurled plastic water bottles at the police.

Then, a police whistle blew.

In an instant, the entire mass of officers surged as one towards the protestors. There were screams and as one, we all immediately fled. Police officers in full riot gear were charging directly at me along with the rest of the crowd. I turned and ran as fast as I could. After a minute, it was apparent that the police had stopped chasing us. The great majority of the force had gone in another direction.

People were arrested. Those who had been detained were yelling out their names and phone numbers to those that were still free who, in turn, were writing them down. I made my way through all of this so I could get uptown of all of it and out of the way. As I did, I saw that the protest group I had seen earlier in Central Park was now arriving from the north. Truly shaken, I left and headed north back home. I've experienced many protests before but never anything like that.

Last night, protests like this happened all around the country. Some were peaceful but many became violent—far more violent than the short moment I witnessed—with looting and arson. Police officers used tear gas and rubber bullets. CNN is reporting that there was violence reported in at least three dozen different communities. 300 people were arrested in New York City alone.

There are multiple reports, in several places, of policemen, themselves, breaking windows and setting fires to trigger the violence. There is video footage of this happening. Last night here in Chelsea, a small group of people on scooters ignited trashcans ahead of the wave of protesters. Journalists and cameramen were shot at in several cities with rubber bullets even after identifying themselves. There are reports of white supremacist groups inciting the violence in the hopes of starting a race war. While there are plenty of protesters who are not engaging in violence and are marching peacefully, we are just not being shown that.

The murder of George Floyd is just the latest in a seemingly endless stream of similar wrongful deaths of black people at the hands of law enforcement officials. People with conflicting agendas seem to be trying to manipulate the very real anguish that we are feeling towards their own ends.

The press, by just covering the violence and the looting, and not the peaceful protest component, are just inciting more of the same. The burning buildings and cars make for very dramatic images, but they obscure what this protest is fundamentally about—rotting systemic racism that has eaten away at the heart of our country for centuries.

Our President is as responsible for this violence as he is for the death rate of our people from COVID-19. He has encouraged this violence by tweeting support for the armed protestors storming the Michigan capital demanding the lock-down be lifted and condemning the George Floyd protesters as being thugs. He is doing nothing to try and re-establish peace. He isn't addressing the nation. He's silent. He is sitting in the White House watching the country burn and, all the while, adding fuel to the fires.

We cannot be silent.

Since I began writing this, I can hear that the helicopters have come back. There have been more sirens and a constant stream of motorcyclists racing loudly through the streets. This isn't over.

Black Lives Matter. That's the slogan we are marching under. George Floyd mattered. The countless others who have lost their lives mattered. Black lives matter.

SUMMER 2020

JUNE—AUGUST

June 1, 2020
374,818 Total Reported Cases in New York. 30,686 Deaths.

A week after the senseless death of George Floyd, another black man was shot in Kentucky last night by the police. Several police officers were suspended in Atlanta over the weekend for the use of excessive force against a couple of black college kids. On the other hand, there have also been reports from many places around the country of some police officers kneeling in support of protesters.

Protests have now occurred in every state of the union. Most have been peaceful, but they are being overshadowed by the ones that have turned violent. The National Guard has been deployed in 24 states as a safety measure to counter the possible violence. Hundreds of people rallied in London yesterday under Black Lives Matter banners calling for an end to police brutality in the United States. They also rallied in Toronto. They rallied in Berlin.

All of this and the President has yet to address the nation. We should probably be grateful for that.

In 1973, the US Department of Justice sued him and his company for housing discrimination against African Americans. He settled without admitting any bias. The DOJ sued him again five years later for the same thing. He was a driving force behind the "birther" campaign questioning whether President Obama was a native-born American. (He is.) He has continually claimed that a group of teenagers of color who came to be known as the Central Park Five was guilty of the rape of a white woman in 1989. (They weren't.) His support of the Ku Klux Klan and other white supremacist groups during the marches in Charlottesville in 2017 is a matter of record, as is his support of the armed white supremacists who stormed the Michigan capital. After coming out of the bunker he was taken to on Friday as protests surrounded the White House, he tweeted that nobody had come over the White House fence. If they had, they would have been greeted with "the most vicious dogs and most ominous weapons." Escaped slaves were hunted with dogs.

To expect any compassion or even understanding from this man is foolish. To expect any sort of meaningful legislation aimed at rectifying the underlying issues of these protests from this man and his supporters is simply delusional. Still, the fact that he has not addressed the country amid all the widespread unrest and national grief we are experiencing is remarkable.

Of course, all of this is happening in the middle of a global pandemic. The press seems thrilled to have something other than COVID-19 to report on. So thrilled, that it is now hard to find any coverage of the coronavirus at all. The White House has significantly decreased the frequency of the COVID-19 task force meetings. Dr. Fauci just reported in an interview that he rarely meets with the President these days. As far as the White House is concerned, it seems that the pandemic crisis is over and done. It isn't.

BOTH the virus and the social unrest are happening at the same time. In a way, coronavirus shutting us down has given us all the time to finally listen to the cries of our brothers and sisters without distraction. We need to listen. We also need to add our voices to the protests because remaining silent is not an option. How we raise our voices, though, is a complicated question and it's one that each of us needs to answer for ourselves.

I hope that in the days to come, our community leaders can start to focus the amazing energy that has been generated these last few days towards the creation and enactment of some positive concrete legislative reforms. We certainly have everybody's attention—let's tell them what we want.

To win this war, both battles must be fought. Achieving some racial reform will be meaningless if we can't get a handle on COVID-19 and move forward towards fully reopening our economy.

A house can withstand dry rot and termites for only so long before it finally collapses. Our house is now starting to show signs of collapse while we are in the middle of a hurricane. We knew the rot and insects were there, but we put off dealing with them. We have nobody to blame for this but ourselves. Now we must fix the problem, remodel, and rebuild at the same time we are riding out a storm.

Grab a hammer and some nails and let's get to work. We need to save our house.

June 2, 2020

375,887 Total Reported Cases in New York. 30,765 Deaths.

Last night, New York City was locked down from 11 pm to 5 am. We were put under an official curfew. It has already been announced that the curfew will be imposed upon us again tonight starting at 8 pm—three hours earlier than last night. It will be in place through Sunday.

I'm trying to remember if I have ever been in a situation before where I was not allowed to leave my home; where doing so could subject me to arrest. This is just one of the many things that I have seen or experienced in New York City for the first time these past few months. I fear that there are more coming.

Throughout Manhattan, yesterday, people were preparing for the night. Stores, already closed, are now being covered up with plywood.

A group claiming to be ANTIFA, issued tweets yesterday calling for violence in all major US cities. ANTIFA is short for anti-fascist. It is a political protest movement of people militantly opposed to fascism and extreme right-wing ideologies. The President is trying to get them labeled as a domestic terrorist organization even though they are not an organization. They are a movement. They're no leaders. They don't have office supplies. They don't have stationery.

You can't legislate against a feeling or an opinion. The people attracted to the ANTIFA movement believe that violence is justified in the pursuit of political aims. Because of that, those people are a perfect target for manipulation by white supremacists who also believe that violence is justified to achieve their aims. The President is trying to get ANTIFA labeled as terrorists because of their political beliefs not because of their willingness to participate in violence. If he was truly concerned about violence, there are plenty of right-wing groups who are bonafide organizations—who do have leaders and office supplies and the stationery—that he could apply that label to, but he hasn't. And he won't.

In Times Square yesterday, I participated in a large, peaceful Black Lives Matter protest. People of all races gathered at the southern end of the square and we listened as people spoke about their pain. Surrounding us, was a massive police force. A long line of Police scooters was parked to the south of the group. To the north, officers stood in three well-ordered lines in front of the Hard Rock café. Each one had a large bundle of zip cuffs tied to their belts.

Afterward, I headed down into SoHo which had been subject to a lot of looting and violence the night before. There was still broken glass in the street and repair crews were doing their best to bring order back to the neighborhood. There was fresh graffiti everywhere. A lot of F★^k 12. 12 is a slang reference to police officers that derives from an old TV series about police officers called *Adam-12*.

The President, after days of silence, finally addressed the nation from the Rose Garden at the White House. There was an odd delay at the beginning and some confusion about when, exactly, he would start.

As the press was focusing on the imminent arrival of the President, there was a peaceful demonstration happening out in front of the White

House in Lafayette Park. It was not a march. Protesters were staying in place. St. John's Episcopal Church which is just to the north of the White House on the other side of the park was operating as a kind of first aid and water station for the protest. The night before, the church had been damaged and vandalized.

When the President finally started speaking in the Rose Garden he said, "I am your President of law and order and an ally of all peaceful protesters." As he was speaking those words, District police officers and National Guard members moved in on the protesters outside with tear gas, rubber bullets and compression grenades and cleared them all out of the Square.

After the President finished his remarks, he walked across into the now empty Lafayette Square for a photo op in front of the church. He held a bible, but didn't seem to notice that it was upside down. He posed with a group of all-white aides. He never went inside the building.

Governor Cuomo did not want to impose a curfew here in New York, Mayor de Blasio did. We got a curfew. Cuomo offered de Blasio National Guard protection last night, de Blasio refused, saying that the NYPD could handle it. They couldn't. Or didn't. There was widespread looting last night throughout New York City. Macy's Herald Square, despite being boarded up, was broken into and looted. There were incidents all up and down 5th Avenue. The New York Police Department was nowhere to be seen in many of these places.

The Black Lives Matter demonstrations happening during the day must be separated from the mayhem that is happening at night. Yes, there is some crossover, but they are two different things—one action is legal and protected by the Constitution, and one is not.

The President reportedly felt that people thought he appeared weak for sheltering in a bunker on Friday night while protests happened around the nation's house. He wanted to show everyone that he was strong. The President did not show any strength yesterday. Instead, he showed us all how very weak he is. Fear is weak. Threats are weak. Hate is weak.

Together, we are strong. Remember your strength. Love will win because love ALWAYS wins.

June 3, 2020
376,676 Total Reported Cases in New York. 30,819 Deaths.

At the Hotel Braddock, up in Harlem, while police were arresting a woman, a guy named Robert Bandy tried to stop it from happening and got into an argument with the arresting officer. The argument escalated and Bandy tried to grab the officer's nightstick, so the officer shot him. Bandy, an army private on leave, was taken to the hospital, where, it was rumored, he died.

This happened on August 1, 1943, and the incident sparked what came to be known as the Harlem riots. Hundreds were injured and six people were killed. Many more were arrested. Stores, mostly white-owned, were looted. Fiorello LaGuardia, the mayor at the time, said that the riots had been sparked by radical agitators. Adam Clayton Powell, Sr. a Harlem activist and church pastor instead blamed "a callous white power structure." LaGuardia imposed a 10:30 pm curfew, but only in Harlem. That was the last time in our city's history that we were put under any sort of curfew.

Private Bandy survived. He'd been shot in the shoulder and made a full recovery. The white officer was placed on probation for a year. Nothing was done to deal with the underlying problems that sparked the riots when he was shot.

There have been other racially motivated riots in our history. A decade earlier, the riots of 1935 were sparked by rumors that a black Puerto Rican shoplifter had been beaten by employees at a Kress 5 & 10 cent store. Lots of injuries resulted and three people died. Many white-owned businesses were vandalized.

Two decades after the 1943 riots, came the Harlem riots of 1964. Those riots were sparked by the shooting death of James Powell at the hands of an off-duty police Lieutenant named Thomas Galligan.

A white building superintendent named Patrick Lynch, who was annoyed by the presence of young black students sitting on the steps of his buildings, turned a hose on them. The angry and wet students started to pick up bottles and trash can lids and then throw them at Lynch. This attracted the attention of Powell and two of his friends who chased the superintendent inside his building. As James Powell exited the building, Galligan shot and killed him.

Six days of rioting followed with multiple injuries, vandalism damage, and at least one other person dead. A grand jury cleared off-duty officer Thomas Galligan of any wrongdoing and all charges were dropped. His claim, that Powell had a knife, despite being challenged by every single witness to the event and the complete absence of any proof of its existence, was believed.

During the Depression, people of color were often the first to be fired and the last to be hired by struggling businesses. In the 1940s, soldiers of color were treated as second-class citizens and segregated into separate units. In the 1960s, the relentless segregation, inequality, lynchings, and overwhelming oppression of the rights of people of color all lead to the rise of the Civil Rights movement.

In 1992 the beating of Rodney King led to riots in Los Angeles. And now here we are again, right on schedule, because despite having made some tiny surface steps forward, we haven't ever changed a thing.

Last night our city-wide curfew went into effect as planned at 8 pm. No vehicular traffic was allowed in Manhattan below 96th Street. From the roof of our building last night, we could see police cars blocking off Columbus Avenue heading south. North of that, there were still buses running and there were more passenger cars than we've seen in weeks. People were out walking their dogs despite the curfew and there were demonstrators. From the roof of our building, we watched as they made their way past.

"Civil disobedience, given its place at the boundary of fidelity to law, is said to fall between legal protest, on the one hand, and conscientious refusal, revolutionary action, militant protest, and organized forcible resistance, on the other hand." So says the Stanford Encyclopedia of Philosophy.

Henry David Thoreau argued that individuals should not allow governments to overrule their moral consciences. He was motivated to write this, in a large part, because of his revulsion from the institution of slavery.

Martin Luther King spent his life engaging in Civil Disobedience despite the inherent danger to himself and his family. When Rosa Parks bravely took her seat on that bus, she broke the law.

I am not suggesting that all laws should be broken. When there are laws on the books that deny segments of the population their basic rights, however, then it behooves us all to resist them. That's why we fought the American Revolution.

From the moment our country was created, we have had to fight to expand upon our founding fathers' narrow initial vision. Where they didn't, we've tried to include women, members of the LGBTQ community, and people of color. We aren't close to being done yet.

Black lives matter. That is a simple idea. Not that their lives should matter more than anybody else's, but simply that they should matter. That's what we are fighting for because under our current way of living, they don't.

An advantage given to me means that something had to be taken away from somebody else. By giving up the advantages I have as a white man, I am not giving up any of my rights. I am just making it possible for everybody else to have those same basic rights. What is being asked is that we give back something that was never ours in the first place. It was stolen.

JUNE 4, 2020

377,888 Total Reported Cases in New York. 30,940 Deaths.

The night of the Presidential election on November 8, 2016, was a gut-wrenching shock for many of us. The following Saturday, Kate McKinnon, as Hillary Clinton, sang Leonard Cohen's *Hallelujah*, simply, at a piano for the *Saturday Night Live* cold open. It caught what we were all feeling, perfectly—a profound sadness that left a pit of dread at the core of all of us who were hoping that the election would swing the other way.

In January, the day after the inauguration, we all headed to Washington for the Women's March. It was the largest single-day protest in the history of the country. It was peaceful and nobody was arrested. The goal of the March was to send a clear message to the incoming administration that women's rights are human rights. Not only had a woman not just been elected President, but a man with a well-detailed history of misogyny had just assumed the office.

Once we got home, there were several additional Marches in New York City. We had our signs—colorful, clever, and eye-catching. As we marched, we joked that we were going to be marching a lot in the coming months. Well, as it turned out, we didn't.

We went back to our lives and tried to ignore what the new administration in Washington was doing. The signs that I had made for the marches sat idle in the entranceway of our apartment until they were finally moved down to our storage space in the basement. They are still there as far as I know behind a shelf unit.

At the time, we all dreaded what we thought was coming. We joked that the country under the new President would end up like Biff's version of the future in the *Back to the Future* films. Despite the fear, we never really believed it.

The mismanaged global pandemic has completely shut down our economy. 42.6 million Americans have filed unemployment claims—that is a number more than the combined populations of the 22 smallest states. Our cities have been boarded up to protect our buildings from looting and arson. We are in our 9th straight day of nationwide demonstrations against the racism that the new Administration has supported and encouraged. In 2016, while we thought the new administration would be terrible, I don't think we ever imagined that they would not uphold and support the basic rule of law.

The remarkable thing about these daily demonstrations is who is out there demonstrating. I have now participated in about six or seven different marches in New York, and I can probably count on one hand the number of people I have seen with any grey in their hair at all. These marches are almost purely made up of young people. Black, White, Hispanic, Asian—the younger members of our community are out there marching. That 18-44 demographic is energized and engaged in a way that my generation feared they never would be.

There are some older Americans participating, but the millions of older people who drew together for the Women's March seem to be largely absent from these current demonstrations. Older Americans are at far more risk to contract the coronavirus than younger Americans are. That may be one of the reasons why the older folk seem to be staying away from the crowds. A lot of older urban Americans have also had the means to shelter during the pandemic outside of the city, so they are simply not here.

These protests are not Parades. The signs being carried are not beautiful in their execution the way the ones at the Women's march were. They are messages and slogans scrawled on anything at hand—cardboard boxes, container lids, discarded paper. Today is the 10th day since the death of George Floyd and the day's demonstrations have already begun. The demonstrators are staying the course. I feel like we, the older generation, somewhat dropped the ball and I am moved to see that the younger generation seems to be picking it up and are running with it.

Do I always agree with what these younger people are saying and what they are doing? No, not necessarily. Did the generation before mine always agree with what I and my contemporaries said and thought? This generation is going to be reckless at times and yes, they are going to make mistakes, but so did we when we had our turn.

These demonstrations were triggered by a single event that was merely one in a long line of similar occurrences. Since they started, however, they have initiated a national dialogue about an even larger issue that is uncomfortable, rancorous at times, and long overdue.

I don't know where we are heading, but we are getting some new drivers. I still have a sense of dread when I think about the future, but from what I've seen over these last few days, I also have a newfound sense of hope.

June 5, 2020
379,011 Total Reported Cases in New York. 30,967 Deaths.

Yesterday, Michael baked some cookies, and we took them to the park. We met up with some friends and had a responsible socially distanced, masked, picnic. We needed a break.

Chris Trousdale, a member of the boyband *Dream Street* passed away yesterday from the virus. He was 34 years old. A friend of mine who is in his 30s has just recovered from the virus after spending many weeks fighting it. During his illness, he had to go to the ER twice with breathing difficulties. He has now tested negative but is nowhere near being fully recovered. Nick Cordero, a Broadway actor that everyone in the entertainment community has been praying for, is still in the hospital after more than two months. He's 41. His condition is still extremely serious.

Yesterday in Minneapolis marked the first of several planned memorials to George Floyd.

In Buffalo, two police officers pushed over an elderly protestor, who fell and hit his head. The initial report from the Department was that the man had tripped. Only when the video, captured by a local news camera, clearly showing the man being shoved out of the way by the officers started circulating did the Buffalo Police Department revise its report. Even with a spotlight shining brightly in their eyes, the first response of the Buffalo Police Department was to deny and cover up the incident.

This isn't a TV series. Everything that we are experiencing seems so far removed from what we think of as reality, that we must constantly remind ourselves that, yes, it is unfolding in front of us.

We are being called upon to help others and we must. We cannot, however, stop taking care of ourselves in the process. It is not selfish to take care of yourself. You are of no help to anyone else if you are not strong. On an airplane, we are always warned to slip the oxygen mask over our own mouths and noses first before we try and help others. That picnic in the park yesterday was exactly the oxygen I needed. I got a nice, deep breath and today, I am good to go again.

June 6, 2020
380,066 Total Reported Cases in New York. 30,988 Deaths.

My cousin in South Africa has been trying, since the pandemic began, to mathematically chart the trends of the virus in his country. In theory that should be a straightforward undertaking. What he's found, however, is that the raw data is hard to uncover and once found, hard to quantify. Different areas are underreporting cases or classifying them in different ways.

Here in the US, that same problem is magnified more than 50-fold. We have 50 separate states, each with its own government, plus Washington D.C. and several protectorates. Each of them has a different mechanism for calculating their data and each of them has a different political filter that their data is being run through before it is released.

So, what is going on? The answer is, I don't think that we know. 23 different states plus Washington D.C. and Puerto Rico are seeing their cases of coronavirus rising. In most of those places, the increase is at least 10%, in some, much more. The case rise is not happening uniformly in any area, but rather in geographical clusters.

Many of the states that moved to reopen the soonest seem to be seeing their numbers go up. Some of them, however, are not. Given the differences in how these disparate areas report their case numbers, it's hard to tell.

More than 1200 medical professionals just signed an open letter that was drafted by the University of Washington stating that the need for civil protest outweighs the health risk posed by the large gatherings. Michael and I are marching today to show our support for the Black Lives Matter movement. We are going to wear a mask and we're going to do everything within our power to maintain social distancing. I'm guessing, we will, ultimately, likely fail at that.

One of the clarion calls at these marches has been, "Defund the Police." It turns out that "Defund the NYPD," is a misbegotten phrase that represents a very interesting idea. It isn't about abolishing the police force, although some are, indeed calling for that. It is, instead, about empowering other areas of the system to handle specific issues.

Public advocates are calling for a 16% cut to the Police Department so that money can be reallocated to the already massively compromised social services arm. What they are saying is that police involvement in areas such as homeless outreach should end and that social services should take over. If more money were put into housing, there would be fewer homeless on the streets. If there is a mental health issue on the street with a homeless person, send a trained social worker, perhaps with a policeman in tow, to deal with it. "Defund the NYPD" is a cry to remove the police department from the aspects of policing the city for which they have no training.

Michael has already left the apartment for the march. Every time one of us leaves the apartment, the other waits for a few moments until they come back having forgotten something. Sure enough, a minute later he was back for his wallet.

Given that we both have antibodies to the virus, there is a good chance that we have some resistance to both transmitting and getting COVID-19. It's not remotely a sure thing, but it seems like it might offer some protection. At the very least, being outside with people seems to be less dangerous than being inside with people. That is how we assess the risk.

We ultimately choose our own paths forward through confusing and terrifying times. Will they be the right decisions? We can't know until we make them.

JUNE 7, 2020
380,923 Total Reported Cases in New York. 31,071 Deaths.

Remarkably, the demonstrations have not only continued since Memorial Day when George Floyd was killed, but they've grown. The Bushwick Daily, a local Brooklyn paper, publishes a list of the day's protests every morning. There are 11 separate marches and rallies planned for today in Manhattan alone. There are 16 others scheduled to happen in the surrounding boroughs.

Michael and I went to a march yesterday that was called The March for Stolen Lives and Looted Dreams. It started at the north end of Central Park and wove its way downtown where it terminated in a well-produced rally in Washington Square Park. Thousands of people marched. As we made our way down 6th Avenue, our crowd filled up about ten city blocks—about ½ a mile. When we got to the Village, we met up with other marches coming in from other directions. Our crowd grew and grew, and, throughout all of it, remained peaceful.

In London, thousands of people peacefully marched on Parliament Square. Thousands more gathered in Manchester and in Cardiff. 15,000 people rallied peacefully in Berlin's Alexander Square. Munich, Frankfurt, Cologne. Several thousand people in Paris defied a ban on assembly to protest peacefully within sight of the US embassy. Still more in Sydney and Brisbane, Australia, and in Seoul, South Korea.

Yesterday, saw marches and rallies the world over. The anger and fear of the early days are starting to be replaced by determination and resolve. These marches are not about looting and mayhem. They are about change.

The President tweeted last night that fewer people than anticipated showed up for the demonstrations yesterday and that we shouldn't believe what we are seeing.

The President, also yesterday, signed a proclamation that will allow commercial fishing to resume in The North Canyons and Seamounts Marine National Monument off the coast of New England. The monument had been created in 2016 to allow marine life there to recover from decades of over-fishing. He signed an executive order that allows companies to ignore long-standing environmental laws to speed up federal approval for new mines, new highways, and new pipelines. Earlier in the week, the EPA finalized a rule that will make it much harder for States, Tribal groups, and individuals to block pipelines that could potentially pollute and destroy their lands and waterways.

While the attention of the country is elsewhere, the government is quietly and efficiently dismantling protections that have taken us decades to put into place. We need to pay attention.

10 days of rioting and looting followed the assassination of Martin Luther King in April of 1968. Did anything change as a result? Given that we find ourselves marching and demonstrating fifty some odd years later for the same thing, my guess would be no. Nothing has changed. I am hopeful, that this time it will.

The White House seems to have overplayed its hand when they attacked the stationary group of people in Lafayette Park with tear gas and rubber bullets to make way for the President's bible photo-op. The President is now claiming that there was no tear gas, despite thousands of witnesses and incontrovertible proof that there was.

Each passing day, as these protests continue to grow, it becomes harder and harder to ignore what is being said. As rational thought replaces knee-jerk reaction, thoughtful conversations are starting. People are starting to tell their stories. Whatever happens, these stories won't ever be untold.

JUNE 8, 2020
381,659 Total Reported Cases in New York. 31,132 Deaths.

It's quiet this morning. No sirens. No helicopters. The nightly curfew was lifted yesterday. It seems to have been a relatively peaceful evening. There are fourteen Black Lives Matter marches and rallies scheduled for today plus two press conferences and a cleanup.

I'm voting today. Because of the pandemic, I was able to get an absentee ballot. I am going to the Post Office to mail it after lunch. It is the Democratic primary election which means that we are choosing which candidate we want to represent the Democratic party for both President and Member of Congress from our district.

The right to vote is still not universal in this country. The true meaning of one man, one vote has long been subject to interpretation. In the 1600s, the Plymouth colony in Massachusetts began by restricting voting rights to male property holders. After about a decade, they added the additional qualification that voting was only open to freemen who were "orthodox in the fundamentals of religion." Quakers were not allowed to vote. Other colonies restricted voting rights to Christians but excluded Baptists and Catholics.

The US Constitution did not, when it was first written, define who was eligible to vote. It was up to the individual states to decide. Originally, several states allowed freed black men to vote as well as women who were property owners. By the late 1700s, however, most states restricted voting to white male property owners, stripping the right from women and free black men. By the mid 1800s the property-owning restrictions on voting were largely lifted, but the racial and gender restrictions were still very much in place.

Starting after the Civil War, amendments were added to the Constitution that expanded voting rights. The fifteenth amendment added in 1870 stated that voting rights could not be denied because of "race, color, or previous condition of servitude."

The nineteenth amendment added in 1920 stated that voting rights could not be denied "on account of sex." The twenty-fourth amendment stated that voting rights could not be denied "by reason of failure to pay any poll tax or other tax" for federal elections. The twenty-sixth amendment set the minimum voting age at eighteen.

Because the Constitution never explicitly stated a universal right to vote, states have still, to this day, even with the amendments, been able to weasel around the idea of suffrage for all. In many states, you are required to register to vote in a set number of days before an election. Convicted felons are not permitted to vote in many places, even after they have served their sentences. People who live in US protectorates like Puerto Rico and Guam, despite being considered American citizens, are not allowed to vote at all in Presidential elections.

Historically, the more people who vote, the worse the Republican party does. Voting by mail means that many more people can and will vote. The President is railing against voting by mail. He is ranting and raving about totally unsubstantiated widespread mail fraud. He is even going so far as to try and defund and close the United States Postal Service to keep people from casting ballots. Not for nothing, the President votes by mail himself. Thankfully, though, none of this is up to him.

In the 1980s Aung San Suu Kyi rose to prominence in Myanmar (formerly Burma), in Southeast Asia. She became the Secretary-General of the National League for Democracy (NLD) a political party that she, herself, helped form. In 1990, the NLD won 81% of the seats in Parliament, but the Military Junta who was in control, nullified the results. For much of the following two decades, Aung San Suu Kyi was placed under house arrest in her home.

She became internationally famous as a symbol of resistance against repression. Time magazine claimed that she was the non-violent spiritual heir to Mahatma Gandhi. Prominent international politicians the world over visited her to seek her blessing. In 1991, she was awarded the Nobel Peace Prize. When she was finally released in 2010, the world waited with breathless anticipation to see what remarkable things she would do.

In 2015, her party won 86% of the seats in Parliament, and she became State Counsellor, a role like that of Prime Minister. Of particular concern to the rest of the world in Myanmar was the genocide being perpetrated against the Rohingya people, a tribal group. It was widely thought that Aung San Suu Kyi would, with her newfound freedom and party position, finally be able to speak out against the massacres.

Instead, she said nothing. The world was outraged. Bob Geldorf called her a "handmaiden to genocide." There were calls for her Nobel Peace Prize to be revoked. In response, she has said, "I am a politician."

She feels that speaking out against the military directly will simply land her back in confinement.

"I am a politician."

The world wanted a saint. What we got was a human being. As a politician, she has had to weigh what she feels that she can accomplish at any given moment, and what she can't. Is it better to speak up and just be imprisoned again, or to largely keep silent and try and effect small changes from within? She chose the latter. It was a political decision—not a humanist one—because that is how she defines herself.

Jimmy Carter might be the best example of someone we have had in office who comes closest to exemplifying the ideals of what a human being could and should be. He is a poster boy for Humanism. He has dedicated his entire life to being of service to others. At 95 years old, the man is still out there swinging a hammer to build homes for those in need. He was arguably not a great president. Great guy—somewhat ineffective politician.

The conservative right-leaning religious groups in this country have based their political aspirations squarely on the moral codes outlined in the Christian bible. They have promoted legislation that they feel follows their traditional teachings. They have supported candidates who will uphold those values and have torn apart those that they feel don't. In 2016, though, they united behind a candidate who embodies the exact opposite of everything they stand for. Why? Because they wanted to win an election.

Our choices come election time come from a pool of politicians, not from a roster of divinely inspired prophets. That doesn't mean we shouldn't vote. It means that we need to be even more vigilant about who we pick.

June 9, 2020
382,257 Total Reported Cases in New York. 31,173 Deaths.

Today is the day of George Floyd's funeral and burial.

An hour ago, a New York city council meeting on public safety and police misconduct started. The demonstrations and marches, and even the riots, seem to have had an effect. The people who can change things have heard enough that they have started some long overdue discussions.

In Minneapolis on Sunday, nine out of their thirteen City Council members stood up in a rally and announced that they intended to vote to dismantle the police department. The Mayor of Minneapolis, Jacob Frey, issued a statement saying that he was all for reform, but would not support dismantling the entire department. Instead, he signed a temporary order banning the use of chokeholds and requiring that other officers intervene and report if they witness excessive force. He was booed.

Seven years ago, Camden, New Jersey dissolved and shut down its' Police Department. Before that, Camden was often listed among the most violent cities in the United States. Since disbanding their Police Department, the crime rate in Camden has dropped by half. Several smaller towns across the country have had to close their policing units because of a lack of funds to pay for them. In Camden, however, that decision was made to root out corruption. Camden has 75,000 residents. Open-air drug markets were common. Violent crime was everywhere, and it was continuing because the Police were being paid off. Lawsuits against the department alleged that officers were routinely planting evidence on suspects, reports were often fabricated, and officers lied under oath when they testified. Camden got rid of its' old Police Department completely and created a new one from scratch. Once the department was disbanded, 88 people were released from prison and their cases were overturned.

Were you to join the police force in Camden, New Jersey today, the first thing that you would be told to do is to go out, knock on all the doors of the people on your beat, and talk with them. This kind of community-oriented policing encourages problem-solving over violence and incarceration. It allows the officers to find out who the people they are protecting are, and what they are concerned about. The officers even host neighborhood barbeques and ice cream parties and, in an area that was once called "heroin alley" show drive-in movies. There has been an attempt at diversifying the force to better reflect the population they are representing.

It all sounds hopelessly too good to be true and lefty-feel-good but disbanding the Police Department and rebuilding it has improved the crime rate in Camden.

Here in New York, Governor Cuomo announced that he plans to sign ten different pieces of legislation that are in the process of being enacted by local lawmakers. These proposed laws will criminalize chokeholds, open police disciplinary records, and require courts to report the racial and demographic data for all low-level offenses. Another would require New York officers to wear body cameras. Some of this legislation has been pushed by reformists for years. Not only could the advocates of the bills not get these laws voted on before this, but they also couldn't even get the sponsors of these bills to bring them up for a vote.

The international reaction to the killing of George Floyd by Officer Derek Chauvin and his partners has changed something.

Mr. Floyd will be laid to rest in Houston today. It seems unlikely, however, that the movement to change that his death sparked will be buried with him. There is only one march scheduled in the city today, but that doesn't mean the fight is over. He will never know it, but George Floyd is leaving behind a legacy that has the potential to change much of how we live our lives.

Trayvon Martin, Tamir Rice, Michael Brown, Eric Garner, Philandro Castile, Breonna Taylor, Ahmaud Arbery, Rodney King, Malice Green, Abner Louima, Amadou Dialo, Sean Bell, Oscar Grant, Laquan McDonald, Walter Scott, Freddie Gray, Antwon Rose, Jr. ...

George Floyd.
Rest in Power.

JUNE 10, 2020
7.2 Million Total Reported Cases Worldwide.

A friend of mine who works in real estate regularly posts a newsletter about the history of New York. The other day, he posted the earliest known photograph taken in the city. It was from 1848 and was taken on the Upper West Side, somewhere near where Michael and I live. It shows a house on a hill with a large fenced-in space and a road. It's a farm. The road is out of sight in a cut and is probably unpaved. The people who lived in that house could not possibly have imagined what their land would look like 172 years in the future. The house is, of course, long gone. The fence is gone. Even the hill upon which they stood, is gone.

25,000 retail stores are expected to be closed for good this year. The hardest hit will likely be the nation's malls which may bear the brunt of those closures. J.C. Penny, J. Crew, and Neiman Marcus have all filed for bankruptcy. Brooks Brothers and the parent company of Men's Wearhouse and Jos. A. Banks are in discussions about doing the same. Other companies are closing many of their store locations. Those retailers include Pier One Imports, Victoria's Secret, and GNC, but there are hundreds of others.

On the other hand, Amazon, Walmart, and Target, all retailers with massive online platforms, have seen their orders surge. After three months of us all living at home, that's now what we've become used to doing. Grocery stores may have continued operating, but we have learned to look online for almost everything else. We have also learned to do without.

The coronavirus case rate remains low here in New York. The state's economy should be able to start opening back up soon. Because the numbers are so low, there is now even a possibility that the city's pools and parks may re-open before the end of the summer.

Will we recognize our city when it comes back?

1848, the year the picture was taken, was also the year of the Seneca Falls Convention that launched the women's suffrage movement. I am sure that many people at the time thought that giving women the right to vote would destroy society. It didn't, but it did change it.

Somewhere around 500BC, a Greek philosopher named Heraclitus said, "The only constant in life is change." He's still right.

JUNE 11, 2020
383,528 Total Reported Cases in New York. 31,246 Deaths.

My maternal grandfather was a regional tax collector in India under the British Raj. My mother was born in Shimla, in the mountains, which was where the British went to escape the heat of the Indian summers. At its peak, just before World War I, the British Empire controlled nearly a quarter of the globe and nearly a quarter of the people living on it. It was proudly referred to as "the empire on which the sun never sets".

During what is called "the Age of Discovery" in the 15th and 16th centuries, Europeans searched the planet for the optimum trading routes and sources of trading goods. They were not driven by the science and curiosity of experiencing new places, they were driven by pure commerce. They wanted tea, silk, rice, porcelain, you name it. Whatever it was, they wanted to get it so that they could sell it and make money.

By the early 1700s, a series of wars with the French and the Dutch plus the English union with Scotland left Britain largely in control of the colonies in North America. By the mid 1700s the East India Company had taken control over much of the Indian sub-continent. At this point in history, having defeated the French in the Napoleonic Wars, Britannia ruled the waves. When the British lost the thirteen colonies in America, they used their navy to concentrate their expansion into Asia, Africa, and the Pacific.

The British did not rule benevolently. When there was resistance to their expansion, they simply massacred that resistance. They considered the inhabitants of whatever lands they took over as being culturally inferior. They were peoples. Not people, therefore expendable. "Don't give in to it, and it will give in to you," was their oft-repeated motto.

The British in India lived well. They surrounded themselves with Indian servants and, using Indian labor, built European-style houses and buildings—some of which are still standing today.

In the 1940s the British exported a massive amount of food staples such as rice out of India for their own use. This resulted in what is now known as the famine of Bengal. Three million Indians starved to death. The great Winston Churchill said this, "I hate Indians. They are a beastly people with a beastly religion. The famine was their own fault for breeding like rabbits."

A growing rise of Indian nationalism led by people like Nehru and Mahatma Gandhi, who, like the Reverend Martin Luther King, advocated non-violent resistance, finally started having an effect and Britain granted India its independence in 1947. It's not as if the British suddenly realized that they were wrong and Gandhi was right, it was mostly because their resources had been used up fighting World War II and they had no choice.

Before that, as the war started, fearing for their safety, my grandfather sent my grandmother, my mother, and her brother and sister to what seemed to be the safest British outpost which happened to be South Africa.

In South Africa, the white Europeans had instituted a system called apartheid to control the black population which outnumbered them 9 to 1. This is a Dutch word meaning apart-ness. Black South Africans were not allowed to interact with white South Africans. They were not allowed to live in the same places. They were not allowed to vote.

When we lived there, as I've talked about before, my grandfather had several black house servants. They all referred to him as Master. "Would Master like lunch to be served now?" At five years old, I was referred to as Master Richard. It never dawned on me that there was anything wrong with that. It just was.

The last time, I think, that we went back to South Africa was in 1980 when I was eighteen. Anti-Apartheid protests were common by that time in the US. I was now aware of what I was seeing. Once there, my sister and I went with our South African friends to Location to see where they lived. We had to duck down in the back of the car so we wouldn't be seen. We created a bit of a stir. Several people asked us to take pictures of them in front of their rondaavels which were mud huts with conical roofs.

I also took pictures of the large signs in train stations that said: "Whites Only" referring to certain platforms. I noticed benches that were reserved for whites. When we went to the butcher with my grandfather, I noticed the separate door for black people and the inferior cuts of meat that they were sold. I noticed all of that, but I didn't do or say anything.

The Americas, once discovered, seemed like a great empty space just waiting for Europeans to move in and make something of. Like the British, the Americans considered the native population of the continent a nuisance. They were in the way. Their lands were taken from them with barely a thought and happily distributed to any European willing to settle on them. It isn't an accident that the great Western US landscape painters created those giant canvases of idyllic-looking land stretching as far as the eye could see and kept them completely devoid of people. By European standards, no people were living there.

European Americans did everything that they could do to completely exterminate the Native Americans. While they were doing that, they brought over African Americans in chains to work as slaves in their newly acquired fields.

On my father's side, the connection that my family has to history is no better. My grandmother's father fought in the Spanish-American War and ended up being posted in the Philippines. When she was two years old, my grandmother and her mother joined him and made their home there. The United States was in control of the Philippines from 1898, the year my grandmother was born, to 1946.

Like the British in India, the Americans in the Philippines lived very well. My great-grandparents had three Filipino house servants as well as a Chinese cook. My family was never able to live with that kind of luxury back in the United States. Not before and not after.

Throughout US occupation, the Filipino people constantly fought for their right to rule themselves. The Philippine-American War was fought from 1899 to 1901. About 4,000 American soldiers lost their lives in that conflict. Nearly 20,000 Filipino soldiers lost theirs in their fight for freedom and famine and disease claimed the lives of at least 200,000 more Filipino civilians.

During the Depression, in Virginia, my paternal grandfather worked as a lawyer in Lynchburg, Virginia. He was often referred to as the N——Lawyer. Most of his clients were, what he called, colored.

He was just starting his life and during the Depression with jobs and money so scarce, African American clients were all that he could find. He needed to put food on the table. Often, his clients would not have enough money to pay him so they would barter with food for his services. Days after the trial, there would be a knock on the back door of the kitchen porch, and somebody would be standing there with a live chicken or a sack of potatoes as payment.

By the time my sister and I came along, my grandfather was already in his 60s. He was a kind man with a deep gravely southern drawl that was wonderful to listen to. He sang bass in the church choir. He was extremely well respected in Lynchburg and some people continued to let him do their taxes even when he was well into his 90s. He maintained relationships with some of his African American clients throughout his life. They always called him Mr. Hester and, to the best of my knowledge, when they came to call, they always came to the back door.

I remember my grandfather talking about one such client with admiration and calling him a good N——. My, by then, Yankee father jumped all over him and asked him not to use that word in front of my sister and me. If I remember this correctly, I think my grandfather's response was, "But he was."

I am a product of these people. Whatever success I have had, began with them. My entire existence in this life and all the advantages I have been given have been built upon a solid foundation of deep-rooted and continuous institutional racism.

That I loved all four of my grandparents is completely immaterial. They didn't create the racism that permeates our society, but as far as I know, they didn't question it much either. They continued driving the machine forward in the same way that their parents and grandparents did before them. And I am its beneficiary.

In 1921, on June 19, Tulsa, Oklahoma was the site of one of the worst massacres of Black people in the history of the United States. A mob of white people attacked and destroyed nearly 35 square blocks of Black-owned residences and buildings from the ground and the air in private aircraft. It is estimated that somewhere between 75 and 300 people lost their lives that day.

June 19, more commonly called Juneteenth, celebrates the day that the people of Texas were told that Abraham Lincoln had signed the Emancipation Proclamation that freed slaves from bondage.

The President has planned his first re-election rally back from the COVID-19 shutdown to take place in Tulsa, Oklahoma on June 19.

We do not need to follow in every single one of our ancestors' footsteps. No matter how ingrained or how easy it might be to just step into those same footprints, we must forge our own paths. We must. The past is the past. We cannot change it, but nor can we forget it. It requires constant vigilance to keep what we were born into from being the only thing that guides us forward in our lives. Nothing we do will be perfect and some of it will be naïve and some of it might cause more offense and some of it will be downright stupid. If we are to face the future with any hope of success, though, we must begin to address the issues of the past that we have allowed to permeate our present.

I will let the great Maya Angelou have the last word, today: "Do the best you can until you know better. Then when you know better, do better."

June 12, 2020
CDC "strongly encourages" protesters and rally attendees to wear masks.

"What fresh hell can this be?" is apparently what Dorothy Parker would say every time there was a knock on her door. Every morning, before I turn on the TV, I find myself taking a deep breath to brace for what I am about to see.

It's tempting to think that everything would have turned out differently had the 2016 election gone the other way. Even had Clinton won, though, the virus would still have emerged from Wuhan. Her response to it would probably have been quite different. Rather than completely ignoring the pandemic response recommendations already in place, Clinton would have likely been far more willing to act upon them. And to react sooner. If that had happened, how different would our current situation now be?

How different would the current racial discussion be?

There is no more and no less racism in the US now than there was under President Obama. Under President Obama, however, racism was considered a shameful, nasty condition that was suppressed. It was undercover. It was still everywhere, just as it is now, but it was out of sight.

Three months after Breonna Taylor died, her police report was finally released by the Louisville police. The report is largely blank. Under injuries, what is written is the word "none". Breonna Taylor was shot at least eight times by the police and died in her hallway in a pool of her own blood.

We need to address excessive force by the police department and eradicate it. That is clear. We also need to address the fact that Black people living in the United States are subject to less obvious injustices and more insidious obstacles during every waking moment of their lives.

We have five more months before the election. Five. Long. Months. There are going to be a lot of knocks on the door before that and a lot of fresh hell out there doing the knocking.

June 13, 2020
385,104 Total Reported Cases in New York. 31,410 Deaths.

As I was walking through Central Park yesterday, I made my way up into Strawberry Fields, and there, sitting on one of the benches near the Imagine mosaic, were two friends of mine. Certainly, I have had a sense of what these two had been doing via social media but seeing them both sitting there in the flesh was a bit shocking and, frankly, a welcome relief.

For the last three months, all of us have been isolated from each other. It doesn't always feel that way because we've all started becoming experts on Zoom and FaceTime. Michael and I have scheduled meals and chats with friends and family. We've both had some business meetings. All of that, though, has been from the inside of our apartment. The people we've been interacting with weren't there with us.

New York is beginning to open back up. The plywood is starting to come down from some of the buildings that were covered to protect them from the vandalism of two weeks ago. More stores are open. You can't go inside, but if you are, say, looking for sheets, you can go to Laytner's now and point to which ones you want from behind the barricade at the front door. People are out and about. Some in masks and some not.

For the last few days, as I walked around New York, even as I marched with the Black Lives Matter demonstrations, there was something strange about the people I was seeing that I couldn't put my finger on. Yesterday, as I walked towards Times Square, it finally came to me. There are no tourists.

Almost all the people I am seeing walking around outside actually live in New York or very close by. Last year, 67 million people visited New York City. We are the most visited city in the United States. For the last three months, however, we have had almost no visitors at all. I knew that intellectually, of course, but yesterday it sank in. Once I realized that all I could see was their absence.

For those of us who live here, tourists are the bane of our existence. They gather in confused groups on the sidewalk, blocking our way. They fill the streets. You get behind a group of them not familiar with American food at a take-out place and you're sunk. In midtown, the lines to get onto tour buses block everything often forcing us into the street to get around them. Well, they aren't here now, and the sight-seeing buses are parked out of sight off the streets.

In the summer after my freshman year in college, I got a job in the gift shop at the American Museum of Natural History. It was a fun job. I got in trouble one day for spending too much time showing an assortment of African carvings to the actress Karen Black who was completely and delightfully bonkers. When the museum closed, we had to work for an additional half-hour to close the shop. Afterward, to leave, I had to walk through the darkened Hall of American Mammals. It was very creepy to be inside the museum without anybody else in there. That's what the streets of the city feel like these days.

Almost all the health professionals around the country feel that a second wave of the virus is coming. While our numbers in New York continue to go down, they continue to rise all around us. In some places, they are dangerously spiking. As much as we need visitors to come back and shore up our economy until the rest of the country gets themselves under any sort of control, they all need to stay away. Our downward trajectory is a hard-won victory that we are not willing to give up. We've lost too many people.

Yesterday, on the fourth anniversary of the horrific massacre of gay people at the Pulse nightclub in Orlando in the middle of Pride Month, the President finalized an agreement that removed protections for transgendered people in health care. Noted.

I was so happy to see my friends yesterday. Strawberry Fields is just inside Central Park across from the Dakota where John Lennon was murdered. The circular mosaic containing the word IMAGINE inlaid at the center of it is by now a beloved and iconic city sight. I hope that, someday, when the tourists start coming back to take pictures of it that they can also hear what it is saying.

Imagine all the people
Sharing all the world

June 15, 2020
384,464 Total Reported Cases in New York. 31,472 Deaths.

It seems impossible, that after more than two weeks of worldwide demonstrations, with everybody's attention firmly focused on the issue of the use of excessive force by our local police departments against people of color, that another black man would be shot and killed by a white policeman. And yet, it happened. Again.

On Friday night in Atlanta, Rayshard Brooks, while he was running away from an officer, was shot, and killed.

The ERA was first proposed in 1923. It was designed to prohibit discrimination based on sex in all matters about divorce, property, employment, and other matters. It would provide for legal equality between the sexes. With the rise of the Women's Movement in the 1960s the proposed amendment was finally introduced in Congress where it passed in 1971 and then went on to the Senate where it also passed in 1972. It was then up to the states to ratify the amendment. 38 states were needed before the ERA could become an official addendum to the US Constitution. On January 15 of this year, 2020, while the first reports of COVID 19 were starting to come in from Wuhan, Virginia became the 38th state to ratify the amendment. Finally, after nearly fifty years, the number of states needed to ratify had been achieved.

Unfortunately, the deadline (1982) had long since passed. So, in 2020, nearly fifty years after the push to correct this, men and women are still not considered equal in the eyes of the law in the United States. Like almost everything else that we are facing these days, support of the ERA splits down party lines. Democrats are for it. Republicans are against it.

This morning, the United States Supreme Court voted on a trio of landmark LGBTQ cases. The rulings on Bostock v. Clayton County, Altitude Express, Inc. v. Zarda and R.G. & G.R. Harris Funeral Homes, Inc. v. Equal Employment Opportunity Commission ruled that both sexual identity and gender identity were inextricably linked to sex, therefore, the Civil Rights Act of 1964 which prohibits sex discrimination also applies to discrimination based on sexual orientation and gender identity.

While this is a massive victory in the LGBTQ fight for equality and cause for celebration, it is merely a step.

Black Lives Matter. Women's Lives Matter. LGBTQ Lives Matter. We are fighting multiple wars on multiple fronts, and we likely will be doing so for the rest of our lives. These wars may never be fully won We have to keep going. We can't ever give up.

Ever tried. Ever failed. No matter. Try again. Fail again. Fail better.
—Samuel Beckett

JUNE 17, 2020
387,384 Total Reported Cases in New York. 31,537 Deaths.

One of the glorious things about New Yorkers is the fact that when faced with miles of raw plywood covering the fronts of our stores, what we see, instead of desolation, is possibility. Miles of raw plywood suddenly becomes miles of blank canvas.

All over the city, artists have transformed these rough surfaces into something amazing. It started with graffiti during the demonstrations—angry, immediate, and direct. Sometimes just somebody's name—George Floyd. Breonna Taylor. Sometimes a sentence or a thought—I can't breathe. Black Lives Matter.

Now, though, people are taking their time and going in deeper. Somebody down near Union Square Park does beautiful line drawings of musicians. A violin player. A jazz musician with a stand-up bass. They look like the wire portraits of Alexander Calder.

Painters are expanding upon the graffiti and adding color and imagery. ABC Carpet's plywood is now a stunning riot of color and defiance. Instead of just saying their names, actual portraits of those we've lost to police violence are all over the plywood in SoHo showing us who they were.

Other artists have added work that has seemingly nothing to do with the lockdown and the protests—landscapes and abstracts and rainbows. Seemingly nothing to do with it, but really, everything to do with it. These artists are creating an idyllic world that we can't be in these days because of the pandemic or one that some have been denied because of the color of their skin.

Last month, the director and actor Tyler Perry announced that he would be reopening his Atlanta film studios and published a document called "Camp Quarantine" outlining how he would do it. Everyone would be tested before they traveled to Atlanta and then again after they arrived. They would all be kept isolated in their rooms while waiting for the results. Anyone who tests positive will not be allowed to remain. Everyone who tests negative will be required to stay on the lot for the entire duration of the shoot. Masks and distancing, where possible, would still be used, but a kind of quarantine bubble would be formed to protect everyone from the threat of outside infection. Testing would continue throughout the shoot regularly. The word that is starting to be used to describe this is "biodoming" as in "We are going to biodome in Atlanta while we are filming *The Bold and the Beautiful*."

In my business, theatre, the way that we tell our stories has its own set of current complications. The main one is that it happens live, in the moment, and requires a lot of people to be present, together, inside, all at one time. Actor's Equity Association, the union governing actors and stage managers has issued a set of guidelines. What these guidelines for all practical purposes mean is that until the virus is under some sort of control, AEA members will not be able to work.

Before these guidelines were published, Barrington Stage Company in Pittsfield, MA announced that they were going to attempt to do a season. Those plans seem to still be on track. Their first production is a one-person play that they hope to open in early August. Having only one actor means that the crew can set up the stage beforehand without him, and then keep away from him during the performance. He can dress by himself and do his own makeup. There will probably be no scene changes. The actor can be isolated out on stage and the crew can keep away from him and each other backstage.

As for the audience, every other row of seats in the theatre has been removed. Seats in the remaining rows will be sold leaving two seats empty between each party. The front row will be 12 feet away from the stage. Different sections of the audience will be required to enter and exit the theatre through specific doors to prevent everyone from coming in together the same way.

Everyone in the audience will be required to wear a mask both as they enter and exit and during the performance. There will be a no-touch temperature check upon entry and any patron with a temperature of 100.4 or higher will be sent home—their tickets refunded or rescheduled. The program will be digital so patrons can access it on their own devices and not have to touch a physical booklet. The play will be performed without an intermission and the concession stand and gift shop will remain closed so that patrons will not congregate together while they are in the theatre.

I am trying to imagine what that experience will be like. Will the result be worth it? Will watching a play under those conditions be satisfying? Will performing it that way be satisfying? Can the theatre make enough money under those conditions to make the whole undertaking worth the effort?

The coronavirus has not stopped our artistic drive. Adversity, instead of thwarting the artistic impulse, tends to engender it. In the worst of the German concentration camps during World War II, Jewish prisoners still made art. Secretly. The art they created survived their awful destruction and still, to this day, remains vibrantly and defiantly alive. It still has the power to move us and draw us in.

COVID-19 is forcing us all to find new ways of expressing ourselves. Obstacles become opportunities. There are plenty of unused plywood panels left on our city's buildings. You can look at them as barriers or you can look at them as an invitation.

JUNE 18, 2020
Governor Newsom of California issues a mandatory mask order.

On the days that I walk or ride downtown, I invariably end up passing through Columbus Circle. It sits at the southwest corner of Central Park.

At the center of the traffic circle, stands a tall column with a sculpture of the man for whom the circle was named atop it, Christopher Columbus.

It was installed there in 1892 and is listed in the National Register of Historic Places.

As time has passed, however, Columbus has come to be regarded as far less saint-like than we were led to believe. What greeted him upon his arrival was an entire culture of people whom he subsequently enslaved and almost drove to extinction in his quest for gold. It turns out that he didn't discover the Americas at all, he was just the first person from the east to invade them.

Statues of Columbus all over the country have been repeatedly vandalized in recent years. Following the killing of George Floyd last month, a sculpture of him in Richmond, Virginia was spray painted, set on fire, and thrown into a lake. Richmond has also become a focal point for the tensions around the country regarding public statues that commemorate leaders of the Confederacy. Monument Avenue has a whole series of statues of so-called Civil War heroes who fought for the South.

The Civil War was fought over the issue of State's rights. Should States be able to decide for themselves how they are governed, or should the Federal government be the ultimate power? The Southern states believed that they should control their destiny, so they seceded from the Union. The specific issue over which they decided to do this was the institution of slavery.

Slave labor was the fuel that ran the engine of the South's pre-war economy. When President Lincoln signed the Emancipation Proclamation on the first of January in 1863, he also signed away the South's prosperity. A hundred and fifty years later, the resentment against him is still very much present in deep pockets throughout the South.

The men who fought against the North are considered heroes and martyrs by many in the southern white population. Statues to those men serve as a reminder to them of what could have been. That the prosperity their ancestors enjoyed came from the blood of enslaved Africans is immaterial. The people who want to keep the statues of these Civil War Generals up, resent the North for winning and they resent present-day African Americans for being free.

Two weeks ago, Virginia Governor Ralph Northam announced that the statue of General Robert E. Lee, the largest on Monument Avenue, would finally be removed. A lawsuit by a man who claims that Virginia promised to guard and protect the statue when the land was annexed by the state in 1890, caused a judge in the Richmond, Virginia Circuit Court to issue a 10-day injunction. A three-foot-high barrier has been erected around the monument, the base of which is now covered with graffiti from the recent Black Lives Matter demonstrations.

Symbols matter. You can say that African Americans are free, but if you keep a statue of a man who led a war against their right for that freedom, you are sending a very clear message that you don't believe what you are saying. Sure, all those fancy words and lip service to the idea of equality are out there floating around, but just drive down Monument Avenue in Richmond and those statues tell you something else.

Just north of Tampa, where we rehearse the Norwegian Cruise Lines version of *Jersey Boys*, at the intersection of two interstate highways, flies a gigantic Confederate flag 139 feet up in the air. The tiny plot of land in the middle of the on and off-ramps where the flagpole stands is owned by a guy who believes he has the right to exercise his freedom of speech by flying it. It is temporarily down because the local chapter of the Sons of Confederate Veterans fears it will be burned during the Black Lives Matter protests.

In 1889, a new pancake mix started to be sold under the name Aunt Jemima. The Quaker Oats Company bought it in 1926 and formerly registered it as a trademark in 1937. Quaker Oats then introduced Aunt Jemima syrup in 1966. As early as 1864, while the Civil War was still being fought, a character named Aunt Jemima appeared onstage in Washington D.C. Aunt Jemima was based on a stereotypical "Mammy" character from the minstrel shows common at the time. Minstrel shows featured white performers in black-face makeup behaving as exaggerated and grotesque caricatures of enslaved people. The inspiration for the brand came from a song called "Old Aunt Jemima" written in 1875.

Aunt Jemima, and characters like her, idealized idyllic antebellum plantation life. Early advertising promotions featured paper dolls of Aunt Jemima and her family all dressed in tattered clothing befitting an enslaved person. In 1890, the R.T. Davis milling company, the brand's original creators, hired a woman who'd been born a slave named Nancy Green, to be Aunt Jemima's spokesperson. In 1893 at the World's Columbian Exposition in Chicago, she cooked pancakes next to what was billed as the world's largest flour barrel. She continued appearing around the country as Aunt Jemima until she died in 1923.

Hattie McDaniel played a character named "Mammy" in the 1939 film *Gone with the Wind* for which she became the first African American performer to win an Academy Award. It didn't happen again for another 24 years when Sidney Poitier finally won his for *Lilies of the Field*. When the film debuted in the South, the black actors were removed from the poster and the promotional materials. Neither Hattie McDaniel nor her fellow black cast members were permitted to attend the film's premiere in Atlanta.

The Academy Award ceremony for *Gone with the Wind* took place at the Coconut Grove Restaurant at the Ambassador Hotel in Los Angeles.

The hotel had a strict whites-only policy, but they allowed Ms. McDaniel in as a favor. She had to sit at the back, against the wall, at a segregated table, with only her escort and her white agent. The after-party was also held at a whites-only establishment and Ms. McDaniel was not allowed to attend.

Hattie McDaniel was and is often criticized by the black community and liberal northerners for helping to perpetuate the "Mammy" stereotype. Her response was usually along the lines of, "I'd rather play a maid than be one." Neither Nancy Green nor Hattie McDaniel had been given a lot of other options.

Last year, I spent a week in Russia. While I was there, I went to an open-air museum called the Graveyard of Fallen Monuments. When the USSR and the communist government collapsed, the Russians took the old statues of Lenin, Stalin, Brezhnev, and other so-called "heroes of the revolution" and put them all together in one area. Today, you can walk through that stone and cement forest of towering monuments. They weren't destroyed, they were just relocated and put somewhere where their history could be contextualized. Why not do the same with the Civil War statues and the monuments to Columbus. We shouldn't forget who those people are, but do we need to keep glorifying them?

Our First Amendment rights to free speech do not apply to everything. The things that aren't covered include obscenity, defamation, fraud, incitement, true threats, and speech integral to already criminal conduct. NASCAR just banned the display of the Confederate flag. What is flying the Confederate flag but incitement? They should all be taken down. The Mississippi state flag includes the Confederate battle flag in its design. Take that down, too, and redesign it.

HBO has pulled *Gone with the Wind* from its streaming service. They say that they are going to create a documentary to accompany it in the future that will try to explain the period of history in which it was made. The Quaker Oats Company, a subsidiary of Pepsi announced just yesterday that they will finally be pulling the logo and will change the name of their Aunt Jemima brand. Cream of Wheat is now also reconsidering the image it uses—a character named Rastus who shares the same minstrel show origins as Aunt Jemima.

At the end of the Christmas special, *Santa Claus is Coming to Town*, the citizens of the town throw away the portraits of the Burgermeister Meisterburgers, who are the central villains of the story. The town should have kept them so that they wouldn't forget and make the same mistakes again.

We are repeating history as it is because we have forgotten things that have happened before. We shouldn't glorify the parts of our pasts that we have fought to overcome, but nor should we hide them. The bottles of Aunt Jemima syrup belong in a museum that explains what they were. They do not still belong on our grocery shelves sending the message to all that pass by them that African Americans are inferior. Dump most of them in the trash but keep one or two around as a constant reminder and as a warning.

Following the murder of George Floyd, we are all being called upon to look deeply within ourselves to identify institutional racism. The more you look, the easier it is to see the symbols of that racism that surround us. They are in our entertainment, in our streets, in our grocery stores. They are in the clichéd phrases we all use without thinking. They need to be changed.

The first step in solving a problem is acknowledging that there is one.

JUNE 19, 2020
388,907 Total Reported Cases in New York. 31,588 Deaths.

It's Juneteenth and an even hundred days into all of this. Our world is starting to look very different after this past century of days than it did when we started.

The President's re-election campaign has made the astonishing conscious decision to appeal right to the center of the most racist core of his base. His campaign has been using an upside-down red triangle in its messaging. That symbol was used by the Nazis in their concentration camps to identify political prisoners. Hitler's political opponents were some of the first people sent to the camps. According to the Auschwitz Memorial, 95% of the prisoners there in the fall of 1944 were political prisoners. A letter inside the triangle would indicate nationality. Social Democrats, Communists, union members—all of them were considered a threat to Hitler and his party and were thrown into the camps.

The current Administration has co-opted the red triangle in recent days to use as a symbol against protesters. The President's base knows exactly what it means. Facebook, yesterday, removed all the advertising on the site that contained the symbol. The campaign complained, saying that they were just using it as an emoji.

After he moved the rally that he'd planned for today to tomorrow following the backlash, the President tweeted, "I did something good. I made Juneteenth very famous. It's actually an important event, an important time. But nobody had ever heard of it." In an interview with the Wall Street Journal, he was told that his administration had put out statements on Juneteenth on each of his first three years in office. "Oh really? We put out a statement? The White House put out a statement? Ok, ok. Good."

Ironically, the recent abhorrent actions of his campaign have brought wider attention to Juneteenth. I thought I knew what it was, but it turned out that I didn't.

Abraham Lincoln's Emancipation Proclamation was formally issued on January 1, 1863. It declared that all enslaved persons in the Confederate States of America in rebellion and not in Union hands were to be freed. The wording was specific. It did not cover slave-holding areas in States such as Missouri, Tennessee, Kentucky, West Virginia, and Maryland or the tip of Louisiana around New Orleans. It also didn't cover the unincorporated territories to the west.

It was a calculation on Lincoln's part that gave the Union some strategic advantages during the war. Slaves from the south who escaped to the north and became free could, for the first time, join the Union army and carry weapons. It also ensured that England and France, both of whom were against slavery, would throw their support behind the Union and not behind the Confederacy.

Many people from the eastern States had moved into Texas during the war with their slaves to avoid the fighting. As a result, the slave population there had grown to about a quarter of a million people. Distances were vast and communication was unreliable. Robert E. Lee surrendered to Ulysses S. Grant on April 9, 1865, but word of that only reached Texas later in the month.

There is a story that a messenger who had been sent to deliver news of the original proclamation was murdered so Texans never knew their slaves had been freed. There is also the very real possibility that the slave owners did know and just didn't tell their slaves. Some historians even think that there is evidence that some in the federal government withheld the information on purpose to ensure one final cotton harvest before farmers lost their source of free labor.

At any rate, On June 18, 1865, Major General Gordon Granger finally arrived in Galveston, Texas and the next day, June 19, publicly read out the contents of General Order Number 3:

"The people of Texas are informed that, in accordance with a proclamation from the Executive of the United States, all slaves are free. This involves an absolute equality of personal rights and rights of property between former masters and slaves, and the connection heretofore existing between them becomes that between employer and hired labor. The freedmen are advised to remain quietly at their present homes and work for wages. They are informed that they will not be allowed to collect at military posts and that they will not be supported in idleness either there or elsewhere."

There were celebrations. The following year, in Galveston, freedmen organized the first of what became an annual celebration called Jubilee Day. By the 1890s the day started to become known as Juneteenth.

In 1938, the then Governor of Texas James V. Allred issued the following proclamation: "Whereas, the Negroes in the State of Texas observe June 19 as the official day for the celebration of Emancipation from slavery; and

Whereas, June 19, 1865, was the date when General Robert S. Granger, who had command of the Military District of Texas, issued a proclamation notifying the Negroes of Texas that they were free; and

Whereas, since that time, Texas Negroes have observed this day with suitable holiday ceremony, except during such years when the day comes on a Sunday; when the Governor of the State is asked to proclaim the following day as the holiday for State observance by Negroes; and

Whereas, June 19, 1938, this year falls on Sunday; NOW, THEREFORE, I, JAMES V. ALLRED, Governor of the State of Texas, do set aside and proclaim the day of June 20, 1938, as the date for observance of EMANCIPATION DAY in Texas, and do urge all members of the Negro race in Texas to observe the day in a manner appropriate to its importance to them."

To date, 49 of the 50 States recognize this day either as a state holiday or a special day of remembrance. Montana is the sole holdout. On Friday, Mayor de Blasio announced that Juneteenth would become an official holiday in the city of New York starting next year. There is now a concerted push to make Juneteenth a formally recognized national holiday.

Interestingly, the slaves in those five Union States plus the tip of Louisiana who were not mentioned in the Emancipation Proclamation were not officially freed until several months later, on December 6th when the 13th Amendment to the US Constitution was ratified.

Today also marks the last of Governor Cuomo's daily briefings. As we head towards reopening, he feels the need for them is waning. In his closing remarks, he asked, "Why does our politics appeal to our fear and weakness rather than to our strengths?" I think, that as we go into our November elections, that is a question that we all need to ask.

There are 28 marches, vigils, and protests in support of the Black Lives Movement scheduled for today in Manhattan, alone. If you participate, please wear a mask. We cannot lose the ground that we have gained during this war with COVID-19.

June 20, 2020
389,602 Total Reported Cases in New York. 31,656 Deaths.

Michael and I are FINALLY taking a road trip today. We are going up to Albany to have a socially responsible Father's Day celebration with his dad.

These days, my suitcase which usually sits partially pre-packed in the front hall is down in our storage unit. For the first couple of months following the shutdown, I was completely content to stay at home in our apartment. Now, I'm antsy. This will be the first time that we will have left the island of Manhattan in three months. As excited as I am to see my in-laws, I am even more excited about getting into a car and going for a drive.

The Supreme Court has been busy. I've been watching to see how individual Justices, vote. The decision in the recent landmark LGBTQ cases before the US Supreme Court was led by a Justice appointed by our current President. The decision, on Thursday, to protect DACA (Deferred Action for Childhood Arrivals) was led by a Justice who had been appointed by President George W. Bush. The decision, yesterday, to deny the Administration's request to block the publication of John Bolton's potentially explosive book about his time in the White House, was handed down by a Judge who had been appointed by President Reagan.

The Judges in each of these cases were making their decisions based upon the law. They were not partisan decisions. The law can be interpreted in different ways, though, and that's where the conflict comes from. Do you interpret the law strictly upon what the original framers of the law specifically intended it to be applied to, or do you interpret it, by considering how society has changed and evolved since it was created?

The three Justices that sided against the LGBTQ cases did so from a strict literalist interpretation of the original laws. The majority decided along more progressive lines. It seems, however, that their decisions were based upon how they were interpreting the law, not on the ideology of the party of the President that appointed them. I find that comforting.

Over the last 16 years, I have spent almost as much time working on publicity events in support of *Jersey Boys* as I have working on the show itself. I traveled nonstop. Those events happened all over the place. Often, in conjunction with a specific production, but sometimes just in support of a producing partner's venture. There is a massive outdoor music festival that happens in Amsterdam every year that we were a part of when we put the show up there. We've appeared on the Tony Awards in New York, the Helpmann Awards in Sydney, and the Olivier Awards in London. We performed on New Year's Eve in Toronto and down under in Australia. We even did a set at the Belmont Stakes horse racing track. Sometimes, though, the events are one-offs and can be just about anywhere. We did one in Berlin, one in Rabat, Morocco, an afternoon in Bentonville, Arkansas, and a huge event in Singapore to open the now-iconic Marina Bay Sands.

In Singapore, the hotel, itself, was still under construction. I remember us all walking down the hall to a rehearsal while workers were unrolling and installing the carpeting ahead of us. After the gala, the building's architects threw a private party on the roof which also marked the opening of that fantastic swimming pool. They invited the six of us to come so, of course, we did. Remarkably, we made it out of the country the next day. Diana Ross, who had also performed that night was on our flight home with us but that's about all I can remember about that morning.

That trip hardly seems real anymore. Neither do any of the others. Albany won't be nearly as exotic, but it will be somewhere other than here.

There is so much noise and confusion out there. We aren't through this by a long shot, but we are still here. We will get through this strange and sometimes terrifying time in our lives. I do believe that.

I do hope that everyone had a great Juneteenth. For a day at least, it was good to celebrate freedom.

June 22, 2020

WHO reported a 183,000 single-day jump in worldwide coronavirus cases.

Apparently, from the moment I was born until about the age of five, I never stopped screaming.

My mother tells stories of having to take me out of stores because she was afraid that other people would think that she was torturing me. One of the only things that would calm me down, from what I have been told, is a car ride. My poor Dad would put me in the car and drive me around for hours on end until I fell asleep.

One of the places he took me was Teterboro Airport which was about an hour away from where we were living at the time in Princeton. He said I liked watching the planes take off and land. I still like doing that at airports all these decades of years later. I like to imagine where they are going and where they have been.

There is a black and white photo of me sitting in my car seat looking like the very picture of happiness. The seat had a little steering wheel attached to the front. I feel like I have a memory of sitting in it, but it may just be that my memory formed around that photograph. I also had my massive fleet of toy cars. When we moved back to the US from South Africa, the first thing I remember about our new house was seeing a large new toy mustang on the bed in the room that my father had set up for me. For Christmas one year, my aunt gave me a beautiful picture book called "The Boy with 100 Cars" by Inger and Lasse Sandberg. I'll have to look, but I think that I may still have it somewhere.

Getting into the car on Saturday with Michael and our nephew, who lives near us in the city, then driving upstate was glorious. After three months without going anywhere, we were on an honest-to-goodness car trip. Because we were with my nephew, we kept our masks on in the car and opened the windows to keep the air circulating.

Last Wednesday, knowing that we were going to be seeing Michael's family, I went to CityMD to get tested for the virus. The whole thing, including the wait, took about an hour. When I got inside the nurse asked me if I wanted both the blood test and the swab. His eyes, above his mask, looked confused when I said that I didn't need the blood test because I already knew that I had the antibodies.

"Why are you here then?" he asked. I explained that I had participated in some Black Lives Matter marches and that I was going to be seeing my father-in-law who was in his eighties, so I just wanted to be sure. I have read enough to know that there is still some question as to whether the antibodies do provide immunity from becoming re-infected. There is also a question about how long the antibodies remain in our systems.

The nurse thought I was crazy but went ahead with the test. Much to my surprise, it was very easy. I swabbed myself. There is some question now, however, given my status, whether my insurance will cover the test. In retrospect, I should have just done the blood test as well and not said anything. In terms of this trip, the whole thing was somewhat moot as I won't get the results for a couple more days.

Navigating through this weekend with the family in terms of COVID-19 was, in a lot of ways a test case. There were 11 of us from four separate family units. Michael's younger sister and her husband have two kids—one of whom is still in high school and the other is set to start college in Arizona this fall. His older sister and her husband have one son—the nephew we drove up with. My father-in-law's partner is younger than he is but still within the most vulnerable age group.

All of us have been careful over these past months. I'm not sure any of us, though, have been perfect. On Saturday, before my father-in-law and his partner got there, the rest of us made the decision not to wear masks with each other. Was that wise? Strictly speaking, no. Practically speaking…?

The longer you spend in the company of somebody who has the virus, the more likely you are to get it. Given that we were all spending about 36 hours together, I don't think that masks were going to stop anything. Deciding to spend the weekend together was the point at which we all accepted that being 100% safe from each other was not going to be possible.

Once Michael's dad and his partner arrived, we all wore masks. Originally, we had planned on eating outside to be safer. It was so hot yesterday, however, that we stayed inside in the air conditioning. When we couldn't understand each other, the masks came down. They came down again when we all ate.

We did the best we could, but really if somebody in that group of 11 had the virus, I am guessing that we all got exposed to it. Driving home, we didn't wear our masks in the car. As our very sensible nephew said, if any of us had it, we would have given it to the others within 10 minutes of us getting into the car right at the beginning of the trip.

We are entering Phase 2 here in New York City today. That means that salons and barbershops can operate at 50% capacity. Retail stores can re-open with limits on how many people can go inside at one time. Restaurants can have outdoor seating. Offices can reopen with social distancing and sanitizing guidelines in place. The city is estimating that an additional 300,000 people will be traveling in the city today.

The President's much-hyped rally in Tulsa ultimately fizzled out. Instead of a packed arena with 19,000 people and an overflow crowd of 100,000, there were only 6,200 people in the arena and an overflow crowd of 25. Not 25 thousand, just 25.

A million people requested tickets, almost none of them came. Some of this was due to a concerted effort among young TikTok users and international K-pop fans who, by the thousands, created fake accounts to request tickets with the intention of not using them. Many older people in the US did the same thing. Two hours before the event when it became clear that the expected crowds were not going to materialize, promoters from the campaign sent out a tweet saying there were still plenty of tickets available and people should come down. While just over six thousand people did go, many more people, even those among the President's supporters, clearly were more than a little concerned about the virus. They stayed away.

The overflow event outside the arena was canceled and the stage and holding areas were quickly dismantled. Hoping for a huge bang to kick off his campaign, what the President got, instead, was a dull pop. The film of him returning to the White House from the helicopter on Saturday night, his tie untied, and his clothes wrinkled and hair flat against his head, is as defeated as I can recall him ever looking. I wouldn't want to be anywhere near him today. Somebody's surely getting well and truly fired.

It's great to say that we are doing well in New York, but if everyone around us doesn't do equally well, it's meaningless. In the coming days, we are all going to be making more and more choices about our own safety and the safety of those around us. We are going to make some mistakes. We are going to take some risks, some of which may end up having some consequences. We need to keep our eyes, ears, and hearts open and do the best we can. That's all. We all just need to do the best that we can.

Spending a Father's Day without my own dad this weekend was bittersweet. His wanderlust is very much a part of me. I'd like to think that he was in the car with us this past weekend, looking out at the endless, rolling, green-covered mountains of upstate New York.

He loved a good car trip as much as I do.

June 23, 2020
391,411 Total Reported Cases in New York. 31,791 Deaths.

For the last few years, the traffic in New York has been slowly and rather erratically redesigned. Bike lanes have been added as have left-hand turning lanes. Some avenues have moved their parking spaces into the street, leaving the bike lane between the parked cars and the sidewalk. Now, some of those parking areas are being taken over by dining tables. Restaurants all along Columbus Avenue are in the process of setting up outside dining areas. They have all been permitted to expand out onto the sidewalks and even, in some places out onto the street.

On, Restaurant Row, a stretch of 46th Street in the heart of the theatre district has been completely blocked off from traffic. Some of the eating places there have started to re-open as well. A few, like Joe Allen's, though, are strongly linked to theatre performance schedules. They are great places to eat before a show and even better places to gather afterward.

It will be interesting to see how these places fare without the Broadway shows. And without the tourists. The subways, while certainly cleaner these days, are very much being avoided. The few times I have been on them in the last few weeks, they've been largely empty. Will people from other areas of the city venture out of their immediate neighborhoods to eat?

It's also very hot in New York this week. Last night it was 88 degrees (31/32C) and very humid. I doubt that anybody is going to want to sit outside until later in the evening when it gets somewhat cooler. Only one person was sitting outside at Don't Tell Mama, a Restaurant Row piano bar.

I headed downtown to Macy's which has just reopened. There are signs all over the place encouraging shoppers to wear masks and keep their distance from other shoppers. There is only one masked clerk at each cashier station and those stations have plexiglass sneeze guards installed.

Macy's is usually one of the worst places on the planet to shop. Crowds of tourists and New Yorkers alike make it impossible to navigate through. Every single time I go in, I instantly regret it and leave. Yesterday, the store was manageable. There were some people shopping, but not many. I had no intention of buying anything but as an enticement, there are some very good deals to be had so I bought some polo shirts. I've been living in them these days and the ones I have are getting a bit worn. Part of the fun of buying new clothes is when other people notice them. I guess that's not going to happen with these.

As some of New York starts opening back up It feels a bit like what we have access to is just a tasting platter of what we once had. Soon I am going to want to order something off the main menu. For now, though, this will do.

June 24, 2020
391,884 Total Reported Cases in New York. 31,813 Deaths.

Every night, for the last few weeks, the sound of fireworks exploding across the city has become ubiquitous. Friends have posted that their dogs are becoming stressed out and asking what other people are doing to comfort theirs. On Sunday, when we were driving back from Albany, a massive firework ignited on the West Side Highway directly in front of us with bright tendrils of light covering the road.

Someone posted a video showing city firefighters setting some off somewhere in the city. Monday night, protestors drove past Gracie Mansion, Mayor de Blasio's home on the upper east side of Manhattan and honked their horns long into the morning and chanted, "We don't sleep, you don't sleep." Our cat, who disappears at the sound of the first raindrop hitting our window air conditioning unit, is thankfully completely unfazed by the explosions. What's going on?

Michael Flynn was the President's National Security Advisor for just the first three weeks of his term. He was forced to resign when it came to light that he had misled the Vice President about his communications with the Russian Ambassador during the campaign. In December of 2017, he formalized a deal with Special Counsel Robert Mueller to plead guilty to making false statements to the FBI—a felony offense. He pleaded guilty again a year later, but then in January of this year, he attempted to withdraw it. In May, the US Department of Justice, led by Attorney General Bill Barr announced that it was dropping all charges against Flynn. A federal judge then stepped in and put the matter on hold.

It was announced last night that an appeals court has ordered the judge to dismiss the Flynn case. They did not say that Flynn is not guilty, they just said that the case needs to be decided by the Department of Justice and not by the court and that the federal judge did not have the right to intervene. It looks very likely that, despite pleading guilty to a felony twice, that Michael Flynn is going to be exonerated by the current US Attorney General. The President has just tweeted that he thinks that this is "Great!"

Twenty-six states are now showing increases in their coronavirus cases. Arizona is 56% up from where it was last week. Violating the city's ordinance, the President rallied a packed auditorium of students in Phoenix yesterday. From the pictures, it is apparent that nobody in the crowd was wearing a mask. He downplayed the virus, even referred to it as the "Kung flu" and railed against safety measures.

The news wants us all to be wound up, anxious and hysterical because we then tune in to watch what is going on. The second that something happens, the newscasters pounce on it. They continually dissect it over several days. Each small new development gets announced as BREAKING

NEWS! Flashing in bright red across our screens. Then they break for commercial.

My daily anxiety is just as high as anybody else's. Wading through the nonsense and trying to put it into some sort of rational order by writing about it is the thing that keeps the terror at bay for me.

The TV is now off, and the windows are open. I can hear the wind through the trees, the tops of which are just under the level of our apartment. It is 82 degrees outside (28C) and the humidity level that was up to 87% yesterday has dropped to 36%. I can hear that there's a good breeze.

I am going to go for a walk. Or a ride.

We are running a bit low on coffee and on wine (the essentials that are my responsibility), so I will do a little shopping as I wander. Maybe Michael and I will take a walk together later. We have been in this apartment together for so long now, that I think we occasionally forget that the other one is here too.

I feel like my immediate mission is clear: enjoy the weather and my partner and chill out. I'll worry about the rest of the stuff later.

JUNE 25, 2020
2.4 million Total Reported Cases in the United States.

Do you want to get something done? Ask a busy person. So goes the saying, anyway.

I am used to dealing with multiple problems on multiple fronts at the same time. Some things invariably slip through the cracks, but the busier I am, the more focused I get. I can be working on a large project, get up to take a break, deal with three other things then go back and pick up where I left off with the larger project. These days, though, as the sun starts to set, I realize that I haven't accomplished much of anything on my very meager list of things to do. Worst of all, I've often completely forgotten what was on the list in the first place.

Australia's borders are closed. Residents returning from international destinations are required to quarantine in hotels. Non-residents are simply not allowed in. The Vienna Convention mandates that diplomats from other countries have freedom of movement and travel and cannot be subject to detention. Diplomats are the only people not required to quarantine although they are at least urged to self-isolate at their embassies or homes for 14 days before they venture out. Flights anywhere within Australia are largely shut down. It has taken a couple of weeks for my friend whose apartment I'm packing up to be able to even FedEx me the keys to the apartment simply because there are so few flights out.

The Arts in Australia, after a long hard fight, have just been given a small reprieve by the government in terms of financial aid. Like here, artists are deemed non-essential workers and, like here, are likely to be among the last people in the country back to work. Much of the health of their city's economies, however, again just like here, rely on performances and exhibitions to attract people to the hotels and restaurants and shops nearby. The Australian government is far more supportive of the arts than ours is, but even they have somewhat ignored the entire sector during this pandemic.

New Zealand, across the Tasman Sea from them, has been largely successful in eliminating the virus within its borders. They currently have only nine active cases in the entire country. All nine cases are from people entering the country who are in quarantine facilities. The military is now overseeing these facilities after two people with the virus were accidentally allowed to leave. People are flatly not allowed to leave the facilities until they have tested negative for the virus. The cruise ship ban in New Zealand was due to expire at the end of this month, but it has just been extended for an additional 60-90 days.

New Zealand and Australia are still looking to create a contained travel bubble between their two countries which could start as soon as September if both country's cases continue at their current very low levels. The island country of Fiji who derives 40% of its economy from tourism, has just made a proposal asking to join in on the bubble.

I was just reading about Cambodia where they have instituted a $3,000 coronavirus deposit for tourists who plan to travel there to see the spectacular temples of Angkor Wat. In addition to that, travelers need to carry at least $50,000 worth of travel insurance to cover healthcare, laundry services, meals. And a funeral. Many in Cambodia are complaining that this is deterring tourists who make up a large chunk of the country's GNP. The extra pressure that foreign travelers could potentially put on the already inadequate health care system, however, makes this a necessity. Cambodia has been spared the worst of the pandemic so far, but officials are already fearing the worst.

My friends around the world are all looking at us here in the US with their mouths agape.

At ANY point in our past, we would be among those counties leading the world towards a solution. Instead, we are now leading the world in the opposite direction—towards an increasing amount of completely avoidable deaths.

The European Union is currently considering banning all travelers from the United States. The US and Canadian border will remain closed for at least another month. The Canadians are in no rush for any of us to visit. It's like living above a meth lab, as somebody down here posted.

I cannot imagine what life must have been like in 1918 during the Spanish flu pandemic. I know that if I had been alive at that time, it is unlikely that I would have had the number of friends that I have now who live outside of the country. During the lockdown of 1918, however, even communication between friends in the same city would have been difficult.

In 2020, I can easily talk to my friend in Australia. We can even see each other on FaceTime or Zoom. How the heck we are going to be able to ship his stuff down to Australia remains to be seen. It doesn't look like my friend and I will be able to be together, though, until at least well into next year.

In a way, New York is a bit like Australia. We each seem to have a handle on our cases, but we are both islands in a sea of COVID. We are safe for the moment, but neither of us can exist indefinitely in isolation. None of us on this planet can exist without the others. We are all inextricably interconnected.

We are eventually going to need to apologize to the rest of the world for our current stupidity and get to work with them on trying to solve it. Until then my Aussie mate, I'm finally heading down to your apartment with a tape measure. Let's figure out how to do this.

June 26, 2020
393,527 Total Reported Cases in New York. 31,869 Deaths.

The Coca-Cola sign in Times Square seems to be having a nervous breakdown. In what appears to be an attempt to cover all bases, Coke has programmed their sign with a continuous loop of reactive imagery. A bright red love heart dissolves to a rainbow-colored bottle of coke and an array of the logo across the color spectrum for Pride celebrations, which, in turn, dissolves to a somber black screen exhorting us all to "share hope, do more, end racism."

Just above Coke, Samsung is thanking Health Care workers and above them, Prudential is bouncing back and forth between showing photos of both front-line masked health practitioners and rainbow Pride images. Throughout Times Square, the LED screens are all trying to pay tribute to everything that's going on around us while, at the same time, doing what they are designed to do: sell us stuff.

On a much smaller level, at all the demonstrations around the city, you can now buy Black Lives Matter t-shirts and buttons from sellers on the streets. As some of the souvenir stores reopen, they, too, are starting to stock BLM shirts and caps. In the early days of the protests, there was a huge variety of different styles and designs available. The most popular of those designs are still available and being copied by different makers, while some of the others have fallen away. We are watching, in real-time, the market adapting itself to new conditions. Supply and demand economics in all its greedy glory.

Much of the advertising we are watching on TV is also starting to embrace various causes. Since nobody knows what the long-term changes are going to be on our consumer habits, companies are doing their best to try and keep ahead of what they think we are going to want and cover everything.

As I am writing this, the Vice President is on TV giving full credit to the federal government for their remarkable work in containing the COVID-19 virus. Where is he getting that idea that it's contained? Yesterday, we hit a new high in the United States. There were 39,327 new cases of coronavirus reported. California, Texas, and Florida all set new records for their largest single-day increases. Ever. Texas is pausing its reopening. They have just re-closed their bars. Seven other states are also pausing.

Governor DeSantis of Florida still refuses to mandate the wearing of masks or to issue stay-at-home orders. Disney World, with 77,000 employees, is one of Florida's largest employers. They are set to open again two weeks from tomorrow. Cast members have been pleading with government officials as well as park officials to delay the reopening out of concern for the safety of both the guests and the workers. As of this morning, a petition on MoveOn already has over 12,000 signatures urging them to stay closed for now.

Michael and I are talking about going out and getting a frozen margarita somewhere. We have been talking about it for a couple of days now. Nothing hits the spot on a hot humid New York day better than a frozen margarita. There was a great place right near us called Gabriella's, but they closed sometime before the virus even hit. We talked about it, but we didn't go yesterday. I'm not sure we are going to go today either. It all seems to be a bit much to deal with now. Maybe, tonight, instead, Michael and I will have a nice glass of chilled rosé at home.

JUNE 27, 2020
394,261 Total Reported Cases in New York. 31,890 Deaths.

Our niece graduated from high school yesterday in upstate New York. Only immediate family were allowed to be present at the actual ceremony. The rest of us were all meant to be able to watch it via streaming on YouTube. Of course, something screwed up and the feed didn't work. We got a scattered bit of *The Star-Spangled Banner* at the very beginning and then the picture froze. Our family, all from different places in the country, were all frantically texting each other. The live stream never recovered.

Somebody though, taped it so we should all get to watch it later. Michael's sister sent us photos of the graduate and her boyfriend. At the end of the ceremony, there was a parade through the town with the graduates in their separate cars. It looks like they all had fun.

It's tempting, I think, to take the idea of our lives being on pause too literally. Our lives aren't on pause. It's just that some of the things that we usually do to fill them have stopped for the moment.

That was our niece's high school graduation. She's not going to get another one when the virus recedes. It wasn't a normal graduation ceremony, but it was certainly memorable. I'm going to guess that forty years from now she will remember it a bit better than I can remember mine.

My dad graduated from high school in 1941. In December of that year, the Japanese bombed Pearl Harbor and World War II began. He went into basic training and was eventually shipped overseas to Europe. He stayed there through the end of the war, fighting in the last major counter-offensive launched by the Germans called the Battle of the Bulge. At the end of the war, his infantry division was one of the first to go into the Bergen-Belsen concentration camp.

That whole journey started for my dad when he was the same age our niece is now. He didn't plan it. It just happened to him. What he went through in the army while the normal course of his life was on hold, and as horrific as some parts of it were, in some way became the defining experience of his life. He met people from other parts of the country who became life-long friends. He told stories about them and about what had happened to him, right up until his passing sixty some odd years later.

When the war was over, he returned to the US and finally went to college. He majored in chemistry. He got a job writing for a chemical magazine. After having been there in the war, all he wanted to do was to go back overseas. Much to his delight, the magazine made him their European correspondent and he was posted in London where he met my mother.

Going to Europe at 19 years old instilled in him a life-long love of traveling that he passed down to both of his kids.

Downtown, in part of the park surrounding City Hall, an occupy Wall Street kind of tent city has sprung up. The young people living in the enclave are advocating for Police reform. They are doing everything that they can to push the "defund the NYPD" agenda forward. They want $1 billion of the proposed annual budget slated to go towards the Police Department to, instead, be siphoned off to other social services. They believe that those social service organizations are far better equipped to deal with some of the issues the Police are currently in charge of.

I was down there yesterday taking some pictures and looking around when I got roped into moving supplies into the food area. Food and medical supplies have been donated and areas for them have been set up. There are social workers onsite who seem to be coordinating the organization and flow. Hammocks have been strung up on fences and between some of the park's trees.

Most of the people there look around college-age to me. The combination of the economic shutdown and the Black Lives Matter demonstrations have created the time and space and spark for these young adults to get energized and focused. Some may eventually drift away, but for some of them, this could be the beginning of what they do for the rest of their lives.

When the AIDS crisis hit us in the early 1980s, I was about the same age as my dad was during the war and just a year or two older than my niece is now. At the time I took it as a cruel joke being played only against me. Just as I was starting to get confident enough to start living inside my gay skin, to do so at that time meant a potential death sentence. I spent years waiting for it to be over. As the years have passed, however, I, along with everybody else, have figured out how to live with it.

Friends of mine, who contracted HIV, were far more impacted by it than I was. Some died, but some survived. And fought. Today, forty years later, they are still fighting and living with it. That "pause" in our sexual lives, in many ways, has made us the people that we are today. The AIDS relief organization, Broadway Cares / Equity Fights AIDS was started out of desperation. Something HAD to change. Without exaggeration, in the last forty years, BC/EFA has raised and distributed hundreds of millions of dollars impacting more lives than there are starfish in the sea. Did the people who started it think that it would turn into their life's work? I sincerely doubt it, but it did. Careers were made. Life-long causes were taken up.

The attention that the gay community, commanded, and demanded, during that time is one of the main reasons that, today, I am sitting in my living room writing this next to my husband.

The whole idea that what we are currently living through is a time that, at some point, will be over, is something that I think we should start moving beyond. We have, throughout our collective history, been continually beset upon by wars, plagues, and uprisings. The coronavirus is just the latest in an infinite series that will continue long after this virus has been either dealt with or absorbed. Rather than thinking of it as a disaster sent from above to end our world, maybe it is better to just step back from it and see it for what it is. Plot. COVID-19 is just the next bend in our story.

It's all about the journey. It always has been.

Our niece's strange quarantine graduation is one of the things that is going to be a permanent marker of her life. Our lives are chugging forward as lives are wont to do. We should enjoy the ride and take it all in because we aren't ever coming back this way again.

June 29, 2020
395,406 Total Reported Cases in New York. 31,948 Deaths.

I slept right through the Pride march yesterday morning.

Most days, I go to sleep after about 1 am and sleep through until about 10 am. It's not necessarily nine straight hours, though, because there are always interruptions. Michael doesn't go to sleep until after I do and then usually wakes up before I do.

In the morning, the cat demands that he be fed shortly after sunrise. Whether there is still any food in his dish or not, the cat requires that attention be paid. He will start reminding us of our duty to him as early as about 5 am (Or so I've been told. I can sleep through most of what he does. Michael, however, can't.) If the sun gets too high into the sky and we are still asleep, he will start knocking things over.

Despite sleeping late, Michael and I decided that it was finally time to go out and celebrate Pride with the frozen margarita that we've been talking about for days. So, we took a walk down Columbus Avenue looking for a place that seemed safe.

I have a scar on the ridge between my eyebrows. When I was quite little, a toddler I think, my mother had to stop the car suddenly and I slammed into the front dashboard. I needed to get seven stitches. I wasn't wearing a seat belt.

On January 1, 1968, a few years after my accident, the US government passed a law requiring that all vehicles, except buses, install seat belts in the designated seating areas. On December 4, 1984, New York became the first state that required people to wear them. Today, in 2020, only 49 out of the 50 states have laws mandating the wearing of seat belts by adults. New Hampshire is the sole holdout. Kids under 17 are required to wear them there, but adults aren't.

68% of adults, according to a Gallup poll in July of 1984 were opposed to being forced to wear seat belts. One of the arguments against them at the time was the belief that it was safer to be thrown from a vehicle than it was to be trapped inside one after an accident. The CDC, however, analyzing data, found that wearing a seat belt reduces the risk of death by 45% and of serious injury by 50%. People not wearing a seat belt are 30 times more likely to be thrown from a vehicle than those who have buckled in. 75% of the people who get thrown from their cars because of an accident die from the injuries they receive. When the law was first passed, people cut the seat belts out of their cars and challenged the laws in court.

According to recent surveys, 90% of Americans now routinely use seat belts. Countless public service campaigns and enforcement of the laws later, it has largely become something that we don't even think about doing anymore. We don't have to. Every single time we get into our cars, we are beeped at until we buckle up. I look at my scar every single morning while I brush my teeth and shave. You don't need to remind me to wear a seat belt.

It took us fifty years as a country to get to the point where most of us routinely wear seat belts for our own safety. Worldwide cases of COVID-19 have now gone past the 10 million mark. We, here in the United States, account for 25% of those cases. How long is it going to take us to routinely wear masks?

Michael and I walked for thirty blocks yesterday before finding a restaurant that we felt comfortable sitting in. The rest of the places we passed were either set up too close together or many of the people gathering there were not wearing masks.

There are risks inherent in almost everything that we do. Over time, we learn to weigh them. We haven't been around COVID-19 long enough to be able to judge the relative risks properly yet. Based on the behavior of similar viruses and from early reports, however, there is a general understanding of relative risk.

Michael and I had a wonderful meal yesterday. No frozen margaritas, after all of that, but I had an excellent Moscow Mule instead. Well, two.

There is no such thing as safe sex. What there is, is safER sex. Wearing a condom is safer. Wearing a mask appears to be safer, too. So, until somebody who doesn't seem like an irrational kook, presents a compelling argument against it, we are going to wear a mask. If we can wear a mask in the 85% humidity and heat in New York these days and have a good night out, then honestly anyone can.

So, pick up some condoms, fasten the seatbelt, and mask up and let's get on with it.

June 30, 2020
395,909 Total Reported Cases in New York. 31,909 Deaths.

Actor's Equity Association is the union that covers actors in the theatre as well as stage managers. You can't be in the union unless you have a union job, and you can't have a union job unless you are in the union. That's the endless conundrum facing all of us when we are starting out. I got into the union in 1985.

The way that I got in was that I had been working for a stage manager and a director as a non-union production assistant for a couple of years. On the kind of shows we did, though, the assistant stage manager position was not a union one. Finally, they hired me in a theatre that was big enough to require that I join the union and I got my card.

The show was called *Just So!* (Complete with the exclamation point.) It was a musical version of Rudyard Kipling's *Just So Stories*. We opened at the Jack Lawrence Theatre on December 3, 1985, which was a Tuesday. We then closed Saturday night after six somewhat dismal performances. We were a bomb, but I finally had my union card.

It was announced yesterday, by the Broadway League, that the shutdown of Broadway theatres is going to continue until January 2. The Broadway League is an alliance of producers and theatre owners. That doesn't mean that Broadway shows are going to start up again on January 2, it just means that you can now get a refund for any ticket between now and then. Once those ticket orders have been dealt with, the League will extend the date forward another couple of months.

So, when is Broadway coming back? The answer to that, no matter who you ask, is always going to be the three scariest words in the entire English language: "I don't know." There are some guesses, but they are all based on what is happening right now and not on what will be happening when we get there.

We must stop thinking about the people we choose to lead us as being these omnipotent beings who know everything. They aren't and they don't. They are just people that we have chosen to be our voices. They are making things up as they go along. Somebody like Governor Cuomo can take in the information at hand and then make the best decision that he can. It's still usually a best guess. Making elderly people who had been hospitalized with the virus return to their nursing homes was a massive mistake. He learned that the hard way. Many people died. He could have shut us down earlier than he did, that was a mistake, too. In both of those cases, he was taking the information that he had at the time and weighing against politics, economics, and everything else and, as a result, made some wrong decisions.

Once he learned more, his decision-making improved and now we are seeing the fruits of that. Our cases are well and truly down. Compared to the rest of the country, we are golden. Before he learned those lessons, though, he just didn't know what to do. It's easy to sit at home and second guess our leaders, but in Cuomo's actions, you can see an evolution happening as time progresses. He knows much more about how to deal with a pandemic now than when we started.

"I don't know," can't be an excuse. It also can't be a lie. The President continually says "I didn't know" when something that he does backfires.

He shared a video on Twitter that had a guy yelling "white power!" at a group of protestors and is now claiming that he didn't know that it was part of the video. The President "didn't know" the significance of Juneteenth or the city of Tulsa when he chose to stage his first rally back there. He "didn't know" that the virus was coming out of China because the Chinese didn't tell him. It has been reported that the Russians have been paying Taliban fighters to specifically target American troops. The Russians are paying out a bounty on American soldiers' lives. The President says that he "didn't know" that was happening.

One of the other characters in *Just So!* was a giraffe. The Giraffe was played by my ex-husband. Yes, in the very short time that gay marriage has been legal, I have somehow managed to already have done it twice. You think gay marriage is hard, try gay divorce. Anyway, that's (possibly) for another time. In the show, the Giraffe knows everything. He is a complete control freak. In his big eleven o'clock number, my ex sang a song that should be called "I Don't Know" but I think was called something else. I've been looking for it, but I can't find it to check, but my memory of it is that the lyrics were just "I don't know" sung over and over again. My ex… well, whatever I might say about him, he could wail. This song was a total anthem of joy where the Giraffe discovered the freedom in being able to say the words, "I don't know".

None of us knows what the future is going to be so all that we can do is prepare for the worst and hope for the best. What happens is going to likely fall between the two. When "I don't know" covers a lie it is extremely dangerous. When it's spoken as the truth it is freeing because it gives us a way forward. It points us on the path of discovery that we need to move ahead on.

When we know the date that performances will start up again on Broadway, we will know. Until then we don't. We will get through this. That is something that I do know. We will get through this.

July 1, 2020
396,456 Total Reported Cases in New York. 31,926 Deaths.

Yesterday was a completely normal and unremarkable day. Today looks like it is going to be yet another unremarkable day. It is dark and gloomy outside, and it has just started thundering. The cat is well and truly hidden somewhere he feels safe. I have a couple of Zoom meetings on my schedule. When the storm passes, I will put on my mask and helmet and go out and take a ride. Riding a bicycle again has been a wonderful addition to my life that has only happened because of what we are all going through.

We are, here in New York, living in a bubble of sorts for the moment. Rather than worrying about our bubble bursting, we should take advantage of this time and enjoy it. We've had more than our share of drama lately. I say, bring on another unremarkable day.

July 2, 2020
397,363 Total Reported Cases in New York. 31,950 Deaths.

I've always been drawn to post-apocalyptic fiction. One of the books that I would want with me on a deserted island is Stephen King's, *The Stand*. I have read it more times than I can count.

What's amazing to me is that the same mistakes that people and governments make in these books are very clearly being made now in real-time. Venal politicians follow their own interests rather than the needs of the people and all hell breaks loose.

Just yesterday, our President said, "I think we're going to be very good with the coronavirus. I think that at some point that's going to sort of just disappear." He said this as we hit the new milestone of 50,000 NEW cases of COVID-19 in a single day. I know that we are getting numb to these numbers, but 50,000 people sick in a single day is a truly huge number.

If health concerns and racial justice concerns were not enough, he now finds himself in yet another quagmire in terms of his relationship with Russia.

When it came to light that the Russians had been putting a bounty on American lives in Afghanistan by offering the Taliban cash in exchange for specifically targeting American troops, the President's defense amounted to saying that he doesn't read his intel, so he didn't know. What started to come out yesterday was that the President reacts so negatively to anything said against Russia that much of the time, such information is kept from him by his handlers.

There is a so-called "Gang of Eight" bipartisan group of Senators—four Republican and four Democrat—who are routinely briefed by the Executive Branch on classified intelligence matters. They knew.

In the last few days, since this information has come to light, the President has made at least 6 calls to the Russian President. There have been no reports whatsoever about possible US reprisals against Russia. The President dismisses the whole matter as a "hoax".

All of this would be right at home in any of the end-of-the-world novels I've read. In those books, when things like this aren't addressed, they never just go away. They get worse. And worse.

While I think that it is important not to stick our heads in the sand about any of this, it's equally, if not more important, not to let any of it keep us from being able to sleep. We have it within our power to get through this safely. We aren't under attack by zombies and vampires, just by selfish idiots. To fight them, we just need to be smart.

Just for the moment, perhaps, stay home and read a good book. It may end up being a quieter 4th of July than most of us are used to, but it will be a much safer one.

July 3, 2020

57,497 New Reported Cases in the United States. It is the largest single-day total to date.

The plywood is mostly down along 5th Avenue now. A week or two ago, almost every storefront along its entire midtown length was completely covered up. The stores, themselves, in that area, are, of course, mostly still closed.

We can finally walk around the outdoor plaza at Rockefeller Center again. The long avenue across from Saks, which is lined with heralding angels during the holiday season had been barricaded off from pedestrians for several weeks. The famous ice rink is covered over with a tarp that says, "New York Strong" in gigantic letters.

In SoHo, which was one of the hardest-hit areas of Manhattan by violent agitators during the recent demonstrations, the plywood was transformed by painters into an outdoor art gallery. It reminded me of the wall in Berlin—a long section of which remained standing after the rest of it came down. The section that stayed up, stayed up because of the artwork painted on it and has become an open-air museum of sorts. Similarly, galleries that have removed their plywood walls of art have taken steps to preserve the pieces and store them. There are still many places down there where the plywood is still up. Every time I bike through there, I see incredible new work appearing on the raw surfaces. A lot of the stores there remain closed, too.

I remember coming into Manhattan from New Jersey in the late 70s when I was in High School. It was not the city then that it is now. 42nd Street was all porno theatres and boarded-up storefronts. I was mugged once in the middle of Times Square by two guys who took my wallet and my gloves. It happened out in the open in broad daylight.

After World War I and continuing into the late 60s and early 70s there was a large movement of poor African Americans from the south who had moved north searching for better lives. When they arrived north, they faced a wall of obstacles from the White European Americans who were already here. Segregation and redlining were common. Redlining is the denial of services to certain segments of the population through the selective raising of prices—a practice that is now illegal but still happens. As they moved into places like Detroit, Chicago, Minneapolis, and New York, the white middle-class in those cities fled to the suburbs.

By the time I started coming into the city, the so-called "white flight" had peaked. There were few jobs available in the city, so unemployment and crime were rife. Tax revenue was way down because nobody was earning any money. Graffiti was everywhere. Subway cars were so covered with it that you couldn't see out of the windows and no light could get in.

In the early 1980s, over 250 felonies were committed every week on the transit system making it the most dangerous in the world. Many buildings throughout New York were just abandoned and boarded up. It was a common sight to see people shooting up heroin out in the open.

I remember when I started going to school here at the beginning of the 1980s that it was not safe to walk the ten blocks north of where I live now, up to Columbia University. Joan Armatrading had a concert at Carnegie Hall that I decided not to go to my freshman year because I couldn't figure out how I'd get back uptown that late in the evening.

Manhattan Theatre Club used to have its offices and rehearsal studios downtown on West 16th Street. I can't remember what show I was rehearsing there, but I remember us all being excited that Stephen Sondheim had paid for them to install a metal gate over the recessed entryway. He was rehearsing the original production of *Assassins* and the trans streetwalkers on the corner used the recessed doorway to defecate in. He was tired of stepping over it on his way to work.

Over time, the city improved. The 42nd Street project slowly started reclaiming the Times Square area and renovating the theatres there. A huge public relations campaign was launched to get people to come back to New York to visit and to live. And it worked.

By the time we hit the last election, 20% of the world's population were living in cities of 1 million people or more. In 2016, New York was thriving.

Since its rebirth in the 1980s, New York City has taken several hits. After 9/11, the destruction erased 30% of the area's office space and displaced 100,000 office workers for many years. My father was one of those people. My father worked across the street from one of the towers. He had been on the verge of retiring when the planes hit. He had argued with his bosses that he could work remotely and still be able to do his job, but they wouldn't hear of it. After the devastation, everybody in the office had to work remotely so my father moved to Florida with my mother and didn't retire at that point after all. He worked, I think, for at least another ten more years from home.

The 2008 financial crisis also restructured the way people in the Financial District worked. Since then, the number of people who work downtown in person had already started to substantially decrease.

5% of the city's population has left during this pandemic. The rate in Manhattan, itself, is more than three times higher than that. Many friends of ours have been sheltering with their families elsewhere. More of our wealthier friends have chosen to ride this out in their weekend or summer homes far outside of the city.

As these people get used to working remotely, are they going to want to come back? Not having to pay New York rents on office spaces is, in and of itself, I would think, a huge advantage. Not having to face a daily commute is something many people thrill to think about. I've talked to several people who are seriously thinking about leaving the city for good and only commuting in as needed.

You might think that wouldn't be possible for those of us in the theatre industry. The truth is that Actors spend most of their time auditioning rather than performing. Auditions can happen from home. Michael has gotten some of his best gigs taping himself here in the apartment. Many voice-over artists have been taping in their home studios for years. Almost none of the creative team I work with on *Jersey Boys* live in New York anymore. One lives in Encino, CA, and another in Edmonton, Canada. Others are in various suburbs around the city. It took a while, but we've figured out how to make it work.

Cities will always provide something that outlying areas can't. Cultural institutions require a certain level of nearby population density to survive. New York supports a wide range of museums and theatres that, regardless of where people reside, attract them to the city. We may start seeing an increase in tourism and a decrease in residential living because of all of this. I think Michael would like to live in a smaller upstate town, but I don't think that I am ready to think about that. Yet.

What will this ultimately mean for New York? Are we going to see another flight?

We are heading out of town today for the weekend to spend some time at a friend's house. We are looking forward to the isolation. Michael's sister and her husband are coming in to stay in our apartment. They are looking forward to being in the city. I'm sending them downtown to SoHo to take a walk through the streets so that they can see some of the spectacular and moving painting that's down there before it all gets packed away.

We will be back.

July 4, 2020

11,458 New Reported Cases in Florida.

New York still holds the record with a single-day total of 11,571 back in April.

Last spring, I was invited by an organization that is roughly the Russian equivalent of our Tony awards, to speak to a group of stage managers in Moscow. This invitation came at the time when the United States was already deep into the investigation and discussion about what the Russians may or may not have done to influence our 2016 elections.

All of that, of course, followed the entire Cold War period between the US and Russia which I was born into and grew up with until 1991. President Reagan famously referred to the USSR as the "Evil Empire" in a 1983 speech to the National Association of Evangelicals. In that same speech, he also said that they were, "the focus of evil in the modern world."

Our relationship with Russia had improved during much of the decade following the coup that dissolved the Soviet Union in 1991. Following the NATO bombing of Kosovo in the Federal Republic of Yugoslavia in 1999, though, it got worse again. The Yugoslavs were perpetrating a genocide against Albanians which was driving the victims of it into neighboring countries and destabilizing the entire region. Intervention by the United Nations was opposed by China and Russia so, NATO went ahead with airstrikes without their approval. The US referred to the action as "Operation Noble Anvil." The Russians condemned our participation in the retaliation.

The antagonism between our two countries further intensified when Russia annexed Crimea in 2014 and then even more during their intervention in the Syrian Civil War.

My mother and father visited Moscow for a short time before I was born. My father's job with a Chemical Engineering magazine had seen him posted in different places all over Europe and they attended a chemical conference there. This was not long after US pilot Francis Gary Powers, flying an aerial photographic spy mission deep into Soviet territory had been shot down. Tensions between the two countries were high, but despite high security, they got in and out without incident. They were taken to Gorky Park where all of Power's belongings, including his wedding ring, were laid out on a long table alongside the plane's wreckage, for the public to view. Powers was ultimately released as part of a prisoner exchange—the Americans traded a Soviet spy, Rudolf Abel for him—on the very day that I was born in 1962.

When I received this invitation to speak, I said yes.

They only asked me to come over for two nights, but I went for a full week beforehand, instead, and spent three days in St. Petersburg before heading to Moscow. The process of getting a visa was extremely involved and took a very long time—over a month. The application was 15-20 pages long and required an endless amount of very detailed information about places I had visited and jobs that I had had. My visit was sponsored, and my expenses were largely covered by the US Embassy in Moscow as part of a cultural exchange program. I paid for the extension into St. Petersburg myself. My payment from them for doing all of this was a small honorarium, but well worth it for a truly unforgettable experience.

So, what was it like being in "enemy" territory? It wasn't like being in enemy territory at all. Russians live their lives the same way that we do. They take the impositions and rules handed down by their government and figure out their daily lives around them—the same as we do.

In the week before my lecture, I visited some of the most spectacular museums on the planet—The Hermitage in St. Petersburg, and Peterhof, the palace of Peter the Great. In Moscow, I visited the Kremlin and saw Lenin's entombed body and St. Basil's Cathedral in Red Square. Every night that I was in Russia I saw a different performance of something. These ranged from a strange abstract multimedia piece in a basement somewhere to the Bolshoi Ballet in the spectacular Bolshoi theatre. Some of it was breathtaking some of it was, well, not all that great. Just like here.

My lecture was given in a large nondescript classroom in a large nondescript building to about 40 Russian stage managers. I spoke for three straight hours without a break via an interpreter. I had prepared a basic outline of what I thought would be interesting but after spending a week there, I realized that I needed to adjust it. The way our two theatres work is radically different.

There are at least 200 theatres in Moscow, and they are all state-funded and state-sponsored. Things don't "run" in Russia. Almost all the theatres I saw operated under a repertory system. That means that one play would be performed on Tuesday and then a different one with a different cast on Wednesday and then maybe a musical on Thursday and Friday and a dance recital on Saturday.

I started my talk by explaining how we do theatre here—the difference between profit and non-profit theatre—how a stage manager's job differs between Broadway, Off-Broadway, regional theatres, and cruise ships. Aside from one guy who fell dead asleep after about 20 minutes (and I mean DEAD asleep), they were very attentive and asked extremely probing questions.

These students were just people figuring out how to be stage managers—just like me. We didn't discuss our Presidents and only discussed our governments in indirect ways in terms of how they influenced our work in the theatre. I think if we had ended up in a bar afterward that a political discussion may have arisen, but I don't know that for sure. There was some healthy skepticism of how their government dealt with the arts sometimes and they were amazed (and maybe a bit jealous) that ours stays out of it.

Despite being under government control, there was a much greater variety in the kinds of pieces being performed in Moscow compared to what we have available to us in New York. Some of what I saw, even in just a week, seemed to criticize the government in a way that surprised me.

We are not our government, I don't think, any more than they are theirs. I enjoyed meeting all of them and talking with them. I remain friends with several of them on Facebook and so we can watch each other navigate through our lives. I did not feel like I was sneaking around behind enemy lines in Russia any more than I did when I was in Malaysia or Dubai which operate under strict monarchies. People in these places, too, are just living their lives as best they can. If we are unwilling to let the actions of our current President define us, then it's not fair to define the Russian people by theirs.

It's our birthday, today. It's July 4th, the day that we celebrate the remarkable document that founded our country. Looking around, I can see that some of the ideals extolled in that document are not being lived up to. With every passing day, we are coming to realize that the men who created it were flawed. They weren't gods, they were just human men.

Michael and I are spending this weekend with a friend of ours who leans to the right. I would say that politics might be the elephant in the room but given that we are the outsiders in the house, maybe it's Michael and me who are the donkeys in the room. There was some somewhat uncomfortable discussion last night and I am sure that there will be some more today. I don't expect that either of us will change our minds about anything this weekend no matter what happens.

One of the things that make our system of government unique, is our legal right to express ourselves under the First Amendment to the Constitution. Michael and I are not here to lecture our friend nor are, we, in turn, being lectured. We will… discuss. I would like to try and see things from their point of view because from mine they just don't make any sense.

That we can still discuss this, is one of the things, as we all look at the chaos around us, that still makes this country great. The *Declaration of Independence* and the US Constitution, with their flaws, are truly unique and spectacular pieces of parchment. Next time you are in Washington D.C. you should go to the National Archives building and have a look at them and marvel at their creation. They need our protection.

Have a safe and happy July 4th.

JULY 6, 2020
400,298 Total Reported Cases in New York. 32,099 Deaths.

We had a late breakfast yesterday with our friend, in a little diner in a small town in Connecticut. We ate outside and were the only party of people there at the time. Our server was young—either late teens or very early twenties at the most. It is a place that we've eaten at when we've been there on other visits—the food is excellent. The server was not wearing a mask.

Well into the meal, the owner came out and said hi. The owner wasn't wearing a mask either. In the county that we were in, there have only been about 100 overall deaths reported from the coronavirus so far. The owner said that they had remained open throughout the crisis and had had no problem. Older customers had eaten inside the small indoor space and been fine. As far as they were concerned, the whole pandemic thing has been overblown. Mask wearing wasn't a law, so they didn't see any reason to do it.

For the last 95 days, all of us in the theatre business have been following the story of Nick Cordero. He's not someone I knew personally, but a huge number of my friends did. I certainly knew of him. I saw him in the musical version of *Bullets Over Broadway* in a role that won him a Tony nomination. I also saw him, several times, in the musical version of *A Bronx Tale*. The latter show was produced by the same office that did *Jersey Boys*.

On March 20 of this year, Nick got sick. He was originally diagnosed with pneumonia, but later, testing revealed that he had COVID-19. His pneumonia became serious enough that he was put on a ventilator within a short time after being admitted to the hospital. He was also placed in a medically induced coma to help him survive. He began having issues with his kidneys, so he underwent dialysis. His heart stopped briefly, and he endured a series of small heart attacks and sepsis, so a specialized heart-lung bypass machine was employed to help keep him alive.

Blood clots developed and the doctors had to amputate one of his legs. A tracheotomy was performed. A few days ago, his wife tweeted that his lungs were so debilitated by the ravages of this virus that he was going to need a double lung transplant when his body became strong enough to handle it. His lungs reportedly looked like those of a person who has been smoking for 50 years.

For many of us, Nick Cordero was the face of this virus. A Go Fund Me page that was set up to help cover his medical expenses has already raised nearly $800,000. We all followed his progress every day on social media—Amanda, his wife, tweeted regular updates. People recorded songs for him and taped messages of support that were played for him as he slept. They recorded songs for his baby son, Elvis. For months, Amanda couldn't see him because of the virus. 79 days into his ordeal, however, he was finally clear of the virus, itself, and she was able to sit in the room with him and hold his hand.

Yesterday morning, after more than 90 days on a ventilator, Nick passed away at the age of 41.

He leaves behind his wife and his son, who just turned 1 last month. He also leaves behind the rest of us who have been pulling for him for three months. He was going to beat this thing—he lasted so long and through so much. But he didn't.

The owner of the diner where we ate yesterday was supremely confident that the virus would not touch him in his little town in his downward-trending state. It's hard to blame him for that. He hasn't yet been impacted by the virus in any way except financially. He works HARD. He's in there at the crack of dawn, cleaning and prepping and cooking. He does that all day.

He's not sitting at home watching the news. He's not sitting at home surfing through the internet comparing one news story to another. The information that he's getting is coming in isolated flashes. He genuinely thinks that he's safe and protected in his little corner of the country. The virus is "out there". It's a big city problem, not a small-town problem. That he was speaking to two strangers, guys from a big city who were sitting directly across from him did not seem to occur to him for a second. We could easily have brought it with us.

Mask-wearing by restaurant workers in Connecticut is a law, by the way. I looked it up. Oh well.

The President in his speech at Mount Rushmore on the 4th referred to the people opposing his views as part of a "new far-left fascism" that wants to wipe out the nation's moral values and erase its history. Then there was a spectacular display of fireworks.

Most of us can see this rhetoric for the nonsense that it is, but if that's all that the owner of the diner in Connecticut happens to catch on the radio on his way to work, then that's what sticks.

It was glorious being out in the country. The breakfast that we had at that diner was delicious. We headed to a farm stand afterward and got some of the most amazing tomatoes you can imagine—big, red, and beyond flavorful.

As gay men, Michael and I have had to live most of our lives visiting places where, on the surface, we were welcomed, but underneath, maybe not so much. We've learned to avoid topics and adjust our behavior, not only in small towns in the US but also in other places around the world. It's part of how we get through our daily lives and it's not anything that we usually consciously even think about. The only time we notice it, oddly, is in places like Provincetown and Fire Island where we don't have to adjust our behavior at all. In places like that, we can just relax and be ourselves. We can act silly and hold hands if we want to and not worry that someone might take offense and beat us up. Gay bars anywhere can provide the same kind of respite from the burden of having to live undercover.

We discussed COVID-19 with the owner of the diner, but we didn't fight about it. At some point, we just let off so that we could enjoy the wonderful meal. Two gay men from New York are not going to change the mind of a diner owner in Connecticut. Two gay men from New York, however, who join their voices together with the voices of millions of people across the country who are tired of all of this, well that's a different story. Under those circumstances, two gay men from New York can help change the world.

As we move forward, all of those that we've lost will be there with us. Every single one of the people who've died from this virus is somebody's Nick Cordero. RIP Nick.

July 7, 2020
400,746 Total Reported Cases in New York. 32,121 Deaths.

Like the end of a relationship, the main thing that happens when a Broadway show closes is the moving out. The set goes into storage if it is thought that the pieces might be useful for a future tour, or they just end up in a dumpster. The lights and sound equipment are returned to the rental company, costumes and wigs are sold to a rental shop or, again, put into storage for a future tour. At the end of it, the theatre is restored to an empty four-walled space ready for the next show. The marquee is taken down and… that's it.

It looked to me like they were loading out the set and lights of the Broadway musical *Frozen* yesterday. Disney closed *Frozen* in anticipation of New York opening back up slowly. Their feeling was that as the first wave of people started returning it would be better to funnel them into fewer shows rather than have them spread out among many. They are banking that their other shows, *Aladdin*, and *The Lion King* will attract more people without *Frozen* to compete with them.

Disney is reportedly creating a quarantine bubble for its NBA players in Orlando. The athletes will remain on the company's resort property for the duration of the scheduled three-month playing season. It all seems fine until you consider the fact that about 5,800 unprotected workers will be commuting every day from areas that have become COVID-19 hotspots to take care of them.

As a company, most of Disney's revenue streams come from businesses that require people to gather. Broadway shows, movies, theme parks, sporting events are all group activities. Yes, they can earn money from online streaming, but nowhere near the same level. They just spent $75 million to acquire *Hamilton* to broadcast. I'd be interested to know if that investment pays off. If you go to a park, each admission ticket costs far more than it costs to stream the Disney channel for years. You pay for parking in their lot and perhaps you stay in one of their hotels. You buy their food. You buy their merchandise.

The money you spend at the park is going to pay the salaries of 78,000 people and still leave the company with a sizable profit. People streaming at home, on the other hand, are not going to spend any more than $84 for an entire year. It is no wonder that Disney is so desperate to reopen in Florida. Unless we start being able to congregate again, they are not going to survive.

When cases in New York were finally starting to trend down a few months ago, the general sense that I was getting from producers was that Broadway would likely start to reopen this coming spring. The big fear, of course, would be to reopen a show too soon and then be forced to close it again. Reopening a show is going to require a sizable financial investment. Some shows have already thrown in the towel knowing that they won't have that cash on hand to be able to do that. Most of the other big shows may be able to afford to reopen once. They won't be able to afford to do it twice.

The process of reopening is going to take a couple of months of advance work—marketing, rehearsals, possible recasting. Until it's clear that we are going to be OK, I don't think that anybody is going to start that ball rolling.

We are all facing the end of our supplemental unemployment payments. As of now, there are only four more of them and then that's it. Regular unemployment will continue but will it be enough? In my business, when we are unemployed, which can be often, there are many ancillary jobs that we can take to make up the shortfall. Many of those jobs aren't there now, either.

Watching the crew outside the St. James yesterday on 44th Street loading out the show and seeing the darkened marquee was a bit of a gut punch. The financial and legislative sectors of our country don't particularly care about the transformative power of the arts on the human psyche. They don't particularly have any interest in our souls. The arts make money. That's what matters to them. Broadway brings in more annual revenue to our state than all our sports teams combined. Theatres all over the country, as well as smaller theatres here in the city, help pump billions of dollars into our country's economy.

We do not need to behave like beggars in a house of plenty. We do not need to hope that some governmental agency will look down upon us kindly and take pity on us and throw us a few bones. The Arts are one of the main financial engines that run this entire city. Countless thousands of businesses can only operate when we are up and thriving. New York City simply cannot survive without the arts. As much as we may need the government to take care of us now, they truly need us to take care of them more.

July 8, 2020
401,314 Total Reported Cases in New York. 32,142 Deaths.

We watched *Hamilton* last night. I've seen *Hamilton* on stage twice. Once with most of the original company a couple of months after it opened on Broadway, and then once again in Chicago when I was there doing some casting for *Jersey Boys*. Sometimes, when a show is as hyped as *Hamilton* is when you finally get in to see it, there is a kind of a letdown. You sit there and think, I just spent a fortune for This? That is not the case with *Hamilton*.

There is an alchemy that happens when the right combination of people, get into a room together, at the right time, with the right story that is truly miraculous. That is what happened on *Jersey Boys*. With zero expectations, a bunch of us—many of whom, including me, were the second or third choices for our positions—showed up in a rehearsal room in La Jolla, CA. After the first read-through of the script, we knew that we were all on board for a kind of a once-in-a-lifetime journey.

A similar thing happened on *Titanic, the Musical*. In the face of enormous public derision, a small group of us did a workshop production of it. It worked. The hairs on the back of my neck are standing up just thinking about how exciting it was to be in that room where we started to put it all together. *Titanic* almost didn't make it. When we got into the theatre, the technical challenges were enormous. Plans that were envisioned in the bare rehearsal studio had to be completely scrapped and rethought once we were on the actual gigantic set. Transition scenes had to be rewritten and made longer to cover up difficult set changes. Whole scenes were tossed out because we couldn't make the physical aspects of them work. The original ideas had taken somewhat of a beating, but *Titanic* went on to win the Tony Award for best musical that year.

It is a far more common experience to start rehearsals for a show and realize that there is a lot of work to do. The biggest flop I worked on was a Broadway show that closed after 51 previews and only five performances. It was six months of the most difficult and grueling work I have ever had to do. The agony of it all was that, in our hearts, we all knew it wasn't going to work from almost the first day of rehearsals.

Hamilton is truly inspired. Like many of the greatest Broadway musicals, it comes from a story that seems utterly unlikely to translate well to the stage. Is *Hamilton* historically accurate? Well, not entirely, no.

Alexander Hamilton was not quite the abolitionist that he is painted to be in the musical. The truth is more complex than that. While it is true that he was one of the few Founding Fathers that did not own slaves, himself, he didn't do much to stop the practice.

He was born out of wedlock in Nevis in the Caribbean. Because he and his brother were illegitimate they were not allowed to inherit a boy that his mother owned. As a teenager, Hamilton ran the operations for an import-export company that traded in sugar and slaves. His wife's family, the Schuylers, owned slaves and Alexander Hamilton helped them to buy and sell them. While Hamilton founded an antislavery group called the Manumission Society, he also supported several slave-holding Federalists when they ran for office. Much is made of the fact in the show that Hamilton was an immigrant, when in fact as soon as the Constitution went into effect, people born in Nevis were considered US citizens.

Like *Hamilton*, *Jersey Boys* is a musical BASED on real people. There are some liberties taken with the facts. The chronology of the show does not always follow the chronology of the actual events. Early in the show, a character mentions the movie *The Blob*. If you do a little research using the characters' ages and figure out what year the scene is taking place in, you will discover that *The Blob* had not been released yet. So why was *The Blob* used? Because it was funny. The clothes in those early scenes reference styles that came a bit later as well. Why was that allowed to happen? Because everybody thought that the later style looked better.

Hamilton, *Jersey Boys*, and *Titanic* are all entertainments. Yes, they are BASED on history, but their stories are being told primarily to entertain. There is always the hope that a larger point might be conveyed that shines a light on who we are and perhaps asks us to look within, but all three are there simply to tell a good story.

When a sculptor or a painter attempts to pay tribute to a historical event or a historical figure, they do the same thing that people who create theatre do. They streamline facts and condense a general sense of actual history into a single static image. Cathedrals are often adorned with sculptures of saints. You can tell who each one is by what they are holding. Saint Bartholomew was skinned alive for spreading the faith, so you look for the guy holding his skin like a coat, and you've found him. In classical paintings, you can tell which figure is a saint, and which ones aren't by the addition of a halo around the heads of the beatified. Their entire lives are conveyed in a couple of symbols that the artist trusts we will pick up on and understand.

When James Earle Fraser was commissioned to create the statue of Theodore Roosevelt that stands out in front of the American Museum of Natural History, he was tasked with figuring out how to encapsulate, in one image, the connection between the man and the institution. He used a traditional triangular shape (think Michelangelo's *Pieta*) and put Roosevelt at the apex atop a horse. He added two figures—one to his left and the other to his right. The two side figures' heads are much lower to conform to the overall structure. To Fraser, they represented the two continents that Roosevelt had led expeditions of discovery through. On the right of Roosevelt stands a Native American man representing the Americas and, on his left, stands an African man representing Africa. When originally erected, this statue conveyed the spirit of the man who was partially responsible for helping to create the institution that is housed in the building behind it. Viewers at the time got it.

This isn't the story that we receive from this statue now. The imagery that Fraser used broadcasts a much different story to us here in 2020—one that he may not have consciously intended to send. Now it looks like the Native American and African man are less than the central figure—that he holds dominion over them.

History happens out of the sight of historians. Monumental decisions are made by a small group of people together or sometimes by one person in isolation and it is then left to historians to imagine what MIGHT have happened at the time. I was actually "in the room where it happened" during the creation of *Jersey Boys* and *Titanic* but even that does not necessarily make me a reliable historical witness. Even inside the room, there were private discussions that happened between actors and between creatives that I wasn't privy to. When I tell stories from that time, I leave out things that I think are too complex to get into, or that I have simply forgotten.

During this pandemic and its shutdown, we have begun re-examining our entire history. Historians who wrote a generation ago were writing with different filters in their heads. If somebody was going to sculpt a monument with Theodore Roosevelt in it to stand in front of the American Museum of Natural History today, it wouldn't look like the one that is there now. The parts of his history that were glossed over or ignored 90 years ago when it was created are very much in evidence today.

I do believe that it is time to take down the sculpture of Theodore Roosevelt. It is also, I think, time to take down the sculpture of Christopher Columbus in Columbus Circle. And the Confederate monuments throughout the South. They reflected a different cultural sensibility than the one that we have evolved into now. I do not think that it all should be destroyed, however. Not at all. These sculptures and monuments, like the people they represent, are themselves a part of our history. We cannot pretend that history hasn't happened. Some of it is unbearably shameful to confront. If the truth be told, a lot of the history of humankind on this planet is unbearably shameful.

If we hide it and forget that it's there, we stand the very real risk of repeating it. We should not be erasing our past, but we should be re-examining it considering what we, as a people, have become. Who are we? How did we get here? Where are we going? Science asks those questions. Religion asks those questions. Art asks those questions. If we are going to answer any of those questions truthfully, we need to be brutally honest with ourselves and face up to all of it.

Hamilton is just a Broadway musical. It represents the work of a group of theatre artists at the absolute top of their games telling a story based on history but also relentlessly about the future. It is a breathtaking artistic achievement. Watch it. Then, at the end of it, ask yourself: Who are we? How did we get here? Where are we going?

It's not about finding the answers. It's rarely about the answers. It's about the asking.

July 9, 2020
3 million Total Reported Cases in the United States.

Self-haircut #3 has been done. #2 was like the second performance of a show. Adrenaline has gotten you through the first one and then, for the second one, you relax and think you are OK. Then it doesn't go so well. #3 isn't that bad. I cut off a hank of hair at the back that felt strange (I couldn't see it, myself.) I've caught Michael looking at it a couple of times, but I think that whatever I did back there, he's gotten used to. I'll get him to fix it with #4. In the meantime—hair gel.

We are now four months away from the last day that everything was completely normal.

There's a quote by Eric Levitz in an early March issue of New York Magazine that says, "What passes for reality in American society is far more malleable than anyone realized." We must figure out how to convince half of this country to accept scientific guidance as the way forward through this crisis. COVID-19 is not a political crisis, although the Administration's handling of it, has made it one.

We have spent four solid months in stasis. Anybody should have the ability to look at the numbers rising at these alarming rates and realize that we are heading in the wrong direction. Anybody should, yet a massive portion of our country either can't or won't. Until we cut the current White House out of our response to this virus, what we are experiencing now, is what we are likely going to be experiencing for months to come. Countries that listened to their medical experts are seeing their curves flatten. We are not.

We cannot fix the economy until we start being able to handle the virus. Both must be attended to but dealing with the economy first is probably going to do more damage to it than is happening now.

It doesn't look like it's going to rain today which is a relief. They are painting "Black Lives Matter" on Fifth Avenue today in front of the President's building. I'm going to shower up now, gel my slightly uneven hair, and head downtown to cheer the painters on.

July 10, 2020
402,999 Total Reported Cases in New York. 32,205 Deaths.

It is pouring down rain outside today. The sky is dark and the trees outside our living room windows are whipping around in the wind.

The cat hates it. As soon as he senses a storm coming, he's out. There are only a couple of places in the apartment where he can truly hide. One of them is inside Michael's grandparent's tall antique standing wooden radio. The cloth covering of the speakers in the lower part of it needs replacing because it is rotting away. The cat has ripped open a flap that lets him squeeze into the base and hide. I assume that's where he is now.

I'm glad that they were able to get the Black Lives Matter painting done yesterday before this started. They oriented the words in such a way that anybody inside the building will be able to read it the proper way up when they look out their windows. There's another one up at 125th Street on Adam Clayton Powell Boulevard. That's written in larger letters that take up two blocks—one running uptown and the other running downtown. The Harlem version is more artistic than the Fifth Avenue one—different colors and some of the letters have images within them.

Civil disobedience is all about drawing attention to something that needs it. While there is certainly an amount of petty gleeful triumph that I feel about this being painted on the street right in front of the President's home, how else can we get his attention? He doesn't want to hear anything about social injustice. He can't miss it now.

The Supreme Court ruled in a way, yesterday, that he cannot possibly have wanted to hear about either. There were two separate cases—the first involved the New York Grand Jury and the second involved Congress.

In the first case, Trump v. Vance, the New York Grand Jury, in its investigation into the President's past financial history, issued subpoenas to two banks, Deutsche Bank and Capital One, and an accounting firm, Mazars USA for them to turn over their records about the President and his companies. Vance refers to Cyrus Vance, Jr., the New York County District Attorney. We don't know how broad the Grand Jury's investigation is, but it probably also extends to Stormy Daniel's case in terms of where the hush money, paid to her to keep her relationship with the President quiet, came from. The three companies were willing to provide the records, but the President objected. He argued that the President is not like an ordinary citizen. While in office, he should be immune to law enforcement and subpoenas.

Cases like this have come before the Court before. In 1974 the Court unanimously ruled that Nixon had to comply with a grand jury subpoena and hand over tapes that were relevant to a criminal investigation. In 1997 the Court ruled unanimously that Clinton had to testify in the Monica

Lewinsky civil sexual harassment suit. In both of those cases, the defense argument was much the same—the President, while in office, should be above the law.

In the case of Trump v. Vance, the Supreme Court yet again disagreed with that line of defense. Justice Roberts, writing the majority opinion, stated "No citizen, not even the president, is categorically above the common duty to produce evidence when called upon in a criminal proceeding."

The second case, Trump v. Mazars USA, involved Congress's attempt through the D.C. Circuit to subpoena the President's accounting firm. In this case, the Justices denied them the right to do that. What they said was that Congress was overstepping its authority legislatively. The case needs to be sent back down to the lower courts to be decided. Justice Roberts wrote, "Without limits on its subpoena powers, Congress could 'exert an imperious control' over the Executive Branch and aggrandize itself at the President's expense, just as the Framers feared."

So, what does this mean? In the short term, it means that we are unlikely to all see the President's tax records before the election in November which is what many people were hoping for. We will likely see them eventually, but that process will now need to play out in the lower courts. In the long term, however, it more clearly defines the separation of power among the major branches of our government and more clearly sets limits on the President's authority. The rulings affirm that the President is not a monarch.

July 11, 2020
World Population Day.

I can't help but notice that there is a new level of righteous anger that seems to be rising across social media. Given that we can't be together, the internet has become the sole way that we are all communicating with each other. Communicating online creates somewhat of a false sense of anonymity and, perhaps protection, that is allowing discussions to go far deeper than I think they would, were we facing each other in a room together.

In my industry, a group called "We See You White American Theatre" has published a vividly strong 31-page list of demands for racial reform in terms of how we operate our theatres.

In 1996 the playwright August Wilson delivered a keynote address at the annual conference of the Theatre Communications Group (TCG) entitled "The Ground on Which I Stand." It was an impassioned stand on black pride and black separatism. He likened the idea of non-traditional casting (think Pearl Bailey in the all-black version of *Hello Dolly* on Broadway) to the practice of slaves being "summoned to the plantation house to entertain the slave owner and his guests."

He pointed out that of the 66 professional regional theatres around the country, only one, Crossroads in New Jersey, was created by and run by black artists. He called for the creation of more institutions where black artists could be nurtured, and their work developed and pushed forward.

In the speech, Wilson singled out the critic Robert Brustein as being at the vanguard of backward thinking. Brustein had long argued that funding agencies were supporting what he felt was mediocre work by minority artists over more accomplished work by white artists. He argued that the work needed to be judged on its own merits, separate from the race of the creator. The counterargument to that, of course, is who, then is making that determination? In most cases, white adjudicators. So, the fight was on. The two men had a very heated back and forth exchange over the subsequent years, largely through written articles.

"We See You White American Theatre" has picked up on Wilson's arguments and has expanded upon them.

A group of older theatre performers has formed another group called "Black Theatre United."

Their mission statement reads, "As members of the Black theatre community, we stand together to help protect Black people, Black talent, and Black lives of all shapes and orientations in theatre and communities across the country. Our voices are united to empower our community through activism in the pursuit of justice and equality for the betterment of all humanity. We will not be silent. We will be seen. We will be heard. We are here. Join us."

Tonya Pinkins, a Tony-award-winning actress, who has a long history of activism within the community has written a piece called "Why I am Fed Up with Performative Activism from White and Black Theatre Makers." In it, she calls for actual action rather than the forming of committees and discussion groups. She has long put herself on the line standing up for what she believes in and has paid the price for it. She is saying that it is all well and good to discuss all of this, but in the actual room where it's happening, do any of us have the guts to be the only person in the room who stands up and says something? When you stand up, you are risking your career and livelihood, in other words, everything. Who among us is brave enough to do that?

A group of international writers and educators signed a piece called "A Letter on Justice and Open Debate." It was published a couple of days ago in Harper's Magazine. The concern is that some of those fighting for change are silencing anyone who isn't strictly following the party line. While stating that the protests for social justice and the demands for police reform are long overdue, the letter says, "this needed reckoning has also intensified a new set of moral attitudes and political commitments that tend to weaken our norms of open debate and toleration of differences in favor of ideological conformity."

Emotional confrontations backstage on a show are extremely common. While a cast may seem unified onstage, they are usually like any other group of people offstage—disparate. People who fall in love onstage can have knockdown drag-out fights seconds before they walk out into the lights together. Producers get into conflicts with actors. Actors get into conflicts with stage managers. Stage managers get into conflicts with crew members. Theatre artists, no matter what department they work in, are rarely shy about expressing their anger.

True righteous anger coming at you can be extremely intimidating. I can think of several times when the entire creative team of a show has been sitting out front while we were teching a show and a leading performer became so angry about something that they left the stage. When that happens, everyone in the room—the director, the lighting designer—the music contractor—you name it, all of them, turn and look to the production stage manager. In a word—Me.

My job, at that point, is to get that person back onstage. How? The only way I know to make that happen is to listen to them. It doesn't matter that 100 or so people are sitting around while the clock ticks by, if the person I am talking to is angry enough to walk off the stage, they have something to say. It is usually about something that started small and wasn't addressed and got bigger and bigger until a breaking point was hit.

You can't do anything about stopping the water when the dam breaks. It floods. Once the water level goes down you can start to repair things and maybe build a better dam, but you can't do any of that while the water is still rushing out of the breach. George Floyd broke the dam. George Floyd broke a dam that should never have been built in the first place.

We have the time now to listen and try to work through it all. If we listen long enough, maybe we will all finally be able to hear what is being said.

July 13, 2020
13 million Total Reported Cases Worldwide.

By next month I would have been working on *Jersey Boys* for sixteen years. We started the show in August of 2004 in La Jolla, California, and then opened on Broadway the following fall. For at least the first year, I was working as the production stage manager, so I was on the eight shows a week, two weeks-vacation cycle. It never hit a routine, though, because we were constantly performing at outside events. When a show is as big a hit as *Jersey Boys* was, the energy around it is indescribable.

After a year and some change, I took a leave from the show for a few months to help get the first National Tour started in San Francisco. Then, just as I thought I would be going back to New York, we had to put the London and Las Vegas companies together at almost the same time. It's been pretty much like that ever since.

While I have indeed worked on the same show for sixteen years, it has never been the same work. Sometimes I am sitting in auditions. Sometimes in rehearsals. Sometimes watching the show and taking notes. Sometimes in the producer's office working on scheduling or plans for future productions. I am always traveling. From show to show, city to city, country to country. The only routine I have experienced on *Jersey Boys* has been the complete lack of routine. Then, like everyone else all around the globe, almost everything in my professional world stopped. My days became indistinguishable from each other.

There is a report about a 30-year-old man who went to a COVID party. The point of the party was to see who there would be the first to contract the virus. Everyone there considered it to be a hoax. This man just died in Texas of complications from COVID-19.

Last night, Michael and I took a walk down to Times Square. We had never taken a pandemic walk after dark together. My craving for a frozen margarita still hadn't been satisfied, so we headed over to 9th Avenue to see if we could find one. Most of the restaurants there were completely overcrowded with people jammed in together—no social distancing, no masks. We ended up at a Mexican restaurant that had outdoor space that was nicely separated. I was surprised because in normal times it is usually the most crowded place on the street.

There's a new rule that you must order food when you order a drink, so we split some tacos, and each finally had an amazing frozen margarita—mine was mango and Michael's was blood orange. It was more than worth the wait.

We need to break many of our routines. I wish I had some idea of how that can happen. We seem to be locked in a cycle where the top health experts in the country are being undermined by the politicians in the country. Their warnings are ignored or discredited. The conflicting information that we are being deluged with is impossible to sort out without really taking the time to read and watch everything. Nobody is doing that, and can you blame them—the reality is almost impossible to face.

As routines go, what Michael and I do with our days is not bad. I'm grateful for that. Lord knows it could certainly be far, far worse. Eight performances a week, however hard it once was to get through, seems like bliss right about now. I'd love to be able to give the company a half-hour warning to start the show.

We'll get there. I just wish that we'd get there sooner than it appears we will. I can already feel the flutter of excitement in my heart when the first notes of the overture start. We'll get there.

July 14, 2020
406,132 Total Reported Cases in New York. 32,265 Deaths.

Yesterday evening, as the sun was setting, I headed into Central Park. It was a perfect night. There were a few clouds in the sky, but it was clear and bright. It was warm but not sweltering and the humidity was low. I walked in and immediately fell in love with New York City all over again. The buildings along Fifth Avenue were glowing in the golden light of the dying sun and perfectly reflected in the still water of the reservoir. People were out walking or riding on the track around it. Ducks were lazily floating in front of me.

The only thing that would have made it the perfect summer night in New York would have been having tickets to see a free Shakespeare in the Park at the Delacourt Theatre. The very first play I ever saw there was *The Taming of the Shrew* starring Meryl Streep and Raul Julia. It was in 1978 and I had just finished my junior year of high school. I came into the city with a friend early in the morning and we waited all day on the impossibly long line around the Great Lawn to get our free tickets.

Before we went into the theatre to watch the performance that night, we had to sign something that permitted them to film us during the performance. Woody Allen was shooting part of the opening montage that night for his film *Manhattan*. *Manhattan* is the movie that made me fall in love with New York. I was already deeply infatuated with the city, but that movie…

Manhattan is scored throughout with the most sublime recordings of George Gershwin's music. Gordon Willis shot the entire thing in deeply contrasted black and white. The opening montage is an ode to New York City set to Gershwin's masterpiece *Rhapsody in Blue*. There are, indeed, some shots of the production of *Shrew* and, if I remember correctly, some overhead shots of the audience, too. The camera never really gets close enough to the actors to identify them probably because Meryl Streep also plays Woody Allen's ex-wife in the movie.

In the movie, Woody meets Diane Keaton's character, and they go to art galleries. There's a wonderfully romantic scene between them where they get caught in the rain and take refuge in the Hayden Planetarium on 81st Street and Central Park West.

Years later, I was walking down Columbus Avenue, and there, on the corner by the museum was Diane Keaton, herself, waiting to cross the street. I have never forgotten it. I chose to go to Columbia, in large part,

I think, because of that movie. I wanted to live on the Upper West Side because of that movie. I still love walking down that stretch of Columbus by the museum which I will forever associate with Diane Keaton because it always reminds me what a magical place this city can be.

The one part of the movie that I wasn't all that interested in at the time was the plotline of Woody Allen's relationship with Mariel Hemingway. Her character in the film is 17 years old. It's strange that I glossed over it because it's the major storyline. I just never thought it was all that compelling, so I guess I just kind of ignored it and deleted it from my memory. While the character she played was 17, Mariel Hemingway, herself, was only 16 when she filmed it. She and I are almost the same age. Woody Allen was, at the time, in his mid-forties.

In her autobiography, she tells a story about how, soon after the film, Woody Allen flew out to Idaho to try and convince her parents to let her come with him on a trip to Paris. She didn't want to go but her parents were encouraging her to. That night she said, "I'm not going to get my own room, am I? I can't go to Paris with you."

About ten years later Woody Allen started a relationship with his then-girlfriend Mia Farrow's adopted daughter Soon-Yi Previn who was 19. There have been allegations by his adopted daughter Dylan Farrow that he molested her, but it's also possible that her mother, furious about Allen and her daughter Soon-Yi, made them up. It's a nasty story any way you look at it and we've all watched it unfold over the years and watched almost everyone involved turn against each other.

Can I still watch the movie *Manhattan*?

We are being tasked, these days, with examining all the aspects of our life where we have allowed social injustice to occur. The #metoo movement has pulled our collective blinders off in terms of how women have been treated in the workplace and society. I'm not sure how I managed to sublimate such a major portion of the plot of *Manhattan*, but I did. I just waited through those scenes until we got to the ones I loved. I can't do that now.

The #blacklivesmatter movement is asking us to do the same thing in terms of how people of color have been treated in the workplace and society. I don't know that it is possible to watch *Gone with the Wind* without cringing anymore. We've all watched it without cringing for years. Hattie McDaniel still lived the life she led and suffered the indignities and slights that she did. We just all turned a blind eye to it and grabbed a bucket of popcorn.

New York City is not an idyll. It never has been. The vision of the city that Woody Allen painted is one without homeless people. It is one without poverty and disease. It is one without violence and despair.

Manhattan is a glorious film in some ways and a not so glorious one in others. Marshall Brickman co-wrote it with Woody Allen and they were both nominated for an Oscar for it. Marshall is also one of the co-writers of *Jersey Boys*, so I have spent 16 years working with him. He is funny, warm, and generous to a fault.

When *Manhattan* came out, the world was ruled by white guys. *Manhattan* is a white guy movie through and through. Now, the rule of the white guy is being challenged. The abuses of power are being spoken of. Truths are being told.

I do not believe in censorship. I want to be able to see the astonishing photographs taken by Leni Riefenstahl at the 1936 Olympics in Berlin even though she was a Nazi supporter. That is a part of her art. People should be able to see *Manhattan* and *Gone with the Wind*.

The difficulty we are all having with these movements is that they are asking us to look at the things we love and really see them. We can't just tune out the parts we don't like anymore. If we are going to watch them, then we need to WATCH them.

When I am looking at the skyline of Fifth Avenue across the reservoir, I may never not hear and thrill to the opening strains of *Rhapsody in Blue*. When I am walking past the American Museum of Natural History, I will probably never not fall a little bit in love with Diane Keaton all over again. I don't think that I can watch *Manhattan* again though. I don't want to have to watch 16-year-old Mariel Hemingway being uncomfortable around 40-something-year-old Woody Allen. I truly do hope that nothing beyond what she talks about in her book did happen. If it did, I feel so terribly sorry and even somewhat guilty. My loving of that film makes whatever pain she went through in the making of it that much worse.

There is beauty everywhere just as there is great ugliness. We cannot ignore the ugliness, but nor can we let it keep us from fully appreciating and reveling in the beauty. Cleaning up even a bit of the mess makes the beauty that much more, easy to see. What we are being asked to do is clear up and fix the things that we are ignoring or haven't looked at close enough, so that all of us can enjoy the beauty together.

July 15, 2020
406,834 Total Reported Cases in New York. 32,284 Deaths.

The White House has just launched a fancy new campaign to encourage us to all get back to work that is being spearheaded by the President's daughter. It's called "Find Something New." Your industry is shut down and you can't find a job? Find something new! There are great new careers just out there waiting for you! Aerospace Engineering Technician! Broadcast and Sound Engineering Technician! Diagnostic Medical Sonographer!

There is a story about Queen Marie Antoinette of France that may or may not be true. When told that the peasants of her country were so poor that they couldn't afford bread, she replied, "Well, then let them eat cake!" It takes a long time to establish a career, even longer if it isn't one that you are naturally called to. It also takes a lot of schooling which costs a lot of money. The President's daughter who, like Marie Antoinette, has been handed everything she has ever had on a golden platter, is possibly the last person on the planet who should be advising the people of the United States on how to find work.

The only way to keep us all afloat until then is to subsidize us. As rewarding as a career in Aerospace Engineering must be, I don't see that, personally, as a way forward for me. I have worked in the theatre for 38 years. It's what I know. I'm confident that Michael and I will figure out how to get through the next year. I'm not quite sure how, yet, but I trust we will be able to come up with something. In the meantime, NASA is hiring for anyone interested.

July 16, 2020
407,724 Total Reported Cases in New York. 32,293 Deaths.

Several years ago, a friend of mine came home from a date and while he was trying to get into his apartment, he fell down a couple of stairs and became a quadriplegic. The work he did in the theatre became impossible. Bedridden, with only minimal use of one hand, what do you do for the rest of your life? What would I do?

While I was in high school and then in college, I thought that I was going to be an actor. I was already working as a stage manager and, by the time I got to college, I was getting paid for it. It never crossed my mind that was what I was going to do with my life. Stage managing was just the job I was doing to make money. As kids, we were all warned against going into acting as a career. "If you can imagine doing anything else with your life, then you should do it." At any given moment in pre-COVID times, up to 97% of the members of the Actors' Equity Association were unemployed. To succeed in this business, you had better be fully committed. However much you might want to do it, there are hundreds if not thousands of people competing against you who want it just as much as you do.

I spent my junior year of college in London. I got to London that fall and I saw an audition posting for an on-campus play and I was determined to get in. The morning of the audition, I got ready and headed over to the theatre building. I got about halfway there when the thought suddenly struck me that if I got cast in the play, that would mean that I wouldn't be able to explore London and the rest of England with my new friends. I'd be stuck in rehearsals.

I didn't audition. There was something that I wanted to do more than act. It took me a couple of more years to fully realize that I wasn't going to pursue acting, but when I look back, that's the point where I made the decision.

What was I going to do? Well, it turned out that what I was going to do was what I had already been doing. Overnight I went from somebody who was working backstage just to make some money, to somebody working backstage as a professional stage manager. Same job—different outlook.

One of the friends I made during my time in London has a mom who is an art dealer. Years ago, when I was fretting about how I was ever going to make enough money to live by working in the theatre, he told me something that his mom had told him, "Do what you love, and the money will follow." I've never forgotten that and, I have to say, it's proven to be true.

So now, with everything shut down, I am confronted with the actual question, what would I do if I couldn't work in theatre? After a couple of months of this, the one thing that I do know that I don't want to do is to retire. I'm not ready yet and, frankly, I can't afford to.

Like my backstage work that I didn't fully recognize as being legitimate work at the time, I guess I don't have to figure out what I would do if I can't work in the theatre. I seem to have been doing it. I have a lot to learn, but it looks like I am going to have a long time to practice. I'm going to write.

July 17, 2020
408,551 Total Reported Cases in New York. 32,320 Deaths.

I was down near the Mormon temple across from Lincoln Center the other day and saw an older woman wearing a mask pushing a grocery cart. Coming towards her were two younger guys not wearing masks. She said something to them, commenting on their lack of mask-wearing and they responded with some derisive remarks. I kept walking. Much like every other argument in our lives these days, I don't think that anybody on either side of the mask-wearing issue is going to change the other side's minds.

On Wednesday, Republican Governor Kemp of Georgia issued an executive order banning the mandating of mask-wearing throughout the state saying it's unenforceable. The Democratic Mayor of Atlanta, Keisha Lance Bottoms defied that order saying that the mask requirements, "are enforceable and they stand." Governor Kemp is now suing Mayor Bottoms and the Atlanta City Council. She responded with "I am not afraid of the city being sued and I'll put our policies up against anyone's, any day of the week."

Both sides of the issue are digging in and neither side is going to give in—not the politicians and not the people walking the streets of

New York. That older woman's mind is made up and the two guys she encountered in front of the temple have made their minds up too.

By last week, the Black Lives Matter Occupy City Hall encampment down near Foley Square had gotten pretty rank. There was a lot of rain last week which didn't help matters. Earlier this week I went down to see what was happening. It's been cleaned up. There's a sense of order to it. The individual tents and tarps that people had erected have been combined to create a single, well-covered area. The library and food distribution areas are still up and running. The large flagstone area is now clear of people, though every square inch of it has been painted with a slogan or an image. An older woman with a broom was sweeping. I hope that the organization that they've brought to the encampment has also trickled down to their actions.

There are now at least three streets in Manhattan that have been painted with giant letters spelling out Black Lives Matter. There's the one uptown in Harlem on Adam Clayton Powell Boulevard at 125th street, the one on Fifth Avenue in front of Trump Tower, and the third is in front of the City Court House down near City Hall. I think that there's one in Brooklyn as well, but I haven't seen it.

As a species, we are nothing if not adaptable. This is good because we seem destined to be living this way for quite a while. I wish I understood why the government seems so intent on prolonging this pandemic. What is their end game? They are so seemingly united in their efforts to make sure that this virus continues to spread. I am truly starting to think that this isn't just stupidity but that they are doing this on purpose. But then the question arises—Why?

I am not at all looking to start a whole new conspiracy theory, but this Administration is moving forward in a way that makes no sense and they are together in this course of action. I don't think that anything anyone says is going to sway them.

Breakfast is almost ready. I can hear Michael scrambling some eggs. Trader Joe's has a great cheese called Unexpected Cheddar. Maybe he will put a bit of that in too. And we will have some of his fresh out of the oven sough dough bread with fennel seeds. How can the world possibly be ending when we have that?

JULY 18, 2020

259,848 Total Reported New Cases Worldwide in 24 hours. The largest single-day increase since the pandemic began.

Refrigerated trucks acting as temporary morgues are being brought into areas of Texas and Arizona to handle the overflow. Ken Davis, the chief medical officer for Christus Health South Texas said yesterday, "There are only so many places to put bodies of the loved ones in.

We're out of space, our funeral homes are out of space, and we need those beds. So, when someone dies, we need to quickly turn that bed over."

We had the morgue trucks in New York City. We needed the trucks when we were completely shut down and everyone was staying home. It took several weeks after we initiated those measures before we started to see our case numbers start to decline. They are ordering refrigerated trucks in Texas and Arizona while the good people of those states are still out and about, still happily spreading the virus to each other.

The only logical conclusion to draw from that, based on simple common sense, is that those places are going to see their numbers rise even higher. Left unchecked like this, the number of cases can only rise. The number of deaths can also only rise.

U.S. Representative from the state of Georgia, John Robert Lewis, passed away yesterday.

He was the last living person to have spoken at the rally at the Lincoln Memorial where the Reverend Martin Luther King delivered his "I Have a Dream" speech.

Congressman Lewis almost didn't deliver his prepared speech that day. Many, including Dr. King, himself, thought that it was too inflammatory. Patrick O'Boyle, the Archbishop of Washington D.C. who was scheduled to deliver the opening invocation objected to Lewis's line saying that patience was "a dirty and nasty word." Patience is an important part of the Catholic church's teachings. Lewis agreed to remove it.

Senator Robert Kennedy had gotten advance word of the speech and he was concerned as was NAACP leader Roy Wilkins. Lewis again modified his speech.

He was originally going to object to President John Kennedy's proposed Civil Rights bill saying that it didn't go far enough towards offering any real protection to people against police brutality. Instead, he said, "It is true that we support the Administration's civil rights bill. We support it with great reservations, however." Instead of saying, "we are now involved in a serious revolution" which the others felt would incite violence, Lewis, instead, said, "we are now involved in a serious social revolution."

His original closing remarks were, "The time will come when we will not confine our marching to Washington. We will march through the South, through the heart of Dixie, the way Sherman did. We shall pursue our own scorched earth policy and burn Jim Crow to the ground—nonviolently." What he finished his speech with that day were the words, "We will march through the South. But we will march with the spirit of love and with the spirit of dignity that we have shown here today."

Congressman Lewis devoted his entire life to the fight for social justice. His speech that day at the Lincoln Memorial began with, "We march today for jobs and freedom, but we have nothing to be proud of for hundreds and thousands of our brothers are not here, for they are receiving starvation wages or no wages at all." We are still marching for that today.

Our country was born amidst a fight for social justice and freedom. The principles that General George Washington and the rest of the Founding Fathers fought for may not have included everyone in the colonies at the time, but what they fought for, and won, provided the groundwork upon which broader freedoms could be added. And we have tried to do that ever since.

U.S. Representative from the state of Georgia, John Robert Lewis, was a great man. In him is exemplified everything that we stand for as a country. His pursuit of freedom and justice was heroic. We should look, hard, at the people that we have chosen to lead us at this point in our nation's life. Are they living up to the ideals that we have been fighting for over the past 244 years? If our leaders are not doing that, then we need to replace them.

Thank you, Congressman Lewis, for everything that you've built throughout your life. Our nation, Sir, will remain, forever indebted to you. Rest in Power.

JULY 20, 2020
410,698 Total Reported Cases in New York. 32,361 Deaths.

Somebody vandalized the Black Lives Matter painting on 5th Avenue. It looks like several somebodies did it at several different times. Some of the letters have had black paint spread over them. Some have had white paint splattered on them. It's interesting that happened given that there is a group of policemen on 24/7 duty right there, guarding Trump Tower. They stand about 10 feet away from the street. It is one of the most, if not the most, protected places in Manhattan.

We, the taxpayers, are paying millions of dollars each year for those guys to stand there. It's not as if the Black Lives Matter street painting is graffiti. The Mayor of New York City, himself, authorized those words to be painted there.

A couple of blocks across town at Columbus Circle, barricades have been set up around the perimeter of the statue in the center of it. Police vehicles guard the statue from vandals around the clock—one on either side of the circle. Inside Central Park, there is a second statue of Christopher Columbus. That, too, has barricades around it, as well as a portable generator and light array and around-the-clock police protection.

Neither of those statues has suffered any vandalism and yet the Black Lives Matter painting on Fifth Avenue has been allowed to be attacked and disfigured. That's a clear message that's being sent by the government of our city. Either the mayor is OK with the destruction, or he doesn't have control over his police force. Neither option instills much confidence.

The continental US is experiencing a weather phenomenon called a heat dome. A heat dome is a strong and persistent high-pressure system. The high-pressure air descends from above and heats up as it gets to the surface. The system is called a dome because it is shaped like one. The high-pressure air keeps a kind of lid on the heat that gets trapped on the surface, like a boiling pot, and causes the heat to build up. It's pretty much as unpleasant as it sounds. As climate change progresses, we are likely to see many more of these.

If our world governments don't start to address climate change it is only going to progress. If our governments don't start taking the issue of social justice seriously then the heat from that will continue to rise as well. If our government doesn't start actively working on flattening the curve of this virus, then the resulting heat from that will engulf us all.

The way to combat fire is to take away the things that feed it. Now, all these fires have far too much raw material to burn. Let's start clearing some of it up.

July 21, 2020
411,398 Total Reported Cases in New York. 32,373 Deaths.

I spent most of yesterday thinking that it was Tuesday when, in fact, it was only Monday. On some level, I guess what difference does it make? But it threw me off all day. I could not figure out what to do. I was lost.

When I was a kid and I'd complain to my mother that there was nothing to do, she'd say, "I've got plenty of things for you to do." Whatever it was that those things might be, I knew I didn't want to do them. I wasn't looking for chores, I was looking for something to engage me. My mother would lose patience and tell me that I was being "bloody-minded" and that I should just bug off and figure it out on my own. Yesterday, trapped under this heat dome weather thing, I was just feeling bloody-minded all day.

The main platform that this President ran on in the 2016 election was his promise to build a nearly 2,000-mile wall to separate us from our southern neighbor, Mexico. In a few short years under this administration, it has become normal for US Immigration and Customs Enforcement agents to show up ununiformed and in unmarked cars to grab suspected illegal aliens off the streets and out of their homes.

The US Department of Homeland Security has deployed undercover troops in unmarked vans to grab suspect anti-racism demonstrators off the streets in Portland, Oregon. The President signed an executive order directing federal agencies to send personnel to protect monuments, statues, and federal property during the ongoing Black Lives Matter demonstrations. The Department of Homeland Security is planning on taking the same actions in Chicago, it was announced yesterday, and the President has pledged to do the same thing in Democratic-led cities across the country.

During dinner last night, I was trying to explain to Michael about feeling "bloody-minded." His response to me was, "I've got plenty of things for you to do." OMG.

Bloody-mindedness is just self-imposed paralysis. I think that we can all be forgiven for a bout or two of it. A lot is going on in the world around us and a lot of it is, frankly, rather awful. It's easy to get overwhelmed by it all. As much as I hate to admit it, the only way through it is to do exactly what my mother would tell me to do, "Turn off the TV and go outside and play." So that's what I did.

JULY 22, 2020
411,954 Total Reported Cases in New York. 32,416 Deaths.

This is, by far, the longest I have been in any one spot almost since I can remember.

Norwegian Cruise Lines had been hoping to start cruising again with *Jersey Boys* at the end of September, but we all just received word that now the earliest that cruises will start up again is going to be the end of October.

The NCL Bliss ports in Seattle during the summer months and cruises up the Inner Passage to Alaska and back. During the week, it docks in Juneau, Ketchikan, and Skagway in Alaska. All three of those towns are only accessible by boat or by plane. There are no roads into them, they are completely cut off. Most of the income for those towns comes from the cruise ships that dock there and spend money. What those towns have is access to some of the most spectacular scenery on the planet and salmon. That's about it.

October is the end of the Alaska cruising season. Whether or not the cruise ships start up again at the end of October is now moot for the good people of Alaska. If the ships do start up again, they will do so on their winter routes. For the Bliss, that means the Caribbean. Nobody will be cruising to Alaska until next season.

The other place that the Bliss stops at on its Alaskan cruise is Victoria in Canadian British Columbia. Putting COVID-19 concerns on a cruise ship aside for the moment, that, I am guessing, more than anything else is why NCL is not going to be cruising in September.

In 1920 a federal law that regulates maritime commerce called the Jones Act was put into place. The Jones Act was enacted to stimulate the shipping industry after World War I. It is named after the Senator from the state of Washington who proposed it, Wesley Jones. Washington has a huge shipping industry and the act, in effect, gave the state a monopoly on shipping to Alaska. Under the Jones Act, cargo freighted between American ports can only be transported on ships built, owned, and operated by American citizens or permanent residents. This applies to both people and goods.

To avoid paying US taxes, most cruise ships are registered elsewhere. NCL's fleet of ships is registered in the Bahamas. So, to comply with the Jones Act, they need to be careful with their itineraries. Foreign ships can embark passengers at one US port and disembark them at another, but only if the ship stops in a foreign location along the way. In other words, when the Bliss cruises between say Los Angeles and Miami, it must stop in places like Cartagena, Colombia, and Mazatlán, Mexico along the way.

They can also start and end at the same port in the US and visit other US ports, but only if they call in at a foreign port as well. So, on our Alaska cruise, we start and finish in Seattle, call in at the three Alaskan cities but we also call in at Victoria, British Columbia to satisfy the Jones Act. If people depart the ship without doing this, the ship is fined per passenger. Ships must be careful that anybody who gets off at a stop along the way also gets back on.

One of the consequences of this act, besides, making it difficult for cruise ships who are trying to avoid paying US taxes, is that US protectorates like Puerto Rico end up having to pay much higher tariffs on imported goods. There are so few US registered ships that the demand for them is high. High demand equals higher rates which are passed on to the consumer—in this case, Puerto Ricans. It was calculated that because of the Jones Act, there were almost $1.2 billion of additional costs to the island last year which works out to be just under $400 per resident.

Last week on July 16, Prime Minister Justin Trudeau of Canada announced that the US/Canadian border will remain closed until August 21 with additional extensions possible. The Bahamas announced that as of today, all inbound commercial flights from the US are prohibited. Grand Bahama is on a full 14-day lockdown since yesterday and its borders are closed to all foreign traffic, sea or otherwise.

So, none of us are going anywhere for a while until we can stop in a foreign port of call.

Some of the *Jersey Boys* company members in other countries seem to be faring better than we are and some, far worse. The South African cast members, for example, are not eligible for unemployment as part-time gig workers. They have had absolutely no income at all for the last several months. They would very much like the option of getting back on the boat.

"What the hell are we doing?" asked Republican Senator Ted Cruz of Texas. What, indeed?

We've all been asking that question for months.

There were 57,777 new cases of COVID-19 reported by the CDC yesterday. That is well more than the combined population of all three of the NCL Bliss's Alaskan port cities. At this rate, we will hit 4 million cases nationally in about 4 days. It took New Yorkers roughly two months after we shut down and all started wearing masks for our case numbers to drop. If everyone across the country starts to practice social distancing and following safety protocols, we may see our numbers go down by the end of September.

I probably don't need to say "wear a mask" to anybody reading this, but I'll say it anyway. Wear a mask. Is it really that hard?

July 24, 2020

413,557 Total Reported Cases in New York. 32,436 Deaths.

Today is my mother's birthday.

She was born between the Wars (closer to the second one) in India to British parents who had, themselves, also been born there. As World War II began, she, her siblings, and her mother were evacuated to the nearest British outpost which happened to be South Africa. She grew up in South Africa until she came of age, then emigrated to England to become a nurse. After giving that a try and deciding that it wasn't for her, she was hired as a secretarial temp by my father. One thing led to another, and they were married. They lived in various places throughout Europe before moving to the States.

I was born in Arlington, VA, just outside of Washington D.C. and, three years later, my sister was born in Princeton, NJ. A few years after that, we moved back to South Africa to live with my grandfather and then finally returned to the US and settled in Northern New Jersey.

My mother had started working as a Librarian in South Africa and continued doing that in New Jersey at two different Libraries. My sister and I grew up, went off to school, and ultimately moved away. After 9/11, my mother and my father moved south to where she still lives to this day. In Florida.

In India, and in all the tropical British colonies at the time, everyone wore topees. We've all seen them in movies—the ubiquitous beige pith helmets. Up until the 1950s, it was readily believed that they protected the wearer from getting sunstroke. My mother and her brother and sister hated wearing them. Mom is the middle sibling and was about five years old when they sailed to South Africa. She remembers that as soon as India disappeared beyond the horizon, the three of them flung their topees into the sea behind the ship—happy to be rid of them for good.

Once it was discovered that they had done this, all hell broke loose. If the Germans saw the helmets, they would be able to deduce that a ship had recently passed by there. The ship ended up having to take a zig-zag course all the way across for fear of being torpedoed by a German U-Boat. Thinking about my mother living in Florida now, makes me think about her on board that ship—dodging danger at every turn.

There is no end in sight to the cases in Florida. They are still spiking—their numbers are heading up at an alarming rate. If they shut everything down right now it would still take them two to three months to get down to where we are in New York. IF they shut everything down, but they aren't. Disney World is still open, bringing in people from… everywhere.

If you look at infection rates around the country, Florida currently has the highest. In a gathering of 10 people, the probability is about 25% that one person in that group would be carrying the virus. By the time you get to a gathering of 100 people, there is a 100% probability that someone in that group will be infected. The Republican convention was expecting 15,000 people to show up. The seven out of ten Floridians who think that they would be safe attending the convention appear to be woefully misinformed.

Michael and I had a nice birthday call with my mother this morning. Thinking about her dodging COVID-19 torpedoes down there in Florida is, frankly, terrifying. I do know that she can take care of herself. I also know that she's being careful. She has a small bubble of people that she plays mahjong with. She's careful when she goes to the store.

My family was all supposed to get on a cruise next week as a kind of birthday celebration for my mother. We were booked on a relatively small ship that was going to sail into Alaskan ports that the Norwegian Bliss is too big to get into. Not this year. We've rescheduled it for next year. Hopefully, by then, we might be able to go.

In the meantime, we are all home and safe and knock wood, well. That's as good a gift as anyone could ask for. Happy Birthday, Mom.

July 25, 2020
414,317 Total Reported Cases in New York. 32,446 Deaths.

I rode a bike down to City Hall yesterday to see how the Black Lives Matter Occupy City Hall encampment was doing. The heat dome that had been sitting over the country must have dissipated because it was about 20 degrees cooler than it had been just a few days ago. The last time I went down there was just this past Monday. On Monday, like the time I was there before that, everything seemed orderly and calm. Food was being distributed, People were talking, and somebody was playing the guitar. Yesterday, the whole thing was gone.

I knew that something was up even before I got there because there were police barricades everywhere. The encampment had been on the east side of the park, but as I approached from the west there was a double perimeter of fencing around the whole thing. Chambers Street to the north of the park was completely blocked off and there were policemen stationed on every corner. To get to where the camp had been, I had to walk north, around the block, and enter from the side. None of the officers stopped me, I am an old white guy after all, so I walked into what had been a thriving protest community just a few days before and it was now… empty.

A friend of mine who is an actor posts pictures online of ghost signs from all over the country. Ghost signs are those extremely faded painted advertisements for obsolete products and services that remain on the sides of brick buildings, seemingly forever. Clothing stores, vaudeville houses, import-export companies, long gone, remain as distant almost forgotten memories to those few people who think to look up and glance at the remains of their old signs as they pass by. It's always a big deal in New York when a building gets torn down to make way for a new one and an old sign is revealed. The last one I remember was, I think, down near Lincoln Center. It announced an establishment that was offering the latest in comfortable horse carriages. There was a lot of press about it until the new building was built up next to it and it got covered up again.

I found out that in the early hours of Wednesday morning between three and four, a whole squadron of police officers in full riot gear descended upon the sleeping Occupy encampment and pulled it apart. Protestors were given ten minutes to gather their things and clear out. Tarps and tents were pulled down and thrown into dumpsters. Tables were over-tuned and tossed as well. Once the area was cleared of people, teams of workers wearing white helmeted suits and carrying hoses came in and water-blasted the paint off the pavement and statues on nearby buildings. The little knoll where the tents had been set up was re-sodded. By the time that the sun came up on Wednesday, it had vanished.

There were no news teams present so there is only one shaky video taken by one of the protestors that shows what happened. The whole thing got very little news coverage.

The sod covering the knoll is still in visible checkerboard squares. As it takes hold, those lines will fade, and the pieces will blend. It will just look like grass that has always been there. The Surrogate Court of New York County across from the park had been completely covered in graffiti. The statues in front of it were painted and their eyes taped over. All of that has been completely erased.

Well, not completely. Underneath one of the Court statues, you can still faintly make out the words Black Lives Matter where the black paint has seeped deeply into the porous stone. You can also still see the very light outlines of the giant BLM letters on the side of the Tweed Courthouse steps.

Many blocks uptown in Washington Square Park, the ghostly remains of a Fu@# 12 scrawl are still visible on the base of the iconic Arch. It was sprayed there during the first night of protests following the murder of George Floyd. Much of the plywood art in SoHo has been taken down, but there is still the occasional door or storefront with a remnant of it left.

Time passes and things change, but traces and reminders remain. It would be a mistake for anyone to think that because a bunch of graffiti and a group of protestors have been made to all but disappear that the issues that caused them to be there have just gone away as well. The scab has been pulled off the ugly wound of this country's racism and discussions have been had that will never be un-had. The fights and the arguments have come off the streets and are now happening inside. We are all thinking about it because we aren't all distracted by the usual noise of our lives.

I'm glad that the ghost signs from these past weeks are there. They need to stay. The real work is happening now in a far more rational and thoughtful way, but we need to be reminded of the passion and anger that sparked it to keep the momentum going.

To quote the final lines of Tony Kushner's monumental play *Angels in America*: "We won't die secret deaths anymore. The world only spins forward. We will be citizens. The time has come. Bye now. You are fabulous creatures, each and every one. And I bless you: More Life. The Great Work Begins."

July 27, 2020
4.2 Million Total Reported Cases in the United States.

Chad Wolf is the Acting Chairman of the Department of Homeland Security. He replaced Kevin McAleenan who resigned, who in turn replaced Kirstjen Nielsen who was fired by the President. There were two others before Nielsen, making a total of five so far in this administration. Wolf is just the Acting Chairman. He hasn't been approved yet. It is Wolf, who at the President's behest, has been sending Federal troops into Portland, Oregon and now into Seattle, Washington to quell the violence from protestors. It is unclear whether as Acting Chairman he is legally allowed to do that.

By all reports from both cities, the presence of these Federal troops is inciting the violence not diminishing it. Local government and law enforcement officials are not happy that these troops are there.

The President is using images of the violence (instigated by his own forces) to terrorize the population of the US. It is another step towards suspending the rule of law. The Mayor of Portland, Ted Wheeler, has demanded that the troops withdraw. "People are being literally scooped off the street into unmarked vans, rental cars, apparently," he said. "They are being denied probable cause. And they are denied due process."

Chad Wolf responded to that in an interview on Fox News. "Because we don't have that local support, that local law enforcement support, we are having to go out and proactively arrest individuals, and we need to do that because we need to hold them accountable." These Federal law enforcement officers are not even waiting until anything happens. They are arresting people before they do anything.

I allowed myself to get dragged into an online exchange yesterday with a sweet-looking grandmotherly woman. She runs a history camp for kids at a Museum in Washington D.C.

Here is a quote from her: "I have decided I am not afraid to speak up now. I am tired of getting bashed for my Judeo-Christian values, my respect for the Constitution, law and order, police reform, not backing Marxist BLM, boycotting the NFL, MLB, and the NBA for pandering. I love and adore my black friends and black God Child and follow Bob Woodson and Thomas Sowell. I will not accept the 1619 Project as it is revisionist's folklore. I do believe in Woodson's 1776 Project. I have many liberal friends, a few transgender friends, homosexual friends and family, and a couple of lesbian friends and a lesbian cousin all of whom I love and respect. I just want love and peace for this country not division and hate."

This is why this President stands a very good chance of being re-elected in November. What a day-long pointless back and forth on social media failed to reveal is how this person saw her Judeo-Christian values being reflected in the actions of this Administration. She seems to have missed the memo outlining the fact that the Black Lives Matter movement is fighting for the very things that she claims to respect. The Administration she so admires? Not so much.

One wonders what this large group of LGBTQ and BIPOC friends that she supports will feel towards her as her fear against speaking up against them subsides. She seems utterly terrified of black people. Not "her" black people, of course, but black people out there in general. That fear has been taught and stoked by those trying to consolidate their own power.

The more we all retreat into our own beliefs and block out streams of information, the more set we are all going to get in our ways. This sweet old lady is never going to see the similarities between what is going on now and what happened in Germany in the 1930s. Millions of sweet old ladies back then voted for Adolph Hitler and cheered him on, too. They thought that he was going to restore their country, ravaged by World War I, and make it great again. They chose to ignore the actions of his Brown

Shirts and then the Gestapo and concentrate on what they felt Hitler was doing to uphold their Judeo-Christian values.

We cannot assume that the President is going to be voted out of office in November. Every single one of us who can, must cast a vote. There is going to be a lot more of what we are seeing in Oregon and Washington in the coming months. And worse. I want to believe that more people believe in the rule of law than don't. I have to believe that.

July 28, 2020
416,085 Total Reported Cases in New York. 32,487 Deaths.

In one of the more surreal events that has happened in the last four months of mind-blowingly surreal moments, the President announced that he had been invited by the New York Yankees to throw out the first pitch on August 15 at Yankee Stadium. He hadn't been invited. It was a lie.

This past Thursday, Dr. Anthony Fauci, threw out the first pitch of the 2020 Baseball season for the Washington Nationals at National Stadium in Washington D.C. Seemingly, the President was so bent out of shape that Dr. Fauci was getting so much attention, that just before it happened the President felt obliged to tell everyone that he was doing the same thing.

While the President did have a standing invitation from the Yankees to throw out a pitch, nothing had ever been discussed about him doing it on August 15. That the President was going to throw out the pitch startled everyone from his own aides with him in the briefing room to the Yankees, themselves. This past weekend, the President tweeted that he wasn't going to be able to do it after all because he was so busy with the "China virus."

The tension between the President and Dr. Fauci has escalated in recent days. It's been there from the beginning of the pandemic. We've all watched Dr. Fauci dance around the President's nonsense the White House has put forth. I have always assumed that he felt being politic at least allowed him to get some of his message out.

Back in April when the CDC first began recommending that we should all be wearing them, the President said, "I don't think I'm going to be doing it. Wearing a face mask as I greet presidents, prime ministers, dictators, kings, queens—I just don't see it."

Under intense pressure to do something, anything at all, to appear to be acting against the spread of the virus, he put one on. "I'm all for masks," he said. He said he kind of liked how he looked in one. He said it made him feel like the Lone Ranger. It seemed like the President was finally conceding to the science.

Then came last night's tweets. The President retweeted several things that promoted the use of hydroxychloroquine as an effective treatment for the complications that arise from COVID-19.

He retweeted something paraphrased from a critic of Dr. Fauci named Dr. Lee Vliet claiming that Dr. Fauci misled the public by dismissing hydroxychloroquine. He also retweeted something else from an account that uses the hashtag "faucithefraud." Finally, he retweeted clips of a video where some doctors make several claims about the virus including their belief that hydroxychloroquine is effective. That video has been removed by Facebook, YouTube, and Twitter for containing false and misleading information.

I truly believe that last night's tweets from the President were in direct response to the attention Fauci got from simply throwing out that baseball.

The American Federation of Teachers announced this morning that it would support its 1.7 million members going on strike to fight inadequate health and safety measures connected with school re-openings if necessary.

That the teachers' union would need to announce that it might come to a strike if basic health and safety measures aren't in place to protect them and the kids in the coming weeks and months is inconceivable. The White House is demanding that schools reopen but they are doing nothing to help this happen safely and they are threatening to withhold funding from schools who won't move forward with the plan. Nobody sane ever went into teaching to get rich, but nobody sane ever went into it expecting to die either.

I hope it gets cooler outside, soon, because we've all got a serious amount of marching ahead of us.

July 29, 2020
The United States surpasses 150,000 coronavirus Deaths.

When I was a kid, I remember being terrified that I was going to be drafted into the Vietnam War. I remember lying in bed at night, not sleeping, and worrying about it. There were so many awful images from the war on TV and in magazines. The 1972 picture of that girl running naked down a road after her village got napalmed was particularly brutal. More horrifying to me, perhaps, because the girl in the picture was nearly the same age as I was.

The same year that the picture was taken was the last year that anyone was drafted. Three years later in 1975, when I was 13, they stopped requiring young men to register with the Selective Service. I missed having to do it by five years.

Not long after that, my family and I spent the summer with our relatives in South Africa. Up until 1993, all white males there between 17 and 65 needed to spend two years in the military. I think I must have been about 16 at the time. I had gotten tall very early and always looked older than I was. We were on a platform somewhere waiting for a train and there was a whole group of young cadets waiting with us. The uniformed guy leading them came over and asked my mother why I wasn't serving. My mother explained that I was an American and underage. He looked skeptical but walked away. My heart nearly exploded out of my chest.

It took me a long time to believe that the US draft was truly over. I imagined becoming a hippie and fleeing to Canada to get away from it all. When tension with another country was reported on the news I thought, OK, here we go, this is it.

The current President of the United States seems to have decided that the only way that he will win re-election is if we are all terrified. His television commercials, filled with footage of protestors being teargassed, warn of a future that looks like a war zone unless he is elected. The footage, of course, was all taken during his own term in office. There's another one where an older woman who is alone in her house, hears somebody breaking into her house and calls 911 only to be put on hold because Joe Biden has dissolved the nation's police forces. It's all nonsense and propaganda that is specifically designed to feed upon every single one of our worst fears.

When will we get back to work? Will there be more PUA payments? Will there be a second wave of COVID-19 in New York City? Will we lose the apartment? Will there be a vaccine? Will the President get elected to another term and start a program to eradicate those who opposed him by tying us to chairs and throwing us off buildings the way the Taliban does to homosexuals?

Anything could happen. But it's not happening now. The energy that we are putting into our fear is taking away our ability to enjoy what we have in front of us. It is also taking away from our ability to do anything constructive in terms of trying to stop any of the bad things we are worried about from happening.

The future will come. James Baldwin said, "There is never a time in the future in which we will work out our salvation. The challenge is in the moment; the time is always now."

Barack Obama said, "The future rewards those who press on. I don't have time to feel sorry for myself. I don't have time to complain. I'm going to press on."

Nearly 2,000 years ago Marcus Aurelius said, "Never let the future disturb you. You will meet it, if you have to, with the same weapons of reason which today arm you against the present."

Michael's just come out of the bedroom. He's making us scrambled eggs, turkey bacon, and toast. Both good and bad things lie ahead of us. For the moment, I'm going to enjoy this breakfast and try to deal with the rest of it when it happens.

July 30, 2020
417,454 Total Reported Cases in New York. 32,505 Deaths.

At about 5 am, the cat who gets bored in the early mornings will start walking across the two of us in the bed. Sometimes we can sleep through this. One of us just kicks him off the bed. Usually, though, Michael gets woken up enough that he will get up and change out the dry food that we leave down for most of the day. Sometimes the cat doesn't even eat it. He just makes sure that the task's been done then wanders off.

The activity around all of that usually wakes me up enough that I go to the bathroom. If something is weighing on either of us, one or the other of us might not then be able to go back to sleep, but on a good day, we both go back to sleep. This morning, we both went back to sleep.

Once we were awake the morning began calmly and regularly enough but when I turned on the TV, instead of the usual discussion about case numbers, every single newscaster across the spectrum of the news was completely on fire leading with the most recent inane tweet from our President. "With Universal Mail-In Voting (not Absentee Voting, which is good), 2020 will be the most INACCURATE & FRAUDULENT Election in history. It will be a great embarrassment to the USA. Delay the Election until people can properly, securely and safely vote???"

The current President's tweet comes as no surprise to anyone who is paying even the slightest attention to what is going on. He is doing everything in his power to delegitimize and undermine these coming elections because he is widely projected to lose.

So, why tweet that today? Well, coincidentally, the US Commerce Department released its quarterly numbers today. His tweet came just minutes after the announcement came that the US economy has shrunk by 32.9%. It is the single worst quarterly drop in our history. By far. The United States is now officially in a recession.

Earlier this week, I took a walk down Madison Avenue. At the beginning of the shutdown, all city stores that did not provide food or other essential products were forced to close. We knew that some of them were going to be gone for good, but because of the shutdown, we couldn't tell which ones. One of the stores on Madison had a living Ficus tree in its display window. As the weeks passed, its leaves started turning brown. Then they fell off. It died. When the BLM demonstrations began, plywood went up covering most of the storefronts from sight.

Well, now the plywood is down. With New York City now in a modified Phase 4 re-opening, real estate offices and retail establishments have been able to reopen. Owners, or creditors, of permanently shuttered stores, have been able to clear out the inventory. In that store on Madison, the Ficus leaves have been swept up and the dead tree has been removed.

I would estimate, just by looking, that fully a third of the storefronts along the retail section of Madison Avenue are now vacant. Many of the remaining stores are advertising sales in the hopes of attracting shoppers. Much of the wealthy population of Manhattan, however, is elsewhere. Add to that, there are no tourists here spending money.

Our President takes everything said against his actions as a personal attack. He doesn't understand why more people like Dr. Fauci than like him. His tweet this morning was solely to divert attention away from the disastrous economic numbers that were announced. He is scared that people aren't going to like him because of them, not that they are going to dislike his policies. He's not a politician. He has no vision at all beyond his own ego gratification.

Watching Representative Lewis's funeral this morning is driving home just how far-off base this President is. Nothing that is happening is about him and yet that is how he is viewing all of it. As I write this, I am watching people who have fundamental disagreements sitting together, united in the celebration of a truly great American patriot. They will get back to arguing later. That's how this should work.

The New York Times published, at his request, Representative John Lewis's final words today. I'll let him finish.

"Democracy is not a state. It is an act, and each generation must do its part to help build what we called the Beloved Community, a nation and world society at peace with itself…

Ordinary people with extraordinary vision can redeem the soul of America by getting in what I call good trouble, necessary trouble. Voting and participating in the democratic process are key. The vote is the most powerful nonviolent change agent you have in a democratic society. You must use it because it is not guaranteed. You can lose it."

JULY 31, 2020
418,144 Total Reported Cases in New York.

I'm exceedingly grateful that five months into this global pandemic that I have yet to leave the house without pants. Yet, I fear, is the operative word in that sentence. I'm living in my underwear. So far, I don't feel that I am in danger of leaving the house without my underwear. But, you know, early days.

When I was in tech rehearsals for the original Broadway production of *Jersey Boys*, I was subletting a friend's studio somewhere out in Brooklyn. American tech rehearsals are a uniquely exhausting and ridiculous series of days that can start from 8 am and continue to midnight.

The unions allow us to work through the last two weeks before the first public performance without a day off, so nothing breaks up the days.

They seem to last forever but even so, there is never enough time. One day bleeds into another. It becomes difficult to remember a time when tech rehearsals weren't happening.

My commute to this Brooklyn studio where I was staying during the *Jersey Boys* tech was at least an hour in each direction. There was never time to get enough sleep. One morning, I walked out of the apartment and out onto the street and something felt odd. I could feel the buckles of my backpack against my skin, and they seemed strangely cold. I had forgotten to put a shirt on.

My shorts are draped over the back of my chair at the dining table. That way, I think, I have a decent chance of remembering to put them on. If, at some point, you do happen to see me out there on my bike without my shorts on, just look the other way. By the time that happens, I probably won't be the only one. We are all in danger of getting a little squirrelly. If you do stare and laugh at me, don't worry, I won't notice at all because I will be off in my own head dreaming about being back in tech.

AUGUST 1, 2020
418,899 Total Reported Cases in New York.

Back in the 1980s, the painter Jean-Michel Basquiat lived and worked in a studio owned by Andy Warhol down on Great Jones Street just off the Bowery. There is a plaque next to the door that identifies it. The front door, itself and the walls surrounding it are completely covered in ever-changing street art.

When Basquiat was painting down there it was a rough place to be. For a while, Basquiat and Madonna were a couple. Attention started being paid to the area. These days it is trendy. New modern condo buildings have gone up along the Bowery and the neighborhood is now popular with young wealthy homebuyers. I rode down Great Jones Street on Wednesday on my bike. In just the last week or so, a chic local restaurant has set up socially distant dining tables on the street leading right up next to the door.

Further uptown, there is a huge mural over the Empire Diner on 10th Avenue. It's visible from the street but you can also see it from the Highline. The mural is of Mount Rushmore as reimagined with artists instead of Presidents in riotous colors. Jean-Michel Basquiat and Warhol are up there along with Keith Haring and Frida Kahlo.

A couple of years ago the Brooklyn Botanical Gardens did a huge Frida Kahlo display. They recreated some of the gardens from Casa Azul, the house in Mexico City that she shared with Diego Rivera. It was a beautiful way to experience her and her work.

When I was going to school at Columbia, the MTA would cover over old ads down in the subway with flat black paint before putting up new ones. Keith Haring, who was just starting, would fill those temporary blank black squares with chalked-in explosions of his radiant baby designs. He drew them all over the city. Eventually, the chalk drawings would get covered up by a new ad and disappear. He drew one at the subway stop up near my school that stayed there for a long time. There were so many layers of old paper and paint underneath it that the corners began peeling up. Pieces got ripped off. For a long time, I had a piece of it, myself. I have no idea what I did with it. At the time, Keith Haring was just a guy who graffitied things with chalk, he wasn't an internationally recognized artist.

While I was still in High School, the New York Public Library would sponsor an event called, "New York is Book Country." They would block off a huge section of 5th Avenue and fill it with author booths. Writers would come in and do readings. There would be events for kids and book signings. The year that I went during high school, Andy Warhol was handing out issues of his Interview magazine. I don't remember there being much of a crowd around him. He signed the magazine for me and then with the gall only possible from a teenager, I asked him to draw me a soup can. And he did. That, I know I still have. Mind you, the scrawl is not at all recognizable as a soup can—it's two curly lines in blue sharpie—but he drew it and he signed it.

New York is a city where, it seems, anything can happen. I have traveled all over the world, and I have never found any other place that I would rather live. There was never a question in my mind that Michael and I wouldn't ride out this pandemic in New York.

The morning of 9/11, I remember my ex and I were out at a house that we owned in Pennsylvania along the Delaware River. The television was on while we were packing up to head back into the city when the news started reporting that there was a fire at the World Trade Center. Nobody knew what was going on. We watched in real-time as the second plane hit the tower behind the reporter who was speaking from the street. Fairly soon after that, there was an announcement that the bridges and tunnels into NY were all being closed. We couldn't get back into the city for about three days. We had to watch what was happening on TV. As soon as we could, I took the train in. As we approached, there was a cloud of smoke over lower Manhattan from the still-smoldering ruins. Suddenly, everything that we had been looking at on TV was real.

In the days and weeks that followed the attack, New Yorkers came together. New Yorkers have a seemingly unique ability to drop their differences and work together to overcome disaster. People around the country were terrified about coming into the city so the entire theatrical community gathered in Times Square and filmed a TV commercial. I was stage managing the Broadway revival of *Cabaret* at the time and Brooke Shields was playing Sally Bowles. She was called upon to do a lot of publicity to help portray the city as a safe place to come to. It was a thrilling and moving time to be a part of our amazing industry in the greatest city in the world.

I don't regret for a second our decision to stay here in the city during all of this. Not being able to get home to the city during those first few days of 9/11 was truly frustrating. I wanted to be here. As the pandemic rages all over the country around us, I don't think that Michael regrets our decision to stay here either. As a city, we had one of the worst outbreaks of COVID-19 in the world and we, as a city, beat it back. Together. Every so often I need a break from it, but I never cease to be grateful that this is our home.

August 3, 2020
420,042 Total Reported Cases in New York.

And we are now on just such a break. I am sitting on a bench in a small shady public park just off Commercial Street in Provincetown, Massachusetts. There's a good breeze coming in off the water and it is a glorious day.

Michael's dad and his partner have a condo share just outside of town in Truro. Nothing fancy, but a view of the bay from the front porch. A friend of ours is happily staying back in the apartment with the cat. So, for the next week, these posts will be coming from the far northeastern tip of Cape Cod.

We were up here on the Cape last summer, although it feels like much longer ago than that. There's, unsurprisingly, a very different feel to it this year. It's far less crowded. There are no tea dances. Provincetown is very serious about mask-wearing. There are signs about it everywhere—far more so than there are back in New York. You honestly can't go more than about 20 feet before you see one. Despite that, people seem more relaxed. It all seems so civilized and reasonable. Wearing a mask doesn't seem to be killing anyone. Nobody is storming the Town Hall.

Provincetown has always been a remarkable mix of people from every walk of life. As you walk along Commercial Street you see everything from leather guys in ass-less chaps to young straight families with kids in strollers. The beauty of the place is that everyone gets along quite happily. I don't see a lot of the former yet, but it is, after all still somewhat early in the day.

I think it's time for a walk on the beach.

August 4, 2020
420,675 Total Reported Cases in New York. 32,536 Deaths.

For the first time in nearly five months, Michael and I went to the movies yesterday. The Wellfleet Drive-In was playing the movie *Jaws* which couldn't have been more perfect. Every other space in the lot was blocked off so that there was at least the width of one car between each vehicle. Masks were required at the concession stand but not while you were around your car.

The last time I remember going to a drive-in movie was in 1971 when I was 9 years old. We were living in New Jersey in an orderly little development built in the 1950s. My friend Solomon Yang lived about six or seven houses just up the street from us. He and his family had moved into the neighborhood from Taiwan. It cannot have been easy for them. Solomon and his brother and sister were fluent in English despite having strong accents, but his parents were much less so.

Solomon's dad was an architectural engineer who was working on the new World Trade Center. One weekend, Solomon and I were allowed to go into New York with his dad and see the building while it was still under construction. While I vividly remember this trip, I didn't realize until now just how young we were at the time.

While his dad was working, Solomon took me into Chinatown for lunch. I had never been there before. We went to different places and had all of Solomon's favorite foods. I wish I could remember where some of those places were and what we ate because it was one of the most incredible afternoons of eating, I have ever experienced. Solomon spoke Chinese with far greater ease than he spoke English and I was completely jealous of him.

We went back to the World Trade Center and Mr. Yang took us both up to the top. It was still being built, so it wasn't finished yet. Each of the floors radiated out from the central elevator banks. We got up to one of the top floors and when the elevator doors opened, we looked out across the plain cement floors to nothing—just open sky. There were no outer walls in place at all yet. It was windy. Really windy.

Solomon and his dad walked over far closer to the edge than I was willing to. I stayed resolutely next to the elevator bank holding on for dear life. According to Solomon, the view was amazing. I took his word for it. I wouldn't see that view for myself until years later when the building was finished.

One night, Mrs. Yang took Solomon and me along with his brother and sister to see *The Omega Man* at a drive-in movie theatre. *The Omega Man* was a science fiction movie starring Charlton Heston as a virologist named Dr. Robert Neville. Because of a vaccine he developed, he is the sole human survivor of an apocalyptic bio-chemical war.

Because of that movie, I used to fantasize about what I would do if I was the only person in New York. I don't remember a lot of specifics, but I think I remember that he had taken a Van Gogh from a museum to put on the wall of his apartment. How I would decorate my apartment if I had everything in New York to choose from has taken up more of my daydreaming life than I should probably admit.

   I thought about that movie all the time back in March and April during the height of the stay-at-home order. Standing in the middle of Times Square completely by myself was, in a way, an actual fulfillment of that apocalyptic fantasy.

   When the movie was made, the Black Power movement was in full force. The screenwriters added a character of color who was played by Rosalind Cash.

   The Black Power movement had started as a response to segregation. It was a push to open black-owned businesses like bookstores, food cooperatives, schools, media companies, and clinics. As time went on, however, impatience grew around how slowly the non-violent forms of protest championed by the Reverend Martin Luther King were in achieving an effect. Malcolm X and others demanded more immediate violent action to achieve their ends faster. When Malcolm X was assassinated in 1965, the movement exploded. It hit a peak in the early 1970s at the same time *The Omega Man* was being made. *Network*, a movie made a couple of years later has a strong cynical Black Power subplot throughout its story as well.

   The kiss between Charlton Heston and Rosalind Cash in *The Omega Man* was one of the first interracial kisses ever filmed for a mainstream movie.

   By the 1980s the Black Power movement had largely dissipated. A great deal of what those involved were trying to achieve remained undone. The current Black Lives Matter movement is a natural resurgence of the Black Power movement all those years ago.

   While some of *The Omega Man* has stuck with me over the years, I will admit, though, that the most vivid memory I have of that night came afterward. It was a double feature and that night the second movie was *The Vanishing Point* which was a kind of a drug-fueled road movie. Mrs. Yang was leery about letting us watch it, but we begged her, and she relented. It was rated R, but I am not sure she was fully aware of what that meant. I remember nothing about it at all except that at some point a little way in there's a scene where a woman is riding a motorcycle across the desert completely naked. Poor Mrs. Yang couldn't get us out of there fast enough.

   There are a lot of contemporary echoes in *Jaws* as well. I can't quite process the fact that the movie first came out 45 years ago. A drunk young woman swims out at night and is killed by a shark. The sheriff wants to close the beaches, but the mayor intervenes and says no. The July 4th weekend is approaching and it's the island's most lucrative time. Nobody knows for sure that she was killed by a shark, even though that's what it looks like. The medical examiner says it was a shark, but the mayor holds onto the idea that it might have just been a boat's propeller.

So, the beaches stay open. A boy on a raft is then bitten and killed in broad daylight in front of a crowded beach. A bounty is put on the shark, and one is caught. Our heroes don't think that it is big enough to be the same shark, but the mayor insists that it is. He will not allow it to be slit open to see if the remains of the boy are inside it, insisting that it would be too grisly a spectacle. He stands firmly by his convictions that the problem is solved, and the beaches can open. I'll say no more, but it doesn't end well.

There is no difference between what the fictional Mayor of Amity Island does in the movie and what the current real President of the United States is doing at this very moment. In their drive to protect their economies, both flatly refuse to accept the scientific facts. In both cases, their communities suffer. Amity Island becomes the scene of many truly violent deaths, and the United States has become an ever-expanding graveyard that threatens its long-term prosperity. In both scenarios, early decisive action would have hugely mitigated the severity of the disaster.

Thinking about those two movies from close to half a century ago with plot points that could be lifted right out of today's headlines makes me wonder whether we are truly capable of change at all. The anger behind much of the Black Lives Matter movement is born out of that very frustration. Why doesn't anything ever change? Why can't people see the effects of the actions they are taking? Why can't the President see the facts that are laid out right in front of him?

It was great to watch a movie with a whole bunch of people and it was great to experience a drive-in again. We are probably going to see more of them spring up around the country as this summer drags on.

Is change coming this time? I hope so. It's long overdue.

August 5, 2020
421,159 Total Reported Cases in New York.

While we have visited friends in other places in the past few weeks, this is the first time we have stayed in another place. I am aware, from the news, that COVID-19 is affecting the entire planet. There is, however, something unreal about the news. It comes out of the television along with the rest of our entertainment. It's sometimes hard not to think of the two as the same thing. Sitting here, just off Commercial Street in P-Town, I am as surrounded by this global pandemic here as I have been in New York, and it drives the reality of what's happening home just that much more.

Everyone and I truly mean everyone, without exception, is wearing a mask. The traffic cops are wearing masks. "Entering Mandatory Mask Zone" signs stand on the streets for cars to see and on the sidewalks to alert pedestrians. You don't want to wear a mask, fine, then you don't come in.

Some places in Europe have made mask-wearing mandatory in all public places regardless of what the set-up is. If you leave your house in Madrid or Hong Kong, you must put a mask on regardless of where you go. The same is true in all of Greece. The thinking behind this is not that anyone thinks that there is a high risk for contracting the virus outdoors in a park. The reasoning, instead is, that there is so much confusion and too many arguments about when you should wear a mask and when you shouldn't, that it's far easier to say just put on a mask all the time. Period. No confusion.

While I am sitting out here under a tree, Michael is rehearsing a Zoom reading back in the apartment. Last night I had a Zoom meeting, myself, about a theatre project that is scheduled to start in March. There are no guarantees that we will be able to do this project in March, but if we can do it then, now is when we need to start planning for it. So, that's what we are doing. There were people on the call from at least three different countries. It's honestly not a bad way to work. That's in March, though. For now, I'm, as we call it, resting.

Choosing between mountains or the ocean, I will always lean towards the latter. Don't get me wrong, I love the mountains, too, but the ocean lets me breathe.

Since I've been sitting here this morning, the street has gotten busier. Shops have started to open. Most of the little art galleries and boutiques are open for business but with limits on how many people at a time can enter. There's plenty of outdoor dining.

People have adjusted to living this way. They all seem to be breathing. I am going to take a walk along Commercial Street in a few minutes. I'm going to buy some stuff I don't need from some local merchants. I am going to trust that everything will work out, because, in the long run, everything always does. And I am going to take in as many deep breaths of ocean air as I can.

And breathe.

August 6, 2020

The Average Rate of Death from the coronavirus in the United States is one person every 80 seconds.

The place where we are staying is about five miles outside of Provincetown on the bay. As the sun was starting to set last night, Michael and I walked into town together along the beach. The tide was well out, so we were able to cut off some of the distance by just walking across the tidal flats. It was like walking from our home in New York down to the Village except we walked the entire way on bare feet.

Michael and I have never spent this much time together at any other point in our relationship. For at least half of the year, in normal times, one or the other of us is working out of town somewhere. It's usually me but sometimes it's Michael too. Even when we are working in town, we still can go all day without ever seeing each other. If Michael is shooting a movie or playing his recurring role on *Law & Order*, he is long gone by the time I wake up. When I'm in New York, I am usually out in a studio downtown rehearsing or in auditions.

These days, we are together all the time. Our apartment is large enough that we can work in separate rooms, but it still means that we are in the same place every day.

Is that good? It's certainly… different. I can't imagine going through this and sharing a living space with anybody else. Thinking about what would happen were I going through this with one of my close friends, makes me even more grateful that I am with Michael. I love my friends and trust that they love me too, but I think that in almost every case after a few weeks that one or the other of us would end up in a puddle of blood on the floor with a taped outline around our fallen corpse.

Every relationship has its issues, but it doesn't seem that Michael's and mine are in any way a threat to us staying together. In pre-COVID times, there are so many daily distractions that it becomes relatively easy to be distracted. Those distractions aren't here these days, so nothing is stopping us from having to confront whatever issues arise. It becomes harder to ignore them. We can't possibly be alone in experiencing this.

I think that perhaps a lot of the rush to reopen schools is happening because of the pressure that people are feeling being at home trapped together. The pressure that parents are under these days must be enormous. I, personally, feel like I am made for uncle-dom. As an uncle, I get all the fun parts of interacting with kids, and then, when things inevitably go south, I can just hand them back to their parents and blithely get on with my day. These days, as a parent, there's no escape.

In a completely unrelated and astonishing development, New York Attorney General Letitia James filed a lawsuit today against the National Rifle Association that seeks to dissolve it.

Wow! That is the only response I have. The NRA is registered in New York as a charity which is what gives Ms. James jurisdiction over it. The suit alleges that NRA executives used charitable funds for personal gain, awarded contracts to friends and family members, and provided contracts to former employees to ensure their loyalty. After an eighteen-month investigation, the Attorney General claims to have uncovered financial misconduct in the millions of dollars. The group, according to her, is "fraught with fraud and abuse."

Trying to dismantle the largely Republican-supported National Rifle Association three months before a national Presidential election is an astonishing plot twist.

I am sure that there are people out there who are navigating through this pandemic alone who sometimes fantasize about what it would be like going through it with a partner. To all of you, I would say that you should know that I think that a lot of us who are going through this with someone sometimes fantasize about what it would be like to be going through it alone. Friends who are stuck at home with their whole families seem to occasionally look longing out from their Zoom boxes at those of us without. Those of us without sometimes look longingly in at those with, envying them the activity and energy.

This isn't easy on any of us. None of it is what most of us would choose. Whatever it might look like on social media, nobody is getting through this without stress. "Compare and Despair" is a perfect phrase. We always seem to want what we don't have.

Given that, though, I don't think I regret a single choice that I've made in terms of how to navigate through this pandemic. I tend to keep to myself a lot as it is, without Michael I would have become a monk. The two of us are wired differently but that's what makes life interesting.

Michael's cooking up breakfast. I am so glad that he's there. After I divorced my ex, I was bound and determined never to get married again. Changing my mind was the smartest thing I've ever done. Most days anyway.

Enough is going on that makes this hard. We need to be kind to each other and cut ourselves some slack. We need to be kind to ourselves.

August 7, 2020
422,479 Total Reported Cases in New York. 32,577 Deaths.

In my experience, everyone wants to be told what to do. Almost nobody wants to be the point at which the buck finally stops. People need to know that there's somebody with the bigger picture in mind who is taking care of things. Somebody must be in charge or else people feel anxious and there is anarchy.

That, in a nutshell, is what my job is. I tell people what to do. Do they always listen? No, of course not. I have worked with plenty of people who want to be told what to do just so that they can do the exact opposite thing. There are also plenty of others who consider being told what to do merely the first step in a negotiation.

The most notoriously "difficult" stars I have worked with all follow the rules to some extent. Almost all of them will listen to reason, but they will certainly question the reason and you'd better be ready with an answer. Invariably, what is easier for me, is not going to be what they want to do. That's why I get paid for what I do.

There is a union rule that requires every actor in a professional production—no matter at what level—to be at the theatre half an hour before showtime. Repeated violations of this can result in termination. I worked with a star on a Broadway show who flatly refused to show up on time. For no reason other than I think they just didn't like being told what to do. They were (more or less) professional in most other ways. Thankfully, they were completely terrified of their co-star and wanted their approval, so never broke any rules too badly.

Star or not, if someone in my position doesn't enforce the rules with one person, you then can't enforce them with anybody. So, we worked out that they could be five minutes late every day, and we got the producers to approve it. That way it was official. If anybody else complained that it wasn't fair that they were late and they couldn't be, I could say that it had been negotiated with the producers. It was granted as one of the perks of having above-the-title billing.

Following the overall rule wasn't going to happen but following a specially negotiated compromise rule was fine. They were rarely late for the new call time. I took it as a win.

Elaine Stritch, who is no longer with us, so I am mentioning her by name, was somewhat in a class by herself when it came to following rules. Elaine Stritch was a Broadway fixture on and off the stage. She was… something. She spoke her mind and lived by her own rules.

I did a production of Edward Albee's *A Delicate Balance* on Broadway with her for about eight months. Elaine could take up a week of posts all by herself, but she very well may be one of the most challenging people to work with that I have ever encountered. It's not that she was mean—she wasn't at all—she had a huge heart underneath it all. It's that she could only thrive in utter chaos offstage. She changed the rules constantly to throw everything and everybody around her off balance.

She was, I think, terrified of being onstage. She was getting older and memorizing lines was getting more difficult. She was an alcoholic in recovery, although after our run and for the last few years of her life she started drinking again because I guess, what the heck. Alcohol had given her the courage to go on stage in the early part of her career but without it, she needed something else, so she created mayhem.

She never actually broke any union rules that I can remember—her terror meant that she was usually at the theatre quite early so that she could review her lines with me. She was a devout Catholic and very much believed in a higher power.

She yelled all the time. She liked me and still yelled at me all the time. Once in the middle of a tirade, she stopped for a second, looked at me, and said, "Gosh, I love yelling at you." I had to laugh. She drove her co-stars insane. Once she had stirred everything up backstage to the level of chaos she needed, she was then able to go out on stage and act. Everybody else would be reeling, but she was ready.

Second-guessing her was impossible. She was much too smart and intuitive for me to be able to do that, so I just went with it. She respected me enough that she complied with some of the things that I asked her to do. I didn't flinch in front of her, and I think she liked me for that.

If you are going to be the President of the United States, you need to be prepared for attacks from millions of people just like Elaine Stritch. You are never going to make everybody happy, that's not actually what the job is. The job is to provide leadership. Leadership rarely makes you popular across the boards. You aren't going to make the right decisions most of the time, but you are going to make decisions that at least start the discussion going. You may end up having to backtrack and rethink what you decided, but that doesn't change the fact that your initial decision is what was necessary to start the process.

Our lack of strong central leadership is the single greatest crisis that we are currently experiencing. Even under past Presidents, the worst of them made decisions that allowed discussions and arguments to occur. Some officials would support those decisions and implement them, and some would try and fight them. Regardless, they would still be obligated to follow those decisions under the law. The country moved forward and with it, we, the people. We weren't always happy about where we were going, but we were at least moving forward.

Our current President is simply not leading at all. He is making no decisions. By all reports, he is not aware of what is going on in the country because he doesn't read any of his daily briefings. He reportedly does not want to know. He does not believe that it is his responsibility. He was more than happy to be the guy hurling criticism at whomever the President was via Twitter, but it appears that he does not want to be the President, himself, at all. Being the point at which the buck stops is a terrifying responsibility. In his heart, I think that what he wants is to be led and then be able to complain about it.

So, here we are with no central leader and, as a result, 50 different leaders running around on the state level trying to figure out how to manage on their own. Some of the Governors have banded together, like ours in the Northeast, to try and make unilateral decisions that are hopefully good for everyone. Some are just out at sea without somebody above to guide them.

Here in Provincetown, somebody in charge has told everyone what to do. People in positions underneath that person are carrying out those orders and enforcing them. There's a level of calm here that doesn't seem to be occurring in many other places. Like it or not, everybody here knows what is expected of them and they are doing it.

Wearing masks is non-negotiable, so rather than obsessing about whether to wear them, they are, instead, focused on other things. And enjoying themselves.

Being told what to do, sometimes, is a freeing experience. Somebody else is worrying about it so that I don't have to. I like being in charge at the level I am usually in charge. There is always somebody above me steering the ship. I respect and admire those people who are willing to be the ones at the top. I hope we get one of them in November.

August 8, 2020

The United States hit 5 million new cases as of this weekend just 17 days after reaching 4 million.

Cape Cod extends eastward away from Boston like a flexed arm with its hand bent back towards the shoulder. Provincetown sits at the tip of its fingers.

I was talking with a local who owns and runs a jewelry store on Commercial Street yesterday. She said that from the point where Provincetown is situated down through the next three big towns, which is about halfway to the elbow, the population tends to skew Democratic. After that, heading towards Boston, they lean more towards the Republican side.

When Europeans first landed in Provincetown in 1602, the area was settled by the Nauset tribe. The sailors caught a huge quantity of cod so named what is now Provincetown, Cape Cod. It wasn't until later that the name got applied to the whole area that it now covers. Eighteen years later, the Mayflower landed here, and this is where the Mayflower Compact was drawn up and signed. Eventually, the pilgrims moved across the bay and settled permanently in Plymouth, but the area remained a popular fishing ground for the colony. In 1654 the Governor of the Plymouth Colony bought this land from the Nauset Chief for two brass kettles, six coats, twelve hoes, twelve axes, twelve knives, and a box.

After the American Revolution, the area grew into a major fishing and whaling center. By the 1890s it had also become popular with writers and artists and had started to become a popular destination for summer tourists. A sizable population of Portuguese sailors from the Azores settled here. The Portuguese Bakery, which catered to the sailors, was opened on

Commercial Street in about 1900. It is extremely popular to this day, and you need to get up early in the morning if you want to get a fresh buttered Portuguese sweet roll before their stock runs out.

In 1898, a huge storm called the Portland Gale largely destroyed the fishing industry. The area was fished out. The town's artists moved into the abandoned fishing buildings where they still are. Contemporary Commercial Street is lined with art galleries housed in all sorts of different-looking buildings. In the 1960s, Provincetown became popular with hippies. Many of them moved out here and opened groovy businesses like hand-tooled leather shops, cafes, and head shops. Many of those are still here as well.

Back in the early 1900s, the area started also started attracting a sizable gay population. Drag Queens were performing here as early as the 1940s. The Provincetown Business Guild was formed in 1978 to help promote gay tourism. Nowadays, more than 200 local businesses still contribute to its ongoing work. The 2010 census showed that there were 163.1 same-sex couples for every 1000—the highest rate in the country.

The Provincetown Players started performing on the porch of a summer rental in 1915. The group of writers and artists who participated returned to New York's Greenwich Village at the end of the season and encouraged a much wider group to return here with them the next summer. Among the people who came up the next year was the journalist and poet John Reed. He invited his friend Eugene O'Neill who, apparently unbeknownst to him, was having an affair with his wife, writer Louise Bryant.

Warren Beatty wrote, directed, and starred in one of my favorite movies of all time, *Reds*, which is all about Reed. Beatty (Reed), Diane Keaton (Bryant), and Jack Nicholson (O'Neill) were all nominated for Oscars in 1982. Almost everything about the movie was nominated including the movie itself. Maureen Stapleton won for her portrayal of activist Emma Goldman and Beatty won Best Director. It's a fantastic film that touches on all of this. I am sure I have seen it at least ten times.

As of 1916, O'Neill had never had one of his plays performed. His famous actor father (James O'Neill who was portrayed in *Long Day's Journey into Night*) had bankrolled the publication of a collection of his, at that point, unproduced work, but the Provincetown Players weren't impressed by any of it. That summer, however, he read for them a play he had written called *Bound East for Cardiff*. In it, a sailor lies dying out at sea on a ship. He talks to his mate, while a storm rages around the two of them. The two sailors' language is crude as befitting who they are, which was something that audiences at the time were not used to hearing.

Susan Glaspell, a novelist and one of the founders of the Players said that when they all heard O'Neill read them the play for the first time that the group finally "knew what they were for". The Provincetown Players occupied a building out on a wharf where the sounds of the fishermen and the waves from the surrounding sea only added to the performance. The company got a little attention from some Boston newspapers and that fall, performed a series of the plays back in New York City including *Bound East for Cardiff.*

In the first two years of the Provincetown Players, Eugene O'Neill had six of his plays performed. They took over an abandoned stable at 133 MacDougal Street in the Village and converted it into a theatre. In 1920, O'Neill's play *The Emperor Jones* premiered there starring the great African American actor, Charles Gilpin. He was the first black actor to ever receive the Drama League award and be listed in their annual compilation of the ten most influential people in theatre of the year. From its founding on, the Provincetown Players was also notable for the large percentage of women that made up its management team as well as those who were represented onstage as playwrights.

The Provincetown Players only performed for two seasons out here on the Cape but lasted for six seasons back in New York. After they disbanded, associates kept the name and mission going until the Stock Market crash of 1929 when they were forced to shutter for good. Despite that, the theatre and its name lived on. Edward Albee's first play to be performed in New York, the one-act *The Zoo Story*, premiered there. Writers such as Sam Shepard and John Guare and David Mamet had premieres of their work in that theatre. Charles Busch's *Vampire Lesbians of Sodom* ran there for five years. In 2008, the original structure was torn down but the new building that went up in its place incorporated a comparable space that is still an active theatre to this day and still called the Provincetown Playhouse.

The Spanish Flu pandemic struck two years after the final performance of the Players in Provincetown. On August 26, 1918, several sailors on Commonwealth Pier in Boston reported in sick. By the next day, there were eight new cases. The day after that, there were 58. Ten days later, on September 7, it was reported that Provincetown had 415 cases. There were no doctors or nurses here because they had all been drafted into World War I. The Unitarian Universalist Meetinghouse on Commercial Street opened its doors and became a makeshift hospital. A total of 47 people in Provincetown died over seven months which works out to be one person every four days in this small town. Local lore says that the ghosts of the victims still roam the halls of the Meetinghouse.

Looking at the news on TV this morning, there seems to be just a lot of the same happening. We are in a sort of holding pattern. The Democrats and the White House are deadlocked over the stimulus plan. The President is threatening to issue some sort of an executive order if an agreement can't be reached, but it is unclear if that will have any legal basis. Meanwhile, we will likely hit five million cases of COVID-19 nationwide by tomorrow or the next day.

Michael's making breakfast. It's a beautiful day. Not too hot. We are looking at a perfect beach day. Later, we are going to have dinner with one of my college roommates and his partner in town. Before that, I will drag Michael down to Gosnold Street, and we will try and see where the original wharf was that held the Provincetown Players theatre. We will also stop by and pay our respects to the specters of the 1918 pandemic at the Meetinghouse. Maybe later, we will re-watch *Reds*.

Out here, we are surrounded by ghosts from the past. I'd like to hear what they have to say.

August 10, 2020
424,272 Total Reported Cases in New York.

I had a dream last night that I was working. In my dream, I was just talking to an actor about a moment in a show. It was all utterly ordinary in every way except that when I woke up it sank in all over again that it's been five months since I've had any such conversation with anyone.

The Senate and the House are still deadlocked over what to do about continuing aid to the unemployed. Bored with this, the man who is currently occupying the White House grandly stepped in and signed four executive orders on Saturday that he swears will fix it all. He rose above the petty squabbling of Congress and acted himself regarding the stimulus package seemingly thinking that it was constitutional that he could. The measures not only fall outside of the purview of his office but even were they enacted would do little or nothing to help lessen our current economic crisis.

It is this issue more than any other that is a real head-scratcher for me in terms of why people support this President and the GOP. These Republicans are desperate to stop Medicare and Social Security completely, something countless numbers of their supporters desperately need and rely on. To be fair, at this moment, the President's fixation on eliminating payroll taxes has little support from either side of the aisle. The President has no power to levy or control taxes.

We are heading back to New York tomorrow. It's hard to believe that a week has already gone by. There's no real reason to go home, it's not like we are going back to work, we just feel ready. I also miss the cat.

The cat, I am sure, does not miss us at all. I do not doubt that our friend who is staying with him is paying him far more attention than we ever do. He is more than happy to give his love and affection to whoever is in front of him at that moment in time. You feed him and he loves you unconditionally. Until the next person comes along.

We had a great day yesterday hanging out at the beach with my junior year college roommate and his boyfriend. It was completely unplanned. We just happened to be going to the same beach, so we all spent the day together. It has been thirty-eight years since he and I first met and roomed together which seems as inconceivable as not working for five months does. We are a little older, perhaps, but nothing else has changed. We just picked back up where we left off.

Thirty-eight years, five months, a week, it's all just time. The person I consider one of my professional mentors once said something to me that changed the way I looked at going through difficult things. I was working on a very complicated show, and I was fretting that we wouldn't have enough time to get it all done. My friend said that whatever happened, good or bad, that at some point it would be the day after opening night. In other words, no matter how difficult it was that there would eventually reach a point when it was all in the past.

What we are going through now is no different. In the future, this will be something that we are all looking back on rather than worrying about getting through. We will get through this, and it will be something that we all share in our collective pasts and tell stories about.

So, it makes much more sense to choose to be interested rather than scared. Just think how it will feel ages from now when we work with somebody younger who hasn't been born as of this year. We'll talk about this with them, and they'll think we are crazy and just smile and nod until they can get away.

You think that won't happen? Just wait.

August 11, 2020

424,854 Total Reported Cases in New York. 32,603 Deaths.

Provincetown has hearts all over the place. Red painted hearts on old wooden pallets and weathered pieces of plywood lean against the sides of trees and houses. Somebody started making smaller versions of them using wooden paint stirrers which are now in the windows of shops up and down Commercial Street. They seem to have started as a thank you to essential workers and health care practitioners but now their mission has expanded. Now the hearts seem to signify a general sense of community—of people looking out for each other and taking care of each other.

This morning, we are heading back down to New York. I am grateful to have been here and already looking forward to coming back. It's been a beautiful break from our break.

August 12, 2020
425,318 Total Reported Cases in New York.

It is good to be home in New York. I dropped the rental car off all the way uptown in Washington Heights then walked back home down through Harlem. Like any summer day, people were out on the streets, A few hydrants were open to provide a cool spray of relief from the heat. Small groups of folks were playing dominoes in shady areas. For the most part, people wore masks. They had them down while they were playing, but when somebody got up to go somewhere, they pulled them back up.

The presumptive Democratic nominee Joe Biden finally announced that Kamala Harris is who is going to join him on the ticket as his running mate. The decision was a long time in coming.

Former Vice President Biden had already told us that he was going to choose a woman. In part because of the Black Lives Movement, it also seemed likely that he would choose somebody of color.

The announcement of a strong, experienced, and seasoned Democratic ticket comes at the precise moment when our current lack of leadership seems to be having its worst effect. As schools reopen at the frantic urging of the White House, reports are coming in about a rise in case numbers among children. One report says that case numbers among kids have risen 90% in the last month. A student was suspended in a Georgia school for posting a picture of a hallway crowded with mask-less kids between classes. Now nine students in that school have tested positive for COVID-19.

The most visible event involving supporters of the current Administration was a giant motorcycle rally in Sturgis, South Dakota that was expected to attract northwards of 250,000 people. Pictures from that event show massive crowds, none of them wearing masks, all crammed in together, partying, on the streets of that small town. At about the same time, Florida broke its record for the most COVID-19-related deaths in a single day yesterday with 132 victims. Georgia saw its largest single-day increase of deaths with 137 people perishing there.

Two weeks ago, businessman Herman Cain who ran for President in 2012 passed away from the virus after attending the President's indoor political rally in Tulsa, Oklahoma, and not wearing a mask.

The President doesn't seem to know what to make of Kamala Harris. In the same breath, he is trying to claim that not only is she too tough on crime but also that she wants to undermine the nation's police departments. He thinks she was "nasty" to Justice Kavanaugh during his confirmation hearings. He is clearly at a loss.

I take a great deal of comfort reading liberal friends' comments that Kamala Harris is the safe choice for the Democratic ticket in the 2020 Presidential election. If an educated biracial Black and Asian female candidate can be seen to be the safest choice that Joe Biden could make as a running mate, then there is hope for us as a country yet.

"I am so ready to go to work" is how Senator Harris responded to Vice President Biden in their taped phone conversation yesterday. Good, because the rest of us are too.

I, too, am ready to work. Five months without an industry to work in has made me realize how much I need it. With the announcement, yesterday, for the first time in a very long while I felt a feeling that I haven't had in quite a while. I didn't realize how much I was missing it until yesterday. The feeling rushed in like the ocean waves I spent last week fixated on.

It was Hope.

AUGUST 13, 2020

Democratic Ticket Nominees Biden and Harris call for all Americans to wear masks.

It's raining. Drops are clattering on the air conditioning units and low rolling thunder is echoing off the tall buildings all around us. It looks like this is going to last all day. The cat, I am sure, is going to remain hidden for the duration.

When retail stores reopened in New York City a short time ago, some people from the surrounding boroughs took trips in to see the city. Stores in Times Square were open, but they were still not getting the massive foot traffic that they had come to expect and rely on in the past. Even so, people had a bit of spending money thanks to the government's weekly payments so some shopped. It's only been two weeks since the extra government payments have stopped, but there is already a noticeable difference in the vibe of the area. Nobody out on the street was carrying a shopping bag.

There is trash on the streets. Food wrappers and old coffee cups blow back and forth in the gutters. Stores are advertising big sales to try and attract the few shoppers that might be out there. Some of those stores have now closed. The huge MacDonald's restaurant on the south side of 42nd across from the New Victory Theatre is completely closed and all evidence of it ever having been there is gone. The PAX restaurant next to the New 42nd Street Studios which was where all of us got coffee and salads when we were rehearsing shows there, is closed for good, too. Nothing much is open along most of the stretch.

As I walked towards 8th Avenue, I passed by a couple of guys leaning against an empty building. One of them spoke out and said, "Hey, you dropped your bag of marijuana," and held up a bag of weed. It felt like I was back in the 1980s.

139 of New York's 700 hotels are now being used by the city to house the homeless. 13,000 people who would normally be accommodated in homeless shelters are being housed in otherwise shut-down hotels throughout the area. The homeless shelters, where everyone is kept together, were all seeing spikes in virus cases.

The mayor and the government of New York are refusing to release the full list of hotels they are making use of, and they won't tell anyone how much it is costing. The Daily Mail in the UK found out from an apparent inside source that this is costing the already strapped city about $2 million a night.

Mayor de Blasio says that there is a strong support structure in place to provide counseling services for these people, large percentages of whom suffer from varying degrees of mental illness, but interviews with residents belie that. There is also no visible police presence around any of these places. Add to this that the city has also released some prison inmates early from Riker's Island because of the COVID-19 situation there and placed them in these hotels, too. It is no wonder that the city is starting to feel like it did when I first started living here.

New York City will survive this. It's nothing if not resilient. We seem to have managed to take everything that's been thrown at us in the past and figure out what to do. I do not doubt that we will be able to do it again, but it would be nice not to have everything thrown at us at once. There is an honest-to-goodness serious homeless problem in the City of New York. Nobody disputes that and nobody wants to see these people just shipped off to somewhere else. This current solution, however, is creating more new problems than it is solving.

We can take the truth. I think that we were so successful at flattening our curve in part because our Governor didn't sugarcoat how serious the situation was that we were in. We got what was going on and reacted accordingly. I wish our mayor had the same faith in us. We can take it.

August 14, 2020
426,610 Total Reported Cases in New York. 32,631 Deaths.

Before everything shut down in March, I was trying to figure out how to slow down the amount of work that I was doing. I was always extremely busy. There were some days that I would wake up in the morning with so many things on my schedule for the day that it seemed impossible that I was going to be able to accomplish everything. Between auditions, rehearsals, meetings, theatre-going, and social engagements there was often no blank space on my calendar at all.

It turns out that the annoying little things that I've spent years thinking, "If I only had the time" could all be accomplished in about two weeks.

My father could never understand how I could stand being unemployed all the time. At some point when my sister and I were kids, my dad lost his job at a company that he had worked at for at least 20 years. I remember it being a big deal at the time and there being a lot of tension around it. He ultimately found another job. One, I think, that he preferred. I don't remember how long he was without a job, but I don't think it was more than a few months. Still, it was traumatic.

When I was working on a show that was closing, there was always a part of me that was looking forward to the break. It was a stressful break because I rarely knew what my next job was going to be. I always had faith, though, that I would eventually get another show. There were always corporate events to do as filler.

I am trying to remember the last time that I had to take a job completely outside of theatre and I think that it was in 1987. It was at an IT company on Park Avenue South. They didn't call it an IT company because it was 33 years ago, and that concept didn't exist yet. They did something like setting up computers in offices, but this was before we all had computers ourselves. Anyway, I worked as a receptionist for them.

It was a tedious place to work. The guys who worked there were all incredibly impressed with their positions and enjoyed hanging out at the front desk and teasing me for being in the "arts". This may be hard to believe but this was before cell phones. We had answering services. People would call into the service and leave a message and then we had to call in to check them. Manning the phones at the front desk of this company was the perfect job in terms of being able to call in and check my messages— something I did about every ten minutes.

On a particularly trying day, I got a message wanting to know how soon I could get to Hamilton, Canada to join up with a tour of *West Side Story* starring soap star Jack Wagner. I assumed that soon meant in a week or two, but I was asked if I could go to the office right away to sign a contract and then fly out that afternoon.

I hung up the phone, picked up my backpack, and walked right out of the office without telling anyone I was leaving. I never picked up my last paycheck and never again talked to anyone there. It was a totally satisfying empowering moment.

The *West Side Story* tour only lasted a few weeks before it folded, and I cannot remember what I did after that. I don't think that I ever had to take another job that wasn't somehow connected to performance in some way. 2005, the year that we opened *Jersey Boys* on Broadway, was the first time in my entire professional life that I didn't have to claim for even one week of unemployment that year. That held true until this past March 16.

I was enjoying not having anything on the calendar for a while. Honestly, I don't need to go back to an over-full schedule. I do need, however, to get back to work on some level.

The Senate is on a month-long break. Four weeks is a long time during a crisis, for them not to be working. While they are kicking back at the beach, let's get busy and give them something truly exciting to come back to.

Loyal opposition.

August 15, 2020
13 New Reported Cases in New Zealand.

Our news is full of events being reported that would have been impossible to imagine even six months ago. While these daily ever more bizarre and extreme stories unfold, the seemingly more mundane aspects of our lives haven't stopped. Bills still need to be paid or put off. Homes are being moved out of or into. People are getting married. People are breaking up. Children are being born and friends and family are passing away.

Earlier this week, my Aunt Barbara lost her fight with cancer in Johannesburg, South Africa.

Barbara was two years younger than my mother and, like her, was born in India. Several months ago, when we knew that her illness was getting serious, I had proposed to her that she let me interview her about her life, but she didn't respond so I didn't push it. Like my mother, she moved to England from South Africa when she was old enough to go on her own. Unlike my mother who had planned on being a nurse, my aunt went to London to study acting. She attended the Webber Douglas Academy of Dramatic Art.

I do wish that I'd had the opportunity to hear about what that was like. As far as I know, she never actually acted professionally. Instead, she met and married my Uncle Carlo. From Naples, he always reminded me of a somewhat less surreal Salvador Dali. They ended up settling and raising their family in South Africa.

My mother and my aunt were close in later years but that wasn't always the case. I remember when my sister and I were still quite young, that we all went to stay with them in Durban. At some point, they fought about something, and my mother packed my sister and me up and we left the house. I don't think that they spoke after that for several years.

Thankfully, they eventually moved past it. Towards the end of the run of *Jersey Boys* in South Africa, my mother took Michael and me along with my sister and her family on an epic safari trip. Along with my Aunt Barbara, we all went to a private game reserve called Thula Thula.

It is a reserve that was established by Lawrence Anthony who wrote the wonderful book, *The Elephant Whisperer*. We had an amazing and memorable time together. My sister's kids called her Sister Grandma.

With my family being so scattered around the globe it's never been easy for all of us to gather. I'm grateful that we all had that time to spend with Aunt Barbara and that my niece and nephew got to meet her and get to know her a bit. The international roll-out of *Jersey Boys* allowed me to reconnect with most of my family including all my first cousins. I've been able to spend time with my Australian uncle's children in Australia and with my aunt's two sons—one who lives in South Africa and the other who lives with his family in Toronto. We are hoping, at some point, to be able to figure out a time when all of us can meet up in one place.

Jersey Boys, in addition, to bringing me together with my family, has also brought me together with an incredible team of truly creative and wonderful people. One of those people was our Tony Award-winning lighting designer Howell Binkley who lost his fight with cancer just yesterday.

Howell Binkley lit some of the most successful shows in Broadway history. When we shut everything down five months ago, he had four shows running in New York—*Jersey Boys*, *Ain't Too Proud*, *Come from Away*, and a little show called *Hamilton*. His list of credits is absurdly long and awe-inspiring. He never stopped working and was usually doing many productions at the same time.

I was lucky enough to be able to work with him on two different shows—*Summer, the Donna Summer Musical*, and *Jersey Boys*. We teched *Summer* together twice and *Jersey Boys* so many times I couldn't possibly be able to come up with a number.

For everyone who has watched *Hamilton* on Disney Plus, I would urge you to go back and watch it again and just look at what he does with the lights. His work, like all of what we do in the theatre, was of the moment, but *Hamilton* captured it on film.

In recent years Howell started posting pictures of paintings online—some well-known, some more obscure—that struck him in some way. Every day he'd post a different picture. All the paintings were united by their celebration of light. He loved light. I miss those daily paintings.

More than just his artistry, Howell was a kind, generous and gentle man. We were supposed to work on a new project together in the spring. It saddens me more than I can say that we won't be doing that now. The sound of that easy southern drawl asking, "Are you waiting for me?" over the headset during tech is something I already miss.

Losing both my Aunt Barbara and Howell within days of each other is sadly overwhelming.

In this same period, however, two of my friends have given birth to beautiful baby boys. These new babies will likely never know a world without COVID-19. They will never know either my Aunt Barbara but maybe one day they will meet her Canadian grandsons. They will never know Howell but maybe one day they will see one of his shows. Life goes on.

People are entering and exiting this world as they always have. Making their debuts and taking their final bows. It's a never-ending performance. I am grateful to have been able to travel through this life for a bit with both remarkable people. R.I.P. Barbara and Howell.

And, welcome to the world kids. Sorry that it's a bit of a mess now. We're a bit distracted these days. Hang out for a second while we try and clean it up.

August 17, 2020
428,385 Total Reported Cases in New York.

Everyone who has been paying high New York City rental and mortgage rates suddenly has no income, so, they are leaving the city—especially if they have kids. They are moving to places where their kids don't have to be cooped up in a small apartment. Some people are even moving back in with their parents temporarily to save money.

Working from home is getting to be more and more popular. I'm not sure that when everything opens again that the current high level of output is going to continue. People are going to get distracted when there are other things to do. Going to a place to work focuses you. Human beings are not solitary creatures. We are not designed that way. After all, the worst punishment you can (legally) give someone in prison is solitary confinement. When someone is isolated for too long, they go insane.

While it may seem that there is no way out of this, there is. Yes, things will change. We, as human beings, however, are just not going to change that much. We will still need to be around each other. We will still need each other's energy because that is how we were created.

Theatre is hard work and, sadly, often prone to devastating failure. What gets us all through it is the fact that we create a family every time we dive into a new project. Sure, there's always a crazy Aunt Betty and nobody likes Cousin Morty, but we all end up being in it together and that communal supportive energy is what allows the success to happen. We all get very close, very quickly.

We can't do that when we are by ourselves looking at the world through a screen.

Some of the people who have moved out of the city will, indeed, find new lives wherever they have ended up. Despite that, there will always be new, excited people coming in—maybe from those very same places—to occupy their empty apartments.

New York is not going to be empty for long.

August 18, 2020
428,923 Total Reported Cases in New York. 32,668 Deaths.

I am writing this morning from a blissfully quiet spot overlooking the Delaware River in New Hope, Pennsylvania. I am on my way to North Dakota. That may be one of the more surreal sentences that I have written in a while. As I think about what we are all experiencing these days, though, perhaps it doesn't even rate.

Of all the states in the union, the single one that I have never been to is North Dakota. That is the sole reason that I am going there. The reason that I am going right now is that I have reached the point where have to go somewhere on my own or else I will lose my mind. "On my own" is the operative part of that sentence.

Traveling on my own has always been something that I've thoroughly enjoyed. I used to dream of hiking the Appalachian Trail solo when I was a kid. Don't get me wrong, I love traveling with Michael and I have several friends who are excellent travel companions—one is great for hiking, another is great for temples in Southeast Asia—but I do love being out on my own.

As I got older, hiking the Trail slowly fell off my bucket list. What replaced that for me is going to places that are as different from where I live as I can find. I love to see how other people work and live their lives. Sometimes I meet people while I am traveling and fall into conversations, but most often I just keep to myself and watch.

Last night was the first night of the Democratic National Convention. For the first time in its history, nobody physically gathered. Instead, it streamed virtually. It was a moving night with inspiring speakers.

The evening, however, belonged to former First Lady, Michelle Obama. In her inspiring and moving 18-minute speech, she hammered home the need for all of us to vote. Her necklace is trending like mad today. It spelled out the word "vote" in gold letters. For somebody who claims that they don't want to be in politics, it was the kind of speech that launches a career.

She pulled no punches in her condemnation of the current President's ability to lead. She excoriated him for how he has divided our country and for his inability to govern. "Donald Trump is the wrong president for our country. He has had more than enough time to prove that he can do the job, but he is clearly in over his head. He cannot meet this moment. He simply cannot be who we need him to be for us. It is what it is," she said. That last line is a reference to the cavalier way he responded to the escalating death toll the virus has taken on our fellow citizens.

As if to prove what she was saying about his inability to bring us together, during the convention broadcast last night, the President retweeted a post that said, "Leave Democrat cities. Let them rot…. [Walk Away] from the radical left. And do it quickly."

I've given myself four days to get to North Dakota and four days to get back. I am interested in seeing other parts of the country and how they are dealing with all of this. This is a unique time in our history. We seem to be as divided a nation as we were leading up to the Civil War. Neither side is willing to budge. I want to see what is really going on.

New Hope is about an hour and a half southwest of New York City. It was considered the halfway point between New York City and Philadelphia. In days past, travelers would stay the night and then be ferried across the river in the morning. Before General George Washington's famous crossing of the Delaware during the American Revolution, he is said to have spent the night here. He then destroyed the ferry so that the British couldn't follow him.

These days it is a quaint little town that relies heavily on tourism. The Bucks County Playhouse is a well-known local theatre situated right on the river. Aside from having North Dakota as my ultimate destination, I have no real idea where I am going. For the next few days, I am just heading west. I'd say that I am enjoying the wind through my hair, but who are we kidding. The windows are up, and the AC is on.

I'm looking forward to missing Michael.

August 19, 2020
429,440 Total Reported Cases in New York.

This morning I am sitting by the harbor right next to the Rock and Roll Hall of Fame in Cleveland, Ohio. It is almost completely devoid of people out here. When I drove into the city during what should have been the height of rush hour, there was almost no traffic.

I spent last night in Youngstown, Ohio at their Downtown Hilton. Pennsylvania is an endlessly wide state, and it takes forever to drive through it. Youngstown is just a few miles over the border, but I didn't want to wake up today and still be in Pennsylvania, so I pushed through to get there.

In the mid-1890s a Jewish immigrant family from Poland settled in Youngstown. The father opened a meat market and a shoe repair shop. His three sons went to school and worked in his businesses in the afternoons and evenings. In 1905, the brothers pooled their resources and bought a projector. They opened a small theatre, the first of several, and started becoming successful. The three brothers—Albert, Sam, and Jack—eventually moved to New York and then to Hollywood. They founded their company, Warner Brothers, in 1925.

In 1931, the family gathered again in Youngstown to open a movie palace in honor of their brother Sam who had passed away a few years before but also to thank the town for giving them their start. The theatre, now called the DeYor Performing Arts Center, is where *Jersey Boys* played once.

When I got to the hotel in Youngstown last night, there were very few people there. The receptionist was behind a plexiglass partition and wearing a mask. I got my bag with two water bottles and my freshly baked cookie and headed up. The room's door had been sealed with a sticker that said, "Hilton Clear Stay" and a had link to learn more about the measures that were taken to sanitize it. They also included the Lysol logo on it.

Inside the room, the TV remote had a cover saying that it, too, had been sanitized. In the bathroom on the mirror was another blue sticker that said that nobody would come into the room to clean during my stay unless I requested it. I came in and left the hotel without ever running into another person.

Last night was the second night of the Democratic Convention. The roll call of each state and territory announcing their delegate counts was particularly moving. Each state and territory chose its own people to represent them. Black, White, Native American, Latinx, and Polynesian citizens created a true rainbow montage of people. In maybe the most moving moment of it, the parents of Matthew Sheppard, the gay University of Wyoming student who brutally tortured and left to die on a fence in Laramie in 1998, read out Wyoming's delegate votes.

As expected, former Vice President Joe Biden secured the nomination.

I have a timed ticket to go into the Rock and Roll Hall of Fame in a few minutes. I am going to pay my respects to the Four Seasons and to Donna Summer whose lives have been the basis for two of my more recent jobs. I am interested to see how they deal with social distancing and everything else that we are figuring out how to adjust these days. More than anything, though, I am looking forward to a trip through a museum.

And then? Back on the road again and heading west.

August 20, 2020
430,123 Total Reported Cases in New York. 32,671 Deaths.

Today, I am sitting in Millennium Park in Chicago, Illinois staring at the Bean.

That's not its official name, of course. When the artist Anish Kapoor finished it in 2006, he, somewhat pretentiously, called it *Cloud Gate*. It's an enormous 66-foot-long and 42-foot-high rounded concave chamber covered seamlessly in highly polished and reflective steel plates.

It looks like an enormous blob of mercury, or, in truth, like a big, mirrored bean.

At first, people made fun of it, but now it is a beloved icon of the city. People flock to it to take selfies. This morning the entire park is completely barricaded and there is only one entrance in. There is a limit to how many visitors are allowed in at any one time. As I write this, I'm it.

Chicago is a great city and one that I have been to many times. I spent two months here with *The Phantom of the Opera* twenty-five years ago and I've been coming back ever since. We did the pre-Broadway run of the musical *Sweet Smell of Success* here. I was here with the first national tour of *Wicked*. I've stage managed both Patti LuPone and Mandy Patinkin's concerts here. We also ran *Jersey Boys* here for two years then returned for several shorter engagements after we closed, so I've been here a lot.

Last week, Chicago fell victim to the same looting and violence that we saw happen in other places around the country. It seems to have been ignited by a false rumor that police had shot and killed a black child. In reality, it appears that they shot and injured a twenty-year-old man who had run from them and had turned to fire a gun. The incident has exposed problems with the city's Police Department policies. For one thing, the officers who shot the young man, Latrell Allen, were part of a special squad who were not required to wear body cameras. The officers claim that they recovered his gun from the area. In the past, there have been reports that the Chicago PD has planted guns to cover up shootings of unarmed individuals, so people are understandably wary of accepting that. Without the body camera footage, it comes down to the word of the officers who nobody trusts these days.

Unsurprisingly, rioting and looting broke out. Drawbridges were raised to keep people from entering the city and freeways were shut down. Hundreds of demonstrators fought with the police on Chicago's Magnificent Mile, the city's premier upscale shopping district.

Last night, as I was walking around, Chicago felt exactly like New York City did when, following our own spate of violence, the curfew was imposed. Many stores up and down Michigan Avenue have been boarded up. There were police cars with flashing lights up and down the entire length from the Water Tower down to the river. There were also police cars parked up and down State Street in front of the Chicago Theatre and down by the old Marshall Field's store. There were a few people out and about and a couple of restaurants were open, but the constantly flashing lights from the police cruisers put too high a charged energy in the air for anybody to relax.

Last night was the third night of the Democratic Convention. President Obama delivered an amazing speech. What a difference it makes listening to somebody intelligent, speaking in well-thought-out sentences. I can't remember him ever being that blunt. I can't remember any ex-President, ever, being so pointedly direct in the condemnation of the current sitting President. It is a measure, of how dire things have become, that we are continually being warned that the very basis of our national Democracy is in danger of being destroyed.

Last night, Senator Kamala Harris of California became the first African American woman to be officially nominated for a major party ticket. Her nomination came a day after the 100th anniversary of the passage of the 19th Amendment to the Constitution that finally gave women the right to vote. While the 19th Amendment in theory made that happen, it wasn't until the Civil Rights movement in the 1960s that any of the women in Senator Harris's family would be able to go to the polls. Poll taxes, literacy tests, fraud, and basic intimidation kept them from being able to exercise their rights as American Citizens until we all stood up and said, "No."

I just walked down State Street back to my hotel to pick up my stuff and head out. There are so many more homeless people out on the streets here than I ever remember seeing. As I was walking, a guy in a rainbow sequined shirt driving a beat-up old car drove down into each block and stopped. He then jumped out and handed every street person he saw a couple of bottles of water. For anyone who doesn't feel like voting, do it for this guy. He is doing everything he can with what means he has, to help. He shouldn't have to be out there doing that.

Chicago has always been one of my favorite cities. Even under these circumstances, I am glad to be back here for a minute. I look forward to coming back and seeing a play at the Goodman or Steppenwolf or Chicago Shakespeare or the Lookingglass or any number of other amazing local theatres. I look forward to walking around in the Art Institute of Chicago and paying my respects to George Seurat's masterpiece, *A Sunday Afternoon on the Island of La Grande Jatte*. I look forward to when the Corner Bakery down the block from where I am staying is open. I look forward to seeing crowds of people reflected in the miraculous surface of the Bean rather than just me and the empty pavement.

We have the power to stop most of what we are all experiencing these days by literally just saying "No". When we vote, our voices are heard. One vote matters a little. Our votes together, matter a lot.

August 21, 2020
430,860 Total Reported Cases in New York.

I spent the early part of this morning at the intersection of 38th and Chicago in Minneapolis.

There's a gas station on one corner and across from it a small convenience store. It's a much nicer area than I was expecting. That is my racial bias showing. The houses and businesses surrounding it look well cared for. This morning people were out working in their yards and walking with their kids.

On May 25, in that same intersection, Police Officer Derek Chauvin ended the life of George Floyd by kneeling on his neck until he suffocated.

For a block or two in either direction, the streets have been closed off and the whole area has been transformed into a vibrant, colorful, messy, and completely heartfelt tribute to Mr. Floyd. In letters about a foot high, the names of other people of color who have lost their lives to law enforcement are painted on Chicago Ave from the blockade up to the intersection.

There are almost too many of them to count. I did my best to read them all.

The gas station has become a sort of open-air teaching area. The business is closed, but this morning somebody was lecturing about how to combat systemic racism. A group of about twenty people stood among the gas pumps, rapt. It looked like Socrates talking to a group of eager students.

In front of the convenience store, a huge memorial has been erected. Thousands of flowers and other tributes are stacked in an orderly pattern radiating out from a central tent. There is a ring of planters with living plants in them surrounding everything. In the center of the intersection is a sculpture of a raised fist. It, too, is surrounded by flowers and stuffed animals, and signs. There are signs and placards everywhere.

The whole thing was not unlike the encampment that emerged in the park across from City Hall in New York City calling for the reform of the NYPD. The difference is that this has an air of permanence about it. While I was there, a Native American man was circling the clenched fist and chanting.

From there, I drove about two miles away to where the Minneapolis Police Third Precinct building stands. It was burnt out and destroyed during the rioting that followed the violence and is now surrounded by high fencing to keep everybody out. The only thing that identifies it is the charred remains of the metal words Minneapolis Police that are still visible along one side.

Joe Biden gave one of the best speeches I have ever heard him give last night during the final day of the Democratic National Convention. It capped off four days of addresses from a diverse and eloquent group of his friends and supporters. It gave me hope that we aren't done yet.

When I first started seeing Michael, he took me to the annual gala of a group called Our Time.

Our Time was founded by Taro Alexander to help kids who stutter. A person who stutters, himself, Taro envisioned a place where kids could get together and be themselves and not worry about being made fun of by anyone. SAY, the Stuttering Association for the Young, as it is called now, works with kids to help them find their voices. They aren't about curing their stutters—nobody knows how to do that. Instead, they give the kids the time and space to be able to express themselves. Posters for the event used to have a line that said, "Running time: 2-6 Hours."

Joe Biden is a person who stutters. Last night, a thirteen-year-old boy named Braydon Harrington from New Hampshire addressed the nation from the Convention. He talked about meeting the former Vice President. "He told me that we were members of the same club. We…. Ssssssss……. ssssssstutter." That singular act of unfathomable bravery by that young man who stood up in front of the whole country to speak was a perfect way to introduce Joe Biden and launch us all into this final election sprint.

I have gotten into the habit of sending my niece and nephew a postcard from everywhere I go. When they were very little, I sent them a laminated map of the world and another of the US so that they could see where I was when the cards arrived. I also started sending one to my aunt who lives in assisted living in Virginia. Then my mother felt left out, so I started sending one to her too. I have also kept a scrapbook since I was ten years old. In it, I put all my theatre stubs, museum admission tickets, fliers from shows I am working on, and postcards. They all end up in one place, so I can remember what I've done and where I've been.

I found a little junk store in Milan that looked like it might have some cards and went in. I could have spent an hour in there. Lots of weird old pieces of furniture and strange machines.

The owner had a small stack of cards but asked me not to buy him out because the guy who printed them had died. Together, we picked out four of them that we each thought were acceptable.

Yesterday, I stopped in De Forest, Wyoming to get gas at a station that had a giant pink elephant in glasses standing next to it. Postcards of the elephant… check. Later in the day, I saw the statue of Paul Bunyan and his blue ox outside of the Logging Museum in Eau Clair, Wisconsin. The museum, itself, was closed but I was happy just to see the big statue. I found some postcards of it at a local gas station.

The intersection of 38th and Chicago here in Minneapolis stands as a reminder of the work that we have as a nation ahead of us. For now, though, I am just going to keep heading west.

August 22, 2020
431,543 Total Reported Cases in New York.

I can finally say that I am now in North Dakota. Mission accomplished! I have visited all 50 of these remarkable United States.

Enough people have North Dakota as their final state to visit that the welcome center in Fargo, has a thing called "Best for Last Club". They gave me a certificate, a sticker, and a t-shirt and took my picture with the medallion on the wall. It was kind of great to have a fuss made over the whole thing.

North Dakota is still in the eastern side of the country. The geographical center of the lower 48 states lies in Lebanon, Kansas. North Dakota, South Dakota, Nebraska, and Kansas are all very roughly the same width and the same rectangular shape, although Colorado cuts a big notch out of Nebraska's southwestern corner. They are stacked on top of each other with North Dakota being at the top of the four and Kansas at the bottom. Lebanon lies on the top edge of Kansas in about the center of the state. Fargo is on the far eastern side of the state. Despite looking enormous on the map, North Dakota is only the 19th largest state in terms of area. It is, however, the fourth smallest in both population and population density. Fargo is the largest city, but Bismarck, in the center, is its capital.

North Dakota was either the 39th or 40th state admitted to the union. Both North and South Dakota were incorporated as states together on November 2, 1889. So that nobody would ever know which one had become a state first, the President, Benjamin Harrison, shuffled the papers as he signed them.

On my way to Jamestown, which is closer to the middle of the state, I detoured up, out of the way, to the tiny town of Blanchard to see the KVLY-TV television transmitting mast. It is out in the middle of nowhere. Flat farmland stretches out as far as the eye can see in every direction. It must be truly awful out there in the middle of winter with all the snow blowing around. The snow would completely cover up what few features there are. The tower doesn't look like much. It is just your basic metal transmission tower sticking up out of the prairie.

What makes it interesting is that up until 2008 when the Burj Kalifa was built in Dubai, the KVLY-TV mast in Blanchard, ND was the tallest man-made structure on the entire planet. The Tokyo Skytree and the Shanghai Tower have now surpassed it as well. I guess I am now going to have to go to Shanghai since I've already visited the other two.

I came to Jamestown to see the world's largest Buffalo. Sadly, it's a statue and not a live animal but it stands 28 feet tall. I can see it from the window of the church where I am sitting writing this, so I'll take a walk over and have a look in a bit. Then I will visit the gift shop. I love a good gift shop. I adore a bad one.

When we were kids, we would go on endlessly long car rides during the summer. How my sister and I survived sitting in the back of an un-airconditioned two-door Ford Maverick, I will never know. We didn't even have windows. The small oval glass would just notch open about an inch.

One summer we drove from New Jersey all the way down to Florida where we got to go to Disney World. Another summer, during the height of the heat, we drove down to New Orleans. We would stop everywhere there was something to see. It would drive my father crazy that my mother, sister, and I would always want to make a beeline for the gift shop. "It's just junk," he would say. He just didn't get it. These days, instead of rubber snakes and pirate coins, I try and limit myself to postcards.

I have already noticed that my postcards to my family are taking much longer to get to them than they ever have in the past. Six states have already sued the United States Postal Service over the diminished services and sixteen more have suits in process. In an address to the Senate yesterday, Postmaster General Louis DeJoy said that all the changes that have been happening were all a normal part of how the USPS does business. The House, however, met today to propose a $25 billion bill to ensure that the USPS stay afloat—especially with the upcoming election just months away. They are going to vote on a bill later today that would provide for all the ballots to be sent first class. The President continues doing everything he can to demonize mail-in voting to keep the communities that tend to use that option the most from voting against him.

There is nothing wrong with voting by mail. It has been around for a very long time. During the Civil War, polling stations were set up in army encampments that would allow soldiers to cast their ballots and six states allowed them to send their votes home by mail. Historically, there has been no more fraud connected with mailed-in ballots than there has been with ballots cast in person at local polling stations.

Yet another crony of the President's has been arrested. On Thursday, his former Chief Strategist, Steve Bannon was taken into custody off a luxury yacht off the coast of Connecticut. He is charged with defrauding the American people by siphoning off donated funds that were meant to build the President's border wall between us and Mexico and then using them for himself. While it is completely unsurprising that Steve Bannon would eventually be arrested for something, it is rather surprising to discover who ultimately arrested him—Postal Workers.

The Postal Service has an armed investigative unit. They typically handle cases that have some connection to the mail service. This isn't new either. The first person in charge of this unit was a guy named William Goddard who was appointed by Postmaster General Benjamin Franklin in 1775 to investigate mail fraud and theft.

Postal workers interviewed Billy the Kid about thefts on the Stagecoach runs—which was how the mail was transported in those days. They interviewed Lee Harvey Oswald about the rifle he used in the killing of President Kennedy because he received it in the mail. They also helped hunt down the mail bomber Ted Kaczynski in 1996. There are about 200 federal crimes that can spark action from the US Postal Service and there are nearly 1,300 inspectors on the force.

Article I, Section 8, Clause 7 of the United States Constitution empowers Congress "To establish Post Offices and Post Roads". Undermining the US Postal service is yet another attempt by this administration to undermine the basic structures of our government. Beyond voting, we rely on the mail for home delivery of our medications, paychecks, unemployment checks, holiday presents, and holiday cards, and, of course, postcards.

Having gotten to my bucket-list goal of stepping foot in North Dakota to complete the set of 50, I now must go all the way back home. I am not going to retrace any of my steps. There are plenty of new things to see out there and to get postcards of.

And I need to find a mailbox.

August 24, 2020
432,558 Total Reported Cases in New York.

I am sitting out in front of the Abraham Lincoln Presidential Library in Springfield, Illinois. I've never been here before.

Our Country's divide is not geographical. It tends to fall more along rural/urban lines with the big cities leaning left and the great open spaces leaning right. That's why we have the Electoral College. It was established by a Constitutional amendment in 1787 to allow states with smaller populations to have equal voting power as states with larger populations. Wyoming with the lowest population in the country, therefore, doesn't get completely marginalized by California which has the largest.

When Abraham Lincoln ran for President in 1860, there were four candidates that year. He ran for the Republicans against John C. Breckinridge who represented the Southern Democratic Party, John Bell from the Constitutional Union Party, and Stephen Douglas who represented the Democratic Party. The country was widely splintered. Lincoln won only 40% of the popular vote. He wasn't even on the ballot in 10 southern states. We think we are a divided nation now, well we actually split in half after this election when the Southern states seceded from the Union.

Going through the Lincoln Presidential Library and Museum this morning was very moving in a way that I wasn't expecting. Up until the point that he was assassinated by John Wilkes Booth in Ford's Theatre, few people much liked Lincoln. The cartoons of the day of him were merciless.

His stance on the institution of slavery made him widely unpopular all over the country—not just in the South. Four slave-owning states did not secede—Kentucky, Missouri, Maryland, and Delaware. Some of their governments split, but they stayed with the North.

Strict abolitionists thought that the Emancipation Proclamation was a pointless exercise. It only applied to the southern states that had left the union. Abraham Lincoln, however, was a politician. He knew he couldn't afford to let those four northern states leave. He was moving forward in steps, and nobody was happy about any of it. Too fast. Too slow. Too strong. Too weak.

Lincoln kept the course. He pushed forward when even his own Cabinet tried to get him to hold off. In his Cabinet were his three rivals for the Republican nomination—William H. Seward (Secretary of State), Salmon P. Chase (Secretary of the Treasury), and Edward Bates (Attorney General). Lincoln united his party and then united a deeply divided United States. Then he was killed, and people were deeply shocked. Their perceptions of him changed.

Springfield, Illinois is a perfect place to visit at this moment in our history. It is a reminder of what this country can be and what we can achieve. If our current President can win the upcoming election through lies and deceit, then what does that say about who we are as a nation now?

August 25, 2020
433,113 Total Reported Cases in New York. 32,715 Deaths.

This road trip started in the middle of the Democratic Convention, and I am ending it up with the start of the Republican Convention. It certainly wasn't planned that way, but the two conventions have been the soundtrack for everything that I have been seeing as I loop around this section of the country. For most of yesterday, I had the radio off. As the sun set, however, and I still had two hours of driving ahead of me, I had to turn it on to keep awake.

It was hard to listen to. Most of the language that the Republicans used throughout the evening seemed to be coded to appeal directly to the President's base. They made the Democrats' plans for affordable housing sound like a leftist plot to destroy the suburbs. They think liberals want to bus in criminals to destroy the property values of wealthy white people.

Listening to all of it sitting alone in the dark was maybe not the best way to end my trip but it certainly kept me alert.

There is a lot to see across this great country. I am glad I took this trip and yes, I do miss Michael. A lot. And the cat. Virtual relationships are only good for so long. It's time to go home.

August 26, 2020
433,595 Total Reported Cases in New York. 32,721 Deaths.

After 3,804 miles in the car, (6122km), I am finally home.

One of the reasons that I wanted to take the trip was to see for myself how people outside of the liberal urban bubble that I have been living in are navigating through these times. In terms of the virus, it is affecting life for everyone, everywhere that I went. Businesses all over were either closed or operating under strong restrictions. People, everywhere I went, were steering clear of each other. For the most part, whether an individual state was mandating masks or merely recommending that they be worn, people were wearing them.

Nightlife is pretty much over everywhere. Very little, if anything, is open after 5 pm anywhere I went. Chicago, which was maybe the biggest city I was in, had some bars that stayed open later, but there were very few people in them. Chicago, of course, is still reeling from their recent spate of violent unrest so people who might ordinarily go out were maybe staying home.

Unsurprisingly, there is very little tourism. Many Museums are still closed. Museums that have opened have timed entries, but not many people seem to be taking advantage of that. The Rock and Roll Hall of Fame in Cleveland which would ordinarily be packed at this time of year had just tens of people inside rather than hundreds. When I went through the Abraham Lincoln Presidential Museum in Springfield, only two other couples were watching the short orientation film with me. We all sat, masked, in a giant triangle about 30 feet apart from each other in an auditorium that had a capacity for several hundred people. I then went through the exhibits basically by myself. Like New York, businesses surrounding these attractions that rely on tourist traffic are either closed or empty.

From the radio I listened to, it is apparent to me that the issues that are of most concern to the general population across the country are our kids going back to school and the sports seasons getting back up and running.

Racial discussions were largely absent from the airwaves west of here. An alarming perception has taken root and is growing, that peaceful protesting and violent rioting and looting are the same things. The Republicans—both their politicians and pundits—are relentlessly pushing this idea. Governor Bill Lee of Tennessee has just signed a bill making it a felony crime for protestors to camp out on state property. A felony conviction means that those people would lose their right to vote.

We live in a remarkable country. It was built on the blood of the Native Americans who were here first and with the blood and agony of the enslaved African Americans who were freighted here to work against their wills. The train tracks that crisscross the vast spaces throughout the continent would not be there without Chinese laborers. Countless immigrants have subsequently arrived here from every corner of the planet—many of whom were persecuted in the places that they fled. We are a people born of trauma.

If the only thing that we judge the success or failure of our country on is our Gross National Product, then we are going to fail. When we broke from England, our *Declaration of Independence* stated that the reason we were forming our own country was that we all felt that we had the right to Life, Liberty, and the pursuit of Happiness.

Our country's people are being routinely killed by law enforcement officers. Our country's people are losing their lives to the coronavirus in unimaginable numbers. Our country's businesses are collapsing, and our people are facing severe economic hardship. We need to help each other heal. Any person's happiness that is built upon the unhappiness of another, is not just. We each have the right to a piece of that happiness. We all deserve a slice of that glorious pie. It's time we make the portions fairer.

I'm glad I took that trip but I'm even more glad to be home. Nothing much has changed here—I was only gone for a week after all—but I was truly reminded that what we have here is well worth fighting for. This country has unlimited potential, but if it is going to continue forward, we will indeed need to fight for it.

August 27, 2020
434,393 Total Reported Cases in New York.

I slept for about ten hours last night. The reason that happened, I think, was a direct result of my decision not to watch the Republican National Convention.

I am not going to watch the Convention tonight either. If I didn't think I could face the Vice President twisting the truth last night, I certainly don't have the stomach to face the President outright lying tonight. While everything that is going on now is dark and anxiety-provoking, there should be some comfort in knowing that history will look back at this with different eyes than people are using to see it now.

Abraham Lincoln was seen as a dangerous agitator who was going to destroy the country because of his stance on slavery. Today, he's a hero. It was thought that the artists who were blacklisted during the McCarthy era were going to destroy the country. They are now viewed as heroes for having stood up for their right to free speech. When Muhammed Ali spoke out against the Vietnam War, he was stripped of his boxing titles and not allowed to fight. It was believed that his views were going to destroy the country. Today he is looked upon as a national icon.

Four years ago, when Colin Kaepernick took the knee, he was a dangerous agitator who was going to destroy football and our country. That opinion is already changing. It's just a matter of time before a huge statue of him kneeling is unveiled—maybe right in front of the football stadium in San Francisco where his team was based.

Mahatma Gandhi, Nelson Mandela, the women who fought for their right to vote, the LGBTQ people who stood up for their right to live as fully recognized people, the list goes on and on and on. History remembers THEM, not the small-minded, cruel, and ignorant people who opposed them. There was also this brown Jewish guy who started preaching a message of love and acceptance 2,000 years ago who was seen as a dangerous agitator. He began a movement that now has 2.3 billion followers around the world.

This Convention will be over tonight, and, in a few days, we will be on to something else, this travesty all but forgotten. I'm going to let it go and get some sleep. I will feel better.

August 28, 2020
435,062 Total Reported Cases in New York.

Hurricane Laura, tied as the strongest hurricane ever to make landfall in the US, has been downgraded to a tropical storm and the Republican National Convention is over. Now we have time to repair, regroup, and prepare for what comes next.

On Tuesday, the Centers for Disease Control and Prevention suddenly modified their guidelines for who should be tested. Asymptomatic people, even if they have recently been exposed to the virus, should not be tested. This goes against all current thinking about the virus and how it spreads. Over half of all infections are thought to have occurred from contact with asymptomatic carriers.

The CDC appears to have bowed to pressure from the Administration to slow down testing.

Gov. Andrew M. Cuomo of New York said, "The only plausible rationale is that they want fewer people taking tests because as the president has said if we don't take tests, you won't know the number of people who are COVID-positive." There is also a very serious backlog in being able to get results from our tests in a reasonable amount of time. This move may have been a way to lighten that load. What it isn't, is a responsible fact and science-based response to the pandemic.

Michael and I really wanted to go to the big Black Lives Matter march in Washington D.C. today, but given my recent cross-country road trip, in an abundance of caution, we decided to stay home.

There are no easy answers to anything that we are all experiencing in these highly charged days. The first step towards solving many of these horrifically complex issues is that our leaders must just simply shut up and listen, themselves. That they can't even seem to do that is, in and of itself, reason enough for a change.

August 29, 2020
435,756 Total Reported Cases in New York.

Yesterday, because we couldn't go to Disney World, Michael and I did the next best thing. We went to the Ikea furniture store.

At any time before this pandemic started, a trip to Ikea would just involve figuring out how to get there. Yesterday, we had to figure out whether we would feel safe going there. Assessing the relative risks of various situations and activities, these days, requires a constant internal and external discussion. It largely falls to us, as individuals, to do the best we can to navigate through these choices.

We know that the virus can be transmitted through droplets that occur when people breathe, cough or sneeze. We now know that the virus can also be transported in the air without being in a droplet—so-called aerosol transmission. The virus can exist for up to 72 hours or even longer on a surface. The only way that the latter can be a problem is if we touch that surface and then physically transport the virus to either our eyes, nose, or mouth with our hands.

The major factors in the transmission of COVID-19 appear to be time and concentration. The longer you are in contact with the virus, the greater the chance that you will become infected. If you spend an hour with an infected person in a small, enclosed room without any air circulation you are almost guaranteed to get it yourself. If you merely pass by that same person outside on the street when there is even a light breeze moving the air around, then you are almost guaranteed NOT to become infected by them. The breeze dissipates the droplets and spreads them around.

Another factor, which is just common sense, is distance. If you talk to someone with a heavy viral load face to face, you are going to be on the receiving end of more of the virus than you would be if you were standing further apart. The recommendation, as we all know, is to maintain a distance of at least 6 feet. "At least," are the operative words. There is no certainty that six feet of distance will keep you healthy. If, say, the air isn't moving, and you are with that person for longer than 15 minutes, you could transmit it.

About three weeks ago, Michael wasn't feeling all that well and decided to get retested. When we finally got the results a couple of days ago, they were somewhat sobering. He tested negative for the virus, but he also tested negative for the antibodies.

Michael and I both had mild cases of COVID-19 back in March. When we were finally able to get tested in May, we did, indeed, both test positive for the antibodies. We have both been navigating through these days with the feeling that those antibodies were offering us at least a layer of protection. If both the testing in May and the more recent testing were accurate then, like the regular flu, finding an effective vaccine for this is going to be more difficult. Many of the vaccines currently in development are being based on harnessing antibodies.

Michael and I are doing our best, as is everyone we know around us, to make responsible decisions about how to live our lives through this pandemic. Maintaining our mental health is as important as maintaining our physical health. We are making choices as best we can, trying to use the information that is at hand and coupling it with common sense. There is no way that we aren't going to make mistakes.

During my trip across the country, I spent most of my days alone in the car. I pumped my own gas. I checked into hotels that were uncrowded and had advertised their COVID policies. The only people I met were the people at the front desk, separated from me by a plexiglass shield and masked. I mostly ate on my own, but the few times I went to a restaurant to eat, I ate outside, far away from everyone else. When places I was eating in got too crowded, I left.

The Ikea store was well set up. There are arrows on the floor and customers walk through the entire thing in one direction. It was like a retail version of Disney's *It's a Small World* ride. Masks are mandatory. The physical space is enormous with extremely high ceilings, so we felt relatively safe.

What we wanted to find was a coffee table that we could put our feet up on while we were watching TV. We spend so much time doing that now, that it was high time we made ourselves comfortable. We looked at about a hundred different possibilities before finally settling on one. Of course, when we got to the end, it was out of stock. We quickly compromised on another one and $30 later we now have what we consider to be a temporary coffee table to put our feet on. We will probably have it for years.

August 31, 2020
437,154 Total Reported Cases in New York. 32,791 Deaths.

There seems to be a perception these days that New York is a lawless hell hole. We are overrun by violent homeless people who are squatting in the city's luxury hotel chains and just waiting to kill us all. Marauding protesters are looting and pillaging our stores on a nightly basis.

If that's what you are thinking, then you are merely buying into the rhetoric of a Federal Administration which has completely abandoned any pretense of truth-telling. They are attempting to terrify us all by lying about everything and anything to scare us into voting for them to fix it.

It's certainly not what's happening here in New York City. Yes, there are issues, as there are everywhere, but honestly, nothing is going on that makes me even question whether I want to continue to live here. People are out on the streets. Walking. Shopping. And eating.

The mayor has initiated a program called "Open Streets" that, to date, has closed off 76 Streets and 9 pedestrian plazas to traffic in favor of dining tables. In some places, musicians have set up speakers away from those who are eating and are filling the area with music.

Tom's Diner, up near Columbia, is famous for being the diner on the TV show *Seinfeld*. Their outside dining area is now partitioned off with barricades with the characters from the show's names on them—George, Kramer, Elaine, and Jerry. Suzanne Vega, who was in school at Barnard at the same time I was there, wrote her song *Tom's Diner* about that very same restaurant.

It is a popular place where all of us went. It was good and it was cheap. Our favorite waitress back then, who must have been in her eighties, had fire-engine red lipstick and a wig of jet-black hair that was always crooked. "Whaddaya have?"

The city's museums have finally reopened. Capacity is limited and you need to sign up for a timed entry. You must wear a mask. Yesterday, while I was walking around in the Village, I passed a store that sells eyeglasses. "Make your mask jealous," was the sales sign printed in the window near their collection of sunglasses.

Retail stores are open throughout the city. Everything else is readily available. On the rare occasion that a store is out of something, the one next door will have it. There is no sense of shortages anywhere.

Even though many people are either not working or working from home, the traffic throughout the city has increased. It's still not at the level it was. There are still no tourist busses. In March and April when you walked outside, you could almost cross the street without looking it was so empty. That's not at all the case now. People are out and about in their cars. Trucks are delivering their goods. These days, you need to wait for the light to change before you cross—something most New Yorkers usually resist doing.

When I first moved to New York in the early 1980s, you really needed to keep your wits about you when you walked around. It was dangerous then. Living here then, you quickly developed an extra sense that kept you from walking down some streets or perhaps crossing to the other side of a particular street. Once I developed it myself, I found that it never fully left me. There have been times in other places around the world when that internal radar has suddenly pinged back in. I always listen to it. So far, for me at least, that has not happened again to me in recent weeks here. Yes, I am aware of a certain rise in that kind of energy, but for me it hasn't been enough to make that significant an impression.

I may take a bike ride downtown today, deep into the city that I love. New York City is stronger than anyone thinks. It has survived through many things and it will certainly survive through this.

FALL 2020

SEPTEMBER–NOVEMBER

SEPTEMBER 1, 2020
437,757 Total Reported Cases in New York. 32,800 Deaths.

And just like that, we are into September.

Back in March, my work calendar looked empty during the summer months but starting right about now through the rest of the year it was already starting to fill up. An incredible amount of juggling was going to be needed, on my part, to get through it. Instead, rather than adding things into the next five months with my yellow plastic mechanical pencil, I am starting to erase them.

When much of Scandinavia went into early lockdown back in the spring, Sweden did not. Sweden stayed open. Schools stayed open. Many people worked from home, but offices were open, and workers were encouraged to go to them to belie the gravity of the situation and many did. To date, the rest of Scandinavia has done moderately well. In Finland, 335 have died of the virus. 264 people have died in Norway and 624 in Denmark. To date, by comparison, 5,800 Swedes have lost their lives to the virus. Economically, Sweden has fared slightly better than some of its European neighbors to the south, but not any better than its Scandinavian neighbors in the north. Their decision to stay open had no appreciable effect on their economy but resulted in the needless deaths of 5,000+ of its citizens.

Here in the US, we followed neither of these paths. Instead, what we did was a messy combination of the two. We shut down but then reopened too soon. If we had ALL shut down for about six weeks early on and mandated social distancing and mask-wearing, we would very likely now be in the enviable position that many other countries are in. The United States might now be in the position that New York state is currently in.

New York has now had 24 straight days of our infection rate being below 1%. One person in New York state passed away yesterday from the virus but nobody in New York City did. There are 109 patients in ICU units throughout the state. These are the lowest numbers we've had since the beginning of the pandemic. Mistakes were made in New York, but the numbers don't lie. What we did here has worked.

Estimates are that 2.3 MILLION people would have to die before any sort of herd immunity could be achieved here. That is far more than ten times the number of people who have already perished. Of course, one of the ways that this kind of group immunity could be achieved would be through the development of a vaccine. If some of the current possibilities being worked on are approved, though, a vaccine will still likely only start to be available to the population in spring.

But there's another problem. A CNN poll this morning reported that 40% of Americans wouldn't take the vaccine even were it available. There is a growing number of anti-vaxxers who simply do not trust vaccines at all. They are not necessarily wrong to be wary. The US government, unfortunately, has a history of rushing vaccines into production before they are ready, with terrible results.

In 1955, the US Government, led by President Eisenhower, announced a new polio vaccine which was rushed into production. One of the companies that produced it accidentally incorporated the live poliovirus into it and 40,000 kids got polio. 10 of them died and hundreds were left paralyzed. In addition to that, 10-30% of the vaccines were contaminated with something called simian virus-40. To produce the virus, it was grown on monkey tissues and some of the monkeys they used were infected with this SV40.

In 1976, President Ford was advised that a pandemic was on its way. It was the virus that came to be known as the Swine Flu. The President was talked into making it mandatory that people get vaccinated against it. The vaccine was rushed into production and about 40 million people were administered it. The vaccine was later linked to several hundred cases of Guillian-Barre syndrome.

Rushing a COVID-19 vaccine into mass production without adequate testing is extremely likely to have similar results. Peter Marks, the Director of the FDA's Center for Biologics Evaluation and Research vowed to resign last week if his agency approves a new vaccine without adequate testing. Allowing 2.3 million people to die through active inactivity is not an acceptable option. We need a well-vetted vaccine and the means to convince everyone to take it.

The heavens have now opened, and it is pouring outside. Rain or no rain, I am going to go out and go for a walk. I'm ready to breathe in this beautiful, slightly damp, totally unscheduled day.

SEPTEMBER 2, 2020
President orders federal funding cut to Democratic cities.

The Museum of Modern Art in New York has reopened and is free to all through much of the month.

It's not going to last very long, but right now there is almost nobody there yet. The experience of being there all but alone is an experience that shouldn't be missed. There is always a crowd around some of their more famous masterpieces such as Van Gogh's *Starry Night*, but yesterday, I had it, as well as the other magnificent paintings surrounding it, completely to myself.

Strangely, the lack of attention to *Starry Night* humanizes it. After all, it's just daubs of paint on a piece of stretched canvas. Seeing it hanging on the wall across a vast empty room makes it easier to imagine the man who painted it. It seems more ordinary when there aren't throngs of people adoring it and taking pictures in front of it.

I've found that when famous people are away from the crowds of people who adore them, they become ordinary as well. The energy of a crowd focusing its attention on one person magnifies that one person into something else.

Sharon Stone came backstage once when I was doing *Gypsy* with Bernadette Peters. She and her companion were waiting onstage and quietly chatting and I didn't recognize her. At the time she was one of the biggest film stars in the country. I walked over to them to ask who they were there to see, and something happened. She immediately changed. She… turned on. She became Sharon Stone—instantly recognizable.

I took her back to see Bernadette and every single other person backstage noticed her. There was energy going back and forth between her and all of us looking at her that wasn't there when she was on her own.

The *Mona Lisa* in the Louvre in Paris is like a painterly version of Sharon Stone. It is a small painting, set by itself in a room with a massive amount of protection around it. Its display case is a vault. Tens of thousands of people crowd into the room every day to look at it. Viewing it is an event. The excitement of being there becomes part of the experience of the work. It's almost impossible to just look at the painting through the carnival surrounding it.

That same thing happens around *Starry Night*, albeit at not quite so high a level. The image of the painting is on everything from socks to cutting boards. It's a commodity. Yesterday, though, standing alone with it, my experience of it was very different.

Working in Europe these past many years, I have been able to travel to most of the places where Van Gogh lived and worked. I've seen Zundert, the small town in the Netherlands where he was born. I stayed right near the Westerkerk church in Amsterdam that he occasionally attended. I've been to the apartments in Paris and London where he lived while he worked in galleries, the French town of Arles where he shared a house with the painter Paul Gaugin for a short while and painted his famous sunflowers, the asylum in Saint-Remy where he battled depression and painted *Starry Night* and the Auvers-sur-Oise town cemetery where he and his brother Theo are buried.

That he died before he experienced any success has always seemed to me to be unbearably tragic. There is an episode of the British Sci-Fi series *Doctor Who*, where the Doctor takes Vincent Van Gogh into the future to a museum where his work is hanging. Van Gogh sees all the people admiring his work. He sees his paintings become… larger… under the frenzy of their attention. His work transforms from daubs of paint on the canvas into… something else. He sees that the devotion to his work that he maintained through his life without any encouragement from anyone else was not misguided. He sees that he was right. That episode always makes me weep.

Perhaps it was watching the President lie through the Republican National Convention while his family rallied around him and lied as well, but something has changed for me regarding how I see this Administration. Both he and it look smaller.

There is an episode of the classic *Star Trek* series where the crew of the enterprise is locked in battle on a planet with the Klingons. Unbeknownst to both sides, there is an alien presence who is feeding off their aggression. This alien is driving the two sides to fight each other so that it can sate itself. When both the Enterprise crew and the Klingons realize what's going on, they unite and laugh at it. In the absence of aggression and fear, the alien cannot survive so it leaves.

Nobody was interested in the paintings of Vincent Van Gogh while he was alive. They were considered messy, amateurish, and garish. After his death, his brother Theo relentlessly promoted them and taught people how to look at them. Within a short time, people started to see in them what Theo saw. Van Gogh's reputation began to grow.

As attention started being paid, the work evolved. The paintings are now entirely something else than what they once were. They aren't real in our perception. Prices of them are so high that they seem otherworldly in some way. Supernatural. Even though what they still are, are just daubs of paint on some cheap stretched canvas.

The President is not some great exalted being. We are making him that, by giving him this attention. We are making him that by panicking and cringing in fear every time he speaks. We need to stop expecting him to tell the truth and just ignore everything that he's saying. To defeat him, we just need to band together and laugh at him.

What Vincent Van Gogh was able to do is awe-inspiring. He was a crazy wild-looking guy who always had his easel and a brush with him and by all accounts, people avoided. Nobody took him seriously, but the paint he was gloriously splattering has real magic in it.

We could all use some magic these days.

SEPTEMBER 3, 2020
439,322 Total Reported Cases in New York. 32,810 Deaths.

These days, when I see the American flag flying somewhere, I think… uh oh. In three short years, this Administration has managed to imbue it with a fascist sense of nationalism that is starting to make me recoil from it.

In 1776, at the request of General George Washington, Betsy Ross sewed the first flag. Thirteen alternating red and white stripes along with a rectangular field of blue in the upper left-hand corner containing a circle of thirteen stars. That's the story. There is no definitive proof that it is what happened although there doesn't seem to be any reason to discount it, either. During her lifetime, nobody was aware of her story. It wasn't until 1870, nearly a hundred years later that her grandson William Canby told the story to the Historical Society of Pennsylvania.

According to Canby, Ms. Ross often told the story of General Washington, who, along with Robert Morris who was a financier of the Revolutionary War, and Colonel George Ross, a relative of hers, paid her a visit and showed her a sketch of what they were looking for. She agreed to make it for them. She claimed it was her idea to arrange the stars in a circle and to make them five-pointed rather than six-pointed. Her grandson's story, which was supported by her daughter, niece, and granddaughter, appeared in Harper's New Monthly magazine in 1873 and thereafter passed into accepted national lore.

According to legend, Washington felt that the red represented the British, the white represented our secession, and the stars represented the stars in the sky. In 1782, Congress chose the same colors for the Great Seal of the United States for the following reasons: red for valor and hardiness, white for purity and innocence, and blue for perseverance and justice.

In 1831, a shipmaster from Salem, Massachusetts named William Driver was about to set sail when friends presented him with a flag to fly on his ship's mast. As the by now 24-starred flag unfurled he called it, "Old Glory!" giving it the nickname that we still use today.

Francis Scott Key wrote a poem called *Defense of Fort M'Henry* inspired by a large flag flying over the fort in 1814 during the war of 1812. From that, in 1931, came what we now know as our country's anthem, *The Star-Spangled Banner*.

Francis Scott Key (I've clearly gone down a research rabbit hole here) was, at the time, one of the richest men in America. He was born in 1779 to a very wealthy slave-owning family in Maryland. He spent much of his life doing everything he could to shore up the institution of slavery. He referred to it as our "peculiar institution".

He helped to shape the US Supreme Court which, in his day, was very strongly pro-slavery. When he was in his 50s, he became an advisor to President Andrew Jackson, himself also a rabidly pro-slavery man. Jackson appointed Key the US District Attorney for Washington D.C. Under him, abolitionists were fully persecuted under the law and any infraction against the racial and slavery laws was harshly punished.

Francis Scott Key convinced President Jackson to name Roger Taney to his cabinet. Taney then became Chief Justice of the United States. Roger Taney is known to history as being the author of the 1857 Dredd Scott Supreme Court decision. The decision stated that all Black people, whether slaves or not, would never be entitled to any of the rights enjoyed by White people. That decision is considered one of the catalysts for the Civil War. Taney, incidentally, was Francis Scott Key's brother-in-law.

There is a third verse to *The Star-Spangled Banner* that Key wrote that we don't sing anymore.

> "No refuge could save the hireling & slave/
> From the terror of flight or the gloom of the grave:/
> And the star-spangled banner in triumph doth wave/
> O'er the land of the free & the home of the brave."

While we don't sing it anymore, it still echoes through whatever hall the anthem is sung in.

Back in March and early April, before the stock market opened back up, a giant flag covered the front of the New York Stock Exchange. At the time it seemed an emblem of hope. When the market eventually reopened, the flag came down. Yesterday, I walked onto Wall Street and saw that the flag was back up. My stomach dropped. It wasn't something that I thought about, it was just my immediate visceral response to seeing it. Instead of it seeming like a symbol of hope, it now seems somewhat like a rallying cry in support of fascistic nationalism.

This current GOP-led Administration has co-opted the flag and is using it in the same way that Adolph Hitler and his National Socialist German Worker's Party used the stolen swastika symbol—to incite intense nationalism and paranoia.

Our country is 244 years old. *The Star-Spangled Banner* has only been our national anthem for about 90 of those years. It is probably time to change it. The man who wrote it was not somebody who we should be lionizing. It's ridiculously hard to sing it anyway. The US flag, however, stands for something and it is not what the man who is currently occupying the White House thinks it is.

We deserve to get it back. And we will when we vote.

September 5, 2020
441,012 Total Reported Cases in New York.

Michael and I are back up in Provincetown. It was one of the easiest drives up here that we've ever had. There was no traffic and no delays. Unthinkable over the Labor Day weekend in a normal year.

The TV is on, and I am listening to everyone talk about the President's disparaging comments about all the people who have served and, in some cases, given their lives fighting for our country. He describes soldiers who have lost their lives in service to their country as "Losers" and "Suckers." He cannot understand why somebody would choose to serve for the low salary that comes with enlisting rather than pursuing a more lucrative line of work elsewhere. The idea of fighting for something greater than yourself is beyond his grasp.

Yesterday, the Pentagon announced, seemingly out of nowhere, that they were going to halt the publication of Stars and Stripes, the military paper that has served our armed forces since 1861. The President quickly spoke up and said, "Not on my watch." He has condemned the move.

This seems to me to be a complete Munchausen Syndrome by Proxy political action. The syndrome is an attention-getting device. Caretakers create a medical condition in someone, either by secretly poisoning them or perhaps starving them so that they can then take care of that person and maybe cure them. They become the hero. Stars and Stripes is an infinitesimally small part of the Pentagon's overall budget. For many service personnel, it is the only news and contact with the outside world they get. Putting an end to it seems like a pointless move unless it was directed to do so, so that the President could swoop in and save it. It gives him something to distract from his painful and disgusting remarks.

I don't know that we should shun the news completely—we owe it to ourselves to stay informed—but it doesn't have to rule our lives. There's a beautiful day out there and for Michael and me, at least for the next few days, a beach, so the TV is going off for now. Maybe for a few days.

September 7, 2020
442,315 Total Reported Cases in New York.

Walking down Commercial Street last night, with all the straight families with kids in strollers, the drag queens and the boys being their loud and out-there selves, seemed so achingly familiar that it almost erased the rest of this whole past odd and overwhelming time.

Today is the end of summer. Technically, that doesn't happen until the fall equinox which this year falls on September 22. Practically, however, today, Labor Day, is the last day of one of the strangest seasons any of us have ever lived through.

Provincetown is much more crowded this weekend than it was the last time we were here. For many people, today is either their last day here or the day that they are returning home. The coffee shops all have long lines of customers, some with their small, wheeled suitcases are waiting for the bus and some are looking like they got up too early so as not to miss a second of this final glorious day.

The gay muscle boys were out in force last night. It almost seemed like a normal evening in P-town except that there were no clubs open, and they were all wearing masks. The dance space at A-House is closed, but their outdoor space is open for drinks. Likewise, the Boatslip was also opened but only for outdoor gatherings.

We ate out at a place called Sal's on the beach itself, where they have set up several tables and chairs. Staring out at the harbor, our feet in the cool sand was just about as perfect a way to dine as I can imagine. As the sun set, the flat water turned almost every color of the rainbow, and, for a few brief moments, just before it vanished, the boats scattered across the water all seemed to glow. That's what today seems like. That last moment where everything shines just a bit brighter before we all start hunkering down for the coming winter.

The US Department of Labor website describes today as: "Labor Day, the first Monday in September, is a creation of the labor movement and is dedicated to the social and economic achievements of American workers. It constitutes a yearly national tribute to the contributions workers have made to the strength, prosperity, and well-being of our country".

I am myself, a proud member of a union: Actors' Equity Association. My union represents professional actors and stage managers in the United States. It establishes working conditions, including the number of hours we can work, as well as base levels to our salaries. I have worked for producers who support the union as well as producers who do everything in their power to undercut the union. I have never worked for the latter twice.

We have a history here in this country of fighting for what we believe is right. People gave their lives to the fight for the eight-hour workday, something we all take so much for granted now that we never even question how it came to be. People are now giving their lives fighting for racial equity.

There are always those opposed to these fights. The opposition seems always to come down to a question of money. The people who stand in opposition to forward movement invariably want to keep as much money as they can for themselves. They never want to share.

Somewhere between when we finished dinner last night and this morning, a small army of people appears to have broken out the chalk and written Black Lives Matter in front of almost every single store along Commercial Street. In fact, anywhere where there was space is now covered in it. In front of the New York store, that sells some of the best ice cream around, on the street, there are thick chalked letters that are six or seven feet tall made up of pink and blue flowers. God bless that loyal opposition. It harmed nothing at all, and, for this morning at least, put the word out there for everybody to see.

Today, on this Labor Day, we should all give thanks to those who have come before us, whose work, struggle, and sacrifice have made our lives in this great country that much better. We should also give thanks to all of those among us who continue the fight every day.

The Great Work is well underway, and it continues moving ever forward despite those who would stop it for their own ends. Happy Labor Day.

SEPTEMBER 8, 2020
442,817 Total Reported Cases in New York. 32,850 Deaths.

It's like the day after the big frat party in Provincetown this morning. Bunting is hanging askew off some places and rainbow flags lie crumpled on the street. The Black Lives Matter chalk markings are still visible in some places but worn off in others. It's cloudy and slightly hazy as if the bleary-eyed weather simply couldn't be bothered to put on something nice.

A friend of ours has come up and is staying with us for the rest of the time we are here. We've created a bubble. Last night we all saw the comedian Judy Gold perform at the Crown & Anchor. It was the first live performance any of us had been to in six months. It was perfection.

There's an extensive open area between the street and the Crown & Anchor building that is filled up with tables. The performance, however, took place in the back, behind the hotel rooms around the pool. Chairs had been set up in short rows, distant from each other. While the tickets were all general admission, somebody had already decided where everyone was going to sit. We were all nicely and evenly scattered throughout the seating area—nobody too close to each other and nobody too far away from the action.

Everybody thinks that when the Pilgrims arrived on the Mayflower that they landed at Plymouth Rock. There's even a cement gazebo built around what people claim is the actual rock. While I am sure that they arrived at that point in Plymouth, that is not where they first landed when they got here after their long and arduous crossing of the Atlantic. They landed in Provincetown and stayed here for five weeks.

Eventually, they realized that there was not enough fresh water available out here and they headed further inland, but this is where they began their lives in the New World. Over a hundred years ago, to set the historical record straight, the town's selectmen decided to build a big, showy monument. Finished in 1910, the Pilgrim Monument is 252 feet and 7 ½ inches tall. It is based on the design of the Torre del Mangia in Sienna, Italy. From where we are staying in North Truro when you look across the bay, it makes Provincetown look like Venice out on the horizon.

In a book he wrote about Cape Cod, Michael Cunningham points out that if you look at the design of it, at the top, you can see that it looks exactly like Donald Duck. I took a good long look at it on Sunday, and it is completely true. It looks just like Donald Duck. And now I can't unsee it.

With the Labor Day partiers mostly gone, Commercial Street is starting to open to regular business. Some stores have started to close for the season. Others will wait until Columbus Day in October and then close. Summer clearance sales are happening all up and down the street. A few hardy shops will stay open throughout the winter. I sense some much-needed retail therapy in my future.

SEPTEMBER 9, 2020
443,409 Total Reported Cases in New York. 32,854 Deaths.

In 1935, under the New Deal program, the Federal Art Project was begun to employ artists and artisans during the Great Depression. Sponsored by the Works Progress Administration, it employed artists to create murals, paintings, sculptures, posters, graphic art, photography, arts and crafts, and theatre design. In the eight years that it operated more than 100 community arts centers were established around the country. More than 200,000 individual pieces of art were created, and about 10,000 artists and craftsmen were sustained during one of the worst economic crises this country had ever experienced. In return, the country gained a treasure trove of art worth far more now than what it spent on it then. The morale boost at the time, as this artwork started to proliferate, was incalculable.

The reopening of Broadway this spring has been the dangling carrot pulling us all forward. That is the thing that many of us have been holding onto. Unfortunately, that's not in any way guaranteed. Nobody knows yet how it's going to happen. Spring is a goal that was set to be far enough ahead of us so that it could be achieved. If what is happening now is still happening around the end of the year, that goal is going to have to be pushed off.

As of now, the Broadway League is saying that Broadway will remain closed until January and that you can get refunds for tickets you already have for performances between now and then. At some point in the next few weeks, they will push that date back. All that they are doing with setting those dates is trying to control the number of people getting refunds at any one time.

When Broadway finally does reopen, hopefully, somebody won't just say, "Go!" releasing producers to restart all their shows again in one weekend. It would be far more helpful to reopen in dribs and drabs. One or two shows at a time. But before even that happens, there will need to be a huge collective campaign to convince people that it is safe to come back to New York and safe to come back to the theatre. Before THAT happens, it is going to need to BE safe to come back to New York and safe to come back to the theatre.

Broadway is not going to be able to operate the way the drag shows, and concerts are operating out here on the Cape. Broadway will only be able to operate when shows can play to packed houses again. And only then. To do that, New York needs its tourists back. Our borders need to reopen. We can't reopen Broadway without the tourists, but until Broadway reopens, what will lure the tourists here? March is still another six months away. Much can and will change between now and then.

In the meantime, we need our government to pay attention to us. This isn't a selfish request. We need some of the energy being directed towards our sports teams directed towards us. Why? Because the Arts sector is a larger part of the economy than the Sports sector is. Our economy needs the Arts to get back to work. Until we can do that, we require the government's assistance to help take care of us. Our Senators need to get back from their vacations and start to work towards getting something accomplished.

We're not asking. We're demanding.

SEPTEMBER 10, 2020
444,071 Total Reported Cases in New York.

Today, the sky is white, and the sea is the color of a warship. The only movement I can see at all outside of our front door is a skull and crossbones pirate flag gently flapping in the light breeze across the street on the front of a little cottage. The flag has three skulls on it, arranged in a row.

The President is still trying to counter the nasty revelations about how he really feels about the armed forces of the country. A couple of news cycles later and it hasn't gone away. While that is going on, the United States Department of Justice is trying to take over the defense of the President against E. Jean Carroll, who is accusing him of having raped her in the 1990s.

Having raped her.

There are going to be three debates between the Republican and Democratic nominees for President. What are those going to look like? How can the Democratic nominee hope to use his vast years of experience within the structures of our government to debate a Republican nominee who knows nothing of how any of it was designed to operate? Not only does he know nothing about it, but he also doesn't want to know anything about it. He doesn't want to be limited by any prior agreement at all.

The two sides are already deeply entrenched. I fear it's just going to end up being a boxing match between two old white men. The fact that one has a moral compass and the other doesn't won't matter in the ring. It's all going to be about who can land the most blows.

Fog is now coming in from across the bay. I can't even tell the difference between the water and the sky anymore. It's all just one big hazy white field.

I cannot imagine why that cottage is flying a pirate flag. We have long glorified the pirate as a noble rebel. Johnny Depp and the *Pirates of the Caribbean* movies even made them somewhat lovable. "Yo ho, yo ho, a pirate's life for me." It's one thing to fight against injustice—in that regard, some pirates of the past have done society a service. It is quite another to just rob and steal and create anarchy and fear. That's criminal.

When our leaders start behaving like pirates, themselves, then they must be stopped. We don't need warships and canons to stop them, all we need to do is vote. And we need to make sure that everyone around us votes, too.

There are still more people out there who believe in the rule of law than don't. The pirates would have you think otherwise, but as we all know, pirates never tell the truth.

SEPTEMBER 11, 2020
445,102 Total Reported Cases in New York.

Last night, in the gravel parking lot behind the Pilgrim House, a white clapboard hotel in the center of Provincetown built in the 1700s, we sat and watched a show called *Drag-a-Maniacs*. Cacophony Daniels and Sutton Lee Seymour, two gloriously insane drag queens from New York City entered wearing plastic shield masks and sequins and officially ended, at least for the moment, the great musical entertainment drought of 2020.

The chairs had been set up outside in groups of twos and threes and were scattered apart from each other across the lot. Because the two performers sing their own material rather than lip-synch it, even though the three of us were sitting in the front row, we were still kept 25' away from the stage. There is no substitute for sitting together with strangers, however distanced, and experiencing a show performed live.

Dr. Anthony Fauci, in an interview yesterday said that, realistically, the live vaccine will need to have been out for a year before it can be deemed safe. "If we get a really good vaccine and just about everybody gets vaccinated, you'll have a degree of immunity in the general community that I think you can walk into a theatre without a mask." Suddenly, reopening Broadway in March of next year seems even less likely than it did before.

There are currently over 150 coronavirus vaccines in development the world over. Here in the United States, Operation Warp Speed has pledged $10 billion to deliver 300 million safe and effective doses by January. The World Health Organization is trying to coordinate efforts across the globe to be able to distribute 2 billion doses of an effective vaccine by the end of next year.

Any vaccine aims to help our body's immune systems create a defense against a given virus that is stronger than what it would create on its own. Some vaccines typically use the virus itself to create antibodies. If you can kill the actual virus, and just send in its outer protective protein shell, the body can attack that and eventually figure out how to beat it. If it fails, there is no consequence because the actual nucleus of the virus has been removed. You can also send in weakened versions of the virus so that the body can essentially practice against a less able opponent. There are other ways as well. All 150 different vaccines currently being developed are trying something somewhat different to see what works.

It can typically take 10-15 years to develop a vaccine to the point that it can be distributed. The current record holder for speed was the vaccine for mumps which took four years. Forty years later, despite a huge global effort, there is still NO effective vaccine for HIV/AIDS.

When we all get our yearly vaccines against the normal flu, they are rarely completely effective. There are so many different strains of flu out there that it is almost impossible to predict which one is going to be the most widespread in any given year. Health officials must guess a full year or so before which of the variety of flu they think it's going to be then they decide to produce that kind of vaccine. I remember my doctor telling me at my last exam that the vaccine from the year before had somewhat missed the mark. It ended up being only about 20% effective. Even 20% effective, though, is better than none.

However impatient we all are for a vaccine to be delivered, steps in the testing process need to be followed. Our President is desperate to get a vaccine out on the market before the election so is pressuring the regulatory agencies to streamline the process and skip some of them. Going down that road will only keep the 40% of Americans who say they won't let themselves be vaccinated firmly against them.

Mistakes have certainly been made in the past, nothing is 100% safe, but by and large, vaccines that have been thoroughly tested, both by the people who created them and by the regulatory agencies have proven to be overwhelming safe to use.

We had a great time at the show last night. You can Zoom all you want, but nothing replaces what we get from a live performance. Nothing. That sense of shared experience and a shared emotional journey is simply not possible in any other medium. We WILL get back to it. We are just going to have to slog through the desert for a while searching for whatever water we can find, wherever we can find it.

SEPTEMBER 12, 2020
446,028 Total Reported Cases in New York. 32,858 Deaths.

If Cape Cod is the flexed arm coming out of the shoulder of Massachusetts as a whole, then Long Point is the very tip of its longest finger. Ever since I first saw the lighthouses that sit out there in the distance years ago, I've wanted to walk out to see them.

During much of the first half of the 19th century, there was a whole fishing village out on Long Point. There was a post office, a schoolhouse, six windmills for salt production, and 38 homes. By the early 1850s, the people living out there decided that it was too difficult to maintain the buildings on the narrow sandy spit of land in the harsh marine weather, so they all moved back to the village proper. Instead of leaving their buildings behind, they just floated them across the bay and set them up in various places around the town. Many of them are still standing in Provincetown to this day. They are easy to find as they are each marked by a blue and white enamel plaque with a picture of a floating house on it.

The only building that was left out on Long Point was the Long Point Lighthouse which was situated right out on the very tip of the entire peninsula. The original building was replaced by the current one which was put up in 1875. The Wood End Lighthouse, less than a mile down the beach from that one, was built three years earlier. It was to that one that I walked today.

A causeway out to it was built by the Army Corps of Engineers in 1911. It is a jumble of gigantic vaguely rectangular boulders. The top stones in the center form a walkable path. More or less. There are places where they've slipped or fallen, and a certain amount of climbing is required at those points. Walking the causeway is a commitment because it's fully a mile long.

Nineteen years ago, to the day yesterday, my ex and I were out at the house we owned on the Delaware River in Milford, PA. It was early in the morning, and we were getting ready to head back into the city. The TV was on, and we were watching a news report about a fire in the World Trade Center. One of the newscasters said there was a report that a plane had hit the building, but nobody could confirm what was going on. As we watched the broadcast, smoke billowing out of one of the towers, a second plane, in real-time, flew right across the live television shot directly into the other tower.

We couldn't believe what we had just seen. Over the next few days, we watched that same footage over and over again. We watched it from different angles. We couldn't stop watching it. A couple of weeks ago, on my way home from my road trip to North Dakota, I stopped at the Flight 93 Memorial in western Pennsylvania. That footage was playing in one of the rooms, and I stood there in front of it for a long time, watching it again. Over and over again. It pulled me right back to that day.

My father worked right across the street from the twin towers. We didn't hear from him until the afternoon of that terrible day. That morning, he had gone into the city as usual and, again, as usual, had picked up a cup of coffee in the arcade below the World Trade Center. He figured that he was in there at about 7:45 am. He worked on the 30th floor of an office building directly across from one of the towers. He had been in that building for some years and had always worried that something bad would happen down there.

On February 26, 1993, a few years before my father started working there, a truck bomb was detonated by terrorists beneath the north tower. They intended to destroy the building, but they failed to do that. Even so, seven people, including an unborn child perished, and over 1,000 people were injured. When my father took the job there, he often said that he thought that it was just a matter of time before someone tried something like that again.

When he heard the first explosion at 8:46 am, about an hour after he'd picked up his coffee, he was startled but not all that surprised. He'd been expecting it for years. After the shock, he along with everyone else in his office were told to evacuate and leave by the stairs. It's worth noting that in September of 2001, my father was already 78 years old. He walked down the thirty flights of stairs and when he got to the bottom, somebody down there with a clipboard and a megaphone was yelling that it was OK, the fire was under control and that everybody could go back to their offices.

He decided that he'd had enough for the day and, instead, headed to the ferry to go home. As he walked towards the Hudson River, at 9:03 am, the second plane flew directly over his head into the South Tower—just 17 minutes after the first one hit.

The one thing that my father always said about that experience was that it felt like being back in the war. My father was in the infantry during World War II and fought in Europe in the Battle of the Bulge. The sound of the 747-jet flying overhead reminded him of the fighter planes in battle because, like them then, it was going full speed when it passed over him. If you go to an airport and a plane coming in for a landing, flies over you, it's slowing down. It isn't going at full speed. The planes that went into the Twin Towers did not slow down. They were not braking. The sound they made was very different.

There are horrific stories of people who chose to jump to their deaths that day rather than be burned alive by the fires. My father always claimed that while he couldn't see that happening, the people he was with, could. He claimed that he'd left his glasses back in his office. I've never fully believed that. I honestly think that he saw all of it.

He made it onto the very last ferry that day and got across the Hudson to New Jersey. By about 12:30 pm he found a working phone to call my mother who then called us. Those were not an easy four hours, but we did not lose my father that day so I will forever be grateful. I know people who lost family members that day. As much as the rest of us may feel something on the anniversary of September 11, it pales in comparison to what they must feel on this day every single year.

I thought about my dad yesterday as I clambered over the stones towards the lighthouse.

Some of the big, broad stones were covered in broken clamshells. I couldn't figure out why until I saw a seagull hovering above me, drop a fresh clam onto one of the stones. The gull then swooped down, picked it back up, and dropped it again until the shell broke and it could eat what was inside.

It was amazing to watch. Only a few of the boulders were covered with shells. The gulls knew which ones worked the best. Many of the ones that they used had depressions in the middle so that the clam was less likely to bounce off back into the ocean. There were a couple of boulders that looked like great potential clamming stones to me, but they were completely clear of shells. Maybe the angle was off or maybe it was a different kind of stone and not as hard. The gulls certainly knew which ones they wanted to use. My dad would have been as fascinated watching them do this as I was. He also would have loved hearing about the houses being floated over the water into town.

The events of September 11, 2001, brought us together as a nation. Policemen and Firemen were heralded as heroes. Even Rudy Giuliani who was the Mayor of New York at the time fully stepped up and led our city through that crisis. The President at the time, George W. Bush, didn't. He was very slow to respond to the nation. Giuliani filled that void when we really needed it.

It is painful to see just how far he has fallen since. The Treasury Department has officially just labeled a man named Andriyi Derkach as an active Russian agent who has been operating in the United States for over a decade. He has been found to have strong ties to Russian Intelligence

Services. Rudy Giuliani has been working with this guy for months. "I have no reason to believe he is a Russian agent. There is nothing I saw that said he was a Russian agent. There is nothing he gave me that seemed to come from Russia at all. How the hell would I know?" Rudy Giuliani was working with this Russian spy to come up with something the President could use to smear Joe Biden with.

Our country was attacked from without on September 11, 2001. Nineteen years later, it is being attacked from within. My father didn't fight the Nazis during the Battle of the Bulge just so that we could just create a new generation of them inside our own country.

We must pull together now the same way that we did nineteen years ago. Over the next few months, the people in power are going to do everything in their power to scare us into believing that we are weak. We are not weak. We survived World War II. We survived 9/11. And we have more than enough strength to survive this, too.

SEPTEMBER 14, 2020
447,524 Total Reported Cases in New York. 32,865 Deaths.

Sometimes in the mornings in New York City, the traffic can sound like the ocean. Cars whooshing by have a similar regularity to the constant waves rushing up on the shore.

Then a truck backs up or an ambulance screams down Columbus and the illusion breaks confirming that we are back at home.

Wildfires north of Sacramento in California are raging. So far this season, 3.3 million acres have burned in the flames. 4,100 structures have been lost. To give you an idea of the size of that, all of Manhattan is only 14,478 acres. In California, 228 Manhattans have burned so far and the fires aren't even close to being contained yet.

The number of people experiencing loss these days is staggering. Maybe people are just posting more, and this is all very normal, but it seems to me as if friends and friends of friends are losing relatives and loved ones at a much higher rate than I ever remember before. Not to the fires and not to COVID necessarily, but everything. How did it get this bad?

Back on February 7, the President sat down with Watergate reporter Bob Woodward for 18 hours of a taped interview over several days. In these tapes, the President clearly states that he knew how serious the pandemic was going to be back in January. He told Woodward that on January 28 he was told by the national security advisor Robert O'Brien, "This virus will be the biggest national security threat you face in your presidency." He knew how serious it was. He knew then that it was aerosol, that you could get it from just breathing the air. He described it as "deadly stuff."

Two days later in a January 30th speech to the American people, he said, "We think we have it very well under control. We have very little problem in this country at this moment — five. And those people are all recuperating successfully. But we're working very closely with China and other countries, and we think it's going to have a very good ending for us. So that I can assure you." When he was asked later in March why he said that, he responded, "I wanted to, I wanted to always play it down, I still like playing it down– because I don't want to create a panic."

He's still denying that there is a problem. 194,000 Americans dead and he held an indoor rally in Nevada, yesterday for thousands of people. Utterly disregarding a Nevada state emergency ban that prohibits gatherings of more than 50 people, the President packed many times that number inside of a manufacturing facility. CNN and other major networks did not send crews because of safety concerns. His last indoor rally in Tulsa killed Herman Cain, it will be interesting to see who dies because of this one.

Outside before the event, a TV interviewer asked a woman if she was concerned about attending the event. She responded that anyone who was sick would stay home, "I'm not an idiot. And neither are any of these people." When the interviewer followed up by asking if she wasn't worried about the fact that asymptomatic people can be major transmitters of the disease and they might not know they were sick.

"…No." That tiny pause. She hadn't thought about it.

We are going to continue to experience loss. We would even without all this hysteria happening around us. Some of it is harder to bear than we ever could have imagined. We need each other more than ever to get through this. Social media is potentially a way to connect, but it also has the potential to be a place where misery feeds off itself and grows. If one person is experiencing a particular day of despair and posts something about how the world is ending, what does that do the rest of us? It may make that person feel better in the moment, but now it has plunged many other people into the same despair.

We always have more power than we think we do. Even though we may feel trapped, there is usually a way out. It may not be a great solution, but it's in there, somewhere. Despair, on the other hand, guarantees to keep that pathway hidden.

Much, if not all our profound national sense of dislocation and uncertainty is being created by the people we have elected to positions in our government. We need our leaders—our President, our Senators, our Governors—anyone we have chosen to lead us—to do their jobs.

They need to tell us the truth and help us figure out a way through the problem. When they stop doing that, it is time to replace them.

Well, they've stopped doing that and the time to replace many of them is coming.

SEPTEMBER 15, 2020
448,213 Total Reported Cases in New York. 32,873 Deaths.

Walking through the theatre district, the further we go into this shutdown, the more those buildings are starting to feel like part of an exhibit from times gone by. It's been six months since any show in the city has had a performance. The theatres where shows have permanently closed like the St. James where *Frozen* was and the Booth where the revival of *Who's Afraid of Virginia Woolf* had started previews are now completely dark. There is no indication, at all, of who their former tenants might have been. The others, where shows are still hoping to reopen, still have their marquees and signage up. You can still see advertising for the revival of Company on the side of MTA buses. *Jersey Boys* posters are still up on the side of trashcans throughout Times Square.

A huge poster advertising *Plaza Suite* starring Sarah Jessica Parker and Matthew Broderick is still outside its theatre. That show never even started previews. The poster, however, has been up so long that it now just seems like a normal part of the landscape. *Plaza Suite* along with *The Music Man* starring Hugh Jackman are two big splashy, starry new shows that producers are hoping will help jumpstart Broadway in March. If Dr. Fauci and other health experts are right, though, that may not happen for as long as another year.

The party atmosphere on a lot of New York streets because of outdoor dining will last if people are willing to put up with falling temperatures. I am sure that there is going to be a shortage of outdoor heaters as everyone starts grabbing them. Two weeks from now on September 30, Governor Cuomo has announced that indoor dining will be able to resume at 25% capacity.

The warnings from health officials about a possible second wave of the virus are springing from what has been observed in similar outbreaks from the past. During the Spanish Flu pandemic in 1918, what happened was that cases started appearing in March, as they did with COVID, peaked, then started to subside as they moved into the summer. The second wave returned and peaked in November of that year. The colder weather had forced everyone indoors which made it easier to spread. It was that second wave that was the deadliest.

We've learned that the large Black Lives Matter demonstrations which happened outside with most people wearing masks did not become super-spreader events. On the other hand, the motorcycle rally in Sturgis, South Dakota which attracted nearly half a million people who did NOT wear masks, did. Where the demonstrators mostly left room between them, the bikers ignored that and gathered tightly together. The spread from that event alone, as people from the rally returned to their homes, is potentially responsible for over a quarter of a million new cases. Those cases could lead to health care costs of over $12 billion.

Indoor church services, parties, and, yes, political rallies have created many super-spreader events. Outdoor distanced versions of the same have not.

Winter is coming. First, though, is fall. Fall is why many of us choose to live in New York City. Clear crisp beautiful days bridge the gap between the hot and humid days of summer and the cold and grey days of winter. Fall days when you might have to wear a jacket but might not. The leaves will start changing very soon, but not quite yet. All the great harvest flavors will start appearing in stores and restaurants. The street markets will become full of apple cider and pumpkins.

We are given these occasional glorious days in New York, and we should take full and greedy advantage of them. For my friends out west, who are suffering from the fires, and my friends down south who are suffering from the hurricanes, please stay safe and well. Your glorious days will come just as ours will pass. It's all part of the same cycle.

Yes, winter is coming, but then again, so is spring.

SEPTEMBER 16, 2020
448,897 Total Reported Cases in New York. 32,877 Deaths.

I am sitting across from Lincoln Center watching all the people walking up and down and all the traffic streaming by. Lots of Moms and Dads are out pushing kids in strollers. People on bikes are swerving around them all. They all look like New Yorkers. Statistically, most of them are likely to be Democrats.

It seems to me that the most basic difference between the Republican and Democratic parties is what they value most. For the Republicans, it is the economy first. Fix the economy, you fix the people. For the Democrats, it is people first. Fix the people, you fix the economy.

We have all the evidence that we need from other countries surrounding the globe, that the path that our President took was the wrong one. For him, it has always been all about the economy. The people be damned. The stock market might be doing well these days, but is the economy as a whole?

The United States is currently carrying a National Debt of $26.70 trillion. We have the largest external debt of any country in the world. Over $7 trillion of that debt is held by foreign nations. Our Gross Domestic Product, meaning what we produced, is $21.44 trillion. Our debt is more than our income.

The President's policy since he took office has been to boost growth using tax cuts and additional spending. Both of those things have significantly increased our debt. Continued growth under these circumstances is unsustainable. He has done nothing to stop the number of people getting sick and dying from rising.

That number is only going to increase between now and November 3. We need to remember what, and more importantly, who they represent. People. They are mothers and fathers and sisters and cousins and aunts and brothers and grandmothers and friends and uncles and grandfathers and nieces and lovers and nephews and exes and idols and sons and neighbors and daughters. We need to say their names. We need to do everything we can to put faces and histories on to the people who are losing their lives to the Police. We need to do everything we can to put faces and histories on to the people who are losing their lives to COVID-19.

The ghosts of the people we've lost are going to be looking over our shoulders as we vote. Let's not piss them off.

SEPTEMBER 17, 2020
449,922 Total Reported Cases in New York. 32,904 Deaths.

The day before yesterday, as I was walking home up Broadway, I came upon a large crowd of people and firetrucks gathered on 78th Street. A whole line of news crews there with their cameras all pointed in the same direction. A small black drone was hovering next to a building just up the street. It looked like a gigantic insect.

Looking up ten stories, I could see that a work scaffold's rigging had given out on one side, and it was now hanging at an extremely precarious 45-degree angle. I missed the actual rescue of the workers, but everyone in the crowd was happily telling new arrivals exactly what had happened. Neither of the two window washers who were on it at the time was hurt. Firefighters had come over the roof and brought the two guys back up with them.

The life and death drama had passed with the rescue of the two men, but now the scaffolding still needed to be secured. The TV crews and, in fact, the crowd, were hanging around hoping for a satisfying crash. I didn't wait to see if that happened, but looking at the news coverage later, it appears that, thankfully, it didn't.

Dawn Wooten who worked at a detention facility in Ocilla, Georgia run by a private firm called LaSalle Corrections claims that she was demoted in July for raising concerns about COVID-19 safety measures that were being ignored there. In her complaint, she describes deplorable living conditions, and she says that immigrant women are being sterilized against their will there.

I took this with a grain of salt until later in the day when I received a bulk email from my congress representative talking about this very whistleblower's report. "The report outlined multiple abuses of immigration women, including mass hysterectomies seemingly performed without the full, informed consent of the women. One woman reported knowing of five detained women who had hysterectomies over a three-month period. Other women reported receiving multiple different rationales for the surgery or having nurses yell at them for seeking more information before surgery. These horrifying allegations must be investigated in full and today."

So, now there is an investigation underway.

Speaker of the House, Nancy Pelosi said yesterday, "If true, the appalling conditions described in the whistleblower complaint—including allegations of mass hysterectomies being performed on vulnerable immigrant women—are a staggering abuse of human rights. This profoundly disturbing situation recalls some of the darkest moments of our nation's history, from the exploitation of Henrietta Lacks, to the horror of the Tuskegee Syphilis Study, to the forced sterilizations of Black women that Fannie Lou Hamer and so many others underwent and fought."

Henrietta Lacks was an African American woman, who was undergoing treatment for ovarian cancer in 1951. Unbeknownst to her, some of her cancer cells were taken and cultured into what is still known as the HeLa cell line. Ms. Lacks unfortunately passed away later that year and it wasn't until 1975 that her family found out that her cells had been harvested. Those cells, to this day, are used by scientists to study cancer and possible treatments for it. The discussion about Ms. Lack's rights, including her right to privacy, continues to this day.

The Tuskegee Syphilis Study was a forty-year study that was formally entitled, *The Tuskegee Study of Untreated Syphilis in the African American Male*. The US Public Health Service started the study with Tuskegee University, a largely black college in Alabama. They enrolled 600 impoverished African American sharecroppers into the study saying that they were treating them for "bad blood". They didn't treat them at all. Instead, they administered placebos so that they could study the long-term effects of untreated syphilis. (That, by the way, can lead to blindness, deafness, mental illness, heart disease, bone deterioration, the collapse of the central nervous system, and death.) About a decade into the study, penicillin became widely available which could have cured these people, but the subjects were never told about it so as not to interfere with the study.

Fannie Lou Hamer was an African American leader in the Civil Rights Movement. When she passed, her eulogy was delivered by Andrew Young who was, at the time, the US Ambassador to the UN. In 1993 she was inducted into the National Women's Hall of Fame. While having surgery to remove a tumor in 1961, she was given a hysterectomy, completely without her consent, by a white doctor. At the time, Mississippi had a compulsory sterilization plan to reduce the number of poor black citizens in the state.

Compulsory sterilization first started to appear in the United States in what is, now somewhat laughably referred to as the Progressive Era which lasted from about 1890—1920. These programs were set up for eugenics. Eugenics is the desire to improve the genetic quality of a given population. While we think of it now as applying just to white supremacy, or indeed any kind of racial supremacy, the arguments for it when it started were aimed more towards those with mental and physical disabilities. Those arguments were often based on economics.

People who were deemed "unfit to reproduce" either had hereditary handicaps or conditions or had low IQ's or were criminals or deviants. Keeping these people from reproducing, so the theory went, kept these traits from being passed on and adding to the burden of society.

Deviancy, in this regard, had an extraordinarily wide scope of interpretation. For instance, it could, and was, applied to women deemed to be promiscuous.

Indiana became the first state to enact compulsory sterilization laws in 1907. California and Washington passed similar laws in 1909. Others followed. There were of course legal challenges. In 1927, however, the US Supreme Court decision Buck v. Bell upheld the idea saying that the forced sterilization of inmates at a Virginia facility for the intellectually disabled was legal.

As a result of that ruling, the practice became much more widespread. The 1942 case Skinner v. Oklahoma added a wrinkle that criminals could only be forced to undergo this treatment if it was done equitably. In other words, if it was done to the general prison population, then it had to be done to white-collar criminals too. While people argued that this saved the healthcare system a fortune in future expenses, forced sterilization, of course, also became a powerful tool for white supremacists.

From 1970—1976, between 25 and 40% of Native American women who sought healthcare from the Indian Health Services were sterilized. The US Government launched programs throughout the south against Black women and throughout the southwest against Latina women. The US protectorate of Puerto Rico had its own sterilization program.

The Oregon Board of Eugenics lasted until 1983. Their last forced procedure was done in 1981. Up until now, it was thought to be the last such procedure performed in the United States.

Over a third of all the procedures performed nationwide were done in the state of California. The information about this program was put together in a book by two eugenicists named E.S. Gosney and Paul B. Popenoe. That book was one of the things that convinced Adolph Hitler's government that a widespread eugenics program was possible. The Nazis used that very book as a blueprint to exterminate 6 million people during World War II. During the Nuremberg trials following the end of World War II, Nazi defendants tried to justify what they had done claiming it was no different from what we, here in the US, were doing.

In 400 B.C. Plato suggested that humans could be selectively bred for the betterment of society. "…the state, if it once starts well, proceeds as it were in a cycle of growth. I mean that a sound nurture and education if kept up creates good natures in the state, and sound natures in turn receiving an education of this sort develop into better men than their predecessors."

For a country founded on diversity, we have a lousy history of acceptance of that diversity. Every single wave of immigration we have ever had has been met with hostility, anger, and fear. Being different, in the United States of America, seems to be the greatest crime anyone can commit. Yet, it is the amalgamation of those very differences that can make us great.

We are standing on a scaffolding of our own doing our very best to keep it all level while we all try to live our lives. Target a particular group of people and that scaffolding loses one of its main support cables. We need to build new and stronger supports that can help pull each of us up. All that we are doing now is looking at the impending disaster with mouths open and waiting for the crash. We have all, hands on our hearts, pledged a lofty ideal, time and time again. "…One nation, under God, indivisible with liberty and justice for all." It's long past the time to make good on that promise.

September 18, 2020
450,753 Total Reported Cases in New York. 32,919 Deaths.

I am back out on another road trip. This time, I am heading to Florida to visit my mother.

Planning this has been a bit more difficult than the last one was. On my previous trip, I didn't stay anywhere for longer than a couple of hours. On this one, I am going to be in two states on New York's restricted list for a few days each so that means a two-week quarantine for me when I return.

This morning, I am in Lafayette Park across from the White House in Washington D.C. I wasn't sure what to expect here. The fact that Lafayette Park is open surprised me. It's open, but there is fencing everywhere. The statue of Andrew Jackson on his horse has a circle of concrete barriers around it and then beyond that, a circle of high black fencing.

St. John's Church, where the President pulled that ridiculous stunt with the Bible is also surrounded by fencing. Three blocks of 16th Street north of the park have been renamed Black Lives Plaza. Black Lives Matter has been painted in giant yellow letters that fill the street. There are other Black Lives Matter signs all over the buildings along both sides of the plaza.

When last I was here, back in December long before the pandemic started, they were in the process of building a much higher fence around the White House. There were construction barricades that almost completely blocked the view. The new fence now appears complete, and the barricades are down. It looks much like the old one, only a few feet taller. You still can't get near it, but now you can see through it.

I've been visiting Washington since I was a little kid. I remember being here with my family and going to the Smithsonian Air and Space Museum. I also remember seeing the cursed Hope diamond which, for some reason, I was a bit obsessed with for a while.

In 1998, we did an out-of-town pre-Broadway tryout of the revival of *Annie Get Your Gun* starring Bernadette Peters at the Kennedy Center. Al and Tipper Gore came to see one of our performances while we were there. The security detail came in earlier in the day and set up metal detectors off stage right and off stage left. Every single time we had to cross over to the other side of the stage or go downstairs, we had to pass through the metal detectors. The Secret Service guys were relaxed and were rather fun. They got to know us during that odd night. The Gores seemed to enjoy themselves, too. Presidents going to the theatre doesn't always end that well.

Each time I've been here, I've walked past the White House. It seems to take on the character of the President occupying it. It felt like a symbol of hope during the Obama years. Now, sitting here looking at it, it feels like I am writing this post from inside Mordor.

Helicopters have been flying back and forth overhead as I have been sitting here. They look like they may be coming and going from the south lawn of the White House. The police have just cleared out the park and me with it. I wonder if the President is heading to a rally somewhere today.

The White House looks different to me now not only because of who is currently living in it but also because of what I've learned about it.

According to a White House history website, building began in 1792. Washington D.C. commissioners initially intended to bring in workers from Europe, but the recruitment response was so meager that they turned, instead, to both free and enslaved African Americans. Enslaved men were trained in the work at the stone quarry in Virginia where much of the stone for the walls came from. They quarried and cut the Aquia Creek

Sandstone that was then shaped and laid by Scottish stonemasons.

The more I read, these days, the more I realize that very little is really what it seems. So much of what we all enjoy in our lives only came into being because of the blood and sweat of people who were denied the opportunity to share in it themselves.

"History is written by the victors" is more apt than we know. Those who conquer get to frame the story. They slowly erase the stories of those they have conquered to legitimize their right to occupy somebody else's land. That's why we need to keep saying the names of those who have lost. We can't let their blood just seep into the ground and fade from view. Our nation's ground is so very bloody as it is.

SEPTEMBER 19, 2020
451,655 Total Reported Cases in New York.

Yesterday, I crossed over the Mason-Dixon line on Delaware's southern border, and I am now in Virginia. I am in the South.

The line was established after a survey by two men named Charles Mason and Jeremiah Dixon between 1763 and 1767. They were tasked with doing it to resolve a border dispute between Pennsylvania, Maryland, and Delaware at the time they were all still just colonies.

It all began because of conflicting royal charters. George Calvert, 1st Baron Baltimore, applied to Charles I of England for the original charter of Maryland. Unfortunately, he died before that happened. The charter was ultimately granted to his son Cecilius Calvert, 2nd Baron Baltimore, in 1632. Father George had been stripped of his title of Secretary of State some years before when he'd announced that he was Catholic. Some think that the charter was granted by way of compensation for this. In theory, Maryland is named after the wife of Charles I, Queen Henrietta Maria, but it is also possible that Calvert named it for Mary, the mother of Jesus.

About 50 years later, William Penn received the royal charter for Pennsylvania from Charles II. The problem was that the two charters described where the borders were in different ways. The two different Kings had used two different maps each with varying degrees of accuracy.

As the states each expanded, the discrepancy was discovered. While it was being resolved, William Penn was given an additional charter of three lower counties along Delaware Bay, called, of course, Delaware, which became a sort of satellite colony of Pennsylvania. Calvert considered that land to be part of Maryland's original charter. All collective heck broke loose.

Violence erupted between settlers of differing allegiances that came to be called Cresap's War. England deployed military forces to quell it, and it took until eight years later for George II to negotiate a cease-fire. The crown then sent in Mason and Dixon to establish the border formally and what they came up with still stands to this day.

Stone markers were placed every five miles along the line with an "M" on one side and a "P" on the other. On the two remaining sides, one has the Calvert coat of arms and the other has the Penn family coat of arms. Many of them are still there, so now, having learned all about this, I am going to have to go and find one.

During the Civil War, the line became the informal border between the Northern free states and the Southern slave-holding states. When the line was first drawn, the Virginias were one unified state with the Mason-Dixon line as its northern border. At the beginning of the Civil War, after Virginia seceded from the Union its northern counties broke away and kept their allegiance to the north. West Virginia was the only new state admitted to the United States during the war.

This morning, I am writing this from what was once the capital of the Confederacy, Richmond, Virginia. While I am in almost every measurable regard a Yankee from the liberal Northeast, I am a Southern boy by birth. Virginia is where I was born. To be fair, Arlington, Virginia where the blessed event occurred, is just a suburb of Washington D.C. It never really occurred to me until yesterday when I was in Lafayette Square, that I was born in the South.

My father's side was mostly all southerners. He was born in Rustburg, Virginia. His mother, my grandmother, was born in Versailles, Kentucky. Kentucky, while it remained in the Union, did not give up its slaves until after the war. Part of her genealogy continues back in Kentucky through many generations. The other part came from South Carolina and other southern states.

My grandfather was born in Russellville, Alabama and his family was southern through and through. Many members of my family fought for the Confederacy.

Driving into Richmond last night, I passed by the statue of Robert E. Lee on Monument Avenue that, in some ways, has been the emblematic center of the Confederate memorial discussion. It's still standing, but from what I could see in the dark, it is covered with graffiti and protest signage.

The more I wander down these historical rabbit holes, the more I realize that none of the stories we have been told are as simple as they've been made out to be. They are complicated, messy, and contradictory. They are much bigger than some would have us all think.

Change comes slowly. When it does come quickly, it's a terrible shock.

Chief Justice of the Supreme Court of the United States of America Ruth Bader Ginsburg passed away yesterday. That was a shock. She was only the second woman in our history appointed to the court. She joined

Justice Sandra Day O'Connor who had been the first. There was a time when having a woman serve would have shocked everyone.

Ruth Bader Ginsburg spent her life working for change. "So now the perception is, yes, women are here to stay. And when I'm sometimes asked, 'When will there be enough women on the Supreme Court and I say, 'When there are 9,' people are shocked. But there'd been 9 men, and nobody's ever raised a question about that." She was a tireless advocate for gender equality, women's interests, civil liberties, and civil rights.

Ruth Bader Ginsburg died doing her job. At 87 years old and suffering from metastatic pancreatic cancer, she did. not. stop. Knowing how important, politically, it was for the ideological balance of the Court to be maintained, she kept going long after most of us would have retired. She spent her life working to make us all stronger—what has that work all been for if we give up now?

Yes, the very Republican Senator from Kentucky who refused to let President Barack Obama appoint Merrick Garland to the United States Supreme Court towards the end of his term is now going to try and push through the current President's choice—whomever that may be—before the November election. Why wouldn't he?

President Obama said this yesterday: "Four and a half years ago, when Republicans refused to hold a hearing or an up-or-down vote on Merrick Garland, they invented the principle that the Senate shouldn't fill an open seat on the Supreme Court before a new president was sworn in. A basic principle of the law — and everyday fairness — is that we apply rules with consistency, and not based on what's convenient or advantageous at the moment. The rule of law, the legitimacy of our courts, the fundamental workings of our democracy all depend on that basic principle. As votes are already being cast in this election, Republican Senators are now called to apply that standard." RGB, herself, on her deathbed, dictated to her granddaughter, "My most fervent wish is that I will not be replaced until a new president is installed."

Yes, we should mourn this great American patriot, but let's all also honor her by not giving in to our fears but, instead, continuing to support her cause. Her passing makes everything we're facing more difficult, sure, I'll give you that, but it also just might give us all that last kick in the ass we need to make it through this election. She left us because she knew we could handle it. And we can.

So says the somewhat honorable gentleperson from the Great State of Virginia.

Rest in Power Chief Justice Ginsburg. You've more than earned it. We've got this.

September 21, 2020
453,142 Total Reported Cases in New York. 32,993 Deaths.

It's morning in Florida. I am sitting in my mother's living room, barely awake, and she has already been up for hours.

The night before last, I stayed in Charleston, South Carolina, a place I'd always wanted to visit. I was able to take a good long walk the evening I arrived and another one the following morning.

Compared to many other places I have been to, there were a fair amount of people out and about on Saturday night in Charleston. Some with masks. Some of the rowdier ones without.

The main population corridor in the northeast stretches from Boston down to Washington D.C. The area that encompasses is largely urban and suburban. Boston, New York, and Washington are the three big cultural centers that anchor it but there are plenty of others within that area, such as Philadelphia and Baltimore, that are almost as big. That sphere of influence overflows south of D.C. into Richmond a bit, but when you leave Richmond and head further south, you have well and truly left that largely liberal northeast corridor.

The first thing that you notice driving along the interstate below Richmond is that they start naming the swamps. Signs for places selling peanuts start appearing. Then pecans. As you get into the lower part of North Carolina and South Carolina, signs for peaches start appearing, and then once you've hit Florida, it's citrus—oranges and grapefruit.

Interstate 95 runs up and down the entire eastern side of the country parallel to the Atlantic Ocean. It begins at the border crossing into New Brunswick, Canada in Northern Maine and runs down to Miami at the bottom of Florida. I don't remember being on it as a kid, but we must have been as construction started on it before I was born. The final leg of it, in central New Jersey was only officially completed in 2018. It is the longest north-south interstate in the country and passes through more states than any other in the system—15 plus parts of the District of Columbia. Only five of the 96 counties it passes through are completely rural. It serves about 110 million people or roughly 1/3 of our total population and facilitates delivery, by estimates, of about 40% of the gross domestic product of the country.

As William Least Heat-Moon wrote in his book, *Blue Highways*, however, "Life doesn't happen along interstates. It's against the law." You're not allowed to stop along the interstate. There are no shops or market stalls. There are rest areas every so often where you can pull off and take a bathroom break, but that's it. To experience where you are, you need to take the exit and drive along some back roads.

On long drives, I try to find interesting places to stop every two hours or so. I am particularly drawn to see what strange and odd things might be nearby—the world's largest or smallest or oldest or tallest whatever. Between Richmond and Charleston, I stopped in the town of Wilson, North Carolina. In the center of the historic center of town is an area called the Vollis Simpson Whirligig Park.

Vollis Simpson was a farm machinery repairman who lived on his family's farm about 11 miles outside of Wilson. When he retired, he started making whirligigs. Simply put, a whirligig is an object that spins or whirls. Often it will have a fan-like part that catches the breeze and, as it spins, causes something else to move. People would put smaller ones on their roofs or their mailboxes. A person sawing logs is a common theme. Steam trains with working wheels is another. Made of wood and wire, they've become collectors' pieces in the folk-art world.

Vollis Simpson's whirligigs are different. He constructed them from metal, and they are huge. Some of them are fifty feet tall. He made and installed them on his farm right up until he passed away in 2013 at the age of 94. Before he died, he agreed that his work would be moved into downtown Wilson and be maintained in perpetuity by the town. Thirty of his kinetic sculptures are now arranged in one central area. They are wondrous.

As you walk through the park, all around and above you, everything is in motion. Wheels turn, pinwheels spin, and yes logs are sawn and trains chug. Some are abstract, some are based on something real, but they are all breathtaking. The constant whirring makes the breezy air sound as if it's full of bumblebees.

These sculptures became his life's work and now they are giving new life to this tiny North Carolina town. Wilson was once an important tobacco-growing center. In the nineteenth century, it was known as "the World's Greatest Tobacco Market." Before Mr. Simpson's work was installed, however, downtown Wilson was well on its way to becoming a ghost town. It has now become a model for what is termed "creative placemaking."

Vollis Simpson's visionary and decidedly quirky work has the potential to draw people to Wilson where they will possibly spend some money. You can see that it is already beginning to happen there. Right across the street from the park, a brand-new brewery called 217 Brew works opened earlier this year. The day before yesterday, its outdoor tables were filled with people who all looked like they had come or were going to the sculpture park. A museum and restaurant are being constructed along another side of the park. Downtown, which is rife with empty buildings there are already a few art galleries occupying storefronts. An art studio, teaching classes, was open down the block. There was a class in session as I walked by.

The National Endowment for the Arts describes the creative

placemaking process like this:

"In creative placemaking, partners from public, private, nonprofit, and community sectors strategically shape the physical and social character of a neighborhood, town, tribe, city, or region around arts and cultural activities. Creative placemaking animates public and private spaces, rejuvenates structure and streetscapes, improves business viability and public safety, and brings diverse people together to celebrate, inspire, and be inspired."

Our President, from the beginning of his administration, has done everything he can to try and eliminate the entire budget for the National Endowment for the Arts. Betsy DeVos, the Education Secretary has also done everything she can to eliminate funding for Arts education in our schools. This incredibly short-sighted systematic attack on the Arts by the current Administration simply doesn't make any financial sense whatsoever. The Arts are a thriving, productive, and, yes, a lucrative part of our economy. Do away with our arts programs and you only cripple our economy.

President John F. Kennedy said, "If art is to nourish the roots of our culture, society must set the artist free to follow his vision wherever it takes him… We must never forget that art is not a form of propaganda; it is a form of truth."

You can see the effect of the Arts on a small town like Wilson just as easily as you can see their effect on a major city like New York. Every aspect of our lives is hopelessly interconnected with every other aspect. Unless all parts of it are equally healthy, the body cannot hope to survive. You cannot start chipping away at one sector like the Arts and think that it isn't going to undermine the rest of it.

It's good to be here in Florida with my mother. After taking three days to get here by car, I should probably think twice before complaining again about being delayed a few minutes by an airline. Of course, like the Interstate, you don't see anything much from a plane anyway.

SEPTEMBER 22, 2020
453,730 Total Reported Cases in New York. 33,097 Deaths.

One of the things that I wanted to do while I was here was to set up an iPad for my mother so that she can FaceTime with the rest of the family. It really should have been easier than it was.

The Republicans in the Senate have predictably decided to push to get a new Supreme Court Justice appointed and approved before the election. All the arguments that they made supporting their decision not to appoint Merrick Garland during the waning months of the Obama presidency have been conveniently forgotten. We all grew up playing with kids who behaved that way. Once they started losing a game, they would change the rules of it so that they could win. As kids, the way we got around that is that we stopped playing with them and found other friends to play with. Hopefully, we will be able to do the same thing with the Senator from Kentucky and his cynically hypocritical compatriots. Truth be told, if the Republicans had any confidence that they were going to win, they would not be doing this.

For the first eighty years of its existence, the number of Justices appointed to the Supreme Court fluctuated several times. It went up and down from a low of five to a peak of ten.

The current number, nine, was ultimately settled on in 1869.

The Founding Fathers didn't provide much in the way of guidelines for appointees. There are no explicit requirements for age or experience, or even citizenship outlined in the Constitution. There is also no discussion about how many Judges there should be. The Judiciary Act of 1789 signed into law by President Washington established the initial court. That Act said that a panel of six Justices would be responsible for making sure that laws enacted by the legislative and executive branches followed what was stated in the Constitution.

It established a tiered system of courts. On the lowest level was a federal judge in each state who oversaw different districts within their state. Then the districts in each state were organized into three large geographical districts where appeals and certain cases could be heard. At the top, were the six justices who oversaw all of it. Those six justices were assigned, two per each of these three large districts. They had to spend a large part of the year traveling a circuit through their given area and adjudicate on the road.

Eleven years later, that changed. John Adams, our second President, signed the Judiciary Act of 1801 into law. That law restructured things so that the Supreme Court Justices no longer traveled around, and their number was reduced from six to five. This law was signed after Adams had lost his reelection bid to Thomas Jefferson. At the time, it was seen as a political move on Adams' part designed to limit the power of his successor to make appointments to the court.

Thomas Jefferson immediately repealed the Act when he took office, and the six Justices were restored and resumed their travels. The number of Justices grew over time as the country expanded westward and more were needed to fulfill the responsibilities in the greater area. By 1837 under Andrew Jackson there were nine.

After the Dred Scott decision which said that Black people were not and could not become US citizens, Abraham Lincoln and the Republicans added a tenth Justice to try and move the court further to the left. When Lincoln was assassinated, his Vice President, Andrew Johnson, a southern Democrat assumed the office. Remember the ideologies of the two parties were reversed from what they are today. Whereas Lincoln was progressive, Johnson was decidedly not.

Johnson tried to veto the Civil Rights Act of 1866 which granted full citizenship to all people born in the United States regardless of race. Congressional Republicans were able to override that veto and to make sure that they weren't overturned by the Court they then passed another Act reducing the number of justices to seven. The hope was to establish more of a balance so that the Court wouldn't sway decisions in favor of the Southern states. The next President, Ulysses S. Grant, also a Republican, then passed yet another act in 1869 that raised the number back up to nine and required a quorum of six to be present to make decisions.

It's been nine ever since. Franklin Roosevelt tried to raise the number to 15 when the Court started striking down his New Deal laws. Everyone, even his supporters, accused him of attempting to pack the court and the Senate voted against him.

Now we are here, yet again, in a fight for the balance of the Supreme Court. The Senator from Kentucky is doing everything he can to try and sway the court to the right while he and his fellow Republicans are still in power. The Democrats are trying to figure out how to stop him.

The current slate of Republican-appointed Supreme Court Justices has not always voted in the way that this current Administration would have liked them to. They have, at least some of the time, voted seemingly based on their interpretation of the law, rather than whatever their personal feelings might be.

The President is betting that his "win" on the question of this appointment will completely distract us from other things. The uproar has already pushed the virus to page two right at the point where we are about to lose our 200,000th citizen to COVID-19. The President is paying attention even while it seems he isn't.

This kind of political battle galvanizes some people but also makes some others shut down. The more intense this gets, and it is going to get extremely intense, the more a lot of people will simply just tune it out. My mother, however, is not going to let this election go down without a fight. I brought her down a facemask with the word 'Vote' on it. Last night she wore it into the restaurant that we ordered dinner from.

"I like your mask," said the guy behind the counter. You'd better.

September 23, 2020
454,299 Total Reported Cases in New York. 33,098 Deaths.

Dead in the center of downtown Fayetteville, North Carolina, there is a traffic circle. Inside that traffic circle sits a very interesting-looking building.

It was built in 1832 on the site of the old State House which had burned down the year before in what the town calls the Great Fire of 1831. The building's design owes more to old English market building architecture than it does to the styles that developed here in the United States.

Fayetteville is where a resolution called "The Liberty Point Resolves" was signed about a year before the *Declaration of Independence* was published in Philadelphia. While not a call for independence *per se*, fifty residents of Cumberland County resolved their hope that Great Britain and the colonies be reconciled. Should that not happen, the Cumberland Association vowed, they would "go forth and be ready to sacrifice our lives and fortunes to secure her freedom and safety." The meeting took place in Lewis Barge's tavern, which stood within a block or two of the current location of the traffic circle. The Old State House, which once stood there, was where the delegates from North Carolina had gathered to sign the United States Constitution.

The Market House, as the odd-looking two-story building in the circle is called, has long been the symbol of the town. It is part of its official seal. It has, historically also been on all sorts of other official documents. There is currently a petition that was begun in June that has been signed by over 115,000 people. That represents slightly more than half of the town's population. They want to tear the Market House building down.

Why? The Market House in Fayetteville, North Carolina, is a place where slaves were once bought and sold.

The petition reads in part: "The reason we are making this petition is for peace and unity within the city. This has been brought up in City Hall meetings many times over the years and ignored. We have peacefully protested against the building being there. It is very disrespectful and fuels hatred for African Americans by people who still believe in the values of slavery and racism. There have even been many attempts to burn this building down and it gets rebuilt every time. People are risking their lives to get rid of a building that causes hate, racism, and is a symbol of injustice."

In 1934, during a surprise stopover in Fayetteville, First Lady Eleanor Roosevelt got out of her train to stretch her legs and expressed her desire to see the "slave market". The Fayetteville Observer representative who had been enlisted to be her guide quickly assured her that the story was all a fraud. No slaves had ever been sold there. He must have been convincing because she got back on the train without ever visiting it.

In 1948, a petition circulated to move the building from its position to somewhere else because it was hindering the flow of traffic. A prominent local who was a member of the United Daughters of the Confederacy said if that happened, she would go downtown and, "sit on top of it with a machine gun."

In 1970 while the Civil Rights movement was still in full force, local officials made a concerted effort to get the words, 'slave market' off some state maps. They were afraid that the city would become a target for protesters. In 1979, the Fayetteville City School Board voted to take the image off their high school diplomas because of complaints from black residents.

In 1988, perhaps hoping to put the matter of whether slaves had been sold there to rest, John Cavanagh, a Duke University professor, studied the building's history from 1790 through 1865. He found that, indeed, about every two months, there were auctions of people that took place at the Market House.

Here are some sale advertisements that the professor found in the Fayetteville Observer's files:

— From 1839, "family of Negroes, consisting of a Woman and Five Children."

— From 1846, "a Negro woman and child, belonging to the Estate of John McArn, dec'd."

— From the same edition in 1846, "Ten Likely Negroes, consisting of men, women, boys and girls," to be sold for cash under a Deed of Trust sale at the Market House

— From 1851, "Sale of Negroes," at the Town Hall, "Ben about 27 years, Tena about 13 and Harriet about 60." Also, that year, "a man by the name of Bill, well known as a boat hand, belonging to the above estate."

— From 1863, an "Administration Sale" at the Market House to include land and "the following negroes; viz: Jim, aged about 20 years, Nancy, aged 17, and child about 18 months old. Terms at sale."

According to the last census, Fayetteville is evenly divided along racial lines. White people account for about 45% of the population and black people about 43%. When I drove into Fayetteville, (and yes, it was to see the Slave Market) I found the building surrounded by black fencing. Painted on the asphalt on the traffic circle itself following the line of the fencing, were the words 'Black Lives Do Matter—End Racism Now' in giant yellow letters. During the riots following the murder of George Floyd in Minneapolis, the Market House had been set on fire.

The presence of this building is causing pain. Its history is a constant reminder to the people who live there of an unimaginably horrific past. It is in the direct center of the town. Can you imagine what it would be like to be Jewish and live in a town that had a Nazi crematorium in its center? To have that crematorium on the seal of your town. On your children's High School diplomas? To have holiday decorations placed on it every year?

I will never advocate for the destruction of something like the Market House. Erasing it is just as bad as glorifying it. Instead of razing the building, however, move it. Put it somewhere where it is not the focal point of the town where it can be used to teach people about their past.

Think about this sale advertisement from 1859 for a minute, "a valuable woman and three children, to close a deed of trust." What is the likelihood that woman was sold together with her children? That sale is probably the last time that any of those people saw each other. Picture that woman, probably in shackles, watching as her children, also in shackles, were sold and torn away from her. Picture what it would feel like, if you were descended from that woman, and had to drive past that building every day.

That is what this whole discussion about Civil War monuments is about. It's not about honoring the Confederate Generals or the southern fighting men. It is about the unimaginable pain and anguish that was visited upon the men and women who were bought and sold as property for much of our nation's early history.

A few days ago, at the National Archives, the President announced that he is going to create a commission that will promote what he calls "Patriotic Education." He said that there will be a grant established to be used to formulate a "pro-American curriculum." He railed against what he called the "web of lies" being taught in our country's classrooms.

"Teaching this horrible doctrine to our children is a form of child abuse, the truest sense. For many years now, the radicals have mistaken Americans' silence for weakness. They're wrong. There is no more powerful force than a parent's love for their children. And patriotic moms and dads are going to demand that their children are no longer fed hateful lies about this country."

Slavery is a disease that isn't easy to cure. The overt symptoms might disappear, but the underlying after-effects linger on. They linger on and get passed down to the victims' children and their children and on and on uninterrupted. The disease travels both through the slavers' lines as well as those of the enslaved, but we're all infected on some level. We need to cure it.

SEPTEMBER 24, 2020
455,400 Total Reported Cases in New York. 33,103 Deaths.

I am in downtown Georgetown, South Carolina. This morning, I had what was supposed to be a fifteen-minute talk with an elderly man named Andrew Rodrigues who runs the Gullah Culture Museum here in Georgetown. It ended up being a truly fascinating and rather moving hour and a half.

The museum is a tiny hole-in-the-wall, and, inside it, the history of the Gullah people is told largely through a series of beautiful story quilts that were made by his late wife. Once he started talking, there was no leaving—both for politeness' sake and because he was riveting.

The Gullah people are descended from slaves from West Africa who were brought here to work on plantations. They retained a lot of their African culture because this area was so secluded. Gullah is a creole language with its basis in English but with many elements of West African languages added in. Even today there are about 125,000 people in this area who still speak it.

Michelle Obama's family traces its roots back to this area. One of the quilts that Andrew's wife Vermelle made was for Barack Obama's inauguration. The quilt tells Mrs. Obama's family story from her great, great grandfather who was enslaved on a farm near Georgetown right down through to the last panel which is the White House. In the middle of it is an almost life-size rendering of Mrs. Obama in a graduation gown with the words Harvard and Princeton on top of it.

I asked Mr. Rodrigues if the First Lady saw it at the time but he wasn't sure if she had. I certainly hope that she did. According to him, it was the only quilt his wife ever needed help with because of the deadline of the inauguration. There are some wonderful pictures of the circle of ladies who helped her sew it. There's an amazing amount of history in that tiny little space. I do truly hope that it can keep going in the years to come.

We don't necessarily choose the people who influence us the most. I learned more today from Mr. Rodriguez than I ever could have imagined. All it took was for me to take the time to listen.

SEPTEMBER 25, 2020
456,400 Total Reported Cases in New York.

On the drive up from Savannah, past Charleston, and on into Georgetown, there are stands set up along the road selling sweetgrass baskets. Each stand represents the work of a different artist. They all look similar—they all use the same materials and the same basic technique—but each of them is unique.

The baskets are a Gullah traditional craft that was brought over from West Africa. Originally enslaved women here made them for their personal use, but they soon became popular with their European captors as well. Now they are a well-respected local craft. An expertly made intricate basket can sell for many hundreds, or even, in the case of some that I saw, thousands of dollars.

While I was in Charleston, I came down into the hotel lobby from my room after dinner to go for a walk. A woman was there and had covered several large tables with baskets. She was sitting in a chair off to the side working on a new one.

None of the materials used are dyed so the finished pieces have a similar array of natural colors. The long interior grass that looks like very long dark brown pine needles is bundled together by the wider outer grass which is lighter in color and wound around it. When it's done it makes essentially a thick cable. Sometimes the outer grass is wound right up against itself, so the cable is a light tan, and sometimes it is wound leaving gaps so that the darker brown shows through. That cable is then coiled from a central starting point and worked outwards and then up depending on the design. Some of the baskets are simple bowls. Some are like round jars with lids and others are like flat platters. Others have more fanciful shapes with strange and unexpected curves.

We fell into conversation as she wove, and I asked her how she'd learned how to do it. She told me that she had come to a difficult time in her life some years before and that a friend of hers had given her the greatest gift she'd ever received—an hour and a half of her time. This friend had shown her how to work the grass. "As soon as my fingers touched this sweetgrass it was as if they'd been doing it forever," she told me.

She experimented with different shapes and styles. She looked at what others were doing and borrowed some of their ideas and then came up with some of her own. Sometimes she starts with a particular shape in mind, and sometimes she just starts. As we talked, she looked more at me than down at the piece she was making. Her fingers were doing most of the work on their own.

As each state starts to grapple with reopening its schools, in addition to how we should be doing it, the questions keep coming up about what education is and what it should be.

My niece and nephew are doing online virtual learning and it is, at best, problematic. Some of their teachers are trying by experimenting with how to do it better, but others are just plowing ahead as if they are in a regular classroom. For the kids, it's like sitting at home alone in your room for hours on end watching an incredibly boring TV show without being able to change the channel.

The passing along of facts and figures is just a tiny fraction of what school is all about. After we leave High School, we may not remember what a Golgi body is or how to figure out the square root of 18x over 3, but we have learned how to get along with other people out in the world. We learn how to make friends and how to handle bullies. There will always be a few kids who are inspired by what they learn in biology classes and math classes who turn that into their life's work, but many will simply forget it all and move on to what they want to do.

How much schooling is necessary? Rachel Perkins is a professional sweetgrass basket maker. She learned that skill from a friend. She became proficient by constantly applying herself to it.

I learned to stage manage by doing it. I worked with people who mentored me, and I made my mistakes on the job. With all due respect to my many good friends and colleagues who teach and my many good friends and colleagues who have studied stage managing at school, it isn't a field that requires a university-level education to do. I cannot imagine what it would have been like starting if I was carrying a crippling college loan debt on my back.

Going to school for me, was a gift from my parents. There was much about it that I liked. I was exposed to many schools of thought in many different areas. While I may not have appreciated them at the time and blown a lot of it off, I have since gone back and filled in the gaps and used what I learned there as a basis for further exploration on my own. While I didn't train to be a stage manager there, what I learned in school certainly helped me become one.

When Rachel Perkins told me about feeling like her fingers already knew how to make a basket, I understood what she meant. I had a lot to learn about many aspects of stage managing when I started, I still do, but even in high school, I felt like I already knew how to do it. In retrospect, I'm grateful that my drama teacher saw that and had me do that rather than play one of the poker players in *The Odd Couple* (even though I had a kick-ass audition).

I feel for all the kids who are having to navigate through this strange time, and I applaud the teachers out there who are trying to make it work. The online thing isn't working for my nephew, and he will often just duck out and go fishing.

We won't tell him, but when my nephew searches online to figure out which fish are which and what habitats they like to live in and what they like to eat, that activity is what we call learning. He may not like school much, but he is a smart kid and he's going to be fine. Maybe this year, it is better that he just goes fishing.

September 26, 2020
457,573 Total Reported Cases in New York.

Justice Ruth Bader Ginsburg is lying in state at the US Capitol building. It seems shocking that in 2020, this makes her the first woman to have ever been given that honor as well as the first Jewish person.

In Kentucky, a grand jury failed to indict the police officers responsible for the death of Breonna Taylor. One of the officers was indicted for wanton endangerment but only because during the raid one of the bullets that he fired into Ms. Taylor's apartment went through the wall into the neighboring apartment. There is a department policy that officers have a line of sight when they are shooting, and this officer didn't. He was just firing away blindly through covered doors. He fired ten shots.

The Democratic Mayor of Louisville declared a state of emergency and ordered a curfew this past Wednesday in anticipation of reaction to the case. A sergeant who was shot in the raid sent an email to his fellow officers that said, "I know we did the legal, moral and ethical thing that night." The night in question, an ambulance attended to the officer immediately but did not give Ms. Taylor any medical attention for 20 minutes even though she had been hit by bullets five times. She died. Ms. Taylor was herself an EMT.

I am at my sister's house outside of Raleigh, North Carolina, hanging out with her and her family. There's a lot of life happening now, all at the same time. The pandemic, the election, and the fact that they are growing up. For my niece and nephew, this is the first election that they are experiencing as almost adults.

Last night, while the country roiled and raged, we all lounged around on the couch and watched TV shows—me, my sister, my brother-in-law, my nephew, my niece, the golden retriever, and the three cats. This is what we are all fighting for—life, liberty, and the pursuit of happiness.

I mourn the passing of Justice Ginsburg and Breonna Taylor, but I am not yet ready to mourn the passing of our great Democracy. It isn't gone yet. And we can still get it back.

SEPTEMBER 28, 2020
459,574 Total Reported Cases in New York. 33,136 Deaths.

Quarantine—Day 1.

The New York state guidelines state "If you have traveled from within one of the designated states with significant community spread as defined by the metrics above, you must quarantine when you enter New York for 14 days from the last travel within such designated state, provided on the date you enter into New York State that such state met the criteria for requiring such quarantine."

I am back in New York City from my family road trip down south. The guidelines that apply to me say, "The individual must not be in public or otherwise leave the quarters that they have identified as suitable for their quarantine." So, I am stuck here for the next two weeks. Michael is staying at the apartment of friends of ours in midtown so that I don't have to be trapped in the bedroom the whole time. He's going to come uptown and drop off groceries and whatever else I need over the two weeks. He'll take away the trash, and I'll be able to hand him out things that he's forgotten.

Even at the worst of the shutdown, right at the beginning, I always left the apartment to go for walks and rides. This will be different. I am in here to stay. A lot of people never left their apartments at all in those early days for much longer than two weeks so I'm not complaining. I am looking forward to it with an equal measure of interest and dread.

There is certainly no dearth of news to watch. We are just about to hit a million deaths worldwide from a virus that the President has dismissed as a hoax. The first debate is tomorrow night. That should be interesting.

The New York Times has gotten its hands on the President's federal tax returns for much of the last two decades. In the days ahead there is going to be a lot of discussion over what they mean. Various financial experts have already flooded the airwaves with theories and ideas.

The immediate and obvious takeaway is that in 2016 and 2017 the President paid a total of $750 in taxes for each of those years. For eleven of the other years, he paid no taxes whatsoever. He seems to have managed to avoid paying those taxes because of staggering financial losses which he was able to write off.

The IRS audit that the President has continually used as an excuse for not being able to release his taxes, turns out to be because of a refund of $72.9 million that he claimed and received.

The IRS is disputing the legality of some of what he's claimed were business deductions. One such claim was $70,000 for hair care. He also paid his daughter $700,000 to consult which he claimed was a business expense. At the time she was an employee of the organization. You cannot hire someone to consult who is already an employee.

The Times uncovered that he is in debt for $421 million in personally guaranteed loans. Those loans all come due within the next four years. The conflicts of interest ramifications are potentially huge. The prospect of creditors suing a sitting US President is somewhat unthinkable, but here we are thinking about it. The conflicts multiply exponentially if the creditors turn out to be foreign nationals.

Predictably the President is claiming that this is all fake news. He is also claiming that the New York Times obtained the returns illegally. If they are fake, why would he say that? These returns could shed light on every single action that this man has taken while in office.

On the way home from North Carolina yesterday, I detoured through western Virginia and drove up on part of the Blue Ridge Parkway. The parkway was established right after World War II and runs for 469 miles through North Carolina and Virginia. It links up the Great Smoky Mountains National Park on the border with Tennessee and with the Shenandoah National Park in Virginia.

It's a stunningly beautiful drive. I entered the parkway at the Peaks of Otter. The Peaks of Otter are three separate mountain peaks. One of which, called Sharp Top, is an almost perfect isosceles triangle. Thomas Jefferson had a rock from the peaks of all three mountains worked into the Washington Monument in D.C. The peaks are located less than an hour away from Lynchburg which is where my grandparents lived. It was a favorite day trip when we went down to visit them.

When I was young, maybe ten or eleven, my grandmother gave me a Brownie Box camera. The first picture I ever took was with this camera and is of Sharp Top reflected in the lake at its base. It's a black and white photo and I have it framed in the living room. I've been drawn to reflections ever since.

After my father died, his ashes sat on top of my sister's refrigerator for several years. We finally decided that we needed to spread them somewhere. He ended up in several places but one of them was in the lake at the Peaks of Otter. Another was at a beautiful rocky overlook along the parkway.

Since I visited my mother and my sister and her family, it seemed only right to swing by and visit my dad as well. I took some pictures, but the one I took forty some odd years ago is still better.

It was good to spend some time with my dad. He would have been disgusted by the man who is now sitting in the White House.

We will be hearing a lot more about these latest revelations and I will be right here on the couch listening. At least for the next two weeks. If it were just about me, I would take the chance and go out. But it isn't just about me, it's about everyone else. So here I'll sit.

September 29, 2020
460,553 Total Reported Cases in New York. 33,144 Deaths

Quarantine—Day 2.

It is a hazy cloudy day that is starting to get windy. Not, of course, that I am going to go out into it, but it's something to look at outside.

Thunderstorms are coming. They should start to abate before the debate begins, but there's likely to be a lot of rumbling anyway.

September 30, 2020
33,158 Total Reported Deaths in New York.

Quarantine—Day 3

City mandated repair work on our building continues. I woke up this morning to the sound of crumbling bricks being drilled out of the building's outer walls. Thankfully, they are not currently working on a wall that is connected to our apartment. Not being able to leave the apartment while that is going on would be almost unendurable.

Predictably, last night's debate was a disaster. It wasn't a disaster for either of the candidates—both turned in performances that their bases could be OK with. It was a disaster for our country.

The President was in relentless aggressive attack mode. Almost everything that he said was skewed or untrue. He was rude and boorish throughout. His opponent withstood him. He even managed to get in a few moments where he looked directly into the camera and talked to us. He didn't rise to the President's bait, for the most part, but nor did he truly prevail.

The moderator was unable to control much of the evening. Whatever rules the President had agreed to, he did not follow. What should have been a thoughtful exchange of ideas and a discussion of policy, was, instead, in essence, an hour and a half-long verbal brawl.

A friend of mine in Australia posted earlier on in the day the channel that people there could watch the debate on. All I could think was, oh no, please don't. It's like the neighborhood getting together to watch your parents have a drunken brawl on the front lawn. We, as a country, should be mortified by what we showed the rest of the world last night.

(Just for the record, my parents never engaged in a drunken brawl on our front lawn.)

In the middle of the debate, the moderator asked the President, "Are you willing tonight to condemn white supremacists and militia groups to say that they need to stand down and not add to the violence in a number of these cities as we saw in Kenosha and Portland?"

He responded, "Sure, I'm willing to do that, I would say almost everything I see is from the left-wing, not the right-wing. I'm willing to do anything. I want to see peace."

The moderator kept going, "Then do it, sir."

Biden prodded him. "Say it. Do it. Say it."

What the President then said was, "Proud Boys, stand back and stand by. But I'll tell you what, somebody's gotta do something about Antifa and the left. This is not a right-wing problem. This is a left-wing problem."

The Proud Boys is an all-male far-right organization that advocates and glorifies violence against the left. Their name comes from the song "Proud of Your Boy" from the Disney animated film *Aladdin*.

Taki's Magazine is an online platform that is paleoconservative. Paleoconservatives support American nationalism, Christian ethics, regionalism, and traditional conservatism. They are largely libertarian. They support immigration restrictions, the dismantling of multi-cultural programs, nonintervention internationally in terms of foreign policy, and a decentralization of federal government to give more power to the states. Taki's Magazine started as a magazine of politics and culture. With a series of articles in support of a Greek neo-Nazi political party, it became obvious that their sympathies were strongly alt-right.

The Proud Boys started alt-right but after the neo-Nazi "Unite the Right" rally in Charlottesville, Virginia in August of 2017 started pulling away from that. Their founder said that the alt-right's focus is mainly race and that what they were advocating was what he called "Western values."

Race, however, is certainly a major part of what they believe.

These people think that there is a plot to dilute the purity of the white race through intermarriage, integration, and abortion. The authors of this so-called "plot" are often said to be the Jews. Officially, these guys reject white supremacy, but they often participate in racist-themed events.

The Proud Boys are profoundly anti-feminist. They believe that women are completely subservient to men. Remarkably, they have a female auxiliary branch that they call Proud Boys' Girls who are completely on board with this.

The Proud Boys glorify violence. Their founder once said, "I want violence, I want punching in the face. I'm disappointed in Trump supporters for not punching enough." In November of 2018 after the Charlottesville rally, the FBI classified the group as extremist with ties to white nationalism.

This is the group that the President instructed to "stand back and stand by." This should clear up any question, once and for all, about what this man thinks and where he stands. Not only is he unwilling to condemn white supremacy, but he is also its most visible and powerful advocate.

The Proud Boys have taken "stand back and stand by" as a new slogan. They are treating it as a call to action. It's trending on Twitter. Newsweek is reporting that they are already selling merchandise with the phrase emblazoned on it. I tried to find it this morning but decided not to pursue it. I didn't want the algorithms to start thinking that I was interested in buying any of them. Fred Perry has stopped selling its black shirts with yellow piping in the US because the group has appropriated it as their costume.

Yesterday, I received a notification that my application to be an Election Day polling worker had been accepted. I have a four-hour training session scheduled for October 17th. Early in-person voting begins on October 24th here in New York. I am willing to do as much as they need.

There is only so much that each of us, individually, can do during this election. If we all do what we can, together, we can do it all.

October 1, 2020

462,861 Total Reported Cases in New York. 33,165 Deaths.

Quarantine—Day 4

The cat is ready for Michael to come home. A day or two was endurable, but four days is already too much. I am not nearly as well trained as Michael is to do his bidding.

The cat believes that his food needs to be switched out as soon as the sun comes up. He is happy to remind us of this. If we aren't already up—and these days, we have not had many reasons to get up that early—then the cat will attempt to get us up. He will jump up on the bed and walk on top of Michael and just sit on him, looking at him, until he wakes up. If that doesn't work, he'll meow. It's almost the only time he makes any noise at all.

Michael is a much lighter sleeper than I am, as the cat knows, and Michael will get up and switch out his food then come back to bed. It doesn't work that well with me. I will sleep through it. I might stir a bit, but I'll just kick him off the bed and turn over without waking up. With me, he will usually give it a shot but then curl up and doze alongside me until I eventually get up on my own.

To be clear, the cat is not hungry in the morning. There is almost always a bit of food still left in his bowl. The cat just needs the attention and the routine. I got the cat's food and water bowls from the gift shop at the Dickens Museum in London. The famous quote from *Oliver Twist* is written around the inside lip, "Please sir, I want some more."

Because the stimulus package failed to pass yesterday, American Airlines and United are going to lay off 32,000 employees today. It is the largest day of aviation job losses in history.

28,000 Disney theme park employees are also being laid off today because help is not coming. That number also includes some workers from their retail and cruise line divisions but most of these people had jobs in the parks in Anaheim and Orlando. These lost jobs range from people who were working part-time on hourly wages up to the executives.

Disneyland in California has not been allowed to reopen since the initial shutdown in the spring.

About 32,000 people worked there and have been on furlough since April. Because of laxer restrictions in Florida, Disney World in Orlando has been allowed to reopen in a limited way, but attendance there has been weak. Just under 20% of their 77,000 regular employees were called back to work when the state of Florida allowed them to. Families, however, have not come. According to travel agents, people are unwilling to risk the flight. They also don't want to pay for what ends up being a limited experience—no fireworks, no interaction with characters, limited dining options, and shorter hours.

The CDC announced today that it is extending its No Sail Order for cruise ships through to the end of October. Part of their statement reads, "Recent outbreaks on cruise ships overseas provide current evidence that cruise ship travel continues to transmit and amplify the spread of SARS-CoV-2, the virus that causes COVID-19, even when ships sail at reduced passenger capacities—and would likely spread the infection into U.S. communities if passenger operations were to resume prematurely in the United States." Originally, they wanted the order to extend through February, but the White House pressured them to shorten it.

The cruise industry generates $53 billion in revenue both from the actual cruises but also from other businesses that are connected to them. Florida's cruise industry is the largest in the country and has been the hardest hit.

Contained within the Democrats' Heroes Act, which didn't pass, is The Save our Stages Act. This provision would provide $10 billion in assistance for live event producers, promoters, and talent representatives whose businesses have been compromised by the pandemic. That money would cover six months of payroll expenses, rent, mortgage, utilities, and PPE.

The President of the Broadway League said yesterday about the Act's failure to pass, "It certainly doesn't save us, because we're not going to die."

I will say that I am surprised that it has taken this long for a stimulus package to pass. A month before the election and they are leaving us all high and dry? That doesn't seem like the best campaign strategy to me.

Well, that's it for now. I must get to work. The cat has a whole list of things for me to do today and I'd better get to it before he wakes up.

OCTOBER 2, 2020
464,620 Total Reported Cases in New York. 33,204 Deaths.

Quarantine—Day 5

Last night, just before 1 am, the President tweeted, "Tonight, FLOTUS and I tested positive for COVID-19. We will begin our quarantine and recovery process immediately. We will get through this together."

My niece has gotten me somewhat hooked on a TV show called *Supernatural*. It is kind of a cross between *Buffy, the Vampire Slayer*, *X-Files*, and *Dukes of Hazard*. I'm not recommending this show to anybody, but for me, it's kind of perfect. It's interesting enough to watch, the two leads are cute after all, but it's not so interesting or complex that I can't do other things while it's on. It's a perfect show to exercise and stretch to. I can sort receipts, pay bills, and go through stuff and not feel that it needs my full attention. The best part of it is that there are 320 hour-long episodes of it, and I am only on about episode 14. I am confident that it will last through to the end of this quarantine.

Michael and I have similar tastes in much of what we watch so there are very few things that he is happy for me to watch without him. Science fiction, horror, and fantasy-based shows hold almost no interest for him at all. I, on the other hand, eat that stuff up. My inner 14-year-old self has never really grown up.

The President and First Lady contracting COVID-19 would be a huge moment on any TV series. We expected that the next month leading up to the election was pretty much going to follow the same path that it has been on. There was still the suspense of not knowing who is going to win and what the players will then do when the results are known, but we were pretty much on a straight line to that end. Their story has now veered off on another completely different tangent and none of us know what direction it is now going to take.

The prevailing sense last night is that nobody trusts this. I certainly don't believe that we have been or will be given the full truth. Between 2 am and 4 am a whole slew of conspiracy theories exploded into being. I finally shut everything down and went to sleep. This morning, in the light of day, it all seems to be somewhat calmer, but there is still no clear answer about what we can expect.

Less than a week ago, the President held a ceremony in the Rose Garden to announce his nominee to the Supreme Court. Five people who attended that mask-less, non-socially distanced event have now tested positive for the virus. Among them is Republican Senator Mike Lee. There is film footage of him greeting and hugging people without a mask.

University of Notre Dame President Reverend John Jenkins who was there has also tested positive. It was also announced that a White House journalist and a press staffer have also tested positive.

The President is reporting mild symptoms. We may never know whether that's true or not. He is in some of the highest risk categories. He is male. He is old. He is obese and he has high cholesterol. Even with that, statistically, he is more likely to survive this than die from it.

There are all sorts of discussions about what could happen if the President should become incapacitated or even perish. If the Vice President should be incapacitated as well then-Speaker of the House Pelosi, in theory, would take over. There are some constitutional law experts, however, who say that the Secretary of State could challenge that and assume the office himself.

Dick Cheney, G.W. Bush's vice president, apparently wrote a letter of resignation that he entrusted to a colleague. If something happened to the President and then to him, his resignation would mean that he would need to be replaced and his replacement would then assume the Presidency. That would bypass having to go to the Speaker of the House.

In terms of the election, should something happen to the nominee, the party could appoint a new candidate, but it is not at all certain how that person would be added to the ballot when the election is only four weeks away. People could continue to vote for him with the understanding that they are, in essence, voting for the party and then rely on the party to choose a replacement. Remember, we aren't voting for the candidates directly, we are voting for members of the electoral college to represent our choice in the final balloting. The members of the electoral college could make that call.

A good TV series keeps you attuned and attentive. Our current national series is, at times, a bit hard to follow. It is filled with characters who lie and deceive so you can never fully trust what is going on. What it isn't, is boring. Relentless and overwhelming maybe, but not boring.

For today, though, I've had enough of it. I am switching over to *Supernatural*. At least there, the demon or evil spirit usually gets vanquished by the end of the episode in a satisfyingly gory way. Unlike our current real-life series, no matter how difficult a position our two handsome heroes get into, we know they are going to get out of it.

How is ours going to end? Who knows? We will just have to wait and see.

OCTOBER 3, 2020
466,307 Total Reported Cases in New York.

Quarantine—Day 6

"What is a weekend?" The Dowager Countess played by Maggie Smith rather dryly asks of the younger members of the aristocratic family gathered around the table in the series *Downton Abbey*. She didn't know.

Notes and Queries is a quarterly scholarly journal that was begun in 1849 and is still published to this day. It is a compilation of articles that are related to the English language and literature. Its primary purpose, according to Oxford University Press, was and still is the asking and answering of reader's questions.

The concept of the weekend as we know it is not that old. The first use of the word weekend comes in 1879. A correspondent from *Notes and Queries* tried to answer the question of what it was by saying that they thought that it was a dialect term from Staffordshire. "If a person leaves home ... on the Saturday afternoon to spend the evening of Saturday and the following Sunday with friends ... he is said to be spending his *week-end* at So-and-so. I am informed that this name for Saturday and the day which comes between a Saturday and Monday is confined to this district."

By the 1920s when the word was being more commonly used, the idea had taken on a somewhat more salacious connotation. When Edward, Prince of Wales asked his dad, George V, for permission to use Fort Belvedere at Windsor, the response was, "What could you possibly want that queer old place for? Those damn week-ends I suppose." It was during one of those wild weekend parties that Edward met Wallis Simpson and sent the entire British monarchy into crisis.

The idea of having a day or days of leisure isn't new. In ancient Rome, there was a market day every eight days when kids didn't need to go to school. The French Revolutionary calendar designated every tenth day as a leisure day.

Here in the US, it wasn't until 1908 that a New England cotton mill instituted a 5-day work week so that its Jewish workers could honor the Sabbath from sundown on Friday to sundown on Saturday. The Christian workers then could honor their holy day on Sunday. Henry Ford started shutting down his factories on Saturdays and Sundays in 1926.

Sitting here in my apartment for these two weeks of quarantine, the fact that it is now the weekend means absolutely nothing to me whatsoever. It is merely day 6 and tomorrow will be merely day 7.

The Rose Garden announcement of the President's choice for the replacement for Supreme Court Justice Ruth Bader Ginsburg on September 26, is starting to look like it's becoming a major super spreader event. Former advisor to the President Kellyanne Conway who attended the event now has it. Her daughter has been posting about it with disgust on TikTok.

Yesterday, we already knew that Republican Senator Mike Lee from Utah and Rev. John Jenkins the President of Notre Dame had become infected. Last night, Republican Senator Thom Tillis from North Carolina announced that he's come down with it as well. Republican Senator Ron Johnson from Wisconsin has also tested positive. He wasn't at the event, but he did attend a lunch with other Senators from his party who did earlier this week. Bill Stepien, the President's campaign manager announced yesterday that he has it.

Three White House journalists who cover the President have contracted it themselves as well as an Administration press staffer who worked with them. Then, of course, there is the President and First Lady.

The President was assuring everyone that he was just experiencing a mild case and doing well. Nonetheless, yesterday, the President was helicoptered off the south lawn of the White House to Walter Reed Medical Center. It has been reported that he has been given an experimental Regeneron drug called Regen CoV2. It is thought that this drug might be effective in helping patients fight off a COVID19 infection in its early stages.

The White House is not being open about what is going on with the President's condition. Health experts reporting from various outlets seem to be unified in their feeling that the development of his symptoms has been unusually fast. If the President is experiencing symptoms that are as severe as they now seem, they feel that his infection probably actually occurred sometime before it was reported. That could mean that he might have already been infected when he debated Joe Biden in Cleveland on September 29—three days after the Rose Garden event.

The President was not tested before the debate. He arrived too late. The City of Cleveland has confirmed that eleven people connected with the debate have now been confirmed to have contracted the virus. They include members of the media as well as people involved in the organization and set-up of the debate. None of those people were present during the actual debate. Former New Jersey Governor Chris Christie who was part of the President's debate prep team just announced an hour ago that he, too, has tested positive.

Just now, the President's physician, Dr. Sean Conley held a press conference in front of Walter Reed. In trying to avoid any real answers, Dr. Conley has, instead, opened us all up to a whole raft of more troubling questions. The first question he dodged was whether the President was on supplemental oxygen. He would only answer, even when pressed, that the President was not on oxygen now.

Then in response to another question, he started his answer by saying that it has been 72 hours since his diagnosis. That certainly helps explain the speed at which the President's condition appears to have deteriorated. All of us only found out about his diagnosis 36 hours ago. Dr. Conley confirmed the 72-hour timeline in a follow-up question.

If the President knew that he had been infected with COVID-19 72 hours ago, then that means that when he had his live on-air chat with Sean Hannity on Fox on Thursday night that he already knew that he had it. "I just went out with the test, I'll see, 'cause, you know, we spend a lot of time — and the First Lady just went out with a test also. So, whether we quarantine, or whether we have it, I don't know"

The White House has been spinning the President being in Walter Reed as a move taken out of an abundance of caution. Dr. Conley belied that statement by confirming this morning that the President is a patient. There is a report this morning from a yet unnamed source who is familiar with the President's health that despite what Dr. Conley just told us that the President is not on a clear path to recovery. The White House's control over their messaging seems to be falling apart.

There is a truly sickening inevitability to all of this. The sheer hubris of the President and his Administration in their blasé response to this pandemic from the beginning has almost guaranteed that this is what would happen. This virus doesn't care if it spreads through a crowd of bikers at a rally in South Dakota or a bunch of Republicans at an ill-conceived Rose Garden event in Washington D.C.

It is beautiful weather-wise outside today. The air is crisp and cool. It is the perfect weekend day. Michael stopped by this morning and left me some coffee hanging on the doorknob. I left him a bag of used kitty litter in return. I'm glad that he can be out and about on a day like this even if can't. It doesn't look like the leaves are changing at all yet, but it's got to be just around the corner. If they could hold off for just another week, that would be great.

Have a great weekend.

OCTOBER 5, 2020

The President is discharged from Walter Reed Medical Center. He re-enters the White House without a mask.

Quarantine—Day 8

I've decided to grow a beard. The last time that I tried to grow one I was in my twenties. It ended up more of a goatee than a beard. The area just below my sideburns is somewhat follicly-challenged so I didn't have a choice. We will see what comes of it.

As I was watching it for signs of growth yesterday, the President took a joy ride outside of the hospital. Not since OJ Simpson's low-speed chase in the white Bronco has an SUV out on the road been given so much coverage.

The reports about his condition have gotten more and more murky and contradictory with each passing hour. The worst part of that is the realization that the White House is so disorganized that it cannot even control the messaging from its own staffers.

There is a long history of Presidents hiding the truth about their medical statuses in the United States. This President is hardly the first. When Woodrow Wilson was elected to the Presidency in 1912, a prominent military physician predicted that he wouldn't last through his first term because of his poor health. He did make it through his first term, but in the middle of his second term, he suffered a series of strokes that ultimately left him partially paralyzed.

Rather than tell the public about his condition, Edith Wilson, his wife, essentially assumed the Presidency behind closed doors and ran the country for the final two years of his term. They managed to keep his true condition a secret. He survived for another three years after the end of his second term before finally passing away.

Franklin Delano Roosevelt was stricken by what was probably polio, in 1921. He became the Governor of New York eight years later and then in 1933 began serving the first of what ended up being three terms as the President of the United States. Remarkably, from 1921 on, Roosevelt did not have use of his legs. He was a paraplegic. He was confined to a wheelchair but still managed to figure out a way to appear to be able to walk. Using specially designed leg braces and relying on a cane and the support of a companion, he could give the appearance of being mobile.

He did not want to seem weak to the public. The press, amazingly enough, largely went along with it. His Secret Service remained on the lookout for anybody who might try to photograph him struggling and stopped them. The overwhelming majority of the country remained unaware of FDR's condition throughout his Presidency.

President Eisenhower, who served two terms beginning in 1952, had a whole list of medical issues, the severity of which was kept hidden. He suffered from painful abdominal adhesions that were the result of an appendectomy. During his first term, he suffered a heart attack that was severe enough that his cardiologist tried to keep him from running for a second term. He ignored that advice and ran anyway. During his second term, he was diagnosed with Crohn's disease, a gastrointestinal condition that required surgery. Shortly after that, he suffered a stroke. Almost all of that was hidden from the American public.

President John F. Kennedy suffered from chronic back pain from the time that he was a student at Harvard. It was severe enough that it disqualified him from military service. His powerful father, however, pulled some strings and got him into the Naval reserves. The back pain stayed with him throughout his life. He also suffered from a painful gastrointestinal condition that was finally diagnosed as being Addison's disease. His perpetual tan could be traced to being one of the side-effects of the steroids used to treat it.

Kennedy's assassination in 1963 led Congress to start drafting what ultimately became the 25th amendment four years later.

President Reagan was diagnosed with Alzheimer's five years after he left office, but his son claims to have seen signs of it while he was still serving as President. There were rumors of his dementia throughout his terms in office. He had several cancer scares while he was in office. He had multiple polyps removed from his colon, one of which was found to be cancerous. After he was shot and survived an assassination attempt, he publicly claimed to be fully recovered from the wound when he, in truth, suffered debilitating effects from it for many years.

Our current President, like some of those who came before him, is also trying to hide the truth about his condition. Unlike his predecessors, however, he is hampered by both an inability to control a completely disorganized circle of supporters around him as well as by an inability to control himself. In the years between Reagan's time in office and the current time, the internet has also made it increasingly difficult for anybody to pull off a cover-up in the way some of those earlier Presidents were able to do.

The White House released two different pictures of the President working in two different areas of the hospital. He is wearing a jacket in one and not in the other. They were purported to be from two different days, but the meta-data contained in the digital images confirmed that they were taken only ten minutes apart. It is also apparent that the important papers that he is supposed to be signing are blank pieces of paper. The photos were staged.

Reading between the lines from what various doctors and staffers have said, the President has been given supplemental oxygen at least twice, meaning that his oxygen levels have dropped precipitously at least two times. His own Chief of Staff announced that the President was in the most critical phase of this disease.

He has been administered two experimental drugs, one of which has up to now only been available for compassionate care—meaning that the patient is facing such serious problems that there are no other options. The other, a steroid he was given, dexamethasone, can have side effects which include mania, impulsivity, and grandiosity. With someone who already has these things, it can amp it up. It is typically administered only when there is an acute respiratory crisis.

Yesterday, the President tweeted, "It has been a very interesting journey. I've learned a lot about Covid." This is from the man that has ostensibly been leading us through this global pandemic. This from the man who should have been attending coronavirus briefings in the White House by the nation's top health Officials for every. single. day. of the last six months. Any other person in this man's position would now be among the most informed people on the planet in terms of what is known about this virus.

He's only learning about it now because it is directly affecting him. 7,423,328 Americans have tested positive for COVID-19. 209,857 Americans have now lost their lives to the virus or complications that arose from having contracted it. Two hundred and nine thousand eight hundred and fifty-seven people dead and only NOW he starts to pay attention and begin to learn about it?

His Press Secretary, one of his most loyal mouthpieces has just announced this morning that she, too, has now tested positive for the coronavirus. Two of her deputies have it as well.

I had no idea when I went into quarantine last week, what this would be like. Would I like to go for a walk? Of course. Doing this, however, is the right thing to do. And, honestly, it just isn't that much of a hardship at all. I have a nice place to shelter in. I have a husband who I love who is taking excellent care of me by bringing me things I need as well as the occasional thing I don't. I have the on and off company of my cat and one of the most extraordinary news cycles I have ever witnessed is unfolding in front of me daily. If I can do this, so can all those idiots in Washington.

OCTOBER 6, 2020
469,989 Total Reported Cases in New York. 33,241 Deaths.

Quarantine—Day 9
Today looks like one of those perfect New York days that make all of us who choose to live in the city want to stay here. The sun is shining through some fluffy white clouds scattered across a bright blue arcing sky. The trees that I can see from our windows are still green, but you can sense that they are straining to keep that up. The yellows, oranges, and reds are building up and waiting to burst. If I were going outside today, I think that I would wear long jeans and a light hoodie rather than shorts.

I haven't worn anything but shorts for many months. My closet door has stayed firmly shut. Throughout the entire summer, I've worn a steady series of the same polo shirts and t-shirts in a seemingly endless cycle.

When we first closed everything down in early March, my work email inbox had well over 20,000 emails in it. I have now gotten rid of most of them and filed the others. The main thing that I felt as I worked through them all was a profound disassociation from the work that all of us used to do. I found email arguments between people. Sometimes they were between others that I was only cc'd on and sometimes they were arguments that I participated in. Some of them stretched over a whole slew of passionate and emotional back-and-forths. There were discussions about technical issues and how they were being fixed. Then there were the endless scheduling discussions. Nearly seven months later, all of it just looks like so much ancient history.

Thousands of instances of communication that seemed vitally important at the time, but looking back on, seem ridiculous, are now consigned to the same ether where old phone conversations and in-person meetings go. As satisfying as that feels, and it feels incredibly satisfying, it all makes me feel like I've moved even further away from the life I was leading earlier this year. I can see how busy I was, but I am starting to forget about what that felt like. The energy I put into all of that is now being pulled in other directions.

According to a National Park Conservation Association study, 96% of our nation's more than 400 parks are plagued by ever-increasing air pollution problems. This Republican-led Administration continues to weaken clean-air legislation in favor of allowing corporations to operate as they please. They have also dismantled Obama-era clean water regulations allowing corporations more freedom to pollute our rivers and streams. More than half of our nation's wetlands, rivers, and streams have had their protections eliminated. That move threatens not only endangered wildlife but also endangers our drinking water.

An area of public lands in the Great Basin, the size of the state of Indiana, that has long been protected, has been offered for oil and gas leasing since this President took office. Some of that land has been leased for as little as $2 an acre. The state of Alaska is pushing forward a proposal to allow private industrial mining concerns to construct a road through Gates of the Arctic National Preserve which will impede caribou migration and threaten the livelihood of Native Alaskan communities.

The ill-conceived and absurd border wall construction has already resulted in the bulldozing of hundred-year-old saguaro cactuses in the Organ Pipe Cactus National Monument in Arizona. Land has also been cleared for it just above Native American graves.

Parts of the Endangered Species Act that preserves ecosystems for imperiled species have been repealed. Environmental laws, that ensure that people have a say in how public lands are used and that governmental agencies consider public and environmental health before permitting projects on federal lands, have been gutted.

The environmental and social advances that have been made in this country took years or decades or sometimes centuries to achieve. Once our protected lands are invaded and plundered, they are gone. There is nothing left. The places in our country of pristine beauty and natural majesty disappear forever once they have been mined or fracked or drilled.

COVID-19 will, indeed, eventually go, or we will figure out how to live with it, but the results of what is happening in our country behind all of it will remain. Those protected and cherished lands are OURS. The hard-won rights that this Administration is trying to undermine and overturn, are OURS.

Voting has started in some places and is about to start in others. That's how this all stops. Ask not what your country can do for you—ask what you can do for your country.

October 7, 2020
Derek Chauvin, charged with killing George Floyd, released on bail.

Quarantine—Day 10

Just before I went to bed yesterday, I finished up working on a portion of a project that I've been avoiding for a few days. It took me about fifteen minutes to get it done. This after two or three days of avoiding it. Not actively avoiding it mind you, just feeling that I could do it… later. I did it, last night, because if I didn't, then it would mean that I wouldn't have accomplished a blessed thing yesterday. For the first time in recent memory, I realize that I didn't even take a shower yesterday.

There is very little busy work left to do in the apartment. The early days of the pandemic took care of that. The projects that I still have left to do are mostly utterly ridiculous.

Michael keeps telling me that he has plenty of things for me to do. I don't know what those things might be, but I am certain that I don't want to do any of them. Honestly, I do believe that there are plenty of things to do. I just need to find the motivation to do them. I promise you; I'm not sitting around moping and longing to break free of this apartment. My issue is just the opposite, I am finding it hard to process just how fast these days are flying by.

Tonight, we have the Vice-Presidential debate to look forward to. I'm not sure if any of us are going to have the strength left to watch it. The Vice President's team has objected to the safety measures that were being discussed for the debate. In particular, the use of plexiglass shields to try and isolate the candidates.

On Tuesday, White House advisor to the President, Stephen Miller joined the ever-growing ranks of infected Republican White House workers. So much for that. At tonight's debate, both candidates will, indeed, be behind plexiglass shields. They will also be seated twelve feet apart from each other. That makes them safer—not safe.

The Vice President by any metric that the White House and the CDC have outlined, should, like me, be in quarantine. He was front and center at the super-spreader Rose Garden event last week at the White House. He came into direct contact with many people who have now been confirmed to have contracted the virus.

I am now going to take a shower, change my clothes and put a meal together. I'm not quite sure what I am going to do today, but I am going to figure it out before Michael reads this and assigns me something to do. This day is going to be over before I know it.

I got a great email from my mother this morning. She lives in Florida which is an important state for the President in our upcoming election. It was a great motivating kick in the butt. "(My friend) told me to go on the county website and find out if my ballot has been counted. They need your date of birth—and my ballot has been counted!!!"

Good work, Mom!

October 8, 2020
473,285 Total Reported Cases in New York.

Quarantine—Day 11

Ernestine Wade became famous playing a character named Sapphire Stevens on the *Amos 'n' Andy* show—first on the radio and then on the CBS television program in the early 1950s.

The original *Amos 'n' Andy* radio show was created and performed by two white men. Freeman Gosden and Charles Correll wrote and played the two lead black men as well as voicing many of the other incidental characters.

During the 1920s the Chicago Tribune ran a comic strip called *The Gumps*. It was one of the first, if not the first, strips that rather than just having stand-alone bits, continued a story from day to day. The Tribune approached Gosden and Correll to create a radio show based on those characters whose story would develop daily. The two men did not think that they could voice female characters well, so, instead, they proposed a series called *Sam 'n' Henry* about two 'colored men' based on stock minstrel characters of the time. The show began in 1926 and became so successful that eventually, the two men pitched an idea that their live show should be recorded on phonograph records and distributed to other radio stations. When the Tribune rejected this idea, they quit.

The Chicago Daily News then hired Gosden and Correll to create a show for them. The Tribune retained ownership of the *Sam 'n' Henry* show and its characters, so they were forced to come up with the *Amos 'n' Andy* show as an alternative. The Chicago Daily News agreed to their plan to distribute the show via phonograph records. That was the beginning of what we now know as syndication.

Amos 'n' Andy ran on the radio from 1928 up to 1960. For the first decade, Freeman Gosden and Charles Correll voiced all the 170 characters. After that, performers of color were brought in to take over. Certainly, by the time the television program began in 1951, black performers were playing all the roles. Ernestine Wade began playing Sapphire Stevens in 1939. The Sapphire character was the wife of George 'Kingfish' Stevens and was described as 'shrewish, demanding and manipulative'.

That portrayal helped to create the stereotype of the emasculating 'Angry Black Woman' in the minds of white America. When the Obamas moved into the White House, they seem to have known that stereotype as well as the corresponding 'Angry Black Man' trope would immediately be wielded against them on the first occasion it could.

It never happened. The entire family, including Malia and Sasha, their two young daughters, maintained a calm and even demeanor for eight, what must have been at times excruciatingly long, years. "When they go low, we go high" was Mrs. Obama's famous rallying cry and the family followed that to the letter.

Women, in general, regardless of their race, are hampered by the stereotype of the angry emasculating woman. Female politicians have had to learn how to modulate their views to appeal to the electorate. During the campaigning leading up to the 2016 election, when her opponent made a forceful remark, he was viewed as being strong. When Hilary Clinton made a similar kind of remark she was viewed as being an "angry bitch." Kamala Harris, when she was running for President, herself, earlier in the campaign, often went on the attack and was, indeed, accused of being and summarily dismissed as an angry black woman.

Last night during the Vice-Presidential debate, when her opponent went low, Senator Harris went high. Rather than overriding her opponent each time he tried to interrupt her, she, instead, turned to him, with a smile, and said, "I'm speaking." Tony Award-winner Anika Noni Rose, tweeted last night, "The smile that Senator Kamala Harris gave with "I'm speaking" is the public mom smile every Black child who has ever messed up recognizes as one step away from annihilation."

Anne Richards, who Governed the state of Texas with a smile, herself, famously described what women have to contend with in their lives, "Ginger Rogers did everything that Fred Astaire did. She just did it backwards and in high heels."

Senator Harris and the Vice President did not go into last night's debate as equals. The Vice President had the home advantage. He is white and he is male. Senator Harris, however, ended up having the real advantage. Senator Harris has spent her entire life learning how to navigate through a world run by smug white men. She has had to develop skills that her opponent has no idea that she possesses. She can dance backward in high heels and keep a smile on her face and make it all look effortless. Oh, for the day, when women and people of color are freed from having to do that.

Last night, Senator Harris proved to the American people that she is more than capable of leadership. She fought for her time, and she got it. There were no flies on her. Even without everything in our cultural history that she had to overcome, she turned in an impressive performance last night. If you include all those stereotypical obstacles in her way, she was astounding.

It's another beautiful day outside. Some of the leaves in the trees across the street are starting to turn yellow. The days are getting shorter and cooler. The election is getting closer.

Time for lunch and another day in quarantine. I do feel better after this debate than I did after the last one. For now, I am just going to enjoy the feeling and hang out with the cat.

OCTOBER 9, 2020

474,894 Total Reported Cases in New York. 33,291 Deaths.

Quarantine—Day 12

The worst part about the lack of responsibility I have these days is that I am getting used to it.

This morning, the Broadway League announced a four-month extension of the shutdown of all Broadway shows until May 30th. I was expecting them to say that they were going to extend it through March, so I will say that the May date was a bit of a surprise. Not wholly unexpected, but still a surprise.

It was announced that the revival of the musical *The Music Man* starring Hugh Jackman and Sutton Foster won't start previews now until towards the end of December of next year and not open officially until the following spring in 2022.

Last month Christopher Wray, the director of the FBI, said that the greatest threats currently facing the United States were from within. American anti-government and white supremacist groups have been responsible for carrying out the most lethal attacks against American citizens in recent years.

Federal and State officials in Michigan just announced that they had filed terrorism, conspiracy, and weapons charges against thirteen members of a militia group. This group planned to storm the Michigan Capitol and kidnap Governor Gretchen Whitmer. They planned on putting her on trial for treason and then possibly executing her. The militia was hoping to spark a civil war and overthrow the government.

This Michigan Militia group had gathered over the summer for shooting practice, combat drills, and explosives training. They had spied on Governor Whitmer's vacation home back in August and even identified a bridge where explosives could be placed to create a diversion. Six of the thirteen men were identified as being members of the group and the other seven were affiliated extremists who were offering material support to the plot. The latter group was gathering the names and addresses of police officers whom they also planned to target. Timothy McVeigh and Terry Nichols attended meetings of this same militia group years ago before they carried out the deadly Oklahoma City bombing.

Yesterday, Governor Whitmer addressed the press and said, "Just last week, the President of the United States stood before the American people and refused to condemn white supremacists and hate groups like these two Michigan militia groups… (they) heard the president's words not as a rebuke but as a rallying cry—as a call to action."

This morning, House Speaker Nancy Pelosi announced a new bill that would give Congress a role in determining the fitness of the sitting President and allow them to participate in the invoking of the 25th Amendment of the Constitution. At this point, it is only the Cabinet and the Vice President who have that power. The proposed bill would add a Congressional advisory body which could help determine the ability of the President to serve. While she made it clear this morning that this new legislation would only apply to future Presidents, it seems designed to throw even more light onto the state of the current President's mental facilities. This is Speaker Pelosi getting under the President's skin. "Poking the Bear" as the saying goes.

May, huh? My schedule for the rest of the day is open. I have about an hour until the cat begins to remind me that he gets a fork full of soft food at 5 pm. There's always the danger that I am going to forget to do it and that he will starve to death in the ensuing hours before the second forkful at 11 pm.

Something else is sure to develop on the news, so I am going to watch something else instead. Sitting and watching television is starting to get on my nerves. I need this quarantine to be over so Michael can come home, and I can get out of here for a while and go for a walk.

The cat just glanced in my direction. Don't even think about it, my furry friend. You have an hour.

OCTOBER 10, 2020
476,397 Total Reported Cases in New York.

Quarantine—Day 13

I slept like the dead last night. At about 3 am, I did wake up briefly when the white noise machine we use whispered "black-eyes" to me. That's a sign of demonic possession on the *Supernatural* show which I probably should not have watched last night before going to bed. Even with that, I went back under and didn't wake up until noon.

If the cat tried to wake me up before that, I was unaware of it. When I came to, he was curled up in my legs. There were still eight pieces of dry food in his bowl so he must have felt that the joy of extra sleeping was worth the risk of possibly never eating again.

Tonight will be the 14th night that I have slept alone in the apartment. Tomorrow, after lunch, I'm out.

Somewhat hilariously, because it shows how desperate the GOP is, Secretary of State Mike Pompeo just announced that he was going to release more of Hillary Clinton's emails. This, of course, a full year after the State Department has already said that there is no evidence of any mishandling on her part at all. The President has been publicly deriding Pompeo for not doing this sooner. So, for no reason whatsoever other than to make him happy, The Secretary of State is going to stoop to this stupid charade. Hillary Clinton has nothing whatsoever to do with this election. Perhaps they will go after Jimmy Carter next for admitting decades ago that he had lust in his heart.

Spending the last two weeks inside on my own has been an interesting experience. As human beings, we are social creatures. Being deprived of direct contact with other people, even given the comfort of my surroundings, has not been easy. I even miss dodging other people on the sidewalk. I'm incredibly grateful for the cat's company, but it's not quite the same thing.

As this virus continues to spread throughout our country unchecked, we are looking at a winter where we may end up back indoors. A model put forth by the CDC says that there could be 395,000 deaths because of the virus or complications that arise from it by February. That's an increase that almost matches the entire total of what we've experienced since this all started.

We can't take for granted any of the freedoms that we have—even something as basic as the freedom to take a walk outside. They can be taken away from us in an instant.

This time in quarantine has honestly flown by. The election still seems endlessly far in the future, but we will look back on the next few weeks as having flown by, too. If you are watching the President's speech, I would suggest that you turn it off. Watch something else. If you don't have a voting plan in place yet, maybe now's a good time to make one.

To be honest, I might be overdosing, just a bit, on the show *Supernatural*. There's just so much of it. Maybe, today I'll just read a book.

October 12, 2020
478,925 Total Reported Cases in New York.

I'm free!

I finished up my quarantine yesterday morning and then I went out. From the local deli, I got a breakfast sandwich and then I headed downtown for a walk. It was a great walk.

From the Upper West Side, I made my way down Columbus Avenue, past the Museum of Natural History, and then past Lincoln Center, down Broadway, and through Times Square. Then I continued down past Herald Square into Union Square. From there I turned into Washington Square Park and walked down through SoHo before I headed west and turned back up north. Near the Whitney, I got a timed entry on the spot and went into the High Line Park. Working my way uptown I exited the park at Hudson Yards and got back up to 36th Street. Then it was up 10th Avenue until I finally met up with Michael at the apartment he was staying in Hell's Kitchen. Ten miles all told, and I have a nice blister on the bottom of my right foot to show for it. It was the first time in two weeks that I'd worn socks, let alone shoes.

Including my actual trip down to Florida and back, it has been over three weeks since I have been able to wander through New York. The city has changed a bit over those three weeks.

Outdoor dining seems like it is now a permanent part of our landscape. Some restaurants have re-opened for indoor dining albeit with a cap at

25% capacity. I didn't, however, see a lot of places where it looked like people were eating inside. Instead, they were out on the street with a vengeance. In some places where the portion of the street where the restaurant is located has been blocked off, the entire street was filled with tables and all the tables were filled with people. In all the times I went out before my trip, I never saw so many people in one place.

For the first time in seven months, I noticed some tourists out on the streets. Some were European. I heard some French and some Russian. Some were Hispanic—there was plenty of Spanish. There were also several Indian families. While I didn't see any of the ubiquitous red tour buses, I did notice a guy in Times Square trying to convince two women to buy a ticket for one. The two women looked like New Yorkers to me. I am pretty sure they were just playing with the guy—pretending to be interested when, in fact, there was no way that they were going to get on board.

Having the freedom to leave my apartment and rejoin my city is wonderful. Freedom, however, is a somewhat relative term. In essence, I have just exchanged my small, somewhat gilded cage, for a larger gilded aviary. I still can't go anywhere. Or do anything. Broadway, and by extension my livelihood, is not going to open back up until May. That's seven months away. That means we are just halfway there. The same amount of time is in front of us that has already passed since this all started.

I may not have the freedom to live my life, these days, exactly the way it was at the beginning of the year. Where it counts, however, I and the other members of my chosen community, live under the umbrella of the grace of some of the most important freedoms there are.

I can love and marry whomever I choose whether they are of my same sex or another. The women in my life can choose what happens to their bodies without a man telling them that they can't. I can speak my mind, freely, without governmental interference. And I can vote. I, like everyone else in this country, can help to decide who our leaders will be.

The current Republican nominee to the Supreme Court of the United States of America grew up in a culture that does not believe in all those rights. I do not begrudge the President's nominee the right to be a part of the community of her choice and to believe in the things that she believes. She, like all of us, is free to do that. If the members of her tribe chose to follow a set of beliefs that I don't believe in, it doesn't matter. It doesn't impinge upon my life at all. She cannot, however, and should not, be able to take away any of my freedom by forcing me to follow those rules as well. Freedom of life, liberty, and the pursuit of happiness is the bedrock upon which our founding fathers based the formation of this greater community that is our country.

OCTOBER 13, 2020
480,129 Total Reported Cases in New York. 33,320 Deaths.

It rained all day yesterday and it's still raining now.

Yesterday was Columbus Day. The parade down Fifth was canceled because of the coronavirus. The steady rain would have made it miserable anyway. Columbus, like many other historical figures these days, is undergoing a re-evaluation of his place in history. He's not being erased as some might claim. He is, instead, being re-aligned into the historical timeline by confronting the facts about his life, not just the ones that people want to hear.

Here in this country, we all grew up knowing that "In fourteen hundred and ninety-two, Columbus sailed the ocean blue." Unfortunately, you could also say, "In fourteen hundred and ninety-three Columbus sailed the deep blue sea." I could never be fully sure which one it was.

For the record, it's the former.

Italian Americans are taking the dismantling of the myth that has grown up around the man personally which, honestly, doesn't make that much sense to me. There are plenty of people of Italian heritage to be proud of. Lifting Columbus out of that august group as being the greatest of them all does a tremendous disservice to the others. Christopher Columbus was a man of his time. He was stubborn, ambitious, and somewhat ruthless. In short, he was a man.

528 years ago, Christopher Columbus, after traveling east across the Atlantic Ocean, landed in the Bahamas. While he explored the coasts of Central and South America and what is now Cuba, Haiti, and the Dominican Republic, he never actually set foot on North America.

The first European who set foot on this continent was likely Leif Eriksson a Norseman who was probably born in Iceland somewhere between 960 and 970 A.D. His father was Erik the Red who founded the first European settlement on what we now call Greenland. There are all sorts of conflicting historical accounts, but most agree that Eriksson ended up in Norway where he served in the court of King Olaf I Tryggvason who converted him to Christianity. The King then tasked him with spreading the word across Greenland to the settlers who were now living there.

Either because he had heard of land there, or because he got blown off course (accounts differ), Leif Eriksson probably ended up landing in what is now Nova Scotia a full half of a millennium before Columbus made his crossing. In 1963, ruins of an 11th-century Viking settlement were discovered at L'Anse-aux-Meadows in Newfoundland. It is now a UNESCO World Historic Site and on my bucket list of places to see.

Despite what people think, by 1492, most educated Europeans believed that the world was round. What Christopher Columbus was trying to prove was that it was possible to sail to the wealthy lands to the east by heading west. His deal with the Spanish monarchy guaranteed him 10% of anything that he discovered and the right of governorship over any new lands he encountered. While he believed that the world was round, he badly miscalculated just how large a planet we are on.

When he landed in the Caribbean, he met the Taino people who were living there. In his diary, he wrote of them, "They were well-built, with good bodies and handsome features ...They do not bear arms, and do not know them, for I showed them a sword, they took it by the edge and cut themselves out of ignorance. They have no iron ...They would make fine servants ... With fifty men we could subjugate them all and make them do whatever we want."

He sent 500 enslaved Taino people back to Queen Isabella who was horrified and refused to accept them. She believed that they were Spanish subjects as the lands Columbus had "discovered" were now Spanish and, therefore, could not be enslaved.

Columbus had left his two brothers in charge of the settlements in the New World as he traveled back and forth to Spain. During one of his absences, the colonists had staged a bloody revolt against them for their mismanagement and incompetence, and the Spanish crown had to send somebody else back to take over.

It is estimated that when Columbus landed in the Bahamas that about 250,000 Taino people were living in the islands. Sixty years later, their numbers were down to only a few hundred. Forced to work on plantations and dig for gold by the invaders and exposed to new European diseases, they didn't survive.

Christopher Columbus's journeys began an era of exploration and colonization in the New World that have led us to where we are now. The legacy of his voyages is not so easy to quantify as our history lessons in school would have us believe. We can't take his very real accomplishment of proving naysayers wrong by successfully sailing across the Atlantic Ocean while ignoring the equally real consequences that resulted. Christopher Columbus, whether he knew it or not, heralded a genocide that leaves the Nazis in the dust. Native Americans were pushed off their lands and massacred by the millions as Europeans moved in.

The historical figures we venerate were just people living in the times that they lived in. Our Founding Fathers owned slaves. Even Mother Theresa was just a person—by some accounts prickly and driven and well-aware of her public image.

In his Columbus Day proclamation this morning the President announced, "I have also taken steps to ensure that we preserve our Nation's history and promote patriotic education. In July, I signed another Executive

Order to build and rebuild monuments to iconic American figures in a National Garden of American Heroes. In September, I announced the creation of the 1776 Commission, which will encourage our educators to teach our children about the miracle of American history and honor our founding. In addition, last month I signed an Executive Order to root out the teaching of racially divisive concepts from the Federal workplace, many of which are grounded in the same type of revisionist history that is trying to erase Christopher Columbus from our national heritage. Together, we must safeguard our history and stop this new wave of iconoclasm by standing against those who spread hate and division."

The land that I can see from my apartment window was occupied by the Canarsee people who were part of the greater Lenape tribe. Famously Peter Minuit and his fellow Dutch colonists acquired the title to it by bartering goods worth about $24. It is unlikely that the Canarsee people knew what the transaction truly meant to the Europeans as their culture did not have a concept of land ownership.

Yesterday, in the rain, I walked down to Columbus Circle. For the last few months, the circle has been barricaded and under 24/7 guard by the NYPD. The day before yesterday, three Native Americans were standing across the street from the statue of Columbus. One was wearing a mask that said, "No one is legal on Stolen Land." Chalk outlines of fallen bodies had been drawn on the pavement with numbers inside them. Numbers of Native Americans who had perished. Numbers of enslaved Africans who had been brought over. Enormous numbers.

The rain may have washed away those chalk markings yesterday but, they nonetheless, still represent part of the truth about our history. It is not the job of history to exalt the past, no matter what our President might say.

The Knights of Columbus have done much to support the very real contributions of Italian immigrants to our society. They might do well to start thinking about a name change that doesn't put the weight of generations of accomplished people on the shoulders of one, merely human, man. None of us are saints. None of our history is free from controversy. For someone to win, somebody else must lose.

I was very excited, yesterday, after my weeks of confinement, to finally be able to go to the bank and the post office. Of course, I had completely forgotten that it was Columbus Day, and they would both be closed. Today, however, is a new day. I'm going to go out after I take a shower and try again.

That's all any of us can do. Keep trying again and again, until we get it right.

October 14, 2020

481,227 Total Reported Cases in New York. 33,330 Deaths.

I have suffered from wanderlust ever since I can remember. My first trip overseas was when I was five and I've been on the move ever since. I don't know if I can point to a single year where I didn't leave the country at least once. These days, there are some places where we might be able to go, but we would need to isolate before we go, isolate when we got there, and then isolate again once we've returned. It's a commitment.

As much as I'd like to go somewhere, I think I'm staying here for the next while and watching my beard grow. It has rounded the corner where rather than looking like I haven't shaved in a while it now actually looks like a beard. At least that's what it looks like to me. When I announced that to Michael, he looked at me carefully and took a moment before saying, "Well… sort of…?"

Wearing a mask with facial hair is a little annoying. On the plus side, one of the advantages of a mask on colder days like these is that it keeps your face warm. It looks like mask-wearing is with us for the whole winter. Even though the President keeps announcing that we are "rounding the final turn" of the pandemic, it doesn't seem like we are anywhere near the finish line.

It is beautiful outside today after several days of clouds and rain. It looks like a perfect day to take a walk in the park. Maybe I'll pack a lunch.

October 15, 2020

482,765 Total Reported Cases in New York. 33,353 Deaths.

I woke up this morning with a headache which, of course, is one of the symptoms of COVID-19. I don't think that I have a fever, but I do have an ache in my shoulder. That could be from starting to do pushups again, but it might also be one of the indicators.

Yesterday at the Duane Reade there was a guy in one of the aisles that was restocking the shelves who walked past me closer than six feet. Maybe I got it from him? We were both wearing masks but still…? I suppose it is possible that I didn't drink enough water yesterday and my headache is a result of being slightly dehydrated, but that seems like a desperate reach. It's far more likely that I've been re-infected with the coronavirus from the guy in the drugstore.

When I wasn't worried about getting sick, I did get a lot done yesterday. Admittedly the bar on accomplishment is absurdly low these days, but even so, it was a banner day.

I dyed my shorts.

Many weeks ago, I noticed that the sweat shorts that I had gotten before everything shut down had faded. I got the idea, once I realized how much they had faded, that I could re-dye them. How hard could it be?

I dimly remember tie-dying t-shirts as a kid. You gather parts of the t-shirt together and tie them tightly with a rubber band. When you dunk the shirt in the dye bath, the color can't get into the parts you've tied off. When you cut off the rubber band, there's a big psychedelic circle of undyed fabric that is wicked cool. If you re-tie the t-shirt in a different area and re-dunk in another color, then the design starts to get far out. It was the late 60s after all.

For my life, I can't imagine my mother agreeing to be a party to it. Even as an adult, it's hard to avoid splashing it. Get a bunch of kids involved in the process and total disaster is almost a given. Spills and stains can remain on the walls or the floors for the rest of the life of the house. I'm going to guess that one of the other mothers in the neighborhood hosted a dye party and they let me participate. Now that I'm thinking about it, I'm certain that I can picture a bunch of buckets outside in a row on somebody's driveway.

The process involved boiling water and carting it downstairs to the basement then rinsing them out in the slop sink. My shorts are now an even dark blue. So are my hands. I am unlikely to wear the shorts again until next spring, but when that day comes, I am ready.

These days leading up to the election are excruciating. I watch the news with mounting terror that something bad is going to happen. Two people connected with Senator Harris's campaign have tested positive for COVID-19. She has stopped in-person campaigning for the moment, choosing to do some virtual events today instead. The virus in our country continues to blaze through the population unchecked. The death rate is climbing.

Throughout it all, the President is out and about attending rallies and spouting lies to his base. He continues to misrepresent the dangers of the virus even as the First Lady announced on her own that their son Barron had tested positive.

In California, the Republicans set up fake ballot boxes to dupe people into placing their ballots in the wrong place. They do not want the American people to have a voice in their futures. On an extremely positive front, over 17 million Americans have already cast their ballots in early voting across 44 states and Washington D.C. In some places, people have waited for endless hours in all kinds of weather to cast their ballots.

This election is not about conflicting ideologies. I wish it was. The discussion inherent in our two-party system is a vital component to all of us getting a better understanding of the issues we are facing. All we are getting now is propaganda and rhetoric.

My headache seems to be gone. Maybe I haven't been re-infected after all. I've had a lot of water and some decaf coffee already this morning. Maybe I dodged the COVID bullet today after all.

OCTOBER 16, 2020

69,000 total new reported cases in the United States in one day. Total US cases now over 8 million.

From the window in our living room, I can look across the street at a building that has floor-to-ceiling windows. None of those windows have blinds on them, so it's easy to see what's going on inside the apartments. I can't help but take a quick look over there in the evenings when I am pulling down our shades for the night.

Let me be clear, I'm not perving on my neighbors. I have never seen anything even remotely salacious going on. All I have ever done is caught sight of the occasional glimpse of their distant lives.

In one apartment there is a couple with a baby. One of them is often walking around the living room with it. In another, the television is usually on. Whoever lives there is usually on the sofa in the middle of a bunch of pillows. Another spends a lot of time sitting at a table working on something. I can dimly see the shape of whoever it is in the light from their open computer.

It's comforting to see that people around us are living their lives in much the same way Michael and I are. New York apartments are made for a pandemic. We might be a city of 8.4 million people, but we are completely isolated from one another.

I can only ever see any of those people in the evenings when it is dark outside, and their lights are on. During daylight hours, the sun or the clouds are mirrored in the windows, turning them opaque. What do they do with the rest of their days? Are they working? Are they stressed? What are they thinking?

We are constantly told that we aren't what we do. That our jobs don't define us. These days, I have to say, I can't stop wondering that if we aren't what we do, then who, exactly, are we?

I have never considered my job a job. I love doing it. I get excited when there is a new challenge ahead of me. I am never happier than when I am exhausted and in the middle of a difficult tech.

There may be days when all I want is a break, but the kind of break that I want is just a breather. I'm always ready to go back.

I was talking to a friend yesterday about how much we used to enjoy a staycation. I never imagined that I would have a staycation that lasted seven months with the probability of at least another seven yet to come. Just because it has gone on this long, doesn't make any of it normal. We should all be forgiven for our anxiety and occasional depression. Just because we have gotten used to all of this doesn't mean that we don't want it to stop.

Nelson Mandela spent 27 years in prison. We visited one of them a few years ago on Robben Island off the coast of Cape Town in South Africa. He spent 18 of his years in prison locked down there. 18 years in a tiny stone and brick cell, sleeping on the floor with a bucket for a toilet. He was forced to do hard labor in a quarry on the island for every single one of those endless years. He was allowed one visitor per year. That visitor could stay for 30 minutes.

I am sure he got used to it, but I am equally sure that he never stopped hoping that it would end. He had a place to sleep and was given food to eat. He survived. Is survival the same thing as living? We are, all of us, infinitely more provided for these days than that. I am not for one second saying that any of us are even remotely going through what he had to endure. Of course not. Like him, though, many of us have been separated from doing the things that we do. We cannot do the things that define us while this pandemic continues to spread throughout our country, not to mention, the rest of the world. We are surviving, often in plenty of physical comfort, but are we truly living?

It's pouring rain outside today, but the last thing that I want to do is stay inside all day.

Michael has a virtual audition for a role on a TV series today. Rather than self-taping, he'll be auditioning live using Zoom. I've promised him that I'll vacate the apartment in an hour so that he can prepare. Even with the anxiety that gathers around the act of auditioning for him, this morning Michael is being his full, committed self. He is doing what he does and what he lives to do.

A salary is nice, but that has never been why I went to work. I went to work because that is where I was able to fully express myself and truly be who I am. Am I the same person without it?

OCTOBER 17, 2020
486,207 Total Reported Cases in New York. 33,376 Deaths.

I woke up this morning, for the first time this season, to the hissing of the radiator. Our building is heated by steam from a big oil-fueled boiler in the basement that looks like something out of a science fiction lab. Like the scorching summers in Arizona, it's an incredibly dry heat.

We rarely have the radiators on. Often it gets so hot that it can be snowing outside, and I have to open the windows. When the temperature drops close to zero and the wind starts ripping down the canyons of our gridded streets, Michael sometimes sneaks it on. We then spend the rest of the winter turning them on and turning them off behind each other's backs.

George Stephanopoulos moderated Joe Biden's Town Hall meeting in Philadelphia. The former Vice President fielded questions from the audience and answered them in depth. In most regards, the Democratic candidate is a moderate to the center candidate. Even so, given how far to the right his opponent is, they are extremely far apart.

I am not sure that there is any real way to have a meaningful discussion about racial issues these days without stepping on someone's toes—whether it be inadvertently or on purpose.

Biden was asked by a guy what he would say to Black voters who don't believe that the basic system is designed to protect them.

Biden gave an extremely long, very detailed, answer. When he finished, he asked the guy if he had said what he wanted to hear. "I think so," the somewhat overwhelmed questioner responded. Biden then said to him, "Well there's a lot more if you want to, if you're going to hang out afterwards, I'll tell you more."

The only real answer possible to a topic like that is to have a discussion. He did, indeed, remain behind afterward, when the cameras were off and continued to talk with some of the people who were there.

It was a thoughtful, not always easy, hour and a half. In contrast, the President's competing Town Hall on a different network was argumentative and rife with made-up facts.

There is nothing else, these days, more important than getting people to the polls. Our strength is in our numbers.

October 19, 2020

CDC recommends that all train and plane passengers wear masks.

At this point in the 2016 election, Hillary Clinton was polling ahead of the President with almost the same margins that Biden is currently leading him with. If that doesn't send ice-water through a Democrat's veins, then nothing will.

To get away from it all and try and burn some of the stress (and weight I've accumulated) off, I took a bike ride downtown yesterday. I rode down to Union Square and then continued further downtown on foot.

The Lower East Side of Manhattan sometimes feels like it is a different country. Orchard Street and the area surrounding the Tenement Museum used to be the hub of wholesale clothing distributors. Even in the days when I first went to school here in New York, it was heavily Eastern-European and Jewish. Today, it is a trendy restaurant and boutique-laden area populated with a whole group of disparate people who seem to be only connected by their ages—young.

Chinatown's touristy area is still concentrated near eastern Canal Street on Mott and Mulberry Streets. Further downtown, though, underneath the access ramps to the Brooklyn Bridge is where Chinatown lies these days. There are no souvenir shops down there. Instead, the streets are lined with grocery stores and fresh fish and produce markets. On the sidewalks, sellers have set up crates of live crabs and freshly caught fish. Shoppers throng the streets and bargain with them in Chinese. Walking down there, you feel like you could be anywhere in the world where Chinese is spoken. And that could be almost anywhere.

English is the most spoken language worldwide. Roughly 15% of people on earth can communicate using it. But, in terms of native speakers, it's not even second. There are about 379 million native speakers of English on earth. For 460 million people, Spanish is their native language. Mandarin Chinese has more native speakers than both of those groups put together, 918 million people identify Mandarin Chinese as their native language.

My goal, yesterday, was to get to Battery Park to see the new statue of Mother Cabrini that the Governor unveiled last week.

Saint Francis Xavier Cabrini was an Italian American Roman Catholic nun. In 1946, she became the first US citizen to be canonized as a Saint by the Roman Catholic Church. She was born in 1850 in Italy. She, along with seven other women who had all taken their vows together, founded an orphanage and a day school. Her success came to the attention of Pope Leo XIII who urged her to travel to the US to offer aid to the masses of Italian immigrants who were arriving here every day.

She came and, facing a lot of opposition, founded the Sacred Heart Orphan Asylum in West Park, NY. It remained in operation until 2011. She also founded a hospital that ultimately became the Cabrini Medical Center that stayed open until 2008. All in all, she founded 67 institutions to help the sick and the poor throughout this country as well as in Latin America and Europe.

Mother Cabrini died in 1917 and was buried in West Park, NY in the asylum she founded. In 1933, as the process of beatification was underway, they exhumed her body. Her head was removed and is now preserved in a chapel in Rome. Her heart is in Codogno, Italy where she founded her missionary order. One of her arm bones is at her national shrine in Chicago.

The rest of her remains lie here in New York. Her mummified body is on display in a shrine up in Washington Heights. I don't know if it is open during the pandemic, but when I lived up there, I went in to see it. She is in a glass reliquary casket under the altar. Most of what you can see is a life-like wax representation of her that covers her actual bones.

Between 1975 and 2008 the Vatican reportedly did a whole series of experiments to figure out ways to preserve the relics and bodies of its Saints. An incorruptible body is supposed to be one of the signs of supreme holiness, but none of the bodies, or bits and pieces, would have survived without some sort of help. The NY Post did a whole exposé on this supposed top-secret operation back in 2014 claiming that the people who did the experiments are now dead. Mother Cabrini's body is reputedly one of the 31 that they worked on.

In 1950 Saint Francis Xavier Cabrini was named the patron saint of immigrants. She is also considered the person that you ask for help in finding a parking space. A priest explained, "She lived in New York City. She understands traffic."

The new statue is beautifully designed. It depicts Mother Cabrini and two children standing in a folded-paper boat. The boat represents a story she once told of being a girl in Italy and setting paper boats adrift with violets in them. She considered them her missionaries. The statue of Mother Cabrini in Battery Park brings the total number of statues erected by the City of New York to honor women up to a rousing seven.

This doesn't include the many anonymous scantily clad women depicting concepts like liberty and justice. This number represents city memorials to actual flesh and blood women who have made an impact on our society. Up near us, there's a statue of Eleanor Roosevelt by Riverside Park. There's also one of Joan of Arc up here somewhere too. There's one of Harriet Tubman in Harlem and one of Golda Meir in midtown. In Bryant Park behind the New York Public Library, there is a statue of Gertrude Stein.

In August, a statue of women's rights pioneers depicting Susan B. Anthony, Elizabeth Cady Stanton, and Sojourner Truth was installed in Central Park. The initial design did not include Sojourner Truth, but she was added after the design was criticized for erasing the contributions of women of color to the suffrage movement.

There has been plenty of discussion about statues that honor men who are less than perfect—Christopher Columbus, Confederate Generals, and others. The continued presence of those memorials creates tension within communities and has ignited a national debate. The absence of memorials, however, is every bit as important to address.

Walking throughout the city and only passing statues of men subliminally reinforces the idea that only men have contributed to our society. It plants the idea that women's accomplishments are not worthy of mention. It's long past the time to put up a few more.

OCTOBER 20, 2020
490,166 Total Reported Cases in New York. 33,412 Deaths.

In March of 1918, there were outbreaks of flu-like illness reported in the United States. The first major outbreak arose in Fort Riley, Kansas where more than 100 soldiers came down with it. Over the following six months, sporadic outbreaks occurred in various places around the country and in Europe, and possibly beyond.

Travel in 1918 was far less extensive than it is now, but the main vector for the initial transmission seems to have been US soldiers who were being deployed all over the world to fight in World War I. Without the war, there wasn't the kind of international travel among ordinary people yet that would have allowed the virus to spread as easily as it did.

In September, a second wave of the virus began in Boston at a training camp called Camp Devens. By the end of September, there were over 14,000 cases and 757 deaths reported.

Then it spread. 195,000 Americans died in October, alone. There was a massive shortage of nurses because so many had been deployed overseas in the war. There were trained African American nurses available, but there was a racist resistance to using them.

On November 11, 1918, when Germany capitulated and signed the Armistice, millions of soldiers then returned home and brought the flu with them. Later that winter and into January of 1919, there was a third wave of the virus. In April, President Woodrow Wilson collapsed at the Versailles Peace Conference in France while negotiating the peace treaty. It is thought that he most likely had the flu.

By the summer of 1919, the virus largely disappeared. By the time it left about 500 million people, about a third of the planet's entire population had become infected. At least 675,000 Americans lost their lives to it and somewhere between 20 and 50 million people around the world lost theirs.

A hundred years ago, there were no vaccines or antivirals to treat the flu. The first approved vaccine for the flu didn't appear until the 1940s. What they had was aspirin. Bayer trademarked aspirin in 1899 and that protection had expired in 1917. Several other companies started producing aspirin during the pandemic. At the time medical professionals recommended a dosage of 30g a day. To give you an idea of what that means, no reliable health professional these days would recommend anything above 4 grams. It is now believed that many of the nearly 200,000 people who died in the US in October of 1918 may have died of aspirin poisoning.

The Federal government offered little or no guidance to its citizens. They did not want to alarm the population who they thought were already over-traumatized by World War I. So, it fell to local governments to implement safety mandates. Unsurprisingly, responses were much the same that we are seeing today. Some were effective and some were not. Some resisted doing anything at all.

After the summer of 1919 when the Spanish flu disappeared, there have been several other flu pandemics. About 70,000 people died in 1957 and

1958 from an outbreak. 34,000 Americans lost their lives in the years 1967 and 1968 from another one. The swine flu pandemic of 2009 and 2010 led to 12,000 deaths.

We have learned a lot about how disease spreads and how it can be treated in the last century. Both the Swine Flu and the Ebola outbreak in 2014 could have been major pandemics but they were able to be contained.

1918 is just not that long ago. All four of my grandparents were young adults when it struck. Our collective memory should be strong enough to be able to recognize that a hundred years later, we are following the Spanish flu timeline beat by beat. Why would anyone expect COVID-19 to behave in an appreciably different manner than its predecessors? We do not know how to cure this virus, but we certainly know how to contain it. We know now that the decision was made not to.

The Washington Post, last month, reported that there have been at least 34 times since this started that the President has publicly said that the virus will "simply go away". He and his Administration seem to be pinning their hopes on the fact that if a third or more of the US population gets infected, as they did in the last century, then they will either perish or survive creating so-called "herd immunity." When that happens, the flu will be over.

This is the President's actual plan. He wants to let people get sick and die so those who are left will survive and move back into their lives. Not only does he not want people to protect themselves, but he also wants people to gather and spread the virus as far as possible. There is nothing random whatsoever about what he's doing. The sooner everyone gets it, in this Administration's thinking, the sooner we will get through this.

In 1918, the population of the United States was 103.2 million people. In 2020, the population of our country has risen more than three times that and is now at 328.2 million people. By following the 1918 template, our government is saying that they are willing to accept about 2 million deaths to get us through this crisis. The big 'if', of course, is that COVID-19 will behave the same way that the Spanish flu did. They are betting that come summer, after 100 million US citizens have become infected with it, it "simply disappears."

We don't have to follow this course of action, even if the rest of the country seems to be OK with it. If 2 million people dying seems like a reasonable cost to get our pre-pandemic lives back, think of it in another way. Instead of the number, think of those people as your friends, your spouse, your parents, or your children. How many of those people are you willing to lose so that you can get back inside a movie theatre?

In 1932, Reinhold Niebuhr wrote what has now commonly come to be known as the *Serenity Prayer*.

"God, grant me the serenity to accept the things I cannot change,
courage to change the things I can,
and wisdom to know the difference."

No matter how hopeless it all may seem, there is far more that we have the power to change than you might think. We do not need to watch our friends and loved ones die. That, we can change.

October 21, 2020
Over 60,000 new cases in the US for 2nd straight day.

I am generally healthy—knock wood—it takes a lot to knock me off my feet. Even so, in a normal year, I would probably have developed semi-permanent rolling congestion about now that I would be blaming on allergies. I wouldn't leave the house without a packet of tissues. At night I would be sleeping on whatever side of my nose was the clearest so that the other side could drain.

My doctor has always said that I don't have any allergies and I've just never quite believed him. Every year at certain times, without fail, I get stuffy, and I've always attributed it to some unknown tree that was blooming. My doctor would smile at me and say no, but I knew better. According to my self-diagnosed schedule, I shouldn't be breathing clearly right about now and yet I am.

Yesterday, at one point in my walk, I found myself far downtown, so I decided to take the subway part of the way home. The first A train that came along was crowded so I waited until an empty E train came and got on that for a few stops.

I can't remember the last time that I was crammed into a subway car crowded with people. Before March, that could happen several times a day. Before March, when I ran into friends we would have hugged and kissed each other. I would have shaken hands with the people that I didn't know as well. When the waiter brought the bread to the table at the restaurant, it would have been in an open basket or on a plate rather than in a sealed bag. The waiter wouldn't be wearing gloves and a mask when he brought us fresh cutlery.

On an ordinary day, before this past March, I would come into direct contact with hundreds of people in New York—whether they were friends or strangers on a subway platform—any of whom could have passed along to me some sort of bug. It's no wonder that I haven't been sick in seven months. I've only come into actual direct contact with a total of about 10 people in all this time.

I remember my sister telling me a story when she was pregnant with my nephew. A friend of hers asked her if she was going to get rid of her pets before she gave birth. My sister was somewhat incredulous that her friend would even suggest such a thing. My sister and brother-in-law each had a dog when they got married and since then have always had at least one dog and a somewhat more fluid number of cats. The friend was concerned about the animals not being hygienic. My sister, on the other hand, was all about her kids being exposed to anything and everything early on so that they could build up their immune systems.

Living in New York City is a constant assault on one's immune system. The upside is that we end up with incredibly strong systems that can ward off most everything that comes our way. These days, as we live our lives in isolation from each other, I wonder what the effect is going to be on our ability to fight off disease. In the face of almost nothing coming at us, and all this cleanliness, will it start to diminish?

In 1989 an epidemiologist named Dr. David Strachan proposed what he called the hygiene hypothesis. In a nutshell, what he was suggesting is that people who were exposed to fewer germs growing up had a higher probability of developing allergic diseases like asthma or actual allergies in later life. A director I have worked with for decades always insists on there being hand sanitizer available on his table in rehearsal. This was long before COVID-19. We used to joke that he was helping to develop a super-bug. Hand sanitizer kills just about everything you could pick up. Some articles came out that said that continued use of products like that would kill everything except for a few truly hardy forms of bacteria which would eventually gain in strength as they adapted to the hand sanitizer and put an end to us all.

One thing that we will all know how to do when all of this is over, is wash our hands. The cast of *Grey's Anatomy* has nothing on us. Even in truck stops along the highway, there are now posted notices about how to wash your hands properly—a full 20 seconds, thoroughly soaping up each finger individually and under whatever rings we are wearing.

Hand sanitizer is everywhere these days. You would be hard-pressed to find a store in this city that doesn't have it available to any customer that walks in. Delis have them at the checkout counter and expensive clothing stores set up discreet tables near their front door. Restaurants sometimes have them on each table. Before this spring, I never used hand sanitizer at all. Now I pretty much grab a squirt every time I see one.

I could use a deep breath of some good, somewhat fresh, city air. Anything, to stop having to watch people endlessly trying to predict the electoral college numbers on TV. It's becoming beyond painful to watch. Let's just vote already so we can begin to recover from all of this.

In the meantime, I need to go out and try to find some more hand sanitizer. We are running low.

October 22, 2020
493,774 Total Reported Cases in New York. 33,443 Deaths.

I just got word that I passed my Election Polling Worker test last Saturday, so I am officially able to work for the next year.

The training session was interesting. Some things now seem obvious about the whole process that I had never realized before. When you walk into a polling place in New York, there is an information desk when you arrive. You then go to the desk of your specific district. At every district's table, two people are sitting there—one checking your name and one handing you your ballot. One of those people will be a registered Republican and the other will be a registered Democrat. During the days I might work, I would arrange with my Republican counterpart which of us would do what. Every couple of hours we are meant to switch which task we are doing. New York City is heavily Democratically inclined, so I am guessing that they are probably short of Republicans at this point.

There are a lot of checks and balances in place throughout the day. We are not allowed to ask anybody for an ID unless the system specifically prompts us to. We are not allowed to deny anyone the right to vote. Some issues might invalidate a vote and you may get sent to a different polling place, but you will still be able to cast a vote on the day you are there. If the system identifies an issue, you will be given an affidavit ballot. That ballot will be adjudicated on a case-by-case basis. Judges will be on call all day to decide whether an individual ballot is legal or not. Some cases may need to be decided later.

The polls will close at 9 pm. If you are on the line by 9 pm, you will still be able to get in to vote. We've been warned that as workers we could be there until the wee hours of the morning. Nothing will start to close until the last person on that line has cast their ballot.

At the end of the day, when all the ballots are officially sealed into ballot boxes and accounted for, they get turned over to a police officer who takes them back to the station house. This is something that was absolutely news to me. It is the police who tabulate the votes and report them in. That's what they are talking about when they say that a certain percentage of precincts have reported in. They are referring to police precincts. Perhaps that information is obvious to everyone and I just never put it together. Everything in the polling place is designed to be done in as bipartisan a way as possible and then all the results get placed in the hands of people who may be strongly biased in one direction or another. There are printouts from the ballot machines that indicate how many people voted for a specific candidate so it's not as if a specific precinct could just fabricate the results without it being discovered. It, nonetheless, seems like a somewhat potentially problematic step in the process to me.

As I am sure everybody knows, we aren't directly electing the President and the Vice President, we are, instead, electing a delegate to the Electoral College, who, then, in turn, elects them. That delegate is meant to then cast their vote in a way that supports who most of us in our district chose.

In the United States, there are 538 delegates appointed to the College. A candidate needs 270 of those votes to win. In 48 of the nation's states and Washington D.C., whichever side gets the most votes, gets all the electoral votes from that state. In Maine and Nebraska, however, only two of the total number of Electoral College delegates need to vote with the majority in the state. The remainder pledge according to the majority winner in their district so the votes in those two states could be split. Some so-called "faithless electors" end up voting contrary to what the majority has decided. Many, but by no means all, states have legislation to try to prevent this.

None of the 14 United States territories have any delegates to the Electoral College at all. American citizens who are from Puerto Rico, Guam, the US Virgin Islands, or the others, are not allowed to vote in Presidential elections.

One of the most contentious issues of the institution of the Electoral College is that the number of delegates each state has is determined by a variety of factors, not just by population. A delegate from rural Montana could represent a few thousand people whereas a delegate from New York could represent hundreds of thousands of voters. That means that an individual's vote in Montana potentially carries far more weight, comparatively, than an individual's vote in New York City.

In 2016, 3 million more people voted for Hillary Clinton than voted for the President. The President, however, received more Electoral College votes than she did so he won the election. The same thing happened in 2000. Al Gore received more popular votes, but G.W. Bush won the College. The Republicans have spent decades gerrymandering the election districts in their favor to make this happen. I don't have the slightest idea why Democrats have never tried to do the same. That manipulation of districts has meant that the Republican candidate has won the national election at least twice so far despite their opponent getting more of the popular vote.

The entire election usually comes down to the Electoral votes in a few pivotal states—Florida, Ohio and Pennsylvania, and a few others. Because of that, candidates end up concentrating on those districts and ignoring some of the others. All of this is why, these days, all anyone is talking about on the news is who is ahead and who is behind in those states. The talking heads try to piece together how each candidate might achieve the needed 270 votes. It is worse than listening to a bunch of people discuss an upcoming sports season.

It is thought that when the Russians interfered in the last election that they concentrated their meddling in some of those key Electoral College states. Ohio was a likely target. John Ratcliffe, the Director of National Intelligence announced yesterday that both Russia and Iran have already begun to interfere in our upcoming election. Both have obtained voter registration information that they can use to target groups of people.

There are so many places throughout the world where people do not have a say in the way their countries are run. We do. If this Administration had its way, that right would be taken away from us as well. This President spends so much of his time speaking to the American people sowing discord and distrust about as many aspects of this upcoming election as he can. It is not a given that we will always be allowed to vote. We need to continue to fight to retain that right for as long as we can.

I hope that I get assigned to a polling station for this voting period, although it is certainly possible that I won't. The city is lousy with Democrats—it's Republicans who are in short supply.

Early voting begins here on Saturday. I will likely try and get in on Sunday or Monday. I'll figure out with Michael when a good day for us to go in together might be. However long it takes, however wet we might get while we are waiting in line to get in, however tired and hungry we might be, we will vote. And then, and only then, will we be able to change things for the better.

October 23, 2020
495,608 Total Reported Cases in New York. 33,454 Deaths.

I am at work. I haven't been able to say that in seven months. I am downstairs at New World Stages on 50th Street and we are setting up for a Patti LuPone concert in a small theatre right across the hall from where *Jersey Boys* performs. Performed. Performs.

The theatre is tiny. The concert is going to be streamed for Performing Arts Center subscribers around the country so there won't be a live audience present. It's not quite a show and not quite a TV program. It's somewhere in between. So far this morning, I have answered a question about where Patti will enter from at the top of the concert. I now have a break.

There is a COVID compliance officer on site. We had an orientation and briefing when I first got here. There are hand sanitizing stations set up at regular intervals throughout the space and plenty of PPE is available. Everybody is in a mask.

When Patti and her accompanist get here to rehearse, they will be in masks but once they are ready to go on stage, they will take them off. All of us who might then encounter them will be given face shields to wear to help protect our eyes. The tech tables and cameras have all been set up to comply with social distancing as much as possible. Rather than sitting in the theatre as I normally would do while a show is getting loaded in, I am sitting out in the lobby where we've each been given a separate station to work from.

These measures should make us all safer over the day but there is still some risk involved. We are going to all be working together all day. Mask wearing does not fully stop transmission it just impedes it. I know what I've been doing these past few weeks, and I am confident that I will not pass along anything to anybody. Whether anybody I meet today or tomorrow ends up passing something on to me remains to be seen.

We are using the back of the *Jersey Boys* theatre as a kind of green room area. Some of the props and furniture from the show are stacked onstage. The ghost light is on.

Most theatres have a standing light that gets placed onstage and turned on at the end of the evening that is called a ghost light. Theatre lore says that the light is for the comfort of the spirits of the theatre or to drive away the more destructive ones. Practically, it keeps people from walking onto a darkened stage and falling off the edge of it into the orchestra pit. The glow from the lamp doesn't light up the whole stage, but I can still make out the outline of the steel bridge that is the *Jersey Boys* main set piece. The stage looks the way it does after the day off. It looks ready for a performance tonight.

Each of the candidates in their final debate last night had a different goal to achieve. Joe Biden just needed to get through it. He did that. The President, on the other hand, really did need to convince undecided voters to swing his way. Whether or not he did that is much less clear. While he was far more restrained, he did little if anything to outline any actual policy plans that he might have for his second term. He continued to claim that the pandemic is almost over despite all evidence to the contrary.

Fact-checkers from all the major networks have all said much the same thing—this was one of the least factual of the President's appearances—ever. Polls that were taken after the debate gave it to Biden, but it is unlikely to change much of anything in either candidate's standing. It's just a relief that it's over.

I'm now being called back into the theatre to look at the lights. We've got about three hours before Patti gets here to run through the concert once before tomorrow. It feels good to be doing something in a theatre again—even under these strange and restrictive circumstances. I'll take it.

OCTOBER 24, 2020
497,732 Total Reported Cases in New York. 33,463 Deaths.

It's showtime!

All of the discussion, the fighting, the thoughtful debate, the slinging of mud, the anxiety, the smugness, the questioning, the fear, the projection, the posting, the Tik-Toking, the Instagramming, the Facebooking, the Snapchatting, the drawing, the singing, the yelling, the speaking, the thinking, the joking, the worrying, the fretting, the watching, the listening, the blocking, the shunning, the ignoring, the drinking, the eating, the sleeping, the changingofchannelling, the checking, the calculating, and all of the deciding has been the rehearsal for today's first preview of what's to come for the next four years and beyond.

51 million people have already cast their ballots nationwide and there are still 10 days left before the actual day of the election. That number is 4 million votes higher than all the early voting in the entire election in 2016. The number of early votes cast in Texas, North Carolina, and California is already more than the number of votes that the President received in total in those states in 2016.

How will it end?

When you are putting a show together, you start with an idea. The person with the idea then gets other people to get on board with them. They can decide to do the early work themselves or they can create a team of writers and composers to collaborate with. The story begins to form. At some point, they begin to take what they have and read it aloud to a few friends and colleagues. They give suggestions. The creator either ignores them or incorporates them into the project and begins to adjust the direction it's taking. A director comes on board. A choreographer is chosen.

The piece gets to the point where it is now ready to present to a larger audience—hopefully one that will get excited about what everyone is doing and offer to finance it. Over a couple of readings, a group of producers, financial investors, and hopefully a regional theatre come on board so that the actual production can be planned.

At that point, hundreds of people start to get involved—the design team, the technical team, the casting team, the promotional and marketing team, the press team all get added.

Momentum has begun. The production gets announced. An opening night is chosen. The designs start being set. Schedules are put together with build dates and load-in and rehearsal dates that all backdate from the announced opening night. The show starts to get cast and the stage management team is put together. Pre-production starts—you've booked rehearsal studios and chosen a prop supervisor who begins to put together rehearsal props or cheap mock-ups of larger set pieces. The wardrobe supervisor starts to pull together rehearsal versions of some of the more elaborate costumes.

The rehearsals start. There is always an argument about how long you get to rehearse. No money starts to come in until you have your first preview, and the audience has been allowed to buy tickets. Before that, everything is coming out of the initial investment, so money is tight.

The longer the rehearsal period the longer you pay all those salaries and rent on the rehearsal rooms out of your investment fund.

If you're very lucky you get six weeks in a studio. Four weeks is the more likely number although smaller theatres often shave even more time off. Union rules dictate that you can rehearse for up to seven hours a day for six days before you need to take a day off. Constant meetings and discussions are happening outside of those hours. The cast all need to be fitted into their actual costumes and wigs.

While the cast is working with the director, and the music and choreographic teams in the studio, the set, lights, sound system, and video systems are all being loaded into the theatre and set up. After the studio rehearsals, everyone then starts working together for the first time on stage in the theatre. Lights, sound, set, projection, costumes, wigs, makeup, along with the band all coordinate together, and slowly, the show starts to come together. This period, called tech, can last a couple of days or, if you have a very complicated and intricate show, it can go on for weeks.

The stage manager, along with the director, pushes everyone forward. Then, when everything is almost ready, you have a final dress rehearsal for family and friends, and colleagues. The 'almost' in almost ready is an extremely relative term. When we had our invited dress rehearsal for the musical *Titanic* we had to stop the show more than twenty times. I'm not sure that we ever got to the end of it that day. Nonetheless, we then started previews the following night.

All during previews, you come in early every morning to start fixing and changing the technical elements of the show. After lunch, the cast then comes in and you work those changes and fixes into the show. You get about four hours with them a day. There is then a dinner break (although some tech departments end up working through it at great expense) and everyone gets ready for the performance that night. The first paying audience starts taking their seats a half hour before the performance. At the same time, the cast is called backstage to start getting into their costumes and makeup.

And then it's showtime. The creative and producing team sits out front and watches the show with the audience and notes the response. Changes need to be made but what are they? There is always a fight about that. ALWAYS.

Changes can go into the show every single day during the preview period. Some big and some small. Sometimes whole new songs get written and whole new pieces of scenery get built. Costumes and wigs change.

Scenes and songs get cut. Sometimes people get fired and replaced. On the musical of *The Red Shoes*, from the beginning of the process, it seemed like somebody was getting fired and replaced every few days—actors, the stage manager, wardrobe supervisor, more actors. The director. We started referring to the show as "The Pink Slips."

Millions of dollars are at stake, not to mention people's reputations—artistic and otherwise—and tensions can run high. You can start thinking that you are doomed, that nothing is working, and then get to opening night and the reviews are raves. Unfortunately, the opposite can happen as well. You can start thinking that because the people you are talking to all seem to love what you have that you are in great shape. Opening Night is a confident celebration and then the reviews come out and it's like you've had your knees broken by a thug with a tire iron. *Titanic*, after all our endless work, got lousy reviews but it didn't matter. Audiences started loving it anyway and it grew and grew in popularity until we won the Tony Award for best musical that year.

Doing this concert with Patti LuPone tonight is all of this on a much, much smaller level. Far fewer people are involved. Most of the material in tonight's show, Patti has sung before, so we know how to light it and mix the sound for it. Some of it is brand new. We've had to make many adjustments to what we usually do to accommodate the fact that it is going to be live-streamed. Usually, we would be doing the concert in a hall that seats thousands of people. Tonight, we are in a space that seats less than two hundred and nobody who isn't working on the show will be in the space with us.

No matter how much you prepare and how much you rehearse and plan, you can never really know how the show is going to go that night. You can never really tell what the response is going to be. I have been wrong far more times than I've been right, so I try not to project. Instead, I try and just do my job the best I can and hope for the best.

We have some technical work to do this afternoon. Patti will come in early for a soundcheck and may run some of the things she wasn't happy with at yesterday's rehearsal. Then we will do the show.

The two candidates that we are about to choose between have each followed a similar path that a Broadway musical takes. They each started with an idea, attracted followers, grew their teams, debated their competitors, won some primaries, and ultimately became the candidate.

They've been performing their shows for months now. On Broadway, the equivalent of where we are right now politically is award season. Which musical is going to win the Tony Award? Some support one, some others. The one that ultimately wins will survive. The ones that don't often will close.

When Julie Andrews opened the envelope onstage at Radio City Music Hall in 2005 and said, "and the Tony Award goes to… *Jersey Boys*," that's the moment that we knew we'd won—not a second before. We aren't any more certain about what is going to happen on November 3rd. I don't even know what is going to happen tonight at New World Stages. I know that we are all going to work hard this afternoon, but how will the show go tonight? We'll know when we know. Until then, all we can do is prepare as best we can.

I am going to vote tomorrow or the following day. Today is about getting the concert done, tomorrow I'll go back to concentrating on the future of the country.

Break a leg, everyone.

OCTOBER 26, 2020
501,197 Total Reported Cases in New York. 33,479 Deaths.

It is a dark, chilly, and rather dreary day here in Manhattan. The grey sky looks as soft as the pillow I left on my bed a few hours ago. I am waiting to cast my vote.

The end of the line where I am now standing is across the street from the building where we vote. To get in, however, I am going to need to follow the line down 102nd to Amsterdam, uptown to 104th, then back over to Columbus and downtown to 102nd again and hang a right. Then back to where I started, on the other side of the street, we'll head to Amsterdam again. Then we turn left, head down the block towards 101st Street, and then I can't see what happens. All told, that's probably about three-quarters of a mile, maybe more.

Michael got here about half an hour before me. He's already around the block from me. I am praying that it doesn't rain and that I won't need to go to the bathroom. There are snacks in my backpack.

We are now truly and solidly at the beginning of the much-predicted second wave of the pandemic. 42 states are seeing increases in their case numbers. Yesterday, the rolling average of new daily cases of COVID-19 in the country hit 69,000. That's the highest it has ever been.

Five staff members in the Vice President's office have tested positive for the virus. Utah Governor Gary Herbert just announced that they may need to start rationing ICU beds. Medical Centers in Kansas City, Missouri this past month have been turning away ambulances because they have no beds left. Some Idaho patients have had to be transported to Seattle and Portland to receive care. Officials in El Paso are urging people to stay home for two weeks to try and stop the spread because their hospitals are at capacity.

Dr. Ngozi Ezike the director of the Illinois Department of Public

Health, broke down this morning when she addressed the people of her state and pleaded with them to fight the fatigue—to continue to wear masks and practice social distancing.

After about two hours of standing in line, it started raining even though my iPhone app assured me that it wouldn't. An elderly lady made her way along the line having already voted. She was stooped over and had to rely on a walker to get by. She had her "I voted" sticker proudly stuck on her lapel. She paused to catch her breath near me, and I gave her an enthusiastic thumbs up. "Oh me," she said, "I just can't believe all these people are out here waiting on these lines to vote. It's the most beautiful thing I've seen in all my days." This is a lady who lived through having to fight to even have the right to vote in this country. She knows, in her bones, what this privilege means.

The last forty minutes of the wait was under a row of trees that stopped the misty rain. At one minute past the 3-hour mark, I got into the polling station. They were extremely organized inside. It took me just nine minutes from the moment I entered the building, stood on the line to get my ballot, got the ballot, filled it out and scanned it into the machine, got my sticker, and left. There were as many people on the line when I got out as there were when I started this morning. That lady is right. That may be one of the most beautiful things any of us could hope to see.

OCTOBER 27, 2020
502,978 Total Reported Cases in New York. 33,495 Deaths.

Michael left early this morning in the rain to go down to the *Law & Order* set to get tested. He is shooting an episode that includes his recurring role as Judge Serani at some point in the next couple of days. Everyone on set must get tested 72 hours before they arrive as well as on the day of. Judge Serani is kind of the perfect role in times of COVID. He sits by himself on a bench. He's already socially distanced.

Last night, as we went to sleep, Michael was muttering his lines to himself as I drifted off. Par for the course when you live with an actor. Very early on in our relationship, he got cast as one of the dads in *Mamma Mia* on Broadway. He had to sing *Our Last Summer* while accompanying himself on the guitar. He doesn't play the guitar, so he had to learn the chords of the song and practice them over and over again. They gave him a beat-up instrument to rehearse with at home. Often, he'd wake up in the middle of the night, and I'd hear him softly pick out the tune a couple of times in the dark before he came back to bed. I don't know that anyone who saw him do that realized just how many countless hours he had to spend practicing so that he could make it look easy on stage. I certainly did.

From what we could tell, Patti LuPone's concert this weekend was a success. While it was done live, only about 5 or 6 friends were sitting in the audience. The rest were in their homes all around the country (and around the world) watching it being streamed online.

Before the concert, Patti asked the people in the theatre not to respond—not to clap and not to laugh. What she was hoping to avoid was the occasional smattering of responses that we have all gotten used to listening to comedians and performers who broadcast from home. No sound, we thought, would be better than that. During rehearsals, there was even some humor to be mined from the silence. Patti belting out *Don't Cry for Me, Argentina*, and being met with complete crickets at the end of it made us all laugh during the afternoon soundcheck.

When I first met Patti, I was the Production Stage Manager of a play by David Mamet called *The Old Neighborhood*. We rehearsed in Boston because the director was teaching up there. Between him and David Mamet and the other actors in the play, there was a LOT of testosterone floating around. I immediately gravitated to Patti. At the time, I joked with somebody that she was the only other gay man in the room.

Once we had opened and were running in New York, Patti had to take off a show because she had a long-standing commitment to perform her concert somewhere. In the days before, she would run through some of the songs in her dressing room. I was (and still am) a huge fan of hers. When I was still in high school, I saw the original production of *Working* which was a musical bomb that I, nonetheless, loved. Patti was in it, although she didn't have a song.

Then I saw *Evita* with the original cast. It is still, today, one of the most remarkable things I have ever seen. I did not only not want it to end, but I also wanted to DO it. Afterward, I went to the stage door to see if I could get Patti's autograph and the doorman let me go up to her dressing room. That would never happen now. I knocked on her door and she opened it. Mandy Patinkin and a couple of other people were in there with her. She smiled and graciously signed my playbill and handed it to Mandy to sign as well. To say that I was over the moon, would be a complete understatement. I floated out of there.

So, fast-forward to *The Old Neighborhood*, and I am now actually working with her. On the Saturday before she took off for her concert, she told me that she was going to sing in her dressing room between shows and to let everyone know to leave her alone.

I went out and picked up some food and came back and sat on the stairs outside of her room while she sang. She went through several songs and then it happened, she started singing *Argentina*. I couldn't believe what I was hearing. Patti LuPone was singing *Don't Cry for Me, Argentina* and I was the only person listening to it.

More than twenty years have passed since that day, and I have now heard her sing it countless times. It doesn't matter. It never fails to bring me back to what it felt like sitting in that stairwell eating my sandwich. This weekend, we ran through the concert twice before we streamed it. Patti sang full out in some places and held back in others. When the time came for the actual performance, the energy changed. Nothing was marked. She was fully committed.

The complete lack of response during our rehearsals was not only expected but, as I said, also somewhat humorous. That same lack of response during the actual concert when Patti was giving it her remarkable all was heartbreaking. There was nothing funny about it at all.

The Performing Arts require an audience. Yes, there was an audience watching our stream, and yes, I know that they were responding well because I saw the text comments flying past when I watched it later. Even so, the direct dialogue between the audience and the performer is where the real electricity happens. That was missing. That's the reason we will always crave being part of a live audience.

Listening to Patti sing through a closed door is one of my favorite memories, but it pales in comparison to watching her sing onstage up on the balcony in Hal Prince's spectacular Broadway production. She shot energy at us, and we all shot it right back at her. I want that back. I need to get that back. Yes, I freely admit it, I'm an addict.

The President has said that New York is a "ghost town" but, like everything else out of his mouth, that is a complete lie. New York is far from being a ghost town. Even in the rain, people are out and about. Shows are filming. People are creating. We are all doing the best we can. There is plenty of time left to vote. Bring an umbrella.

OCTOBER 28, 2020
504,689 Total Reported Cases in New York. 33,505 Deaths.

Yesterday, I made like a tourist and went up to the new observation platform called "The Edge" in Hudson Yards. The Edge claims to now be the highest open-air platform in the western hemisphere. It is nine feet higher than the CN Tower in Toronto. With the opening of The Edge, the CN Tower gets pushed down to number 12 on the list of the world's highest decks. Many of the ones that are higher than that are in China where I've never visited. I have been to the Burj Khalifa in Dubai, which is the tallest building in the world, but its observation tower isn't at the top, so it comes in at number three. I've also been to the Tokyo Sky Tree which is 9th.

I should have started by saying that I don't like heights. At all. I got hired to be the Assistant Stage Manager on the Broadway production of *The Phantom of the Opera* way back in 1993. It was beyond thrilling. I was so excited to start working. On my first day there, I followed the Stage Manager around during the show to start to learn it. Towards the end of the first act, we made our way out into the house under the stage right box which was curtained off from the audience. There was a straight ladder there, going up.

"Go ahead," she said. I laughed and then saw that she was serious. I told her to go first and that I'd follow. My hands were sweating. They are sweating now as I write this. She started up and I took a moment then decided. I wanted the job much more than I feared going up. So, I followed her up.

At each rung, I held on so tightly that my fingernails made deep red grooves in my palms. My hands were so slippery with sweat that I was terrified that they would just slip off. We climbed up to the proscenium—the top of the stage. At the top, there was not anything to hold on to, to pull yourself up with, but I got up there somehow.

Once we were up, we had to crawl out on the gangway to the center of the stage. By crawl, I do mean crawl. The facing was only a couple of feet high and if you didn't crawl the audience could see you. The whole thing moved. The Phantom and his dresser came on from the other side. That made it move more. The floor was slatted which meant that you could look down onto the stage. I had to pretend that it was solid.

In the audience, when you watch the show, the whole proscenium arch looks very fancy. It's all gold and ornate and at the top in the center is a gold angel. The Phantom gets into that angel. Our job was to make sure he was in and set and, once he was, to call "clear" to the stage manager who was calling the cues. The calling stage manager, knowing he was safe, then cued the angel to drop, and the Phantom rode it down, singing the end of the act which is when the famous chandelier falls. All that action, by the way, made the platform shake and shudder even more.

Then, in the dark, the angel comes back up and the Phantom gets out and goes off left again with his dresser and then we have to crawl back to the ladder and go DOWN. It was even more difficult to go down because at the top of the ladder, as I said, there was nothing to hold onto. Also, by that time, water was visibly dripping off my hands. The structure was jiggling so much that I thought it was going to collapse into the audience.

I got through it. I ended up doing that several times a week for about six months. *Phantom* then offered me a job on the road as Stage Manager and I took it and ended up touring with it for two years. The ladder on tour was upstage of the proscenium, it had thicker rungs and it had a cage around it. On tour, however, we also had to bring up the Phantom's water bottle as well as his large wide-brimmed black hat.

I got to the point where I could go up and down that ladder without thinking about it. I almost enjoyed it. I thought that I had cured my fear of heights. I was wrong. I had cured my fear of that height. The rest of them were still just as bad.

If there is a lighthouse or an old church tower to climb, I will do it. If there is an observation deck, I'm there. I always regret it, but I'll always do it. I've even been hot air ballooning twice. Once in the Maasai Mara National Reserve in Kenya and once in the Yarra Valley in Australia. Both trips were terrifying and amazing at the same time. Breathtaking in the truest sense of the word.

There is a perspective that you can get from great heights that you cannot get in any other way.

At the top of the Westerkerk in Amsterdam, which has a terrifyingly old and narrow stone staircase up to the top, you can look down on the building that Anne Frank and the others hid in and see how they were able to do it. The annex that they were hidden in, is truly separate from the buildings that line the canals in front and behind it. You can't see that from the ground.

At the top of The Edge, you can look out over the entirety of New York City and even out across New Jersey. You can easily see that we live on an island. Central Park stands out as a green rectangle in a dense forest of steel and concrete towers. All those towers are teeming with people. We are all on top of each other. All eight million-plus of us.

Looking out across all of that, the fact that most of us joined together, wore masks, and followed social distancing becomes even more remarkable. You can see just how many people had to come together and agree to do the same thing to make that work. Yet, we did it.

Going up to The Edge was a distraction. We are six days away from the election. Having my heart pump for something besides the anxiety I have around what the results are going to be was lifesaving.

The glass walls on the outdoor platform tilt away at an angle. To take a picture without glare, I had to put my phone against the glass which meant I had to reach over the edge of the roof. (I think that my sister, who suffers this fear worse than I do, has just stopped reading.) Like the CN Tower, there's an inset glass section of the floor that you can walk on and look down between your feet at the city 100 floors below. One couple was letting their baby crawl around on it. The baby seemed fine, but I couldn't get anywhere near it.

I probably should have saved the Edge for a few days from now when I am going to need it. I'll have to find something else to distract myself today. And tomorrow. And for the few days after that. I don't know what's going to happen on November 3rd. At least whatever it is, it isn't going to be this endless waiting.

Once we've voted, there is nothing more that we can do.

Except hope.

OCTOBER 29, 2020

New Record high of 90,000 new cases in a single day reported in the United States.

It is well and truly raining here today. It's meant to last all day and continue into tomorrow. And it's cold. Another perfect day for the couch, but I think I'm too restless to stay inside all day.

Michael is heading downtown for his *Law & Order* shoot so it will just be me and the cat, as it was when we were quarantining. Michael will have to take a second rapid test before he's allowed onto the set. He tested negative two days ago so I am sure he will be fine.

Over the last few weeks, I've been working on a new virtual project and one of the people involved has been living in France since all of this began. In a televised address yesterday, French President Emmanuel Macron announced that he was shutting the country back down starting on Friday. "The virus is circulating at a speed that not even the most pessimistic forecasts had anticipated. Like all our neighbors, we are submerged by the sudden acceleration of the virus. We are all in the same position: overrun by a second wave which we know will be harder, more deadly than the first. I have decided that we need to return to the lockdown which stopped the virus."

Angela Merkel, the German Chancellor, also announced strict measures yesterday. Bars, restaurants, and theatres in Germany will be closed. Stores will be able to stay open with strict limitations and, again, like in France, schools will stay open.

The Italian Premier, Giuseppe Conte, shut down gyms, pools, and theatres on Sunday for at least a month. He imposed a curfew on restaurants and bars. He has also instituted a national mask-wearing mandate. As opposed to the initial shutdown which was crippling to their economy, this time around, the moves in Italy are designed to hopefully strike a balance between economic safety and personal safety.

All three countries have earmarked billions of Euros in governmental aid to offset the losses.

Rather than shutting down the entire country again, England is trying to institute a regional three-tiered system. Instead of a national blanket policy, each region will impose restrictions based on their specific numbers.

All these European countries are attempting to get through this crisis by implementing policies that try to balance the safety of the individual with the health of their economies. Not everyone is happy with it, but, for better or for worse, these European leaders are trying.

Our system of government is different from all of theirs. Great Britain is an uneasy alliance of England, Scotland, Wales, and Northern Ireland. Then there are other regions such as the Isle of Man, Jersey, and Guernsey. Each of those areas has a certain amount of autonomous power but they are still under one umbrella. France, Germany, and Italy are each a single unit. The United States, however, is a union of 50 separate governments. National mandates can be more difficult, if not impossible, to impose. The President often must lead by example rather than by imposing actual legislation.

As a country, we can do better than we are doing now. We are doing nothing now. Anything has got to be better than that. As Americans, we have never avoided a fight. That's not who we are. We've stood up to everybody and everything that has ever threatened us. Until now. This President waved the white flag before he fired a single shot. Putting aside everything else you can say about this man, he is simply a coward. Americans are many things, but we are not cowards. We should not be being led by one.

The rain is clattering down on the air conditioners. I can hear the traffic down on the street motorboating through the water. I can also hear the wind. The trees outside our windows are in constant movement. Their leaves have just started to turn yellow. The rain is bringing down the ones that have already turned. There are going to be solid masses of soaking wet leaves on the sidewalks for weeks. So much for the joy of kicking through them. Maybe I'll just stay in.

OCTOBER 30, 2020
509,368 Total Reported Cases in New York. 33,553 Deaths.

In normal times, I would invariably have needed to go to work on a cold and wet day like this. I would leave the apartment looking longingly at my folded-up sweatpants and want nothing more than to get back in them. Of course, I don't get to choose, but there are far worse things than being stuck at home on the couch with the cat and a warm blanket on a day like this.

OCTOBER 31, 2020
511,761 Total Reported Cases in New York. 33,559 Deaths.

The dusty smell of fallen autumn leaves is truly one of my favorite smells. By the time I catch a whiff of it, summer, invariably, has gone on much too long. The thrill of those first wonderful warm early spring days after an endless winter has long since flattened out in the endless monotony of long summer days that are far too hot and far too humid.

In my early days, of living in New York, I used to dread summers. The off-Broadway theatres that I routinely worked for in the city, closed in May and didn't start back up again until September. Finding theatre work was difficult. As New Yorkers fled to cooler places, tourists moved in to replace them. Making my way through the crowds of people from other places, made me feel like a visitor to my own city.

For two summers in those early years, I got to do summer stock in upstate New York. I was able to escape.

Cortland Repertory Theatre is a beautiful old wooden theatre sitting in the middle of a cornfield. That's not just a flowery description, it really was surrounded by growing corn for as far as you could see. It would be about a foot tall when we started and by the end of the season it was over our heads, and we were eating it. A lot of it.

A whole army of us was brought in to fill out the ranks of the people in the town who worked at the theatre every year. We stayed in beautiful old ramshackle Victorian houses in town and rehearsed in buildings downtown. We would tech and open whatever show it was and once that one was up and running, we'd start right in on the next one.

I was hired to go up there to stage manage because I often worked at Manhattan Theatre Club in New York. Shelley Barclay was the head of props, and we did a million shows together there. One year, she asked me if I would be interested in coming up and I said yes. Shelley was the production manager in Cortland and her wife, Mona, often acted in the productions. I stage managed Mona up there in *Company* and *Steel Magnolias*. I'm sure there were others, but those are the two that immediately come to mind.

Mona was as tall as I am, with beautiful short blindingly white hair. She had spectacular white teeth that were always in view because she was always smiling. Mona passed away last week. It wasn't from COVID.

Another friend of ours, Dee Cannon, passed away in London recently. She, also, did not pass away from the virus. She was a friend of Michael's who, over the years, I had come to know as well. Like her mother before her, she was a respected acting coach. She taught at RADA—The Royal Academy of Dramatic Arts—but she was also often hired to work with actors on films. She taught Cynthia Erivo who won a Tony for *The Color Purple* and was nominated for an Oscar for *Harriet*. She also taught Eve Best, an Olivier award-winning actor who we probably know better over here from her co-starring role with Edie Falco on *Nurse Jackie*.

Dee was prickly, opinionated, and, by all accounts, spectacular at her job. She was also kind and lovely. We saw her several times in London and several times here in New York when she came here to work. Michael was often sent, by her, on a treasure hunt for vintage American candy for props on a play she was doing or for an old tin advertising sign for the fence in her back garden.

It's hard to process the people that we are losing these days. What we want to do is draw together and keep them alive for at least a day more of remembrance. Yet, we can't. There was a virtual funeral service for Dee. The camera was in the back of the church. Unfortunately, not everyone was mic'd so they couldn't be heard when they were speaking. I didn't watch.

Two of Howell Binkley's lighting design associates put together an amazing tribute to him, after his passing a few weeks ago, that was streamed last weekend. Many people from different walks of his life, spoke. They included me in it as well. There were clips from his work as well as clips from interviews that he, himself, had given. It was almost as good as actually being in a room together, mourning his loss. Almost, but not quite.

Mona and Dee were people I loved but rarely saw. We stayed connected on Facebook. They, along with Howell, were treasured strands of the fabric of my life.

Sean Connery also passed away yesterday at the age of ninety. I didn't know him at all, but we once sat at a table next to him at an opening night party. For my life, I can't remember what it was. I do remember trying to overhear what he was saying. Not to spy on him, mind you, but just to hear the wonderful sound of his Scottish brogue.

I didn't want to face up to either Howell, Mona, or Dee's passing, but somehow losing Sean Connery, who I only knew from his films, made it all seem a bit more real. Maybe it is just a function of my age and the huge amount of people I have encountered over my working life, but three friends in as many weeks seem excessive.

I have friends who have lost their close friends and parents and spouses in these past months. The people I've lost left behind friends and families. My heart goes out to all of them. None of us should be reduced to saying goodbye via FaceTime or Zoom and yet that is what is happening. Everything in us wants to physically connect in times like these, and yet we are separated by everything from thousands of miles to a quarter-inch thick pane of glass. Separation is separation. The distance doesn't matter.

Today is Halloween. It is arguably the beginning of the holiday season. From here we have a few weeks to go until Thanksgiving and then on to all the holidays in December—Hanukkah, Kwanza, Christmas and from there it is just over a week until New Year's Eve. All of these are days that traditionally involve us all getting together.

We can't this year. The CDC is warning that even small family gatherings pose a sizable risk for the transmission of the virus. We are all going to have to spend these holidays anywhere from thousands of miles away from each other to just a pane of glass apart.

Next year at this time, if we correctly choose three days from now, we should be able to see each other in person. If you vote for no other reason than that, that is enough.

November 2, 2020
33,593 Total Reported Deaths in New York

The city is starting to prepare for the election. Stores have begun putting up plywood over their windows in anticipation of the election results tomorrow. Several stores in Times Square have covered up. So has Macy's and some of their neighbors in Herald Square. Downtown in SoHo, which was hard hit by the post-George Floyd murder protests, the sound of sawing and hammering was coming from every direction. The trendy Louis Vuitton store down there has put up what seems to be a permanent outer covering to the store. Corrugated iron panels, painted bright yellow, sheath the entire ground floor. The plywood elsewhere is so fresh, that nobody has painted on it yet.

In the last week or two, I have tried to stock up on everything that we ran out of during the lockdown in spring. I think that we now have about a three-month supply of paper towels, toilet paper, rubbing alcohol, and hand sanitizer. I even found a few cans of spray sanitizer. I would like to think that there is a difference between stocking up and hoarding and that what we are doing is the former. We will eventually use everything that we now have. There may be no issue with any of it, but given what happened a few months ago, I figured it couldn't possibly hurt to be prepared.

Michael and I are also having discussions about having an overall escape plan just in case. Michael thinks I am being a bit extreme, but I can't help but think about all the people in Germany who didn't try and leave before the War until it was too late. Better, it seems to me, to have a plan that we don't ever use than to be caught unaware.

I didn't see them myself, but friends reported yesterday seeing pick-up trucks covered in flags driven by radical supporters of the President riding around the city. A group of them shut down the Tappan Zee Bridge—parking their trucks to block traffic and getting out and waving flags. On Friday, a whole fleet of MAGA trucks, flags a-waving, surrounded a Biden/Harris campaign bus in Texas and tried to force it off the road. This group of trucks has been following the bus all around the country. The President praised this group in a rally speech saying, "I LOVE TEXAS!"

As Hitler was coming to power, he encouraged a group of supporters who came to be known as the "Brown Shirts." Made up of mostly disaffected lower-middle-class Germans who had lost their jobs, they were put into place to guard Nazi meetings, but they eventually turned into the Nazi army. They were antisemitic and anti-democratic and being a part of

Hitler's army gave them a purpose and a focus. They terrorized Germany for two decades and Hitler adored them and they, him.

"These patriots did nothing wrong," the President tweeted yesterday. Right out of the Nazi playbook.

I don't know what's going to happen tomorrow. None of us do. The people who are covering their stores with plywood here in New York have no idea what is going to happen, either. Whichever way the election goes, we could see people out in the streets over the next few days. I'm not confident enough in how any of this will go to say that they are being foolish.

I've never felt this way before. I have truly never envisioned the collapse of our Democracy before this. I have never worried about what would happen if our country drowned in a sea of radical populism. The continued influence of the Russians on this Administration would have been unthinkable before 2016. In 2020, it is a given.

It seems as if minute to minute I am veering between cautious optimism and deep despair. I know that I am not alone in this. There doesn't seem to be anything to do except to plan for the worst and hope for the best.

The Right is as scared of living in a country run by the radical Left as the Left is of living in a country run by the radical Right. The relentless disinformation campaign that has been pushed upon the country by the President and his supporters has genuinely convinced many Republicans that the Democrats are a satanic-worshiping coven of liberal pedophiles. Democrats went into the last election worried, certainly, but also over-confident. This election feels nothing like that at all.

Whatever tomorrow brings, it is probably not going to be anything that we are expecting. Nobody should give up. No matter what happens. The President could win again but lose the Senate and the House. He could win all three. He could lose all three. He thinks he's going to lose. He keeps saying it. What will happen when I lose? Can you imagine me losing to Joe Biden? Where will I go? What will I do?

There is no real way to plan for the worst, so why don't we all just spend today hoping for the best. Hope is what President Obama ran on in 2008 and that worked out quite well for him.

NOVEMBER 3, 2020

517,822 Total Reported Cases in New York. 33,603 Deaths.

Election Day.

Since the beginning, the virus, its spread, and how it has been managed or mismanaged, has been a constant in our lives. Friends, family members, and strangers have died by the hundreds of thousands in the United States. The murder of George Floyd by a policeman in Minneapolis in May brought to the fore the racial tensions in our country that have been there from our inception and that have never been properly addressed.

For the last few months, the closer we have come to today's election, the more that politics started to take up the bulk of our waking lives.

Like the day that we shut down and the day that George Floyd died, today is going to change the narrative. The first two events caught us by surprise. This one, the election, we have seen coming for a very long time. Jimmy Kimmel said that last night felt like "somewhere between Christmas Eve and the night before a liver transplant."

Despite my training session, I was never called upon to work the polls today. Instead, I got a good night's sleep. More than 100 million people had already cast their ballots before the polls opened this morning. A federal court overturned a Republican attempt to discard over a hundred thousand drive-by votes in Texas. It could take days to fully tabulate the results.

Michael and I are sitting on the couch with the cat. I think that we will be here on and off for the rest of the day.

A couple of months ago, I helped produce a virtual version of *Broadway Barks!* our annual animal shelter adoption event that I have done for over twenty years with Bernadette Peters. In a few days, we are going to stream a new British spin-off of that event called *West End Woofs!* We have been actively working on it for about two months. Bernadette is going to co-host it with Elaine Paige who is a major West End star. She has originated roles in everything from *Cats* to *Evita*. Animal shelters from all over the UK will be introduced by theatre stars, writers, and producers from the West End as well as by British film and television performers.

I don't think that any of us truly imagined when we were putting together the first version of *Broadway Barks!* in 1999 in New York that we would still be doing it twenty-one years later. Realizing that we could do it virtually, was very exciting. It allowed us to include some shelters far away from New York's theatre district. A whole array of celebrities that might not have made the trip into the heart of Broadway were more than happy to film something from their homes. We hoped to bring in the virtual version at about an hour and a half and instead it was well over three hours long. Someone in London reached out to us about doing a version of *Barks!* there and, after a lot of discussions, we decided to go for it. *West End Woofs!* was born.

Shelters across the Atlantic have experienced a similar rise in dog and cat adoptions during the pandemic that we have over here. Having a companion in lockdown has proven to be a lifesaver for countless single people wherever they live.

Today is not going to be an easy day for many of us. This election will dictate the direction that this country takes over the next four years. Four more years of this Administration is, frankly, unthinkable. We will know what's going to happen soon enough and this election, like every other election we have ever had, will slip into history.

It's going to be a long night. Hunker down and stay safe and warm. See you tomorrow.

November 3, 2020 (Later in the evening)

I am going to bed. I don't think anything more is going to happen tonight. We have the House, so we are at least no worse than we were.

All the important states that are in play and are leaning red still have a massive amount of uncounted mail-in and early ballots. The counts they have so far are from today's in-person voting. We've been told all along that the in-person will probably trend right, but the early stuff trends left.

In 2016 we went to bed right around this time having lost. That is not what's happening now.

November 4, 2020

519,890 Total Reported Cases in New York. 33,623 Deaths.

I slept like the dead last night. It was about 1 am when I went to bed.

At about 5 am, I woke up briefly. I checked my phone for alerts and the only thing on it was a confirmation from other outlets that the early announcement from Fox News that Biden had won Arizona was correct. The bulk of the uncounted votes in Arizona was from Maricopa County which is where Phoenix is. It is a dense urban area and, true to form, trends left.

Fox was early but proved to be correct. The President had been demanding that they rescind the projection.

I went into the living room where Michael was still watching TV. Well, the television was still on, but Michael was fast asleep on the couch. There was nothing more to be done so I went back to sleep. Sometime after that, Michael came to bed as well.

The President wants to stop the count. He is already threatening lawsuits and claiming fraud so it's easy to see what he and the GOP think is going to happen. In terms of the popular vote, Joe Biden is on track to receive more votes than any other candidate in the entire history of the United States. That's not going to be what decides this election. It's going to come down to the Electoral College.

Time magazine published a very interesting piece on the College last week. When our system was being constructed in the late eighteenth century the College was put in place because it was felt that most Americans across the continent would lack sufficient information to make an informed choice. The Founding Fathers didn't foresee the emergence of political parties which somewhat took care of that. People could figure out what local candidates stood for by knowing which party they aligned with.

The 12th Amendment was passed after the election in 1800-1801. It allowed parties to designate which candidate would be President and which one would be Vice President. In theory, at that point, the Electoral College should have been obsolete.

When it was proposed by James Wilson of Pennsylvania that voting be one man, one vote, James Madison of Virginia objected, saying that the South would never agree to that. The reason that the College was kept was that in a direct one-on-one election, the North would outnumber the South in terms of free men who could vote. The Electoral College allowed the southern states to count their enslaved people as being part of the population. They couldn't vote and they were each only considered 2/5ths of a human being, but their vast numbers ensured that the South would get a larger portion of Electoral College votes.

Perversely, the more slaves they brought in, the more Electoral College votes they would get. The result was that Pennsylvania had 10% more free people than Virginia but got 20% fewer potential votes.

Thomas Jefferson would not have become our third President without the extra Electoral College votes from the south which, of course, were based on the enslaved African population. It was also Jefferson, who recognized that different parts of Virginia would likely vote in different ways. It is he is who pushed through the idea that rather than having Electoral votes split between candidates, that the winner of the state would take all the votes. He was sure that there were districts in Virginia that would not support him, so he rewrote the law and got around it. People, it seems, have been trying to manipulate our elections from the very beginning of our existence as a country.

Neo-Nazis and White Supremacists are standing by. "I'm ready," posted one of the President's supporters along with a picture of three rifles and a handgun. "Get the guns and the amor ready," posted another. The spelling mistake was theirs.

The President is going to continue to bluster and stir the pot all day. He and his enablers are not going to go gently into that good night. They are going to rage against the dying light until the bitter end. Frankly, it's long past the time for all of them to just shut the f%$# up.

I, for one, am going to go out and take a walk through the park and I am going to try and force Michael to come with me. It is a perfect fall day outside. The sky is blue, and the air is crisp and clear, and it is just out there waiting for us.

NOVEMBER 5, 2020
New Record high of 121,000 new cases in a single day reported in the United States.

Votes are still being counted.

In much the same way that we have adjusted to life with COVID, we are starting to get used to living with the uncertainty in this election. We may have an answer later this evening. And, then again, we may not.

The election appears to have gone smoothly in almost every regard except one. The one, of course, being the President, himself. Thus far, it appears that the only interference in the election has been from the President and his immediate circle of cronies.

He has initiated lawsuits to stop the vote in states where he is ahead and continue the vote in states where he's behind. They were a bit confused in Michigan where a suit to stop the vote was filed on his behalf even though the President was trailing in the count.

There is still a path forward for the President amidst the multiple paths forward for Joe Biden. I have been through this feeling before.

About nine years ago, my annual checkup showed that my PSA levels were up. PSA stands for prostate-specific antigen. I needed to get a biopsy. And then I had to wait for the results.

Results of medical tests are among the hardest things we will ever need to wait for in our lives. In my case, the results came back positive. I had prostate cancer.

Once that diagnosis came in, waiting for results, waiting for appointments, waiting for surgery, and waiting for my body to heal became a part of my life. I ultimately survived prostate cancer. My poor prostate, alas, did not. It is lying in a landfill somewhere, but the rest of me eventually continued forward with really the most minor of adjustments to how I live my life. Luckily for me, it doesn't even cross my mind most of the time.

Whatever else might happen today, the results are in, and the United States has tested positive. Over 68 million people have voted for a man who exemplifies the worst in all of us. He is an actual living embodiment of the seven deadly sins: pride and greed and lust and gluttony and wrath and sloth and envy.

Like the worst bully any of us have ever had to endure in school, our President has mocked and belittled all of those who are in any way 'other' to him. He has publicly said that he does not respect women. He has publicly supported those who would willingly subjugate anyone who wasn't white, elevating themselves in the process. He has publicly stated that he has no respect for the people who have served in the military. He has publicly shown his disdain for the disabled. 68 million people who live in this country have decided that they are fine with that.

Whoever ends up winning this election, on some level all of us have already lost. We will either get four more years of sinking ever deeper into this mire, or we will be facing a long hard battle to start putting things to rights. This President has broken open a door that we have spent generations trying to shut. Like the evils that escaped from Pandora's box, the collective hate from the people of this country has been allowed to fly back out and intensify. We are not going to be able to put it back in anytime soon.

Whoever gets these agonizingly slow-in-coming final votes, the damage to We the People has been done. Make no mistake, I am still pulling for Joe Biden to win. With every fiber of my being, I am still pulling for him, and I will not stop. More people than have ever supported another single person in our history agree with me. Whatever happens, I will stand, proudly and unwavering, with them. Always.

NOVEMBER 6, 2020
526,318 Total Reported Cases in New York. 33,702 Deaths.

There's a scene in the movie *The World According to Garp* where the hyper-paranoid and doom-fearing character of Garp, played by Robin Williams, is looking for a house for his family.

While he's standing outside talking to the real estate agent, they notice a small two-seater plane sputtering and stuttering in the sky above them. In front of their eyes, the tiny plane nosedives into the house and explodes.

"I'll take it!" Garp says looking at the burning wreckage with enthusiastic relief. Whatever happens to him and his family while they are in that house moving forward, the chances of a small plane crashing into it again have been reduced to almost zero. One less thing to worry about.

We are now on the third day of vote counting following the election. I went to sleep with the President ahead in Pennsylvania and Georgia and I woke up this morning to him behind.

These days have been a lesson in patience. It's like watching a movie on Netflix with a poor internet connection. We get a minute or two of the story, then it freezes, and we watch the spinning ball until enough of it loads to lurch the story forward a little more.

The Stock Market has been all over the place. The Stock Market fluctuates because investors try to predict what the future will be. When there is a national event as big as a Presidential election, there is a lot of speculation of what the future economy will look like under each of the candidates. The erratic numbers are not surprising.

The store owners in New York City who covered up their windows with plywood before November 3rd are looking as if they overreacted. Before November 3rd, however, their reaction did not seem that far off the mark.

Groups of armed MAGA supporters have created disturbances at vote-counting centers in the last few key states, but there is nothing concrete for them to protest. They want the count to stop. They are claiming fraud. Different states have different laws, and it seems, from all that we are hearing, that the counting is progressing as it should be. Joe Biden is ahead. If they did stop counting now, then he wins. These protestors are complete idiots.

It took me a long time to get to sleep last night. I kept running different scenarios in my head and trying to take them to their logical conclusion. The truth is that there is no way of knowing what's going to come. There's nothing much we can do to plan for it.

In my professional life, I have never really gotten a job that I've actively gone after. My jobs tend to fall into my lap. Lincoln Center did a revival of *A Delicate Balance* in 1996 and when it was announced, I wrote to every single person I could think of connected with it to make my interest known. I wanted to do it. I got no response at all from anybody, so I gave up and started looking elsewhere.

A few weeks later, I got a call from somebody offering me a job on the show. Not because of anything I had done, mind you, but because my name had happened to come up during a meeting about something else. Somebody connected with *A Delicate Balance*, who was there, got the idea to hire me and gave me a call. I worked hard to get that job but, in the end, none of that mattered. It just fell into my lap.

We plan and try to make things happen regardless of what our past track records are of doing it successfully. We are constantly told to live in the moment and live for the now, but we can't help ourselves, we plan and worry anyway. We get encouraged by things that happen that we take as signs. Garp believed that his house was safe because the unimaginable had already happened to it. Well, who's to say that there might not be another plane circling right behind the one that crashed? His comfort was just an illusion, but one that helped him move forward.

I'm not interested in living fully in the moment. I am interested in living mostly in the moment. I like to know where I've been and where I'm heading so that I can be fully open to what is happening now. Many times, the most exciting parts of the journey are when you veer off the path and get lost.

Whatever the future holds in store for us, it's not going to be what we think it is going to be. And really, who would want it any other way?

NOVEMBER 7, 2020

Joseph R. Biden is declared the winner of the 2020 Presidential election.

We are now into the fourth long day of counting. I suppose that there is something to be said for this endless, drawn-out process. By the time we get to the inevitable conclusion, it won't be a surprise.

Before we got the cat that Michael and I are living with now, I had another cat named Wart. Wart traveled all over the place with me. He came with me on the road when I was touring with *The Phantom of the Opera*. He was a perfect companion to travel with.

When I started working on *Jersey Boys*, the two of us ended up in San Francisco where we were putting up the first National tour. Wart had suffered from kidney issues for a while by then and I had learned how to give him an IV of saline to keep him hydrated. At first, I didn't think that I was going to be able to bring myself to do it, but I got used to it—both of us did. I'd hold him still with one hand and insert the needle into the scruff of his neck with the other and he'd sit patiently while it drained. It became a part of our daily routine. Afterward, we would both just get on with our days.

Near Thanksgiving, he started failing. He started having difficulty using his back legs. We went to the vet out there and he said that he would likely not get better and that I should bring him back when things got too difficult. I was sure that we had plenty of time left. Within a few days, though, it became apparent that Wart was not comfortable at all. We went back to the vet, and I left him there overnight.

I started to realize that he wasn't going to get better. The next day, the vet called and described his condition to me, and I accepted that it was time. I went to the vet, and with Wart sitting on my lap, the vet injected him with something which slowly allowed him to slip away. Wart was ready and I was ready. I was not ready for how emotionally wrenching it was, but I had gotten to the point where keeping him alive was just selfishness on my part. It was by no means an easy decision to make, but over the last few days of his life, my shock and denial dissipated and were replaced by understanding and acceptance.

Something similar happens when you have worked for months if not years on a new show and the reviews come out and they are devastating. You end up going through much the same steps of grief before you ultimately come to terms with the fact that the show is going to close. The producers and investors do everything they can to save it, but ultimately the decision needs to be made.

The longer it takes the results of this election to be announced, the more everybody will be used to the way that it is trending. In the last four days, Democrats have gone from nauseating despair beginning that first night to a kind of cautious optimism. I imagine that the President's supporters have taken the opposite journey. It's hard to hold on to extremes of emotion for a drawn-out period. Full-fledged anger and fury flare up but then dissipate into sullen resentment. Anger and fury lead to rioting, sullen resentment does not. Certainly, if the election is ultimately called for Joe Biden that resentment could flare up again, but after these last few days, the wood is somewhat wet.

Of course, the election isn't over. There is still a chance, though diminishing with each new batch of votes that get reported, that something will happen that will radically change the outcome. The President is tweeting up a storm—he sent a whole new batch out into the ether this morning—but he seems to be howling into the wind.

The White House Chief of Staff Mark Meadows who two weeks ago announced to the nation that his Administration, "is not going to control" the growing pandemic, has now tested positive for COVID-19. This is a man who has refused to wear a mask. He has been to all the President's recent rallies and there is video of him fist-bumping the President's supporters. He has free range of the White House—both in the West Wing as well as in the residence. The massive spikes in virus cases that we are seeing around the country are almost all in places where these rallies have taken place.

I don't know what the next two months will be like under an erratic, infuriated President who cannot process losing. Delaying the announcement is not going to make it any easier. The President is apparently on his way to Pennsylvania to make yet another lie-filled rant to the American people this morning. It is at the point where we need to call it, preferably before he arrives.

We need to move forward. It's time.

NOVEMBER 9, 2020
537,243 Total Reported Cases in New York. 33,755 Deaths.

What a difference a few days makes. On Saturday I was on the couch. The TV was on, but it was muted, and I wasn't paying any attention to it.

As I was working, Michael came into the room and said something that I didn't catch. I was deep into what I was doing. I did notice then, however, that there was a great deal of noise coming from outside the window that I had unconsciously been blocking out for a couple of minutes. It sounded like the 7 o'clock pot-banging and applause for our health care workers. Looking up, I saw a big picture of Joe Biden on the TV screen, but I couldn't fully process what it meant. And then it all came together.

Joseph R. Biden is now President-elect Joseph R. Biden. Senator Kamala Harris is now Vice President-elect Kamala Harris.

New York City erupted. After screaming out of the window and banging pans, ourselves, we headed up to the roof. The sound of cheering was deafening and coming from everywhere. A garbage truck going down the street blasted its horn non-stop. We decided to go out. People were dancing in the streets.

On August 15, 1945, Imperial Japan surrendered and thereby brought World War II to a close. New Yorkers took to the streets then, too. That famous picture of the sailor dipping his girlfriend and kissing her was taken on that day in Times Square. After four years of a war that took the lives of over four hundred thousand Americans and wounded over six hundred thousand more, it was time to celebrate.

I wasn't there in 1945, but Saturday is what I imagine it must have felt like. It seemed like the entire city just exhaled after everything that we've been through. From four years of this President's inaction amidst countless hundreds of thousands of lives lost to COVID-19 to, well, everything else.

As he used to do in the early days of the pandemic, Brian Stokes Mitchell leaned out of his window a couple of blocks over and sang, *The Impossible Dream*. People gathered at the intersection outside of his building and cheered for anything and everything that happened. Taxi cabs lurched down the street honking their horns. People with sunroofs stood up in their cars as they drove down Broadway holding up Biden/Harris 2020 signs.

Michael and I walked down into Times Square. Every ten or fifteen blocks or so there was a gathering of people cheering and, yes, dancing. At Columbus Circle, in the shadow of the President's hotel, there was a larger group that got more and more organized as the day wore on. More and more homemade signs started appearing. Times Square was also full of celebrating people.

The President, unsurprisingly, refuses to accept the results. The President's Press Secretary looking out from the White House at similar celebrations in our Nation's capital called what she was seeing, "super-spreader events." From behind our masks, we could only laugh.

In the 48 hours since the election was called in his favor, the President-elect has already announced a bi-partisan coronavirus advisory board made up of actual health experts. Biden said, "We'll follow the science. Let me say that again, we'll follow the science and adjust according to what data comes in."

He warned that we have a long dark winter ahead of us. He was honest and direct—something we have yet to experience from the current Administration. It was a palpable relief. "We could save tens of thousands of lives if everyone would just wear a mask for the next few months… Do it for yourself. Do it for your neighbor… The goal of mask-wearing is not to take something away from you, it's to give you something back—a normal life."

President-elect Biden has already done more in one speech to lead the fight against this virus than the current President has done in his entire term in office. The President, who has spent the last two days golfing, continues to tweet completely unfounded claims about election fraud. Georgia's Lt. Governor, a GOP ally of the President has said that he has seen no "credible evidence" of any of the sort of fraud that the President is referring to.

Before the announcement came in on Saturday, there was a report that the President was going to hold a press conference in Philadelphia where the count was slowly trickling in. After Pennsylvania was called for his opponent, and thereby ended the race, he changed his mind and sent his lawyer Rudi Giuliani there instead.

The President thought that they had booked the Four Seasons Hotel in Philadelphia. The truth was what they had booked was a small business called Four Seasons Total Landscaping on a run-down street in Northern Philadelphia. It was right next to an adult bookstore and across the street from a crematorium. It was a perfectly fitting end to their regime. Four Seasons Total Landscaping has already become a major sight-seeing spot. They are planning on selling "Lawn & Order" tee shirts.

Pfizer announced this morning that they have had a 90% success rate with their new vaccine. The vaccine, if approved, would be a sequence of two shots taken three weeks apart. Even after it is approved, if it is approved, it will still take many months to produce and distribute the vaccine. The difficult thing about this vaccine is that it needs to be stored at -103 degrees to remain viable. That is going to make it challenging to get out there. Then people are going to need to be convinced to take it.

The President's campaign team has put out pleas for donations so that they can fight the election results in the courts. What his supporters might not notice, unless they have sharp eyes, is that the team is reserving the right to use up to 60% of those donations to try and pay down their massive campaign debt.

There will be a transition of power, it is just not going to be easy. Emily W. Murphy currently serves as the head of the General Services Administration. An appointee of the President, she is refusing to sign off on releasing transition funding to the President-elect. It is also through her agency that the incoming President and his team are given access to current officials, office space, and equipment to help facilitate the transition. In any other election, this would be automatic. Not this one.

Ever since the results were announced on Saturday, the weather in New York has been glorious. It's warm and clear and bright beyond belief. After the ecstatic joy of Saturday, yesterday settled into a different kind of joy—the joy of knowing that more people in this country believe in the rule of law than don't. Yesterday, it felt like the city was breathing normally for the first time in four years.

Maybe the most exciting thing was the realization that it feels like we've got the flag back. In the last two days seeing Old Glory being waved from windows up and down Broadway, made my heart beat faster and gave me hope.

November 10, 2020

New Record high of 139,000 new cases in a single day reported in the United States.

The hardest thing about leaving an abusive partner is deciding to do it. Once that decision is made, there are plenty of awful days ahead, but at least you can meet them with a clarity that you didn't have while you were still in the relationship.

I was with my first husband for nearly twenty years. We were only married, however, for the last couple of months of that time. Technically, after we separated, it took me another decade to get the divorce. I was afraid to poke the sleeping bear.

My ex and I were in the first wave of people who got married when it became legal in Massachusetts. To get married there, we had to say that we intended to live there—which we didn't have any intention of doing. New York, at the time, did not yet recognize same-sex marriage so when I made inquiries about getting a divorce, I was told that I didn't need to because I wasn't legally married in New York. Later, when I finally found a divorce lawyer who specialized in same-sex marriage law, she told me that was not strictly true.

The relationship had started well but the last few years of it had become progressively more problematic. I had started to spend a great deal of time daydreaming about being single.

I was never physically harmed, but there was a point that I felt that I was under enough of a threat that I called the police to intervene. At any rate, it wasn't long after that, that we were having a conversation on the phone that was rapidly escalating in tension and volume and I blurted out, "I don't want to be a couple anymore."

My mouth just said the words without checking in with my brain first.

This happened while I was working on the very first production of *Jersey Boys* in La Jolla, California. Not long after that, I went on the road with the *Wicked* First National tour. Splitting up was a slow process for both of us to digest and accept. Some days were fine, and some weren't. At one point, late at night, he called me and told me that he had burned all my books and destroyed my belongings back in our apartment. Alone in my room in Toronto after fuming for a while, I came to terms with it.

I came to accept that it was all just stuff and that it didn't matter. Ending it with him was more important, than any of my physical belongings. It turned out that the only thing he'd tried to destroy was a carved wooden Cherokee mask I had in the shape of a fox. When I was on the road with *Phantom*, another of the stage managers and I had gone hiking in the Great Smoky Mountains and I had bought it from a shop in the Cherokee reservation there. It meant something to me.

Later, after I had finally moved out and put my things into storage, I took the pieces of the broken mask and glued them back together. You can still see the cracks, but only if you look very closely. It was the first thing that I hung up on the wall of my new apartment.

I left the *Wicked* tour to start rehearsals for the move of *Jersey Boys* to Broadway. After we opened, I met Michael, or to be completely accurate, I re-met Michael. We clicked, but I was in no rush. The fact that I was still technically married was a convenient reason for me to not get married again. In my head at least. It took me a long time to trust that Michael would not behave like my ex. Finally, I did.

So, I prodded the bear, woke up the ex, and initiated divorce proceedings. It wasn't easy, my ex refused to accept that it was over. He wanted to punish me. Having a great lawyer guiding me took the fear out of it. It was a slog to get through it all, but we did get through it and then it was done.

The President refuses to concede. He doesn't need to concede. It would be nice if he did, but there is nothing that will keep him in charge if he refuses. He could even barricade himself inside the White House. It won't matter. It's just a house. The President-elect could stay at a nearby Motel 6 for all it matters. The General Services Administration may refuse to turn over funding and office space to Joe Biden's transition team, but that's not going to stop the transition from moving forward.

In 2008, when Barack Obama was elected President, Kentucky Senator Mitch McConnell made it his mandate to ensure that he was only there for one term. In an interview two years after that, the Senator explicitly said, "The single most important thing we want to achieve is for President Obama to be a one-term president." Well, that didn't happen. Throughout President Obama's entire eight-year time in office, though, the Senator from Kentucky did not legislate. He obstructed.

Yesterday, he signaled that he plans on doing the same thing under President Biden. In a speech from the Capitol, he threw his complete support behind our current President's refusal to concede. This, even though there is no evidence of any tampering or confusion in terms of the election results at all. The Senator does not want to give up his power any more than the President does. Because of the run-off Senate elections in Georgia, the balance of power in the Senate is in question which means his leadership is in question. If those two seats go blue, then he becomes Minority Leader rather than Majority Leader. He has just this morning been re-elected Leader of the Republican side of the Senate.

He is not going to do a single thing that might stop the President's Georgian supporters from coming out and voting red in January. He is going to stick fast to the President to the bitter end, whatever the harm is done as a result. He is not, and has never, acted in the best interests of the country. He has always acted in what the best interests of the good Senator from Kentucky were. He wants those two seats more than anything else.

Senator Lindsay Graham from South Carolina, who just narrowly won his re-election recently said, "If we don't do something about voting by mail, we're going to lose the ability to elect a Republican in this country."

Attorney General William Barr, in support of the President, has authorized investigations of "specific allegations" of voter fraud before the election results are certified. By doing this, he is subverting long-standing Justice Department policies designed to keep law enforcement away from affecting the results of an election. In the weeks before the election, his department lifted a prohibition they had on investigating voter fraud before an election. He doesn't want to lose his power either.

Michael and I got married on November 9, 2015. Yesterday was our fifth wedding anniversary. Wood is the traditional gift for five years together. Salacious comments aside, it signifies the strength and durability of a union. Like a tree, the relationship has begun to develop strong roots. I don't regret marrying my first husband if only because of what I needed to learn while I was divorcing him.

As a nation, we needed to learn what the last four years have taught us. We live together in profound inequality. Like termites boring through wood from the inside, racism and bigotry have weakened the structure of our great nation. We have learned that what we once thought was immeasurably strong, is, in reality, quite fragile. We need to tend to it and take care of it.

The next two months before this Great Divorce are going to be difficult and, at times, scary. We will get through it. We have chosen a capable leader. Whatever gets broken, we will glue back together as best we can. We have taken that first and oh so important step. We have stood up and said "No."

Happy Anniversary, my love.

NOVEMBER 11, 2020

545,453 Total Reported Cases in New York. 33,794 Deaths.

In the nineteenth century, people started using the phrase 'Indian summer' to describe this late period of unseasonably warm weather. It feels like summer's last gasp before winter begins to settle in. In eastern Europe, this period is called 'old woman's summer. In Gaelic in Ireland, it is referred to as 'little autumn of the geese'. Turkey calls it 'pastrami summer' because it is the best time to make pastrami. It looks like ours is about to be over. The temperature is dropping today, and we are expected to get some rain later.

Today is also Veterans Day. It is a day put aside to honor all of those who, living and dead, have served in our armed forces. It also marks the anniversary of the end of World War I. The armistice with Germany went into effect in the eleventh hour of the eleventh day of the eleventh month in 1918. Most federal holidays fall on a Monday. Veterans Day, however, lands on November 11, wherever it occurs in the week.

My father-in-law never actually fought in a battle, but as a member of the reserves, he was prepared to at a moment's notice. Michael's youngest sister is married to an ex-Marine. My brother-in-law served several tours in Iraq. My father was part of the 87th Infantry during World War II and fought in the Battle of the Bulge.

The Battle of the Bulge was the last major German offensive on the Western Front. It was also called the Ardennes Counteroffensive. The Germans were trying to stop the Allied forces from being able to use the port of Antwerp in Belgium. The battle was fought largely in the Ardennes region of eastern Belgium, northeast France, and Luxembourg. What the Germans hoped to be able to do was divide and encircle the four allied armies and destroy them.

The Americans got the worst of it. There were more US casualties in this engagement than there were in any other of the war. The 87th fought in Belgium. Conditions that day were awful—snowy and foggy. There was no shelter. People died horrible deaths all around my father. He watched as his friends were ripped apart. Afterward, he was awarded the Bronze Star. The medal was given to any person who distinguishes themselves by heroic or meritorious service. I am not sure what he did to get it, he never said. He always said that it didn't mean anything because so many were given out—everybody got them. I recently found a list of those who had been awarded them in his division and that was simply not true. There were not that many given out at all. Maybe all he did was survive, but, knowing my father, there was more to it than that.

The 87th was one of the youngest divisions that fought in the war. During the Battle of the Bulge, my father was twenty-one years old.

The President avoided the draft for the Vietnam War five separate times. In June of 1964, on his eighteenth birthday, he became eligible for the draft and registered. Five or six weeks later he received his first deferment because of college. In December of 1965, he received his 2nd 2-S college deferment. When that deferment expired, he was reclassified as 1-A, or able to serve, in November of 1966. The following month, however, he was given a third 2-S deferment. In January of 1968, he then got his fourth and final college deferment. By June of that year, he had graduated from Wharton. He was out of the college that he had gotten into by paying somebody to take the SATs for him and could no longer use that as an excuse. After a physical examination in September of 1968, he was reclassified as 1-Y—qualified for service only in a national emergency. He spent the rest of the war working for his father.

My father didn't have the means to avoid fighting in World War II. I'm not sure that my father would have considered not fighting even if he could have avoided it. The men he fought alongside were largely working-class. They were first-generation immigrants who were sent to the front lines in droves. My father was a relatively poor kid from Virginia. He met his first New Yorker in Belgium—a tough Italian guy from Brooklyn with a thick accent. He talked about him for the rest of his life.

The President laid his hands on a wreath in Arlington Cemetery this morning. This is a man who has referred to members of the armed forces as "losers" and "suckers."

The President seems to think that the armed forces are his. Like a character in *Game of Thrones*, he seems to feel that he can just wield them at will. It looks like he is going to try and do just that. As he tries to create his personal army, his loyal enablers continue to rally around him. One Republican Congressional representative tweeted that Mississippi should "succeed" (his spelling) and form its own country rather than work under a Biden presidency.

There is, however, a small but growing group of Republican officials who have started to break with the President and congratulate the new President-elect. Former Republican President George W. Bush said, "I know Joe Biden to be a good man, who has won his opportunity to lead and unify our country. The president-elect reiterated that while he ran as a Democrat, he will govern for all Americans. I offered him the same thing I offered Presidents Trump and Obama: my prayers for his success, and my pledge to help in any way I can."

Joseph R. Biden, the President-elect, is not going to magically fix everything that his predecessor and all of those around him have broken. What Joseph R. Biden can hopefully do is to create an environment where the rest of us can push up our sleeves and get to work ourselves.

The members of our armed forces will need to stay strong over these next two months and remember the oath that they all took when they started: "I, (name), do solemnly swear (or affirm) that I will support and defend the Constitution of the United States against all enemies, foreign and domestic; that I will bear true faith and allegiance to the same; and that I will obey the orders of the President of the United States and the orders of the officers appointed over me, according to regulations and the Uniform Code of Military Justice. So help me God."

It looks like the rain is starting. On this damp day, we should all take a moment and extend our gratitude out to all the people who have served in our armed forces over the years who have kept us and continue to keep us and our country safe.

Thank you for your service.

NOVEMBER 12, 2020

New record high of 164,405 new cases in a single day reported in the United States.

Countless things have needed to be done around this place since before the election. Clothes are draped over the backs of chairs all over the apartment. Receipts are in messy piles on the dining room table. Halloween decorations need to be put downstairs in our storage bin. We need to vacuum, and we certainly need to dust.

I gave myself another haircut yesterday. I've gotten pretty good at it if I do say so, myself. And more efficient. Even my new beard got its first much-needed trim.

There's a lot of noise coming from the departing President. Most of the President's lawsuits against the election results are just being thrown out. In one case, one of the President's lawyers tried to claim that Republicans had been barred from observing results at a polling station in Philadelphia. The Judge in the case kept trying to get to the actual evidence that the lawyer had for his allegation. Finally, the lawyer was forced to admit that the Republicans had "a nonzero number of people in the room." Kellyanne Conway, who gave us all the President's "alternative facts" couldn't have said it any better.

We are, as a nation, leaderless at a moment when we need somebody to guide us the most. The man who is ostensibly our leader for the next two months is not leading. He is sulking. And tweeting. And golfing. The man who is going to be our leader is being kept, from nothing more than pique, from being able to start his work.

One of the theatre projects that I was meant to start working on in the spring has just been postponed. Like walking through a desert, I keep seeing that distant promise of a job on the horizon that could be just over the next dune, or it could be countless miles away. Or it could just be a mirage. The only thing to do is to keep heading slowly towards it. The reason it's been put off, of course, is the soaring COVID-19 numbers.

Here in New York City, our positivity rate has risen to 2.93%. The goal was to keep us below 1.5%. Thanksgiving is two weeks away. In anticipation of that, Governor Cuomo has tightened restrictions on gatherings of more than 10 people.

Back in the spring, the rest of the country looked down on New York and Seattle and San Francisco with a mixture of pity, disdain, and revulsion. As COVID-19 raged through our communities, the feeling that we got from middle America was that liberals deserved it in some way. Well, now the tables have turned. Wyoming and Idaho are experiencing a 40% positivity rate. South Dakota is clocking in at a whopping 55% positivity rate. The mask-less motorcycle rally in Sturgis back in August suddenly doesn't seem like it was such a great idea anymore.

All eyes are on the Senate run-offs in Georgia. If both of those seats go Democratic, then there will be a chance that some meaningful stimulus legislation will be able to be passed. If they don't, then this endless stalemate that we are slogging through will just continue until the midterms. You think you were sick of hearing about the Presidential election? Take a deep breath.

In the meantime, the cat needs brushing and the rugs need vacuuming. And the receipts need filing. And everything needs to be put away. We need to clean up and move forward. Whatever the future holds, it's ahead of us and not behind.

November 13, 2020
556,344 Total Reported Cases in New York. 33,827 Deaths.

A man fell to his death, yesterday, from high in the grid above the stage of the Winter Garden Theatre, here in the heart of the city's theatre district.

When you are sitting in the audience and watching a show and look up and see all the lights shining down, those lights are all hanging on a latticework of pipes and supports. Motors that can raise and lower props and curtains are also hung from it. I can probably count the total number of times that I have been up in a grid in a theatre on the fingers of one hand. It's terrifying to be up there and look down on the stage far below.

At the beginning of June, well into the pandemic shutdown, the producers of *Beetlejuice, the Musical* announced that they were closing for good. The theatre had already been reserved for the incoming revival of *The Music Man*. While that production has now been pushed off for another year and a half, there were still the remains of the old show to load out of the theatre. This man was working up in the grid removing some of that. There is no reason why he should have fallen. He had lived high above the stage throughout his working life. That's what he did.

The news is not releasing his name yet and so neither will I. But I knew him and had worked with him. Always a smile. Never a complaint. And he was amazing in his job. A career stagehand—one of the finest in New York. Just like that, he's gone. He was a couple of years younger than me and leaves behind a wife and kids.

Did he do something wrong up there? Did he miscalculate something? Was there a pipe that was improperly installed that he shouldn't have trusted? Or did it just happen?

He left his family yesterday morning and did not come home.

The people who are dying from COVID-19 around our country are dying deaths that are just as senseless as this. Most of them aren't doing anything dangerous. Quite the contrary, what they are doing should be safe. They are going to parties. They are hugging their friends on the street and then going home and having dinner with their families. They are working out at the gym or taking in a film in a darkened movie theatre surrounded, as usual, by an audience of strangers. They are going to the White House, one of the most secure residences on the planet, and toasting a new Supreme Court nominee outside at a garden party.

Had they been well informed they could have perhaps saved themselves and their loved ones. They would be going home to their families tonight. They would be starting to think about what to get their grandkids for the holidays. They would be dreaming about the future. Instead, they are gone.

There will be an investigation into why the stagehand fell. Authorities and his fellow union members will scour that grid to look for a reason for his untimely death. That will not happen with the army of citizens who have fallen before this virus. We already know why they are gone.

As angry and shocked as I am by the death of the man who was working up in the grid, it seems to have been an accident. I'm not ready to accept it—I am sure I am not alone in that by any stretch of the imagination—but I will, eventually. Some things happen to people in our lives that are beyond anyone's real control.

I'm angry this morning. The COVID-19 pandemic is not an accident. Perhaps its creation and initial release were, but the resulting response is not. I'm angry that we have allowed this inept, unqualified conman to lead us for as long as he has. I'm angry that we are sitting around waiting for him to concede and get out of the way. I'm angry at all the Republicans who have gathered around him and continue to support him as he circles the drain.

Election officials have called this election, "the most secure in history." The President lost. We chose someone else. Let's move on. Let's take up arms against this sea of troubles. And by opposing end them.

November 14, 2020
561,982 Total Reported Cases in New York. 33,844 Deaths.

Today feels like a strangely calm day. Even on the news channels. CNN is doing everything they can to try and get me interested in the Master's golf tournament, but I just can't engage. It's like, as a country, the medication has just started to kick in.

The time after an operation can seem endless while you heal. You are given drugs and therapies that move you forward step by step, but it isn't a straight path. Sometimes it feels like it's one step forward and then two steps back.

It was months after my prostate surgery before I felt normal again. There were things, thankfully minor, that changed for me forever, but I eventually got back to a completely normal way of life. I'll spare you all the grisly details, but it was a slow slog at times.

The first time that I went back to work was when I went up to Providence in Rhode Island to check up on the tour of *Jersey Boys*. Because of my surgery scars, I wasn't allowed to lift more than ten pounds, so I had to pack a very light bag on wheels. Michael was dubious about my making the trip, but I figured out how to get into Providence and back without ever having to lift the bag.

At the time, I lived in midtown on the second floor. That morning, Michael carried the bag out onto the street and kissed me goodbye. I wheeled the bag behind me down to Penn Station and took the escalator down to the main concourse. I then took the escalator down to the track and wheeled the bag onto the train, leaving it down by my feet. Once I got to Providence, I wheeled the bag off and took the escalator up to the street. From there I walked to the hotel and took the elevator up to my room. No lifting at any point. I then did the same thing coming home. Michael met me outside of our building and carried the bag up the last flight of stairs.

It was several weeks before I could start to lift things on my own and many more weeks until my strength was fully back. During that time some days were good and there were some days where it felt that I had lost much of what I had gained.

The last states have finally been called. North Carolina, as expected, went to the President. Arizona and Georgia went to the President-elect giving him a grand total of 306 electoral votes. This is the same spread that happened in the 2016 election only reversed. In this election, five states flipped from red to blue—Arizona, Georgia, Michigan, Pennsylvania, and Wisconsin. No blue states flipped to red.

Yesterday, nine more of the President's attempted lawsuits alleging fraud in the key states where he lost were thrown out. As of now, these cases aren't getting anywhere near the Supreme Court. They aren't even getting past the first step.

The President tweeted something that pretty much sums up the absurd contradictions of the last few days. "For years the Dems have been preaching how unsafe and rigged our elections have been. Now they are saying what a wonderful job the Trump Administration did in making 2020 the most secure election ever. Actually, this is true, except for what the Democrats did. Rigged Election!"

So, we heal. And we wait. The infection may flare up again, but the antibiotics will eventually take care of it. We can't do any heavy lifting until January 20th but that doesn't mean that there isn't plenty we can do in the meantime.

This morning the tree was set up in Rockefeller Center Plaza for the holidays. It is a bright and glorious day here in the city. Life awaits.

November 17, 2020
574,935 Total Reported Cases in New York. 33,985 Deaths.

I try not to pay any conscious attention to Christmas or Hanukkah until at least Thanksgiving. When Santa arrives at the end of the *Macy's Day Parade*, then I'm fine. Christmas can start. Before that, we have the harvest to celebrate. My feeling has always been that things should be celebrated one at a time.

New York at Christmas time, I have to say, can be quite wonderful. Even when it gets cold and snowy, there's an anticipation for the holidays that, despite the horrendous crowds, gives the city an exciting energy. Like anything, of course, too much of it makes you want to scream, but a little of it is great. This year, I am willing to give a little on the start date, but it still seems much too early to begin. To my enormous surprise, however, as Michael and I were going over our schedules after breakfast, I discovered that Thanksgiving is already next week. How did that happen?

November and December are typically among the most lucrative months in the theatre. Everybody wants to see a show. Each year, Radio City Music Hall puts together its *Christmas Spectacular starring the Rockettes*. In an ordinary year, it would be just about to start performing. This year, though, it's been canceled.

Broadway shows which might be struggling, try to hold on for this season where they have the potential to make up for some of their summer losses. June, July, and August can be a brutal time for the theatre—everyone wants to be outside, not in. So is the period after New Year's when everybody has finished celebrating. Many shows post their notices and close in the first week of the new year. As great as these current two months usually are for sales, is as awful as January and February can be. Producers will try and quit while they are ahead—or at least less far behind.

Actors and stage managers working under union contracts are entitled to two weeks of vacation a year. That's it. Some shows will not allow people to take those weeks consecutively and some, to avoid infighting, won't allow anyone to put in for a vacation over Thanksgiving or the last week of December. If you are on a new musical show and you are a hit, you may even end up performing in the *Macy's Day Parade*. That means that instead of sleeping in on Thanksgiving morning and lazily turning on the TV to watch the parade, you are up before the sun and down in Herald Square rehearsing in the dark.

In 1999, when we were doing *Annie Get Your Gun*, we were invited to participate in the parade. It was freezing. It had been raining and the ground was wet and icy. Nobody in the cast—men or women—was wearing all that much. The women put on several layers of pantyhose over their bare legs to try and keep warm but after a split or two on the slippery wet ground, they were soaked through. The men were in open leather vests—not much warmth there either. Some years later, we were there for *Jersey Boys* as well, but it was a much nicer day.

Civilians will have had their holiday meals and then start looking for entertainment. Those of us in the theatre almost always end up having to perform on Thanksgiving Day. For Christmas, there is usually either a performance on Christmas Eve or one on Christmas Day. It is extremely rare to get both days off. You plan your family celebrations as best you can—a grabbed meal here, a little get-together there. Sometimes there's a potluck dinner at the theatre with the entire company—onstage and off—in the alley outside and you make do with that.

Then there is New Year's Eve. *Annie Get Your Gun* was at the Marriot Marquis hotel right on Times Square. We had a matinee that day and needed police escorts to get out of the theatre to go home through the crowds who many hours before midnight had already made the area impassable. On top of everything else, Y2K was a very real fear that year. Everyone was terrified that the world was going to end at midnight on December 31, 1999. Some years later, the Toronto company of *Jersey Boys* performed outside on New Year's Eve. We all gathered around a fire burning in a metal barrel to warm up while we waited as if we were living in a dystopian future. I thought I'd understood what cold was. It turned out that I didn't. I do now. And I wasn't in one of the ultra-short white sequined finale dresses.

Walking around the city today and looking at the lights going up was bittersweet. For the first time, many of us have nothing scheduled that will conflict with our celebrating the season. Most of the people who will be performing on streamed events are taping those things now. They'll be able to sleep in and turn on the TV to watch along with the rest of us. There is nothing to stop us from getting together this year except for the virus.

The next few weeks are not going to be what we are used to, but that doesn't mean that they are going to be bad. Quite the contrary, I am very much looking forward to them. Our family has decided that we are all going to gather in our own homes and hold a big Zoom meeting while we eat. People can cook, eat, and come and go as they please.

This year's holidays will be like no others in our memories. We may find that some parts are better than we think they're going to be. There is plenty to celebrate and loved ones to spend time with, if even just on a screen.

NOVEMBER 18, 2020
579,811 Total Reported Cases in New York. 34,016 Deaths.

Between Michael and the cat, I wake up several times each morning. When I am finally ready to get up for good, the two of them are usually elsewhere, so I make the bed. The extra pillows we throw onto it are stacked on a rocking chair in the corner. They had been stacked there, by me, some hours before we turned in. The time between the stacking and the unstacking and the stacking again seems to get shorter and shorter.

These days, the news is the same, day in and day out. It's like the screen has frozen. "States tighten restrictions as cases, hospitalizations surge." Every single day without change. Cases on the rise. Unchecked.

The Republicans refuse to accept the election results. The President's $20 thousand/day lawyer Rudi Giuliani is not faring very well in the courts trying to get them overturned. Arguing in generalities rather than specifics, all he is doing is delaying the inevitable. And driving up his billing hours. In Pennsylvania yesterday, a Judge said to him, "You're alleging that the two individual plaintiffs were denied the right to vote. But at bottom, you're asking this court to invalidate more than 6.8 million votes, thereby disenfranchising every single voter in the Commonwealth. Could you tell me how this result could possibly be justified?"

Chris Krebs, a senior Department of Homeland Security official, said that the 2020 election was the most secure in American history. So, yesterday, the President fired him.

Throughout all of this, the Senate and the House remain completely deadlocked on approving a new stimulus bill. More and more, it is starting to look as though there will not be any sort of meaningful legislation passed until after January 20th. So, we wait.

I used to think that there would be a point at which even the President's most loyal supporters would finally have to say enough. I no longer think that. Even after he left the office in complete disgrace, President Nixon still had 25% of the country behind him. They aren't going to give up.

In the past, I used to dream of days like this. Days that were unscheduled where I could go where I want and do as I pleased. Days where I could clean out a closet or reorder the office supply drawer or go through my books. Days where nothing was required of me. Be careful what you wish for.

Change will come. The transition will start. One day, the news will report it and all this waiting will be in the past. As comfortably warm as it is on this couch, I need to get up and take a shower and go out into the day. It doesn't look like I am going to miss anything on the news.

NOVEMBER 19, 2020
585,635 Total Reported Cases in New York. 34,044 Deaths.

By the time I woke up this morning, Michael had already been up for an hour or two. He's shooting another episode of *Law & Order* later this afternoon, so I went to sleep listening to him muttering about due diligence and remanding someone to Riker's. He also has an audition for something else that seems to involve a warm chuckle. I woke up to him alternately chuckling warmly and remanding in the living room.

Neither Judge Serani nor the warm chuckler seems to have a cat in their back story because when I went into the kitchen, I saw that the cat's morning routine had not happened. He had not been fed.

The cat was lethargic. The end was near. He seemed to have accepted the fact that he would never be fed again. An hour or two living without his morning food had allowed him to come to terms with the last moments of life as he's known it. As I got my vitamins out of the fridge, he looked at me in profound yet resigned despair. The delicate supply line had been broken, forever.

There was, of course, still food left in his bowl. As I changed his water and replaced the dry food he sat and watched. Once it was in front of him, he inspected it out of habit. He ate one or two pieces with barely disguised disdain, then slowly made his way to the couch to sleep off the after-effects of the near tragedy.

I've noticed while walking around that many restaurants have enclosed their outdoor spaces to keep them warm. I'm not sure how this is a good idea. An enclosed outdoor space is, by definition, an indoor space albeit with less effective insulation.

Some places have enclosed three sides of their space and left one open. One place I saw had an individual standing heat lamp at each table out on the sidewalk. Several places have erected individual tents or enclosed bubbles around each table. That works for people who are living together, but not for friends from different households who are meeting for a meal. Being locked in together would seem to guarantee transmission if one of them is ill. The reason that dining outdoors is safer is that air is circulating freely. You are less likely to transmit or receive the virus if there's a breeze to dissipate the particles. The more you start to enclose a place, the more you are impeding that air circulation. The more dangerous it gets.

Nothing is ever purely safe. Looking at each place objectively, it seems obvious which ones seem less dangerous than others. I find myself walking down the street and as I pass each restaurant I think, "yes," "no," "no," "really no," "maybe," "no."

I don't know if the city is paying attention to any of these individual sites to see if they are complying with any sort of safety rules. It doesn't look like it. I'm not even sure there's even enough clarity about what those rules are. How do you protect your customers from something that even the so-called experts don't fully understand?

I took a friend's recommendation yesterday and went across the East River to Roosevelt Island. Roosevelt Island is a long thin island in the middle of the river between Manhattan and Queens. It's about 40 city blocks long and about one long block wide. The 59th Street Bridge passes over it. There is a bridge to the island from Queens, but not one from Manhattan. From Manhattan, you can access it via an aerial tram that runs alongside the 59th Street Bridge. Built in 1976 it has the distinction of being the first commuter aerial tramway in North America.

I don't think that I had ever been to Roosevelt Island before. I have the dimmest possible glimmer of a memory of possibly taking the tram over and back when I was in college, but I really can't be sure.

At the southern tip of the island is the Franklin D. Roosevelt Four Freedoms Park. Designed by Louis Kahn, it was dedicated in October of 2012. It commemorates the Four Freedoms that Roosevelt outlined in his 1941 State of the Union Address. The words he spoke as World War II was starting in Europe are no less applicable today.

"In the future days, which we seek to make secure, we look forward to a world founded upon four essential human freedoms.

The first is freedom of speech and expression—everywhere in the world.

The second is the freedom of every person to worship God in their own way—everywhere in the world.

The third is freedom from want—which, translated into world terms, means economic understandings which will secure to every nation a healthy peacetime life for its inhabitants—everywhere in the world.

The fourth is freedom from fear—which, translated into world terms, means a worldwide reduction of armaments to such a point and in such a thorough fashion that no nation will be in a position to commit an act of physical aggression against any neighbor—anywhere in the world.

That is no vision of a distant millennium. It is a definite basis for a kind of world attainable in our own time and generation."

First Lady Eleanor Roosevelt used these four freedoms as the basis for the United Nations Declaration of Human Rights. The UN's North American headquarters is across the river on the eastern shore of Manhattan. Another former First Lady, Hillary Clinton, officially launched her 2016 Presidential campaign from the park.

In 1941, when Roosevelt made this speech, the war was coming. We weren't in it yet, the attack on Pearl Harbor was still almost a year away. In 2020, the war is here. It is raging all around us. Those Four Freedoms are still worth fighting for.

November 20, 2020
591,368 Total Reported Cases in New York. 34,082 Deaths.

For the moment, at least, Michael has become the sole breadwinner in the family. For the first decade and a half of our relationship, I had the steady income and his was erratic and yet constant at the same time. Some years he was on Broadway and some years he was doing the occasional regional job and teaching. Michael is almost the textbook definition of a successful New York actor. That's what life in the theatre looks like.

He acts. He directs. He teaches. It took me a long time to convince him that he didn't need to decide between them—that there was plenty of space to do them all. He's great at all of it. He has still managed to do a lot, on some level, during the shutdown of our industry.

Actors Equity Association, the union of theatrical actors and stage managers, has finally agreed with SAG/AFTRA, the union of television and motion picture actors over the issue of who has jurisdiction over certain streaming events. This is good news for almost everyone. It still, however, doesn't help stage managers. The work that we would normally do in terms of scheduling and coordination is being done in recent days largely by others on the producing team.

In my personal experience, almost every time there has been a conflict between actors and stage management, the union has sided with the actor. I suppose that is inevitable given that we are a decided minority within the organization. I am grateful that the protections offered to me by the union rules are there. I know that my basic work conditions will not be compromised and that things like travel and housing will at least be of a certain caliber. I've just never felt like a full member of the union because I feel as if so many of its rules and basic focus simply don't apply to me.

I think that there are a lot of people living in the United States who feel the same way about living under our government. Equal protection under the law is all well and good to speak of, but it doesn't mean much if it isn't put into actual practice.

While this agreement between the two unions is likely to be a positive thing for Michael, it will probably not change much for me in terms of my current state of non-employment. Non-employment is a much better description of what we are experiencing these days than un-employment is.

There have been times in the past where Michael has been working a job that doesn't pay anything near what mine did and he felt guilty about it. These days, whatever money that is being added into the pot is coming in from Michael. Perhaps I will feel guilty about that in the future but for now, I am fine with it. I think.

NOVEMBER 21, 2020
597,680 Total Reported Cases in New York. 34,126 Deaths.

Maybe it is the nature of the material and the story, but the cast members of *Jersey Boys*, over the years, have tended to be overwhelmingly straight. That has never been a factor in the casting decisions. There are plenty of gay people in both the straight and gay roles. Much of the cast, however, was usually made up of straight men and women in their twenties and early thirties—the perfect age to start a family.

I remember as a kid seeing a live-action Disney movie called *The Living Desert*. I don't know why it made such an impression on me, but it did. There may have been a book version of it that I had as well. The film was a documentary that explored how life survives in a desert. After long periods of drought, there will suddenly be a period of intense rain. When the rain comes, the desert explodes. Long dormant seeds quickly sprout and grow. They flower, get pollinated, and die in a remarkably short time. Animals, who have been in a kind of hibernation themselves, burst out into the world, mate, bear their young, and store as much food as they can before the rains finally pass again.

For a lot of these actors, *Jersey Boys* was like those sudden rains. It was a steady gig with a steady income, and it allowed many young couples the security to start their families. That is a decided rarity in our business. Most gigs are short and intensively work-concentrated, or they involve going out of town and only making enough money to get by. Years into the juggernaut that has been *Jersey Boys*, we figured out that there had been at least 250 babies born to people working on the show around the world in some capacity. That was years ago. We have long since left that number in the dust.

No friend or family member of mine, to the best of my knowledge, has ever actually regretted their decision to have children. Yes, there are days when they seem much too close to the breaking point for comfort, but if they could go back would they change their minds? I don't think so. Even those friends of mine who have tragically lost children, I do not think, would have missed a single moment that they had with them—good and bad.

A million years ago, Michael and I were standing in line at the Magic Kingdom with my sister and her family. It was later in the day and my nephew was tired. I can't remember how old he was, but he was still young enough to carry. I was holding him and talking to my sister. To keep him still, I was rubbing his back and rocking back and forth a bit. At some point in the conversation, I looked over at Michael who was looking at me with a look of beatific bliss on his face that a Hallmark movie director would have sold his soul for. Without missing a beat in my conversation with my sister, I said to him, "Don't even think about it."

This new crop of children is going to replace us. We replaced our parents, and they will replace us. That's how it works. If nothing else, within a few more months there should be plenty more of them to keep the process going.

November 23, 2020
609,797 Total Reported Cases in New York. 34,177 Deaths.

If the news coming into our living rooms today came in this past March, we might have taken to the streets in response. Today, however, after everything that's happened, we are, instead, staying on our couches and just flipping the channels looking for something better to watch. We've become numb to it.

The President is behind in the popular vote by over 6 million votes. He has lost the electoral college. He is not appearing in public. He is not governing. He is attempting to pressure State officials to overturn results. His lawyers are being rebuked by judges in many states and seeing their baseless claims thrown out. Only five Republican Senators have acknowledged that President-elect Biden has won. The rest are standing firmly behind the President even as he disintegrates.

We are truly switched off. It's not that people don't want to hear about what's going on anymore, it's that they can't. The COVID numbers simply don't mean anything. They are so big and have been repeated so often that they've just become scribbles on a page. When somebody begins to speak about them, their voice becomes less distinct until they start to sound like an adult in a Peanuts cartoon.

There's a story this morning that management at one of the Tyson meatpacking plants in Waterloo, Iowa was placing cash bets on how many of its workers would test positive for the virus. So far, five of the workers at that plant have died. Five people who were working long hours in one of the worst jobs imaginable just to put food on their family's table and clothes on their kids' backs. Gone. And management treated it all as a joke and a game.

There's another story that a third pharmaceutical company, AstraZeneca, in conjunction with Oxford University, has just announced that they, too, now have a viable vaccine. They claim it has an average efficacy of 70% in large-scale trials.

That so many companies seem to be creating vaccines with such a high rate of success should be a case of some cautious optimism. Some people could be given one of these vaccines as early as next month. Initially, average people will have no access to any of them. Frontline healthcare workers and those most at risk like elderly patients in nursing homes will likely be first in line.

Getting these vaccines out to the rest of us is not going to happen during this President's term in office. The average American may not be able to get one until May. As things stand now, however, most states do not have the funding or infrastructure to distribute the vaccine at the level required to make even that happen. All the vaccines need to be stored in chilled conditions. One of them will require complex refrigeration units to keep it at the proper temperature. The others will require dry ice which is currently not readily available.

The very first apartment that I lived in by myself was in Long Island City. It was a strange apartment in that the front door opened right onto the street rather than into a hallway.

It was right near the tollbooths leading into the Queens midtown tunnel. Many of the buildings around me were abandoned or converted warehouses and workshops.

The 7-train used to let me off very near my building. It was the first stop out of Manhattan.

I could get to Times Square in about 15 minutes. IF the train was running. If the train wasn't running, I needed to take a long hike over to another line that was near the 59th street bridge. It could take me over an hour or two to get to work when that happened.

The sculptor, Isamu Noguchi had a studio just north of the bridge. I knew it was there, but I had never been. He died, I think, a year or two before I moved out there. As a sculptor, Isamu Noguchi was interested in the natural world. His work was often monumental in size. His pieces were usually abstract. He used a lot of stone some of which was highly polished and carved and some of which was left raw. On Friday, the First Lady unveiled a piece of his entitled "Floor Frame" in the Rose Garden. It marks the first time that an Asian American's work has been included in the White House collection. In 2020, that's hard to comprehend.

"Floor Frame" looks like a series of long rectangular black steel shapes on a white stone platform. Noguchi described it as the "intersection of a tree and the ground, taking on the qualities of both an implied root system and the canopy."

Noguchi's father was Japanese, and his mother was American. During World War II, when Japanese Americans were being interned in camps, he went into one voluntarily in support. While there, he used his skills to help redesign the camp to be more efficient. He spent much of his life attempting to promote better relations between the two countries, even when hostilities were at their worst.

I went to his studio the day before yesterday. It is just a coincidence that I went there the day before his sculpture was unveiled at the White House. It was a museum that was open that I could get into. I've spent a lot of time at the MET, MOMA, and the Whitney in recent days, so having a different art museum to explore was a treat.

For me, museums have become a refuge where I can be in a world that hasn't been compromised by COVID-19. There will be a whole wave of art that will come out of what we are all experiencing now. Look at the art that was created around World War II, the Holocaust, the war in Vietnam, and every other period of strife and tension in our country.

Someday we will all be able to walk around a museum looking at the current work that artists are creating. Maybe some of what is happening now will make more sense with that perspective. It certainly doesn't make much sense now.

November 24, 2020

New record high of 173,000 new cases in a single day reported in the United States.

I spent much of yesterday trying not to crawl out of my own skin.

The day began wet and cold and then cleared up, but aside from a visit to the post office, I stayed inside. I didn't want to go out and I didn't want to stay in. I don't know what I wanted to do, but whatever it was, it wasn't among the options I was presented with.

So, in desperation, I opened our storage unit again.

I'm the end of the line for the Hester branch of our family. In recent generations, there has always been one boy and one girl born. My grandfather was a twin. His sister took her husband's name when she married. My father has one sister who is still alive, but she never married. I have one sister but she, too, has taken her husband's name. After me and my aunt and my mother, who took the name when she married my dad, the Hester name will only live on as my nephew's middle name. All the Hester stuff, however, will remain.

A lot of my father's, grandparents', great-grandparents' and even great-great grandparents', personal effects are sitting in these boxes. I have an endless array of eyeglasses, pocket watches, and military ribbons. I also have weird objects from fraternal organizations and a slew of desk accessories. I have a pretty good idea of what interested my father. A lot of what interested him, honestly, also interests me.

I remember my father telling me a story about when he and some of his fellow infantrymen came upon the bodies of some German soldiers during World War II. At the urging of their platoon leader, they all took some of the insignia pinned on the dead men's uniforms as souvenirs—spoils of war, I guess. I think that my father always felt guilty about doing that. In the box along with all the others, I found the two pins that he kept. One has an eagle with a swastika on it and the other is an enameled red circular pin also with a swastika on it.

They are awful little things, but I am keeping them because of the emotional connection my father had to them. I can picture him taking them off his fallen opponent, but I can also feel the years of guilt that followed. Having taken them, I think it's incumbent on me to keep them for him as a kind of penance. There's an energy around them that just isn't there with most of the other stuff. Even if I could sell them, I wouldn't.

The objects in the boxes are easy to go through and sort out. What isn't easy to go through is all the paperwork. I came upon an envelope with a pile of ancient receipts and empty envelopes in it. Two of the receipts were from the company store at Camp Lee, Virginia. Camp Lee was a big training camp for soldiers during World War I. My grandfather, according to the receipt, was 2nd Lieutenant in the Infantry. He spent $27.50 on a new trench coat. The receipt is dated November 20, 1918—which was the height of the Spanish flu pandemic. I wonder what that was like for him?

It is customary for Presidents to create a Library that documents their legacy. All the gifts given to the Administration by foreign powers and important documents created get housed in them. They become centers of learning and a repository for research material surrounding the person in office. I cannot begin to imagine what a Library dedicated to our current President would look like. Perhaps it will contain some old red baseball caps and a bound copy of all his tweets. Even Richard Nixon who left the office in disgrace has a legacy of accomplishments that his library celebrates. Not this guy.

I say just put all his stuff into boxes, stick it somewhere and let someone else deal with it down the line. In another hundred years, maybe there will be another global pandemic, and somebody will be bored enough to find the time to go through it all.

The events of these past months have been "history in the making". That is true of every time, but these days have been so remarkable and so unlike anything most of us have ever experienced. Hopefully, Joe Biden's term in office will be boring. The less interesting it is, the more that all of us will be able to lead interesting lives.

November 25, 2020
620,712 Total Reported Cases in New York.

The lines at COVID testing centers in the city, yesterday, stretched completely past their storefronts, around the corners, and out of sight down the side streets. People are trying to get tested before they gather with family members for Thanksgiving tomorrow. Even if the results come in before they leave to visit their loved ones, and the tests are negative, it still doesn't make for a safe get-together. In my experience though, it is extremely unlikely that anyone who got tested yesterday will get their results before the holiday's over.

I know from friends and family who have decided to travel this week that some people, at least, are going into this adventure with a clear-eyed understanding of the risks. They are doing everything in their power to make it as safe as possible with the understanding that complete safety is impossible. There are always mitigating circumstances around decisions like this.

There seem to be plenty of people, however, who are just doing it because they want to. A click around the channels gets you interviews with any number of travelers who just don't believe that they are posing a risk to anyone. Fox, CNN, BBC, MSNBC—they are all talking to people with similar views. It's Thanksgiving and they can't take it anymore.

While I have spent plenty of Thanksgivings with family, I have also spent plenty of them away from them out on the road. I have spent at least two of them in the same restaurant in San Francisco with different *Jersey Boys* companies. I think we were even in South Africa for one a few years ago. No other country but the US celebrates Thanksgiving at the same time we do. Canada has a Thanksgiving, but they celebrate it earlier in the year. When Americans are out of the country on the fourth Thursday in November, you make do with what you can find.

That so many people are flying home to gather with their families is inevitable. Given the President's repeated belittling of the dangers of the virus, why wouldn't the people who listen to him and believe him not travel? Poor Dr. Fauci is doing everything that he can to warn people against gathering with their elderly relatives but since the science behind what he is saying has been undermined, the message is falling on deaf ears.

This year, Michael and I are going to celebrate together—apart. Just this year. Next year… we'll do it up with our families. Wherever you are and whoever you are with or not with, may everyone have a happy and safe Thanksgiving.

NOVEMBER 26, 2020
628,024 Total Reported Cases in New York. 34,282 Deaths.

A few days ago, our neighbor down the hall told us that she had bought an 18lb turkey.

Michael offered to cook it. That's how it started.

He then decided to bake some bread. Two loaves to eat and two to cut into cubes to make sausage stuffing with. Then our neighbor's daughter announced that she was going to make cornbread. And some mashed potatoes. Our neighbor's son is making a vegan casserole. Our neighbor, herself, is making some cranberry sauce. I picked up a sour cream apple walnut pie from the Little Pie Company on 43rd Street and Michael decided to bake a peach pie to go with it.

We are going to set up a table in the hall where the two of us with our neighbors will all leave what we brought or made. Then, we'll take turns serving ourselves and bring it back to our respective apartments where we can zoom with our families as we eat. Some neighbors from the first floor are going to join in, and as of last night, one from the fourth floor is making a sweet potato mash.

The Macy's Parade is on television this morning. Most of it was filmed over the last few days down in Herald Square in front of the store. I think that the floats are going past it live this morning but without spectators present. In a normal year, last night, the streets surrounding the American Museum of Natural History would have been filled with the giant balloons being inflated for this morning's parade. Instead of that, they secretly inflated the ones that are going to participate downtown near the store. They are only going to travel them down the one city block between the two avenues.

The feast that we have come to think of as the first Thanksgiving happened in Plymouth, Massachusetts. It was prompted by a good harvest and a desire to thank the Native Americans who had helped them get through the previous winter. This morning during the parade, a group of tribespeople from the Wampanoag Nation offered a land acknowledgment and a blessing to honor the Wampanoag and Lenape people—the traditional owners of the land on which New York City stands. This kind of gesture is a normal and expected part of Australian life regarding the Aboriginal people. This is the first time that I have seen it done here. It was beautiful and moving. A step in the right direction and long overdue.

Abraham Lincoln was the person who established Thanksgiving as a national holiday in the United States in 1863. Before that, it was celebrated haphazardly on different days in different states. A woman named Sarah Josepha Hale had been badgering politicians for over forty years at that point to make it an official day. Some of that pressure may have influenced the President to finally make it happen. Lincoln set the day for the final Thursday in November specifically to celebrate the Union's successes in the war. It took seven more years until after the reconstruction for the holiday to be properly incorporated. In 1939 Franklin Roosevelt moved the day to the next to last Thursday in November but then two years later changed the day to the fourth Thursday where it has remained to this day.

The first Macy's Thanksgiving Parade happened in 1924. Store employees marched in colorful costumes and enthroned Santa on the balcony of the 34th Street entrance. 250,000 people attended and it was so popular that it became an annual event. The first balloon, which was Mickey Mouse, was added in 1934. The parade has happened every year since except for 1942-1944 because rubber and helium were needed for the war effort.

We have lost so many people and so many more are sick. More of us than ever before are without jobs—whole industries are at a standstill. Nonetheless, today is a day for gratitude.

Yesterday, President-elect Biden addressed the nation with a Thanksgiving message of optimism and hope. The day before he introduced his initial cabinet picks and they each spoke. It was hard not to cry watching a team of people vowing to put the needs of the country ahead of their own. They committed to us, the American people, and our safety and well-being. They committed to re-establishing our presence on the global stage and to rejoining the climate and military treaties that we have strayed from. Included in the group of experienced professionals were several firsts in terms of gender and ethnicity.

Attacks on our democracy and social norms, on simple basic decency, seem to have been beaten back—at least for the moment. The war isn't won yet, but nor was it won in 1863 when Lincoln set the holiday. It wasn't won either when those first settlers celebrated. They still had years of hardship and toil ahead of them.

Taking this day to celebrate everything that we have achieved over these last few weeks seems to me to be perfect timing. There is cause for optimism. Change is on the horizon. We may not all be able to gather today, but we are all still all together regardless. Let's take the day to celebrate and be grateful for what we do have, rather than focus on what is missing.

Michael is clattering around the kitchen in a frenzy. There's a lot of muttering. I think he's enjoying the heck out of himself.

Santa just arrived in front of Macy's. The holiday season has begun.

NOVEMBER 27, 2020
636,302 Total Reported Cases in New York. 34,320 Deaths.

The dishes are done. The leftovers are in the fridge. I slept for about ten hours last night so this morning I still feel sleepy.

Our building meal turned out better, I think than any of us expected. Michael's first-ever turkey was perfectly cooked, and all the sides were delicious. The feeling of community that we generated was far better than anything we ate, as tasty as it all was.

The President, while continuing to deny that he lost the election, is back on the golf course. At a news conference yesterday, one of the first times he has taken questions from reporters since the election, he somewhat lost his mind when Jeff Mason of Reuters questioned his claims of voter fraud, "Don't talk to me that way. You're just a lightweight. Don't talk to me that way. I'm the President of the United States. Don't ever talk to the President that way."

There are stages of grief. Some say seven, some say five, but they all boil down to much the same thing. The first stage is shock and denial. We have certainly seen plenty of evidence of that from the President. The second is pain and guilt. I imagine that in these days where he has been largely absent from public view that he has experienced a lot of that. Given his pathology, as recently outlined by his niece in her tell-all book, I am sure that he is experiencing a massive amount of shame as well.

Some will skip over stage two and go directly to the next one. Stage three is anger and bargaining. That appears to be where we are. His outburst to the reporter yesterday is indicative of that. He also tweeted after that, that he will leave the White House if President-elect Biden can prove that his 80 million votes are not fraudulent. Bargaining. President-elect Biden does not need to prove any such thing, it is up to the President to prove that there was. Even his own lawyers say there wasn't. Denial.

He did tweet that he'd leave office if the Electoral College votes for Biden. More bargaining. If he continues to follow the steps, depression is next, followed by an upward turn that will lead to reconstruction and working through which should finally end with acceptance. So, while we wait for the Electoral College to cast their votes on December 14, the president will continue to lurch through his grief while we are all forced to watch each bloody step. All of us will keep paying for him to play golf while nobody leads the country.

My favorite thing to eat after Thanksgiving is dry white turkey on white bread with a light scraping of butter. The worse the bread, the better. I like it when you take a bite and it all compresses into the roof of your mouth, and you can't get it out. I don't know why I like that, but I do. Candy Corn for Halloween and a dry white turkey sandwich on white bread for Thanksgiving. Nothing better. Michael keeps asking me if I want cranberry sauce or anything else on it. No. Just dry. He appears to have decided to just let that just happen despite how horrified he is. His sourdough bread is far too good for my ideal sandwich, but we are all called upon to make sacrifices these days, so I have.

November 30, 2020
656,413 Total Reported Cases in New York. 34,454 Deaths.

It seems like the first COVID-19 vaccines are going to start being given out by the end of December. The CDC's Advisory Committee for Immunization Practices is meeting tomorrow to vote on who gets it first. Whatever they decide will be a recommendation rather than any sort of hard and fast rule. They don't have the authority to legislate how it is distributed.

They have already decided that the first group, that they are calling Tier 1A, should be frontline health care providers and support personnel. That group would probably also include nursing home residents as well as those in other long-term health care facilities.

The CDC estimates that in this country that there are 21 million healthcare practitioners. In addition to that, 87 million essential support workers are surrounding them. Then there are 100 million adults with high-risk medical conditions and 53 million Americans who are 65 years or older. The head of Moderna says that they are going to be able to provide 20 million doses of their vaccine by December. Each person requires two doses a couple of weeks apart so that would cover 10 million or about 10% of just the doctors, nurses, and support workers.

Pfizer believes that it will be able to create 50 million doses of their vaccine by next month, with half of those going to the United States. That leaves us 25 million doses that, with two going to each person, covers another 12.5 million people before the end of the year. Pfizer thinks that it can vaccinate 75 million more Americans by the end of March. Even with that, that still only gets us halfway through the Tier 1A group by the end of March. It doesn't begin to touch the general population. It is going to be a while before the ability to get vaccinated against the virus trickles down to the rest of us.

The longer it takes to get the vaccine out there, I think the better off we will all be. It needs to become separated in people's minds from the Republicans and the President. The more it becomes a health matter and not a political one, the more people will start to be willing to take it.

There are also many aspects of a vaccine that simply need time to be able to explore and figure out.

Outside today, it is gloomy and rainy. The cat is curled up in a tight ball on my backpack. I'm not sure what he likes about that backpack, but wherever I leave it he will go to sleep on it. And leave a solid circle of fur on the front. While all I want to do is lie down next to him, I need to get it together and go out into the wet to run some errands.

Over the weekend, I started putting things away and moving some furniture around so that we can bring in a Christmas tree. One of the things that sold us on this apartment was that there is a perfect place to put a tree right between our two living room windows. Rain or no rain, Michael and I are going to go out and get our tree later today.

It looks like we will have plenty of time to enjoy it. Unlike a usual December for me, it doesn't seem like I'm going to be traveling anywhere. Thanksgiving this year, turned out to be one of the more memorable ones we've ever had. Christmas will, hopefully, be the same.

I'm not a religious person, but I truly love all the goodwill that is generated around this time of the year. Candles in the window or candles being lit on a menorah. Whether gifts are given on Christmas Day or the seven days of Hanukkah or on January first for Karamu Ya Imani, it's all the same to me. Each celebration is about gratitude and community. They are about home and each other. They shine a light of hope that dispels the darkness that sometimes seems to envelop us.

If these vaccines do get approved and start doing their work, then that will be the best gift of all. Let's hope.

WINTER 2020-2021

DECEMBER—FEBRUARY

DECEMBER 1, 2020
663,500 Total Reported Cases in New York. 34,513 Deaths.

I knew where I was this morning when I woke up.

It wasn't until I was in the kitchen that I realized how odd that was. For the last decade and a half, I have often woken up without the slightest clue where in the world I might be. Lying in a strange bed, I'd try to figure out which direction the bathroom was to orient myself. OK, it's on the right, which means that I am in Detroit. What am I doing today? Oh, right, rehearsal isn't until 1 pm so before that I can go to the Art Institute and see the Diego Rivera murals.

Throughout my working years, I have woken up in some extremely strange places. Some of them have been bland hotels alongside freeways in the most unremarkable places imaginable. There have been times, however, when I've woken up in some spectacular places such as the Peninsula Hotel in Hong Kong, the Raffles Hotel and Marina Bay Sands in Singapore, or a lodge in the middle of the bush in South Africa. In northwest Australia, in Kakadu National Park, I woke up one morning in a rather ordinary-looking room in a hotel that, from the air, was shaped like a crocodile.

While we were putting *Jersey Boys* up in the Netherlands, I lived in an apartment for many weeks in Amsterdam just off one of the canals. It was right around the corner from the Anne Frank House. Every day, on my way to rehearsal, I rode past it on my bike. In Tokyo, Michael and I lived for some months in a completely ordinary apartment in a residential district of the city that was completely unvisited by tourists. For us, though, there was nothing ordinary about it at all. There was an owl bar just around the corner. It was an actual bar with owls that you could interact with. In my apartment in Singapore, the entire bathroom was also a clothes dryer.

I've had great extended experiences living in Johannesburg, La Jolla, and Auckland. There are places like London, San Francisco, Los Angeles, Las Vegas, Sydney, Melbourne, Chicago, and Toronto that almost feel like second homes to me because I have spent so much time there.

Given what a major undertaking it is to get to Australia, I know that I have flown there and back nineteen times. I couldn't begin to count how many times I've been to the other places.

With all the traveling, I have often woken up in my bed at home and not been able to figure out where I was for a good minute or two.

These days, as I come to, I know exactly where I am. I don't even need to think about it. There is no anxiety about what I might have to do that day because there is almost always nothing that I'm going to have to do. While I certainly miss the traveling, this experience of being home for all these months has developed its own pleasures.

Our apartment is slowly being made more efficient. Michael rearranged the kitchen drawers last week so that they make sense in terms of cooking. He has always cooked but never with the regularity that he is doing it these days. I was gone sometimes as much as five months out of a year, so he often didn't cook a whole meal for himself. Now, he cooks two meals for the two of us almost every single day.

We gave away an antique factory stool that looked great in the corner of the kitchen but didn't do anything except attract extra stuff. It's been replaced by a new small simple white cabinet, bought online two weeks ago, that has changed our lives. All the stuff like dishtowels and extra dishwasher pods that were left stacked around the apartment and on the old stool are now put neatly away in our new piece of furniture. After all these years, our apartment is starting to function as a home.

Sitting in our living room and watching the President flailing around these days is certainly worrisome. I cannot imagine, however, what these days would be like had he won. Four years ago, when he was elected, we knew that the four years ahead were going to be bad. I don't think that any of us had the slightest idea how truly bad it would be.

Our standing on the global stage is compromised. We have cozied up to dictators and oppressive regimes and alienated our allies. We have withdrawn from long-standing international treaties. We have seen environmental regulations dismantled and discarded. Clean air, clean water, and pristine wilderness areas have all been threatened. Offices in our State Department remain vacant and unused as we've shunned global diplomacy.

We have seen immigrant children taken away from their parents at the border with little hope of reuniting them. Ever. While those children languish in cages, the First Lady walks the halls of the White House somberly showing off her cold, elegant Christmas decorations. The official video tour is barely a minute long. That's all the time FLOTUS could spare for it. As she famously was recorded saying to someone she thought of as a friend, "Who gives a f%$k about Christmas stuff?"

As President-elect Biden's Cabinet and staffing choices are announced, we are beginning to see an Administration that looks far more like America than anything in the last four years has done. His entire communications team is made up of women. They are experienced, qualified, and able. Janet Yellin is his pick for Treasury Secretary which, if confirmed, will make her the first woman in that role. The rest of her team are equally as qualified and diverse in terms of race and gender. This country just might start being able to function again.

We are in the middle of decorating the apartment for the holidays. Our decorations may not be as fancy or as elegant as the ones in the White House, but they are certainly much warmer. A star mobile that our nephew made when he was nine is one of my favorites. It's on an old wooden hanger with silver stars on it that we put on the hall mirror every year. Thinking about it, I can't help but be reminded again of all those terrified children at the Federal detention facilities along the border.

After the First Lady visited them, she said, "The kids, they say, 'Wow I will have my own bed? I will sleep on the bed? I will have a cabinet for my clothes.' It's so sad to hear, but they didn't have that in their own countries. They sleep on the floor. They are taken care of nicely there. But you know, yeah, they are not with parents. It's sad."

A bed and a cabinet do not make a home. Nor does an Executive Mansion filled to the brim with perfectly cut trees bedecked in steely holiday ornaments. May we all be lucky enough this year to spend these holidays in our sometimes messy but very human homes.

December 2, 2020
671,635 Total Reported Cases in New York. 34,573 Deaths.

The Pfizer vaccine was approved for use in the United Kingdom today. Vaccinations could start there next week.

There were 2,600 deaths from COVID-19 here in the US yesterday. On average last month, 51 people died every. single. hour. Every minute or so last month, somebody in this country lost a family member or a friend. That's on top of all the people that we lost to everything else.

After revealing the decorations in the building on Monday, the First Lady hosted a thank you get-together for everyone who helped put them together. People flew in from all over the country and gathered tightly together in the foyer. Pictures from the event show little social distancing and few masks.

There are currently nineteen other White House parties scheduled. Invitations to them make no mention of the virus. At a reception last night for Republican National Committee members the President said, "It's been an amazing four years. We're trying to do another four years. Otherwise, I'll see you in four years."

As recently as last week, the President's lawyer Rudi Giuliani reportedly discussed with the President the idea of him getting a pardon. Giuliani has been under investigation this summer for his business dealings in Ukraine and what his role may have been in the ouster of our ambassador there. It certainly looks like a pardon might come in handy for him.

There are rumors that the President is also considering pre-emptively pardoning some of his family. His name-sake son was under investigation by Robert Mueller for contacts he may have had with the Russians over getting access to Hillary Clinton's emails during the 2016 election, but he was never charged. The son-in-law gave false information about his contact with Russian nationals when he was seeking security clearance early in the President's term, but he was granted the clearance anyway. An investigation into the President's organization shows millions of dollars of questionable tax write-offs—some of which were paid to his daughter. There is even an investigation being done into allegations that money is being funneled into the White House in exchange for potential pardons.

I can't imagine another four years of this.

December 3, 2020
681,783 Total Reported Cases in New York. 34,635 Deaths.

That these vaccines are coming out at all is still miraculous. Back on January 10, before the virus had even been named, a team of Chinese scientists uploaded its entire genetic sequence to a public site. The posting was coordinated by Edward C. Holmes an Australian from the University of Sydney on behalf of the team of Chinese scientists led by Professor Yong Zhen-Zhang from Fudan University in Shanghai. They shared it with everybody.

Frederick Sanger was born in England in 1918, coincidentally, at the height of the Spanish flu pandemic. He won his first Nobel prize for developing a method to read the amino acid sequence of insulin. He won his second for developing, with his colleagues, what is now called the Sanger Sequencing method. Beginning in the late 70s, he used that method to partially sequence a human virus called phiX174. It took him about three years. One of Sanger's doctoral students, George Brownlee, then started sequencing the virus that causes the flu in humans. In 1981, for the first time, a significant portion of a virus was able to be sequenced.

Scientists divide the flu into three basic categories, A, B, and C. Brownlee studied a subtype, H1, of the most virulent type which is A. Influenza's genome is made up of several RNA strands rather than one continuous one. One of the aims of Brownlee's study was to find the mechanism by which the interaction of these RNA strands, contributes to the creation of influenza pandemics.

All that mishmash means that if you can identify all the individual pieces of these strands, you can then pinpoint the ones that are responsible for specific things and target them. Each of the vaccines that are coming to the market now, focuses on a slightly different part of the genome sequence. None of this technology was available in 1918 during the Spanish flu pandemic. The first vaccine to fight the Spanish flu didn't come out until 1942, twenty-four years later. That vaccine was developed without any access to this kind of technology.

Since the creation of the Sanger Sequencing method, other, even more sensitive ways to map DNA have been developed. The amazing pace of the creation of the COVID-19 vaccine is largely a result of that work. Add to that, that this type of virus luckily tends to be a much easier target for vaccines than other human pathogens.

By making the sequencing of the virus public, multiple groups of scientists were able to sink their teeth into the problem at the same time. By the time the President announced his Operation Warp Speed in mid-May, scientists had already been working on it in multiple countries around the world for four months.

There's a saying that crops up when you are doing a home renovation; twice as much, twice as long. Whatever you think it's going to cost and however long you think it's going to take, double it.

When we bought our apartment, we felt like we had gotten a great deal. The guys who had lived here before us had lived here for several decades. They'd renovated the bathroom, but they hadn't touched the rest of the apartment at all. We couldn't believe our luck when we found it. We had far less competition to buy it than we would have if they'd updated it. We also bought it for less than we were planning on spending but knew that we were going to make up the difference in the work that we were going to put into it. And we did. And then some.

Most of the work was concentrated in the kitchen, which we rebuilt. We opened one entire wall, which meant, among other things, that the entire electrical panel needed to be relocated. Another mini wall needed to be constructed. Twice as much, twice as long.

Everything is more complicated in New York City. You need permits for everything. There is so much work available that good contractors can get booked months in advance. At the time we were living in Michael's old apartment in midtown. The landlord let us stay there month to month after Michael's lease was up. I have no idea what we would have done or where we would have gone if they hadn't done that.

The work on our new apartment started. Then it stopped. Then it started again. The old kitchen floor was pulled up and we found that half of the floor underneath it was rotten. We now needed to replace the floor.

How much was that going to be? The work stopped again. It started again. Something else came up. If we were doing this, we should probably do that. How much? How long? Do you know that your electricity to the bathroom is not up to code? Really? How much? How long?

There are already some side effects being reported from the vaccine—fatigue, headaches, and muscle pain. The fear is that this is going to keep people from getting the second shot. Without the second shot, it won't work. The first primes the body, so to speak, and the second boosts the anti-viral load. Nobody knows yet, how long it's going to be effective. How will they find out? They will keep testing people and when they no longer have the antibodies, they'll know. That information is months or years away.

As wonderful as the prospect of the vaccine is, it doesn't seem like we should be sitting around waiting for it to happen. There's likely to be a lot of time—maybe a full year—before ordinary folk can get it. A lot can happen in that year and there are going to be hiccups along the way.

Twice as much, twice as long.

As opposed to the first months when we were trapped at home and waiting to be released, we are now just living our lives. I find that while there are certainly many things that I miss about how our lives were being lived in February and March, there are also plenty of things that I am not in any hurry to return to. Working 24/7 no longer seems as interesting to me as it once was.

Traveling I miss. Getting on a plane once or twice a week, every week, I don't. I miss working on a show, but I don't necessarily miss working on seven shows at the same time. If life went back to the way it was, I would miss being at home with Michael. I would miss the clarity I have found just being still.

The low-level anxiety that suffused my pre-COVID life is gone, and I am fine with that. Mask wearing can be annoying, but honestly, I don't even really notice it anymore. There's a whole winter to figure out what I want to do once our lives begin to open back up again. I don't need to decide now. We've all been given the chance to be still and truly listen to our hearts.

It does look like the vaccine is coming. It will be nice when it gets here. We don't, however, need to wait until then to get our lives back. We never actually lost them.

December 4, 2020

693,629 Total Reported Cases in New York. 34,693 Deaths.

The November employment numbers are out and, unsurprisingly, they are bleak. The number of new jobs fell for the fifth straight month. More than half of the people who lost their jobs at the beginning of the pandemic have been rehired, but there are still 10 million more people unemployed than there were in February. If the level that jobs are being added remains constant it will take us about two and a half years to get back to where we were at the beginning of this year.

What is most worrisome is that the number of long-term unemployed has dramatically risen. Some have given up looking. There were some hard lessons learned after the 2008 recession which was the last time in US history where there was a comparable rise in long-term joblessness. The longer someone is away from what they do, the rustier their skills get.

Then there are the psychological implications. By 2010, after the 2008 financial crisis, there was a marked rise in opioid addictions. The despair that many felt led to all manner of mental health issues. Then, the longer people remained away from the workforce, the harder it became for them to rejoin it.

COVID-19 vaccines could change that depressing picture. If they do what they are supposed to do and if they become readily available, there could be a dramatic rise in the reopening of businesses and the rehiring of workers. The long-term effects after only a year, would not necessarily be as bad as they were a decade ago.

But. People are going to have to be able to get the vaccine. And they are going to have to want to. If these vaccines are going to be effective, a coordinated public relations campaign is going to need to happen. Presidents Obama, Bush, and Clinton have already said that if it is approved that they will be vaccinated publicly to help show that it's safe. That won't be enough.

After 9/11, people were terrified to come to New York. All of Broadway joined together and did a massive commercial in Times Square to assure the rest of America and the world that New York was safe to visit. I was doing the musical *Cabaret* at the time with Brooke Shields. Brooke was constantly being called upon to make public appearances to promote New York and she was more than game for it. Ultimately, the campaign worked. Tourists started coming back.

We are in uncharted territory. There are going to be missteps and mistakes. We should be copying the best of what our global neighbors are doing and avoiding the worst. That others got there "first" is utterly immaterial. This isn't a race. Bragging rights shouldn't be about the first jab, they should be about the last. We all need to get there eventually, and we all need to get there in our own way. Together.

DECEMBER 5, 2020
275,000 Total Reported Deaths in the United States.

Yesterday, was cold and threatening rain, but Central Park was still grimly beautiful. I walked down Madison Avenue to see the Christmas tree in Rockefeller Center. All the stores that are still open these days along the way are tastefully decorated. Tiny white lights cover the trees outside and discretely outline some of the windows. Little holiday accents, like a miniature Santa hat on a table-top sculpture or a little white deer in among the antiques, pop out here and there, but rarely anything too garish or showy.

Fifth Avenue, on the other hand, is another story. A whole collection of light-covered mostly non-denominational holiday sculptures line the street from the park down to Rockefeller Center. There's a big bright yellow New York taxi in front of the Plaza and a red wagon piled high with presents across the street on the corner of 57th Street. There's a teddy bear with a red Santa hat and a blue dreidel each sitting in front of boarded-up properties. There's a big red mailbox with a pile of shiny white letters next to it further down and in front of the Microsoft store is a snowman sitting in a cherry-red single-seater airplane. Bergdorf Goodman has filled each of their windows with saturated jewel-toned letters spelling out uplifting words. Cartier's has made their entire multi-story building look like a wrapped present.

At Rockefeller Center, the tree is now fully lit. It is an 80-year-old, 75-foot-tall Norway Spruce that was donated by Daddy Al's General Store in Oneonta, New York.

In 1912, because many people couldn't afford the expense of having a tree in their own homes, the city put up the first public tree in Madison Square Park. In the middle of the Great Depression nearly two decades later, workers who were helping to build what is now Rockefeller Center, pooled their resources and put up a tree to raise their spirits. Their families all joined in together to make ornaments and garlands of cranberries and paper. Two years later, in 1933, a publicist grabbed onto the idea and turned it into an annual tradition.

During World War II you couldn't use anything that might be able to be used in the war effort, so a giant tree was out. The lumber was too valuable. Instead, in 1942, three smaller trees were put up—one red, one white, and one blue. In 1944, blackout regulations kept the tree dark.

Kate Smith first televised the lighting of it on her show in 1951. Because it would be getting national attention, the decorations got more elaborate. In 1969, a sculptor named Valerie Clarebout created the now-iconic row of trumpeting angels that lines the plaza leading up to the rink. They've been installed there every year since.

In 2004, a 550-pound Swarovski crystal star was added to the top of the tree. In 2018, an architect named Daniel Libeskind designed the one that is up there now. It weighs 900 pounds and is over nine feet wide. By

2007, the tree's lights were switched to LEDs. They are partially powered by solar panels on the roofs of some of the surrounding buildings.

Daddy Al needed to take this year's tree down anyway. It was, reportedly, in danger of falling. By donating the tree, the city assumed the cost of its removal. A win-win for both parties. After the Christian Epiphany on January 7th, the tree will come down and, for the 14th year in a row, it will be donated to Habitat for Humanity. The wood will be milled so that it can be used to build homes for the homeless.

That the tree is up at all is a testament to our need for tradition. This year, instead of being able to gather around it, strict social distancing measures have been put into place. 50th Street between 5th and 6th Avenue on the north side of the plaza where the tree stands has been blocked off. Large 6-foot circles have been laid down on the asphalt spaced six feet apart. To view the tree, you enter the street and stand in line on one of the circles. Monitors keep you moving forward and then allow you to enter the mezzanine that surrounds the skating rink in front of the Lego store. There are more circles along the north side of the area for observers to stand. You have up to five minutes to be able to take pictures or just take it in before you need to exit on the other side.

Because it was cold and wet yesterday, there were very few people there. I only waited for a couple of minutes before I could go in. The set-up was a bit weird, but it did my heart good to be there and see it.

By the end of the day, today, we are likely to reach 280,000 people dead from the virus.

We have well over 14 million cases in this country and we added over TWO HUNDRED THOUSAND NEW CASES to that count yesterday alone.

Hospitals all over the country are seeing their beds fill up. Many are reaching or have reached capacity. And still, more are coming. All over the country, healthcare workers are reporting that people who believe that the virus is a hoax are taking that belief with them to their graves. Even as they die from the virus that they don't believe in, their faith in what the President has assured them doesn't budge.

It might even be too cold and too wet for me to venture out today. We need to clip the cat's claws today. He can't even walk across the carpet without getting stuck. It's going to be an unspeakably awful job. All three of us are going to need a drink before we get to it.

Afterward, and later tonight, Michael and I will decorate our own tree. We will put on either *A Charlie Brown Christmas* or one of the Rankin-Bass movies—*Rudolph* or *The Year Without a Santa Claus* and drink some hot cider. The holidays are coming regardless of the virus. The holidays are coming regardless of the President. That we all know that, is a testament to our collective faith.

The cat just tried to jump up on the coffee table and got his claws caught on the carpet, so he never left the ground. (Sigh). It's time.

D<small>ECEMBER</small> 7, 2020
723,287 Total Reported Cases in New York. 34,904 Deaths.

The President has now lost the election in Georgia yet again. The state is about to re-certify the election for President-elect Biden. On Saturday, the President called Republican Governor Brian Kemp and attempted to pressure him to call a special legislative session to overthrow the results. Governor Kemp refused.

A survey by the Washington Post has found that only 27 Republicans in the House and the Senate combined acknowledge that Joe Biden won the election. Two of them, despite all evidence to the contrary, believe that the President won. The 220 remaining senators and Congresspeople will not commit.

There have been indications, however, that the Administration is finally seeing that they have exhausted their legal challenges. There is word from White House aides that the President may travel to Mar-a-Lago, his Florida home for the holidays, and not ever return to Washington. He may be starting to think that if he resigns that his Vice-President might be able to pardon him.

The President's attorney Rudi Giuliani has contracted COVID-19. There are no reports on his actual condition, but it is serious enough that he has been admitted to a hospital. Bill Barr is reportedly considering stepping down as the United States Attorney General. The President is upset with him for saying that the elections were fair and secure. We are truly seeing rats scrambling to find a way off this ship. It is taking on water and listing badly.

The President fired Defense Secretary Mark Esper on November 9th. He then fired three more top officials and is now targeting the military's advisory boards. Past Secretaries of State Madeleine Albright and Henry Kissinger have been jettisoned. All these people are being replaced with people loyal to the President. The inmates are taking over the asylum. The Republican Party is taking all of this in and accepting it.

We can't expect our leaders not to make errors, but we absolutely can expect, if not demand, that they learn from them. We can demand that they tell us the truth even if it is hard to hear. We can demand that they put the needs of all of us before their own needs. That, in plain and simple terms, is their job. That's what we've hired them, as Public Servants, to do: Serve.

December 8, 2020
731,722 Total Reported Cases in New York. 34,994 Deaths.

The cat couldn't be less interested in the Christmas tree. As a tiny kitten in San Francisco when I first got him, he would climb up into my artificial tree and sleep inside in the branches. After that first year, however, once we were back in New York and he had gotten bigger, he has never paid any Christmas tree we have ever had the slightest bit of attention. He is, however, obsessed with our crèche.

As I've said before, I am not a religious person, but around the holidays, I at least become drawn to what the world religions are teaching. I like the idea of a crèche and the coming together and awakening that it represents even if I don't necessarily believe in it.

The crèche that Michael and I put up every year is a complete mishmash of international characters. In the center of it are a beautifully and somewhat abstractly carved pair of figures that represent Joseph and Mary. I got them for Michael, along with the crib and the figure of baby Jesus that go with them, in Vienna, Austria one year when I was there scouting out a potential theatre for *Jersey Boys*. Somebody gave us a set of ceramic folk-art nativity figures from Mexico that we use to populate most of the rest of the characters. The Three Wise Men come from that set, and we use the Mary as an extra angel in with the others that are beaded figures from Kenya. The Joseph from that set has become a shepherd with three little white sheep.

The Italians have a wonderful tradition of making these enormous extensive crèches that contain figures of people from ordinary walks of life all rendered completely realistically. Three years ago (I had to look that up) Michael and I went to Italy on the day after Christmas and stayed there until the Epiphany at the end of the first week of January.

Christmas in Italy is utterly glorious. There are crèches set up everywhere and some towns even have competitions over who can present the best one. One town did a live presentation of Jesus and Mary arriving in Bethlehem that neither of us will ever forget. The entire place was turned into Bethlehem. The main street had stalls set up selling loaves of bread and other foods that were being made right there. You could put together a hot meal by going stall to stall.

Everyone was dressed up in period clothes. In the town was a facility for disabled kids, and they were all very much a part of the festivities. For the kids who really couldn't get around there was a Bethlehem school set up in a garage with their minders playing the teachers.

For the presentation itself, a manger area had been built in a large parking lot nearby. As people started gathering, a local farmer drove a small herd of sheep into the staging area. Musicians from the town played instruments and there were several singers and a small choir. Other animals were led in who were, in turn finally followed by Joseph and Mary who made their way slowly in. The rest of the town came in after them. The woman playing Mary was confined to a wheelchair.

When they got to the manger and took their places facing us, a recording of Andrea Bocelli singing started, and one of the most spectacular fireworks displays that either of us have ever witnessed exploded behind it all. Michael and I were sobbing. We had been a little choked up during our wanderings through the town but when Mary wheeled in pushed by Joseph and holding the baby Jesus in her lap, we fell apart and didn't stop crying until the end.

There are now a couple of Italian crèche townspeople around the edge of our display along with a small carved wooden figure of St. Francis that we got in Assisi. He stands opposite three comical plump plastic wind-up reindeer.

To hold the whole thing together, we bought a small slab of raw Italian olive wood that had been fashioned into a cheeseboard. During the year, we use it as a cheese board, as it was intended, but at the holidays, it becomes the base for our eccentric nativity scene.

The cat cannot resist the olive wood. He will lick it and rub up against it for minutes on end. We have a small hand-carved wooden bowl that we got in South Africa that we keep on the coffee table to hold the TV remotes in. He likes that one too. He will fall asleep with his head in the bowl. He likes that bowl, but he loves the cheeseboard somewhat obsessively.

In July, the New York Times published an article titled, "Gotham Refuses to Get Scared," by Laura Collins-Hughes. During the pandemic of 1918, it seems that New York kept its theatres open. The city's health commissioner at the time was worried about the psychological effect that closing them would have on New Yorkers.

He coordinated with individual venues and got them to stagger curtain times to keep crowd size out on the street down. There was no standing room and no smoking. Ushers and attendants could bar entry to anyone with symptoms and use force if necessary.

For the most part, he was able to keep the city open during much of the pandemic that year.

Just about the same number of people died of the Spanish flu in New York City then as have died from COVID-19 so far this year. Would the actions that they took in 1918 have worked now?

In 1918 people just died. It seems to me, that by taking away or finding cures for so many of the things that can lead to our demise, that we have changed our relationship to death. I would venture that we are probably a bit more scared of death now in 2020 than our counterparts were in 1918. In 1918, almost anything could kill you. In 2020, it usually needs to be something serious. In 1918, living with the risk of infection was a normal part of daily life. There were no flu shots in the years before 1918. It came, it killed, it went. Life went on. The President's seemingly blasé response to hundreds of thousands of people dying today seems outrageous. In 1918, maybe people wouldn't be so horrified.

This spring, a survey about what would keep people from returning to the theatre now showed that the main deterrent was "a lack of trust that others in the audience will adhere to safety protocols."

After a couple of mornings of having to find all the scattered creche figures from the board, I got an idea. The cat now has his own little olive wood bowl that we leave on the floor. It is from the Holy Land. It is a low bowl, more of a deep plate, and it's about 6 inches across; the perfect shape for him to comfortably sleep with his head inside it on the floor. Since we got him his own dish, he has miraculously left the crèche alone.

I am not religious, but I am, nonetheless, moved by the teachings of many of the world's religions. Do unto others as you would have them do unto you is a good one. Peace on earth and goodwill towards others is another.

In the years to come, we will hopefully be able to add more figures to our Nativity set. One of the Angels might be Muslim, I can't tell. The Hindu cow figurine that I picked up at a festival during a trip to India is too big to fit in with the rest of the figures. I'll have to go back and find a smaller one.

There's always room for more. Peace on earth, indeed.

DECEMBER 9, 2020
740,980 Total Reported Cases in New York. 35,062 Deaths.

These days are going by very quickly. As we get deeper into the end of the year, the hours of daylight are getting shorter. Beyond that, we just seem to be going week to week to week at a much faster pace than we did even a short time ago. It seemed inconceivable when all of this began that almost nine months later, we would still be in the throes of it.

My body's clock has changed. I'm going to bed later and then waking up later. Michael has settled into his own busy which keeps him occupied for much of the day. He works all day then after dinner, he will work for another hour or two, and then we will watch a couple of episodes of whatever show we happen to be following. After that, I go to bed and read for a while. He keeps watching other things because he finally has a break. By the time he comes to bed, I am long out.

These days, while there are many different projects that Michael, as an actor and a teacher, is being called upon to do, there are almost none for me as a stage manager. The tide has turned. The new show that I was meant to start working on in March has been indefinitely postponed. Others keep getting pushed off. I'm watching this happen as if it's happening to someone else.

Do I want to get back to work in the theatre? Of course, but I realize that recently I have stopped feeling like I am just filling time waiting for it to come back. I'm working. I'm living my life and I am making plans regardless of whether Broadway is open. I'm not counting off the calendar anymore. The only calendar that I am counting off these days is the great Advent calendar that a friend of ours gave us. It is a library, and each day has a different literary character in it.

I wonder who will be behind that little door today…

DECEMBER 10, 2020
752,104 Total Reported Cases in New York. 35,149 Deaths.

Seventeen states, via their Republican Attorneys General, have indicated their support of the absurd lawsuit that Texas has lodged to try to get to the Supreme Court to overthrow the results of the election in Georgia, Pennsylvania, Michigan, and Wisconsin. Seventeen.

Those states are currently being overwhelmed by COVID-19. Five of them have the top ten worst case rates in the country. Indiana, alone, is averaging nearly 7,000 new cases a day. Five of them are experiencing the highest death rates in the nation. Yesterday, South Dakota was the leader.

When South Dakota allowed its annual Sturgis Motorcycle Rally to happen back in August, nearly half a million people showed up from all over the Midwest. 34% of Minnesota's 87 counties later experienced outbreaks of the virus that could be traced back to the rally. Many of the people affected in Minnesota didn't even go to Sturgis, they just got it from someone else who brought it back.

Throughout our history, we have experienced many deadly days on American soil. The number one deadliest event that the US has experienced was the hurricane that hit Galveston, Texas on September 8, 1900. 8,000 are estimated to have died that day. The second deadliest day was on September 17, 1862, during the Battle of Antietam during the Civil War where about 3,600 people lost their lives. The third deadliest day, in the history of the United States, was yesterday when 3,100 people lost their lives to the coronavirus.

Five of the top ten deadliest days in our history seem to have occurred just this year and over this last week.

Not everything is on that list. Real numbers aren't available, but nearly 200,000 people are estimated to have died of the Spanish flu in October of 1918 which would average out to over six thousand people a day. The three-day-long Battle of Gettysburg likely had at least one day of over 3,000 fatalities and it is estimated that 3,000 people died during the San Francisco earthquake of 1906. Just under 3,000 people died on September 11, 2001, when terrorists flew their planes into the Twin Towers, the Pentagon, and the remote farmer's field in Shanksville, Pennsylvania. The death toll from the Japanese attack on Pearl Harbor on December 7, 1941, was about 2,400 people. This month, we are experiencing a national calamity of these proportions Every. Single. Day.

If you compare our actions with the actions of other countries around the world, you can see how badly we have responded to this crisis. South Korea is currently experiencing a surge in its new cases. Since Thanksgiving, they have had about 7,000 new cases. Their case totals now number just over 40,000. As a comparison, as I write this, we are at 15,412,133 cases. We will add a number comparable to their TOTAL number to that in less than two weeks.

South Korea has been successful largely because their society is very different from ours. In South Korea, the government can track its citizens in invasive ways that would drive Americans to the streets in protest. In South Korea, the government has access to its citizen's cellphone location information as well as their credit card transactions. They can get a complete print-out in as little as ten minutes. Americans would balk at the very idea of that.

Without submitting to that level of oversight, we can, nonetheless, learn much from what they have been able to do. We have never been able to implement even the most rudimentary contact tracing measures here. When Michael and I were up in Provincetown a few restaurants took our name and number so that they could contact us if any cases were reported from people who had eaten there on the same day that we had. The US federal government never even tried coordinating something like that on a national level. They never provided individual states with the funding so that even those states who might have been inclined to do it could afford to.

We shouldn't look to the government to keep us safe. It's up to us to keep each other safe. Ignore the politics and listen to your heart. It can be hard to hear it with all the noise and nonsense that's raging on around us, but it's there and it's beating.

December 11, 2020
763,228 Total Reported Cases in New York. 35,247 Deaths.

One of the things that has been noticeably missing from the city this season is the little Holiday Villages that spring up every year in places like Columbus Circle and Union Square Park. Made up of lines of covered stalls, with holiday music piped in, they showcase craftspeople from all over the country. Invariably, I can find something in one of the shops that makes a perfect gift for somebody hard to buy for. At the very least, walking through one can jog my mind into coming up with other ideas. Some of the stalls sell hot cider and homemade baked goods, which is yet another incentive to visit.

Walking through Columbus Circle on my daily walks around the city, my heart always sinks a bit when I realize yet again, that it isn't there this year.

Yesterday, I had walked into Times Square for the millionth time, and I decided to take a left to see if the library had been decorated. Lo and behold, as I got to 6th Avenue, there were the familiar brightly lit white vinyl roofs scattered in between the Park's trees. There are fewer booths than usual, and they are set somewhat further apart, but, like always, they encircle a seasonal skating rink. Rather than one big Christmas tree, there is a grouping of smaller ones towards the east end.

Everyone was wearing a mask, even the people out on the ice. Only one or two people at a time are allowed inside the little stores and everybody seemed to be well spread out and moving. Because there are no tourists, the usual crowds are much thinner. It felt comfortable to be there. If an area seemed too packed, I simply went to another one and waited for it to clear out. And yes, I did get some shopping done.

Today is likely to be the day that the FDA approves the Pfizer vaccine. Today is also likely to be the day that the Supreme Court decides whether to take up the inane lawsuit from Texas challenging the election results in other states. It appears unlikely, however, that there is going to be any agreement at all on a possible stimulus deal out of Washington today.

Michael has left for the weekend to visit his aunt in the Berkshires in western Massachusetts. Among other things, he is going to set up an iPad for her so that we can all Zoom in together for the holidays.

The cat and I now have the entire apartment to ourselves. This has been the longest time in our entire relationship that Michael and I have been in the same place at the same time. The last break that we had from each other was when I visited my family down south over the summer. I won't say that it was time for another one, but... Suffice to say, I am looking forward to missing him again. In a day or so.

In the meantime, I am going to wrap the things I bought yesterday and try and get them into the mail today. It's sunny and not too cold outside so I will probably take a walk. On the other hand, with the apartment to myself, I may just loaf around inside with the cat all day. I am looking forward to seeing how long it takes the cat to realize Michael's not here and try to jump up on the dining room table.

December 12, 2020
774,228 Total Reported Cases in New York. 35,335 Deaths.

As much as I enjoy shopping for Christmas presents, the feeling of getting my family's gifts wrapped, boxed, and into the mail is the same one that I experience in April when our taxes are finally done and filed. I woke up this morning alone and freezing. I crawled out of bed and went straight to the Post Office with all my boxes before it got too crowded. It's done.

The second that Michael left yesterday, the radiators were turned off and the windows opened. Last night was perfect. The cat was curled up tightly against me. He was so warm and comfortable this morning that he was even a little reticent about getting up to be fed.

Like many apartments in the city, we have steam heat from a giant boiler in the basement that looks like a component from a spaceship in one of the *Alien* movies. You can turn the radiators on, or you can turn them off, but you can't regulate the temperature. It's almost always too hot for me. So much heat comes up from the apartments below that, except on the coldest days, the apartment is usually warm even when everything is off.

We spend all summer trying to get the apartment to a comfortable 68 degrees. I don't understand why that shouldn't be the same goal in the winter. Some feel that it is completely acceptable for the apartment to get up well into the 70s when it's cold outside. Not this weekend!

The Supreme Court has rejected Texas' suit to overthrow the results of the election. The case that the President has been referring to as the "Big One" was thrown out as having no merit. Under whatever circumstances these Justices got to the bench and regardless of who appointed them, they are sending the clear message that they aren't puppets. While they all have biases they are, nonetheless, following the rule of law. I take some comfort in that.

We still have forty-some-odd days left before the transition of power. The President is going to continue to try and throw the results out, but this case does seem to mark the end of his chances to do that through the courts. The single case that he did win was over a minor procedural matter that had no bearing on the election results. I think that we can look forward to some other attempts on the Republican's part before January 20th, but they are likely to be even further outside of the box than this latest one was.

While the President rants and raves and digs in his heels, the First Lady has been quietly overseeing the packing up of their personal furniture and belongings and the shipping of them down to Florida. His foolish supporters might believe what he's saying, but despite giving lip service from the sidelines to what he's screaming about, she seems to be moving on.

There is less than a month left before the Senate runoffs in Georgia. The Republicans are, unfortunately, favored to win, but it isn't, by any means, a sure thing. The President's continued undermining of the election results has somewhat muddied the issue. On top of that, some Republican lawmakers are urging voters NOT to vote because they believe the system is rigged. On the other side of the aisle, there are Democrats like Stacey Abrams who are firing up people to get out and vote. She has been lauded as somewhat of a hero for her efforts in the main election which helped turn the state of Georgia blue. The hope is that she will be able to help that happen again on January 4.

Now that I'm up, the cat is sleeping next to the kitchen sink. There is a hot water pipe right underneath the floor there that makes a warm spot. He can tell that there is some kitchen activity about to start. For the first time since I was in quarantine, I'm going to have to make my own breakfast.

It is dark and gloomy outside but it's perfect inside. Our new remote-control candles are each set to 'flicker' and the Christmas tree lights are on. Having sent the family's presents out, I can now clean up the apartment before Michael gets home. I think I'm still a couple of hours away from missing him, but I wouldn't mind hearing his voice on the phone right about now.

December 14, 2020
794,953 Total Reported Cases in New York. 35,529 Deaths.

December used to involve more traveling for me than any other time of the year. US tours of Broadway shows tend to sit down for longer stays around the holidays which makes it the ideal time to head out and visit them and do a bit of rehearsing. There are also often a lot of holiday events like parades or tree-lightings with performances attached to them that need coordinating. Between all of that, I needed to schedule some time to just sit back and allow myself to get into the holiday spirit. Some years, the holiday was over before I knew it.

It always seems like Christmas is upon us before I am ready for it. I am continually finding myself rushing around these days for no reason at all and I stop and remind myself to take a deep breath and slow down. This year, there are plenty of hours in the day and almost no distractions. I've already spent more time sitting by our tree than I have in any year in memory, and we are still ten days away.

Across the country, the first Americans are receiving the vaccine today. Sandra Lindsay, a frontline health care worker was the first person in New York to get it this morning. She got her first shot on camera.

The Washington Post has an interesting article by Ronald G. Shafer about an early smallpox vaccine that was developed by Cotton Mather in 1720. It was somewhat dangerous as it involved infecting the recipient with a mild case of the disease. People receiving this treatment would have a small section of their skin scraped off and a serum containing smallpox would be applied. When successful small pockmarks would occur near where the procedure had been done. That's where the name of the disease, 'smallpox' came from.

Cotton Mather's procedure was considered so dangerous that several states banned it. Over 100,000 people in the colonies had already lost their lives to smallpox so people were desperate to get it anyway. The demand was so high that Massachusetts eventually repealed the ban.

People flocked to Boston. Future First Lady Abigail Adams took her four children there in 1776 and submitted them all to the painful and dangerous operation. One of her kids had to have it done three times before it worked. General Washington, in 1777, gave the order that his troops submit to the inoculation.

In 1798, a British doctor, Edward Jenner, created a vaccine that didn't require the live virus, and Cotton Mather's method could then be abandoned. Abigail Adams and her family survived the earlier method although Abigail, herself, would eventually lose her life to yet another disease for which there was no vaccine yet, Typhoid fever.

The other long-awaited event that is happening at the same time this morning is that the Electoral College is convening around the country to formally cast their ballots. The process started this morning when Vermont cast its three votes for the Biden/Harris ticket and will conclude at 7 pm EST when Hawaii cast its votes. If all goes well, President-elect Biden should pass the 270-vote threshold at about 5 pm when California casts their ballots.

It is extremely unlikely that anything that happens today will change the outcome of the election. It is still rather nerve-wracking to watch it all unfold. I don't remember ever paying attention to the Electoral College casting their votes before. Today, there are cameras and reporters galore in every place around the country that it's happening. The news outlets are carrying it live all day.

32 states plus Washington D.C. have laws in place to discourage "faithless-electors" meaning electors who end up voting for the opposite party. This summer the Supreme Court ruled on a case that upheld their right to do that. Even given that there is the potential that the remaining 18 states could switch their votes, it is extremely unlikely that they would.

Before the election, each party nominates its slate of electors. So, in Vermont, for example, the Republicans had three and the Democrats had three. The Democrats won the popular vote in Vermont, so the three democrats are the ones who cast their ballots today. It would be remarkable for electors to vote for someone who didn't win the popular vote, to begin with, but extremely remarkable for electors to go against their own party.

In the last election, three electors in the state of Washington switched their votes to General Colin Powell instead of Hillary Clinton. A fourth cast their vote for Faith Spotted-Eagle an anti-Keystone Pipeline protester. They were each fined $1,000 and the appeal on that is the case that the Supreme Court ruled on when they said that states had the right to set their own rules around the process.

Republican state representative Gary Eisen announced on a Michigan radio station this morning that he was part of a group that is organizing a protest today against the casting of the Electoral College votes. He said that he couldn't rule out violence. In response, his fellow Michigan Republican legislative leaders removed him from his committee assignments. The Capitol was closed to visitors today because of these credible threats of danger.

On Saturday night, crowds of the President's supporters, in response to the Supreme Court throwing out Texas' bid to nullify some election results in other states, clashed with Police in Washington D.C. 8 officers were injured and 33 of the protesters were arrested. By evening, counter-protesters far outnumbered the President's people. Even so, members of far-right groups like the Proud Boys, kept the violence going through the night.

There have been countless reports of threats being made to Democratic electors across the nation ranging from violence against them and their families to actual death threats. The few Republican voices that have spoken up against this have been drowned out by the silence from the White House. The President not only stands by this unlawful and dangerous action, but he's also encouraging it.

On a trip to Norway some years ago, Michael and I drove through the Laerdal tunnel on our way to Bergen which lies to the west of Oslo. Laerdal is the longest traffic tunnel on the planet. It is just over 15 miles long. Entering the tunnel, you cannot see the light at the other end of it for a very long time. But you know it's there ahead of you.

The time we are in seems endless, but we are getting there. There is reason to be hopeful at the beginning of this, yet another, strange pandemic post-election week. The vaccine has begun being administered. The Electoral College vote will be done in a few hours. If that wasn't enough, early voting began today in Georgia for the Senate runoff race.

We are moving through this tunnel. Tonight is the 5th night of Hanukkah. The Festival of Light. Let's light another candle against the darkness and celebrate.

חמש הכונה

December 15, 2020
803,917 Total Reported Cases in New York. 35,653 Deaths.

We may get slammed with some snow starting tomorrow evening. I almost hate to admit that I am looking forward to it.

If you don't have to go anywhere, New York when it snows can be fantastic. Especially before the holidays, it creates the perfect backdrop for all the decorations up and down the avenues. Piled up on cars and air conditioners, the snow muffles the jagged edges and jarring sounds of the city and makes everything seem softer. The beauty of it, alas, doesn't last very long.

My mother and I were coming back from a trip years ago and got stuck in Los Angeles because of a big New York snowstorm. Since we had the day, we went to Disneyland and rode the Indiana Jones ride three times in a row while drifts accumulated on the streets back east. By the time we were able to fly out the next day, the snow had already started melting and forming giant lakes of brown and grey slush on every street corner. Then everything froze again, and the sidewalks and streets became lethal skating rinks. We'd completely missed the good part.

The Electoral College vote concluded yesterday without incident confirming that our next President will be Joseph R. Biden. Some Republican Senators grudgingly admitted that he won once the College votes were finally cast, but the Senate Majority Leader hasn't said a word.

Yesterday, it was reported that Russian intelligence agencies had engineered a massive hack against the Pentagon, our intelligence agencies, nuclear labs, and many Fortune 500 companies. The State Department, the Department of Homeland Security, as well as the Treasury and Commerce Departments all appear to have been compromised.

We didn't discover this. A private cybersecurity firm named FireEye did and spoke up. It is reported that over 18,000 government and civilian users downloaded a software update that acted as a Trojan horse for Russian malware. That gave the Russians access to these systems. It is still not clear what the extent of the damage from this attack is.

Whatever this Administration's actual ties to Russia are, are not going to be discovered while this President is holding office. The State Department is refusing to directly acknowledge that Russia is responsible.

Remarkably, the Senate Majority Leader has just this moment delivered a speech on the Senate floor congratulating Joseph R. Biden on winning the election to become the next President of the United States. He said that the Electoral College, "has spoken". What can we now expect in response from the President?

There is a storm coming. It could rage and do some real damage, or it could just blow itself out. Who knows which it will be? We will just have to hunker down and wait.

DECEMBER 16, 2020
813,336 Total Reported Cases in New York. 35,761 Deaths.

This morning seems to be heralding winter's early arrival. The temperature here is 30 degrees (-1C) and the heavy grey sky seems ominously still. Officially, the season doesn't begin until Monday, but the weather is ignoring the calendar.

A nor'easter is a non-tropical cyclone whose winds come in from the northeast. They typically form when cold arctic air meets up with the somewhat warmer air over the Atlantic Ocean. The northeast coast of the US is where they tend to strike but they can also plow into the Atlantic maritime provinces of Canada. The one that is heading our way is currently dumping a lot of rain on my sister in North Carolina. As it continues to move north that is almost certainly going to change to snow.

It took over half the day, but the President finally tweeted a response to the Senate Majority Leader after he broke ranks and congratulated the President-elect on his election victory. "Mitch, 75,000,000 VOTES, a record for a sitting President (by a lot). Too soon to give up. Republican Party must finally learn to fight. People are angry!"

The Republicans are becoming more and more divided over whether to continue supporting the President or to concede that they lost the election. The Senator in question must be betting that he has a better chance of holding onto his power without the President than he does with the support of the President-elect. It is a bet, not a sure thing. If he is wrong and his colleagues continue to throw their support behind the President, then he could end up by himself out in the cold.

While the President digs in his heels and rails into the storm to feed his deluded base, the President-elect made an announcement this morning that I never dared to hope would happen in my lifetime. Joe Biden presented his choice for Transportation Secretary to the nation. Pete Buttigieg is not only the youngest person ever nominated to a cabinet position but also the first openly gay person put forward. The fact that both the President-elect and the Vice-President-elect talked in such glowing terms about both their nominee for the position, as well as his HUSBAND, was, frankly, mind-blowing in the best possible way.

This morning Pete Buttigieg, speaking to the nation, spoke about how important transportation has been in his life. He told a story about proposing marriage to his husband in an airport. When I was growing up, I never heard anything like that. Ever. From anyone. It remains to be seen what happens during the Senate confirmation hearings next year, but today the world changed a bit. For young LGBTQ people, seeing that kind of acceptance and inclusion from the highest elected officials in the country might not seem so remarkable. For anyone older, however, it is almost unbelievable. There were a lot of happy tears in our home this morning.

Mayor Pete, in addition to being the first LGBTQ nominee to the Cabinet, is also the first Millennial. He is the ninth person that the President-elect has announced for a leadership position that has broken some sort of a barrier. We are moving forward.

This morning, shivering, Michael finally figured out that I had turned off all the radiators while he was gone. To be fair, even I will admit it is cold in here. FaceBook ads lured me into buying a long almost robe-like sweater for exactly this kind of day. It is finally chilly enough for me to wear it inside.

I will concede that we should probably turn on at least one of the radiators before it gets any colder. The snow hasn't started yet, but it's just about to. We are going to go out and get enough fresh food to get us through the next two days just in case. Yesterday would have been a smarter time to do it, but the time got away from us.

The wind is picking up. The trees are moving outside and it's rattling the windows as it whips past our building, but none of that matters because one of our own was nominated to the Cabinet.

December 17, 2020
825,059 Total Reported Cases in New York. 35,889 Deaths.

The snow is still falling this morning. While places outside of the city got as much as two feet, it looks like we got considerably less than that here. Because of the wind, none of it has accumulated evenly so it's hard to tell. Looking out the window, I would say two or three inches, but according to the weather service Central Park has had accumulations of 10 inches with up to 2 more expected before it all finishes up later today. It is well below freezing this morning so none of it is going to go anywhere anytime soon.

The Pfizer vaccine rollout is underway. Two people in Alaska have reported an allergic reaction to the vaccine. Both are fine, but one had a more serious response than the other. Both were healthcare workers. There are reactions like this expected with any vaccine. So far, there are so few of them that they are notable enough to report. That's a good sign. It looks as if the FDA is going to give emergency approval to the Moderna vaccine later today. That will certainly speed up the number of people who can be inoculated on any given day.

I'll admit that I've been as suspicious about these vaccines as anybody. These days, the messaging on the virus is no longer coming from the President which has relieved a lot of the anxiety around it. Even though amid his insensible rants about election fraud and other nonsense, he occasionally touts his great success with the vaccine, nobody seems to be paying any attention to that anymore.

COVID-19 might not be our biggest problem anymore. The extent of the damage done by the Russians to our security systems via their latest hack is only starting to be understood. Even though it has only come to light in the last day or two, this hack happened months ago—possibly as early as March.

The insidious nature of these attacks is that the Russians, if it is indeed them who perpetrated this attack, will be able to monitor all the efforts to investigate it from within those very systems. What they are likely to do with this access is to use their ability to control these networks to disseminate false information. This will have the effect of further undermining Americans' confidence in the government—something this President has been doing ever since he took office.

The President has yet to utter a word about it. The White House Press Secretary said that they are taking a "hard look" at the data but left it at that. This President is far too in the thrall of the Russian President to take this seriously. You know that things are dire when over breakfast you have a serious discussion with your partner about how likely is it that the current President of the United States is a Russian state operative.

The snow has stopped. The sky is now a brilliant blue although it looks like clouds are moving back in. Despite the brightness, however, it is seriously cold out there. Time to break out the Timberlands and the parka and venture out. I'm not sure how far I'll get, but I am going to give it a shot. If worse comes to worst, I'll just head over a couple of blocks to the new Krispy Kreme Doughnut Shop that opened on Broadway and 96th Street.

Nothing is so bad that it can't be made better by a Krispy Kreme doughnut.

December 18, 2020
837,711 Total Reported Cases in New York. 36,018 Deaths.

Some states are complaining that they aren't getting the amount of vaccine that they were promised. The Federal Department of Health and Human Services, however, says that Pfizer hasn't provided as much as they promised. Pfizer, in turn, says that there are millions of doses sitting in warehouses for which they haven't received any instructions or authorizations to ship.

We are still waiting for a response to the massive cyber-attack. The National Cyber Security Division (NCSD) is a division of the Office of Cyber Security and Communications, within the United States Department of Homeland Security's Cybersecurity and Infrastructure

Security Agency. Nobody is currently heading this department.

Chad Wolf has been the acting Secretary, but he's never been confirmed. Wolf was appointed by the President to replace another acting DHS chief named Kevin McAleenan. McAleenan resigned after he complained in an interview about the "tone, the message, the public face and approach" of the Administration's immigration policy. McAleenan had replaced Kirstjen Nielsen who, herself, resigned after a meeting with the President where he announced that he wanted to go "tougher" on immigration.

Back in August, the Government Accountability Office said that both Wolf and Ken Cuccinelli, the acting deputy Secretary, were serving in their roles in an "invalid order of succession" and were in those positions illegally. Democrats have called upon the two men to resign but they've refused. The GOP has ignored it. Not only are the two people ostensibly in charge of our nation's security doing so in an unlawful manner, but the President has surrounded them with unqualified supporters in many other key roles.

To sum up, in the face of what appears to be the most effective cyber-attack on our nation to date, nobody, from the President on down, seems to be interested or capable or even allowed to deal with it. There is a military spending bill up for review that contains measures to strengthen cyber defenses against just the sort of attack the Russians have allegedly perpetrated against us. As recently as yesterday, the President has threatened to veto it.

I had to switch the cushions on the couch around this morning. There is a truly distinct dip in the one that I have been sitting on all these many months. The one on the opposite end from where I usually perch that doesn't get sat on at all, is much, much higher—by a good couple of inches. The one that Michael usually sits on is somewhere in the middle.

I certainly spend more time on the couch than Michael does. It's my Command Central. There isn't space in the living room for other chairs, nor is there room anywhere else in the apartment for us to each have a proper desk, so the couch it is. Michael lives on a rocking chair in the bedroom that he found in an antique store at least a decade ago out in New Jersey. Before all of this, we certainly sat on the couch occasionally, but by no means every day. As far as I know, neither of us had ever sat on the rocking chair.

A long time ago, my ex, who was—is—a writer, was working on a screenplay about Hugh Hefner for Imagine films. He spent a lot of time at the Playboy mansion while he was working on it and we both ended up being invited there for Hef's 75th Birthday Party.

The party was, of course, at the mansion, and, under attire, the invitation said, "pajamas mandatory". We had to go shopping. I got a pair—top and bottom—that was cream-colored with bears on them. I have no idea why. We were staying at the Beverly Wilshire and had to drive over to UCLA to park in our new pajamas, then take one of a line of shuttle buses that had been arranged to get us all to the house. It felt strange to be outside in pajamas until we got to the parking structure and saw that everybody else was in them too. We got on the bus right behind Weird Al Yankovic and headed over.

The Playboy Mansion was not nearly as large as I had imagined it would be. The party was mostly outside. This was the era when Hefner was "dating" about seven women at the same time. They all looked exactly like Pamela Anderson. The backyard was packed with every minor celebrity you could think of. Rod Stewart was there. Scott Baio. Kato Kalin from the O.J. Simpson trial and almost the entire cast of *Buffy the Vampire Slayer*. Everybody was in pajamas.

Brian Grazer from the production company had come and wanted to do some work, so my ex went off with him and I was on my own. I ran into a friend who was there with Jane Krakowski and we all went off exploring. We all knew that this was a once-in-a-lifetime event. Peacocks were strutting around the grounds and there was a small zoo in one corner. And then there was the famous grotto. We spent most of the night on mattresses inside the grotto watching people cavort with Bunnies in the hot tubs.

It was a fantastic night. When I told straight guy friends about it later the response was almost always, "what a waste!" I don't know what happened to the tops of those bear pajamas, but I am wearing the bottoms of them now. Every. single. day.

It is unconscionable that we are going to have to wait for another month for our government to begin to operate properly. The man who so desperately wants to keep his job does not appear to have any interest in doing it in the time that he has left. So, we wait. On our couches. On our chairs. In our homes. In our pajamas.

Hugh Hefner once said, "I have about 100 pairs of pajamas. I like to see people dressed comfortably." I think he was on to something. If we can't fix what is going on outside in the world, at least we can make the worlds we are stuck in the best that they can be.

Tonight, is the eighth and final night of the Festival of Lights. Happy Hanukkah! and Chag Urim Sameach! to all.

DECEMBER 19, 2020

847,778 Total Reported Cases in New York. 36,142 Deaths.

Michael and I ate dinner outside last night with his sister and her family. It was well below freezing.

We made our way down to an Italian restaurant which is a few blocks south of us. They have a particularly deep patio area with an overhang in front. This outside structure has been there ever since Michael and I have lived up here, but they've recently added plexiglass below the railing while keeping the space above it open. Piles of snow were packed up against it on the other side.

We sat at one of the outer tables and while there were some other people at the other end of the space, by the time our meal was over, we were the only diners there. I left my parka on for the whole meal. The cutlery was ice-cold, but it warmed up as we started eating. We joked about avoiding putting our tongues on it for fear they'd get stuck.

As Michael and I navigate through the city, we are trying to be aware of which restaurants seem safe so that we have options. The place where we ate last night is very lucky to have so much outside space because of how the building that rises above it was designed. I would be interested to know whether the restaurant felt that being open last night was worth it. It doesn't seem possible that with the few people who were there when we arrived that they would have even really covered their operating costs.

A study released this week by the universities of Chicago and Notre Dame shows that over 8 million Americans have fallen into poverty since June. At the same time, the wealthiest 643 billionaires in this country have seen their fortunes grow by 29%. Collectively, these people have earned $845 billion since the pandemic started. Mark Zuckerberg has made nearly $46 billion this year. Jeff Bezos, the founder of Amazon, alone, has seen his net worth gain over $70 billion in the last few months. Robert Reich tweeted back in September that Bezos could give every single Amazon employee $105,000 and still be as wealthy as he was before the pandemic began.

Republicans have long advocated the idea of trickle-down economics. By creating tax cuts for the wealthy, the idea is that money would eventually "trickle-down" through businesses and, therefore, jobs being created.

A paper that was just published by two economists from London explored what happened over 50 years here from 1965 to 2015. They looked at 18 developed countries, including the United States, and found that, after five years, whether the wealthy were taxed or not, per capita gross domestic product and unemployment rates remained pretty much the same across the board. The difference between what happened in these nations occurs when you look at what happened to the wealthy. In countries where the tax rates were cut for the top income earners, the rich just got richer. The only thing that changed was the disparity between the rich and the poor. That gap just widened. There was no demonstrable "trickle-down".

The period of history when we taxed the rich the most—the post-World War II era—turns out to be the period we saw the highest growth and lowest joblessness. In 2017, our President radically slashed taxes on the rich. Three years later, we can see the effect that has had. 643 families are partying on their yachts and 8 million families are scrambling to find food. We need the stimulus deal currently being argued about, to pass. Taking anxiety and terror out of it and just looking at it dispassionately, there is no way for our economy to improve without priming the pump. People need money in their pockets to be able to spend it.

I never imagined that I would look forward to eating outdoors in the snow. Spending the evening, relatively safely, with our family, was more than worth any of the adjustments that we had to make to do it. We are going to keep it up for as long as we can. As Elsa sings in *Frozen*, "Let the storm rage on. The cold never bothered me anyway." Remind me that I said that in a month or two when it starts to get very cold.

December 21, 2020
866,888 Total Reported Cases in New York. 36,389 Deaths.

We are meant to visit a friend of ours who lives out at the Actors' Fund Home in Englewood tomorrow. They are scheduling visits for residents in 20-minute timeslots. Visitors sit outside and residents stay in. An intercom has been set up so that we can speak through the window. Anything that we bring our friend needs to be sealed in plastic and left on a table where it will be disinfected before it goes in.

London has been closed again. A mutated strain of COVID-19 that is reportedly 70% more contagious than any we have seen is ripping through the population there. 30 countries, including France, which lies right across the channel at the other end of the Chunnel, have cut off all land, sea, and air links.

It's still too early to tell, but it does not appear that this new strain is either more lethal or in any way resistant to the vaccine. It just appears to spread much faster than the strains we have seen so far. Of course, nobody knows for sure yet.

In a replay of the United States government's delayed action at the start of the pandemic, the US is not one of the 120 countries that have now banned travel from the United Kingdom. According to our Governor, even with the sharply reduced travel, there are currently six flights a day arriving in New York from the UK. There are no health screening facilities set up at any of the airports. Travelers from Britain just arrive and either head into our city or continue to other parts of the country.

Instead of worrying about the virus, according to White House staffers, the President has been sending out feelers about how to get an airport named for him. Reportedly, he wants to make sure that whichever one gets chosen doesn't have, "a bad reputation or crumbling infrastructure." He has also floated his desire to get an aircraft carrier commissioned and named in his honor.

Today is the first day of winter. It is also the winter solstice. It is the day of the year when the north pole is at its maximum tilt away from the sun which results in the shortest length of daylight for all of us in the northern hemisphere and our longest stretch of night. Many cultures, some stretching far back into prehistory, viewed today as the end of one year and the beginning of another—the symbolic death and rebirth of the sun.

Stonehenge, built during Neolithic times on Salisbury Plain in England, is aligned with tonight's sunset. The Great Trilithon, the largest of two standing stones with one lying on top of them, faces out from the center of the circle to catch the full blast of the winter sun.

For the next six months, rather than getting shorter, our daylight hours will now start to last a little bit longer. While the worst of winter is still ahead of us, just behind it is spring, the time of renewal and strength. As of today, we are finally starting our long trek back towards the light.

Tonight, after sundown when the dying rays of light align perfectly with Stonehenge, Jupiter and Saturn will, themselves, align in the southwestern sky. It will be the first time that this has happened since the Middle Ages—March 4, 1226, to be exact. They will be so close together that they will appear as a bright Christmas star in the sky, apparently much like the miraculous one that was reported on the day that Christ was born in Bethlehem.

NASA claims that the fact that this extremely rare event is occurring on the Solstice is just a coincidence. I believe them. This coincidence, nonetheless, ignites a glimmer of completely non-scientific hope in my heart.

DECEMBER 22, 2020

876,281 Total Reported Cases in New York. 36,547 Deaths.

The Christmas tree lights in the living room are lit. It's otherwise dark and silent. The cat is curled around his olive wood dish from the Holy Land and Michael is still asleep. It's all so still.

I tend to thrive in a busy environment. I'm used to blocking out conversations around me so that I can focus on whatever I happen to be doing. Sitting here this morning in the dead quiet, I wonder if I will still be able to function in mayhem when we all go back.

This being New York City, dead quiet is, of course, relative. I can still hear a garbage truck outside. Some sort of emergency response vehicle with a siren went by just now. They must have been blocked in traffic because they were broadcasting someone speaking. I assume it was some variant of, "get out of the way" but from up here it sounded like the garbled wah-wah of adults in a Peanuts special.

We will brave the crowds once during the holiday season. When we finally decide to do it, we grit our teeth and just dive in ending up with a selective memory of the experience. We try and remember the lights and how beautiful everything looked over the heads of the dense throng of people, and we try to forget all the pushing and shoving and unpleasantness around it.

This year, I've been drawn back to the places that are usually overcrowded because they feel like they belong to us New Yorkers. Nobody much is around. There's no shoving at all. This year, we can experience something that will unlikely be repeated in the future.

Rather than winding up as a series of obligatory stops that can be checked off a rushed holiday list, during this holiday season those places seem to be more like symbols of our resilience. Walking near them, you can see that people have gotten used to keeping their distance from each other. Certainly, there are always people who seem either clueless or actively defiant, but they do appear to be the rare exceptions rather than the rule. I've gotten adept at looking at the sidewalks ahead and changing direction if things look too crowded. I rarely even notice that I'm doing it these days.

When I drive a long distance, my mind starts to wander after a while. It's not that I'm not paying attention to the road, it's that a different part of my mind takes over with the driving, and I can think about other things. The same thing is happening these days out on the city streets. I can navigate through them almost unconsciously—keeping my distance and avoiding groups that have stopped somewhere while my mind is a million miles away.

Historically, about 2.8 million people pass away in this country every year. That's without COVID-19 as a factor. As of this morning, we have lost 319,466 loved ones to the virus alone. There's a United States Death Clock online that ticks up every couple of seconds indicating the speed at which people are dying. It's somewhat gruesomely mesmerizing.

It is possible this year that the rate of death from causes other than the virus will go down. Social distancing measures are not only keeping the virus from transmitting, but they are also keeping everything else from transmitting, too. Even if only half of the country is respecting those mandates, that is still a lot of people being responsible.

The stimulus bill has passed through both Houses and now only needs the President to sign off on it. Will he, I wonder? He is so off the rails these days that anything could happen.

It's brightened up considerably. Michael has gone out shopping and the cat has finished his nap on the bowl and is now sleeping on the bed. Construction work started up outside a few doors down. Horns are honking and I can hear a plane flying overhead. In other words, it's another peaceful winter's day here in New York City.

December 23, 2020
886,813 Total Reported Cases in New York. 36,697 Deaths.

Over the last few weeks, I have been sorting through boxes of stuff that have been kept, in some cases for decades, in storage. While most of it are things that various members of my family decided to keep, some of it is certainly my own.

As a kid, I collected almost everything at one point or another—coins, stamps, rocks. If I happened to get more than one of anything, it would inspire a new collection. When we started expanding *Jersey Boys* beyond New York, I thought it would be fun to get a Starbucks mug from every city we worked in. "Don't do it," said a friend of mine who was also working on the show. Some of the best advice I've ever gotten.

My grandparent's basement in Virginia was a veritable treasure trove of things that nobody but me needed—my grandfather's World War I uniform, a selection of my grandmother's dolls, old kitchen things from early in the last century. Each time we visited them, I would go down the creaky wooden stairs and root around.

I'd discover some treasure and ask my grandmother if I could keep it and she almost always said yes. I think she was happy that I was interested. Sometimes, I'd see something in a history museum and wonder if there was one like it in the basement. One time I was on the hunt for an old candlestick phone. When I couldn't find one, I asked my grandmother why she hadn't kept one. You can't save everything is what she told me.

When my grandparents passed away and my aunt finally moved into an assisted living facility, my father went through the basement and saved some things. He then hired a removal service to just clear out the rest of it and cart it off. At the time I was somewhat agonized by this. Given what I am sorting through now, though, I am grateful that he had the wherewithal to do that.

My grandmother's brother, who died before I was born, was a wealthy, rather dandy, gay man. He lived on Park Avenue up here in New York and would often send his southern yokel sister expensive sophisticated gifts. She wouldn't always realize what they were. Under the sink in the kitchen, my father found an old vase stuck in the back of the cabinet with a dried sponge stuck inside it. He asked me if I wanted it and I said yes. In between stage management gigs, I'd sell things on eBay to make my rent. I shared the proceeds from the family stuff with my sister. I figured I could see if it would sell. The vase, which listed to one side a bit, turned out to be a genuine, signed Tiffany piece. My great uncle had sent it to my grandmother who didn't care for it, so she'd found another use for it.

It sold for a lot. My father was dumbstruck. Both my sister and I paid our rent on time that month.

Yesterday, going through my stuff, I decided to shred a pile of my old driver's licenses and other old IDs. I decided, however, to keep my canceled passports. I have about six or seven of them. The first one I had, I shared with my sister. I was about five and she was probably two when we got it to travel to South Africa. The things that I am keeping as I sort through it all are things that I think help tell my story—my passports, my old calendars, old journals. I've had most of my old photographs scanned and then I destroyed the hard copies of them. There were albums upon albums of them—all sitting in boxes, unseen. I had old VHS tapes and home movies and family slides digitized and then destroyed or recycled the originals of them as well. They now exist virtually, backed up in several places, but the many boxes that held them have been emptied and broken down.

My goal is to scan all the old family photographs and letters and put them into some sort of clear order. At the end of it, rather than a truckload of boxes, I hope to be able to hand my nephew and niece each a single hard drive with the entire history of their family on them. There will be one or two small plastic crates with the originals of things like my father's letters home during World War II and the photo albums my great-grandmother put together in the Philippines in the early 1900s, but that will be it.

The few other things that we've kept, are practical. My grandmother had an old kitchen timer from the 20s or 30s that still works. Michael uses it in the kitchen. Getting rid of the stuff I don't want is every bit as satisfying as gathering it up in the first place was. It's like a tide of junk. It all flowed in and now it's flowing out.

What will we remember from this year? What will end up in the boxes that the following generations will need to sift through?

As much as I admire the simplicity and starkness of Japanese design, I will always tend toward the Victorian. I like being surrounded by things that remind me of past experiences. Getting rid of all the things that either remind me of things I'd rather forget or that I have no associations with at all, clarifies and focuses the things that I treasure.

Maybe that's something that we will all walk away with this year. A better sense of what's important and what isn't. That may end up being a somewhat backhanded gift from the pandemic this year. Clarity.

DECEMBER 24, 2020
899,837 Total Reported Cases in New York. 36,846 Deaths.

About a year after I graduated from college, I got a job as a production assistant on a reading of a one-act musical called *The History of the American Musical Theatre*. Charles Strouse, who wrote *Annie* and *Bye Bye Birdie* was the composer. I can't remember anything at all about it except that there was this incredibly beautiful girl in the cast. Almost the same age as me, she looked a little bit like a blonde Julie Andrews.

I couldn't take my eyes off her which annoyed the heck out of my then-girlfriend who was in the cast, too. (In retrospect, my then-girlfriend need not have worried about THAT.) This girl looked as if she were from another time, which was mesmerizing enough, but her voice was what was truly remarkable. Clear and pure beyond measure.

I think that the musical might have been performed during a festival somewhere—I want to say Hartford Stage but I may be making that up. Wherever it was, I only worked on the rehearsals for it in New York and then never heard another word about it again. I looked it up just now and can't find any record of it—Charles, himself, doesn't even mention it on his webpage.

Several years later, I got hired to be on my first Broadway musical, *The Secret Garden*, as the Assistant Stage Manager. Mandy Patinkin had already been replaced by Howard McGillin and Daisy Eagan, who won a Tony as Mary Lennox only overlapped with me for about a week or two before she left as well. Starring as Lily, however, was the same angelic woman that I had worked with on the reading, Rebecca Luker. At that time, we were both about 30 years old.

I was completely starstruck by the entire experience of working on a Broadway musical. I loved everything about it and couldn't wait to get to work every day. It was impossible to be star-struck around Rebecca, though, because she was never anything but completely open and friendly.

At the very top of the show, the curtain raised to reveal an arrangement of picture frames, the largest of which was a kind of swing. Rebecca sang the first lines of the show from that frame as the ghost of Mary Lennox's aunt.

At the places call, Rebecca would come out, we'd lower the frame, which we all called the Egg, to the deck and she'd get into it. While we were waiting for the overture to start, we'd chat. About anything. Everything. We always laughed a lot. Inside the Egg where nobody else could see it, she had taped a picture of her very-handsome then-boyfriend—naked. (My ex-girlfriend had long since figured out what it was that she needed to worry about in terms of me.) As the overture started, I'd take her water bottle from her and signal to the calling stage manager that she was ready to get raised, and up the Egg would go in time for her to be revealed.

One day, Rebecca and I got into a deep discussion about something that made us both laugh. I was a few seconds later than usual giving the signal to raise the Egg. As I scurried away to get offstage and the Egg started up, she whispered something, but I couldn't hear her. There was only the front curtain between us and the audience, so we had to keep our voices down.

"What?" I whispered back.

In a louder whisper, she said, "What's my first line?"

"Clusters of crocus," I whispered back.

"What?" she asked?

"Clusters of crocus!" I answered as loud as I could from near the wing. We were almost at the point in the overture where the curtain would fly out to reveal her.

"WHAT?!" she asked as loud as she dared over the orchestra.

Now, the curtain was starting up so I had to be offstage or else the audience would see my feet.

"CLUSTERS OF CROCUS!!!" I barked out in a hoarse yell. JUST in time. She glanced at me off stage left after she sang the line and I mimed wiping sweat off my brow. She smiled and gracefully turned back out front to continue, the audience none the wiser.

After that, every day that I was on the deck, no matter what we were talking about, I'd pointedly look at her just before I left and she'd say, "Clusters of crocus," and we'd both laugh.

Last year she was diagnosed with ALS and yesterday, she passed away. I have been lucky enough to work with some truly lovely people and she may have been one of the loveliest. We never worked together again after that show, but we ran into each other from time to time over the years. If there is anyone in show business who is nicer than Rebecca it might be her husband, Danny Burstein. The outpouring of love for the two of them from the Broadway community over this last day has been remarkable and entirely fitting. They are an indelible part of all of us. In many ways, she was spared the worst of that horrible disease by passing before it progressed to the end. If there is any comfort to be taken from her early death, it is that.

At one point in the show, she had to sing a duet with the boy who played her son. The boys who played the part were all at exactly the age when their voices would start to change. When that change was fully underway, they, wrenchingly, would have to be replaced by younger boys. Rebecca would always do her best to harmonize with the increasingly bizarre notes that would start to come uncontrollably out of them at the end of their runs to help keep them in the show for as long as possible. It can't have been easy.

What I remember most of all, though, is the sound of her singing the opening of the show by herself. Perhaps it was because, after that near-miss, I felt somewhat responsible for it. More likely, though, it is because the combination of Lucy Simon and Marsha Norman's beautiful writing and Rebecca's lovely voice is just unforgettable.

Listening to it on Christmas Eve seems exactly right somehow.

Clusters of crocus,
Purple and gold
Blankets of pansies,
Out from the cold.
Lilies and iris,
Safe from the chill.
Safe in my garden,
Snowdrops so still.

December 25, 2020
912,885 Total Reported Cases in New York. 36,978 Deaths.

It is Christmas morning on the Upper West Side of Manhattan. Michael was up late, so he is still sleeping. The cat is snuggled up with his wooden bowl.

Last night, it was as windy as I ever remember it being. Our windows rattled as if they were going to blow into the room. This morning it's calm, though rainy and grey. Inside the living room, it's warm and cozy. Maybe a little too warm. We have the windows open.

Plenty is going on around the world, but today is about family and friends and celebrating the season, so the heck with all the rest of it.

The Christian holiday of Christmas celebrates birth. The early Christians attached this celebration to an already established pagan holiday that celebrated the solstice—in itself a rebirth. Both are about new beginnings. Another chance to get it right. The coming of the light.

For today, the year ahead doesn't matter. There's plenty of time to think about it tomorrow. This past year doesn't matter either. Sure, there are lessons to be learned from it, but not today. Schools are officially on a break. Today is a day for hope.

A very merry Christmas to everyone from me, Michael and, of course, the cat.

December 26, 2020
924,014 Total Reported Cases in New York. 37,108 Deaths.

In countries across the historical reaches of the British Empire, today is Boxing Day.

What this refers to is not at all clear. In the days when it was common for households to employ servants, the day after Christmas was typically when employers would allow their servants the day off to go back to their families. On Christmas Day, itself, the servants would have had to work overtime to keep up with the festivities. The next day, employers would give the servants a box with leftover food and maybe gifts and a holiday bonus to take with them back to their homes.

It also could refer to the custom of giving people that have worked throughout the year doing something that affects the giver in some way a tip or 'Christmas box'. This would apply to people like those who collect garbage or deliver the mail or some service like that who wouldn't necessarily be paid directly by the person giving the tip. Samuel Pepys refers to this practice in his diary in 1663.

Then again, it could also refer to the practice of churches opening their alms boxes on the day after Christmas and distributing the contents to the poor.

These days in the places that recognize it, Boxing Day is a major shopping day, comparable to our Black Friday after Thanksgiving. It is the day when retailers can expect their greatest revenues. This year, with the UK in a strict general lockdown and all non-essential businesses closed, that is not going to happen.

A whole slew of French and other European truck drivers went into the holiday trapped and not being able to drive through the Chunnel back into France. Troops were sent in to organize them. Thousands of trucks, or lorries, had logjammed. The troops sent the overflow into a local airport and parked them on the runways. It was referred to as Operation Stack. Testing protocols for the drivers were put in place to help unsnarl the mess, but there weren't any tests available. As of Christmas eve, France relented and began to allow their drivers to return. As of today, most of it has been sorted out. This, even though there are now reports of the new strain of the virus having been identified in several European counties.

We never left the apartment yesterday on Christmas. We connected with family and some friends over the day. By no means were we able to do that with everyone, but we made a good stab at it. By the time we went to bed, we felt that we'd been talking all day.

Zooming, unless it is controlled as to who is speaking at any one time can devolve into a wall of noise very easily. My elderly aunt who is in Assisted living in Virginia is hard of hearing, even with her hearing aids, so our conversation with her was just yelling.

At the end of the day, when everything was done, the dishes put away, and the wrapping paper folded in the recycling bag, we settled in on the couch and watched *Holiday Inn*.

Holiday Inn has always been one of my favorite films. Except, of course, for the sequence on Lincoln's Birthday when Bing Crosby and Marjorie Reynolds perform in blackface. I don't remember seeing that sequence when I first started watching it on TV as a kid. I think that it was just cut out. I'd be interested to see how they cut it so that the story made sense. Bing loves Marjorie and is scared that Fred Astaire, who is coming to see their show, is going to fall in love with her too, so he "hides" her from him by putting her into blackface.

The scene was uncomfortable but also sort of fascinating. Many movies that I have seen repeatedly have sequences that I either don't like or find somewhat boring, so when re-watching them, I just let my mind wander or get up and go to the bathroom or get a glass of water during them. The Lincoln's Birthday number was one of them. Last night, I watched it.

What's truly astounding about the whole sequence is just how unremarkable it all is. It's not just Bing and Marjorie who are in blackface, but the whole band is as well. The people playing coat check people and waiters are also all in blackface. Nobody notices. Everyone behaves so normally around it, that I had never really noticed all the other characters. People enter the inn chatting with each other, hand their coats over to the attendants who are in blackface and never even so much as glance at them. In 1942, there was nothing unexpected about it.

Marjorie's outfit is particularly grotesque. Her blond hair is done up in exaggerated braids. Even then in 1942, I think that she was supposed to get a laugh for her appearance. Bing, however, is done up as an elderly black man with white mutton chops and a top hat. I may be wrong, but aside from the fact that it is Bing Crosby, and he has bootblack on his face, I don't know that it was done for a laugh. The song that they sing is a song about freedom and a tribute to Abraham Lincoln. It is sung sincerely. So sincerely, that Mamie, the black maid played by Louise Beavers, sings a section of it back in the kitchen to her two kids as if she's teaching them a lesson.

It seems clear that the filmmakers thought that they were sincerely creating a moving number. There's a film montage dedicated to the men fighting in World War II which, at the time the movie was released, was well underway. Of course, there is not a single person of color in any of the footage.

What must have been going through Louise Beavers' mind as she worked on this film? Like Hattie McDaniel, I am sure that she thought being paid to play a maid was a step up from having to be one. Watching the movie last night, all I could think about was how she had to sit there during the filming watching a whole lot of white people dressed up as gross parodies of the very people who were out there fighting for freedom, sing about freedom.

That's how racism endures. People don't notice it.

The sequence in *Holiday Inn* was not in support of white supremacy, it just was white supremacy. That it might be offensive doesn't seem to have occurred to anyone at all in 1942. Marjorie Reynolds objects to the blackface makeup because she wants to look pretty, not because she finds it offensive.

That level of racism has not changed. It's just gotten more subtle. It is such a part of everyday life that we don't notice it any more than the performers in the film being led to their tables by other white performers covered in bootblack do. How many white people watching and enjoying *Holiday Inn* wonder how black people would feel watching it?

Louise Beavers was, initially, not interested in acting. "In all the pictures I had seen… they never used colored people for anything except savages," she once said. In the movie, *Imitation of Life*, which was the first time that she broke through, she played Claudette Colbert's maid. Her character's story, however, is an actual subplot of the film. It was the first time that a black woman's struggles were given any weight in a major Hollywood film. As she became more successful, she began speaking out against the portrayal and treatment of African Americans. When she was criticized for playing subservient roles she said, "I am only playing the parts. I don't live them."

I don't think that we can just cut out that scene from *Holiday Inn* and pretend that it didn't happen. What happens in that scene is underneath every other scene in the film. It's underneath every scene in every other film made during that era. It's underneath everything that happened in this country. Cutting the scene out whitewashes the film. How is whitewashing any less offensive than blackface?

Yesterday was a Christmas that we will never forget. I hope that, despite the challenges, it was a good day for everybody. Sure, there were some adjustments, but at the end of the day, I think it ended up quite well.

So much has changed in our lives over this past year. If we are lucky, there's a lot that we've learned recently that we won't forget. There are stories embedded in everything and every aspect of life around us. Here's to being able to hear those stories.

DECEMBER 28, 2020
940,290 Total Reported Cases in New York. 37,364 Deaths.

That yesterday was Sunday, caught me completely by surprise. I didn't just think that it was Saturday, I knew that it was Saturday. When Michael tried to correct me, I pulled out my phone to prove him wrong.

I'm still not sure when I lost the day. Christmas Day seemed twice as long as a usual day so maybe that's when it happened. Not, of course, that it mattered, but I was planning to go to the bank and the post office but they are closed.

Early yesterday, I registered for what I thought was my final unemployment check. The President, who spent the day much as he had many others recently, golfing, had dug his heels in against signing the stimulus deal. Many of the things he particularly objected to in the bill were things his staff had put in there on his behalf. The government was facing an imminent shutdown.

There is always somebody worse off than you are, and I know that Michael and I are extremely fortunate in that we still have several options ahead of us. Many Americans who are also relying on these payments do not. For a sizable percentage of the US population, these payments are the only thing that is putting food on the table. The eviction protections that have been put in place were also due to run out. Millions of people who have had their rental payments deferred were going to need to pay up on Friday. Without income and protection, we were about to see an unprecedented wave of evictions at the worst time of year possible.

I didn't panic yesterday because I'm just not sure I have much of that ability left.

Many years ago, my mother took my ex and me on a trip to Namibia. Namibia used to be called Southwest Africa. It had been colonized by the Germans during the mad European scramble for Africa. The Germans were driven out by the South Africans in 1915 and after World War I, the League of Nations placed the area under South African jurisdiction. In 1990, they gained their independence.

Namibia is a strange and wondrous place. While many Nazis fled to South America after World War II, many also made their way down to the former German colony. When we were there, Hitler's birthday was still being celebrated by some. With the growth in their international tourism and the passing of that generation, that part of the culture seems, thankfully, to have somewhat subsided.

It is the driest sub-Saharan country in Africa and the desert is one of the oldest on the planet.

When you see giant orange-red sand dunes with razor-sharp crests that stretch for miles in 4x4 TV commercials, chances are you are looking at Namibia.

Part of our trip was a week-long flying safari up Namibia's northern area along the Atlantic called the Skeleton Coast. We were a small group—the three of us and just four others and our guide.

To get around, we had two tiny 6-seater planes. The three of us were in one with everybody's luggage and the food and the four others and the guide were in the second. At the time, I was a nervous flier. I flew all the time, but I couldn't help worrying about everything that could go wrong.

On a 747, you can usually stop thinking about the fact that you are flying through the air in a metal tube. In a tiny plane, that's impossible. Our pilot was an enthusiastic twenty-something-year-old guy who had just left the air force.

The Namib is the only desert in the world that is right up against an ocean. It is called the Skeleton Coast because ships would wreck off the coast and survivors would make it to shore only to find thousands of miles of sand between them and any hope of salvation.

We had to meet our planes at the airport in Windhoek, the capital. They were late in coming. The only airport people that seemed to be around were all up in the control tower, so we went up the stairs to find out what was going on. One of the air traffic controllers asked us to keep a lookout for them in one direction so that he could keep concentrating on his screen.

Finally, they arrived. They were SO small. All of us were anxious about getting in them. Even so, we loaded everything in and took off. The initial flight was about 500 miles over nothing but sand towards the sea. The planes were so little that every single air pocket caused them to drop or bump. We all thought we were going to die. The pilot, however, was completely upbeat. At one point he handed over controls of the plane to my mother. It was then that we knew we were going to die.

From then on, we had near-death experiences about every three or four minutes. For an entire week. We landed on anything and everything except a runway. Sometimes the landing strip was a place that had been previously cleared and was marked by stones, but sometimes it was just a place that looked flat. We all got good at being able to point such places out.

We landed near a seal colony once and got out to have a look at them. Getting back in, we couldn't take off because the wheels had gotten stuck in the sand. All four of us had to get out and pull and push the plane onto firmer ground before we could get back in and take off.

There is an odd weather event that happens there in the mornings where a cloud bank settles in about 100 feet off the ground, goes up to about another 100 feet before the sky above it clears again. By afternoon, this layer burns off. Taking off in the morning, however, means that once you enter the cloudbank, you can't see the other plane at all. We were all on plane spotting detail. Sometimes they were far away and sometimes they were almost on top of us.

Landing through it was a whole other proposition. More times than I can remember, we'd descend through the cloud layer and there'd be something in the way. A giant dune would appear right in front of us, and the pilot would have to suddenly swerve up to avoid hitting it. Once, when the layer was lower than usual, we broke through and there were fences right in front of us, so up we went again.

In the beginning, it was all beyond terrifying. Lots of yells and gasps and clutching of each other. As the week wore on, however, we just got used to it. "Rock!" we'd say and up we'd swerve. "Dune!" and he'd bank to the right. The time we broke through and the fences were in front of us, is the only time I remember the pilot saying, "oh, sh@#". The rest of the time he'd just laugh. By the end of the trip, so would we.

In 2016, when the President won the election, I feared for the worst. On the day after his inauguration, we went to Washington D.C. and marched in the Women's March. We anticipated being out on the streets all through his Administration, but that didn't happen. We just got used to it.

We didn't march when he pulled us out of the Paris accord. We didn't march as the country's education system got gutted. We didn't march for any of the hundreds of other despicable things that happened, any of which under previous Presidents would have driven us out into the streets in protest. There was just too much. We didn't march for anything until George Floyd was killed in Minneapolis and then we marched. A lot. Until we stopped.

The weeks leading up to the election and now the weeks leading to the President-elect's inauguration on January 20, are and have been maybe the most fraught politically in any of our experiences. There is nothing comparable to it in our conscious memory. Even everything that roiled the nation around Richard Nixon's crimes doesn't begin to compare with what we are seeing now.

I don't know who or what convinced the President to sign the bill at the last minute, last night. I don't care. I'm sick of thinking about him. I'm sick of worrying about him. I'm just relieved he did it.

Glinda said it best in *The Wizard of Oz*. When confronted by her sister, the Wicked Witch of the West, she said, "Oh, rubbish! You have no power here. Be gone, before somebody drops a house on you, too." Ultimately, all it took to get rid of the Wicked Witch was a bucket of water.

It's long past time for all of us to get ourselves some buckets.

DECEMBER 29, 2020
950,473 Total Reported Cases in New York. 37,505 Deaths.

The city feels as if it is still a bit groggy from the holidays. In Times Square before Christmas, the giant 2021 that will sit atop One Times Square for all next year had been sitting down on the street below. People lined up to take their pictures in front of it. Yesterday, it was gone—presumably, it's now up on top of the building where it will be revealed at midnight on New Year's Eve.

This year, while the year counts down, there will be live performances from several stages in Times Square, but there won't be any spectators allowed in the area. Like the *Macy's Thanksgiving Day Parade*, we will all be watching from the comfort of our own homes.

I don't think I have ever personally been in Times Square at midnight on New Year's Eve. In recent years the crowds have been overwhelming. The city has taken to putting up a maze of police barricades that funnel spectators into specific areas—getting them there through incomprehensibly roundabout routes. I've always worried what would happen if some idiot shot off a gun or, God forbid, detonated a bomb. The barricades would simply ensure that nobody could get out safely.

That won't be a problem this year. At the pace we are currently going with rolling out the vaccine, it will take us ten years to get to the point where 80% of the population has been vaccinated. Only 2.1 million doses have been administered so far which is far short of the projected 20 million that the President's Administration promised to have done by the end of the year. To the surprise of absolutely nobody at all, there have been hiccups in distribution and storage. 500 doses of the Moderna vaccine had to be thrown away in Milwaukee after somebody forgot to put them back into the refrigerator.

From his golf course in Florida, the President is fuming. Not about the vaccine rollout. Not about the thousands of people who have died on his watch. Not even about potentially losing control of the Senate. He is still just irate that he lost the election.

I saw that there were already Valentine's Day chocolates and stuffed animals on display at the drug store yesterday and my eyes rolled. What I realized, though, is that by Valentine's Day, we will be nearly a month into a new Administration. This President's term will be in the past. All those red-plastic stuffed-plush and chocolate hearts will mean something else this coming year. A new beginning. A new start. Maybe it's not too early to start putting them out after all.

December 30, 2020
963,390 Total Reported Cases in New York. 37,658 Deaths.

Something that is happening on a construction site near us makes a sound like the one the cat makes when he's barfing up a hairball. That's what I woke up to this morning.

Michael, enslaved to his sourdough starter, was asleep on the couch when I woke up and the cat was with him, so, happily, there was no slimy surprise to be found. I dimly remember Michael's alarm going off while it was still dark outside, but I went right back to sleep. The leaven was ready—it seems to rise faster in the dry warm environment inside the apartment—and could not wait. Once Michael had done whatever the next step in the bread-making process was, he conked out again on the sofa.

That these days, Michael gets into his zone of creativity kneading bread and I do it sitting on the couch with my computer and a variety of news stations on, in front of me, I think has surprised us both. Neither of us planned on doing what we are doing, but this is what we've fallen into.

Both of us are also doing other things. I don't want to suggest that Michael spends all his days pummeling dough in the kitchen any more than I spend mine typing, but both of us seem to have found something that we enjoy doing. Both of us also seem willing to keep at it, too—both when it's working and, maybe more importantly, when it isn't.

The more contagious UK mutation of the coronavirus has shown up here in the US in Colorado. The victim, who is in his 20s, hadn't traveled anywhere which means that he got it from someone else in Colorado who had. Our surveillance system for being able to detect different strains is woefully undeveloped compared to other countries so it is likely already made some solid inroads into multiple areas all over the continent.

The United States has now reached 19.5 million cases of the virus. That's the entire population of Chile or Romania. There are 82 million cases of it worldwide. We have seen 338,742 deaths. That's almost the entire population of Honolulu—wiped out.

California's healthcare system is so overtaxed that it seems certain that they will need to start rationing services. They are going to have to move into critical crisis mode and hospitals are going to need to start pooling their resources. Patients, who desperately need care, are going to be turned away.

It doesn't look like this will be over soon. Rather than planning on going back to work in theatre in March, then having it pushed off until May, then to August, and then to next winter, I am just going to assume that we have another year ahead of us without it and behave accordingly. If things do open sooner, then it will be a pleasant surprise. If not, that will have to be fine too.

I learned while traveling like a lunatic that if I downloaded enough entertainment onto my iPad and brought my own food with me that I'd be happy. There are always delays in air travel—it's inevitable. Taking on all the responsibility for making myself comfortable meant that I never needed to get anxious when I got stuck somewhere. I always had something to eat that I liked, and I always had something to watch or do that I enjoyed. Making myself responsible took all the stress out of it. I could leave the house and despite almost anything that cropped up, I'd be fine. I simply stopped expecting the airlines to take care of me.

In two days, we will be living in a new year. In less than three weeks we will have a new President. As exciting as both of those things are, neither of them is going to change anything about how we are living day to day now. At least not right away. We may someday be able to look back and pinpoint a time when things started to improve, but it is going to take a long time before we start to experience those improvements in our lives. In the meantime, we are on our own.

We are all more than capable of taking pretty good care of ourselves. We've already been doing it.

DECEMBER 31, 2020
978,783 Total Reported Cases in New York. 37,799 Deaths.

During the first two and a half months of this year, I spent 44 days working out of town. For most of January, I was in Tampa rehearsing a new cast of *Jersey Boys* for the Norwegian Bliss. Then for the first two weeks of February, I was aboard the ship while it cruised the Caribbean and we got them up and running. I came home from that and immediately, we put a new actor into one of the lead roles on the Off-Broadway company. I then attended two Board meetings—one for our apartment building and one for Broadway Cares—and had a day of rehearsal towards the end of the week.

The whole last week of February was taken up with a workshop of a brand-new musical in a studio near Times Square. We did a final presentation on that Friday and the next day, I flew to London.

After spending the first two days of that trip on my own exploring the Isle of Jersey in the English Channel, we then spent the rest of the week in a church across from the Drury Lane theatre auditioning people for the next *Jersey Boys* company aboard the ship. After work, every night, I went to the theatre. I saw two Caryl Churchill plays, Tom Stoppard's remarkable new play, *Leopoldstadt*, Beckett's *Endgame* starring Daniel Radcliffe and Alan Cumming at the Old Vic, a moving John Kani play produced by the Royal Shakespeare Company and then, finally, a beautiful production of *Uncle Vanya* at the Pinter Theatre.

On Sunday, the 8th of March, I flew home and the next night Michael and I went to a gala in a restaurant under the 59th Street bridge. We were the guests of the producer of the musical we had workshopped the previous month and, we spent the evening shoulder to shoulder with many people from that experience as well as other friends. Ethan Hawke along with his and Uma Thurman's kids performed a couple of songs on a little makeshift stage that had been set up in the center of the room.

For the whole week following that, the week beginning March 9, I was scheduled to be in auditions. All were for *Jersey Boys*, but the first four days were for Norwegian Cruise Lines with one casting team and the Friday ones were for an Off-Broadway replacement with another team. Everything was set but by Tuesday of that week, Michael wasn't feeling well.

While I am occasionally ill, Michael is almost never ill. He had a headache and a fever and weirdly, he had lost his sense of smell and taste. By Thursday, I wasn't feeling all that great, myself. I got through the day, but afterward, I sent out an email to the second team. I said that while I wasn't sick enough not to work the next day, but considering this odd new virus that maybe we should postpone?

The immediate response was that everyone felt it was fine to just go ahead and do the work. Then, after an hour or two when everyone had a chance to think about it, we all decided to put them off. I was somewhat relieved because as time passed, I was getting more and more uncomfortable. That night the aches in my back were so severe that I couldn't sleep.

That weekend everything shut down. All work stopped. Except for the one-night virtual Patti LuPone concert that I did a few weeks ago, I haven't done anything that's produced income since.

Nine months later, millions of people have been infected. Hundreds of thousands have died. Unemployment has soared. Food banks across the country are seeing daily lines of hundreds and thousands of people who have become food insecure. Businesses have closed—some permanently.

As the virus traveled, it became apparent that people of color were suffering more than their share of the impact. The murder of George Floyd by police officers in Minneapolis sparked a reaction that led to the largest series of Civil Rights protests in history. The marches shone the brightest light we have seen yet on the systemic racism that has infected our country since its founding.

Throughout it all, we have watched our government fail to address any of it. So, we voted the person in charge out and chose someone else. In three weeks, we will have a new Administration.

The election results are due to be certified next week. A Republican Congressman is going to hold them up. Not for any other reason than he wants the attention. He wants to run for the office of President, himself, in four years and he wants people to know who he is. It will not stop President-elect Biden from being inaugurated on January 20th. It will just create a delay in one step of the process along the way.

That's my experience of the year we are leaving behind.

We've lost a lot of people. I don't know that I will ever forget the sight of the make-shift morgues that were set up outside some hospitals around the city this past spring. I will also not ever forget the sensation of being the only person standing in Times Square—in total silence—no traffic and none of the usual underlayer of sound that comes from air handlers and the other machinery that keeps this city running. Standing there with nothing but the sound of my breathing and the occasional chirp of birds in one of the busiest intersections on the planet was as surreal a moment as any I have ever experienced in my life.

Many endured loneliness this year in a way that, perhaps, they had never imagined before. I was lucky enough to spend the year with my husband. And my cat. I honestly can't think of anyone else I could have gotten through this with. That we have figured out how to maneuver around a one-bedroom apartment and still give each other some space, seems miraculous.

Parts of this year were truly awful, and parts of it were rather wonderful. It was, in short, a year. Much of it was unlike any other year that most of us have ever lived through. We were challenged to figure out how to survive in extraordinary circumstances and, if you are reading this, we did.

Whatever this new year brings is going to be different, too. If this waning year has taught us anything at all it is that we can live with change.

David Shire and Norman Gimbel wrote a beautiful song for the film, *Norma Rae*.

And maybe what's good gets a little bit better
And maybe what's bad gets gone

Really, what more can we ask of the new year?

JANUARY 1, 2021
995,816 Total Reported Cases in New York. 37,973 Deaths.

Rabbit, Rabbit.

A friend of mine posts the words "Rabbit, Rabbit" at the beginning of every month. It's meant to bring you good luck if it is the first thing that you say when you wake up in the morning on the 1st. If I don't see her post right away, I start to get nervous.

Nobody seems to know how or why this superstition started. The first time it was ever recorded seems to be in 1909 in *Notes and Queries*, which if you remember, was essentially the Victorian-era version of Wikipedia. People would write in with obscure questions, and the answers would get published. The author of this entry said that it was something his daughters did. President Franklin Roosevelt used to say it. He also carried a rabbit's foot around with him. British pilots used to say "white rabbits" every day for luck during World War II. Some people say it three times.

Like most people, I think, I am superstitious about some things. I tend to operate under the. "Well, it couldn't hurt," umbrella. If I find a penny, I pick it up for luck. I'll only do that if it lands heads up. If it lands tails up, I flip it and leave it there for somebody else to find. I've been doing that for as long as I can remember. In a crowd, it can be a little embarrassing so I'll pick up the tails-up penny and carry it for a while until I can unobtrusively put it back down heads-up.

Back in high school, when we were driving and went over train tracks, I had a friend who'd say, "lift your legs or lose your love." We'd all dutifully lift our feet off the floor until we were over them. We'd always make fun of her for doing it, but we'd always do it with her. I don't always do it now, but I will say I can still hear her in my head every time I drive over some tracks.

I have a little pre-flight ritual that I do. While I know intellectually that air travel is far safer than most other forms of travel, it still involves an enormous leap of faith. People you don't know and can't see are taking you up into the atmosphere in what is essentially a tin can with wings. You put your trust in them to get you back down on the ground again. When she was young, my sister worked on *Good Morning, America*. She often found herself at plane crash sites. She learned a lot about what can go wrong during a flight. To this day, I can hear her saying the words, "wind shear" in my head when I'm flying. When I fly, I make a conscious decision to give that trust and control over to whomever to be comfortable for the duration of the flight.

We have a lot of famous superstitions in the theatre. As much as we may all scoff, we do tend to take them seriously.

You are never meant to whistle onstage. This dates to the early days when sailors were often hired to work up in the flies. On a big sailing ship, sailors would communicate over the roar of the wind up in the rigging by whistling to each other. If you whistled on stage, therefore, that could accidentally signal one of the ex-sailors above you to fly in a set-piece or a painted drop on top of your head.

Green onstage is meant to be unlucky. I had to look this up to find why. When spotlights were first invented, they worked by using a chemical called quicklime that was burnt. The light they threw was somewhat greenish, so wearing a green costume would wash out the performer rather than highlight them. There's another story about the great French playwright and actor Moliere who died a few hours after a performance while still wearing his green costume. In truth, nobody looks good reflected in green light. It makes you look ill.

In a theatre, anything that is green is meant to be kept in one place. Hence, the common room where a company meets and maybe gets coffee in the theatre is called the green room.

Macbeth is considered an unlucky play. There are endless stories about disasters that have happened in conjunction with various performances of it. If you accidentally say the name of the play backstage, you are supposed to turn around three times, leave the room, and wait to be invited back in. I have seen that happen several times throughout my working career and had to go through the ritual once, myself. We made Rosemary Harris do it once on our Broadway production of *A Delicate Balance*. We were all doing a jigsaw puzzle downstairs in the basement between cues, and she casually said it out loud. She, herself startled and we made her do the ritual. It gave me pause just now even writing the title down, but it's only unlucky if spoken aloud and inside a theatre. There you should refer to it as the Scottish Play or sometimes Mackers. I think I'll be OK. But I don't want to jinx it.

While there are only 20 days left until President-elect Biden's inauguration, I am afraid to tempt fate, by making any assumptions. 140 House Republicans have indicated that they intend to challenge the election results when they are due to be ratified on the 6th. It does not appear that there is enough support, even among Republicans, for this to be any real threat.

These next weeks are going to be very tricky for a lot of Republicans who are trying to balance their political futures while the current President continues to crazily try to destroy his.

Without the distraction of the holidays, now, what we can all now look forward to are the Georgia Senate run-offs, the election certification process in the House and the Senate, and the Inauguration of President-elect Biden and Vice President-elect Harris.

All of it is somewhat nerve-wracking. Some of this is going to go smoothly and some of it is going to be bumpy. There will be delays, cancellations, and rescheduling, but it won't be any different from any other trip that any of us have ever taken. So, sit back, relax, and try to enjoy the flight.

I might do my pre-flight ritual here on the couch before we take off. I won't describe what that ritual is because then it might not work again. I would hate to lose its protection when we start flying and I'll need it. There's plenty left to watch on my iPad, I think. That's good because it's probably going to be a very long time until we land.

Welcome aboard and please buckle up.

January 2, 2021

1,011,665 Total Reported Cases in New York. 38,093 Deaths.

The time has come for us to put the Christmas decorations away.

The cat will miss the tree. He doesn't have the slightest interest in the ornaments, but he likes drinking the pine-infused water from its base. We leave a little opening in the tree skirt so that he can get to it. Yesterday, I re-oiled his wooden bowl as he was starting to ignore it. Sure enough, he spent the entire afternoon with his head in it.

Yesterday, I walked down to Times Square to see the New Year sign lit up. We missed the actual ball drop at midnight on New Year's Eve because we were zooming with some friends. In the afternoon, I went down to see what the set-up looked like and couldn't get anywhere near it. From 49th street to 42nd street and from 6th Avenue to 8th Avenue the entire area was blocked off. Three garbage trucks formed an impenetrable blockade against all comers on 7th Avenue and every other street had at least one large truck and a police car blocking them. Whole infantry divisions-worth of police officers swarmed the area. Nobody was getting in there.

Yesterday, in one of my big boxes of papers, I found a copy of a letter that my grandfather had written to his father in February of 1920. At the time he was attending Law School at Washington and Lee University in Lexington, Virginia. He wrote it from his fraternity house. In among the general news that he shared, he wrote this: "We had three sad deaths in Lexington yesterday; Mayor Jackson died of heart trouble and pneumonia, Henry Boley's sister died of influenza, and a Mr. Harper, the jailer, also died of influenza... One of the boys in the house was taken sick yesterday with the influenza but is not very bad off." It's the only reference to the Spanish flu I've been able to find anywhere in the family's letters.

The early part of 1920 saw the final big wave of the pandemic. People, at the time, don't seem to have been quite as terrified of it as we have been about COVID-19 today. Maybe it's because there were so many other deadly diseases out there as well. It was just another thing on a very long list that could kill you.

My elderly aunt does not recall my grandfather ever talking about the pandemic. He lived well into my adulthood, finally dying at a ripe old age, and I don't remember him ever talking about it either. He told stories and reminisced about everything else, but not that.

Thanksgiving, Christmas, and New Year's Eve have all now slipped into the past. The election was a constant source of anxiety and maybe even terror for weeks if not months and now it is mostly in the past as well. I think we all harbor a small but nagging fear that something awful is going to happen between now and January 20th. With each passing day, however, it seems more and more unlikely. But, of course, not impossible.

Once we are finally past all of it, what of this will we remember? One of the things that allow us to survive through hardship is our capacity to forget. We might recall that there was pain, but we won't recall the actual pain. We may not be able to imagine forgetting this past year now, but in time, I think we will.

January 4, 2021
1,035,139 Total Reported Cases in New York. 38,417 Deaths.

"So, look. All I want to do is this. I just want to find 11,780 votes, which is one more than we have because we won the state."

The transcript of the hour-long plus phone call that the President made to Georgia's Secretary of State on Saturday in his attempt to change the election's outcome, has now been published everywhere.

Adolph Hitler made liberal use of a propaganda technique called "The Big Lie." He believed that the Jews used the Big Lie to blame the German loss of World War I in 1918 on the antisemitic general who led the country's forces. He made no secret of his admiration of this technique.

In *Mein Kampf*, Hitler says: "All this was inspired by the principle—which is quite true within itself—that in the big lie there is always a certain force of credibility; because the broad masses of a nation are always more easily corrupted in the deeper strata of their emotional nature than consciously or voluntarily; and thus, in the primitive simplicity of their minds they more readily fall victims to the big lie than the small lie, since they themselves often tell small lies in little matters but would be ashamed to resort to large-scale falsehoods.

It would never come into their heads to fabricate colossal untruths, and they would not believe that others could have the impudence to distort the truth so infamously. Even though the facts which prove this to be so may be brought clearly to their minds, they will still doubt and waver and will continue to think that there may be some other explanation. For the grossly impudent lie always leaves traces behind it, even after it has been nailed down, a fact which is known to all expert liars in this world and to all who conspire together in the art of lying."

This is how Hitler, and his government, paved the way to exterminate Jewish people throughout Europe. The German propaganda machine claimed that there was an international coalition of Jews in Europe, England, and the United States who started World War I. They claimed that the Jews wanted to exterminate the German people so exterminating them was a justifiable act of self-defense.

The Nazis made use of the term "Lebensunwertes Leben," which translates loosely as "life unworthy of life," to label people that they wanted to get rid of—the mentally ill, people who did not conform to strict heterosexual sexual norms, anyone of a race other than the pure Aryan strain of the Germanic people, and anyone who could in any way be termed an enemy of the state.

They concocted false scientific studies to prove that these people were inferior. Skulls were measured and noses were measured as if that data had any pertinence to anything. So-called scientists and so-called doctors were employed to make the so-called research seem as if it had truth behind it. Over time, the Nazis used the Big Lie to wipe out over ten million people including over six million people of the Jewish faith.

During World War II, the United States Office of Strategic Services put together a psychological profile of Hitler and included this: "His primary rules were: never allow the public to cool off; never admit a fault or wrong; never concede that there may be some good in your enemy; never leave room for alternatives; never accept blame; concentrate on one enemy at a time and blame him for everything that goes wrong; people will believe a big lie sooner than a little one; and if you repeat it frequently enough people will sooner or later believe it."

In 1990, our President's first wife, Ivana, told a reporter from Vanity Fair that her then-husband kept a collection of Hitler's speeches near his bed. When the same reporter asked him about that without saying who had told her about it, the now-President said, "Actually, it was my friend Marty Davis from Paramount who gave me a copy of *Mein Kampf*, and he's a Jew." Davis, who is not Jewish, later confirmed that he had given him a book about Hitler.

In 2011 our President joined in on the completely unfounded birther movement against President Obama which tried to sow doubt about where he was born. "I have some real doubts. I have people that actually have been studying it and they cannot believe what they're finding. Maybe it (Obama's Birth Certificate) says he's a Muslim."

The Republican Party has been using this technique for decades. Their systematic dissemination of lies against the Clintons is likely the single major factor that led to Hillary Clinton losing the 2016 Presidential election. To this day, there are perfectly reasonable and thoughtful people who find her "untrustworthy." While they may discount the more extreme parts of the lie, such as the part that says she was responsible for a Democratic-led child pornography ring that operated out of the back rooms of a Washington D.C. pizza parlor, they still believe that she did something.

President Clinton lying about his affair with Monica Lewinsky was seen as proof that he was just generally untrustworthy across the boards. If he lied about that, he must be lying about everything. As Hitler said, "For the grossly impudent lie always leaves traces behind it, even after it has been nailed down, a fact which is known to all expert liars in this world and to all who conspire together in the art of lying."

The Big Lie. Endlessly repeated. Never deviated from. A sizable portion of the Republican party is standing behind this President and giving voice and fuel to these spurious lies. They claim that the election was fraudulent. Not their own, mind you, just the President's. That they were elected themselves in the same election doesn't seem to occur to them.

The Big Lie. Endlessly repeated. Never deviated from.

Look for the truth. You will not find it in what either the President or his ardent supporters are saying. The President is on the way out. Let's ensure that he gets all the way out. He will leave many of these supporters behind him—still in office and still in positions of leadership. We cannot forget who those people are.

January 5, 2021
1,048,281 Total Reported Cases in New York. 38,563 Deaths.

The streets of New York are strewn with dead Christmas trees. During my walk, yesterday, all I could hear echoing in my head was the clanging of the bells and the shouts of "Bring out your dead" from the movie of *Monty Python and the Holy Grail*.

Today is the twelfth and final day of Christmas. Tomorrow feels like it's going to be the day that begins the next era of our political life. The Vice President, in a joint session of Congress, will announce the results of the electoral vote. Several times this morning, I have heard newscasters describe what he is going to do as being the same thing that presenters at the Oscars do when they announce the winners. The votes have been cast, Price Waterhouse has tabulated the results and Julia Roberts is merely going to announce the winner.

In 2016, when announcing the Best Picture of the year, Warren Beatty and Faye Dunaway were handed the wrong envelope. Instead of Best Picture, they were handed a copy of the envelope that awarded Emma Stone the Best Actress award for the movie *La La Land*. Somewhat confused, Dunaway announced *La La Land* as Best Picture, but then the mistake was caught and the correct winner, *Moonlight*, was announced. Similarly, the Vice President cannot announce something tomorrow that isn't in the envelope. He can say anything he likes but anything other than what's in the envelope won't stick. The results are the results, and we all know what they are.

Republicans have already challenged the results in a myriad of specious lawsuits that have all, except one, been thrown out by the courts. The one that wasn't thrown out, has no bearing on the final tally. Like the Academy Awards, tomorrow's exercise is a ceremony. Period. *La La Land* did not win Best Picture and the President did not win another term.

I am always of two minds when it comes to using a live tree. It is, after all, a living thing. But an artificial tree requires plastics and mined minerals to create it. When they are discarded, they don't decompose, they just add to the ever-growing mountain of garbage on our planet. A real tree, while it is growing, adds oxygen to the atmosphere. It helps scrub the air of its impurities. It offers shelter to other creatures. Land that might otherwise be developed is kept clear for them to grow. Given the years necessary for them to get big enough, growing trees ensures that jobs continue through good times and bad. Once the holidays are over and the trees are mulched, those same trees then help the next generation grow.

The storms we have ahead of us will eventually subside. Spring is coming. In more ways than one. The next few days will, at the very least, be extremely interesting.

JANUARY 6, 2021
1,064,297 Total Reported Cases in New York. 38,729 Deaths.

The Rev. Raphael Warnock has won the Georgia Senate seat from the Republican incumbent. Only 11 African Americans have ever been elected to the Senate and Warnock is only the second to have been elected from the south since the end of the Civil War.

The other race has not been called yet, but Jon Ossoff, the Democratic challenger is ahead. We may not get the result until later today. With Warnock's victory, the Senate now stands at 49 Democrats and 50 Republicans. Should Ossoff win, that will mean an evenly divided chamber which would put Vice-President-elect Harris in the position of casting the deciding vote in the case of a tie.

The Senate has only been this evenly split three times before. In 1881 for two years, in 1954 but just for a few months because a Senator died and was replaced, and in 2001 but again only for a few months. In both 1881 and 2001, the two parties reached a power-sharing agreement whereby if a bill was deadlocked in committee by a vote divided along party lines that it would still be brought to the floor. In normal times, the party in control could effectively kill such a bill and keep it from ever being voted on. In 2001, the two-party power-sharing agreement lasted until the Democrats convinced a Republican Senator to switch parties and they, then, got complete control of the Senate with a clear majority.

The President has convinced crowds of his supporters to descend on Washington D.C. today to protest the election results. In a meeting yesterday, the President attempted to convince the Vice-President to overturn the election results during the certification process today. Reportedly, the Vice-President told him that he did not have the power to do that.

There have been calls for violence. As terrifying as this might be for people living there today, in the long run, what this is going to do is drive even more moderates away from the President. Whatever violence happens today is squarely on the President's shoulders. Huge crowds of his maskless supporters have already gathered and he is due to address them soon.

Today is going to be a very interesting day. We will see what happens at the President's rally. More election results will come in over the next hours and will hopefully solidify Ossoff's lead and put him over the .5% threshold that will protect him from a recount. In an hour or two, the Vice-President will start to read the Electoral College results from the election.

To object to the results, one Senator and one Congressperson need to do it in writing. Once the objection has been lodged then a debate that is limited to two hours will take place. Each person in the debate can only speak once and can only talk for a maximum of five minutes. After that two-hour debate, the chambers then need to vote on the objection.

All three of these events could drag on all day. In the meantime, it looks like a perfect day for a good long walk.

January 7, 2021
1,081,885 Total Reported Cases in New York. 38,933 Deaths.

There's a joke that's been circulating: A Black man and a Jewish man walk into a bar in the South. The bartender looks at them and asks, "What can I get for you, Senators?"

In the middle of the insurrection, yesterday, I went out for a walk to buy some jam. We had reached the point that occurs in any crisis where nothing new was happening. It was hard to keep still. In the face of everything that I was seeing on television, going out to get jam was the only constructive thing that I could think of doing.

Any addict will tell you that you must hit rock bottom before you can truly start to recover. Rock bottom is the point at which it is not possible to sink any lower. The only way from there is up. Or out. Yesterday, the United States of America hit rock bottom. At least I hope that what happened yesterday was rock bottom because I cannot imagine what could happen that would bring us any lower.

At a rally of white supremacists and QAnon believers in the afternoon, the President of the United States incited a mob to storm the Capitol to attempt to take control of the government of the country as elected officials were certifying the results of the election. Before he got there, one of the President's sons along with his lawyer Rudi Giuliani stoked the crowd, adding fuel to the fire. Giuliani screamed out, "Let's have trial by combat!"

At the point in the certification process when Republican Senators and Congresspeople had lodged the first of their baseless objections to the electoral college results—in this case, those from the state of Arizona—the mob of domestic terrorists that the President unleashed, broke through the perimeter of the Capitol building.

For the first time since the war of 1812, over two hundred years ago, forces hostile to the US government occupied the building that is one of the central symbols of our Democracy. While windows were smashed and doors broken into, it also looks like some of these people were invited in. American flags were taken down and replaced by the President's flags. While legislators sheltered in place or cowered in balconies, armed terrorists took selfies of themselves everywhere from the Senate dais to inside House Speaker Pelosi's office seated at her desk. Files were vandalized and objects looted. Shots were fired.

Capitol police were unprepared, outnumbered, and overwhelmed. Where was law enforcement? Where were the legions of police officers in riot gear? This is the Capitol of the United States of America and there was nobody there to defend it.

Nothing about yesterday should have been a surprise. The President's attack against the legitimacy of the election has been going on for weeks if not months. That he viewed the certification process yesterday as his last chance to overturn them was not a secret. The rally he attended and began his coup attempt had a permit. If even a fraction of the law enforcement response we saw happen against the largely peaceful Black Lives Matter protests had shown up, none of this would have occurred. This mob, however, was almost completely White. None of the participants were shackled and dragged away. Instead, they roamed the halls freely.

The President refused to call in the National Guard. Ultimately the Vice President did that but only after the Governors of Virginia and Maryland had sent in theirs. The President did not want the insurrection to end. Insiders report that he was "borderline enthusiastic" about the carnage. When he finally issued a video message to try to halfheartedly break it up, it ended with him saying, "So go home. We love you. You're very special."

Four people died. One woman was shot and killed by the police and three others died from other medical issues somehow connected to the events of the day. Once law enforcement had finally cleared the mob from the building, they swept it and the buildings surrounding it for explosive devices. Two pipe bombs were found—one each in the RNC and DNC headquarters—as well as a cooler full of Molotov cocktails in the back of a vehicle.

After 8 pm, the Senators and Congresspeople returned to their work of certification in the chambers. The objection to the Arizona results was voted down. Even after the shocking events of the day, and even though several other Republicans decided not to proceed with their objections to the election results, a small group of them nonetheless persisted. Even after the President's attempted violent coup, seven Republican Senators still stood solidly by him and objected to the fair and secure results of the Pennsylvania vote.

Their meritless objections were also summarily overruled. Some minutes later, with Vermont's three electoral votes, Joseph R. Biden and Kamala D. Harris officially crossed the 270-vote threshold. It was just after 3:30 am. A short while after that, the process was finished, and all the results were certified.

As of this morning, Joseph R. Biden and Kamala D. Harris are officially and irrevocably, the President and Vice-President-elect of the United States of America.

There is a lot to fix. The broken glass and jimmied locks will all be replaced in short order. What is going to take much longer is the damage that has been done to our trust in our government. Not only our trust in it but also the trust of the people over the entire rest of the planet in it.

I fell asleep early last night—right after the Arizona objection discussion started up again—

I then woke up a few hours later just after the Pennsylvania objection was voted down. Michael and I watched the rest of the process until the end. Then, we went to bed, but I couldn't sleep, so now I'm up very early.

I still can't believe what we all saw yesterday. One of the images that keeps flashing into my mind is the one of the white guy carrying a confederate flag through the Capitol rotunda.

If we did hit our rock bottom yesterday, and I pray that we did, then there is hope this morning that things will finally start to get better.

In the middle of all the mayhem, Jon Ossoff's win in the Georgia Senate race was finally confirmed. He won by .8% so there is no avenue for his opponent to demand a recount. A Jewish man and an African American man—both Democrats—are now the Senators from Georgia. Democrats, at least for the next two years, will have control of both houses, if only just.

Yesterday was a long day. We all deserve something for getting through it. If I were in that bar in Georgia, I'd put the two Senators' drinks on my tab and offer them a toast for the future.

January 8, 2021

1,101,445 Total Reported Cases in New York. 39,098 Deaths.

Can it be said that you overslept if there is nothing that you needed to wake up for? Regardless, after a couple of days of anxiety-provoking national events that kept me awake, I finally slept like the dead last night and didn't wake up until noon.

What I've woken up to is a strong, though largely uncoordinated, discussion about how to keep the President from being able to take any further destructive action over the next two weeks that would put more

Americans in harm's way.

With the departure of the Attorney General, there is a lack of coordinated leadership at the Department of Justice. There is also still no official leadership at the Department of Homeland Security. Under pressure from Democratic leaders, the US Capitol Police Chief has now resigned, and, at the behest of the Senate Majority Leader, the Sergeant of Arms of the Senate has also resigned.

Two members of the President's Cabinet have now resigned as well—Elaine Chao, the United States Secretary of Transportation, and Betsy DeVos, the United States Secretary of Education.

It is not unreasonable to look at the departure of Chao, who is also the wife of the Senate Majority Leader, and DeVos as a way for them to avoid having to weigh in on invoking the 25th Amendment against the President. As a newscaster so aptly said this morning on CNN, "These are not patriots. These are people leaving the arena early to avoid the traffic."

On Wednesday, Democrats on the House Judiciary Committee sent a letter to the Vice President urging him to invoke the 25th. As of this morning, at least 200 legislators, 37 Senators, and 191 House members have signaled that they would support this move. While he hasn't responded to the letter, reports from within his circle are that he won't do it. He is reportedly worried about creating even more chaos.

The second option to remove the President from power is to impeach him. Again. Yesterday, Speaker Pelosi sent a letter to the members of the House. In it, she said that should the Vice President not proceed with removing the President using the 25th that they should initiate an unprecedented second impeachment proceeding.

There is a remarkable paragraph included in the Speaker's letter: "This morning, I spoke to the Chairman of the Joint Chiefs of Staff Mark Milley to discuss available precautions for preventing an unstable president from initiating military hostilities or accessing the launch codes and ordering a nuclear strike. The situation of this unhinged President could not be more dangerous, and we must do everything that we can to protect the American people from his unbalanced assault on our country and our democracy."

The President has already tweeted that he will be going to Mar-a-Lago on the 19th and will not attend the inauguration. He at least seems to realize that his term will end. White House advisors, however, say that he has no intention of resigning before then.

I got so much sleep last night that I still feel groggy. Having to work through all of this and make some sense of it should have woken me up but I think it's done the opposite. I need a nap.

JANUARY 9, 2021
1,119,284 Total Reported Cases in New York. 39,288 Deaths.

It's cold this morning. Clear and bright, but very cold. Our building was built in 1941, so when it is this cold and breezy, the cold finds its way in. Especially around the air conditioners, there are tiny little frigid drafts that creep into our rooms like icy tendrils.

For me, I am more than happy to curl up in a couple of layers. For Michael… not so much. The cat, if he's not already sleeping on one of us, keeps his eye on our comings and goings from in front of the TV. If one of us gets up, he knows that we are going to leave a warm spot behind us, so he'll jump up and curl up into it as soon as he can.

More and more video that was shot inside the Capitol during the coup attempt is coming to light. While the footage we all saw on the day seemed to focus on the lunatic fringe of the mob who were posing and grandstanding, the video we are all seeing now shows the underlying core group of people carrying weapons who seem focused and intent on doing some real damage.

There are pictures and footage of armed rioters, in full body armor, with supplies of zip tie restraints hanging from their belts, breaking down doors as they hunt for legislators and confront law enforcement. They planned to detain the Vice President, try him, and hang him. Where once he might have been admired by these agitators, he is now reviled by them for not overthrowing the election results.

The Anti-Defamation League published a dire warning on January 4th that extremists were mobilizing. They reported that organizers from events such as "Stop the Steal/Wild Protest" had applied for four different permits to rally and that a fifth one called, "Operation Occupy the Capitol" was also being planned. They published some of the chatter that they had found on extremist platforms. "Please, I dare them (Congress) to defy the constitution while millions of patriots are anxiously waiting to hang them and gun them down in the streets like the tyrants they are." "My truck is lifted, and I have a plow on it right now. What do you need Mr. President?" Nobody seems to have paid any attention to these warnings.

Twitter, yesterday, suspended the President's account indefinitely. Congress is moving forward with impeachment proceedings against him. In response, the White House issued a statement yesterday that said in part, "A politically motivated impeachment against a President with 12 days remaining in his term will only serve to further divide our great country." That hardly seems possible.

The CDC is warning that the mob attack on the US Capitol will likely be a super-spreader event. No masks, no distancing and they were indoors. In the last few days, the participants have dispersed back to their homes all over the country.

Michael is cooking breakfast. For the moment, that is what I am going to concentrate on. This has been some week.

JANUARY 11, 2021
1,149,771 Total Reported Cases in New York. 39,650 Deaths.

On a zoom call, yesterday, with some friends from various places around the country, I was asked to describe what was going on in New York. What was it like being in the city?

It's a question that comes up all the time and I haven't been able to put my finger on what the difference is. As I was trying to articulate what's odd, I suddenly realized what it was.

Nobody's rushing.

Nobody's late for anything. There isn't anything to be late for. The service industry and retail workers get to where they need to go in the morning and stay there. White-collar jobs are largely happening from home. There are no midday meetings to not be on time for. Working lunches are eaten in solitude in kitchens and living rooms. After work, there are no curtains to miss. There's none of the panic that comes with navigating through midtown traffic to get to a pre-theatre dinner reservation in time to catch a show. With far fewer people flying, worrying about missing a flight isn't a thing anymore.

People aren't fighting over taxis. People aren't cramming onto subways. People aren't jostling for space on sidewalks. The constant incessant blaring of impatient car horns that always dominates the melody of New York City life is no longer there. The music has changed.

Dr. Fauci, in a virtual conference with theatre professionals on Saturday, said that he believed that performing arts venues could reopen as early as the fall if everything went right with the vaccine roll-out. If the distribution of the vaccine succeeds, then he saw no reason why theatres with good ventilation couldn't reopen with minimal restrictions. Audiences could reach near-capacity levels with mask-wearing being the only inside measure needing to be taken.

That sounds great and hopeful until you begin to parse it out. "If" everything goes right with vaccine distribution. That hasn't happened yet—at all.

The federal government had estimated that 20 million Americans would be vaccinated by the end of last month. They missed that mark by a very wide margin. Two weeks after that deadline, only about 8 million people have received their first shot. Without any guidance for the rollout, states have had to figure out how they do it themselves. Unsurprisingly, some states have been better at it than others. Without the resources to accomplish this at the state level, much of the burden of figuring out how to do this effectively has fallen even further down the ladder onto individual counties.

Theatres with good ventilation are another flag. Our Broadway theatres are not huge open spaces. They were largely built at the beginning of the last century and theatre owners have filled them to bursting with the greatest number of seats possible. It's even worse in the UK where many theatres are older and even smaller. The Lunt-Fontanne Theatre on 46th Street still has the remnants of a mechanism in its roof that, when it was originally built, allowed them to roll it back and expose the audience to the night sky. I don't know if they ever really used it, but these days, the whole thing has been tarred over and is inoperable.

Near capacity is a vague measure. The economics of Broadway are ruthless. Shows can survive at 70% capacity for a while but that would mean 70% at every performance. When a show is operating at 70% usually what that means is that the weekends are full, and the weekdays are much emptier. We will need to get the audience to spread itself out over an entire week in a way that they have never done before. None of that will happen before people begin working downtown again and tourists start returning to the city.

The bottom line is that getting people vaccinated is the only way that I think the entertainment industry will get back up and running. We will come back. It won't be like a light switch turning back on. It will be slow and uncertain. Some shows will open too early and not survive. Some will get it right.

At some point, we will find ourselves sitting in a meeting that's going too long and fretting about when it will be done. When it's finally over, we will then rush out of the building to elbow our way into a taxi so that we can get to midtown in time to grab a bite of something from the Deli on 44th Street before showtime. On the way down, we will sit in the backseat of the cab and urge the driver to go faster, or maybe take another route. More for our benefit than theirs, the driver will honk at all the other people trying to do the same thing and yell out obscenities at the ones who cut in front. We'll get within a block or two of where we are going and tell the driver to just let us out there. If we're lucky, there'll be a deli open without a line and we'll grab a protein bar, and rush to the theatre where our companion will be impatiently waiting outside.

"Where were you?"

"Sorry, the meeting ran late, traffic was hell."

The usher at the door will then scan the tickets as the bells inside chime. We will get to our seats just as the lights go down, take a deep breath, and try and calm our beating hearts. We will be back in a theatre, with a show about to unfold. We will be in that glorious moment just before a performance where it feels like anything is possible.

And then the overture will start.

January 12, 2021
375,000 Total Reported Deaths in the United States.

I am watching the House Rules Committee discuss a 25th Amendment resolution. They are discussing, seriously, whether the President of the United States is fit to hold office. Both sides of the debate are being argued passionately and thoughtfully. It seems as if most of the House feels that the President is, indeed, unfit.

It's all so monumental and unthinkable and yet in a few minutes, Michael's going to make breakfast as usual and I'm going to turn off the TV. Afterward, I'll clean up. At some point today, I will try to install a new hinge on one of our kitchen cabinets. It took days to find the stupid thing. Of course, the original hinge that broke had been discontinued so, after much research and a trip to the east side to get a comparable replacement, I finally have one that may work.

How can I worry about a hinge when we may be attacked by white supremacists at any moment? What we are looking at these days, few of us white folks have ever had to deal with before. Not being of color myself, I can't begin to know what living in this country feels like for those who are. Having large parts of the country willing to commit violence against you for no other reason than you exist? Well, now there is a large part of the country that wants to attack the liberal left for no other reason than we exist.

People of color have lived with that fear and that stress for centuries. The difference is because white people are now on the receiving end of some of this, the government is debating what to do about it. That, right there, is some white privilege. Attention is being paid. Imagine all this happening and nobody doing anything about it. I'm guessing half the population can do that very easily.

Fear about what might come to be cannot keep us from living our lives in the moment. We must eat our breakfasts and change our hinges. The goal of terrorism is to disrupt our lives. We can't give into that.

I realize that everything is collapsing, but I need to go. The breakfast table is not going to set itself.

January 13, 2021
1,179,266 Total Reported Cases in New York. 40,005 Deaths.

Last night the House adopted a non-binding resolution to call upon the Vice President to invoke the 25th Amendment to remove the

President from office. The vote was largely symbolic because earlier in the day the Vice President had already said that he would not support it. The resolution passed in the House but almost completely along party lines. The Democratic majority voted yes and the Republicans, with one exception, voted no. If the impeachment passes in the Senate, the Senate can then vote to bar the President from holding any further office in his lifetime.

They are all playing politics and jockeying for position. It is the Game of Thrones television series but with a cast of people that nobody wants to see naked.

It's one thing to watch events like this play out on a television show and quite another thing to have to live through it. What we are seeing now is going to change the course of our country's politics for years if not decades to come. This is a pivotal moment in our history and it's happening right in front of us. The insurrection of January 6 is going to be something that historians will continue to refer to.

We can't fast forward. We can turn the TV off, but events are going to keep on moving regardless of whether we pay attention to them or not. I would rather know what's going on than not. I have a rather vivid imagination, so I continually must stop my trains of thought from derailing me.

There are currently 6,600 armed National Guardsmen in Washington. By the inauguration, that number will rise to 15,000 people. The Capitol Building is now surrounded by a wide perimeter of fencing keeping all but the lawmakers and staff out.

We are a week away from the inauguration of the President and Vice-President-elect. We should be prepared for more nonsense before then, but we shouldn't let the fear of what might come, deter us from living our lives. If we do that, they've already won. There are more of us than there are of them. That's something we should all remember.

JANUARY 14, 2021

President-elect Biden proposes a $1.9 Trillion Coronavirus Stimulus Relief Package.

There are three layers of fencing around the US Capitol in Washington D.C. now—an 8-foot fence on the outside, a 12-foot fence based in concrete within that and then within that, another fence topped with razor wire. 5,000 more National Guardsmen have been deployed to the capital with another 1,000 authorized by the Army Secretary bringing the total up to 21,000.

State Capitols around the country are also blockading themselves. In Harrisburg, PA, the streets are being closed surrounding the Capitol, and

450 National Guard troops are being deployed. The Capitol in Richmond, Virginia has been boarded up and a perimeter erected. In Lansing, Michigan where armed militias stormed the Capitol in April, a 6-foot-tall fence has been put in place surrounding the building. The concern that some states have is that with the increased security around the US Capitol local militias may instead choose to target places closer to home.

In the first year of this President's term, a white gunman in Las Vegas murdered 58 people and wounded 850 others in the deadliest mass shooting in US history. A month later another white man shot and killed 26 people in Texas while they were at worship in their church. The following year, a white former student shot and murdered 17 students and adults at the Marjorie Stoneman Douglas High School in Parkland, Florida. In 2019, a fourth white man opened fire at a Walmart in El Paso, Texas, and took the lives of 23 people.

Four of the deadliest mass shootings in our nation's history have happened during this President's watch. After the shooting in Parkland, the President met with a bipartisan group of legislators who were proposing a system of universal background checks for people attempting to buy guns. At the time, the President nodded and smiled, but later, after meeting with the National Rifle Association, he, instead, passed the Fix NICS act. This appropriations act did not create a federal mandate but rather set up a structure by which individual states had to report what they were doing on their own. In 2018, he recommended that instead of trying to curb gun sales, that teachers and school staff should be armed.

The inauguration of Joseph R. Biden and Kamala D. Harris is going to take place on Wednesday on the steps of the Capitol. The Mall, which lies between the Capitol and the Lincoln Memorial will be kept clear. It is already off-limits to the public. We will be able to watch the proceedings on TV or our computers, but only a very tightly controlled group of people will be allowed to be there in person.

The FBI is doing what they can to monitor online chatter among the particularly virulent militia groups, but with so many platforms shut down or restricted, much of that chatter has been forced onto fringe encrypted sites that are harder for outsiders to get into.

Thomas Fuller was a seventeenth-century English theologian and historian. He wrote a religious travelogue called "A Pisgah-Sight of Palestine And the Confines Thereof." Within that, he is credited with expressing a now-common idea for the first time. "It is always darkest just before the Day dawneth."

Last week, during the insurrection, rioters were met with little or no resistance as they breached the Capitol's perimeter. We are now seeing law enforcement preparing to meet any comers with full force. As terrifying as some of this looks, the fact that it is being done so openly and publicly will hopefully deter any sort of similar attack. Over 200 of last week's marauders have been arrested. Their ranks have been diminished.

I think that we are going to stay home all day on Wednesday. On my daily walks until then, I am probably going to veer away from visible New York City landmarks. Earlier, I said that was amazed. What I am most amazed about is that these threats are coming from my fellow Americans. We are not under attack by a foreign power. No, this attack is coming from within. Like it or not, these people are us.

It's getting darker, but it will get lighter again soon. Having passed the solstice, our days are now getting incrementally longer and incrementally brighter. Dawn is on the way.

January 16, 2021
1,228,867 Total Reported Cases in New York. 40,621 Deaths.

When the President won the election in 2016, he seemed as surprised as the rest of us. Without any political experience at all, he seemed to have no idea how to set up a government and how to run it. As he prepares to leave in 2021, he still seems to have no idea how to set up a government and how to run it.

The Health and Human Services Secretary, Alex Azar has, rather pointlessly resigned his office effective January 20. Azar blames the slow rollout of the vaccine on Governors. He blames the FDA for not approving the virus sooner. In short, he blames everyone but the federal government and his own department.

On Tuesday, Azar announced that rather than stockpiling doses of the vaccine that were to be used for the second of the two shots required to achieve immunity, that the Administration would release them immediately. A health director in Oregon wrote to Azar demanding to know what was going on because he had just been told by the chief operating officer of Operation Warp Speed that there was no reserve of doses. Yesterday Azar announced that, indeed, the US did not have a stockpile after all.

The Vice President called Vice-President-elect Harris yesterday and congratulated her on the election win. The Vice-President has his eye on the future. From refusing to contest the results of the Electoral College vote, it's clear what he views that future to be—one without the current President.

His recent actions have made him as unpopular with the radical and weaponized right as some Democratic leaders are. I'm no fan of the Vice President at all, but he is one of the few members of this Republican administration who seems to be trying to maintain our political norms. It's hard not to look at his actions as being anything but self-serving given his unfailing support of the President up until now, but at least it's something.

This Administration is splintering apart. While they were riding the crest of their power, they protected each other. Now all of them are trying to save their own skins. The people who get hurt in all of this, are all of us.

JANUARY 18, 2021
1,255,971 Total Reported Cases in New York. 40,991 Deaths.

I spent a good portion of yesterday doing what I imagine Republican aides were also doing throughout Washington D.C.—shredding. At the beginning of each year, I pull out the oldest accordion tax files in the storage unit, empty them and relabel them with the current year. 2012 is now mostly consigned to the recycle bin in indecipherable pieces.

The anxiety surrounding the inauguration on Wednesday is truly excruciating. There is now a greater military presence in Washington for the inauguration than there currently is in Iraq, Syria, and Afghanistan—combined.

We are poised for a monumental change in our government and a sizable portion of the people of this country don't want it to happen. The current President and Vice-President's terms are officially over at noon on Wednesday. The President and Vice-President-elect will be sworn in before noon so that there is never a moment when the country is without leadership.

I don't recall ever being aware of timelines like these, in any prior election. I feel like I am aware of every minute that passes. It's the not knowing what is going to happen over the next 48 hours that makes this all so fraught. I'm on the edge of my seat. What little bombs and booby traps are the departing legislators going to leave for their successors?

In the last moments of her tenure as Secretary of Education, Betsy DeVos issued a memorandum encouraging further discrimination against transgender students. She did this, minutes before she walked out the door.

Among other last-minute moves, last week, Secretary of State Mike Pompeo added Cuba to the list of states that sponsor terrorism. This action against Cuba runs completely counter to the work that the Obama administration had tried to accomplish there during his two terms.

This ruling opens Cuba up to lawsuits initiated by opportunists here in the US that they would not be able to defend. Raúl Castro is nearing the end of his time as Cuba's ruler—a new generation of leaders will be taking over. Pompeo's move is going to ensure that they hate us. He is salting the earth ahead of the Democratic takeover. Pompeo was scheduled to make a final trip to Europe this past week but had to cancel it when leaders there refused to meet with him.

The current President is planning on departing Washington on Wednesday morning. The Pentagon has refused to give him a big military send-off. His approval rating is currently the lowest that any President has ever had at any point in their administrations since the metric started being calculated.

Seven or eight years from now, I'll be shredding documents from this year. At least I hope I will be.

Here we go.

January 19, 2021
1,268,692 Total Reported Cases in New York. 41,184 Deaths.

The other day, having finished a book, I was on the prowl for a new one. Nothing in the stack by my bed caught my attention, so I started looking through a cabinet in our front hall where I keep my overflow of unread books. The first book that caught my eye was a book that I found too slow the first time I tried to read it, so I decided to give it another try. I figured that if I couldn't get into it again then at least I could get rid of it and clear out some more space.

In the days before digital, we had records. Most albums were on vinyl that had to be played at 33 1/3 RPM. Single songs were on much smaller disks that had to be played at 45 RPM. There were older records that were thicker and had to be played at 78 RPM. RPM, for those younger than me, stands for rotations per minute.

Every so often, you'd forget to change the speed and what came out was gibberish. Either your album was set at 45 or 78 and it sounded like Alvin and the Chipmunks, (That was how Alvin and the Chipmunks were created—normal voices were recorded and played back at a faster speed.), or your 45 was set at much too low a speed and a low droning dragging monotone came out of the speaker. To come out clearly, you had to set the machine to the right speed.

Over the last few years, I was continually on the move. My speed, at the time, was set at 78 RPM. The book that I hadn't been able to get into was set at 33 1/3. I couldn't read it. Right now, my body's internal rhythm is now set to exactly the right slower speed to be able to read it.

A lot of the last fifteen or sixteen years is somewhat of a blur. Don't get me wrong, I loved every second of it. I worked with some truly wonderful people—many of whom I am still friends with now. I wouldn't trade a single second of any of it. In between work sessions, I tried to take advantage of every moment I could to travel and experience everything. At the beginning of one week, I could be in a jeep in South Africa looking at giraffes walking against the setting sun. By the end of the very same week, I could be in an art gallery in Cleveland looking at a Van Gogh.

I kept up a ridiculous pace.

Even at the time, I knew that all of that wouldn't last. Knowing that it would end someday, is what kept me going. If I had thought that was what the rest of my life would be, I might have slowed down considerably. But I didn't.

When everything shut down, I felt the loss of that velocity. I wanted to keep moving. Looking back over this last year, much of the time during those early days I felt trapped and restless. I started walking to burn off all that energy.

In the late 80s, I stage managed a play called *A Piece of My Heart* that was about women during the Vietnam War. It was a series of extremely short intense scenes of nurses and officers talking about the horrors and challenges that they faced, all done in rapid-fire succession. At some point in the run, a small group of women who had been nurses in the war came to see the show. None of them were still in the military. Some had become housewives, and some had had careers in various professions. They all, however, suffered from a certain amount of PTSD and spoke openly about it.

After the performance, they talked with us and shared some of their stories. They wouldn't let us go home. As they told the stories, they got more and more drawn into it. As horrific as much of what they had experienced was, the adrenaline that had been produced had addicted them. By reliving what they had been through, you could see that they were getting a fix. They had sped up to 78 during the war and never been able to truly slow back down.

My father talked about World War II all the time. It was the most exciting time in his life. He loved to talk about it. Much of it was horrific. He usually glossed over those parts. But when the adrenaline is flowing, you don't notice the hard parts. He liked getting a fix, too.

I can't say that I miss operating at the speed I was going at before everything stopped. I'm finding 33 1/3 RPM to be kind of a great speed to be in. Sure, I'd like to get back to work whenever that happens, but there's plenty to do before then. I don't feel restless these days. I feel like I'm in my own body. I don't think that I want to go back to being played at that speed again. I'm not a chipmunk.

JANUARY 20, 2021
1,279,811 Total Reported Cases in New York. 41,399 Deaths.

On the Saturday following the election in 2016, Kate McKinnon, as Hillary Clinton, sang Leonard Cohen's *Hallelujah* for the cold open of *Saturday Night Live*. She sat by herself at a piano and the song caught the feeling of the moment and maybe even helped to define it.

Last night, in front of the reflecting pool between the Lincoln and Washington Memorials, Yolanda Adams sang the same song in memory of the now over 400,000 people who have lost their lives to COVID-19. Standing near President-elect and Dr. Biden and Vice-President-elect Harris and her husband Mr. Emhoff the song, for me, marked the end of these past years in the same way that it marked the beginning of it four years ago. It closed the circle.

The memorial last night was for us all. Not just for Democrats or Republicans, it was for all of us together who have suffered an unimaginable loss of friends, family, and neighbors. After these last fraught four years, I felt myself begin to exhale.

I'm watching the inauguration unfold on the television. President and Mrs. Obama have just arrived at the Capitol. Before them, Sonia Sotomayor, who will be administering the oath to Vice-President-elect Harris arrived with fellow Supreme Court Justice Elena Kagan. Now, President and Secretary Clinton have pulled up and walked in.

The soon-to-be-former Vice-President and the soon-to-be-former Senate Majority Leader have also arrived along with some Republican Senators who as recently as a few days ago were arguing against the results of the election.

President and Mrs. Bush have just walked into the building that two weeks ago, was overrun with white supremacist insurgents who brought with them a Confederate flag and spread their feces on the walls. As the Bush's enter the retaken seat of our government, the US Military Band is playing patriotic marches behind them. Vice-President Dan Quayle is there.

Capitol Police Officer Eugene Goodman who is the person who put himself in harm's way by luring rioters upstairs and away from the location where the Vice President was sheltering, is, today, escorting Vice-President-elect Harris through the Capitol. He has been newly appointed as Acting Deputy Sargent of Arms in the House of Representatives. There is a bipartisan move afoot to award him the Congressional Medal of Honor.

It's snowing in Washington D.C. as the Inauguration Ceremony is underway.

Lady Gaga is singing *The Star-Spangled Banner* in a gigantic red dress with a golden dove of peace over her left breast. It is thrilling.

Kamala Devi Harris is now the Vice-President of the United States of America.

Jennifer Lopez is singing *This Land is Your Land*, Woody Guthrie's critical response to *God Bless America*. She then added in some of *God Bless America*. She is thrilling, too.

Joseph Robinette Biden, Jr. is now the 46th President of the United States of America.

All around us here on the Upper West Side of Manhattan a wave of sound has erupted. People are cheering with sheer joy and relief and banging on pots.

In his inaugural address, President Biden calls for unity. He says that the dream of justice for all will be deferred no longer... He says that unity is the path forward and we must meet this future as the United States of America. He says that we must end this uncivil war. He says that joy cometh in the morning.

Garth Brooks is now singing *Amazing Grace*.

The 22-year-old Inaugural Poet, Amanda Gorman is reciting a poem. She is blowing everyone else off that stage. Remarkable.

Following the final benediction, the President and Vice President of the United States of America are making their way back inside the building so that they can now head over to the White House, after laying a wreath on the Tomb of the Unknown Soldier, at Arlington Cemetery, and finally begin the job of leading this country.

In the Hebrew tradition, the word hallelu means "to praise joyously." "Yah" is a shortened form of the unspoken name of God.

Hallelujah, indeed.

January 21, 2021

1,293,719 Total Reported Cases in New York. 41,599 Deaths.

The new Administration has immediately ceased construction on the Mexican border wall. Funds that had been directed to it will now be directed elsewhere.

Immigrants who had been brought to the US as children now have a clearer path to citizenship. The Obama-era DACA program will survive and be strengthened. Non-citizens will no longer be excluded from the census count. Aggressive efforts to deport undocumented immigrants have been halted. The ban on travel from several Muslim nations has been lifted and the harm that those bans may have caused will be addressed.

The United States has rejoined the World Health Organization. Dr. Anthony Fauci will head the American delegation to the executive board. Jeffrey D. Zients, who under President Obama was the head of the National Economic Council, has been made the official COVID-19 response coordinator whose first duty will be to raise the level of the nation's response to the pandemic. On all federal property throughout the US and its territories, mask-wearing and social distancing are now mandatory.

The United States of America will re-enter the Paris Accord in thirty days. We will rejoin the nearly 200 countries that are working together to move away from the use of fossil fuels. The Keystone XL pipeline permit has been revoked. A temporary halt to oil and natural gas leases in the Arctic has been extended. Vehicle emission standards that had been rolled back have been reinstated. Bears Ears National Monument and Grand Staircase-Escalante National Monument have been restored to their former sizes, with development within their borders prohibited. A group that will work together to examine the social costs of greenhouse gases has been formed.

The 1776 Commission, created to rewrite and distort US history from a white perspective, has been disbanded. Federal agencies and their contractors will now need to resume diversity and inclusion training. Susan E. Rice, who, as of yesterday, now heads the Domestic Policy Council, has been put in charge of an intra-agency effort to combat systemic racism in the way that these agencies currently operate. They have 200 days to review and report on the equity within their structures.

Title VII of the Civil Rights Act requires that the Federal government not discriminate based on sexual orientation or gender identity has been reinforced.

A federal moratorium on evictions during this crisis is now on the way to being extended. The Departments of Agriculture, Veterans Affairs, and Housing and Urban Development have also all been asked to extend their moratoriums on foreclosures on federally guaranteed mortgages.

There is a movement towards a continuation of the temporary halt to the accrual of interest on student loans with the hope that it will continue at least through September. There is a discussion about possibly forgiving a portion of every student's debt.

The new appointees in the executive branch of our government have been ordered to sign an ethics pledge. A clear set of ethical rules has been set.

Every one of the executive orders that were signed following the election on November 6 has been put on hold until they can be reviewed and evaluated. Those without merit will be discarded.

All of that happened just yesterday afternoon. Over one-half of one day, the government of the United States finally began to operate again.

This morning, there are reports that when the Biden administration officials were finally able to investigate the COVID-19 vaccine distribution plan yesterday, what they found was that there wasn't one. Today, a distribution plan for the coronavirus vaccine is beginning to be built from the ground up.

In my career, I have worked with directors who rely on the people they hire to run the different parts of their productions. They issue the mandates and all of us then march off to fulfill them. Much of what happens is then taken care of within our various departments. This type of director is focused on the endgame, and they are not concerned with the minutiae of how we get there. When an issue comes up that affects the final product, then and only then is the matter brought to the director's attention. The rest of the time, they forge our path forward and the rest of us do our jobs to make that possible.

I have also worked with directors who don't trust the people they've hired to be able to make even the most mundane decisions on their own. Invariably, easily solved issues become more complicated and more fraught because of the director's involvement. They lose track of the bigger picture and the endgame. They don't trust discussions that happen outside of their earshot so they keep everyone who works for them as much in the dark about the plan as they can. Nobody, as a result, can do any work on their own because nobody knows where they are going.

I don't work for that second kind of director twice.

I wouldn't have stayed with *Jersey Boys* for a decade and a half if Des McAnuff weren't one of the former. He knows that I know what he wants and trusts me to give it to him. Sometimes I make mistakes. Sometimes he changes his mind about something. Sometimes I disagree with him. At the end of the day, however, it's his show. If he wants something a certain way, that's how it's done. He will, however, always, and I mean always, hear me out. Occasionally, not often mind you, but it has happened, he will say, "You were right."

This, from what I can see, is the kind of leader we now have in President Biden. He has thrown a lot of balls up into the air and he is trusting the remarkable people he has chosen to support him to do the actual juggling and keep them aloft. He will continually throw more and more balls into the mix. When some of them drop or when something happens to make the juggling that much more difficult, he will step in and help. Otherwise, he will leave them alone to do their jobs and they will report back on how things are going. Yesterday, I breathed a huge sigh of relief as I realized exactly who we had elected to run this country.

It feels like we are back. It feels like it is safe to come out of our houses. In short, it feels like, once again, we are living in the United States of America.

January 22, 2021
1,309,403 Total Reported Cases in New York. 41,786 Deaths.

We are in debt.

I can't say that I know what that means. The little I know is probably worse than knowing nothing at all. From a very early age, I have had an accountant do my taxes just so that I didn't have to know. About a decade ago I decided that I should learn how to take care of myself financially, and resolved to start doing it myself. That resolve lasted for just under an hour.

In that short time, I learned that to truly understand how to follow it all, I would need to go back to school.

By next year, our debt will surpass our GDP (Gross Domestic Product). That means that more money will be going out that will be coming in. The last time that happened was in 1946 after World War II. About $7 trillion of that debt, about a quarter of it, is held by other countries. The five countries that hold most of it are, in order from the top, Japan, China, the United Kingdom, Ireland, and Brazil. It is in those countries' best interest to lend us money. The stronger the dollar, the cheaper their goods are for us so the more we buy from them. Their economies need us to import their goods.

The higher the debt, though, the more uncertainty there is over whether we will be able to repay it. That can affect the markets and the confidence of investors. A certain amount of debt is seemingly good for everybody. How much, though, is too much? That is one of the endless debates that have been discussed since time immemorial.

The United States, as a country, has been in debt since 1790. In recent times, we have seen an almost predictable cycle of Republican administrations raising it and Democratic administrations lowering it or at least trying to. Republicans tend to cut taxes and then increase spending leaving it to the Democrats to have to re-raise those taxes to pay for it.

Under Reagan, the debt which had largely stabilized in the mid-70s in terms of its relative percentage of the GDP rose sharply to over 48%. Clinton got it back down to about 31%. It then went back up again under the second George Bush, who, of course, had cut taxes and then had the 2008 economic crisis hit at the end of his term. To combat that, the Obama administration was somewhat forced into raising the debt. It was at 43.8% when he entered office and at 75.9% when he left.

Then came the last President. His Tax Cuts and Jobs Act diminished revenue by easing the tax burden on the rich. As a result, our debt rose 4% in the first three years of his term, and then when the pandemic hit and the economy shut down, it ballooned up to where it is now at just about 100%.

There are four ways that the government can pay down this debt. They can cut government spending, they can raise taxes, they can speed up economic growth or they can shift spending to areas of the economy that will create more jobs. There is, of course, a fifth way, the country can default. Nobody wants the fifth way. Some combination of the other four is where the magic number lies.

The current push for the $1.9 trillion stimulus bill, while further raising the debt in the short term will hopefully lead to its lowering in the long term. It is designed to put more money into individual Americans' pockets which will allow them to spend it on goods and services which will then allow the providers of those goods and services to pay their employees who will then, in turn, use that money to buy more goods and services. And so on.

At some point, the Biden administration is probably going to have to raise taxes. In a way, they've been set up to have to do this by the previous administration. Presidents Clinton and Obama were put in the same position. Republican legislators are already hilariously starting to squawk about the ballooning debt. Last week it was all fine, but this week...? It looks like that the only way out of our current debt spiral is to dive deeper into it.

A friend of mine posted something online about how President Biden's Executive Order revoking the Keystone XL pipeline was a disaster because of the thousands of jobs that will be lost.

The reasons to quash the pipeline are good ones. Environmentally, pipelines are brutally destructive. Potential spills are a constant threat and are a danger to both wildlife and to the people who live near them. Add to that the availability of extra crude oil from Canada will only increase our reliance on fossil fuels and further slowdown our transition to alternate greener sources of energy.

There is, indeed, a cost to the President's decision and my friend is not wrong when he says that jobs will be lost both here and in Canada. In addition to jobs lost, one of the first things that our new President has done is take away a potential market from our neighbors to the north who need it badly. That is going to hurt their economy.

President Biden is due to make his first call to a foreign leader today. That call is going to be to Prime Minister Trudeau of Canada. I bet that this pipeline is going to be a major topic of conversation. Yes, there is a price to be paid for getting rid of Keystone XL and we are going to have to figure out a way to pay it.

It is so much better to be watching our government work, albeit in its usual slow and somewhat plodding way than it was worrying that we were going to be overrun by radical-right terrorists and shot on sight in the streets. We have lived with an overriding sense of that fear for so long that I feel somewhat adrift in its absence. While I know it isn't gone, and those people have not magically seen the light and converted to a less virulent form of thinking, it does seem that they have been somewhat sidelined—if only for the moment.

QAnon supporters who were all counting on the "storm" that was promised would unfold on January 20th are reeling. Q had told them that the former President was going to rain down his might and expose and bring down the deep state ring of child-trafficking Democrats. A new state was going to be born from the ashes and they would all rule.

Well instead, Q remained silent. Instead of raining down anything, the former President just slunk away down to Florida where he has been spotted playing golf. Quietly. Hundreds of insurgents from the January 6 uprising have either been arrested or are under investigation. Their friends, family, and neighbors are turning them all in.

The militias have been banished from popular social media sites and are trying to reach out to each other on other fringe sites. The founder of a message board called 8chan, who many suspect as possibly being the infamous Q, told believers to keep their chins up and get back to their lives.

The Proud Boys, the white supremacist misogynist militia who were among the staunchest supporters of the ex-President have now turned on him. Calling him, "extraordinarily weak," and saying that, "Trump will go down as a total failure," they seem uncertain of where to go next. Other militia groups, the Oath Keepers, America First, and the Three Percenters have also risen against him on the far-right messaging platforms.

We haven't seen the last of these groups by a long shot. We need to remain vigilant against the rise of another charismatic leader who could emerge to re-unite them. For the moment, though, they've at least been stunned. The former President is now facing a seemingly insurmountable wall of lawsuits. As he starts trying to get past them all, his former followers are going to be on the lookout for a new leader.

Like the lights in our apartment and the computer that I'm typing on, the government and our economy seem to function without me fully understanding how. I'm going out now to get coffee and dishwashing liquid and leave it to the people we just elected to figure out the details.

January 23, 2021
1,323,312 Total Reported Cases in New York. 41,950 Deaths.

It seems hard to believe that the inauguration was only three days ago. Everything seems to have become so normal so quickly.

At the beginning of the week, I was watching TV on the edge of my sofa completely convinced that some white cracker was going to try and take out our newly elected leaders before they could get into office. All through the inauguration, every single time the President or Vice President seemed to be out in the open I would grit my teeth until they got to someplace that seemed safer. I still can't believe that the whole thing went off without a hitch. But it did.

For the last couple of nights, I have slept very well.

This month is set to be the deadliest month of the pandemic that we have experienced so far. We will hit 25 million cases this weekend and we are already at well over 400 thousand people dead. New York state ran out of the vaccine yesterday although the Governor says more is coming.

Yesterday, British Prime Minister Boris Johnson announced that there is some evidence that the UK strain in addition to being easier to transmit, may also be deadlier. Danish scientists have discovered that the variant is already widespread in Europe, and it seems that it is probably here, too. Our testing levels are far too low to be able to truly tell.

Our new health officials are formulating a vaccine rollout plan. Imagine that.

JANUARY 25, 2020
1,347,667 Total Reported Cases in New York. 42,357 Deaths.

Friends of ours who were supposed to have been married overseas this past June have just pushed off their wedding until September of next year.

In a press release last week, Norwegian Cruise Lines announced that their suspension of global cruising was being extended until April 30th. As opposed to the airlines who are getting some business these days, albeit, at a far lower level, Norwegian and its sister companies are not able to operate at all during these suspensions. For them to get up and running, international travel is going to need to resume, and borders are going to need to be reopened.

President Biden has just announced that he is extending the ban on travel from all non-US citizens from The United Kingdom, Ireland, and 26 countries in Europe as well as instigating a ban on travelers from South Africa. US travelers coming from those countries will still need to have taken a COVID-19 test within three days of their flights and have the paperwork proving that they have tested negative. The last Administration had added a two-week waiver from having to do this that countries without adequate testing capability could apply for. That waiver option has now been taken away.

Moderna has said that their vaccine does appear to be somewhat less effective against the South African version of the virus. Reports are that its efficacy reduces from 95% to somewhere between 70 and 80%. In response to this, Moderna is developing a booster to specifically protect against it. That would mean a third shot might be necessary for each person.

Rochelle Walensky, the new Director of the Centers for Disease Control and Prevention has been at work now for six days. This is what she said in an interview on Fox News yesterday:

"I can't tell you how much vaccine we have and, if I can't tell it to you, then I can't tell it to the governors, and I can't tell it to the state health officials. If they don't know how much vaccine they're getting, not just this week but next week and the week after, they can't plan. They can't figure out how many sites to roll out, they can't figure out how many vaccinators that they need, and they can't figure out how many appointments to make for the public."

While her honesty and openness are beyond welcome, what she is saying is not necessarily easy to hear. The CDC Director was very blunt, "The fact that we don't know today — five days into this administration and weeks into planning — how much vaccine we have, just gives you a sense of the challenges we've been left with."

My mother had planned on taking the whole family on an Alaskan cruise last August. We were booked for a trip on a small 250 passenger ship which would have allowed us access to areas that the larger ships can't get to. In comparison, the Bliss, which is the ship *Jersey Boys* is on, holds 4,500 passengers. It's one of the largest passenger ships on the planet and, therefore, is limited in where it can go.

Our cruise was postponed until this June, but I cannot imagine a scenario that will end with us getting on board a ship in June. I am ready for at least another road trip, but not until the country gets its collective wits about it first. For the moment, I am just going to curl up on the couch with the cat and plan where I'll go today on my walk. I'll take advantage of the bright and clear day ahead of me and get out there and make my own adventure.

January 26, 2021
1,358,707 Total Reported Cases in New York. 42,537 Deaths.

We are due to get some snow flurries any minute. Outside, it is dark and rather dreary. Inside the apartment, it is chilly enough that the cat has forsaken me and is curled up against the radiator.

The cat can count on one of us being in the apartment nearly all the time. There are moments when he seems sick of us, but for the most part, he seems happy to have us as permanent laps to sleep on. I have a bit more patience for him than Michael does. I'll adjust my position either in bed or on the couch to make him more comfortable, Michael usually won't.

The cat is not the only one who seems happy with our routines. I think that both of us are too. Periodically, discussions about various work projects pop up and my first thought is, "oh I hope that this doesn't happen too soon." Not that I wouldn't take a job now, but if it doesn't happen until spring, or summer, or next fall, then that's OK, too.

The news about our government gets more complicated the further we get away from the simple good vs. evil paradigm that we lived under for so long. There were no gray areas then, but now it all seems to be gray.

When the Founding Fathers created the Constitution, they envisioned that most of the business of the House and the Senate would be passed by a simple majority of its members' votes. There are several exceptions to that which they stated explicitly. Conviction on impeachment charges, expelling a congressional member, overriding Presidential vetoes, ratifying treaties, and Constitutional amendments would all require a 2/3 majority in both houses to pass.

Alexander Hamilton fought against the idea of the 2/3 majority, or super-majority, requirements in other regards. "The public business must, in some way or other, go forward. If a pertinacious minority can control the opinion of a majority, respecting the best mode of conducting it, the majority, in order that something may be done, must conform to the views of the minority; and thus, the sense of the smaller number will overrule that of the greater, and give a tone to the national proceedings. Hence, tedious delays; continual negotiation and intrigue; contemptible compromises of the public good."

The very first US Senate created a rule that a simple majority could vote to end a debate and therefore vote on the question. Aaron Burr, however, argued that it was an unnecessary and redundant rule and convinced his fellow Senators to vote against it.

This then left open the possibility for a filibuster. A filibuster is when a Senator tries to block or delay a vote by extending the discussion of it. Senate rules allow any Senator to speak on any topic for as long as they choose.

In the classic film, *Mr. Smith Goes to Washington*, Jimmy Stewart, who plays a naïve Junior Senator from an unnamed western state who is unfairly thought to be guilty of graft, famously filibusters for 25 straight hours before he passes out. His doing so eventually leads the actual corrupt Senator to finally admit his guilt regarding a fraudulent land scheme.

The filibuster is a favored tactic of the Republican Senate Minority Leader. He used it countless times during Obama's terms in office to obstruct and delay legislation.

Going into this new Administration, Republicans, who had been in the majority still controlled the Senate committees. The now-Senate Minority Leader was unwilling to give that up, in large part because he was afraid that if he did, Democrats would vote to abolish the filibuster.

Yesterday, after two Democratic Senators signaled that they would not support abolishing the filibuster, the Senate Minority Leader agreed to implement a power-sharing arrangement like the one that had been established in 2001.

The Senate committees will now be evenly divided which, maybe more than anything else, will require them all to work together. Moving forward, both sides will want to achieve things and this, at least, ensures that they will need to compromise on some things if they want their own legislation to get through the process. Abolishing the filibuster is not off the table, but for now, there do not appear to be enough votes to do so.

The snow has started. It's going to start to warm up a bit this evening, so I don't think that any of it is going to stick. The trees outside our windows are waving in the wind and the flakes are swirling around like mad. The cat is back in his usual midday spot on the bed near where Michael is working. He knows that I am going to leave soon, and that Michael will still be here. He doesn't always need to be on one of us, but he does like being at least near one of us.

He can sleep through almost anything. Most of the normal noise we make doesn't bother him at all. Even when we get loud, if it is something that we do every day, he doesn't even twitch an ear. It's only if something out of the ordinary happens, like one of us dropping something, that he'll startle.

Nothing much startles me these days either. Very little keeps me from following the same schedule every gray day. There's comfort in that. As days like this accumulate, I can see the trend of things being accomplished continue. Slowly but surely. It's satisfying and I'm fine with doing it for a while longer.

January 27, 2021
1,369,072 Total Reported Cases in New York. 42,699 Deaths.

Wearing a mask outside during these very cold days has proven to be a great way to keep warm. I have a distinct memory of a Halloween when I was young, and I dressed up as Casper the Friendly Ghost. I must have been seven or eight years old at the time. My store-bought costume came with a molded plastic face mask. I remember trick or treating with that mask and having the chin continually fill up with the condensation from my breath. Periodically, I would need to empty it. It was so warm and uncomfortable with the mask on that I ended up keeping it up on top of my head and only brought it down when we got to someone's front door. Almost every time that I am out walking, that memory comes back to me as I often find myself needing to lift my mask over my bearded chin to cool down and dry off.

Last night I had a dream where I was the only person present not wearing a mask. In the dream, I was driving an electric convertible through the carpeted back hallways of some sort of large church looking for the box office. As one does. There was going to be some sort of performance and the cast, all dressed in grey knitted robes that looked like armor were all lying around on the carpeting waiting for the show to begin. I had to get them out of the way so that my car could get through. All of them were wearing masks and I wasn't, so I kept trying to hide the fact by covering my mouth and nose with my hand, but it wasn't working. And then I woke up.

As I walk around the city, I rarely come across anyone who isn't wearing a mask. The actual mandate says that you are required to wear a mask anytime that you are unable to maintain proper social distancing. In my experience, though, most people are just wearing them all the time regardless of how many people are around them.

Dr. Deborah Birx was interviewed on Sunday by Face the Nation. In the interview, she dropped several bombshells.

She said that despite assurances to the contrary, that she was the only person working full time on combating the virus. She said that she would see charts and graphs get distributed that she had nothing to do with. Many times, that material contradicted the facts that she knew, at the time, to be true. Her ideas and strategies were disregarded. She said that she was routinely prevented from sharing what she knew with the American public.

As alarming as all of that is, the response from many people has been to condemn her for not speaking up sooner. She is being blamed for helping to enable the former President and his supporters from doing anything to fight the pandemic.

You are invaded. Do you collaborate or do you resist? It turns out that none of the choices, in either direction, are good. The answer isn't at all clear. If Dr. Birx had spoken up last year and been replaced by someone like Scott Atlas would that have helped anything? Was it better to have someone like her in there or should she have left?

When I think of Dr. Birx, I think of the press conference during which the then-President suggested that injecting bleach might be a way of cleansing the body from infection. Dr. Birx, who was sitting on the sidelines, jumped a little but did everything she could to remain neutral in the face of such an idiotically dangerous suggestion. In a way, that is what she did the whole time she served. We had to try and glean the truth from what she wasn't saying.

Was it better to have her in there or did her position give legitimacy to a group of people who should have been exposed? Dr. Birx was in an impossible situation and regardless of how it played out. I don't know that the question is answerable.

However late it is, I am so grateful that we now have seemingly honest reporting coming to us from our health officials. We can thank ourselves for that. It's one of the things we got when we went out and voted. We have the power to take care of ourselves and each other. Wearing a mask is one of the simplest and easiest things that we can do. Does it solve the problem? No, not by a longshot, but the data suggests that it helps, and we should all be willing to help.

JANUARY 28, 2021
1,382,055 Total Reported Cases in New York. 42,905 Deaths.

Michael's out for a walk this morning.

We've hit that point in winter where the trees are completely bare and there's very little color to be seen anywhere. The city looks like it's been filmed in black and white. Not like the lush and saturated palate that Gordon Willis used in *Manhattan*, but more like a color picture whose colors have just faded out. Central Park is a spectrum of greys that range from a dull sepia brown to a dark shadowy grey that has somewhat yellowed over time.

New York City will look like this for months to come. Occasionally there will be a day amongst the endless cloudy ones where the sky stretches overhead in an unreal photoshopped blue, but that only seems to highlight the fact that nothing below it has any real color.

This time of year, in theatre, is usually one of the busiest. Shows that were just holding on for the holiday bump would have closed and new shows would be starting to be rehearsed to open within the next few weeks before the award-eligibility window closes. Existing shows would all be rehearsing new cast members to replace those who had left to work on the ones coming up. Old marquees would be coming down and new ones going up replacing them.

We wouldn't notice the starkness outside because we would all be inside darkened theatres or brightly lit rehearsal studios focused on the worlds of our plays. We would be aiming for spring and the excitement of the many opening nights ahead.

This time last year, I was in Tampa where we were doing run-throughs with the newest cast of the Norwegian Cruise Lines version of *Jersey Boys*. On this same day, while I was in the studio in Tampa, a delegation from the World Health Organization was traveling to China to meet with its leadership about a new virus that had been detected in the Wuhan province the month before. They were there to gather information about it and to offer their assistance. On that day, the first report of limited human-to-human transmission had been reported outside of China.

After that meeting in China, the WHO Emergency Committee recommended to the Director-General that the outbreak be termed a Public Health Emergency of International Concern or a PHEIC. Their report which was published two days later said that there were 7,818 cases of the virus worldwide—82 of which were in 18 countries other than China.

On this day, a year ago, the rest of us were all blissfully unaware of what was to come.

The new President's honeymoon appears to be officially over.

Republican lawmakers are, unsurprisingly, now attacking him for the Executive Actions he has been issuing. I cannot imagine that President Biden expected anything less. He's worked in Washington for decades. He understands its machinery. Republicans wouldn't be attacking him if he wasn't being effective.

The long-overdue raising of the minimum wage is particularly sticking in the GOP's craw.

Their panicked objections make it sound like the minimum wage will rise to $15 an hour tomorrow and bankrupt small businesses. Instead, the proposal is to raise it slowly and steadily over the next several years. The last time it was raised was in 2009, nearly twelve years ago. Twelve. Cost-of-living expenses have certainly skyrocketed over that time. It's time we kept up.

The South African variant of the virus has now been detected in South Carolina. The people who got it are not travelers, so they got it from somebody else. That means that it is already circulating through the population.

Michael is back from his walk. My turn next.

JANUARY 29, 2021
1,395,806 Total Reported Cases in New York. 43,090 Deaths.

It is truly cold this morning. Seriously cold. Alert on my phone cold. Cat refuses to leave my lap cold.

The White House COVID relief team has just begun their morning presentation. Dr. Fauci went on for at least ten minutes about mutant strains of the virus and the effectiveness of the various vaccines that are out there against them.

In essence what he seems to be saying this morning is that, yes, the virus is mutating and yes, some of the new strains are somewhat more resistant to existing vaccines. The new Johnson & Johnson vaccine is not as effective against preventing infection from the South African variant, but it is still quite effective at keeping those who do contract it from becoming seriously ill and or hospitalized.

The tone of these briefings is remarkable. They are thoughtful and calm. You can hear in the reporters' voices that they are no longer scared that they are going to be cut off. They aren't fighting for position with their fellow reporters knowing that only one or two carefully chosen questions are going to be allowed to be asked before everyone vanishes. They aren't going to be personally belittled. Their publications aren't going to be mocked.

In my position on a production, I am often privy to information that the cast and crew aren't.

I try and be as honest as I can with everyone, but sometimes I am just not allowed to say what I know. On one occasion, I had to deal with some cast members on a show who were extremely angry about the way something was being dealt with by the powers that be. They did not want what was happening to continue as the show moved forward and wanted to know what I was going to do about it.

What they didn't know was that by the end of the day it was going to be announced that the show was closing in two weeks and the whole situation would be moot. I wasn't allowed to tell them before the producers announced it themselves.

The best that I could say to them was, "I'll see what I can do," which was a less than satisfying response at the time.

It is remarkable to me how remarkable I continue to think it is that the President is allowing the people who work with him to do their jobs. He sees these people as working with him and not, as was the case with his predecessor, as working for him. The President has yet to publicly interfere with how those around him are working. He has also yet to go golfing.

In short, the machinery of our government seems to be moving forward. We won't all agree with what they are doing, but at least they are doing it. The best thing of all, and we should be truly, truly grateful for this, is that the whole thing is just, gloriously, a little bit boring.

January 30, 2021
1,408,698 Total Reported Cases in New York. 43,268 Deaths.

The first full week of the new Administration has now drawn to a close.

In Washington D.C., there are still fences and barricades up around the White House and the Capitol building. There are discussions in progress about whether they should all remain.

With members' safety a serious concern, law enforcement is hesitant to remove them.

Remarkably, it is still not illegal for Representatives to have firearms within the Capitol. Many, however, are concerned about optics. Do we want to be seen as living in a police state?

I've wondered when all the security around the ex-President's buildings here in New York would be taken away. For the first few days after the inauguration, I walked past them hoping to see it being dismantled. That hasn't happened yet. The answer I got from the officers standing there when I asked when we could expect it to go, was that they didn't know. It seems that the Secret Service and NYPD are going to evaluate the ongoing concern. At one point during the last four years, security around those buildings was costing the city over $300,000 a day.

I remember when I was a kid, and we went to London. At that time, you could walk right into Downing Street and knock on the Prime Minister's front door if you wanted to. Somewhere, I am sure that I have a picture of me standing right in front of the door. Now, of course, you cannot enter the street at all. There is a large iron gate and sentries posted next to it around the clock.

After the election of 2016, the iron fence around the White House was replaced by one that was higher. I watched it going up. As the election of 2020 drew closer, that fence was then covered up with panels that shield the building from the street.

Abraham Lincoln said at Gettysburg that, "the government of the people, by the people, for the people, shall not perish from the earth." That, of course, remains to be seen. What I don't think that even he imagined, was that the government would need to be hidden from the people and need to be protected from the very people who should be fighting for it.

Almost all the last President's legislation that he enacted during his Presidency was erased last week with a few simple strokes of President Biden's pen. The only thing that he can point to that still stands, besides a few uncompleted sections of his Mexican border wall, is a tax break for his wealthy friends. His legacy is a United States that is now faced with having to protect itself from itself.

After the IRA assassinated Lord Mountbatten in 1979, Margaret Thatcher increased the security on Downing Street that then prevented ordinary people from entering. I don't know that young Britons even realize that you could once freely walk in there. We may be living with the same kind of security measures here for a long time to come as well. It's probably going to be a while before any of us can take a selfie in front of the White House from anywhere nearby. The security measures around 10 Downing Street were never relaxed and I fear that these won't be either.

I do look forward to being able to walk down 5th Avenue without the mess surrounding the ex-President's tower in the way. I am sure the businesses nearby do too. They've all suffered from the reduced access. Thankfully, that building no longer has anything to do with our government so maybe once we are past the impeachment trial, it will clear up a bit.

In the meantime, I guess, I'll just walk elsewhere.

FEBRUARY 1, 2021
1,428,839 Total Reported Cases in New York. 43,622 Deaths.

As I was setting the table for dinner last night, I couldn't believe that I was already setting the table for dinner. Again. What happened to the day?

This feeling of being trapped in an endless repetitive loop comes in what I now see as a repetitive cycle, itself. I'll feel stuck one day, then be fine for a week or two and then I'll feel stuck again. Something that I put off until tomorrow, can sit around for a week before I get to it, and yet it feels like, when I do, that I had just set it aside the day before.

There are some days when I feel like there are things that I can point to that I've accomplished. Then there are others where I find myself setting the table—the beginning of the finale of the day's ride—and I don't seem to have a single thing to point to that I've done.

Groundhog Day isn't until tomorrow. It's hitting me a day early.

Today's iteration of the schedule has been somewhat thrown off by a massive snowstorm that slammed into us last night. When I went to sleep, there was some accumulation in protected areas around our building, but the streets were still clear. I expected to wake up to a few inches of snow on an otherwise clear day, but instead, it's a full-out storm. It's meant to continue all day and into tomorrow.

It is coming down. The weather forecast says we could see it fall at rates of as much as 2 inches an hour before it stops. Looking out, this morning, I believe it. Usually, flakes of snow flutter somewhat slowly down to the ground. This morning the snow is dropping like it is rain. Gusts of wind blow them around for a moment but then it just dumps.

I do love mornings like this when it's dark. Michael was prepping bread to bake last night and was up at all hours, so he is still asleep. When I woke up and got out of bed, the cat looked at me for a moment but then curled up tighter against him. I don't hear traffic noise or sirens outside because the streets are largely impassable.

As I was walking yesterday, I suddenly came across a small crowd loosely gathered in front of a storefront window across Broadway from Lincoln Center. Inside, two musicians, one on the piano and the other with a viola, were playing a duet. They are part of a series called *Musical Storefronts* presented by Kaufman Music Center. I know that because, instead of a program, it was written right on the glass. They were wonderful. At the end of their piece, we all clapped. It was a bit muffled because we were wearing gloves and mittens, but it was heartfelt.

Live music is a rare commodity these days. Every so often there will be a small group performing at an outdoor restaurant, but as it's gotten colder, that's become much more infrequent. I didn't realize how much I miss it.

I never would have imagined that a time would come when we would all willingly sit outside at a restaurant in the dead of winter and eat a meal with our coats on and be happy about it.

Even during this past week when the temperatures were routinely below freezing, there were people outside chatting and enjoying a meal. Huddling around a central heat lamp to eat seems to be an accepted part of our lives now. Our prehistoric ancestors did much the same thing around their campfires for millions of years, so why shouldn't we?

This weekend, the President's lawyers all quit. He has found two more. Planning for the second impeachment trial which starts a week from today continues in full force. The guy from the insurrection in the war paint and horns seems to be desperate to testify against anything and anyone that will save his hide.

There are reports that there has been a military coup in Myanmar. Nobel laureate Aung San Suu Kyi has been taken into custody.

The snow is coming down so thickly that I can barely see across the street. On days like this, it is easy to feel that all of "that" is happening in a nebulous "out there" place. In here, in the warm, as we get more and more snowed in, all of it seems a bit unreal. Thankfully, it vanishes when the TV is turned off. Click.

FEBRUARY 2, 2021
1,436,788 Total Reported Cases in New York. 43,793 Deaths.

Tom Stoppard, the playwright, gave a lecture that I went to at the American Museum of Natural History way back in the dim and dusty recesses of time. It must have been when I was working there in the gift shop in the very early 1980s. At the end of his talk, somebody asked him if he minded when a production of one of his plays veered from what he originally imagined and was presented differently from the original one.

He responded by saying that, in some ways, he felt that his job was more like that of an architect than anything else. Like somebody who designs a house that may get replicated many times in a development, he felt his task was to create a sound structure that could stand on its own. After that, how it got decorated was somebody else's job. If its bones were sturdy, it didn't matter what color its walls were painted. Part of the joy of the experience for him was seeing what furniture people choose to move into the house and what art they hung on the walls. Sometimes they put up additional partitions inside that made two rooms where one had been intended. Sometimes they added in a picture window.

Hamlet, he said, has been done a million different ways over the last centuries. Despite being set in outer space or a brothel, the play has endured unscathed.

That discussion came into my mind as I was trudging through the snow out on my walk yesterday. For the first time in my memory, we have all, the world over, been handed the same obstacle to deal with—in this case, a new virus that spreads easily through the population—but we have all reacted differently to it and had to figure out a way to live with what it's wrought.

Our individual experiences since last March have been radically different. Even Michael and I, who have been living together in the same apartment this whole time are forging our unique paths through it.

I had a phone conversation with a friend of mine who has been remarkably busy through all of this—completely online. Together with other friends on Zoom, she wrote a play. She has created a popular YouTube channel. My friend has had what looks like a very successful year without her ever having left her apartment. Despite that, it is, quite simply, as my friend said, lonely.

We are designed to be social creatures. The insidiousness of this virus is that it is that very need that we all have, to physically connect, that allows it to spread. The AIDS virus stopped us from having sex for a while until we figured out how to protect ourselves, but this one is stopping us from shaking hands with each other. Even the act of breathing near each other is potentially dangerous.

From inside our bubbles, we can look out at others who seem to have it all and compare it to what we have and despair at the difference. They are probably, however, looking out from where they are and doing the same. The people who have been with their families in the same space since March are likely just as desperate to reconnect with other people as those who have been on their own.

Michael and I have now been together more than we ever have over the entire decade and a half that we've been a couple. We eat almost all our meals together. We watch TV together and we sleep together. The rest of the day, we are by ourselves. Even if I can hear him in the other room, we have figured out how to have our own spaces.

I was with my ex for nearly twenty years and now I've been with Michael for over fifteen years. If I wanted to live completely by myself, I would not choose to be in these relationships. My job took me away from home for sometimes months at a time. In all that time Michael and I can probably count on the fingers of one hand the days that we didn't talk or text or FaceTime with each other at least once.

I like being alone. I'm usually happy with my own company. Up to a point. Most of my time away from home these days has been spent walking around the city. I enjoy being part of a crowd without being part of the crowd—not an actual crowd, mind you, I have very little patience for that, but the normal crowds that you encounter, in daily life. I like the energy of people around me who are living their lives.

It's still snowing outside this morning, but only in flurries. Punxsutawney Phil, the Pennsylvania groundhog, saw his shadow this morning, so we are getting another six weeks of winter. He was awoken at 7:25 am and made his prediction in front of a small group of the Punxsutawney Groundhog Club at Gobbler's Knob. I did take a long walk yesterday. Central Park in the snow is truly lovely. There were a lot of families out with their kids sledding down the few small hills that weren't flattened out by the people who first built the city centuries ago.

I look around at how everyone else is getting through this time and sometimes I am somewhat envious and sometimes, not at all. None of our lives are all that similar even though we have all been subject to the same overall restrictions. I'm happy, though, with the straw I've pulled. I'm grateful for it. New York City, even with its issues, has proven to be the best place for me to watch the events of this past year unfold. It probably wouldn't be for everyone.

The cat woke Michael up early this morning to be fed even though there was plenty of food still in his bowl. Michael had to get up and rearrange the food to the cat's liking. After that, he couldn't get back to sleep. He's somewhat annoyed. He's in the kitchen, now, making breakfast and he and the cat are exchanging words. In its own way, it's everything. Despite it all, I'm, indeed, utterly grateful. Grateful for him, grateful for the cat, even grateful for this time.

FEBRUARY 3, 2021
1,443,942 Total Reported Cases in New York. 43,959 Deaths.

The cat is sitting under the dining table staring at me in utter confusion. I've thrown him this morning by waking up before he could wake up Michael. He's now been fed, and he has nothing left to do until 5 pm when he will get fed again. He's at a total loss.

The news channels are gearing up for the impending impeachment trial by re-showing clips from the rally where the ex-President incited his followers to storm the Capitol. I don't want to look at footage of the man. I want to move on. It's only been a couple of weeks, but I already cannot believe that he was our President.

During World War I, the Allies came up with the idea that at the end of the war, defeated enemy leaders should be held accountable for international law violations. At the Paris Peace Conference, they established a Commission of Responsibilities to recommend how best to do that.

In 1921, the Leipzig War Crimes Trials were held. Only 12 defendants were charged and only some were found guilty. At the time, the trials were considered a failure, but they did establish a precedent that was then expanded upon in World War II.

In 1943, during the new war, the US, along with the UK and the Soviet Union published the "Declaration on German Atrocities in

Occupied Europe." In it, they warned the Germans that when the Nazis were defeated that they would, "pursue them to the uttermost ends of the earth ... so that justice may be done."

The first of the Nuremberg Trials was held in 1946. Twelve more followed. By the end, 199 people were accused. 161 were convicted and 37 were sentenced to death. There were subsequent tribunals set up in Russia and Japan. Some argued that the trials were unfair because in several cases the Nazis were being accused of crimes that weren't formally established as crimes when they perpetrated them. Nonetheless, the trials were a turning point in international law. For the first time, it was decided that individuals could be held responsible and punished for their participation in state-sponsored crimes.

At the end of Apartheid, South Africa chose to do something completely different. They established a Truth and Reconciliation Commission. Victims of human rights violations under the ruling White government could give testimony as could the perpetrators of those violations.

In large part, the TRC is considered to have been effective. The question as to whether its restorative justice was more successful than the retributive justice of the Nuremberg trials remains an open one. And that's what we here in the United States are grappling with now as this 2nd impeachment trial gets underway. What is this trial going to do for US? What are we going to get out of it?

A few weeks ago, Senator Rand Paul of Kentucky warned that a third of Republican voters would leave the party if Senators voted to impeach the former President. A week ago, he forced a vote on the Senate floor to decide the simple question on whether the impeachment trial against the former President was Constitutional. 45 Republican Senators voted that it was not.

As much as I would rather that all of this was over, I will admit to being intrigued to see just how deep these GOP Senators are going to dig themselves in. I don't want to even look at pictures of the ex-President anymore, but I guess we should get ready to watch it. I don't know if this impeachment trial can bring this era in our history to a close, but it will certainly have some lasting effects.

Michael's popping some corn. We're going to need snacks for this.

February 4, 2021
1,450,912 Total Reported Cases in New York. 44,109 Deaths.

Yesterday turned out to be a day of pulling things together. Something must have triggered it, because suddenly we were organizing receipts, putting things into storage in the basement, bringing down the garbage, and recycling, and I cut my hair again.

As we tidied up, Republicans in Washington were deciding how they are going to move forward.

In an op-ed piece, Mark Sanford, the former Republican Governor of South Carolina made a clear case for where he believes they need to go. Calling the last four years, "an unmitigated disaster," he outlines five things that he believes Republicans need to do if they are to survive. Adhere to the truth and reject the acceptance of so-called "alternate facts." Establish a tone that is not tone-deaf. Re-embrace reason, faith, and common sense. Re-embrace science. Re-embrace math. Not only do these proposals seem reasonable they also all seem blatantly obvious. There is, however, no indication that the Republicans, as a Party, are going to embrace any of them.

President Biden is planning on visiting the State Department today to outline his foreign policy objectives. Refreshingly, he hasn't sent out a single tweet insulting anyone. Not today and not at any time since he was elected.

Maybe he'll be able to get some things done, today, too.

FEBRUARY 5, 2021

1,458,809 Total Reported Cases in New York. 44,277 Deaths.

The sound that the boiling water from the electric kettle makes when it pours into one of the chrome coffee-presses that I bought on sale for Michael for his birthday one year, is the sound that, for me, heralds the beginning of a new day.

Michael's and my gifts to each other tend to be completely hit or miss, but those two coffee presses were a hit. I found them one day when I was walking to work in London. Just down the street from where I usually stay near Covent Garden is a strange little shop that sells a lot of sailing supplies. I have no idea what it's doing on Shaftsbury Avenue hidden in a small row of little places or how it's been able to survive, but it always makes me happy when I see that it's still there.

That day, as I was walking by on my way to some auditions, I saw the coffee presses in the window at about 10% of their usual price. Not 10% off, 90% off. The only problem with them is that one had a baby blue handle and the other one had a baby pink one—not our colors. Regardless, we love them, and we've used them almost every day for at least a decade.

Several times over the years, Michael and I have walked past the shop, and I never fail to say, "That's where I got the coffee presses." We always stop for a moment to look in the window just in case there's another treasure waiting in there among the weird collection of yachting cleats and ropes.

Yesterday, the Republicans formerly chose the direction that they are going to head in for the coming years. While the motion in the House passed to strip Marjorie Taylor Green of her committee assignments, 199 Republican Representatives voted against it. 199 Republican lawmakers wholeheartedly threw their support behind antisemitism, QAnon conspiracy theories, 9/11 denial, school shooting denial, and the Big Lie of election fraud.

With the support of 199 of her fellow Republicans, Marjorie Taylor Green has now become a celebrity and a symbol of victimhood by oppression from the left. She has been catapulted into the national spotlight. She claims to have raised $1.6 million from her followers over the last week or so. Far from being chastised by this move, she is elated. "How stupid they are. They don't even realize they're helping me. I'm pretty amazed at how dumb they are," she said of the Democrats in an interview a couple of days ago.

Whatever happens in the future, yesterday was the moment that she and the ex-President could have been stopped. And they weren't. Oh well.

There is now a whole symphony of sounds coming from the kitchen. Michael's cracking an egg into a small enamel bowl that I found somewhere in Provence. The plates that we were given as a Christmas present one year by Michael's family clatter together as he takes them out of the cupboard. The high notes of the cutlery in their drawer sing in counterpoint to the clanks of the glass lids of Michael's cooking pots.

In traditional Japanese meals, a multitude of food is served in small, mismatched bowls and plates—all beautifully designed and crafted. Over the years I have picked up so many bowls and plates from so many different places that we end up doing the same. Michael had several of his own that he got long before he met me. None of them match, but each one has its own story, and they all go together in their own eccentric ways.

Every one of those bowls and each dish makes a different sound when Michael sets them down on the table, brimming with the day's food he's made. My husband conducts a mean symphony in the kitchen. It's the sound of our lives and however it goes, it begins every morning with some variation of the same thing.

Where will this morning's music take us? We'll have to see.

February 6, 2021

1,470.301 Total Reported Cases in New York. 44,478 Deaths.

On top of one of the low white storage units along the wall of one side of our front hall, we have a very heavy carved wooden, seemingly old, Chinese duck.

I say it's Chinese, but in truth, I have no idea where it's from. Rather than being depicted realistically, it is somewhat abstract with distinct sharp angles and it is carved with a saddle on its back. In the Hindu religion, there is a bird called a Hamsa which translates from Sanskrit, from what I read, to mean some sort of bird of passage like a goose or a flamingo. It is believed to be the vehicle of Brahma and others. So, I guess it could depict one of those and be from India. At any rate, this solid and weighty wooden duck sits in our front hall and I'm embarrassed to say that it's where I usually hang my bicycle helmet.

The duck was a gift to Michael from Christopher Plummer.

Michael appeared in the play *Barrymore* with him back in 1996 up in Stratford, Canada, and then again on Broadway and, then briefly on tour. *Barrymore* was ostensibly a one-man play about the actor John Barrymore rehearsing a revival of his big hit, *Richard III*, but Michael played a second character—the offstage voice of a stage manager named Frank. He was invisible for the entire show except during the curtain call when he would join Chris on stage for a bow.

They worked together for over a year, but I only met him once long after. We saw the revival of *Inherit the Wind* that he did on Broadway with Brian Dennehy, who, himself, passed away last year, and we went backstage afterward to say hello. Chris was very fond of Michael and seemed very happy to see him. When we got there, he was already talking to a somewhat stooped and elderly lady. After she left, he told us, with a twinkle in his eye, that she had played a vestal virgin in one of his very early films, *The Fall of the Roman Empire*.

Aside from *Inherit the Wind*, I saw him on stage in *Macbeth* alongside Glenda Jackson and then again up in Stratford in a truly wonderful production of *Caesar and Cleopatra* opposite Nikki James and as Prospero in *The Tempest*. The latter two were directed by Des McAnuff. Des and Chris had a long and happy working relationship and were good friends.

In the last weeks, we have lost several other spectacular actors—all of whom were in their nineties. Cloris Leachman, Hal Holbrook, and the incomparable Cicely Tyson all passed in the last two weeks. All of them, along with Mr. Plummer, created unforgettable characters that are an integral part of our cultural life. All of them enjoyed careers that spanned almost countless decades. Between them, they are responsible for some of the most indelible performances I have ever seen.

There is a lot that remains unknown about both the virus and now, the vaccine. We won't know how long it remains effective until enough time passes, and it stops being effective. It seems that having COVID gives you antibodies for just a few months. When Michael was tested a few months ago, there was no evidence that he still had them from our bouts with it back in March of last year. On the other hand, we have some friends who still have the antibodies many months after having come down with the virus. The simple truth of the moment is that nobody knows for sure what, beyond, throwing some obstacles in the virus's way, these vaccines are going to do.

Given that we now have a President, whose policies are rooted in science, we are finally getting some leadership by example. The anti-vaxxers will not get the vaccine but maybe natural selection will take care of that.

In the meantime, life continues its steady slog forward. Even though we are due for another round of snow tomorrow, it is a beautiful day out there today. Today, a walk. Tomorrow, when it snows, might be the perfect time to re-watch *The Sound of Music*. Christopher Plummer didn't care for it very much, but despite that, as he feared, it was in the headlines of most of his obituaries.

Michael has some wonderful stories about working with Christopher Plummer, but they are his to tell, so I won't repeat them here. Unfortunately, when it came time to film *Barrymore*, Michael was no longer doing the show, so another actor played his role. He does, however, mention Michael several times in his autobiography, *In Spite of Myself*.

I know I should find another spot for my helmet, but really, the duck is the perfect place.

RIP Christopher Plummer.

FEBRUARY 8, 2021
1,489,196 Total Reported Cases in New York. 44,781 Deaths.

Central Park was as beautiful yesterday as I have ever seen it. It snowed for most of the day in big sticky flakes that clung to everything. The whole park was outlined in white making a stark contrast between the bright fluffy snow and the dark outlines of the leafless trees. Had we gotten any more snow everything would have just been covered. Had it been windier or warmer, nothing would have stuck. As it was, conditions were perfect, and photographers were out in droves. As much as I didn't want to go out in the storm, once I did, I was more than happy to be there.

We don't get this much snow in the city in most years. Yesterday's snow was the third of the season and we are already meant to get some more starting tomorrow and then again later in the week.

I've only been cross-country skiing once and that was when I was in college, spending my Junior year abroad. I went with some friends over a break to a small ski resort in Switzerland. The conditions there were much as they were here yesterday—a fresh dusting of snow over packed older snow. We had a blast skiing on picture-perfect trails through the Alps.

Everywhere we were looked like the picture on a tin of Swiss chocolates. As fun as it was, cross-country skiing is exhausting, and I ached for days afterward. Central Park was every bit as beautiful as the Alps, yesterday, more so, maybe, because it was so unexpected.

The ex-President's impeachment trial starts tomorrow. It's going to suck a lot of air out of the room. As their main argument, his defense team is likely going to focus on whether impeaching a President is constitutional.

As much as we are all sick of hearing about the insurrection and even about the ex-President, himself, the results of this trial must be definitive. In 1923, Adolph Hitler attempted to launch a revolution in what was called the Munich Putsch. The country was suffering from deprivation due to hyperinflation. The Nazi party, at the time, had over 50,000 members. Like what we are experiencing here in the US, different geographical areas of what was then the Weimar Republic had different political views. The majority of Bavaria was Catholic and conservative. They saw the Weimar Republic as being weak.

Hitler plotted with two nationalist politicians to take advantage of this and take over Munich, the capital of Bavaria, using his loyal followers. At the last minute, the two politicians changed their minds and called the whole thing off. Hitler then broke into a meeting and holding them at gunpoint, forced them to change their minds. Hitler and his brownshirts marched on Munich but the two politicians had alerted the police and army to be ready and he was defeated.

The response to this was to ban the Nazi party and prevent Hitler from speaking publicly until 1927. He was sentenced to five years in prison. He only served eight months of the sentence in a relatively comfortable prison during which he wrote *Mein Kampf*. That book was subsequently read by millions of Germans.

The leniency shown to him indicated that there was support for him among the higher authorities.

Once out of prison, Hitler changed tactics. Instead of armed revolution, he figured out how to gain power using the political system. He rearranged the Nazi party, and we all know the rest. It is possible to look back at that trial in 1923 and see that had he been more forcibly punished and removed from the public eye and his revolution taken more seriously, that history might be very different.

I suppose I should mention the Super Bowl. We didn't watch it. We did, however, watch the opening. Amanda Gorman became the first poet to perform at a Super Bowl when she spoke at the beginning of the game. She was thrilling. I am guessing that Michael and I are in the decided minority of people who tuned in to the biggest football game of the year only to see the poet.

FEBRUARY 9, 2021
California surpasses New York as the state with the highest number of COVID deaths.

Zoochosis is the word that is used to explain the repetitive pacing that large animals do in captivity. It is a repetitive behavior pattern without a goal. In zoo animals, it can be a sign of stress or depression. Back and forth, back, and forth, a caged tiger will walk in a never-ending circle around its enclosure—up on a rock, off the other side, around the corner, along the glass, across the back, up on the rock, off the other side, around the corner, along the glass, across the back, up on the rock, off the other side, around the corner, along the glass, across the back, up on the rock… endlessly.

In the wild, these large animals can range over hundreds of miles. In their tiny enclosures, there are only so many places that they can go. New York City is now starting to feel like a cage. It is becoming harder and harder to see it because it feels like on some days that I am just pacing through it.

When the museums reopened, there was finally a destination to go to. Sure, I had to get to the museum, but once there, I could be inspired by what was within and take a journey beyond myself. Unfortunately, museums don't turn over their exhibitions all that often. Once they have been curated and installed, the same paintings and sculptures remain in place for many months. Walking through familiar galleries starts to feel like its own kind of pacing.

Even as I write this, I am telling myself to just wander further afield. Why follow familiar paths when there are still many parts of Manhattan that I have never visited before?

The physical exploration of a place is just half of the reward of a journey. It's what you find once you get there that makes the journey complete. For nearly a year now, at the end of almost every physical journey in New York, what I have found is closed doors and vacant arenas. Yes, there is plenty to see, but these days, there is very little to do.

So, I walk and make my way downtown, taking several different routes, reaching some sort of goal then turn around and head home. Every day. Without fail. In the rain, in the snow, or the bright crystal-clear winter sun, I walk.

Michael can go days on end without ever leaving the apartment. That, I fear, would send me completely over the edge. I'm never sure what he is doing, but his days are full. He is far more social than I am and has a far greater tolerance for virtual communication than I do. I am physically incapable of sitting still for that long. After a few hours, every morning spent sitting on the couch writing, I need to get up and go somewhere.

I will say that the few hours that I spend writing every morning are effortless in that regard. Hours can go by without my noticing at all. Even on the days where I sit down and don't have the slightest idea where it's going to go, once I start, I just get taken away. When I'm done, though, I'm done. As wonderful as it is to escape into the writing, I can't stay in it all day. It's a bit like being in the silent bliss of swimming underwater. Eventually, it's time to come up for air. And then I need to figure out what to do with the rest of the day.

Throughout this past year, we have been confronted with the most remarkable series of unfolding historical events. As much as none of us wants to delve into anything and relive the events surrounding this impeachment trial, this may be the most important moment that we will face as a country during this entire year.

With each showing of the footage from the January 6th insurrection attempt at the Capitol, the enormity of what happened that day sinks in a bit further. That serious harm did not befall any elected officials seems incredible. Representative Alexandria Ocasio-Cortez released a video in which she described being right behind a door that one of the insurgents had opened while looking for her. What would have happened had these people found her? What would have happened had these people discovered the Vice-President?

It's one thing to look back at remarkable events and quite another to live through them. For every monumental occurrence, there is an endless amount of waiting that the historians gloss over when they look back upon them and tell the story.

Historians won't look back on the endless days where we paced back and forth and waited. They'll only look back on the result. They will sum it up in one sentence—they voted to convict, or they voted to acquit. What follows will be where the story lies. Do we continue forward as a democracy, or do we take another step towards a Republican-led dystopian future where populists and extremists rule outside of the confines of the Constitution?

While we wait for these events to unfold today, I will pace the city. Relentlessly.

February 10, 2021

1,504,059 Total Reported Cases in New York. 45,123 Deaths.

Yesterday, the Senate voted to proceed with the trial that begins today. After a compelling case from the Democratic side and a rambling, incoherent defense from the ex-President's new team of lawyers, 44 Republican legislators still voted against the trial proceeding. Only 6 Republicans sided with the Democrats.

In this trial, the Senators are the jurors. Jurors are meant to be impartial. How can Senators, who are, themselves, on opposing teams, hope to be impartial especially since half of them are on the team of the accused?

Just hours before the impeachment trial starts, the district attorney of Fulton County in Georgia has announced that they are opening an investigation into the phone call where the ex-President tried to pressure the Georgia Secretary of State into "finding" a few thousand extra votes to tip the Electoral College votes in his favor.

The timing of this announcement cannot be an accident. The greatest pressure possible to convict the ex-President is going to be brought to bear on this jury of Senators. This investigation in Georgia only supports the Democrats' case that the President's incitement of his followers to violence did not just occur on the spur of the moment last month. It was meticulously laid out months before, planned so that the ex-President merely had to pull the pin at the rally on January 6th. Senators who are going to stick by their party and vote to acquit the ex-President are going to have to do so right out in the open.

Michael is cooking breakfast in the kitchen. It's my birthday, today, so I got to choose what we're having, so this morning we are having scrambled eggs and waffles. Michael's even put out the whipped cream. One of my very best friends in the world also has her birthday today so later the three of us are going to go out to have dinner together. We're having Mexican food. Nothing sounds better to me right now than a frozen margarita out in the snow under a heat lamp.

Birthdays may, after all, just be days in the calendar, but they are milestones. Another lap around the sun has been completed. Each birthday is a chance to look back, roll your eyes and say, "oy" before gearing up to start the next trip around.

The impeachment trial is a strange gift to get today, but it is a gift. I, somehow, don't think that it's going to just end up in a drawer with some of the other things I've received over the years. Let's see what we can do with it.

FEBRUARY 11, 2021
475,000 Total Reported Deaths in the United States.

A year ago, today, I was clambering over Mayan ruins in Mexico. The cast on the Bliss had a full day of onboard training scheduled, so we couldn't do anything with them on stage. Instead, we joined a small group of hardy ship passengers and took a bus deep into the jungle and explored several different sites. I had been to several other Mayan cities in the Yucatan before, maybe twenty years before, but not to these, which were further afield.

At one point during the day, somebody climbed to the top of the largest pyramid in the complex and blew on a conch shell. The blare from that shell echoed off all the other ruined buildings and spread out through the surrounding jungle. It was an ancient sound brought forward from centuries before. For just a moment, the ghosts of the people who had lived there woke up and repopulated the entire city.

That day seems like an experience from another lifetime.

I have kept scrapbooks since I was ten years old. In them, I have put the tickets from every piece of theatre I have ever witnessed. I've listed the books I have read and the movies I've seen. Every time I go somewhere, I try to find a postcard from that place and add it to the book.

In recent years I was traveling so much and to such a disparate group of places, that it seemed to me to be the only way that I would ever be able to remember where I had been. At this point, there are probably about twenty full books. They originally used to last for years, but by the time everything shut down I was filling them up every eighteen months or so.

I don't look at them. They are all, except for the current one, in plastic crates in our storage unit, but knowing they are there takes the pressure off my having to worry about forgetting.

About two months ago, Norwegian Cruise Lines started signing up crew members again from India and the Philippines. That seemed to indicate that they were planning to resume sailing in the spring. Two weeks ago, however, they sent the crews back to their homes. Financial analysts and port authorities do not seem to think that there is any way that the first cruises will start up again until midsummer at the earliest. Once they start, it could take many, many months for them to get up to full speed.

Whatever you think about cruising, itself, countless port cities around the world rely on those passengers visiting them to get by. Part of our global recovery depends on those ships getting back out there.

Day two of the impeachment trial has just gotten underway. While repetitive and, at many times, harrowing, yesterday's presentation by the Democratic trial managers was, nonetheless, riveting. Whatever the result of this trial, the Democrats' outlining of events and their arguments connecting the then-President with what happened on January 6th, was devastatingly thorough. Their organization of footage from the Capitol's security cameras, tweets, and statements from the ex-President as well as video clips from the insurrectionists themselves into a coherent timeline creates a narrative that is nothing short of jaw-dropping.

An anonymous computer programmer, fearing that much would be lost when the social media site Parler was shut down, downloaded nearly 30 terabytes of the posts by individuals who participated in the attempted coup. The programmer describes herself as a "hacktivist" but everything she downloaded was freely available on public platforms. The trial managers have made good use of that footage.

Stacey Plaskett is a Democratic Congressional Representative from the United States Virgin Islands. Because the Islands are a territory and not a state she was not allowed to vote for or against the impeachment of the ex-President in the House. She made history yesterday when she became the first nonvoting delegate to Congress to serve as an impeachment manager. She was also the only Black woman in the room.

Even during the pandemic, I've added a few things to my scrapbook. In November, I put in my "I voted early" sticker. Souvenirs of these last many months, however, are few and far between.

Instead, I have these posts. I will probably just write in "Pandemic March 12, 2020—_____" in the scrapbook and then, hopefully, continue forward with the postcards and ticket stubs when we start up again. Remembering the past is important. Memory is such a fickle thing.

I am struck by how watching videos that were taken at the same time but from different locations during the occupation of the Capitol changes what I thought the story is. Seeing footage of lawmakers inside their chambers from the building's security system next to footage taken by the insurrectionists themselves at the same time is truly chilling. The people attacking the Capitol were out for blood and the interior video shows just how very close they came to getting it.

The Democrats have created an extremely thorough scrapbook of the events leading up to, during, and following the violence on January 6th. Long after clear memory has become clouded and fragmented, what they have amassed will remain to tell the story. How do you defend the indefensible? The only way to do it is to refuse to look at the truth. To lie. The more scraps of video, film, and photos we find, the harder that will be to do.

February 12, 2021
1,522,785 Total Reported Cases in New York. 45,410 Deaths.

The defense team is going to present their arguments today. They have already said that they are only going to use 3-4 hours of their allotted time. Each side has been given 16 hours, but they have decided that they don't need all that. Their mandate today is to provide the Senators who are going to vote against convicting the ex-President with some sort of hook, no matter how flimsy, that they can use as justification.

We have just started watching *The Plot Against America* which is a series that explores what would have happened had the United States not entered the war in Europe. It centers on a Jewish family and what happens to them when the country elects an anti-Semitic and white supremacist aviation hero: Charles Lindbergh instead of Franklin Roosevelt. Lindbergh, historically, thought that the US should remain neutral during the war and not get involved. Whether he supported the Nazis is a matter of conjecture, but he, along with his friend industrialist Henry Ford, was an avowed anti-Semite and a white supremacist.

World War II brought the entire planet to a crossroads. Had it ended differently, and it very well could have, what would our lives look like today? I would say that I might be writing this in German, but I don't know that I would be allowed to be writing anything like this at all.

In much the same way that families huddled around their radios listening to news about the war back in the 1940s, this year, we have all been huddled around our televisions. The pandemic has kept us at home and the news has been much harder to avoid. Last month, we hit the point where more people had died because of COVID-19 than were killed in battle during all of World War II. Except for the attack on Pearl Harbor, World War II did not happen on American soil. Until last month, the US Capitol had never been breached by enemy combatants.

The most effective opposition to the populist movement is always going to be competent governance. While all of this has been going on, President Biden has been running the country. We need to move forward.

FEBRUARY 13, 2021

The former President was acquitted by the Senate in his second impeachment trial: 57-43.

Every day when I leave the apartment, I pass families with kids heading towards Central Park. Inside the park. Within its low walls, every hill is covered with people. Blanketed in white under cloudy skies, the park, itself, looks like a faded and blotchy photograph from the beginning of the last century. Brownish gray trees and lampposts, fences, and rocky outcrops are the only breaks in the endless expanse.

With the kids and their families, however, come bright speckled blotches. Their coats and plastic sleds are so vividly colored that they are visible from extremely far away. It makes the park look like it is frosted with vanilla icing and decorated with rainbow sprinkles—or hundreds and thousands for my friends in Britain and her colonies.

Anyone who has walked the streets of the city has long gotten used to seeing the enclosures that restaurants have put up outside on the street. Yesterday, restrictions were relaxed so that indoor dining at up to 25% capacity can resume. Despite the official permission to proceed, there are still many people who won't do it.

Some restaurants have chosen to build what looks like old-time train cars divided into a series of separate compartments. You and the people you are with end up in an enclosed space, but you are separated by either wooden or plastic walls from everybody else. Other places have chosen, instead of that, to build an open enclosure putting up a roof and surrounding the tables on three sides with walls, leaving the fourth side, the one facing the sidewalk, and the front of the actual brick and mortar building, completely open. In those, diners can safely eat together with strangers, albeit at a distance. Heaters either to the side or above the tables keep diners somewhat warmer than they would be if they were just sitting outside in the snow.

In recent weeks, it seems like some restaurants have discovered that the reddish-orange light that comes from the heaters looks far more inviting on cold days than just normal lighting. I am starting to see enclosures where the usual run-of-the-mill lightbulbs have been replaced by reddish-orange ones. They don't provide any additional heat, but even from a distance, they make their dining areas look like a little warm and inviting oasis out on the bleak and icy city streets.

There are still restaurants that seem to have missed the point completely and have put up enclosures that are not divided inside and have all four walls in place. I have no idea why the city has allowed those kinds of enclosures to remain in use. Four walls and a roof, no matter what they are made of, are the definition of indoor dining. The whole point of outdoor dining is to encourage air circulation. Enclosures like that thwart that goal completely.

Investors will tell you that the only thing that is riskier than investing in a Broadway show is investing in a new restaurant. Like Broadway shows, almost all of them close, losing their entire investment. When they hit, though, they hit.

In the 1950s Joe Allen started working as a bartender at P.J. Clarke's on the Upper East Side. In the 60s, he opened a place of his own on 46th Street that he named after himself. At the time, the entire area was somewhat derelict. From the beginning, Joe Allen's Restaurant hit. It attracted actors and others who were working in theatres nearby.

As a somewhat inside industry joke, he lined the inside of the restaurant with posters from Broadway shows that had flopped. To this day, you don't get on the wall of Joe Allen's unless you closed on opening night and lost at least a million dollars.

Only one of my shows is up there. The musical *The Red Shoes* is right in the corner. For whatever reason, possibly because they were hemorrhaging money, the producers of that show never really made a poster for it. Before we closed, though, they made an extremely limited number of them—about ten—and one of them was for the wall at Joe Allen's. I am always happy to see it up on the wall when we eat in there.

Joe opened a fancier restaurant next door called Orso's, and a wonderful kind of inside-industry speak-easy called Bar Centrale just upstairs between them. Elaine Stritch ate at Orso's all the time. I never got the full story from her, but at one time she and Joe Allen were engaged to be married. Whatever happened to end that relationship, he let Elaine eat there for free for the rest of her life.

At the end of the run of *A Delicate Balance*, she took everyone in the company that she could still stand out to dinner at Orso's as a thank you. The party was made up of me, the Company Manager, the Wardrobe Supervisor, and her dresser. That was it. We were seated at a table right in the middle. A guy was sitting behind me by himself at a table and another guy sitting by himself with his back to us opposite from where I was sitting, but Elaine was the undisputed center of the room.

That night, both Lauren Bacall and Stephanie Powers had come to see the show. As we ate, Elaine told some truly wonderful and utterly salacious stories about Ms. Bacall. They'd known each other for decades, had slept with some of the same people, and we heard about all of it. And she wasn't whispering.

As she was holding forth, Lauren Bacall, herself, walked into the restaurant. Seeing Elaine, she came over to our table and said hello. They chatted for a bit while the rest of us, of course, looked at her with mouths agape after all the stories that we'd just heard about her. As the chat ended, she introduced her son, who turned out to be the man sitting with his back to us at the table right behind me. It wasn't possible that he hadn't heard every story out of Elaine's mouth and Elaine knew it.

Rather than being in any way chastened by this, Elaine merely changed direction. Ms. Bacall sat down with her son and Elaine continued telling the stories but pretended that, all along, she had been talking about Stephanie Powers. The two of them had also known each other for decades, so she also had some pretty great stories about Stephanie Powers.

As she was gossiping, who, of course, should walk into the restaurant but, Stephanie Powers. She, too, came up to the table and said hello. After a few pleasantries, she introduced her husband who was the man sitting with his back to us at the table across from me. He, too, had heard every word that Elaine had said.

After she left, Elaine shrugged and said, "What can you do?" We all fell out. As quietly as we could. It was one of the most memorable meals I have ever had.

Michael and I have had hundreds of meals in Joe Allen's and spent countless nights up in Bar Centrale either with friends or by ourselves.

Often, Joe would be sitting at one of the bars. He was a constant fixture there. He lived in an apartment above them.

Early on, he had the chance to buy the buildings that his restaurants are in, and he did. When he bought them, the area was so depressed that he got them for a very good price. This summer, they were able to open for business for a few weeks. When it got colder and the case numbers went up again, though, they closed back down. Because they don't have to pay rent, they will be able to remain closed as long as necessary and re-open when it is safe to do so.

Joe Allen's is a genuine Broadway fixture. Certainly, some tourists make their way there, but it belongs to our community. In *Applause*, the musical version of *All About Eve*, Joe Allen's restaurant figures prominently as a location where everybody in the show within the show meets up. That Joe, himself, will not be there when Broadway finally reopens is tragic. So far, though, it appears that the restaurant that bears his name should still be there for us to gather in again.

While I will likely spend much of today glued to the television, I would much rather go down and have the chopped La Scala salad or a burger at Joe's. I guess I'll have to wait until spring.

RIP Joe Allen.

February 15, 2021
1,546,408 Total Reported Cases in New York. 45,816 Deaths.

Among other things, St. Valentine is also, fittingly, one of the patron saints of plagues.

There are three saints in the Catholic Encyclopedia that share February 14 as a feast day: one in Africa and two in Italy. Nothing much is known about the guy in Africa, and the two in Italy may be competing versions of the same person.

The two Italian Valentines share the same basic story. While under imprisonment for preaching Christianity, their captors told them that if they could cure their family member or members of what ailed them—blindness, or what have you—that they would then, themselves, convert. The Valentines, of course, made with the healing, and the captors did, indeed, then convert and free them. Later, not being able to keep their mouths shut, the Valentines continued to proselytize, got caught by somebody else, and were both put to death in gruesome ways.

Relics from one or the other are scattered throughout Europe.

It is thought that Valentine may have been a physician, what with the curing and all, so, after sainthood, he started to be called upon whenever a plague descended on a community. It was only much later, probably with Geoffrey Chaucer, that St. Valentine started being associated with courtly love. That then led to the exchanging of valentines and our custom of giving our beloveds roses and chocolates which gave shopkeepers something to pin a few sales on in the depth of winter.

Shakespeare mentions him. Ophelia, having been abandoned, sings a little song about his feast day in *Hamlet*.

> *Tomorrow is St. Valentine's Day betime,*
> *And I a maid at your window,*
> *To be your Valentine.*
> *Then up he rose, and donn'd his clothes,*
> *And dupp'd the chamber door;*
> *Let in the maid, that out a maid*
> *Never departed.*

The superstition was that if you were the first person that someone saw on Valentine's Day that said person would fall in love with you. The maid, or, in other words, the virgin, having been espied, would go into her beloved's chamber, and once in, her virginity, haven been taken, would never come out. Having been so used and abandoned, Valentine's Day for Ophelia becomes the opposite of a day meant for celebration.

This year, maybe more so than any other year, many people must have had a rough day of it yesterday. The isolation and separation that we are all feeling just seem more pronounced on a day when everyone is posting pictures of their families and loved ones.

Lysander, in *A Midsummer Night's Dream*, says, "The course of true love never did run smooth."

Too much of anything, be it separation or togetherness, is not necessarily a good thing. Maybe I should speak for myself, but most years, we probably find ourselves moving from one of those states to the other, trying to land on that sweet spot in the middle. This year, of course, we are all pretty much stuck in just one of those conditions trying to figure out ways to achieve a balance.

The impeachment trial already seems like something from the distant past. At the trial's conclusion, which happened surprisingly quickly, 57 Senators, including 7 Republicans, voted to convict and 43 voted to acquit. Even though it was the largest percentage of the chamber to ever vote for impeachment, it was not enough to carry the vote and the ex-President was acquitted.

The GOP had their opportunity to move forward without him, and they chose not to take it.

Whatever happens as we move forward, is firmly on them.

This morning, I was able to schedule an appointment to get my first dose of the vaccine. It's not until April 2 and it's over four hours away upstate in Syracuse, New York, but it's a start. I could use the road trip. Monitoring and refreshing vaccine scheduling websites have become a blood sport.

While there are massively huge inoculation sites set up all over the state, there is not enough supply of the vaccine to make them useful. Here in Manhattan, the Javits Convention Center has been organized to look much like the customs hall at JFK. Endless stanchioned paths wend their way back and forth through the gigantic open space to private screened-off areas where the shots are administered. There are only a handful of people there, though. Not nearly enough to warrant that massive array of barriers.

A couple of days ago, President Biden announced that we would be buying an additional 200 million doses of the vaccine from Pfizer and Moderna by the end of July. This will go a long way towards ensuring that most Americans be inoculated by the middle of summer. The vaccine does not mean that the pandemic is over. It just means that we are being provided with a better weapon to fight it. We are going to need to remain vigilant against this virus for many years to come.

What that future existence will look like is anybody's guess. Perhaps we should call upon St. Valentine to intercede in his plague capacity now that his feast day duties are behind him for another year.

FEBRUARY 16, 2021
108.2 Million Total Reported Cases Worldwide.

During a crisis, time flies by. Without bombs falling all around us, which is what the last few months have felt like, we are now, sitting in the silent and smoldering ruins wondering what to do next. The loud and dramatic wave of war has seemingly passed over us and in its wake, our government is knuckling down to the hard and largely silent work of actual governance.

In an article from last year in Psychology Today titled, "Is Peace Boring?" Dr. Betty Luceigh points out that it is far easier to bomb a building than it is to build one. Building one takes time, moves slowly, requires a lot of effort, and is, well, largely dull.

We are going to need a push to reconstruct our pre-pandemic lives. They won't just start up again as quickly as they shut down.

This weekend, a new state initiative called NY PopUps is going to start presenting 300 free performances over 100 days throughout the city. To prevent crowding, nothing will be announced beforehand—not what or when, or where. The Governor has promised that there will be people like Hugh Jackman, Sarah Jessica Parker and Mandy Patinkin involved. The program is designed both to employ New York arts workers but also to begin to pave the way for more traditional and established venues to reopen.

It still seems unlikely that anything on Broadway will reopen before September. If, as the federal government is promising, most Americans could be vaccinated by midsummer, then things might start in the fall. Smaller venues could, however, could begin to open before that. Broadway relies on tourists, but not-for-profit Off-Broadway shows appeal more to New Yorkers. We are here. We are ready to watch some theatre in no matter how eccentric the venue.

I spent the better part of this morning on the phone. As a result, I now have a vaccine appointment at the Javits Center here in the city at the end of next month. I canceled the one that I previously made up in Syracuse. I may be back at work before that, but I'm not counting on it.

These next few months will see the beginning of our slow march forward towards reopening.

There will, of course, be obstacles, setbacks, and delays. What we end up with probably will not match what we had, but whatever it is, it will be something.

As Sam says to Frodo when he is in deep despair in the middle of *The Lord of the Rings*, "How could the world go back to the way it was when so much bad had happened? But in the end, it's only a passing thing, this shadow. Even darkness must pass. A new day will come. And when the sun shines it will shine out the clearer."

It may still be night, but it feels like we might be at that dark moment just before the first light of dawn appears on the horizon. If I'm wrong, I'm wrong, but if I'm right, when it starts, it's liable to come quickly.

FEBRUARY 17, 2021
1,559,042 Total Reported Cases in New York. 46,075 Deaths.

The President of the United States held a Town Hall last night during which he answered questions from citizens. Actual questions. Actual citizens. It was strange. Where's the drama? Where are the protests? What happened to the daily barrage of lies and angry filth emanating from the White House?

Instead, he showed empathy. He comforted a little girl and told her not to be scared, "You are going to be fine, and we are going to make sure mommy is fine, too." To a woman who wasn't having any luck finding a vaccine for her son who has a pre-existing condition, he said, "But here's what I'll do. If you're willing, I'll stay around after this is over and maybe we can talk a few minutes and see if I can get you some help."

If this were an episode of *Supernatural*, as soon as the Town Hall was over and the cameras shut off, the President's eyes would have turned black and fangs would have emerged from his teeth and he'd drop to all fours, eviscerate the little girl and feast on her entrails.

Instead, the little girl just went home, presumably somewhat comforted, and President Biden met with the concerned woman and has likely put someone onto the task of helping her to get her son vaccinated.

My niece put me onto *Supernatural* and I am now coming to the end of season twelve. It is, apparently, endless. These are full old-school seasons with 23 episodes each. It finally finished shooting after fifteen seasons and its finale aired this past year.

Every time Michael walks into the room while I am watching it, somebody is screaming and there is blood everywhere. It disturbs him to no end. He won't watch. The cast, of course, is very attractive so he always at least stops and asks what is going on. I then go through the complicated demonology chronology that has unfolded up to that point. It's so confusing that it eventually causes him to lose interest and walk away.

When I was my niece's age *Star Wars* is what I watched obsessively. In many ways, it turned out to be my way into beginning to see the underlying structures of religion. *Star Wars* director, George Lucas, when he was writing the story, followed the general outline of the world's mythology that Joseph Campbell discussed in his book, *The Hero with A Thousand Faces*.

Comparing the stories of the world's religions and mythologies, Campbell found that almost all of them share many similarities. In his introduction to the book when describing what he calls the hero's journey, he says, "A hero ventures forth from the world of common day into a region of supernatural wonder: fabulous forces are there encountered, and a decisive victory is won: the hero comes back from this mysterious adventure with the power to bestow boons on his fellow man." Watching the *Star Wars* saga unfold helped me as a young teenager put what I was seeing around me in the world into perspective.

The two leads of *Supernatural* fight evil and the darkness in an epic journey that leaves Odysseus in the dust. Michael worries about the level of violence that my niece is watching. I, on the other hand, am thrilled that she is getting a small window into what is a much bigger picture. That it comes with a certain amount of decapitation is beside the point.

None of what we are watching is as violent as the original *Grimm's Fairy Tales* are. In their original story, the princess turns the frog into a prince by hurling it against a wall, not by kissing it. After he turns into a prince, she then sleeps with him.

In later editions, the Brothers Grimm toned down the sex but amped up the violence. In a story called *The Robber Bridegroom*, bandits drag a girl into their cellar, force her to drink wine until her heart bursts, rip off her clothes and then hack her to pieces. In their original *Cinderella* story, the stepsisters saw off their toes so that their feet can fit into the slipper. In *Snow White*, the evil queen dies after being made to dance in red-hot iron shoes. Lots of kids bite the dust in the stories and several are eaten by their murderers.

The collection of stories that the Grimms put together was originally an attempt on their parts to preserve the Germanic oral tradition. The finished product was intended for adults as well as children. As they became more and more popular, the stories became tamer so adults would feel more comfortable allowing their children to read them. The Victorians added moralizing lessons to them and replaced their raw sexual aspects with more flowery depictions of chaste romantic love. Disney then Disney-fied them.

The first movie that I was ever taken to was Disney's *Bambi*. Not in its initial release, thank you very much, but about twenty-some-odd years later when I was about 4 or 5. I was so traumatized by Bambi's mother getting shot that my mother had to evacuate me from the theatre.

Bruno Bettelheim, a world-renowned psychoanalyst who died in 1990, was critical of the move away from the violence. He felt that it weakened the stories' usefulness in allowing readers to symbolically work through their own internal issues. Carl Jung felt that fairy tales were spontaneous expressions of the soul. He said, "In this pure form, the archetypal images afford us the best clues to the understanding of the processes going on in the collective psyche." In other words, by experiencing these stories' conflicts in their most extreme forms, the child's subconscious can use them to resolve its own more mundane and, hopefully, much less extreme, conflicts.

In *The Princess Bride* Peter Falk, who plays a kind and direct grandfather, reads a bedtime story to his young grandson played by Fred Savage who is at home sick in bed and bored. The grandson doesn't want to hear the story but eventually, the grandfather wears him down and he gets pulled into it. At a particularly tense moment in the middle of the tale, the grandfather sensing his grandson's anxiety offers to stop reading. The grandson begs him to continue to the end. Afterward, he gives his grandfather permission to come back and read it to him again. If he wants.

It feels like over the last four years that we have all lived through a violent and extreme thriller. That said, we now have a President who is the living fairy tale embodiment of the kind and gentle grandfather. Even though what lies ahead of him seems daunting and possibly unsolvable, there is something about his easiness and elderly confidence that inspires trust that he will be able to fix it. Everything will be OK because he says so.

The story of the January 6th insurrection is almost certainly going to pop up in many of our narratives moving forward. Nothing that we experienced through this past administration was as tailor-made for storytelling as that was. Good guys, bad guys, and extreme violence. It has it all. A cautionary tale if there ever was one.

Today, my niece went back to in-person schooling for the first time in months. I am oddly comforted by the fact that she has watched almost the entire *Supernatural* saga. It seems to me, that getting through all of that will make what she is sure to face moving forward just that much easier to deal with. She has watched two guys give it their all fighting against unimaginable horrors. They literally both go to hell and back. Several times. Dealing with mere high school students can only pale in comparison.

I trust that she won't decapitate anyone who gets in her way, but if she can do that figuratively, then those stories will have done what all the stories we tell each other should do—give us the objectivity and strength to confront what comes up in our lives.

President Biden is not going to fix everything, but wow does it feel better listening to him than it did listening to the last guy. After the horrifying story that we've just lived through, having Grandpa Biden now staying with us lets me sleep better at night.

February 18, 2021

Senator Ted Cruz (R-Texas) returns from his Cancun vacation while millions in his state are without power or water.

Michael gave me a large coffee thermos for my birthday last week. While that may seem like a strange gift, I love it. I drink decaf all morning while I'm writing. After it's been made in the press and the first mug is poured, the rest starts to cool off. To be honest, it has never been a problem. I never gave it a second thought. It's just what it was.

I never mentioned it. It was never discussed. Michael just noticed it on his own and, quietly, did something about it. It wasn't necessary, it was just a very kind and thoughtful gesture on his part. In and of itself, the thermos is not a remarkable object. It's brushed stainless steel to match the rest of our appliances with a black plastic lid and handle, but it makes me feel taken care of every time I use it. It was the perfect gift.

My mother got her first vaccine shot. Her neighbors took her to her appointment and brought her home. So far so good.

A very long time ago, my mother and my ex, and I went on a multi-day hike through the wilderness on Irian Jaya. Irian Jaya is the western half of the island of New Guinea with Papua New Guinea being the eastern half. It lies just above Australia.

Once away from the tiny port, there was almost nothing of the modern world around us. The Papuan people live much the same way that their ancestors have done for millennia. Once out into the countryside, it felt like we had completely been taken to another time. For one thing, the women wore only hand-woven skirts, and the men were almost naked except for a long, pointed gourd that they wore on their penises. Their 'meat' was therefore covered, but their 'potatoes', as it were, hung free. The gourd pointed straight out and thin strands of twine attached to the pointed tip tied behind their backs to keep it on. In addition to the gourds, the elders of the community wore what looked like beaded ties around their necks and the leaders had curved boar tusks through their noses.

A small army of villagers accompanied us on the hike. Instead of the slim gourds, these guys wore larger gourds that were kept straight up against their stomachs. These larger gourds also served as a kind of suitcase, holding things like fire-making kits and other tools. When we tipped them at the end, that's where the money went.

We were a small group and we carried everything we needed on our backs. My ex is very tall, much taller than me, and he towered over the tallest of these guys by nearly a full two feet. We were out there with these men for several days. At one point we got to a substantial stream, and they carried us across—they insisted. Strong as they were, it took four of the guys to get my ex over the water. One of them carried my mother over piggyback.

Anyway, at one point, my mother fell against some rocks and ripped her leg open. There was truly blood everywhere and she had a huge flap of skin that had been torn away. We were several days of hard trekking away from anything that could be thought of as civilization. The Papuan men swarmed around her and with the help of our guide, patched her up with whatever they had at hand, and we kept going. I am sure my mother must still have the scar from that, but it didn't stop her for a second. It's no surprise that the vaccine didn't stop her either.

It was reported this morning that, because of the pandemic, the average life expectancy in the United States has fallen by a full year over these last 12 months. That, number, however, is just the average.

Life expectancy for white people fell just 0.8 years. If you are white, it is expected that, on average, you will live to be 78 years old. If you are black, however, the expectancy for the length of your life is much, much lower. Over this last year, life expectancy for African Americans has fallen by 2.7 years. If you are black you can expect to live to the ripe old age of 72, shrugging off this mortal coil a full six years before your white neighbors do.

The system in this country does much what that small army of guys in Irian Jaya did for me and my family. It carries us white folks over obstacles and takes care of us when we falter. The system is often not there for people of color so they are left to get by on their own as best they can.

Snow is falling. I can feel the cold creeping in around our air conditioners, but my coffee is still hot. Thank you, Michael. Thank you, Michael, for the gift that you give me every day by just waking up beside me. At the end of the day, whatever happens, that's all that truly matters.

And I'm glad that you didn't notice that the cat barfed off the end of the bed last night.

FEBRUARY 19, 2021

1,577,197 Total Reported Cases in New York. 46,400 Deaths.

As of today, the United States is officially back in the Paris Accord. The agreement is a commitment from countries across the globe, signed in 2016, wherein the countries who participated, pledged to work together to reduce climate pollution.

189 nations from the 197 members of the United Nations Framework Convention on Climate Change have ratified the agreement. The countries that haven't are either major oil exporters like Iran, Iraq, and Libya or are nations that are being torn apart by conflict like Yemen and South Sudan. The most recent country to ratify was Angola this past August. Our former President had pulled us out of the agreement.

The United States is behind only China in the total amount of $CO2$ emissions that we release every year into our shared atmosphere. The pollution from our two countries does not just hover above our territories, of course, it is released into the air and every other country on the planet suffers as a result.

This morning, President Biden also firmly re-avowed America's commitment to the North Atlantic Treaty Organization—a mutually beneficial military alliance between 30 European and North American governments that was created after the end of World War II. Our former President had no understanding of what any of these agreements meant. He didn't understand their purpose. He didn't even know who many of our allies were or where on the globe they were located.

There is a phrase known as the Peter Parker principle which is, "With great power comes great responsibility." Peter Parker is Spiderman's alter-ego. The concept, however, is much older than Stan Lee's comic book. Luke 12:48 in the Christian bible says, "From everyone who has been given much, much will be demanded; and from the one who has been entrusted with much, much more will be asked."

Why us? Well, for one thing, we are among those who have been most guilty of creating the global climate problem in the first place. Every single person that we share this globe with is breathing the air that we have helped to make dirty. The garbage that we dump into the ocean washes up on the shores of allies and enemies alike. The plastics that we helped create have been consumed by almost every creature in the world. A brand-new shrimp-like creature that was just discovered in one of the deepest ocean trenches on earth was named Eurythenes Plasticus after the man-made particles that were discovered in its digestive system.

Yesterday, NASA successfully landed its rover, Perseverance, on Mars. As exciting as that is, we must not make the same mistakes up there that we have down here. Whatever problems we face, working together with our allies is the only chance we have to keep our ship from sinking.

The person who delivered the news of the landing to the rest of the world was an Indian American woman named Swati Mohan. Inspired by seeing her first *Star Trek* episode when she was nine, Dr. Mohan studied mechanical and aerospace engineering at Cornell University and then got her master's and a doctorate in aeronautics and astronautics at M.I.T. in Boston.

One of the things that made *Star Trek* notable at the time it was created was its multi-racial cast. NASA seems to be doing its best to try to catch up to them. Yesterday, the scientists in the NASA control room could easily have all been together on the bridge of the USS Enterprise.

The landing on Mars is as remarkable an indication of where our future may lie as anything we have seen for a long time. In honor of the event, Krispy Kreme has created a special Mars donut. It is filled with chocolate cream and covered in swirled red and orange caramel icing with a sprinkling of Oreo cookie crumbs. It seemed un-American not to try one, so yesterday, out on my walk in the sleeting rain, I aimed for the new Krispy Kreme megastore in Times Square and got one. I mean…

FEBRUARY 20, 2021
1,585,435 Total Reported Cases in New York. 46,512 Deaths.

I don't remember my pre-pandemic life. Of course, I remember what I did, I just don't remember what it felt like.

Yesterday in Times Square, it hit me that I couldn't recall how it felt to be anxiously rushing through the crowds late to a day of auditions or a rehearsal and being annoyed because of the wide-eyed throngs of tourists blocking my way. I could remember that I felt that way, but what that felt like…? Gone.

Offhand, I would say that the worst pain I can ever remember experiencing was when a nurse yanked out the catheter that I had been forced to have in for about two weeks following my prostate surgery. She told me she was going to do it on 3 and, of course, tore it out on 2. The searing pain blanked out my vision. Everything went white. I vividly remember every single detail about that moment except for the actual pain itself. That, mercifully, I can't recall at all.

I'm fine with that. Experiencing it once was plenty. About a year after that I had a much less serious follow-up procedure and again needed a catheter during it. The first time, the catheter had been put in while I was out cold on the operating table, so I didn't have to experience it. This time, though, I was wide awake. While every fiber of my being tensed against what I was sure was coming, it was at worst unpleasantly uncomfortable. It wasn't nearly as painful going in or subsequently coming back out.

I would say that on any given day that I walk between 6 and 10 miles. From here where we live down to Battery Park at the lower tip of Manhattan is about 6 ½ miles. It is just under an 8-mile walk from here to St. Anne's Warehouse in Dumbo across the Brooklyn Bridge. Rarely do I walk in a straight line. I wander. When I get to an intersection and the light is against me, I will change course and head off in a new direction. After I get diverted a few times and see generally where I am being taken, I will then sometimes set a destination and try to make my way there more directly. Or I won't. I will just go wherever the traffic lights take me.

If it's snowing or if I think I'm going into the park I'll wear my ancient and well-broken in Timberlands, otherwise, I will just wear sneakers. After it has snowed, sneakers keep me from being able to cross certain streets or walk down some un-shoveled sidewalks, so that can further alter my daily trek.

I am thankful that during this extremely strange year that we are living in a big city. If we weren't here, I would want to be out in the wilderness somewhere. I wouldn't want to be somewhere in-between.

My relationship with walking and exploring has changed this year. Covering the same ground day after day has forced me to look more at the details than at the whole. Now I walk through the city trying to be alert to what looks different. So much changed so quickly last spring that it was easy to see what was new. After months of the same thing day in and day out, these days, it's not nearly as easy.

What I notice, more than anything else is the move towards making the changes to our daily lives more permanent. The other day I was walking through a shopping complex looking for a restroom and I passed a sign near the entrance that said, "Please observe respiratory etiquette." We've been doing this for so long that it is a given that anyone reading that sign would know what it means.

A year ago, everything changed overnight. It was sudden, shocking, and disorienting. It feels to me that we are on the brink of things changing again. This time, I think, the change is going to be much more protracted and incremental. It might take a couple of years.

For the first time, some of the work projects being talked about around me feel like they could happen. Some are developmental and some are aimed towards virtual presentation so they could be done because the issue of an audience wouldn't need to be faced.

When does Broadway reopen? When do cruise ships start sailing again? Those are questions that still don't have anything close to a firm answer that I can see. I take whatever dates that I hear or am told with a grain of salt. There are still too many obstacles ahead of us to keep them from happening on a firm schedule.

Once some of that work does start back up again, all of this will start to become hard to remember. I think that I can now see how almost everybody was able to forget all about the Spanish flu pandemic. It was too much of the same thing for too long a time.

I know that so far there have been 346 separate days since we stopped. Having written these posts, I can personally account for all of them. Each of them, though, is stored in one folder on my desktop. Together they are all just one single file.

I think that we are all going to look back on this year as a singularity, not as 365 separate events. That is what is going to make it easy to forget. I might guess that the truly shocking things like the death of a loved one or even the January 6th insurrection are going to be remembered on their own. I don't think that we will remember them in the context of this incredibly strange year.

Looking back on my life, I remember the jobs, and the adventures, not the gaps of waiting in between them. However long this period lasts, when it's done, I don't think that we will be able to recall the tedium and repetition of this endless string of somewhat empty days. This time will just be remembered as a gap.

Maybe after work one night, we will get together and become a bit nostalgic and try to remember what it was like. Whatever's new, though, will be awaiting us the following morning so maybe we will decide that we should call it a night and go home and get some sleep.

After all, tomorrow is coming. It always does.

FEBRUARY 22, 2021
1,597,969 Total Reported Cases in New York. 46,729 Deaths.

We've been in this apartment for several years and even though it is only a one-bedroom, there were still parts of it that we weren't using. I couldn't have told you what some of our cabinets had inside them. We'd put things in them when we moved in and then never looked inside them again. I used about 4 or 5 scattered places, mostly just surfaces, and that was about it.

Some years ago, we were casting in Cape Town, South Africa and the producers of the show put me into a large two-bedroom apartment with a full kitchen and a dining room. It was enormous. Rather than spreading out, however, and taking advantage of the space, I only used about 10 square feet of it. In the morning when I woke up, I'd laugh because only a small sliver of the gigantic King-sized bed far off on one side was rumpled, the rest of it was untouched.

Traveling as much as I did (do?), I resisted fully unpacking in a new place because I didn't want to then have to find everything again when it was time to pack to leave. Usually, I would just hang up my shirts and leave my underclothes in the suitcase which I would put on a stand in the bedroom. When it was time to leave, even though I checked every drawer and closet, all I needed to do was pull my toiletries together from the bathroom, fold whatever clean shirts that were left hanging onto the top of everything else and I was ready to go.

Back in New York, between trips, my suitcase remained packed with essentials and sat in the front hall ready for the next trip. The things that I needed for daily life here in New York were all concentrated in a few places so that I could keep track of where they were. I rarely spent much time in the apartment except to sleep.

These days, my suitcase is down in the storage unit. Over this year, I've raided it for supplies that we've run out of. A pair of batteries that have been in a side pocket of it since time immemorial got used when one of the Christmas LED candles needed them. A roll of packing tape that I used out of town more times than I can count got used up around the holidays as well when I was mailing gifts to my family. My suitcase is, for the first time in over a decade, now actually in a state that might be able to be described as unpacked.

A few days ago, I bought us a drying rack. There are a whole bunch of shirts and jeans that we don't put in the dryer. Instead, we drape them over the backs of our six dining table chairs. Yesterday, Michael walked into the living room and saw all the damp clothes on the new rack rather than the chairs and his eyes went wide. "Honey—this is amazing. Are you going to write about this?"

Our current apartment is arguably the nicest place that either Michael or I have lived in during our adult lives. Our walls are lined with art that I've picked up over the years from all over the world. We don't have any show posters or other work-related material up, but in the bedroom, we do have a framed ticket from the night of Michael's Broadway debut in *Love!*

Valour! Compassion! as well as a beautifully drawn series of caricatures of him from several other shows. We have furniture and other objects from both sides of our family throughout our living space and things that we each had in prior apartments.

Truthfully there's far more of my stuff than there is of Michael's, but Michael doesn't accumulate things the same way that I do. There is also a fair amount of stuff that we have accumulated together. As a shell, I think it well represents who we are. After several years though, it is only in these last few months that we have started fully inhabiting this shell together. We've adjusted where things go and how we use them. The white enamel kettle that has sat on the stove for years because it looked good was given away because we never used it and it was constantly in the way.

Yesterday I did a massive clean-up of the top of the table. We eat at one end of it which we keep clear and use the other two-thirds of it as a catchall for our lives. After the clean, I can now see the piles of stuff that are sitting on it. We USE the table. My great-grandfather originally bought it from a department store in Virginia well over a hundred years ago. He used it in his law office to spread out his books. My grandfather eventually shared the office with him, and my great-grandfather would complain that my grandmother would come in and clean up the table so that he couldn't find anything that he needed. A century later, nothing has changed. If Michael moves my stuff or I move his, we can't ever find what we need either.

Yet again, it is snowing outside today which makes the apartment seem even more of a Hobbit hole—snug and comfortable. I know I travel a lot so I'm not always here, but this seems like a great deal more snow than we usually get here in the city. It's going to be a challenging walk, today.

I feel fortunate to have a place to shelter in that has heat, electricity, and running water. As has been driven home by the crisis in Texas this past week, even here in the United States of America, that is not, by any means, a given.

We all deserve a place where we feel safe and welcomed and protected—a place that we yearn to return to when we are away from it. I'm grateful that I've always had such a place and even more grateful that this year has allowed me to move into it.

FEBRUARY 24, 2021
1,611,031 Total Reported Cases in New York. 46,960 Deaths.

The cat can, again, no longer walk across the carpet without getting stuck on it. When he gets to the wooden part of the floor he clicks. When he yawns and stretches out on my lap if I'm not careful he can draw blood.

I cannot believe that it is claw-clipping time again. It's been nearly three months, but it seems like we just did it last week. Aside from a zoom call late tomorrow afternoon, I have nothing at all scheduled for weeks to come so I don't have any excuse whatsoever not to do it.

Last night I finally broke the silence on the topic and mentioned it out loud and Michael abruptly said, "I know," before I'd even finished my sentence. He needs to film another audition sometime today, so I will wait until he's done before I bring it up again.

At best, auditioning is an awful process. Actors spend a huge percentage of their lives preparing material that nobody will ever hear or see. I've spent months if not years of my life sitting behind a table watching a steady stream of nervous, resentful, hopeful, angry, anxious, confident, desperate, defiant, prepared, unprepared, busy, skillful, and green and experienced performers parade in front of us all with the hope of getting a job.

We give them pages and pages of material to prepare that we may never ask them to do. When they walk in the room, we might dismiss them before they even start—too tall, too short, too old, too young, too fat, too thin, too attractive, not attractive enough, too this, too that.

Sitting behind the table, we pray that everyone does well because we need them to be good. So many people are undone by their nervousness, or they don't prepare the material well enough. Sometimes they fall apart in front of us. But then, somebody comes in, and everything clicks. They may have been new or may have been in several times before but for whatever reason, this time they were exactly who we were looking for. Plenty of ridiculously talented and completely prepared actors have come in over the years and have blown us away and then never gotten the gig.

Living with an actor, especially one like Michael who works his tail off to prepare, has made me aware of what it is like to be on the other side of the table.

Actors rarely hear how they did in an audition. A good audition or bad audition the response is either a crushing silence or, very occasionally, a job offer. There's rarely feedback. Feedback isn't all that useful because it is not honest, just polite. Someone auditioning may spend hours and hours working on a particular song with a coach who is charging them $120 an hour. Me asking them to sing something else just because whatever song they've chosen bores me is nothing short of cruel. I have a job and they have a job. I'm not there to be entertained. I'm there to listen.

The advantage of auditioning from home is that Michael has control of what the people who he's auditioning for, see. In an in-person audition, you have one shot. Countless outside forces, the subway, the weather, a competitor in the waiting room can throw you off. At home, Michael can keep filming until he's happy with what he's done.

We are relying on Michael getting television and film work, so whatever it takes, it takes. He feels guilty about having spent money on a new phone but if it makes his audition look better, it is well worth the investment. As much as I'd like one of the new phones, myself, I don't need it, he does. I can wait for mine until I am back to work, and we have more money coming in.

Maybe because it is suddenly a beautiful sunny day, but I feel like I want to go to work this morning. There's a weight that the cold grey wintry weather adds to the day that makes me glad to stay home on the couch. When it's this nice outside, though, I don't want to do that as much. I would be more than happy to spend today inside a rehearsal studio listening to a steady stream of songs that I am completely tired of listening to.

A friend of mine and I went to the Museum of Modern Art yesterday and aside from Van Gogh's *Starry Night*, I couldn't tell you anything else that we saw. We wandered around and talked about stupid things. And we laughed.

It seems to me that our so-called "normal life" is still at least a year away. But it feels like there is something new on the horizon—not our normal life and not what we've been experiencing for this past year but something in-between. Maybe not everything we had in 2019 but with luck, more than we had in 2020. I'm ready for it.

In the meantime, I have the rest of the day to get ready to clip the cat's claws. He's curled up against the radiator and twitching in his sleep. He has no idea what's ahead of him.

FEBRUARY 25, 2021
1,619,924 Total Reported Cases in New York. 47,065 Deaths.

I now have a vaccine appointment for this Saturday instead of the one I had at the end of next month. Yesterday afternoon, I was this close to getting one right away, but as I was filling out the website form, somebody else grabbed it.

A friend of a friend is who ultimately found me the one I got. She is a stay-at-home mom who started taking referrals from her friends. She keeps various sites open and keeps refreshing until appointments become available. It shouldn't be that hard.

I have the time, resources, and contacts to figure out how to play this absurd game. What happens to the people who don't? What happens to the elderly people who may not have access to the internet or the facility to navigate through it. What happens to the people who may be vaccination hesitant in the first place who, when confronted with this byzantine structure surrounding the process, simply give up.

The vaccine rollout started without any real guidance at all. What's being attempted now is a kind of retroactive re-jiggering of a deeply flawed system already in place. People, like the woman who helped Michael and me, are stepping in to fill the void.

MSNBC interviewed a 14-year-old kid in Chicago who has already helped hundreds of seniors find appointments. As he was helping his grandparents in Florida get one, he realized how impossible it was for most people to navigate the system. He started helping others and now has a large group of volunteers who have joined with him. They all keep multiple computer screens open and keep refreshing them until appointments crop up and then they swoop in and grab as many of them as they can.

It's like trying to get tickets to a Beyoncé concert. You can't just buy them. They're gone within minutes of being put on sale with most of them seemingly going to ticket agencies who then resell them at a substantial mark-up. Die-hard fans wait on their computers for the exact time of the release and then refresh like mad until they find them. After the first ten minutes of the sale, if you can find them at all, it's usually through a third party. I am not interested in navigating through all of that, so I don't ever even try.

I did get to see Beyoncé in Las Vegas a few years ago when I just happened to be in the right place at the right time. A small group of tickets that had been held back was suddenly released and I happened to be at the box office getting tickets for something else when it happened.

The person behind the counter who was helping me looked startled and suddenly said, "Oh wow. Beyoncé tickets." I asked if I could get one. Much to my surprise, the answer was yes, and I got in. The tickets had been reserved for the press, so it was a great seat, too.

I wasn't looking for a Beyoncé ticket. I knew she was playing and when I saw the billboard, I thought, "that would be nice," and never gave it another thought. If I was desperate to see Beyoncé, that never would have happened. It was just luck.

It was a fantastic concert, of course. She is an incredible performer and the energy in that arena was unbelievable. I left, though, feeling angry that events like that are so hard to get into.

Eventually, people who want the vaccine will be able to get it. There are probably going to be instances where if you can't prove that you've been vaccinated that you aren't going to be allowed to participate in whatever it is—be it a job or an event. There are going to be countries that will not let outsiders in who cannot prove that they've been inoculated.

It makes sense that when Broadway starts up again that the casts and crews of shows may need to show proof of vaccination before we can all interact together. We will need to be together in close quarters every day, whereas the audience will only gather for one performance.

Hopefully, sooner rather than later, the people in our industry will start to be considered essential workers. If we are all vaccinated and can work together, then the audience can be dealt with separately. Most of the effort seems to be going towards making the audience safe. That thinking is misguided—they need to start with us.

I am happy that Michael and I have been able to schedule our appointments sooner rather than later. When work does start to happen again, the fewer obstacles in our way, the better.

That said, there is no real need for an immediate rush towards being inoculated. The overwhelming majority of the people in my industry are younger and healthier and, as a result, are much further down the list. They might be many months away from being able to get it. I can't get back to work before they can so all the vaccine will give me at this point is a little more peace of mind in my daily life. For the moment, that will have to be enough.

FEBRUARY 26, 2021
1,627,998 Total Reported Cases in New York. 47,190 Deaths.

We are waking up.

Lincoln Center just announced that it is planning on creating 10 different outdoor performance spaces on its property. They are looking to start presenting dance pieces and chamber concerts outside beginning in April. In conjunction with the New York Public Library, they are also going to build an open-air reading room.

A new play called *Thoughts of a Colored Man* installed its marquee at the Golden Theatre yesterday even though they haven't set a firm opening date. It's the first new marquee of the season. It's impossible not to feel a butterfly or two of excitement.

The danger ahead of us, of course, is that as the weather starts to improve and things start to open back up that we will all rush to get back to our full lives too quickly. According to Dr. Fauci, two fully inoculated people should be able to get together with minimal risk. Not with no risk, but, instead, with greatly reduced risk.

I can already see those boundaries getting blurry. If four friends want to hang out and three of them are fully vaccinated and one isn't, I can see people making the rationalization that it should be safe for all of them to meet. The vaccine isn't a wall, it's just a very sturdy fence. The more fences in place the harder it is for it to freely travel. Harder, but not impossible.

If you want any sort of proof about how effective our current social distancing and mask-wearing protocols have been, all I would say is how many of us have gotten sick with our usual winter colds and flu this winter? During my annual exam on Tuesday, my doctor told me that ordinary flu cases have dropped by 90% this year.

Moving forward, if we adopt the same habits that many of our Asian neighbors have done and wear masks when we feel unwell, regardless of what we're sick with, we could keep those numbers much lower than what we had gotten used to.

I am cautiously excited about some of the new performance ideas being developed. Broadway may not reopen for a while, but that doesn't mean that we can't tell our stories in other ways. All the world's a stage, or can be, with a little effort and ingenuity. My fellow theatre professionals are nothing if not ingenious. This spring should bring some very interesting performances.

We didn't quite get to the clipping of the cat's claws yesterday. It got dark. And cold. We started watching TV. I had a glass of wine. In short, we chickened out. If we are smart, we will do it before breakfast today and just get it over with. We just need to commit.

We all need to commit to just getting through the final major part of this pandemic without sinking any further into it. It would be a shame to swim across the Atlantic only to drown in the surf on the other side.

Spring is on the way, but it isn't here yet. That I can feel it starting is going to have to be enough for now. I'll take it. I'll be keeping my eyes open for those first new green shoots poking up from the dirt. It won't be long now.

FEBRUARY 27, 2021

1,636,040 Total Reported Cases in New York. 47,300 Deaths.

This morning I drove out to Martin Van Buren High School in Queens and got my first shot of the Pfizer vaccine.

Martin Van Buren was, until the last guy, considered to have been one of the worst, if not the worst presidents that the United States has ever had. I'm sure that wherever he is, he must be thrilled that he's no longer scraping the very bottom. I am supposed to be related to Martin Van Buren in some way. I think that one of my Great-Great-Grandmothers may have been his niece. That's the family lore at any rate.

Why anyone felt compelled to name a High School after him, is beyond me. Some rather distinguished people went there, though. They've had a couple of Nobel laureates. Both Madeline Kahn and the photographer Robert Mapplethorpe attended the school. When Kahn was a senior, Mapplethorpe was a freshman. I wonder if they knew each other.

The vaccine site was extremely well set up and organized in the school's gymnasium. The whole process couldn't have been simpler. Once

I checked in there were two rows of chairs set at distanced intervals to wait in. Then I was processed and sent into a cubicle where a health practitioner gave me the shot. After that, I was sent to another area with rows of distanced seats to sit and wait for 15 minutes to confirm that I wasn't going to go into anaphylactic shock. They then scheduled my second shot for three weeks from today and sent me home.

It was a very wet morning. Driving home on the Cross Bronx Expressway in heavy rain was no fun at all. I have a slight ache in my arm where I got the shot, but it's already going away.

A year ago, I was finishing up a developmental workshop and about to leave on what would turn out to be my last overseas trip before we shut down. There were reports in the news about the virus but mostly they were about how Italy was getting swamped by it. We were fine and England was fine. A year later, we seem to have passed through it. That there is already a vaccine available would be a miracle if it wasn't so firmly based on actual science. Nothing supernatural was required.

The world has changed a lot in a year. So have we all. For the better?

SPRING 2021

MARCH–MAY

MARCH 1, 2021
1,650,303 Total Reported Cases in New York. 47,519 Deaths.

Michael reacted to his vaccine. I wouldn't say that it knocked him on his butt so much as it kicked him in the shins. He's fine now but he didn't feel all that well this weekend. My arm ached a little for a bit after mine, but that was the extent of it for me. He got vaccinated on Friday, so I'm a day behind him. Last March, when both of us had COVID, he had it worse than I did, then, too. Yesterday, we both planted ourselves on the couch for the day.

Over 96% of American households have television sets. It is an expected appliance in the same way that a sink, stove, or refrigerator is. Some people leave their sets on all day and some never watch, but the set is sitting there. It tends to be a passive way to hear a story.

Live performance takes storytelling to a whole different level. The action unfolds a few feet away from you. You hear and sometimes even feel the vibrations from a dancer's feet on the floor. The power behind an opera singer's voice is evident with their every controlled breath.

I remember when I was still in High School seeing a production of *Once in a Lifetime* at the Circle in the Square Theater and sitting in the front row. During a performance of a play or a musical, you can often see the droplets of moisture coming out of an actor's mouth caught in the beams of light. John Lithgow, who was in *Once in a Lifetime*, is an impressive spitter. I remember having to move my head to avoid it when he was standing near me. He was right there. Ben Platt in *Dear Evan Hanson* was himself, a veritable fountain.

At a live performance, the audience becomes a character in and of itself. Unlike watching a movie, the audience's reactions influence the performance. A responsive house can ignite the evening and one that isn't, can flatten it.

Part of the actor's job is to reach out to the audience and guide them in the right direction. A good director will design the performance to train the audience to react the way they want them to. In *Jersey Boys*, there are moments when the action is crafted to move forward and not allow the audience to applaud something so that after a later moment the applause that finally happens ends up being that much bigger. You can store up an audience's energy. You can also keep the audience from responding in some places when you want to change the emotional temperature onstage and maybe make it darker and more somber.

Television shows or a movie can't do that. Sure, a director can try to manipulate the response through careful editing, but the action is fixed. Movie actors can't adjust what they are doing to either reign in an audience or set them free. Their performances have been captured and they are what they are regardless of who is watching.

This year the storytelling that we have witnessed, has been very different. Instead of an array of experiences open to us, everything, and I mean everything, that we have seen this year has come from our television sets. Whether it was a dance performance, an opera, a Broadway play, a lecture or a movie, or a television show, all of them have been filtered through our individual screens into our living spaces. The Broadway musical sensation *Hamilton* was converted into just another television presentation. Even our social interactions are televised these days, albeit as interactional events, on Zoom. Whatever it once was, everything is now just becoming a television show.

Our televisions and computer screens are both the only things that are keeping us all together as well as being the medium through which we are being separated. Finding the balance between engaging too much and not engaging at all is not easy. Instead of the shows featuring our politicians, I much prefer the shows that feature our friends.

For now, though, all our screens are off while we get ready to eat our first meal of the day. After Michael works with a few students on screen, of course, and I take my walk we are going to get down to the business of living during a pandemic. Food shopping, laundry, and taxes are on the docket for today.

And no, we still haven't clipped the cat's claws yet. It's on the list.

MARCH 2, 2021
Governor of Texas ends mask mandates and allows businesses to fully reopen.

According to popular thought, it takes 21 days to form a new habit. It is a generally accepted idea without any actual scientific study behind it. In 2009, four researchers at University College in London decided to investigate whether it was true or not and wrote a paper called *How are habits formed: Modelling habit formation in the real world*. They published it in the *European Journal of Social Psychology*.

In an earlier 1960 book, Dr. Maxwell Maltz had referenced the 21-day idea and based on his casual observance, given it some credence. The UK psychologists wanted to see if they could back it up. What they found was that the time it took from the initial moment of planning an action through to the point that the action became automatic, or, in other words, a habit, could take anywhere from 18 to 254 days.

Starting with the idea that a repeated action is the basis for forming a habit, the researchers asked 96 participants to, "repeat a behaviour of their choice, in response to a cue, in an everyday setting, and complete a measure of automaticity on a daily basis."

The subjects were asked to carry out the new behavior in the same situation each day. Instead of doing whatever it was at a certain time, they would do it, say, after they had eaten or before they worked out so that it started to become associated with that activity. Drinking a bottle of water with lunch or running for 15 minutes before dinner were two of the kinds of things that the participants chose to do.

Previous studies seemed to indicate that some sort of reward was necessary to incentivize the creation of the habit. Given that the participants chose their habit to form, the leaders of the study assumed that achieving it would be reward enough.

There are three main features of habits—lack of awareness, lack of control, and efficiency. In addition to those, there are two others—a history of repetition and identity. Unsurprisingly, simple actions, such as eating and drinking, were found to create habits faster than more complex ones like exercising.

When everything first shut down almost a year ago now, we all started engaging in new activities. We were all put in a new situation and we had to figure out what to do. We got used to doing certain things at certain times and even had to figure out how to do some new things. Nearly a year has passed at this point and given the length of time it takes to make something an actual habit, we will likely never lose some of the new behaviors we have created.

In the first few months, the running joke was the COVID 19—the extra pounds that everyone put on while stress-eating. We all needed immediate comfort and food was the easiest path to that goal. At the point where the anxiety of being locked down was starting to let up, the election process started which kept everything at a fever pitch and the comforting behaviors kept going and got more entrenched.

In recent weeks, with the election and inauguration behind us, I have been able to make the conscious decision to change some of the habits that I've created. I have been trying to eat better and carry the behavior through. The weight is starting to come off and I find myself within spitting distance of where I'd like to be.

In normal times, my schedule was so unpredictable and erratic that coming up with any sort of exercising or nutritional routine was almost impossible. I would start to get into a groove in one situation but then it would completely change, and I'd have to start all over again in a new place.

We are not living in normal times. My schedule is nothing if not utterly routine. Writing these posts every day started as a conscious decision on my part to try and put what was going on around me into some sort of context. That people started reading them was both gratifying and alarming in equal measure. When there started to be an expectation that I would post every day, I started to worry about how I would be able to keep going. I decided to keep going as long as I could and told myself that I would stop when I ran out of things to say.

That "out" that I gave myself took away the anxiety and allowed me to form what is now very much a habit. I spend the first 2-4 hours of each day writing and I don't have to think about doing it at all.

For the most part, I have no idea what I am going to write about until I sit down and start. Sometimes, when I am about halfway through, I think, "Really? This is what you are going to publish?" but I honestly have stopped worrying about it. I think about the writing as I am doing it, but I do not think about the act of it at all. It has very much become an actual habit.

So, has walking. The only thing that I think about around walking is how to protect myself from the elements. Pouring rain is no fun to walk in at all, but I am pretty much driven to do it regardless.

Michael and I have long gotten into the habit of only eating two meals a day and it never crosses my mind to add in a third. I am now firmly in the early days of attempting to form new habits around what, specifically, I am eating. I want to take advantage of what looks to be a stretch of time ahead of us where I will still be on the same schedule to let the behaviors truly sink in.

I have been trying to drop 10 pounds for a decade. Whatever weight your body stays in for a period, your body adjusts to and starts to believe that is its proper weight. Diets fail in large part because when you lose that weight, even if it is just fat, your body thinks that it is in distress and does everything it can to convince you to put it back on. I found it easy to lose the extra COVID pounds but not these last 10. The COVID pounds were new, the 10 not so much. The trick is to get to your goal weight slowly and methodically and then to stay there for a few months.

I have been successful at the first part several times. I have not been successful at all in the second part. If the conservative right doesn't try to stage another coup, I'm feeling confident that I might be able to do it this time. Should be able to.

In a far more practical vein, no, we again did not get to the cat's claws yesterday. I know that we truly need to get into the habit of doing it. The more we do it, the less traumatic for all three of us it will be. It will start to become normal for him and maybe, as a result, less of an assault.

Michael is humming Sondheim which usually means that he's done with what he needs to do and is relaxed. The cat is curled up next to me and oblivious. Oh, too late. Michael has just now started making breakfast. Maybe after.

March 3, 2021
1,663,248 Total Reported Cases in New York. 47,733 Deaths.

My walk yesterday took me across the Manhattan Bridge, through Williamsburg, Brooklyn, and then back into Manhattan via the Williamsburg Bridge. All of it was new territory to me. While the Williamsburg Bridge was fun to walk over, the Manhattan Bridge wasn't. Several subway lines run over it and the walkway is right alongside it. It was deafeningly noisy the whole way.

The Manhattan Bridge and the Brooklyn Bridge are right next to each other although they come into Brooklyn from slightly different directions creating a triangle when viewed from above. Between where they end in Brooklyn, lies the DUMBO area which is where many artists fled as SoHo became gentrified and they could no longer afford to live there. Unsurprisingly, DUMBO, itself, has now become gentrified. Its abandoned warehouses now house expensive condominiums. High-end clothing boutiques and trendy restaurants and coffee shops line the streets. St. Ann's Warehouse, one of the best Off-Broadway theatres in the city, sits in its latest renovated home on the banks of the East River just a stone's throw away from Jane's Carousel—a beautifully restored 1920s Merry-Go-Round.

Rather than going into DUMBO, I instead ventured north into Williamsburg. Like walking into Chinatown, walking into Williamsburg feels a bit like going into another country. The area is largely inhabited by tens of thousands of members of various Hasidic Jewish communities.

Living under strict religious rules, the people there have their own modes of dress. The women wear wigs and modest dark skirts, and the men wear long black coats and brimmed black hats and keep their hair and beards long. In the early afternoon, when I was there, school was letting out. Older kids walked together in small groups chatting and laughing like kids everywhere. Younger kids walked with their parents—often with a couple of mothers strolling together. Men were largely on their own or in pairs, intent on getting to wherever it was they were going in good time. It's a bustling area with a lot going on. People seemed happy and often greeted each other as they passed. Stores were doing a brisk business. Nobody was wearing a mask.

Not one Hasidic person that I passed yesterday had a mask on or was observing any kind of social distancing at all. I would occasionally see a person who was not a member of the community—a police officer or bus driver—and all of them were wearing masks—but nobody who looked like they lived there was. If you want to know what life was like before the pandemic struck, you need only head across the river.

It's not that the virus isn't there—it is and at much higher rates than anywhere else in the city.

It is largely Hasidic areas that make the average of our city's positivity rates as high as they are. Everyone there just seems to be ignoring it. Large Orthodox community events, especially funerals, have become super-spreader events, allowing the virus to spread like lightning.

A Jewish journalist named Louis Finkelman tried to answer why this is in an article he published in The Jewish News. He was a bit confused as well. The main tenants of Judaism all require their followers to put their health above even their customs and codes. An observant Jew must use a phone to call a doctor even on Shabbat, eat during a fast day, or do any number of other things that ordinarily would not be allowed if doing so will protect themselves or another from harm. Jewish law also encourages the following of civil laws to respect those others with whom they live.

That is not what is happening now in Williamsburg. Regardless of how it looks to others or sickens their members, the Orthodox communities are living by their own rules. The Hasidic people consider themselves an insular community. Separate from the rest. They believe that laws that keep them from worshiping as they choose should be ignored. Elders rely on a strict interpretation of Jewish teachings and will dismiss so-called scientific experts with a wave of the hand, often without any consideration whatsoever.

Then we get to the crux of the matter. Orthodox Jewish communities tend to overwhelmingly vote Republican. In our last election, 83% of surveyed Hasidim said that they planned to vote again for the ex-President. Given the party's embrace of Anti-Semitism and the use of Nazi-era imagery, I find this hard to reconcile. Nonetheless, the whole not wearing a mask thing then becomes somewhat less surprising.

Republican Governor Greg Abbot of Texas announced yesterday that he is lifting his state-wide mask-wearing mandate and is going to allow businesses to reopen at full capacity. As of now, only 6.57% of Texans have been vaccinated. The only likely result of this decision is going to be a spike in new cases, hospitalizations, and deaths. Texas, the Lone Star State, is the one state in the union that, at one point, was its own country. It takes pride in being separate from the rest of us. In his announcement yesterday,

Governor Abbot said, "People and businesses don't need the state telling them how to operate."

Both the Jewish community in Williamsburg and the state of Texas share a desire to be left alone by the rest of the country. They are, however, very much a part of the rest of the country and they each derive protections and advantages from their memberships in our collective society. As dispirit as these two groups are, they share something with all the rest of us—we are all Americans. As trite as it sounds, we are all in this together.

"America, Love it or Leave it" was a popular bumper sticker in the 1970s. It was directed against the lefties who were protesting our involvement in the Vietnam War and other governmental policies. The idea being, that if you were critical of the government then that meant that you didn't love the country. Anyone who tried to alter the insular, racist, and unfair policies of various American communities, the people who displayed the sticker thought, should just get out and go somewhere else. The same stickers could be printed today with Texas and Williamsburg replacing the original word, "America."

I don't plan on going back to Williamsburg anytime soon. It's a fascinating area, but watching an entire community reject simple and basic commonsensical measures to protect themselves just because they resent somebody else telling them to do so is tragic. When I was a kid and being stupid, my mother would say to me, "You are cutting off your nose to spite your face." In other words, doing something out of spite or revenge causes YOU more harm than it does anyone else.

There are plenty of people in Texas who will continue to wear masks and keep their distance from each other, but there are also plenty who won't. I cannot begin to fathom why wearing a mask makes so many people recoil in the way that they do. It is just not that big a deal. Is it a guaranteed solution to the problem? No, of course not, but it helps. It may not help you as much as it will help your neighbors, but shouldn't that be how we live with each other anyway?

The reaction some people have against wearing a mask seems as absurdly out of proportion as our cat's reaction to getting his claws clipped.

We finally knuckled down and got at the cat's claws yesterday. I think that when all was said and done it took just about three minutes. The yowling and spitting and hissing were completely off the charts. The second we were done, he calmly and, with great suffering dignity, made his way to the kitchen to wait for the treat that he knew was coming. To soothe his ruffled feathers, he got a whole extra portion of soft food.

I missed one claw on his front left foot which I discovered later when he curled up on my lap. We waited until just before he was due to get his second round of food at 11 (we call this, his "elevenses"), clipped it quickly and all was well. One yowl and a hiss and we were done, and he could eat. We have vowed to try and do the stupid clipping every couple of weeks in the hope that he will just get used to it. The whole thing is ridiculous and I'm just glad that it's over for now.

Loving our individual views of America has sort of led us to where we are now. So, maybe, instead of loving, what we should be doing is simply respecting America. Right now, we need to respect each other far more than we need to love each other. Let the love come later. For now, some basic simple respect would be enough.

It is a stunning day out and I am very much looking forward to today's walk. My journey through Williamsburg made me realize just how unfamiliar I am with Brooklyn, so that's where I'll head.

March 4, 2021
Vaccinations in the United States reach an average of 2 million a day.

Congress is not in session today because of fears that there might be some sort of attack against members from the Republican far right.

Back in 1790, using land donated from the states of Maryland and Virginia, a federal district was formed to create a capital for the new country. Included in the area were the port city of Georgetown, Maryland, and the Virginia town of Alexandria. The new city was named in honor of President Washington.

Both Maryland and Virginia continued to govern parts of the new district. A levy court with 7-11 Justices of the Peace who were appointed by the President governed the rest. To make things even more confusing, the two individual cities that had been incorporated into the new district retained their individual municipal governments.

After the Civil War, the population of the federal district exploded. Newly emancipated former enslaved people were drawn to the area searching for work. By 1870, there were over 130,000 residents—three-quarters more than had been there a decade before. Most of the district still had dirt roads and lacked basic sanitation facilities. Even though some in Congress thought that since conditions were so bad that the capital should be moved, President Ulysses Grant, instead, passed the District of Columbia Organic Act of 1871.

In it, the individual charters of Georgetown and Alexandria were revoked and combined with that of Washington county to create a unified territorial government. There have been other changes to how Washington D.C. is governed since then, the last major one being in 1973 with the passage of the District of Columbia Home Rule Act which provided for an elected Mayor and a Council, among other things, taking local governance away from Congress.

The reason that I went down that rabbit hole is that conspiracy theorists believe that the Organic Act of 1871 turned the district, and therefore, the entire United States of America into a corporation. They believe this because the words Municipal Corporation were used in the language of the Act. It is simply a legal term for any local governing body, whether they control cities, counties, towns, townships, charter townships, villages, or boroughs.

QAnon conspiracists believe that no President since then has been legitimate nor has any federal legislation. This includes the passage of the Twentieth Amendment in 1933 which moved the date for the incoming President's inauguration to January 20 from, yes you guessed it, March 4. The extreme right-wing Republican supporters of the ex-President believe that after another insurrection today, March 4, that their leader will be reinstalled as the 19th President of these United States. This threat is so credible to law enforcement agencies, that members of Congress have taken today off.

Q followers find clues to support their lunacy just about everywhere. If you add up the numbers in 1871 you get to 17. What number is Q in the alphabet? It's 17! That can't be a coincidence, so it proves that it's all true! There are even conspiracy theories around the conspiracy theories. Some Q members are saying that the March 4th conspiracy theory was created by the Deep State of the far left to discredit QAnon. As if running an international child trafficking ring from the back rooms of a pizza parlor wasn't time-consuming enough.

Should the overthrow of the government of the United States of America not happen today, Q followers have a plausible reason, in their eyes anyway, why and they will be able to move on to the next coming of the righteous wrath of truth. Whoever the actual Q is or was, they have been silent for months. The goal of terrorist organizations is to disrupt. Today, they have succeeded. Calls on the ex-President to tell his followers to stand down have fallen on deaf ears.

It seems to me, that the drive necessary to become powerful often comes along with the less desirable side effects of bad behavior. Where does controlling leadership behavior end and bullying behavior begin? People in leadership positions, and I will include myself, have a certain amount of ego and desire for attention. Even the very shy directors that I have worked with are completely confident about their visions and become relentless while pushing them forward.

I can look at a problem and think, "I can fix this." There is a cost, however, to every solution. Some people are happy with the result, and some are not. As the saying goes, you can't make a cake without breaking some eggs. When, however, your solutions end up with the same people being unhappy time and time again then it is probably time to come up with another solution. We are in a unique position in our society. We can change. I certainly include myself in that as well. There are plenty of recipes for egg-less cakes. Some of them are quite good.

We cannot expect our Politicians to be better than anybody else. We can, however, expect them to act better than anybody else, at least around the responsibilities that they agree to take on when they assume their offices. At the end of the day, they are all just people with the same driving passions as the rest of us. When they get into office, they take an oath to put our needs ahead of theirs.

We need to move forward, and we need the people we chose to be at the head of the line to choose the direction that we go in. We trust that they will do a better job of it than we would, ourselves. If they don't, then we choose someone else.

At some point, while I was writing this, without my noticing it, the cat curled up next to me. He's dreaming about something because his paws are twitching. I hope it's a good one.

March 5, 2021
1,678,867 Total Reported Cases in New York. 47,951 Deaths.

Michael has another audition to film this morning, so the living room is, again, being converted into a television studio. When filming gets underway, I will get out of his way.

New York City has initiated a new permit for outdoor performances called "Open Culture" to try and jumpstart the performance industry. People can apply to the Mayor's Street Activity Permit Office to get permission to stage ticketed events at over 100 outdoor locations throughout the five boroughs.

To receive one of these permits, the applicants must prove that they are connected to a bona fide art or cultural institution. "A theater, music venue, comedy club, or similar venue that has regular live performances could qualify," says the description on the city website. "A residence that hosts performances (e.g., poetry readings) or a film production facility that is used to film shows before a live studio audience would not qualify."

Yesterday, we all received an email from the Actors' Equity Association President warning that this program does not meet basic union requirements regarding either salary or COVID-19 safety measures. In addition, there is nothing that mandates that performers and other workers receive unemployment insurance. There is nothing that mandates testing or social distancing between performers and the audience or between the performers themselves. There is no requirement for a COVID safety officer.

This is a completely different program than the state program called

NY PopsUp. In the same email to us, AEA's President says, "Equity staff and your elected leadership have been in ongoing dialogue with state leaders about this (NY PopsUp) program since it was announced in January. As a result of those conversations, we have signed an agreement allowing for Equity members to be paid for NY PopsUp performances with a living wage and health and pension payments. The NY PopsUp team has also incorporated our feedback into their safety plan, improving the safety for everyone associated with the project."

It took me many years of working to convince my father that working in the theatre was more than just a hobby. It wasn't that he thought that the work was somehow "less than" it is just that I don't think he thought that it was actual work at all.

I spent much of my time in High School working on plays and musicals while I was also studying. When I was initially starting in professional theatre here in New York, I often had to work non-theatre jobs during the day to pay the bills. The theatres that I was working in were tiny and the jobs only lasted several weeks so, I think, in his head, it was a continuation of what I had been doing in school—working by day and doing theatre for fun in my extra time. My theatre work seemed to be on top of my money earning, not money earning in and of itself.

I was finally able to join the union and start qualifying for health insurance about three years after I graduated from college. It wasn't until three or four years after that I got a regular job on a long-running Broadway musical. While that job certainly paid better. I still don't necessarily think that the perception of it was as serious employment. After all, what I help create is called a "play" and not a "work."

The advantage of working on Broadway is that when people ask you what you do, they have often heard of your project. When you tell strangers that you are stage managing a three-character Strindberg play at a small downtown Off-Broadway theatre, the reaction is completely different. You can see people's eyes glaze over and something between pity and embarrassment creeps into their expressions. "Oh… Hmm…"

The Strindberg play was very much a bona fide job. The performers and stage managers were working under union contracts, and we were earning both unemployment and health insurance weeks. To the greater world, however, working in a small theatre, I think, seems as if we are doing it for love rather than for money. Certainly, we are putting up with low pay and weird working conditions in part for the love of it, but we also have rent to pay and groceries to buy.

Just like everyone else.

There are moments of glamor and flash while working in the theatre. There is nothing like an opening night on Broadway when you are working on a hit. Despite how boring it can be to sit through the entire thing, I wouldn't trade the few times I've put on a tux and gone to the Tony Awards for anything. I have traveled all over the country and all over the world and seen some remarkable things.

Most of the time, however, I, along with my fellow industry members am simply working.

Sometimes it's rewarding and sometimes it's tedious. Working in the theatre ensures extremely long hours and erratic schedules. We work when everyone else is resting. Nights and weekends mean extra work for us, not time off. We work through weddings, funerals, baptisms, and holidays. Sometimes we are very well paid and sometimes not so much.

What most people don't see when they tune in to watch *Law & Order SVU* and see Michael sitting behind his bench for a minute or two is the hours and days and weeks and months and years and decades that he put in to get there. It looks like fun—he gets to hang out with Marishka Hargitay and Raúl Esparza and kibbutz with them between shots. All of them, however, are working just as hard if not harder than anyone else in any other job.

Yes, we love it. You cannot work as hard as we do and not love what you are doing. But we don't need anyone's pity, nor should anyone be embarrassed for us. This is the life that we all chose.

Broadway, alone, when it's functioning, brings in $12.6 billion to the city's economy on top of ticket sales. Broadway, alone, provides direct jobs for 12,500 people and indirect jobs for 74,500 more. When you then add in every single other venue in the city and what they generate, you end up with a sizable chunk of our economy accounted for. An analysis by the US Bureau of Economics found that arts and culture, pre-pandemic, accounted for 3.2% of our country's entire Gross Domestic Product. In dollar terms that equals about $504 billion. To put that into some sort of context, the entire US tourism and travel industry only accounts for 2.8% of our GDP.

After this past year, we are all more than ready to be entertained again. We are all starved for it—I'm starved for it. Despite that, we are not going to do it for free. We are not members of a charitable organization. This is our work. Would anyone ask a meat packer or a bus driver or a stockbroker to work for free? Of course not. Those are "real" jobs and people who do them should be paid for them.

Whatever it might look like to outsiders, I, along with my colleagues, have spent my entire professional life working real jobs in the arts. Sometimes I've been on Broadway or at Lincoln Center and sometimes I've been in an empty unfinished loft in the middle of nowhere or even out in a field.

Our industry needs to come back. Whether or not you work in the performing arts, we all need it to return. All the souls on both sides of the footlights need it, and all our bank accounts need it too. Our country's economy cannot recover without it.

Programs like the ones being initiated by NY state and the city are probably a great way to start. That said, all of us who are out of work cannot be called upon to participate in these for free or for vastly reduced wages and without complete and proper health guidelines being followed. We are trained, skilled and experienced workers at the top of our crafts and deserve nothing less.

Nothing in the performing arts industry is coming back until we can beat this virus back to manageable levels. We aren't there yet. The Biden COVID response team is warning of a possible fourth spike in the virus. If the city and state want us back, then performers and crew members need to be all reclassified as essential workers and be allowed to get vaccinated. Yes, protocols for audiences need to be figured out, but long before that, protocols for the theatre workers themselves need to be created and put in place. There is nothing frivolous about the work that we do in arts-related jobs. It is hard and, at times, completely thankless. Despite that, we are happy and committed to doing it with our whole hearts. We will be back, but not before our safety and financial well-beings are ensured.

As somebody wrote on the sidewalk in front of the Martin Beck Theatre in the early days of the pandemic, "You want a live performance? Wear a f&^%ng mask."

I need to get out of Michael's way, now, and go out for a walk. He's working.

MARCH 6, 2021
1,686,993 Total Reported Cases in New York. 48,045 Deaths.

Exactly a year ago today, I was in London. We were on our last day of auditions there for the Norwegian Cruise Lines production of *Jersey Boys*.

A year ago, tonight, in London, I went to see Tom Stoppard's new play. It never crossed my mind at that point that my flight home two days later would be the last time I'd be on a plane for at least a year. Why would it?

The museum that I went to on that last Saturday was the Hayward Gallery on the South Bank of the Thames. In it, there was a wonderful exhibition centered around trees.

Everything in the exhibit referenced trees in some way—from photographs and paintings to huge installations with some containing actual parts of fallen branches and trunks. At the time I was reading *The Overstory*, Richard Power's book that would go on to win the Pulitzer in May.

The whole narrative of his wonderful book revolves around five trees and some of the people who interact with them over the centuries.

The combination of both seeing that exhibit, and reading that book woke me up to a new way of seeing. I cannot walk through New York City these days without being aware of all the trees living among us. Nearly 600,000 of them line our streets. From those whose canopies lie just below our living room windows to their wilder cousins out in our parks, we live in a city of trees.

5.2 million trees grow on the land that encompasses New York City. That number seems more remarkable given that, unlike us, they can't live on top of each other. Each one of them needs its own patch of land.

As of this past year, there are 168 different species of tree known to reside in this city. The ten most prevalent are the London Planetree, the Littleleaf Linden, the Norway Maple, the Green Ash, the Callery Pear, the Red Maple, the Honey Locust, the Silver Maple, the Pin Oak, and the Ginkgo.

In the gift shop at the Hayward Gallery, they were selling some beautifully designed and made eco-friendly items. I bought us two rechargeable battery-powered LED lamps made of sustainable wood. They have become such an integral part of our life around the dining table that I can't quite believe that I only got them a year ago. I remember on that long-ago Saturday in London carrying them with me in their boxes to meet up with my cousins for lunch before we went to see a play.

I think I contracted COVID-19 sometime that weekend.

We are now entering into a time where we are all going to be aware of anniversaries.

A year since we last worked.

A year since we saw our last performance of a show.

A year since we went anywhere.

A year since we experienced an unimaginable loss.

A year since the birth of a child.

A year since… fill in the blank.

Trees live on a different timeline than we do. There are Bristlecone Pine trees in California that are over 5,000 years old. There are other trees in Italy, Japan, Brazil, Wales, and other places that are almost as old.

As endless as this year has felt, it is just a mere fraction of our total lives. It's been an important year in many regards, but it's still just a year. In the life of one of those ancient trees, it is nothing more than a relative minute.

Many of the trees in Central Park were placed or planted there in 1857 by landscape architects Frederick Law Olmstead and Calvert Vaux. Not all of them have survived and, over the years have had to be replaced. Of the 18,000 trees currently in the park, only 150 were already there when the park was created. The oldest tree in the park is a London Plane tree on the Bridal Path right near our apartment at 96th Street.

The trees that canopy the Literary Walk constitute the largest grove of American Elms in the world. American Elms were largely decimated by Dutch Elm disease. These hardy survivors are one of New York City's greatest treasures. Another beautiful American Elm, with a canopy wider than it is tall stands in the cobbled plaza across from the American Museum of Natural History. Yet another one also dating from the 1800s stands by the western 97th Street entrance to the park.

We aren't trees. The passage of time impacts us far more than it does them. Storms and glorious weather come and go. Like them, our lives are punctuated with periods of plenty and periods of want. Are we currently in a period of plenty or one of want? I would argue for the former.

That it took a global pandemic for me to even notice these remarkable trees, some of which stand less than a block away from where I live, tells me that maybe this pause was long overdue. It is a little too early to stop and smell the flowers, but now, just before their leaves return and begin to hide them, is a perfect time to stop and look at the trees.

MARCH 8, 2021
1,700,091 Total Reported Cases in New York. 48,198 Deaths.

The northern end of Manhattan is far less tame than its southern part is. Starting uptown at about where we are, the mostly flat landscape starts to roll so that by the time you get to the top of the island, you've had to climb some actual hills.

Large outcroppings of glacial rock separate some streets from others, enough so that if you've chosen to walk in one direction instead of another, you are out of luck if you change your mind. You either need to keep going north and hope that you will be able to walk around it, or you need to retrace your steps downtown for a few blocks and start up again on the other side.

The original Dutch city of New Amsterdam was founded on the southern tip of the island. The city sprang up there and slowly crept uptown as more and more people arrived. Surrounded on three sides by water, the only direction that new people could settle in was to the north. As waves of people arrived the settlement started to fill up the rest of the available acreage like water being poured into a glass. The rising tide of people flattened the land and sent rivers and streams underground to get them out of the way of everything that was being constructed.

The oldest photograph known to have been taken in Manhattan dates from 1848. It shows a small, comfortable-looking farmhouse perched on top of a hill encircled by a white picket fence.

Between that enclosure and the camera is a deep gully that must have had a stream rushing through it.

This house was somewhere along what was then called Bloomingdale Road and is today called Broadway. Bloomingdale Road was the main thoroughfare from the city below up to the farmland and the northern tip of the island which, of course, was as far as you could go then. There were no bridges to take you further north into the Bronx. Instead, there were just extremely steep cliffs falling into the Hudson that stopped you in your tracks. The highlands stayed cool in the summer, so it was a popular place to take a day trip to, to escape the city's heat and noise. Somewhere around 100th Street was a small village, also called Bloomingdale, and then a couple of miles to the north of that was Washington Heights.

In 1848, when the photograph was taken, downtown did not look all that dissimilar from how it looks today. Another photograph taken in 1850 at a point near Broadway and Franklin Streets shows multi-storied tenements that may still be standing down there today. It is recognizable to our contemporary eyes as lower Manhattan. Nothing in that 1848 shot of the farmhouse, however, looks like anything you would see, today, in the city.

Above 190th Street, lies Fort Tryon Park and in the middle of it stands the MET Cloisters Museum. Built around sections of four different actual medieval French cloisters, the museum houses much of the Metropolitan Museum of Art's collections from that time. The buildings, themselves, sit atop a steep hill that commands a breathtaking view of the Hudson River and New Jersey beyond.

The cloister buildings were purchased by American sculptor George Grey Barnard. People in France were already starting to use the building's stones for other things. Barnard claimed that one of the tomb effigies that he bought was found face down across a stream functioning as a bridge. He purchased the structures as ruins, gathered up the pieces he could find and had them transported to New York. John D. Rockefeller then bought them from him for the museum. Rockefeller also bought the land along the Palisades Cliffs across the river in New Jersey and donated it to the State to preserve the view.

One of the pieces in the Cloister's collection is a carved ivory cross called either the Cloister's Cross or the Bury St. Edmond's Cross. It is about 2 feet tall and beautifully made. Walking through the treasury section it has a position of relative prominence but aside from a basic description, there is little to differentiate it from the other treasures surrounding it.

In 1981, Thomas Hoving, who was an Associate Curator of the museum at the time that they acquired the cross, published a book called *King of the Confessors*. The book is all about the cross and its creation, its imagery, and, most of all, the adventure that Hoving went through in the process of buying it. It would make a spectacular movie. The book goes into depth about how museums work—how they raise money, how they compete—all the nasty little things that happen behind closed doors.

The cross, itself, is not all that it seems on first viewing. While nobody knows who made it, there is a lot about it that suggests that there are decidedly anti-Semitic aspects to the imagery. It is thought that the piece was made somewhere during the 12th Century in England. At that time, the tide of public opinion was rising against the Jewish people to the point that by the end of the following century they were all expelled from Britain. The cross may have been made to help that process along. Most of the population in those years was illiterate. The carver of the cross may have been trying to tell a tale that would help sway the population to their way of thinking.

To a casual observer, the Bury St. Edmond's cross is a beautiful object, but it likely wouldn't be the piece of art that person would remember the most after they left. I read Thomas Hoving's book when I was still in High School so for, me, that carved cross is the most vivid thing in the entire place. Yes, much of what I know of it came from one person who certainly told his story to benefit himself in some way. Regardless, his story adds remarkable dimension to what would, ordinarily, just be two or three dry lines of description on a card posted next to it.

Strolling through the ancient stone buildings up there is as close to being in Europe as we here in the states can be these days. Around each corner, it seems, is another columned courtyard, each with a garden. It's as far away from New York City as you can go and still be on the same island.

The city, itself, though, has so many stories to tell, that it seems a far better use of my time to go out and track some of those down than it does to sit home and watch television. People come and go, but the city, at least during this current epoch, endures. It was here before us and, God willing will be here long afterward. The city has nothing to gain and nothing to lose in the telling of its tales. They're just stories. And I am always hungry for a good story.

MARCH 9, 2021

1,706,924 Total Reported Cases in New York. 48,277 Deaths.

I started to laugh this morning as I made the bed. The action of pulling up the covers and smoothing them out has been repeated so many times this year that the sheer repetition of it suddenly seemed absurd. I tossed the pillows that I stacked on the rocking chair last night back onto the bed knowing full well that in just a few hours that I will toss them back on the rocker.

Small, Dark, and Furry, as we sometimes refer to the cat, was sitting by the bedroom door and batted at my leg as I walked past him with such a complete lack of any interest or intent, that I had to laugh again. Even he knows that there is almost nothing that will break up the routine of the day. No food is due to come his way for hours.

It looks like our unemployment payments will continue until September. The Stimulus bill passed through the Senate on Saturday and then went back to the House to get some changes to it approved. It is not expected that any of those will fail to pass. After that, the bill will head to the President for signing in a few days and payments should, in theory, then keep coming uninterrupted. The final Congressional vote on it could happen later tonight but it's more likely that it will happen tomorrow.

The CDC announced its new vaccination guidelines yesterday, saying that fully vaccinated people should be able to finally meet up with other fully vaccinated people without masks and distancing, but in small groups. Fully vaccinated people will also be allowed to meet up with a single small unit of unvaccinated people, either friends or family, in private as well. Those meetings will all need to happen inside homes and not just out in the crowded world. The CDC defines fully vaccinated as being two weeks after your final shot. Michael and I will be considered fully vaccinated by the middle of next month.

It feels like Spring has already begun. This is the time, of course, when we are going to need to be the most vigilant regarding the virus. Cracking the door open a bit doesn't mean that we can all just rush out together at the same time. Given how badly some groups have followed the guidelines thus far, it is almost guaranteed that those groups will do everything too quickly and that we will see another spike.

Going back in time to the Spanish flu a hundred years ago, a final spike is exactly what happened during this time, then, too. It happened at exactly this time of year, when people, desperate for the end of winter and the shutdown, tried to get back to some sort of normal too soon.

In 1919, the third wave started at the end of that winter and the beginning of spring, and then ultimately subsided during the summer. After that, there were periodic annual outbreaks that were all very much smaller and isolated. The Spanish flu, of course, never fully went away. It still recurs sometimes during regular flu seasons, but it has never raged through the population again the way that it did.

So far, COVID-19 has pretty much followed the Spanish flu's trajectory beat for beat. If we are lucky, it will continue to do so. That we could have avoided much of this journey seems clear but that will be endlessly debated by historians in the future. For now, though, it doesn't look like we did any better or any worse than our ancestors did a century ago. A shame, really. We should have learned something from 1918.

There are still very few tourists, if any, in the city these days. As the weather has gotten better, there have been more people out in the street. They are shopping and walking and eating out in restaurants. With so many people working from home, the steady deluge of commuters has dwindled to a fine trickle. More and more people are returning to the subways, but still at nowhere near pre-pandemic levels. I have yet to see anyone run to catch one.

There are no squads of grey-suited men and women out on the streets in midtown on their way to business lunches or meetings. The entire theatre district becomes dead silent and still every day at just the point that it should be at its busiest and most chaotic.

The city feels more crowded now but not yet anywhere near the levels it once was. There are still plenty of moments, even in Times Square, when you can walk out into the street without there being any traffic coming at you at all.

I can tell how anxiety-provoking living under the last Administration was, by how much lower my anxiety level currently is. We aren't through this, but it feels like we are at least heading in the right direction.

Breakfast is close to being served and I've promised to get out of the house again so Michael can film yet another audition. There are still several hours ahead before I need to take the pillows back off the bed and stack them on the rocking chair, turn down the covers and get ready to go back to sleep.

You have to laugh.

March 10, 2021

Brazil surpasses the United States as the country with the highest daily rate of COVID-19 infections.

Both Michael and I have spent a sizable amount of time this past year searching for things that we've lost.

I'm not talking about anything on an existential level like our reasons for being, the spark that drives us forward, or the actions that we used to think defined who we were, I'm talking about actual objects in our apartment.

This morning, Michael lost his mug. He spent a solid minute searching for it. He had just poured himself some fresh coffee. It's not as if he left it somewhere last night. He had just had it in his hand. Last night I lost a glass of wine. Once I finally found it on the sideboard in the front hall, I could then piece together how it got there. I had started cleaning up the coffee table and I went to put some used empty envelopes into our recycling bag by the front door. When I got there, two other bags of stuff had fallen over so I set down the wine and picked everything up. When it was all put back together, I put on a mask and took a lot of it down to the basement to get rid of it. When I got back, I went back to the couch, plopped down, and reached for my glass of wine and it wasn't there.

"Where is my glass of wine?"

"I didn't take it. Where did you have it?"

"Right here."

My phone has been irretrievably lost inside this one-bedroom apartment this past year more times than I can count. Its case is similar in color to both the couch and the cat. Once or twice, after searching high and low, I have found it under the sleeping cat, but out of the hundred times that I've lost it, that has only ever happened twice. Regardless, if the cat is sleeping on the bed or the couch, he is always my first stop.

Before this year, losing my phone would immediately make me worry that I had left it backstage at a theatre or that maybe it had fallen out of my pocket while I was watching a show. In my mind, I would immediately launch into the worst-case scenario involving buying a new phone and getting it operational in time to get to work the next day. These days, I know it's in the apartment and that makes losing it all the worse.

The trial of Derek Chauvin, the ex-Police officer from Minneapolis who is the person who was kneeling on George Floyd's neck as he died, is underway. Chauvin has been charged with second-degree murder and second-degree manslaughter.

The fear is that though the possibility of justice being served is being dangled in front of us, that the system behind that justice is so corrupted by systemic racism that, somehow, he will get away with it. For Derek Chauvin to be convicted, the jury, who is being selected now, is going to have to be convinced that he broke the law.

We can look at the video of what happened and say that he's guilty of killing George Floyd. Given existing laws and police department practices, though, did he? Is he legally guilty of overreach? The jurors being chosen this morning will be tasked with deciding Chauvin's guilt or innocence based purely on the existing laws and not upon what is morally right or wrong. The pressure on this jury, however, is going to be the almost certain wave of protests that are going to erupt again if Chauvin is acquitted—no matter how "legal" that decision might be.

Meanwhile, Republicans in Georgia are passing laws specifically designed to restrict voters of color from casting their ballots. After a much larger Democratic turnout in the Senate run-off election resulted in Republicans not only losing the two seats but also losing their majority in the Senate, Republicans are trying to ensure that it will not happen again.

On Monday, they approved a bill that repeals no-excuse absentee voting. 1.3 million Georgia voters used that during this past election—including 450,000 Republicans—to vote by mail.

Last week, they passed a bill that cuts weekend voting days. "Souls to the Polls" was a popular way for Black churches to get their parishioners out to vote following Sunday services. They are now going to restrict the use of drop boxes and no longer allow non-profits to donate to community centers that help to get voters to the polling sites. It will even no longer be legal in Georgia to hand out food and water to people waiting in long lines to vote.

Jim Crow was a well-known character in Minstrel shows whose name became synonymous with a whole series of vile legislation. Directly following the end of the Civil War, white legislators started passing laws to keep the newly emancipated enslaved population from ever gaining any power. African Americans were kept from voting, attending schools, or working in some jobs that Whites wanted to keep for themselves. The most egregious and visible of these laws were overturned during the Civil Rights movement in the 1960s, but much of it continued.

As obvious as the new Georgia laws are in terms of them targeting voters of color, the laws surrounding the events that led to George Floyd's death in Minnesota are just as clearly biased.

This so-called fair trial is already weighted heavily in the defendant's favor. Centuries of racial discrimination will be standing there beside him supporting him throughout the entire trial.

One of the things that I lost this year was my political innocence. I knew that things that were happening were bad, but my sense of those things was far more general than it is now. Having the time to take in what was being fought for during the Black Lives Matter demonstrations and during the national elections last year, filled in the details of a picture that before this year was for me, just an outline. I would never sell myself as an expert, in fact, one of the things I have discovered this year is how much more I need to learn. Like any student, though, I know more now than I did then. Once shown how complex, interwoven, and, yes, rotten much of what rules us is, I find that I can't unsee it.

Change is painful and difficult and not everybody can do it. That doesn't mean that we shouldn't do everything that we can to try and help to bring it about. We can't unsee what we have all seen this past year and nor should we be trying to. Instead, we should be doing everything that we can to take the lessons of this year and turn what we have into something better. The power to do that lies within every single one of us.

And I'm going to get right on that as soon as I find my phone.

It was right here because I know I used it to look up something. Then… I got up to get some more coffee…

March 11, 2021
1,720,199 Total Reported Cases in New York. 48,486 Deaths.

It's been a solid year since I began writing this.

A year ago, today, the World Health Organization declared COVID-19 a global pandemic.

A year ago, today, in New York City, the St. Patrick's Day Parade was canceled. We had recorded 216 cases of the virus but so far nobody had died from it. It was announced that SUNY and CUNY classes would begin distanced learning for the rest of the semester.

A year ago, today, the White House held its first public news conference on the virus and announced that all flights from Europe were going to be canceled a couple of days hence. Later in the day that was amended to exclude cargo planes from the ban. Then it was further amended to exclude Great Britain from the ban. Then it was further amended to exclude American nationals from the ban. By the end of the day, there wasn't much of a ban in place at all—there were plenty of people still traveling for the virus to hitch a ride on. And it did.

As we looked on, Italy was drowning in the virus, and we pitied them. They were in lockdown and barred from traveling from region to region. Some of them were even wearing masks when they went outdoors. We all rolled our eyes thinking it was all an overreaction.

The NBA had just canceled the rest of its season and in the first of these posts that I wrote that I feared that Broadway would be next. The next day, Broadway shows played their final performances.

A year ago, today, I wasn't feeling well.

Except for the virtual Patti LuPone concert that I was on for two days several months ago, it's been a year since I last worked.

The cat has had a year of us always being here all the time.

A year after all of this began, however, there is some reason for a bit of optimism. There are three vaccines against the virus that are approved for emergency use in this country. More people in the United States have now gotten vaccinated against the virus than have gotten the virus itself. Nearly 33 million people have now been inoculated compared to the 29.3 million cases of the virus that we have registered as of this morning. With the former number accelerating and the latter slowing down, we seem to be heading in the right direction.

Sadly, in the last year, on top of all the people we lost to all the things that we usually lose people to, as of this morning, we have lost 531,865 additional people to COVID-19.

Yesterday, looking back, infectious disease expert Dr. Anthony Fauci who has become a virtual member of our family this past year said, "If you had turned the clock back a year … even though I've been through multiple outbreaks of different diseases, the thought that you would have 525,000 people in America to have died and about, you know, 28 million infections in this country, would have really been unimaginable."

President Biden is vowing that every adult American who wants one, will be able to get vaccinated by May. Despite a rocky start, it is looking like what will stop many Americans from ultimately getting one is not a supply or distribution issue but rather a disinformation one.

The last Administration downplayed the severity of the virus to such an extent that there are still sizable sections of the population who believe that the virus is a hoax. Joining in with the existing anti-vaxxers is a whole new group of conspiracy theorists who seem to believe just about anything that they read. None of it is rational. I am not sure why I would need a microscopic tracker injected into my bloodstream when I'm not going anywhere. If Big Brother wanted to find me that badly these days, all they would need to do is knock on our door.

Four former Presidents and First Ladies have joined together in a video testimonial urging people across the country to get the vaccine. The Carters, Clintons, Bushes, and Obamas have all shared films of themselves receiving their shots. Our last President and his wife did not participate. Even though it has now come out that they did receive the vaccine before they left the White House, there is no visual record of them having done so.

President Biden's $1.9 trillion stimulus relief bill called the American Rescue Plan has now passed through both the Senate and the House and only needs the Presidential signature attached to it to become law. One Democrat, Maine Representative Jared Golden, voted against it claiming that there was already plenty of money left in prior stimulus bills to cover Maine's problems. Every single Republican in the House also voted against it.

Over this last year, we have seen the Republican party disintegrate in front of our eyes. Led by an incompetent pathological liar in the person of our ex-President, the GOP has not taken advantage of a single moment when they could have separated themselves from him. Instead, they have doubled down on their support. A large majority of Republican citizens across the country supported the stimulus bill. The Republican lawmakers who voted against it did so purely so as not to give the Democrats a "win". That their constituents need what's in this relief package did not enter into their decision on the vote. The GOP in their desperate drive to win have completely lost sight of the fact that their jobs are to lead and to fight for what those who support them want.

It is hard to look back on the former Administration and be able, after four long anxiety-ridden years, to point to a single constructive accomplishment. The rich got richer and all the rest of us did not. The virus raged unimpeded. The former President's approval rating never rose above 50% for the entire time that he was in office. President Biden's overall average approval rating this morning is at about 54%—nearly ten points above the highest rating the former President ever got. 70% of all Americans approve of the passage of the American Rescue Plan.

That today is day 365 since this truly started seems beyond comprehension. We have learned a lot this past year about health, but we have also learned a lot about racism and gender bias. How will we incorporate that new awareness into how we do what we do? The one thing that I am certain about is that whatever it is that we all think we are going to do is not going to be what we end up doing.

With every year that passes, we all change and grow. This year has been unique in that suddenly we all were taken away from our busy lives and, like it or not, we've all been forced to sit back and think. How have we changed? Until we are further away from this, I'm not sure that we will be able to tell.

I'm grateful for having found this outlet to work through everything that I experienced.

I ended my first post by saying:

Be safe.

Be kind.

Be smart.

We still have a lot to face together as we move forward, and make no mistake, we will move forward. Our theatres will reopen. We will be able to start congregating together again. When? That's the big question. I don't have that answer—nobody does—but I know that it's coming.

Until then…

Be safe.

Be kind.

Be smart.

And thank you.

MARCH 15, 2021

1,748,482 Total Reported Cases in New York. 48,815 Deaths.

As I came up from the subway station on our street yesterday, a woman was crossing out of Central Park towards me ringing a bell. She was both deliberate and completely nonchalant in how she rang it and met my eye for a second as she passed without any sense of self-consciousness at all.

Thinking how strange this was, I headed towards home and slowly realized that it was 7 pm. She was applauding our health care workers. Even after all this time, the 7 pm neighborhood twilight barking in support of them all still happens in some fashion. I walked towards home and saw that an older couple was standing on their front steps applauding. I could hear someone else banging on a pot from an apartment above me, so I started clapping, too, as I went home.

On Friday, the greatest number of people who have traveled since the pandemic began passed through our nation's airports. There were still nearly 40% fewer people flying than usual, but it was a notable milestone.

Europe, largely because of the spread of the new UK variant, is heading into what they believe is the third wave. Severe restrictions have been reimposed in Italy as of this morning to try and stop it. The entire nation is going to be considered a "red zone" over Easter to keep people from gathering and spreading the virus during the holiday. Cases are climbing in Germany. Hospitalizations are up in France. Overcrowding is such a problem in Paris health care facilities that patients there are being evacuated to other places around the country to relieve the pressure.

The UK variant contributed to Great Britain holding the record for the highest number of COVID-related fatalities in Europe and the rest of the continent is taking that threat very seriously.

Nearly a dozen countries have just halted their use of the Oxford-AstraZeneca vaccine after it was discovered that it might be causing sometimes fatal blood clots in some people. That still hasn't been confirmed, but the already slow vaccine rollout in some of those places has just gotten noticeably slower.

We haven't approved that vaccine over here yet in part because the FDA was concerned about transparency from the manufacturers. There were reports that some severe neurological complications arose in a couple of trial patients, and they were improperly reported and accounted for. Still, that vaccine's efficacy does seem to have turned the tide of new infections in England. The company is standing by their vaccine saying that the few cases of complications out of millions are still at a rate well below that of any vaccine.

Two weeks ago, the Dutch health minister assured the Netherlands that there was nothing to worry about with the Oxford-AstraZeneca vaccine. This morning their vaccination program has been halted for two weeks to make sure.

I am not comfortable yet with some of the easings of restrictions here in New York. Michael and I met up with some friends that we hadn't seen in a year on Saturday for a walk. We waited until we found a restaurant with well-spaced outdoor seating before we sat down for a meal. They were open for limited indoor seating but none of us were ready for that.

The AMC movie theatre near us on Broadway has reopened albeit with limited seating. The yellowing and dusty movie posters announcing the opening of new movies last March were finally replaced with new ones. I don't know what happened to all those other movies. If they got released anywhere, I wasn't aware of it. I don't think that I could watch a movie for several hours indoors and not worry about the virus. I'm not ready to take that chance. Yet.

Last month, the "Coming in March" taglines suddenly started to seem relevant again. There are still *Riverdance* posters in the subways announcing March performances. It's only because of how old and faded they now look that I can tell that they were from last year.

I'm finding that time isn't passing in hours these days so much as it's passing in weeks. That my second shot of the vaccine is already scheduled for just a few days ahead seems inconceivable.

On Sunday, we met up with a couple of other people and went into Central Park with our beach chairs and thermoses. We sat in a nice, wide circle. We've been doing that regularly throughout this past year. Our little gatherings lasted well into the fall but, except for one bright snowy day last month, we pretty much put them on hold for the winter.

Yesterday was a beautiful day—chilly but not freezing and very sunny. It was nice to be back outside together. As we talked, the conversation came around to a discussion about whether we were ready to go back. What would that look like? What did we want it to look like?

After a year without being able to do much of what we had been doing before, we all agreed that while we were ready to get back to work that none of us wanted things to return exactly as they were. Time off the hamster wheel has made us all a bit leery of getting back onto it.

This coming summer, I am sure that we will begin to see smaller theatres and the not-for-profits begin to present some material, but I remain certain that Broadway is not going to reopen in any meaningful way until it can fully reopen. That means full houses. Full houses mean that tourists will need to be able to freely come back to New York.

That time will come, but not if we rush back into all our pre-pandemic lives all at once. Doing that will only prolong the time that we wait. I am eager to work, but I find myself unwilling to contemplate fully giving up all the daily routines that I've created for myself this last year. I've always tried to live my life by saying yes rather than no. Much of what I have agreed to do over the years that fell out of my comfort zone at the time, turned out to be great heart and mind-opening experiences. Moving forward, I will likely still say yes to those new things that seem challenging. Yes, but…

This year has shown me that I can exist without working seven days a week and being available at all times of the day and night. I've been rewired. I don't think I'll mind being crazy busy for bursts of time, but I don't want it to grow back into being all the time the way that it was.

My wanting or not wanting that may be moot. When we reopen our industry, it isn't going to be the same industry that we closed. We need to do it by letting more people into the club. As more people get a voice, what and how we do things will change and grow. We need to teach ourselves how to widen our expectations and then we are going to need to teach our audiences how to do the same. If we are going to remain viable and relevant, we are going to have to figure out how to attract a more diverse crowd of people into our performance spaces.

And we will. I am very much looking forward to being a part of that, but that is all still to come. For now, we just need to keep doing what we are doing. We need to follow the mandates as best we can and keep being patient. We need to get to the point where our health care workers can get off their own hamster wheels. There is a limit to how long we can expect these incredible people to be able to keep spinning.

MARCH 23, 2021
1,788,874 Total Reported Cases in New York. 49,262 Deaths.

The cat caught a mouse.

Michael was on a zoom call when suddenly the cat was fully engaged. He flattened himself out and crawled under the long low metal cabinet that our television sits on. After some thrashing around, a mouse ran out from underneath it and scurried along the wall to the other corner of the room where it got into a bag with some empty binders in it.

I'm not quite sure how, but some combination of the cat and Michael dislodged the mouse from there and the cat ended up with it in his mouth. He carried it into the bathroom and Michael shut the door on the two of them so that he could finish his call. When he later opened the bathroom door, the mouse was nowhere to be seen and the cat just wandered back into the living room as if nothing had happened.

I slept through the whole thing. The after-effects of my second dose of the Pfizer vaccine on Saturday had kicked in and I could have slept through anything.

Neither of us is at all sure where the mouse could have come from and, perhaps, more importantly, where it could have gone. We fully renovated the entire apartment before we moved in and there were no holes when we were done. The room that we didn't touch was the bathroom so maybe the mouse escaped through the grate under the tub. It must have come in from somewhere behind one of the radiators in the living room.

As far as I know, the cat has never laid eyes on a mouse before, let alone caught one. Cats that we had growing up would catch and kill any number of creatures and then often lay their dead bodies outside the back door as a gift to the house. We had a Maine coon cat who caught everything from blue jays to baby rabbits. He was lethal. Other of our cats would catch things and then let them go without killing them, but not him.

I suppose that this is the year for all of us to scratch a few things off our bucket lists so I'm glad that the cat had the opportunity to check one off his too. I'm also glad that the mouse seems to have gotten away.

The aftereffects of the vaccine left me a little achy and tired, but not so seriously so as to keep me from going out. After a full year of not feeling anything but fully healthy, it was interesting to feel a little ill. I headed into the park thinking that it was close enough that I could always just turn around and come home if I started to feel worse. The more I walked, though, the better I felt, so I just kept going.

This year, we have been given the distance to look at what our lives are and how we are living them. It requires outside observation to fully appreciate something. The view from within lacks scope. The cliché of not being able to see the forest for the trees has a great deal of truth to it.

Over this past year, some former employers have stayed in contact and sent out regular updates and some have just vanished. Where I work, and who I work for, and maybe even what I do moving forward is probably going to be different from what it was that I did before. A year ago, that made me anxious. A year later, I find myself feeling excited about what might be on the horizon ahead.

I want whatever work lies ahead of me to add to the lives we have renovated, not replace it.

More and more, signs are cropping up that this fall is when we will start to see Broadway begin to reopen. That feels right. By the fall, everyone who wants a vaccination should have been able to have gotten one. The work I thought I had in spring has been canceled or pushed off. I cannot say that I am surprised. I think that some things will begin to happen in mid to late summer. If there is one thing that I've learned this year is that what seems to be impossibly far away simply isn't.

Time shoots forward like an arrow after it's left the bow. Rather than keeping my eye on where we might be going, I am more than happy to keep it here, looking at what we have. What I'm seeing isn't always pretty, but it's real and wonderful in its own way.

Two songbirds just had a tuneful argument on the air conditioner outside the living room. The cat ran in at the first scratch of their claws on the metal, fully ready to pounce. Sadly, they flew off before he could.

Seeing that in addition to being the purring furry hot water bottle who curls up in my lap every night, that the cat is also a ruthless predator makes him more than in my eyes, rather than less. If he gets the mouse again, I will certainly do everything that I can to save the little thing and release it outside. If the mouse makes the mistake of coming into the apartment again and letting the cat catch him, though, there is very little that I can do about it. The cat is just being true to who and what he is. Sorry mouse.

Every morning as I look in the mirror as I am brushing my teeth, I see a guy looking back at me with grey hair and some wrinkles. I used to say that my hair only started to turn grey after I worked with Elaine Stritch. Whether or not that's true, I can't honestly remember, but at any rate, I've earned all of it. If I look into that guy's eyes, though, I can usually see who he is with a bit more clarity.

Our bodies and our faces are the scrapbooks of our lives and, god willing we keep adding to them. We are who we are, and we shouldn't feel the need to hide it.

I will say, however, that I am long overdue for a good beard trimming.

MARCH 29, 2021
1,859,474 Total Reported Cases in New York. 49,955 Deaths.

Flowering trees and shrubs have started to bloom in Central Park. A few days ago, when I was in the park, their branches were still bare, but yesterday, even in the rain, there were finally some lightly shaded swaths of color to be seen.

We had forsythia bushes alongside our driveway at the houses that we lived in, in New Jersey when I was growing up. Their yellow flowers always seemed to herald the end of the winter for me. For a moment, that yellow is the only other color in an otherwise black and white landscape. Then, slowly at first, it is joined by the purples and pinks of the crocuses and flowering trees, and before you know it, everything is out and loud and green and new.

Last year at this time, by the time I started to be able to see what was going on around me, everything was already out. I missed this moment of beginning. This year, I've been waiting for it.

We celebrated our second virtual Passover Seder last night with much the same group of friends and colleagues that we celebrated with at this same time last year. The Seder ends with the wish, 'Next year in Jerusalem.' Last year that didn't seem likely. This year, it does.

Last year, George Floyd was still alive. He had just about two more months left to live. This morning, the trial of the officer charged with killing him begins in Minneapolis. It remains to be seen whether everything that we have learned about the flaws in the very fabric of our society over this past year will finally allow a measure of justice to be served. George Floyd was not the first man of color to lose his life at the hands of a white law enforcement officer. He was, however, the first to have been murdered when all of us had nothing else to do other than watch and listen.

Michael got his second jab of Moderna on Saturday. I got my second shot of Pfizer a week ago. As of this morning, 143,462,691 Americans have been given at least their first shot of one of the vaccines. As of this morning, 15.5% of Americans have been fully vaccinated and 28.2% have been partially vaccinated. The CDC released a study this morning saying that two weeks after the first shot of either vaccine, people are 80% immunized, and two weeks after the second that rises to 90%.

By the end of this week, vaccinated New Yorkers will be able to pull up a certification called an Excelsior Pass on their phones. The Excelsior Pass will be proof of either having been vaccinated or having recently tested negative for the coronavirus. When you go to a theatre or sports event, or, indeed, an airline flight, it is envisioned that this app will function in much the same way as an airline boarding pass.

There are going to be hiccups as this app rolls out. Connecting all the data from individual pharmacies and national chain stores that are providing the vaccine along with state-run testing centers is going to be challenging. There are going to be lawsuits. Many are going to argue that forcing people to reveal their COVID status is an invasion of privacy. The Excelsior Pass, anticipating that, will not distribute any information other than a simple OK to enter. IBM, the company that created the system, will not have access to anything other than a yea or a nay from the testing and vaccine centers.

Will airlines and theatres and sports arenas and cruise ships turn people away who have not been vaccinated? If those people have tickets, will those tickets be refunded? Will we need to get COVID insurance when we purchase our tickets?

As our society begins to open back up, the people who have been the loudest in their protests of shutting down in the first place are likely going to be the very same people who will refuse to be vaccinated. To them, the virus is a hoax, and the current federal government is illegitimate.

The case rate here in New York City while not rising is not appreciably declining either. It is still very much out there and very much still spreading. More than a dozen other states, including our neighbor New Jersey, are seeing rising case numbers. Nationally, we are now at over 30 million cases. In a very short time, we will reach 550,000 people dead. We are not through this yet.

In a televised interview a couple of days ago, the former director of the CDC, Robert Redfield, said, "I still think the most likely etiology of this pathogen in Wuhan was from a laboratory, you know, escaped. It's not unusual for respiratory pathogens that are being worked on in a laboratory to infect a laboratory worker." He, however, can provide no evidence for this scenario at all.

Blame.

Dr. Birx, who was the virus response coordinator for the former Administration, is speaking out about what she witnessed now that she is free of governmental pressure. She says that, in her opinion, after the first wave of 100,000 deaths that the rest could have been largely avoided or at least contained at a much lower level. The lack of action on the part of the former President and the Republican-led government made that impossible.

Blame.

Dr. Birx has been criticized for not speaking up while this was happening. Should she have? Was it better to have her in the White House and muzzled than it would have been to have her get fired for speaking the truth? She is being blamed for being a collaborator.

Having a person as respected as she was standing silently next to the former President as he lied to us, gave what he was saying some credibility that it may not have had for some people. At least in her we now have a credible witness to what was going on inside the White House last year.

Blame?

President Biden called President Putin of Russia a killer. To be fair he didn't say the words himself but, when asked by an interviewer if he thought that Putin was a killer, he replied, "I do." On the other hand, he refuses to say the same thing about Crown Prince Mohammed bin Salman of Saudi Arabia. This is despite a report from US intelligence that the Crown Prince is responsible for the 2018 death of journalist and dissident Jamal Khashoggi.

Blame is a useful and powerful political tool. Unlike our former President, President Biden so far has said nothing that appears not to have been fully considered. We need to maintain a relationship with the Saudis, calling the heir presumptive to the throne a killer will only jeopardize that. We do not need to maintain a relationship with Russia, and, in fact, we need to defend ourselves from their attacks. Acknowledging Putin as a killer puts him on a global defensive. It was a concerted retaliatory shot of blame and, judging by the angry and indignant response from Russia, an effective one.

I had a meal on Saturday with two friends that I hadn't seen in over a year. They have been fully vaccinated as have I. We decided to hug each other. It was a calculated risk, but one that we discussed and agreed to accept. Those hugs felt good.

As much as assigning blame can be a way to avoid personal responsibility, it is also necessary for us to be able to move forward. The only way that true reform will start to happen in our law enforcement agencies will be if someone like Officer Derek Chauvin is blamed for someone like George

Floyd's death. If he is let go, with all of us being convinced of his guilt, the message will be that others can do the same. Our former President must be blamed for his criminal inaction so that future leaders don't do the same as well.

Blaming the Chinese for the virus without any evidence, however, does nothing more than increase an already lethal level of anti-Asian bias. If any evidence ever does surface that the Chinese allowed this virus to escape—either on purpose or accidentally—then the balance of power on the entire globe changes. China opens itself up to an unimaginable backlash—both politically and financially. That the former director of the CDC said this, himself, seems the height of irresponsibility. That level of blame is not his to assign.

I am going to download the Excelsior Pass and sign up for my passport. I don't want to go into a crowd of people without knowing their statuses, so I am more than happy to provide them all with that information myself.

I may be greedy, but after two great hugs, I want some more. Next year in Jerusalem? I honestly don't much care where I am next year. If I can hug my friends and family then anywhere is fine.

Chag same'ach.

April 4, 2021
1,905,737 Total Reported Cases in New York. 50,432 Deaths.

As of yesterday, I am officially vaccinated AF.

It's now been two full weeks since my second jab so, theoretically, the vaccine is now at its most effective level. There are reports that because I've had COVID before that I could be up to ten times more resistant to the virus now that I've been vaccinated. That remains to be seen, but for now, I am at least as resistant to it as any of us can hope to be.

Having this viral passport still doesn't mean that I can go anywhere. Whatever obstacles that were in place before are still very much in place now. If Michael and I went to Mexico, we would still need a COVID test with a negative result 72 hours before returning home before we would be let in. Our vaccine cards wouldn't affect that requirement.

Governor DeSantis of Florida just signed an executive order prohibiting the use of such passports in his state. The White House Press Secretary said recently that there are no plans for a federal mandate. I guess that without such a mandate, all of this is going to be moot.

We have tended to trail Europe by about a month in terms of how we are affected by the pandemic. They are currently very much in the middle of a fourth wave fueled largely by the highly contagious B.1.1.7 variant. The alarming thing about this variant is that it is driving up the infection and hospitalization rates of young people.

While the United States is far ahead of Europe in our vaccination rates, we still have not yet allowed our younger population to be eligible. About a fifth of all American adults have now received either both doses of the Moderna or Pfizer shot or their single shot of the Johnson & Johnson one. While some of the country is seeing a decrease in cases, many places are seeing their cases rise at an alarming rate. Overall, our cases are at best plateauing.

Yesterday, Michael and I joined five friends at a restaurant for brunch. The seven of us ate indoors and then two of our group left early to prepare for a show. The remaining five of us then finished up and went downtown to watch them perform inside a small cabaret theatre.

This was the first weekend that indoor theatres have been allowed to open in New York City, so the show was completely sold out albeit at just a third of capacity. We all had our temperatures taken when we checked in. The five of us sat at one table which was separated by a comfortable amount of space from the surrounding tables. Everybody, except for the performers, wore masks inside during the concert. The show lasted just over an hour.

It was glorious to be back inside a restaurant and to be back inside a theatre. Both places felt large enough and ventilated enough that we were comfortable. There have been plenty of places that I haven't gone into in recent days because my newly developed sense of COVID claustrophobia kicked in and drove me out. Was it safe? Were we safe? Who really knows? The safest option, of course, would have been for all of us to stay at home. If we chose to do that, what then would be the marker that we would use to decide to start back?

We are going to make mistakes as everything starts to reopen. It is inevitable. Yesterday, we did not throw off our masks and pretend that there wasn't still a problem. We asked every single person who waited on us whether they wanted us to put our masks on when they were there or if we could leave them off. Every single time one of us got up from our table, we put our masks back on to move through the restaurant.

Throughout the day, we all mostly followed the recommended guidelines. Mostly. Yes, there were times, when we didn't or couldn't, but we all remained as vigilant as we could. The alternative to not creeping forward is to just stay in place where we are. I don't see that as an option. Doing that in an as informed and responsible manner as possible is the best that any of us can hope to do.

We are moving ahead. It isn't always easy or quick. We may have a long way to go before we are all sitting together in a theatre laughing and crying without our mouths and noses being covered by masks, but we need to start along the road to getting there. The first step towards that is to try and take some tentative baby steps.

Yesterday, Michael and I took our first couple of steps. It felt good—a bit nerve-wracking at times maybe, but still good.

April 10, 2021
1,949,964 Total Reported Cases in New York. 50,835 Deaths.

These days are almost stranger than the days we experienced last year when we were still at the beginning of everything.

The strangeness is that they are starting to feel not so strange. As temperatures start to rise, more and more people are venturing outdoors. I ran into some friends downtown yesterday on the street and we hugged.

After having had our first meal inside last weekend, Michael and I have now had two more. Both were with vaccinated people, and both were in restaurants that seemed open and well-ventilated.

We are trying to use common sense, and keep the science in mind, but really, we are operating on gut instinct. Watching how people behave out on the street is fascinating. Some are terrified, and some seem completely unconcerned. Everyone is still wearing a mask, but the level of social interaction has risen markedly. For everybody hugging a friend, there is also somebody else desperately trying to skirt around them and give them a wide berth on the sidewalk.

Theatre work is starting to happen again, though very slowly. Most of the available work is small in-person performances for a limited audience. I have had some meetings and discussions about future work in recent days which I am encouraged by, but there are still so many unknowns ahead of us to be fully able to fully count on any of it yet. Most of the work that I think is most likely to happen is still going to be for things that don't require a big in-person crowd to watch.

An immigration ban to protect us from the virus only works if it is an actual ban on everyone entering the country. If you start saying that say American nationals can come in, then it is no longer a ban. The same thing happens with the vaccine. If you start saying that you need to be vaccinated to work but if you choose not to be vaccinated then you can work anyway, then the whole purpose of vaccination is sidestepped.

Not everybody gets an annual flu shot. Thousands of people die every year from the flu, and we don't particularly worry about it. COVID-19, however, is not the flu. Over the years most of us have built up a tolerance to many strains of the flu. Sometimes we get it and sometimes we avoid it. The difference is that none of us had a tolerance to COVID-19 until we either got it and survived or got vaccinated against it. Our bodies don't have a history of fighting it.

What feels strange about these days is that while there seems to be the great promise of forward movement, there isn't any in evidence. I do think that we are working towards the goal of getting back and, in many cases, doing many positive things to accomplish it. Practically, though, we are still in the same state that we were in six months ago. That's what feels strange. Nothing has changed except our outlook.

My days are pretty much locked into the same solid routine that I have been doing for a year. My mornings are filled with work. Then we eat. Then I take a walk and then I come home and maybe work some more and then we eat again and then we watch something on television and then we go to sleep. Certainly, eating out with friends occasionally breaks the repetition somewhat but without a steady income, we can't afford to do that all the time. None of the work that I am doing at home these days is bringing in any income. It's satisfying, certainly, but not generating anything financial. Yet.

Seeing that the end of this strange time may be in sight, I am trying to finish up the projects—both the artistic ones and the ones that are pure maintenance—that need finishing. We have already done a lot. We have cleared a lot of excess stuff out of our home this past year to the point that I still occasionally open my closet and revel at how organized and spare it looks compared to what it once did.

My effectiveness in accomplishing tasks like that, though, comes in waves. I have tried to ride those waves when they come and accept the lulls when I simply can't face doing anymore.

Having had a whole year to finish these projects has made me realize that completing everything is an impossibility. There are simply not enough hours in a day—even when I'm not working. Not only is it an impossibility but I realize that I shouldn't even necessarily have had it as a goal in the first place. Life is messy. My instinct always pushes me towards trying to control and organize everything, but this year has truly shown me that, at best, that's a fool's errand.

We are in the part of the flight where after taking off late and then circling the airport endlessly we have finally landed but we are now sitting on the tarmac because there isn't a gate available for us to disembark through. It's the part of plane travel that makes me the craziest. When you can see the end of the trip, but you just can't get there. They never just pull up a staircase and let you get off that way. They keep you sitting there—sometimes for hours—trapped within touching distance of the end.

We are going to forget all of this.

However long we are stuck in this last kink of the trip, the door is eventually going to open and let us all out. A gate will eventually be cleared. A ground crew will be located, and we will all get off the plane, collect our luggage, and head home. We will be annoyed by the delay until bedtime, but when we wake up the next day, aside from telling one or two people about it, we will likely never think about it again.

We are going to forget this past year because when all is said and done it was just a year out of our lives. I never understood before how the Spanish Flu could have become the "Forgotten Pandemic," but while hugging my friends on the street yesterday, it became crystal clear. When we start to move on, we are going to lunge forward, and we are not going to look back.

Part of what is making this all seem endless is that we don't know when the gate will be cleared. The not knowing makes it seem that much longer, and more fraught than it is. This past year, when I look back at it, seems to have flown by. It certainly didn't seem that way as it was unfolding, but it does now. So much of it already seems like history from another era.

I'm not the person that I was when all of this began last March. I don't think that any of us are. There is no way for us all to collectively go through an experience like the one we have just all shared and not be altered by it.

The people that we have become over this past year are facing a future of possibility. For a while, when we all get together, we might ask each other, "What did you do during the pandemic?"

Soon, though, we are going to have other things to talk about.

April 16, 2021
1,986,681 Total Reported Cases in New York. 51,270 Deaths.

There's a trace of desperation that's becoming noticeable in Michael's voice when he says, "so what should we have for dinner?" A week or two ago, he made artichokes for the first time and got excited. They were a wonderful novelty. They'd caught his eye in the store and he bought some on an impulse. They were something that we hadn't had before. We've had a rotating cycle of asparagus, broccoli, brussels sprouts, green beans, cauliflower, and other vegetables but as we are now 400 days into this pandemic, that cycle has repeated itself more often than either of us can count.

Michael has always been a very good cook and I think he enjoys it. At least he used to enjoy it. I am guessing that at times he does and at times he wishes that he didn't have to do it. Over this year, he has gotten to be very good at it.

400 days into this pandemic there are very few parts of New York City that I have not walked in now. I readily admit that I've covered downtown far more thoroughly than I've covered uptown, but I've done a pretty good job of hitting most of it. I often tune out as I'm walking and find myself drawn to familiar paths so when I'm alert, I will purposefully try and veer off in an unlikely direction.

In August of last year, I was desperate to travel somewhere. Anywhere.

I'm not feeling that kind of pent-up energy now. I'm just ready to be doing something else.

Having been vaccinated, there doesn't appear to be anything more that we can do other than wait for everyone else around us to catch up. After lagging behind the world in everything having to do with containing this virus, we seem to be ahead of most other places when it comes to getting inoculated. Countries that were beating down their curves seem to be struggling to distribute enough jabs for their citizens.

I'm not sure that we will fully know what we've lost this past year until we are back up and running without it. When you start something new, the first day is always nerve-wracking. You don't know what to expect and you don't know who all the new people are. You look out at a sea of strange faces and you think that they won't possibly ever be as good or as fun or as close to you as that last group was. Then you realize that you thought the same thing about that group when you first saw them.

We are, all of us, the sum of our choices. It's often the time when you least want to do something or change something or repeat something, that you break through into something new. In my experience, the best choice is just to say yes. Before it all starts up again, how many walks can we take and how many meals can we possibly eat?

All of them.

May 6, 2021
2,064,530 Total Reported Cases in New York. 52,368 Deaths.

Broadway to reopen on September 14 at full capacity!

61 years ago, just 19 days from the day, President John F. Kennedy announced before a joint session of Congress that we were going to land a man on the moon. Were we ready to land a man on the moon? Not really.

A month before, Yuri Gagarin from the Soviet Union had become the first person in space when he successfully orbited the earth in a Russian capsule. We sent Alan Shepard up a few weeks later, and he became the first American in space, but he only achieved a short sub-orbital flight rather than being able to orbit the earth the way the Russian had.

While Gagarin was up above us, Kennedy was embroiled in the Bay of Pigs fiasco. He needed something to turn the tide of public opinion. He consulted with his Vice President as well as with NASA administrator James Webb and decided that even though nobody yet knew how that this was an achievable goal, landing a man on the moon before the Russians did would send a clear message of United States superiority. Project Mercury was then adjusted towards this goal and the Gemini and Apollo programs were initiated to finally achieve it. On July 20, 1969, just over eight years later, Neil Armstrong took his first step on the lunar surface.

Between 1960 and 1973, the United States spent $28 billion to land men on the moon. In today's adjusted dollars that amount would be $283 billion. There were setbacks and accidents including a fire that killed the three Apollo 1 astronauts.

Was it worth it? The moon is a desolate rock. Nobody quite knows what, if anything, to do with it. After the Apollo program was discontinued, nobody has been back. Eugene Cernan was the last person to stand on its surface in 1972 which is now fifty years ago. John F. Kennedy was assassinated long before Apollo 11 fulfilled his dream, but it remains one of his greatest legacies. The moon race did, indeed, turn the tide of public opinion and became an immense point of pride for the country that endures to this day. Kennedy is considered by many to have been one of our greatest Presidents.

The announcement that Broadway will be back in September has been met with both elation and utter skepticism. The question on every skeptic's mind is, how?

A couple of days ago, Governor Cuomo announced that theatres and other indoor businesses can reopen at full capacity as of May 19. This followed an announcement from Mayor de Blasio that New York City would fully reopen by July 1.

In recent days, Michael and I have been dining out with friends in person and indoors. A month ago, we would never have considered doing that.

Over the past year, there have been all sorts of discussions about how handshakes and hugs were going to be things of the past. After the pandemic ran its course, people said we would move forward with less physical contact. That is not going to happen. It is already started back up again. There is always a slightly awkward conversation before about whether we are each open to a hug, but as more and more people in our orbit become vaccinated and we get used to being back in the world, that's going to pass.

As of this morning, 32.3% of Americans are fully vaccinated. Nearly half of all eligible New Yorkers have received both doses of their vaccines. For any sort of herd immunity to be in place, however, we will need to get to somewhere between 70% and 80% of people inoculated. The concern in New York is that the number of people seeking the vaccine has dwindled. Too many people are choosing not to get the vaccine.

Neither Michael nor I have anything beyond the most rudimentary understanding of the virus and how it is spread. We get a general idea, but do we know enough about how air circulates and what the risks truly are? Of course not. We are operating on almost pure gut instinct.

There is a risk every single time you step onto an airplane. Do I know how an airplane works? No, I do not. I have a vague idea from having visited the Wright Brothers' museums around the country and the National Air and Space Museum in Washington D.C., but I can't look at an aircraft and know whether it is flight-worthy or not. Even when I get on one that seems a bit suspect to me for whatever reason, I just take my seat, buckle up, and hope for the best. Eventually, that's what we are going to feel about COVID.

So, back to Broadway. Am I willing to sit shoulder to shoulder with the rest of a sold-out crowd in a crowded theatre? Not yet. Will I be willing to do that in September? I don't know. I am far more comfortable being near members of my community who tend to be more informed than I am with the population at large. Unless the theatres are extremely strict about checking tests and vaccination cards, I'm going to be selective in what I choose to see at first.

The United States floundered badly under the previous Administration in our response to the pandemic. We have almost completely reversed that trend with the efficiency of our vaccine rollout. Other countries have not been nearly as lucky. Nobody in the Japanese government seems to have ordered any vaccine. The Japanese inoculation rate is just 1.6%. That's among the worst rates on the planet. India is drowning in COVID cases. Brazil is still suffering badly.

For a Broadway show to be successful, we need an influx of foreign people from all these places and more. Will they be allowed into the country in four months? What will happen if *The Phantom of the Opera* reopens, and not enough people come? By September, it will have been six months since I was vaccinated. Will the vaccine still be as effective then? We don't know yet.

Phantom is not alone. Other shows have announced that their performances will resume before the end of the year, too. Some have delayed their starts until next year. Certainly, at first, there will be a limited pool of people for these shows to pull from for their audiences. Most of the travel-related articles I have read are not expecting a return to pre-pandemic tourism levels until well into 2023. This rush to reopen everything runs completely counter to the slow and measured rollout that was being discussed last year.

When John F. Kennedy announced that we were going to the moon, nobody was fully sure that we could do it. In his speech, he said, "We choose to go to the Moon. We choose to go to the Moon... We choose to go to the Moon in this decade and do the other things, not because they are easy, but because they are hard; because that goal will serve to organize and measure the best of our energies and skills, because that challenge is one that we are willing to accept, one we are unwilling to postpone, and one we intend to win, and the others, too."

As many obstacles that are in our way, we are going to have to bite the bullet and go back sometime, so why not September?

A good friend and mentor once said to me that however impossible it seems that your show is ever going to get to opening night, at some point, you will wake up the day after opening and it will have been done.

We know that Broadway will reopen. Right now, the 'how' of it all seems insurmountable, but we will figure it out. The first time back might be nerve-wracking and uncomfortable, but the second time will be better and by the fifth or sixth time it will just feel normal.

If we can land a man on the moon, we can reopen our theatres.

May 17, 2021

For the first time since the start of the pandemic, infection rates are down in all 50 states.

This past Thursday, the Center for Disease Control announced that fully vaccinated people no longer need to wear masks or social distance. Curfews on restaurants are being lifted. Over the next couple of weeks, more and more guidelines will be lifted. By July, New York will be fully reopened with no restrictions. Life can go back to normal.

I can't take my mask off.

I know it doesn't make sense. Having had COVID a year ago combined with the Pfizer and Moderna shots Michael and I got should make us ten times more resistant to the virus than somebody who never became infected.

I still can't take my mask off, nor do I want to be near people that I don't know who are not wearing masks. I'm comfortable going to a restaurant with friends and sitting at the table with them without our masks on, but up until now, we have always discussed it first.

Our cloth face coverings were never designed to keep us from getting infected ourselves, they were supposed to keep us from spreading it to others. The official mandate was never that we had to wear a mask all the time outside, only when we couldn't observe social distancing. It became much easier to just wear a mask all the time than it was to keep thinking about it. Over time we all forgot what the real mandates were.

I've been out and about throughout this entire year. That is not true of a lot of people I know who are truly isolated. I don't think that I was reckless, I kept away from other people, and I didn't go into crowded trains or cramped stores. Knowing that I survived the virus once probably gave me more confidence than I should have had, but I've never felt terrified of getting it. Concerned, certainly, but never terrified. Many others in our social orbit were and maybe still are very anxious around it.

After 14 months of making my own schedule, I am working again. We are still in preproduction, so my salary hasn't kicked in yet, but it looks like before the end of the month that I'll be getting on a plane. Nobody is sure what protocols will be in place for this job and which of them can now be set aside.

A groundswell of reaction from health experts around the CDC's lifting of the mask mandate has been concern that the new measures may have come too soon. In their rush to share some positive news, they may have jumped the gun.

The CDC, along with their headline, released some caveats but how many people will read beyond the headline? This new mandate ONLY applies to people who are two weeks past their final shot. They are saying that schools should keep masking for at least the rest of this school year. Pfizer is now authorized for kids 12-15 years old, but nobody younger than that is eligible yet. Businesses, they say, should keep the mask mandates in effect at least until all their employees have been fully vaccinated.

The Director of the CDC said that Americans are going to need to take responsibility for themselves when it comes to getting vaccinated and following precautions. Not to be a naysayer, but we don't have a great history of following the honor system about anything. And that's just here. The CEO of the airport in Dubai, which is the busiest international hub on the planet said that he does not think that anything other than a vaccine passport is going to work for us to be able to resume any sort of regular travel.

The European Union is planning on letting vaccinated people from outside their borders come in this summer if they can prove that they have been fully vaccinated. The Equality and Human Rights Commission warns that while vaccine passports work in principle, they are also going to create a two-tiered society where some have the right to go and do what they want, and some don't. It would be easy to say that is fine and the people who are refusing to get vaccinated need to accept the consequences of that choice, but some people are medically unable to be vaccinated. What about them? Does that mean that somebody who's had an organ transplant can't fly anywhere?

Many places around the globe are still drowning in COVID cases. India is in the middle of an unimaginable crisis. People are dying because they can't find oxygen. Poorer undeveloped countries are going to need us to step in and help them achieve some sort of immunity wall themselves. Having one here won't do us any good if nobody else has one. Even Canada which led us for so long in their response has fallen behind in the vaccination process.

I can see past all of this. I know we will all be trudging through airports, maybe even the one in Dubai, that is crowded with people in the not-too-distant future. We will line up to get into clubs and theatres and restaurants that are packed to the brim with maskless people. We will walk into stores without giving their architecture a second thought. All of that will happen. I can see all of that. It's the next couple of months that I cannot figure out.

I've gotten used to wearing a mask. In places like Japan where people have been wearing masks for years, they only wear them when they, themselves, are sick. I hope that we, here in the United States, can keep that going. How many cases of the regular flu and other colds would we avoid getting if people did that for each other? I know that there is no reason for me to wear a mask now. Whatever it is that I could transmit to someone, it is almost surely not going to be COVID. I'm about as unlikely a vector for that as anyone is.

I'm just not ready yet. It doesn't make any rational sense, but there you are. I'll get there, but I'm going to do it in my own time. I would rather be too safe than too reckless. I'm not looking forward to being locked down when I start work again or having to keep a mask on in whatever bubble we create, but if that's what it is, then I'm not going to be the one to put my foot down against it. I'll roll my eyes a little, but I'll do it until we all don't have to.

May 31, 2021
2,102,404 Total Reported Cases in New York. 53,098 Deaths.

At 5 am on Saturday, for the first time in well over a year, I woke up to the alarm from a deep sleep so that I could get to the airport. The first flight I took after fourteen months on the ground, was out of LaGuardia to get to an in-person meeting in Cleveland. While I was prepared for anything, aside from mask-wearing, there was nothing much out of the ordinary that happened to me at the airport. My frequent-flier status, much to my surprise, was still intact even without there having been any activity on it during the pandemic, so I got through security easily. Even without it, there were not very many people traveling.

Had I not been specifically looking for things that were different from the last time I was in an airport, I probably would not have noticed all the signs about mask-wearing. They have become so much an expected part of our lives in New York, that they don't register anymore.

Even though I am almost certain that everybody else present at the Cleveland meeting had been vaccinated, we were still required to take a specific COVID test before arriving. The project has hired a COVID-compliance officer whose sole job is to maintain protocols. They arranged for my test in New York and then required me to fill out an online questionnaire that morning. The meeting was conducted with us all in masks. I knew some people there and was introduced to some others for the first time that day. Later, the director and I joked about how surprised we were by what some people looked like when they took off their masks to eat lunch.

After the meeting, we headed back to the airport and continued to Los Angeles, to do some more preliminary work for a few days before we eventually head home. We had to take a puddle-jumper to Detroit before getting on our flight onward to Los Angeles. The experience before both of those flights was much the same as the first one- normal, except for mask-wearing. The flight to LA was full. The flight attendants paid a lot of attention to the mask mandate and throughout the trip asked people to make sure that their mouths and noses were always covered.

As of the middle of the month, federal employees who have been vaccinated no longer need to wear masks in federal buildings. The mask mandate on interstate public transportation, however, has been extended into September. In New York City, the limits on how many fully vaccinated people can be present inside an establishment have been removed on a state level along with social distancing guidelines, but businesses, themselves, can still choose how they want to operate in that regard. Stores still have signs requiring people to wear masks and many smaller stores still have capacity limits.

So far, I have never once been asked about my vaccination status by anybody. Ever. It has had no impact at all on workplace safety that I can see. There are reports that the entertainment unions are working towards easing and updating their protocols based on vaccinations, but for the moment, everything is operating as if the vaccines don't exist.

Over the last fourteen months, I have watched New York shift and change daily. Here in LA, I am seeing the city for the first time after the fact. I walked down Hollywood Boulevard yesterday. The Farmer's Market was in full swing. Plenty of people were out and about buying produce and homemade food. Along the Boulevard, itself, though, many stores were shuttered and dark. There were far more homeless people camped out than I ever remember seeing before. Up near Grauman's (now TCL) Chinese Theatre, there were many tourists out and walking, but most of them seemed American. I heard a lot of English and Spanish, but not much of anything else.

Later, I met up with some friends at the Grove, a high-end shopping mall to the south, and aside from mask-wearing, everything there seemed to be as I remembered it the last time I was in town. I ate lunch at the Farmer's Market adjacent to it and it was as crowded as it usually is. People wore masks but there was no distancing.

I heard that I may not get a job that I was approached about doing next year because the theatre in question is hoping to hire somebody of color for the position. Part of what theatres are up against in their attempts to diversify is that there are a limited number of people of color with the experience necessary to be able to do the job at the level required. It is going to take a few years of concentrated effort on everybody's part to bring others forward to the place where they can fill these positions. If the theatre can find someone who can do it, then they should. There is a huge difference between getting fired from a position and just not getting hired in the first place. It's not my job until it is my job. It's not something that I might lose, it's just something that I might not get.

I am looking forward to getting deeper into the job I am currently doing. It has a beginning, middle, and end. It's not a show that is going to run. The whole experience will be about six weeks and then I'll be unemployed again. I am fine with that. One of the projects that I am supposed to be doing later in the year might end up as a show that runs, but certainly for the next year or two most of my work is going to be on exploratory and developmental workshops that are finite periods. I am fine with that.

I have friends who are starting back up in shows that are going to resume their runs from where they left off. From fourteen months off back to eight shows a week almost overnight seems daunting to me. There have been times in my life where I could do many push-ups and sit-ups at one time, but it would take me a few weeks to be able to get back to that point now. (Truth be told, I should get back to that.) If I tried to do that now, without building up to it, I would hurt myself. It takes longer to build up to where you can do something like that than it does to lose it. I know that I could build back up to eight times a week given some time. What I am asking myself, though, is, do I want to?

Poor Cleveland is the undeserving butt of many jokes. Still, it does seem like a punchline that after 14 months of not being on a plane that the first place I end up flying to is, indeed, Cleveland.

The circle of these last fourteen months is starting to come back around to itself. By the time I got onto my third flight on Saturday, it already felt completely normal to be flying again. After the first few minutes of our production meeting, the fact that we were together, in-person, albeit wearing masks, seemed normal, too. I was acutely aware of how abnormal the feeling of feeling normal felt.

It was not until several months into the shutdown that the overall tension in my body that had accumulated over my professional life started to dissipate. This was a tension that I wasn't even aware was there. As excited as I am to be working on something, I do not want to let that tension start to creep back in again. After working today in Los Angeles, I will admit that I find myself becoming excited about the project that we are about to begin, but I can't help worrying that I am letting myself get dragged back onto the hamster wheel.

What will this job be like? I don't have the slightest idea. It's when you can answer that question that life becomes boring and predictable. When that happens, I will stop. But until then, I guess I'm going back to work.

JUNE 10, 2021

2,107,831 Total Reported Cases in New York. 53,296 Deaths.

The other day, as I was walking through Washington Square Park, I came upon a woman dancing in the rain.

The rain was really coming down, so nobody else was out in the park. I had nowhere much to be, so I didn't care if I got wet. I'd been out on a walk when it started, and I just decided to keep going.

I'd seen the woman in the park before. She was always in the same place by the fountain and always dancing. She had a box out for tips but the fact that nobody at all was out there with her didn't seem to have stopped her resolve to keep at it. When I'd seen her before on other days, there was enough noise around her that I couldn't hear her music very well. That day, out there in the rain, though, I could hear it plainly and follow how she was interpreting it and reacting to it, through her body.

We all make things. We make shows. We make deals. We make stories. We make agreements. We make paintings. We make decisions. We make friendships. We make money. We make dinners. We make photographs. We make children. We make art. We each, hopefully, decide to make the thing that fulfills us the most. As things begin to reopen, I find myself faced with the question, what do I want to make?

I couldn't write without also working at my job in the theatre. That I mostly love what I do in the theatre is a boon that I am beyond grateful for. The success of *Jersey Boys* and all the other commercial theatre shows I have worked on has provided me with the prospect of a comfortable retirement pension, but I'm not there yet. I've still got some time ahead of me where I need to work to pay the bills. Artistically, I may have found something new and satisfying to do this past year and a bit, but practically, I still need to mind the business that pays me.

I think that the dancer in the park understood how much I loved what she was doing when I dropped the money into her collection box. Our eyes met for a moment, she smiled, and then she kept on dancing.

We all need to keep on dancing.

AFTERWORD

During one of the early days of the pandemic, while I was out walking, I ran into Rick Elice, one of the writers of *Jersey Boys*. Neither of us had seen many friends in person for quite a while so, after bumping fists, we both happily chatted at a responsible distance out. Rick had been reading the essays that I was posting, and at one point he asked me, "At what number post did you think, oh f—, I'm going to have to do this every day?" Trying not to miss a beat and hoping for a laugh I responded, "Thirty-two." By that point, I think I was up to nearly a hundred, so I did, indeed, get a chuckle out of him.

The impulse to write and publish an essay every day came from a desire on my part to make sense of what was really happening to us. The first few days of the crisis were extremely anxiety-provoking and people were posting all sorts of crazy things online filled with nonsense and rumors. (Little did I know where THAT would lead.) At first, my attempts to make sense of it all were mostly for myself but then, I realized that I was being read by an ever-increasing group of people. I started getting nudging texts if I was late in getting one of them up online. After a couple of months of doing it every day, I went down to a more manageable six times a week and took Sundays off. On Sundays, instead of an essay, I published whatever photographs I had taken that week.

I may not have consciously decided to start writing them, but somewhere around the nine-month mark, I did consciously decide to stop. One full year from the beginning seemed like the perfect ending time to me. I was sure that I'd be back at work by then and that things would be starting to return to normal. Well, I am writing this afterward close to another full year after that and the world has yet to return to whatever that normal was. I have worked sporadically, but at nowhere near the level that I did before this all started. I have, however, continued to write and publish past the point that I decided to stop, albeit not nearly as frequently, and I imagine that I will continue.

It turns out that novelist Emily St. John Mandel was right. Disaster does get a bit…well… boring after a while. After a year that saw COVID-19 explode across the globe, George Floyd murdered in Minneapolis and a fraught Presidential election, the likes of which we have never experienced before in this country, this past year has been one of us slowly, sometimes glacially slowly, and often painfully, trying to build ourselves back up. Plenty has happened this past year and I am sure we have plenty ahead of us, but it seems as if we have all built up a resistance to being as shocked by any of it as we were in 2020.

I chose to stop where I stopped because that final June 2021 post felt hopeful. This new chapter life has given us is certainly strange and somewhat unpredictable, but it's not all bad—not by a longshot.

This past January, the woman I saw dancing in Washington Square Park in the rain six months before was out there dancing again in the frigid winter weather. She was in bare feet on a thin white cloth spread out on the icy pavement blissfully moving to something she felt deep inside herself.

If she can keep going, we all can.

ACKNOWLEDGMENTS

I have spent much of the last two years holed up in a one-bedroom apartment with my husband Michael and our cat, Ziggy. That they have both put up with me in such close quarters for so long, never ceases to amaze me. For that I am forever grateful.

Throughout the pandemic, there have been several constant groups of people that have sustained Michael and me no end—The Merri Band of Players: Merri Sugarman, Jack Cummings III, Barb Walsh, Ann Nathan, Adam Heller and, (occasionally) Beth Leavel. Our trips to the park and incessant texting were everything. Merri, Tara Rubin, and Rick Elice—our dinners and your friendships mean the world to us. And the Gypsy group? All of you? You are the most insane, loving group of people on the planet. I am so grateful for all of you. The Ex-Libris group, some of you I still haven't ever seen in person: Alison Boden, Henry Ferris, David Highfill, Vincent X. Kirsch, Anne Hopewell, Cindy Kubik, Kathy Milne, and Matthew Moross. Zooming with you all every week gave a shape to what otherwise would have just been just a limp watery collection of endless days.

To Peter Gregus, Chris Messina, and Danny Austin—I would not have gotten through any of this without you idiots. Likewise, among many others, James Mellon & Kevin Bailey and Heather Lee & Greg Thirloway and Jenna Gavigan & Kevin Fugaro and Joe Brancato & Andrew Horn and Joe Danisi & Adam McLaughlin and Daniela & Shaun—whether in person or on Zoom, your constancy sustained us. Stewart Shulman, Doug Keston, Richard Alfredo, and especially Nyle Brenner for being such a great Uncle to Ziggy—thank you. Pat, Shumei and Jose Sebastian, our neighbors here in New York, along with everybody else in our building—especially my fellow board members—Thank you. And David Petrarca and Cece DeStefano our new neighbors in Italy—every time we think, "What have we done? "we think of you and relax a little! Here's to more time together. And Henry Gibson and Michael Fulmer—wow. Just wow.

To Bernadette Peters, Scott Stevens, Patty Saccente, and Paul Wonterek—being able to do Broadway Barks! virtually twice here and once in England almost made up for not being able to do it in person. You are the most generous and giving people imaginable. Tom Viola—all I can say is anytime, anywhere. You lead, we'll follow.

Patti LuPone, for nearly a year there, you were my one paying gig and, of course, I love being with you so much, I would have done it for free.

To Kumiko Yoshii and Brendan Walsh, you two along with the entire team of The Karate Kid have been and continue to be, our light at the end of the tunnel.

To that most constant of my readers, my mother Angela, and my sister Sue along with Will, Wyatt, and Izzy—you are all part of who I am. Mom, you rock for reading all of this. And the endless and glorious stream of Mastrototaros —both legally linked and permanently committed - I have been blessed with a whole second family that I adore—thank you to all of you - from Ben and Karyn all the way down through the second cousins fifteen times removed who Michael quizzes me on before every gathering.

To Rick Sordelet and David Blixt at Sordelet Ink: I truly cannot begin to thank you enough for going on this adventure with me. I dreamed of doing this someday in the vaguest of ways and you made it a reality. I will be forever grateful. Rory Max Kaplan for the endless hours I've spent with you and Chelsea reading this aloud, I don't have the words. For the endless work you've done when I'm not there—I can't begin. To Michael Lomenda for your cover design—truly, thank you, my friend. To Charles Chessler who photographed me all over Times Square—I loved every second of it—thank you for your consummate skill and boundless enthusiasm. To Judy Katz and Sean Katz, thank you so much for helping to get the word out. To my sister Sue who painted the picture based on one of my photographs that we used on the cover—simply, thank you.

To everybody who read my posts on FaceBook and Substack every day and encouraged me to collect them into a book, this is all on you. I wish I could say that this book is just mine, but it isn't, it's yours, as well. If I listed you all by name, this book would double in length. I will, however, give Giselle Libertore a special shoutout. Thank you for all the support. You will never know how much it has meant to me.

Michael Mastro. I thanked you first and I'm thanking you last. I have absolutely no idea what I've done to deserve you. Thank you, my love, from the bottom of my heart.

REFERENCES

Hold, Please: Stage Managing a Pandemic is not a scholarly work. My intention, as I was writing it, was to try to synthesize, for myself at first, and then as people started reading the posts, for anyone else who was interested, what was going on during one of the most chaotic and confusing periods many of us have lived through. There were many times when I believed one thing on a certain day only to have my understanding change a few days later. Any errors in factual reporting are strictly mine.

As I was writing, I often consulted sites such as Wikipedia.com, History.com, and Smithsonian.com for facts such as specific dates and other basic information as needed. In addition, I consulted United States government websites and state-level websites as specific events unfolded to see what their response to them was. In the cases when I did a deeper dive into a historical event or referenced a specific person's writing without stating the source of the information in the text, itself, I have tried to include a list those sources below.

I am indebted to Heather Cox Richardson who, like me, wrote (and continues to write) about unfolding political events. Each day, since before the lockdown began, she has brilliantly tried to put everything that is happening in the news into its proper historical context. While I did not consult Ms. Richardson's work before publishing an installment of my own, I did often check in with her a day or so later to see if I was on the right track or not. It was she who inspired me to publish my daily blog on Substack.com.

Her blog, Letters from an American: A newsletter about the history behind today's politics, is available at: https://heathercoxrichardson.substack.com/?utm_source=discover_search. I would urge anyone with an interest in history and politics to read what she has to say.

What follows is a list of many of the sources that influenced the writing of the pieces in my book.

Daily COVID-19 Statistics
(2020-2021) Impact of Opening and Closing Decisions by State—A look at how social distancing measures may have influenced trends in COVID-19 cases and deaths—New York, Johns Hopkins University of Medicine Coronavirus Resource Center. Available at: https://coronavirus.jhu.edu/data/state-timeline/new-confirmed-cases/new-york

Daily News Updates
When not specifically noted in the text, the following television news channels, among others, often contributed to the daily news updates:

BBC America (BBC Studios and AMC Networks)—New York, NY
Cable News Network (CNN)—Atlanta, GA
Fox News Channel (FNN)—New York, NY
MSNBC News (NBCUniversal News Group—Comcast)—Philadelphia, PA
Spectrum News NY1 (Charter Communications)—New York, NY

In addition, news reporting from the following agencies also influenced the direction that some of the pieces took:

The Guardian/The Observer (Guardian Media Group)—London, UK
Los Angeles Times (Nant Capital, LLC)—El Segundo, CA
The New York Times (The New York Times Company)—New York, NY
Politico (Axel Springer SE)—Arlington, VA
The Washington Post (Nash Holdings)—Washington D.C.

For basic information about the virus itself and our response to it, I often consulted the following:

—Centers for Disease Control and Prevention (CDC—https://www.cdc.gov/)—Atlanta, Georgia
—World Health Organization (WHO - https://www.who.int/)—Geneva Switzerland

What follows is a (by no means complete) list, organized by entry date, of work that I referenced:

April 4, 2020
—1918 Pandemic Influenza Historic Timeline (2020) Centers for Disease Control and Prevention. Available at: https://www.cdc.gov/flu/pandemic-resources/1918-commemoration/pandemic-timeline-1918.htm
—The History of Vaccines (2020) The College of Physicians of Philadelphia. Available at: https://www.historyofvaccines.org/timeline/yellow-fever
—Rapid Response was Crucial to Containing the 1918 Flu Pandemic (April 2, 2007) National Institutes of Health—US Department of Health & Human Services. Available at: https://www.nih.gov/news-events/news-releases/rapid-response-was-crucial-containing-1918-flu-pandemic
—A Timeline of HIV and AIDS (2020) HIV.gov. Available at: https://www.hiv.gov/hiv-basics/overview/history/hiv-and-aids-timeline

April 15, 2020
—Durkheim, Émile. The Elementary Forms of the Religious Life, (1912, English translation by Joseph Swain: 1915) The Free Press, 1965: ISBN 0-02-908010-X; HarperCollins, 1976: ISBN 0-04-200030-0; new translation by Karen E. Fields, Free Press 1995: ISBN 0-02-907937-3

April 16, 2020
—President Obama Provides an Update on the US-led Response to Ebola: (October 25, 2014) (Obamawhitehousearchives.gov) Available at: https://obamawhitehouse.archives.gov/ebola-response

April 22, 2020
—Chidi, George. Dear Decaturish—Governor's decision to reopen businesses is political murder (April 20, 2020) Available at: https://decaturish.com/2020/04/dear-decaturish-governors-decision-to-reopen-businesses-is-political-murder/

May 10, 2020
—Bromage, Dr. Erin, The Risks - Know Them - Avoid Them (May 6, 2020) Available at: https://www.erinbromage.com/post/the-risks-know-them-avoid-them

May 13, 2020
—Greenblatt, Stephen. "What Shakespeare Actually Wrote About the Plague." The New Yorker, May 7, 2020. Available at: https://www.newyorker.com/culture/cultural-comment/what-shakespeare-actually-wrote-about-the-plague
—Grisar, P.J. "The 1918 Marx Brothers musical stopped short by the Spanish Flu." (March 30, 2020) Available at: https://forward.com/culture/442738/the-1918-marx-brothers-musical-stopped-short-by-the-spanish-flu/
—Knox, Bernard M. W. "The Date of the Oedipus Tyrannus of Sophocles." The American Journal of Philology, vol. 77, no. 2, Johns Hopkins University Press, 1956, pp. 133–47, https://doi.org/10.2307/292475.
—Schwarz, Michael. "A plague on both your houses." (May 21, 2020) Available at: https://beguidedbyart.com/a-plague-on-both-your-houses/

May 18, 2020
—Marineli, Filio et al. "Mary Mallon (1869-1938) and the history of typhoid fever." Annals of gastroenterology vol. 26,2 (2013): 132-134. Avilable at: https://www.ncbi.nlm.nih.gov/pmc/articles/PMC3959940/

June 3, 2020
—Britannica, The Editors of Encyclopaedia. "Harlem race riot of 1935". Encyclopedia Britannica, Avilable at: https://www.britannica.com/topic/Harlem-race-riot-of-1935.
—Britannica, The Editors of Encyclopaedia. "Harlem race riot of 1943". Encyclopedia Britannica, Available at: https://www.britannica.com/topic/Harlem-race-riot-of-1943.
—Clark, Alexis "How the Police Shooting of a Black Soldier Triggered the 1943 Harlem Riots." June 5, 2020. Available at: https://www.history.com/news/harlem-riot-police-1943
—Prison Culture.com "The Burned Down Harlem in '64..." Available at: https://www.usprisonculture.com/blog/2012/08/02/they-burned-down-harlem-in-64/

August 8, 2020
—Provincetownplayhouse.com "A History of the Provincetown Playhouse." Available at: http://www.provincetownplayhouse.com/history.html
—Ptownie.com "How Did the Spanish Flu Affect Provincetown." (March 27, 2020) Available at: https://ptownie.com/spanish-flu-provincetown-history/

September 1, 2020
—Christensen, Jen, "Past vaccine disasters show why rushing a coronavirus vaccine now would be 'colossally stupid'" CNN Health (September 1, 2020) Available at: https://www.cnn.com/2020/09/01/health/eua-coronavirus-vaccine-history/index.html

September 22, 2020
—McKeever, Amy, "Why the Supreme Court ended up with nine justices - and how that could change." National Geographic.com (September 20, 2020) Available at: https://www.nationalgeographic.com/history/article/why-us-supreme-court-nine-justices?loggedin=true

October 5, 2020
—Porterfield, Carlie, "These Four Presidents hid their Health Problems from the American Public." Forbes.com (October 4, 2020) Available at: https://www.forbes.com/sites/carlieporterfield/2020/10/04/these-four-presidents-hid-their-health-problems-from-the-american-public/?sh=37ea04c87e27

December 3, 2020
—The College of Physicians of Philadelphia, "The History of Vaccines." Available at: https://www.historyofvaccines.org/timeline/all

December 5, 2020
—Schulz, Dana, "The history of the Rockefeller Center Christmas Tree, a NYC holiday tradition" (December 2, 2020) Available at: https://www.6sqft.com/the-history-of-the-rockefeller-center-christmas-tree-a-nyc-holiday-tradition/

December 19, 2020
—Han, Jeehoon (Zhejiang University), Meyer, Bruce D. (University of Chicago), Sullivan, James X. (University of Notre Dame), "Real-time Poverty Estimates During the COVID-19 Pandemic through November 2020." (December 15, 2020) Available at: https://harris.uchicago.edu/files/monthly_poverty_rates_updated_thru_november_2020_final.pdf
—Hope, David, Limberg, Julian, "The Economic Consequences of Major Tax Cuts for the Rich." The London School of Economics and Political Science (December 2020). Available at: https://eprints.lse.ac.uk/107919/1/Hope_economic_consequences_of_major_tax_cuts_published.pdf

February 4, 2020
—Sanford, Mark, "How the Republican Party can find its way." InsideSources.com (February 3, 2020) Available at: https://greensboro.com/opinion/columnists/mark-sanford-how-the-republican-party-can-find-its-way/article_621eba82-64f0-11eb-8fa4-d7b4ce254fd6.html

March 2, 2021
—Lally, Phillippa, van Jaarsveld, Cornelia H.M., Potts, Henry W.W., Wardle, Jane, "How are habits formed: Modelling habit formation in the real world." European Journal of Social Psychology (July 16, 2009) Available at: https://onlinelibrary.wiley.com/doi/abs/10.1002/ejsp.674

March 4, 2021
—Narea, Nicole, "QAnon believers think Trump will be inaugurated again on March 4." Vox (March 3, 2021) Available at: https://www.vox.com/policy-and-politics/22280323/qanon-march-trump-inaugration-conspiracy-theory-militia

ABOUT THE AUTHOR

Richard Hester's career as a stage manager and production supervisor spans forty years. His credits include everything from the off-Broadway premiere of Harold Pinter's *Mountain Language* to the hit Broadway musical *Jersey Boys*. For the latter after serving as its original Production Stage Manager in La Jolla, CA, and in New York, he spent sixteen years staging and maintaining productions of it both in the US as well as all over the world. After more than two decades, he continues to tour with Patti LuPone as well as with Mandy Patinkin for their concerts, both nationally and internationally. Twenty-three years ago, with Bernadette Peters and Mary Tyler Moore, he helped found and produce *Broadway Barks!* an annual animal adoption event that ever since then, has helped thousands of dogs and cats find forever homes. This is his first book.

MORE FROM SORDELET INK

PLAYSCRIPTS

ACTION MOVIE—THE PLAY BY JOE FOUST AND RICHARD RAGSDALE
ALL CHILDISH THINGS BY JOSEPH ZETTELMAIER
CAPTAIN BLOOD ADAPTED BY DAVID RICE
THE COUNT OF MONTE CRISTO ADAPTED BY CHRISTOPHER M WALSH
DEAD MAN'S SHOES BY JOSEPH ZETTELMAIER
THE DECADE DANCE BY JOSEPH ZETTELMAIER
EBENEZER: A CHRISTMAS PLAY BY JOSEPH ZETTELMAIER
EVE OF IDES BY DAVID BLIXT
FRANKENSTEIN ADAPTED BY ROBERT KAUZLARIC
THE GRAVEDIGGER: A FRANKENSTEIN PLAY BY JOSEPH ZETTELMAIER
HATFIELD & McCOY BY SHAWN PFAUTSCH
HAUNTED BY JOSEPH ZETTELMAIER
HAWK'S TAVERN BY LORI ROPER AND RICK SORDELET
HER MAJESTY'S WILL ADAPTED BY ROBERT KAUZLARIC
IT CAME FROM MARS BY JOSEPH ZETTELMAIER
THE LEAGUE OF AWESOME BY CORRBETTE PASKO AND SARA SEVIGNY
THE MOONSTONE ADAPTED BY ROBERT KAUZLARIC
NORTHERN AGGRESSION BY JOSEPH ZETTELMAIER
OEDIPUS ADAPTED BY ANNIE MARTIN AND TONY CASELLI
ONCE A PONZI TIME BY JOE FOUST
THE RENAISSANCE MAN BY JOSEPH ZETTELMAIER
THE SCULLERY MAID BY JOSEPH ZETTELMAIER
ANTON CHEKHOV'S THE SEAGULL ADAPTED BY JANICE L BLIXT
SEASON ON THE LINE BY SHAWN PFAUTSCH
STAGE FRIGHT: A HORROR ANTHOLOGY BY JOSEPH ZETTELMAIER
A TALE OF TWO CITIES ADAPTED BY CHRISTOPHER M WALSH
VOICES IN THE DARK BY JOSEPH ZETTELMAIER
WILLIAMSTON ANTHOLOGY: VOLUME 1
WILLIAMSTON ANTHOLOGY: VOLUME 2

WWW.SORDELETINK.COM

WORKS BY NELLIE BLY

JOURNALISM
Ten Days in a Mad-House
Six Months In Mexico
Nellie Bly's Book: Around the World in 72 Days

NOVELS
The Mystery of Central Park
Eva the Adventuress
New York By Night
Alta Lynn, m.d.
Wayne's Faithful Sweetheart
Little Luckie
Dolly the Coquette
In Love With a Stranger
The Love of Three Girls
Little Penny, Child of the Streets
Pretty Merribelle
Twins and Rivals

NOVELS BY DAVID BLIXT

THE ADVENTURES OF NELLIE BLY
What Girls Are Good For · Charity Girl · Clever Girl

STAR-CROSS'D
The Master Of Verona · Voice Of The Falconer · Fortune's Fool · The Prince's Doom · Varnish'd Faces: Star-Cross'd Short Stories

WILL & KIT
Her Majesty's Will

COLOSSUS
Stone & Steel · The Four Emperors

Eve of Ides – a play

NON-FICTION
Shakespeare's Secrets: Romeo & Juliet
Tomorrow, and Tomorrow: Essays on Macbeth
Fighting Words

SORDELET
ink